Labor's Untold Story

D1488793

By Richard O. Boyer

MAGICIAN OF THE LAW

THE DARK SHIP

JOHN BROWN: PROFILE OF A LEGEND

By Herbert M. Morais

THE STRUGGLE FOR AMERICAN FREEDOM: THE
FIRST TWO HUNDRED YEARS

DEISM IN EIGHTEENTH CENTURY AMERICA

GENE DEBS: THE STORY OF
A FIGHTING AMERICAN

THE HISTORY OF THE NEGRO IN MEDICINE

LABOR'S
Untold Story

by
Richard O. Boyer

and
Herbert M. Morais

United Electrical, Radio & Machine Workers of America
Pittsburgh, PA

All rights reserved, including the right of reproduction
in whole or in part in any form

Copyright © **1955 by**
Richard O. Boyer and Herbert M. Morais

FIRST EDITION
Published by Cameron Associates
100 West 23rd Street, New York, N.Y. 10011

SECOND EDITION
1965 Marzani and Munsell

THIRD EDITION
Twentieth Printing, 1988
Twentyfirst Printing, 1991
Twentysecond Printing, 1994
Twentythird Printing, 1997
Twentyfourth Printing, 2000
Twentyfifth Printing, 2003
Twentysixth Printing, 2005
Twentyseventh Printing, 2009
Twentyeighth Printing, 2014
Twentyninth Printing 2019

Published by
United Electrical, Radio and Machine Workers of America (UE)
www.ueunion.org

Library of Congress Catalog Card Number: 76-347
ISBN Number: 0-916180-01-8

MANUFACTURED IN THE UNITED STATES OF AMERICA

Contents

CONTENTS

THE AUTHORS

A happy collaboration between Richard O. Boyer, author of *The Dark Ship*, a study of the Maritime Union, and Dr. Herbert M. Morais, formerly of the history department of the College of the City of New York and a specialist in American history, produced this long-needed book. Mr. Boyer, as a member

of the staff of *The New Yorker*, was one of the most successful practitioners of the *Profile* of that magazine, a technique which he employed to good advantage in *Labor's Untold Story*. He wrote *John Brown: Profile of a Legend*. Dr. Morais was the author of *The Struggle for American Freedom*, *Deism in Eighteenth Century America* and *The History of the Negro in Medicine*.

CHAPTER I

"Be Jubilant, My Feet!"

"All that harms labor is treason to America. No line can be drawn between these two. If any man tells you he loves America, yet he hates labor, he is a liar. If a man tells you he trusts America, yet fears labor, he is a fool."

"I am glad to see that a system of labor prevails under which laborers can strike when they want to. . . . I like the system which lets a man quit when he wants to and wish it might prevail everywhere."

"The strongest bond of human sympathy, outside of the family relation, should be one uniting all working people of all nations, tongues and kindreds."

FROM THE SPEECHES OF ABRAHAM LINCOLN

1. In the Beginning

Labor's story, still untold and largely missing from textbook and conventional history, is more than an account of strikes, spies, and frame-ups, of organizing and building unions, of men and women fighting and dying for better lives in a better America. It is more than the grim drama of Big Bill Haywood shooting it out with hired gunmen in the mine wars of the Rockies; or of Parsons crying with his last breath as he stood on the gallows, "Let the voice of the people be heard!"; or of the sit-down strikers at Flint whose bravery fanned the flame of CIO sweeping across the land with the speed of a prairie fire.

Fundamentally, labor's story is the story of the American people. To view it narrowly, to concentrate on the history of specific trade unions or on the careers of individuals and their rivalries, would be to miss the point that the great forces which have swept the American people into action have been the very forces that have also molded labor.

Trade unionism was born as an effective national movement amid the great convulsion of the Civil War and the fight for Negro freedom. From that day to this the struggle for Negro rights has been important to labor's welfare. Labor suffered under depressions which spurred the whole American people into movement in the seventies, in the eighties, and in the nineties. It reached its greatest heights when it joined hands with farmers, small businessmen, and the Negro people in the epic Populist revolts of the 1890's and later in the triumph that was the New Deal.

For labor has never lived in isolation or progressed without allies. Always it has been in the main stream of American life, always at the very crux of American history, with none more concerned than it at the ever-increasing concentration of American corporate power. Labor's story, by its very nature, is synchronized at every turn with the growth and development of American monopoly. Its great leap forward into industrial unionism was an answering action to the development of trusts and great industrial empires.

Labor's grievances, in fact the very conditions of its life, have been imposed by its great antagonist, that combination of industrial and financial power often known as Wall Street. The mind and actions of William H. Sylvis, the iron molder who founded the first effective national labor organization, can scarcely be understood without also an understanding of the genius and cunning of his contemporary, John D. Rockefeller, father of the modern trust. In the long view of history the machinations of J. P. Morgan, merging banking and industrial capital as he threw together ever larger combinations of corporate power controlled by fewer and fewer men, may have governed the course of American labor more than the plans of Samuel Gompers.

It is of all this, then, that labor's untold story consists. It is a story of great gains won and of labor's rank and file; of the sobbing desperation of Mrs. Munley as she shook the gates of Pottsville Prison where her husband and other Molly Maguires were being hanged as foreign agents because they had formed a trade union; of the railroad strike of 1877 and of how it was broken with the charge of Communist conspiracy.

It is the story of Eugene V. Debs running for the Presidency from a prison cell in his fight for world peace and of the movement for amnesty that grew until it freed him. It tells of the great love of Lucy Parsons and of her lonely fight for the life of her framed husband. In its pages are men and women, unknown to history but the very heart of the labor movement, distributing leaflets, arranging meetings, collecting dues, and spreading the word and the seed which built the trade union cause. It tells of the millions of immigrants arriving in steerage on a strange American shore; of the singing Wobblies, a union on wheels, the iron wheels of speeding freights; of the bloody struggles of the unemployed which were climaxed by the triumph of the CIO and New Deal.

It is a long story and an exciting one. In the beginning there was the country-shaking struggle of the Civil War. Out of its fat war contracts for the instruments of mass killing came the great American fortunes and the beginnings of monopoly. Out of its hardships on the civilian front, out of the poverty, starvation, and exhausting labor fastened on the North's working class, came the first successful national trade unions and, in 1866, the National Labor Union, the first effective nationwide federation of labor.

2. Mr. Ruffin Starts a War

The American Civil War began on April 12, 1861, amid a gala atmosphere in the jasmine-filled air of Charleston, South Carolina. At celebrations of the event ladies in crinoline with gaily colored parasols crowded around old Edmund Ruffin, who had asked and received the honor of beginning the bloodiest war in the Western Hemisphere. Because of his long advocacy of treason, slavery, and secession, he had been permitted to fire the first gun at the Union's Fort Sumter in Charleston Harbor. There had been, as he fired the shot, a long hissing suspense and then a hollow boom swelled out over the quiet blue bay toward the federal fort and the American flag gently stirring in the sweet air of early morning.

The old man saw neither past nor future as his shot went echoing out over the sea, putting forces into motion that he could not comprehend. In the sudden silence there was a little burst of cheering, almost instantly engulfed by an iron roar as battery after battery joined in the cannonading, signaling war, but signaling too the swift growth of an industrial order destined to revolutionize American life.

But Edmund Ruffin, unconscious of this, stood uncertainly for a moment or so at the center of history, and then went his way to a series of Charleston receptions where he was hailed as a hero. There was no thought then of decaying corpses strewing miles of field, of legs and arms blown from bodies until the earth was red and wet, and the dainty belles of Charleston were lovely in minuet and reel as toasts were drunk to Edmund Ruffin, the savior of the South.

All about the savior were the slaves who served him but apparently he sensed nothing of their writhings and strivings for the liberty that 186,000 Negroes would fight for in the Union Army. We can see him down the years, patting his lips with a snowy napkin, filled with wine and certitude and never a single hint of the defeat and death before him.

A great surge of patriotic feeling swept the cities and farms north of the Mason-Dixon Line at the news that the flag and American troops had been fired upon by slaveholders, the most rabid of whom were frankly intent upon fastening their system of unpaid, driven labor upon the entire nation. The *Charleston Mercury,* for example, had declared just before the war's beginning, "Slavery is the natural and normal condition of the laboring man . . . and the Northern states will yet have to introduce it. The theory of a free society is a delusion." When President Lincoln called for volunteers the entire membership of trade union locals enlisted in single groups, knowing well that there would be no free trade union movement if the slaveholders triumphed.

Seldom in all history had there been such a war, not only for bloodiness, bitterness, and far-flung battle line but for the momentous issues involved. As it swayed back and forth across half the country, men dying by the scores of thousands at Wilderness and Shiloh, Chickamauga and Antietam, many trade unionists felt that the issue being decided was not only whether 4,000,000 Americans should continue in Negro slavery but whether there was to be any freedom at all for working-class Americans, black or white, North or South.[1] As the war increased in ferocity along a thousand miles of battle front, on mountain top and prairie, in swamp, forest, and burning towns that extended from the Mississippi to the Atlantic, the whole world watched in awe and even "the workingmen of Europe felt instinctively that the Star-Spangled Banner carried the destiny of their class."[1a]

3. The Second American Revolution

When Edmund Ruffin fired his shot across Charleston Harbor he was supremely confident of a slaveholders' victory and his confidence seemed amply justified by the facts. For more than a quarter of a century the slaveholders, through their economic and political allies in the North and their own iron regime at home, had owned the national government. They had dominated the Presidency, directed the Supreme Court, managed Congress, held both major political parties to their will, and controlled to large degree the press, the school, and the pulpit. For more than a quarter century they had passed the laws, formulated the nation's policies, and balked the rising industrial capitalist economy of the North.

Always bold, audacious, confident, they had progressed from victory to victory. As the area of slavery steadily increased, they threatened the great West, which had almost doubled in size after the seizure of nearly half of Mexico in 1848 and which was so necessary for capitalist expansion. And in 1857 their United States Supreme Court declared in the Dred Scott decision

[1] The *Iron Platform*, a New York labor paper, indicated, for example, in November, 1862, that if the slaveholders won the war "all laborers, white or black" would be "and ought to be slaves." It said: "There is one truth which should be clearly understood by every workingman in the Union. *The slavery of the black man leads to the slavery of the white man.* . . . If the doctrine of treason is true, that 'Capital should own labor,' then their logical conclusion is correct, and all laborers, white or black, are and ought to be slaves."
[1a] Address of the International Workingmen's Association to President Lincoln, London, Jan. 7, 1865.

that slavery was legal in all the territories of the United States.[2] They were the ruling class, and their power was founded on property, on 4,000,000 human beings, owned as cattle are owned and valued at two billions of dollars.

Through their influence upon the press they had convinced much of the public, even in the North, that the Abolitionists were not primarily concerned with the elimination of Negro slavery but were instead a treasonable conspiracy to overthrow the government by force and violence for the benefit of "our hereditary foreign enemy," Great Britain.[3] For almost thirty years the Abolitionists had been described as "Communists and Socialists" using the cry of Negro liberty as a shield to hide their plot of Socialist insurrection. Typical of the diatribes against them, as frequent as similar attacks against labor today, was that of George Fitzhugh, Southern sociologist, who declared in 1857:

"We warn the North that every one of the leading Abolitionists is agitating the Negro slavery question as a means to attain their ulterior ends . . . Socialism and Communism . . . no private property, no church, no law . . . free love, free land, free women, and free children." [4]

[2] Northern labor was particularly alarmed by the Dred Scott decision, in which Chief Justice Taney declared in effect "that Congress had no power under the Constitution to prohibit or abolish slavery in the territories of the United States anywhere at any time." The decision seemed to mean that free labor would have to compete with slave labor in all the great area of the West, from Washington and the Dakotas to Arizona and New Mexico, from California to Kansas. The Dred Scott decision was only one of a long series of victories won by the slave power in the critical decade leading to the Civil War. In 1850 the slaveholders pushed through Congress the Fugitive Slave Act which provided for federal government assistance in the return of runaway slaves from the North. There were thousands of runaways each year, aided in escaping on the so-called Underground Railroad, by thousands of otherwise law-abiding Negro and white citizens of the North as well as of the South, despite the violation of federal law.

[3] In 1835 Harrison Gray Otis, former Senator from Massachusetts and a leading citizen of Boston, told a huge pro-slavery audience meeting in Boston's Faneuil Hall that the American Anti-Slavery Society was "a revolutionary society for the purpose of undermining . . . the government of our sister states." He further declared the Abolitionists were a conspiracy "to trench upon the provisions of the Constitution by overt acts." As a result of these charges, often repeated in the public press, the Abolitionists were exposed, according to the sons of William Lloyd Garrison in their biography of their father, "to public odium, as disorganizers, seeking unconstitutional ends by unconstitutional means, aiming to excite a servile insurrection . . . and calling to their aid the hereditary foreign enemies of the republic. . . ."

[4] Another typical utterance was that of Dr. James H. Thornwell, a religious and educational leader of South Carolina, who declared in 1850: "The parties in this conflict are not merely Abolitionists and slaveholders—they are atheists, socialists, communists, red republicans, Jacobins on one side, and the friends of order and regulated freedom on the other. In one word, the world is the battleground—Christianity and atheism the combatants; and the progress of humanity at stake." The words somehow have a modern ring.

The slaveholders had diverted attention from their own treasonable designs by hanging John Brown and his men for treason even as they themselves were plotting it. Prime movers in Brown's execution on Dec. 2, 1859, for his attempt to free Virginia's slaves were Jefferson Davis, soon to be president of the slaveholders' Confederacy, Governor Wise of Virginia, and Senator Mason of that same state, all three of whom were leaders in the treasonous assault less than two years later against the Government of the United States.[5]

Reactionaries, both North and South, concealed their own plans by charging that the foreign-born, particularly the Irish, were plotting to seize the White House and the nation under the leadership of agents of the Papacy.[6] As for the young labor movement, it had been charged many times with being a foreign, un-American conspiracy, since 1805 when the Philadelphia shoemakers' union had been held to be "a design against the freedom of the nation."[7]

From the organization of the very first local trade unions in the United States in the 1790's, it was found difficult to raise wages for shoemakers, shipbuilders, and bricklayers when a few hundred miles to the south shoes were made, ships were built, and bricks were laid for no pay at all to the slave worker. It was difficult to gain shorter hours in Rhode Island when in Maryland a worker might be driven until he fell exhausted, only to be whipped to his feet again. As early as 1844 textile workers in Fall River,

[5] In October, 1859, John Brown led a band of twenty-two men, five of whom were Negroes, in an attempt to capture the United States government arsenal at Harper's Ferry, Virginia. The raid, which was part of a much larger plan involving the destruction of slavery by the arming of its victims, was unsuccessful. Brown and six of his followers—ten were killed during the raid—were hanged for criminal conspiracy and treason against the Commonwealth of Virginia. On Dec. 2, 1859, Brown was executed.
[6] In 1835 Samuel F. B. Morse, the inventor, published a book, *The Foreign Conspiracy Against the Liberties of the United States,* in which he charged that Catholics were foreign agents conspiring to overthrow the United States government. This book, and similar agitation, was used to distract attention from the main issue, slavery, diverting it instead to the foreign-born. Under the stimulus of such propaganda Catholic churches were assaulted, incited mobs declaring that they contained arms and ammunition for an uprising. So general was the feeling that Catholics were foreign agents that it was proposed that they be excluded from holding public office. During the 1850's a political movement, confined to the native-born and called the "Know-Nothings," became widespread in the East, its chief article of faith opposition to Catholics and foreign-born.
[7] From 1805 when eight shoemakers were indicted by a grand jury in Philadelphia for "a combination and conspiracy to raise wages," employers with the help of pliant courts repeatedly branded the labor movement as a conspiracy using force as its method of subverting society. Judge Edwards declared in New York in 1836, for example, that trade unions were un-American. "They are of foreign origin," he said in holding New York's tailors guilty of conspiracy, "and I am led to believe mainly upheld by foreigners." Similar charges were prosecuted against trade unions in 1821, 1823, 1827, 1829, 1834, 1835, and 1836, union tailors, hatters, spinners, shoemakers, and carpet weavers being the victims.

Mass., were told, "You must work as long and cheap as slaves in the South." Two years later the New England Workingmen's Association resolved that "American slavery must be uprooted before the elevation sought by the laboring classes can be effected."[8]

But through the decade before the Civil War, that time seemed far removed. So unbroken was the series of victories enjoyed by slavery that Wendell Phillips, leading Abolitionist and champion of labor, wrote:

"The Government has fallen into the hands of the Slave Power completely. So far as national politics are concerned we are beaten—there's no hope. We shall have Cuba in a year or two; Mexico in five. . . . The future seems to unfold a vast slave empire united with Brazil. I hope I may be a false prophet but the sky never was so dark."

The proponents of slavery agreed with Phillips—but to them the sky was bright. They felt that their system was as permanent as gravity. They did not know that the world was changing under them, that the precepts of liberty and the force of steam and industrial power driving the North's emerging capitalism were soon to engulf them; rather they felt that chattel slavery was everlasting and never dreamed that the very air they breathed was revolution which would change or kill them.

The revolution had begun, in a sense, when Jefferson wrote "All men are created equal," and a great revolutionary war was fought for freedom and independence which had left millions of Americans with neither; which had left the Negro people, who had arrived on these shores as early as the Pilgrims, still in slavery. Also it had left the North's advancing capitalism the prisoner of a hostile ruling class, the Southern plantation owners, who ran the national government, framing policies which attempted to straitjacket and confine the North's growing industrial power. If Northern enterprise had thrown off British tyranny, it had gained another. An explosion was inevitable.

But a revolution, the ousting of one class by another, is not fought by war alone and because the First American Revolution of 1776 had been uncompleted it continued in a gradually rising day-to-day conflict of competing social systems. It continued, sometimes quietly, sometimes with all the clatter of the ever-expanding factory system, not infrequently breaking out in slave insurrections, often marked by conflict in Congress between slave and free forces which were contesting also for the vast territories of the West. It was this continuing conflict over the long years, and not Mr. Ruffin's little shot across Charleston Harbor, that had exploded into the beginning of the Civil War, into the Second American Revolution.

[8] Despite many differences, slavery was the same kind of brake on the young labor movement as the unorganized, low-wage South is at present on today's labor.

4. Blood and Gold

The trade union movement, slowly growing in strength through the fifties until the depression of 1857, almost ceased to exist when Lincoln issued his call for volunteers. Between 500,000 and 750,000 men left Northern industry, until more than fifty per cent of the nation's working force was on the battlefield. In Massachusetts a company of Lowell textile workers received a prize for being the first company mobilized and ready to march to the defense of menaced Washington. Trade union members joined the colors so unanimously that many locals in all parts of the country were dissolved for the duration. In Wisconsin, for example, the National Typographical Union had to disband Local 23 when virtually all of its members left for the front. The Spinners Union of Fall River practically disappeared during the first few months of the war because of enlistments. Entire companies of Illinois volunteers were composed almost exclusively of members of the Miners' Union and in Brooklyn the Painters' Union resolved to fight as a unit against the slaveholders' conspiracy and "for the maintenance of the flag of our country."[9]

The dying began at Bull Run in July, 1861, with a terrible Union defeat.

It continued for four years until more than 600,000 young men, mostly workers and farmers, had been killed and more than 400,000 had been wounded, maimed, crippled, and burned.

It continued at Fair Oaks, Gaines' Mill, Malvern Hill, Fort Wagner, Fredericksburg, Fort Donelson, Murfreesboro, Perryville, Vicksburg, Chattanooga; in 2,400 battles which have received the honor of names; in thousands of crossroads skirmishes and chance encounters where men were killed but which never received the recognition of designation. Trade union papers of the time were edged in black, issue after issue carrying casualty

[9] The foreign-born, long the target of discrimination and repression, the butt of the powerful Know-Nothing movement of the fifties, had an extraordinary record of heroism in the Civil War. The Irish, over 900,000 of whom had immigrated to this country in the 1850's alone, enlisted by the thousands, entire regiments being composed almost wholly of Irishmen who had a battle record second to none. The Germans, too, many of them veterans of the Revolution of 1848, formed whole regiments and from the first won important victories in Missouri and Arkansas. Exiled Poles, Jewish scholars, English Chartists, Welsh miners joined the colors. More than 40,000 Canadians enlisted in the Union army. The Garibaldi Guard, made up of Italian workingmen of New York City, also veterans of the Revolution of 1848, was one of the first regiments to leave for Virginia. They were followed by the DeKalb Regiment of Germans and the famous Phoenix Regiment of the Empire Brigade, composed almost wholly of New York Irish.

But of all the troops that served none surpassed the 186,000 Negro soldiers, many of them escaped slaves; to them the war was indeed a revolution. John Worthington Ames, who had led the bravest of white troops, wrote after assuming command of a Negro regiment in August, 1863: "Until I joined the Negroes, I never saw the enemy's works carried by assault, I never saw guns captured and never knew of captured guns to be used against the enemy; our Negroes have never failed in all these things."

lists of fallen brothers. The fighting and dying continued until Washington, menaced with capture for almost two years by continuing victories of the slave forces, was one great hospital.

The poet Walt Whitman had gone there to help. Although he was only forty-two, his hair and beard turned white as he labored day and night, feeling as one man fighting an army of pain. His journal, which he kept throughout the war, is a catalogue of death. "In one of the hospitals," he wrote, "I find Thomas Haley, 4th New York Cavalry. He is a fine specimen of youthful physical manliness, shot through the lungs and inevitably dying. Next to him is Thomas Lindy, 1st Pennsylvania Cavalry, shot very badly. . . . Poor young man, he suffers horribly, has to be constantly dosed with morphine, his face ashy and glazed bright young eyes . . .

"Opposite an old Quaker lady is sitting by the side of her son, Amer Moore, 2nd U.S. Artillery, shot in the head. He will surely die. I speak and he answers pleasantly."

As Amer Moore lay dying, young J. Pierpont Morgan, magnificently whole and completely healthy, stood in his Wall Street office, calculating the profit he would make from his speculation in gold. There had been another Union defeat, which, by depressing the nation's currency, would bring him a pretty penny since it had driven up the price of his hoarded gold.

Chesty and imperial for all his youth, and he was only twenty-four at the war's beginning, Morgan perceived from the first that wars were for the shrewd to profit from and poor to die in. When thousands of less calculating young men, their "hearts touched with fire," in the words of one of them, marched off to Bull Run and the defense of Washington, young Morgan advanced on a government arsenal in New York City. He had received a tip that a store of government-owned rifles had been condemned as defective and with the simplicity of genius he had bought them from the government for $17,500 on one day and sold them back to the government on the next for $110,000.

He had a kind of phlegmatic aplomb, unusual in one so young, and he did not seem bothered when a Congressional committee investigating his little deal said of him and other hijacking profiteers, "Worse than traitors are the men who, pretending loyalty to the flag, feast and fatten on the misfortunes of the nation."[10]

---

[10] Commodore Vanderbilt, then one of the richest men in America, was another named in Congressional investigations of wartime fraud. Particularly mentioned was his leasing to the government at between $800 and $900 a day a decrepit lake steamer, the *Niagara,* used to transport troops on the Atlantic to New Orleans. Senator Grimes of Iowa declared that "in perfectly smooth weather with a calm sea, the planks were ripped out and exhibited to the gaze of the indignant soldiers on board, showing that her timbers were rotten. The committee have in their committee room a large sample of one of the beams of this vessel to show that it has not the slightest capacity to hold a nail."

When the Draft Act was passed in 1863 Morgan purchased a young man to go to war in his stead as he would purchase a sack of flour. The price for a substitute was $300 and more than one young entrepreneur found that it paid off handsomely when in scanning casualty lists he found that the poor boy who had gone in his place had been killed. Three hundred dollars was a cheap price for life, particularly when life was daily growing more profitable with millions on millions of dollars being awarded in war contracts.

Morgan's action in buying a substitute was neither illegal nor unusual, it being provided in the Draft Act itself that substitutes could be purchased. Among those who availed themselves of this provision was a large-headed, thin-lipped youth, one John D. Rockefeller, who, as others were dying in Virginia, was prowling safely enough about a forest of derricks in western Pennsylvania, his small eyes alight with dreams of oil and empire.

"Only greenhorns enlist," wrote Judge Mellon of Pittsburgh to his son, James. "Here there is no credit attached to going. All stay if they can and go if they must. Those who are able to pay for substitutes do so and no discredit attaches." An advertisement appearing daily in New York City newspapers announced, "Gentlemen will be furnished promptly with substitutes by forwarding their orders to the office of the Merchants, Bankers and General Volunteer Association."

If there were many young men who died expressing such plain, old-fashioned sentiments as "Tell mother I did my duty," or "Tell father I died for my country," there were other more practical youths who lived for the mammoth plunder in ventures which ranged from profiteering war contracts to the Congressional bribery necessary to gaining railroad rights-of-way. So it was with Philip Armour, James Hill, Andrew Carnegie, Jay Gould, and Jim Fisk, all in their early twenties, who, like Morgan and Rockefeller, did not go to war. While staying safe as others died these men laid the basis of the great American fortunes, some of which still dominate American life. Matthew Josephson writes of them:

"The young men who were to form the new nobility of industry and banking had, most of them, reached their prime of youth or manhood when Lincoln issued his first call for volunteers. Jay Gould, Jim Fisk, J. P. Morgan, Philip Armour, Andrew Carnegie, James Hill and John Rockefeller were all in their early twenties; Collis Huntington and Leland Stanford were over thirty, while Jay Cooke was not yet forty. In the ensuing years all the members of this band of youth would meet with their first 'windfalls'; sure-footed they . . . would take their posts in the economic revolution which rose to a climax in the war; and the end of the war would see them masters of money, capitalists equipped to increase their capital. In the hour of danger it was as if *they alone were prepared*. It was as if the Second American Revolution had been fought for them."

As the Second American Revolution progressed and "the new nobility of industry and banking" were thrust into seats of power, the country presented a picture of astounding contrast and colossal energy. Titanic battles raged while men were getting rich beyond the dreams of avarice and a whole people, 4,000,000 Negro slaves, were wandering over thousands of miles, uprooted, homeless, and often starving as they followed the increasingly victorious Union armies. As Sherman's army burned Atlanta and swept toward the sea, a stream of white-topped wagons moved to the West, the thoughts of their occupants far from war as they took the trail for Oregon and Washington, Montana and Wyoming, intent on new lives and new land under the Homestead Act of 1862. While Grant's army hammered toward Richmond, suffering appalling losses, 10,000 Chinese laborers and 3,000 Irishmen were throwing track eastward from California over the Sierras and the Rockies, their casualties almost as numerous amid the icy peaks and burning deserts as those of the fighting armies. They were working east on the first transcontinental railroad.

The rising industrial class of the North had already ousted the old rulers of the South as the country's dominant group. All the pent-up energy of years, like a flood bursting through a crumbling dam, inundated the country with enterprise. More than a million dollars a day, most of it raised by the rising banker Jay Cooke, who acquired a fortune of $20,000,000 in commissions, was being spent by the federal government for the huge paraphernalia of war. Thousands of miles of railroads, needed for troop transport and supply, were being built; thousands of miles of telegraph wire, needed for military communication, were being strung.

The great new factories, their belt lines and looms clattering day and night, were using new methods of mass production, particularly in the manufacture of uniforms, army shoes, canned goods, and agricultural machinery. The water wheel, whose slow ponderous turn had so recently been the general source of power, was fast becoming a relic of the past. The revolutionary power of coal, steam and iron had released energies which by the middle of the 1890's would make the United States the world's first industrial power, creating one-third of the earth's manufactured products.

Western Pennsylvania was gushing with oil and millions as the youthful Mr. Rockefeller, "low-voiced, deft-footed and humble," was making plans to capture all of both; Pittsburgh was flooding the country with iron rails, girders, and rolling stock while twenty-nine-year-old Andy Carnegie was repeating softly to himself, "Oh, I'm rich! I'm rich!" Chicago was becoming the center of railroads, wheat, and meat as twenty-six-year-old Philip Armour made $2,000,000 by selling pork short to the army, buying at $18 a barrel and selling at $40. Young James Mellon, who had taken his father's advice and had not enlisted, wrote admiringly of friends who were making millions through speculations in wheat. "They continue growing richer," he wrote his father, "and don't care when the war ends."

Despite the mass dying everything would have been perfect in a perfect world had it not been for certain unfortunate aspects of the rising industrial system. On the one hand it produced mass poverty and on the other it created a troublesome labor movement. At first the new tycoons were unperturbed. They had a country to plunder and they could not be disturbed. They owned the young Republican Party and they owned the government. They were hungry for money and not to be denied. Within a short time Congress, many of its members rewarded by bribes, had given the youthful robber barons, as they were later described, almost half the nation's natural resources. During the fifties and sixties Congress turned over to the Union Pacific, Central Pacific, Northern Pacific, and other western railroads 158,-000,000 acres of land, an area almost as large as New England, New York, and Pennsylvania combined, while the states turned over 167,000,000 acres, a domain nearly the size of Texas.[11]

This colossal land grab withdrew from circulation a considerable portion of arable land which might otherwise have passed into the hands of working farmers under the Homestead Act of 1862. As originally enacted, this law was designed—or so the public thought—to assure ownership of the West to the millions of average Americans. The labor movement had agitated for the act for a generation. Under it the government pledged itself to give a farm to every man who would improve the land upon which he settled. But this and other land acts also endowed Congress with the power to reward its friends and bribers with huge public grants. Soon the young promoters owned the best parts of an area half the size of the present United States. Not only did they own the rich and fertile land itself, pasture and forest, but they also owned the incalculable wealth beneath it, all the iron, coal, copper, gold, silver, and oil; owned it all and forever, in perpetuity for themselves, their assigns and heirs.

But in Virginia the golden years of mammoth theft were bloody. "In one corner of the woods," wrote a young officer, "the dead of both sides lay piled

---

[11] It is estimated that the public domain turned over to the railroads was worth $335,000,000. Actual money subsidies given by the government to the railroads were even higher; a conservative estimate puts them at $707,000,000—in all, a billion-dollar grab. By 1870 sixty per cent of the cost of building the railroads had been provided by public authority from lands belonging to the American people and from taxes taken out of the pockets of the American people. And that was not all. The robber barons controlled them as the principal stockholders. In this way the Credit Mobilier, the Union Pacific's construction company, received $73,000,000 for construction which, according to a later Congressional investigation, would actually cost $50,000,-000. The Croker Company, one of the Central Pacific's two construction companies, took $100,000 a mile on the average for laying down the road's tracks, the actual cost being no more than half that amount. Besides profiteering, there was graft attending the building of the railroads. In this connection Senator George Hoar of Massachusetts said at the completion of the first transcontinental railroad in the United States: "When the greatest railroad of the world, binding together the continent and uniting the two great seas which wash our shores was finished, I have seen our national triumph and exaltation turned to bitterness and shame by the unanimous reports of three committees of Congress that every step of that mighty enterprise has been taken in fraud."

in the trenches, five or six deep, the wounded often writhing under super-incumbent dead. The losses of our corps in nine days are 10,547. . . ."

The dark dead lay in windrows before Fort Wagner where Negro troops had made one of the most gallant assaults in the history of the war. A Negro woman, Harriet Tubman, "the Moses of her people," then acting as a scout for the Union army, was bending over the dead and dying. She had seen the battle and later was asked to describe it.

"And then we saw the lightning," she said, "and that was the guns; and then we heard the thunder and that was the big guns; and then we heard the rain falling and that was the drops of blood falling; and when we came to get in the crops, it was dead men that we reaped."

5. Sylvis

William H. Sylvis, one of the great names of American labor, was a small peppery man with large ideas, flowing blond sideburns and the muscular arms and shoulders of an iron molder. His bright blue eyes seemed to flare with hotness when he was angry, which was most of the time, and he found it difficult to sit or be silent. A founder of one of the first national unions, the Iron Molders, as well as of the first national labor federation, his energy was such that it was to wear him out and kill him by the time he was forty-one. Suffering from permanent indignation, he was not a cautious man and if he thought a thing he would say so.

For him, to think was to act. Despite his impetuosity, he was a genius at organization and administration, bringing thousands into the trade union movement and initiating trade union practices in the collection of dues, the sale of charters, the establishment of adequate strike funds, card index systems, and centralization that are still in use today. Throughout his adult life this dynamo of the labor movement bummed his way over the country in repeated organizing tours, wrote articles, speeches, and resolutions, and endlessly buttonholed his colleagues, urging them to accept his ideas. Among the principles to which he devoted his life and energy were Negro-labor solidarity; equal pay for equal work for women and their admission into trade unions; independent political action by labor, farmers, and the Negro people; and international labor solidarity.

Born in Pennsylvania in 1828, one of ten children in a poverty-stricken family, his years had been filled with little besides work and resentment un-til he joined the union of the Philadelphia iron molders in 1857. To an-other it might have been only a method of obtaining a raise, but the idea of trade unionism blazed in Sylvis' mind until it became a religion and a way of life, a standard of conduct and a philosophy. Something of his feeling may be gained from his exclamation, "I love this union cause! I hold it more dear than my family or my life. I am willing to devote to it all that I am or hope for in this world." From the first he agitated for a national organization of iron molders and in 1860, the year after it was formed, he was elected treasurer.

Sylvis and his family, to the time of his very death, were dogged by bill collectors and poverty. Often there was not enough food in the house for his five hungry children. His wife was always worried and frequently ill. Sylvis gave all his time to "the cause." He liked to be where things were happening, at the center of events. Thus it was natural that when the Civil War broke out he organized a company of volunteers, made up mostly of trade union members from the iron molders. He was elected a lieutenant and was about to leave when his wife managed to gain his attention amid all the excitement. They had no money. There was no food for the children. How were she and the children to live? And so, with the bands playing and the crowds cheering as Sylvis' company embarked, the lieutenant went back to the foundry and family life.

But he could not stand it. He organized another company, this one of militia, and when Pennsylvania was threatened with invasion in 1861 Sylvis took the field as a sergeant. However, after three months of service Sylvis was forced to return to support his family. He was not a very happy man then. All of his friends were on the battlefield. The Iron Molders, so recently formed into a national union, had virtually disappeared as its membership went off to the war.

His indignation found plenty to feed upon as he looked about the country. If there was extraordinary bravery on the battlefield, there was extraordinary knavery behind the lines. As Southern spies and Northern traitors known as Copperheads plotted to seize Detroit and Chicago, Indiana and Ohio, Fernando Wood, Mayor of New York, was engaged in an equally abortive conspiracy to take the North's largest city out of the Union, to secede in the wake of the Southern states. While the new fortunes pyramided thousands of women and children were forced into factories, hunger the spur, their fathers and husbands at the front, the new tycoons using the new labor to cut wages. In September, 1864, a leading Republican newspaper was forced to admit that "there is absolute want in many families, while thousands of young children who should be at school are shut up in work that they may earn something to eke out the scant supplies at home."

Free Negroes, hitherto excluded from Northern industry, were being hired at reduced wages while the ports of the North were becoming busy with ships, their steerages packed with many arriving as contract laborers. These were the equivalent of indentured servants, unable to make a decision or have the slightest voice in their movements, wages, or occupations until they had paid corporations for their passage and livelihood at the cost of incredible toil.

The cost of living was increasing out of all proportion to the rise in money wages. Between 1860 and 1865 wages rose 43 per cent and prices soared 116 per cent. While the purchasing power or real wages of workers was thus being drastically reduced, new speed-up techniques were being introduced to increase production. To add to the workers' burden, the hours of labor were long. Although the average working day was eleven hours, twelve to fourteen hours a day was not uncommon.

As Sylvis fumed and fretted and worked himself an exhausting twelve hours daily for about $12 weekly, he read articles in the *New York Tribune* and the *New York Herald* which told of girls working from six in the morning until midnight for three dollars a week. As he read of women fainting beside their looms, of children falling asleep exhausted beside the machines they tended, he himself was having a desperate time supporting a family of seven—butter having risen in price from four cents to twenty-four cents a pound, milk increasing from four and one half to ten cents a quart, beef, bread, and other food similarly soaring. The slums were growing along with the fortunes; with rent doubled, ten and twelve were sleeping in a single room in the spreading tenements of the growing cities.

But every new factory produced workers, potential union members, as inevitably as it did profits, the number of factory workers mounting from 1,300,000 to 2,000,000 during a single decade. By 1870 the industrial section of the population was already in excess of those engaged in agriculture. In addition to the 2,000,000 factory workers there were 3,600,000 other wage earners—5,600,000 in all.

Sylvis was goaded almost to frenzy when he read that he and other workingmen could live adequately on their wages if they would only economize. "And what if the husband and father should be sick?" he burst out. "The body prostrated by racking pain and the mind frenzied with apprehensions of a starving family? Who shall describe his agony? Who can comprehend his misery?"

The breaking point was reached late in 1862 when it was equally manifest that life could not be supported on wages paid and that employers, although prosperous beyond precedent, would not raise them unless forced to. Early in 1863 strikes began breaking out everywhere. With these strikes came wage increases and more trade unions. The *Springfield Republican* declared on March 26, 1863, ". . . the workmen of almost every branch of trade have had their strikes within the last few months. . . . In almost every instance the demands of the employed have been acceded to. The strikes, which have all been conducted very quickly, . . . have led to the formation of numerous leagues or unions." And the San Francisco *Evening Bulletin* of Nov. 6, 1863, reported that ". . . striking for higher wages is now the rage among the working people of San Francisco."

Sylvis exploded into action, writing to molders all over the country, proposing that the National Molders Union be reconstituted at a convention in Pittsburgh in January, 1863. At this convention Sylvis was named president and assigned to bring back into being what was largely a paper organization. As he set out on the first national organizing tour in American history, he had only $100 with which he was expected to travel some 10,000 miles. His money soon gone, he progressed from city to city by begging rides from railroad engineers. Everywhere he preached the gospel of union organization. He was often hungry and his clothes were in tatters but he said later that he was never happier, for he was doing what he had long wanted to do. His brother wrote of him then:

"He wore clothes until they became quite threadbare and he could wear them no longer. The shawl, which he wore to the day of his death, was filled with little holes burned there by the splashing of molten iron from the ladles of molders in strange cities, whom he was beseeching to organize."

Everywhere he went, he reported, workers asked him, "Why does capital roll in luxury and wealth while labor is left to eke out a miserable existence in poverty and want?" And everywhere he replied, "Single-handed we can accomplish nothing, but united there is no power of wrong that we cannot openly defy." He was a man inspired and factory after factory was organized by him on a closed-shop basis. Never known for patience, he was spurred to particular fury by those who said that capital and labor had a common interest and he denounced the theory as "mere humbug" in many a long speech in which he asked his listeners why they had to fight for a living wage if their interest was their employers'.

By the end of the year he could report: "From a mere pigmy our union has grown to be a giant." At the beginning of 1863 the Iron Molders had had 2,000 members in fifteen locals with $1,600 in the treasury. At the conclusion of Sylvis' organizing tours of 1863, in which he ranged from Pennsylvania and Ohio to Missouri, Canada, Michigan, and New York, the union had 6,000 members, fifty-four locals, and $25,000 in the treasury.

Everywhere workers were flocking into the revived unions and everywhere other laboring men were taking to the road as Sylvis had done. Ira Steward was reorganizing the Machinists and Blacksmiths and already talking of the eight-hour day, an evangelical gleam in his eye as he claimed it would solve most of mankind's problems. Richard Trevellick, "a tireless labor lecturer and organizer," was rebuilding locals of the Ships' Carpenters and Calkers; Robert Schilling, active in the labor movement for more than thirty years, was reconstituting the Coopers' Union, while the National Typographical Union, first of all the national unions, was being restored to life by J. C. Whaley and A. C. Cameron. All of these unions, and others, had been born during the fifties, suffered the depression of 1857, and practically disappeared at the beginning of the Civil War as most of their members left for the field. Now they were enjoying a glorious resurrection, with the labor movement growing from a few thousand members in 1861 to 200,-000 members by the end of 1864.

By 1864 employers were determined to break the growing labor movement. They themselves began joining together on a citywide basis to counteract the city labor councils everywhere being organized. Owning the Republican Party and with a large influence over the Army, they sought to impose a 25 per cent pay cut in 1864 at the point of bayonets. When strikes resulted troops were recalled from the field and thrown against strikers in New York, Tennessee, Pennsylvania, and Missouri. Other strikes and use of the military were averted by the intervention of President Lincoln on the side of the workingman. He told one labor delegation, "I know that in almost every case of strikes, the men have just cause for complaint." At the same time employers were frequently declaring they would settle with labor after the war. One of them told Sylvis: "The day is not far distant when the condition of workingmen will be worse than ever before. The day will come when men who are now active in the labor movement will be forced upon their bended knee to ask for work. . . . A spirit of retaliation has been aroused in the bosom of every employer, the fruits of which are now being manifested in the widespread and universal organization of capitalists for the avowed purpose of destroying your unions."[12]

6. "Be Jubilant, My Feet!"

Lee's shattered army surrendered at Appomattox on April 9, 1865, and a nation's long and terrible agony was over, or so the American people believed. Thousands, millions, rushed through the streets weeping, shouting, laughing, the great weight of blood and death suddenly lifted from them.

The newspaper reporters tell of seeing, pushed and borne on the wave of hysterical people, a woman whose husband would not return, a mother who would never again see her son, trying to extricate herself from the crowd, her face contorted and wet, alternately weeping and trying to join the general joy. Farmers and their wives went out on porches of houses twenty miles from nowhere, fired old squirrel guns into the air, and, with tears streaming down their faces, scanned the roads as if they half expected to see their sons already returning to them.

In Charleston, proud Charleston, where the slaveholders had begun their war with Edmund Ruffin's shot, the famous Fifty-Fourth, the Negro regiment from Massachusetts, marched past the stately mansions singing *John Brown's Body,* while in their wake came thousands of Negroes, terrible in their joy and strength at being free. They surged into the mansions and slave pens shouting "Liberty!" They burned the auction blocks, destroyed whips and branding irons, wrecked the stocks which had held them, shattered the many specialized tools of torture with which they had been cut, maimed, twisted, and flogged for more than two hundred and fifty years. Four million slaves all over the South, Americans once sold like cattle, were doing similarly, remembering their many martyrs and their two hundred and fifty bloody revolts, their two hundred and fifty smashed efforts at freedom.

[12] As quoted in P. Foner, *History of the American Labor Movement,* New York, 1947, p. 360.

And as he heard their cries of joy upon the evening air old Edmund Ruffin went into his garden and put a bullet through his head. . . .

Just after Lee's surrender Abraham Lincoln, whose patient, melancholy strength had somehow wrenched the country's heart, was slain by John Wilkes Booth. It did not seem as if victory could be enjoyed with Lincoln dead, and Whitman wrote of the great tide of grief that swept the nation as Lincoln's coffin returned him to his Springfield home in Illinois, of the "coffin that passes through lanes and streets, through day and night with the great cloud darkening the land. . . ."

As Lincoln was lowered into his grave the plain people remembered his words at Gettysburg, pleading that "these dead shall not have died in vain" and for "a new birth of freedom." They were determined that both should become fact. Labor served notice that in the future it would expect more of the wealth it produced. At Faneuil Hall in Boston at a great mass meeting of Massachusetts workers it was resolved that:

"While we rejoice that the rebel aristocracy of the South has been crushed . . . we yet want it to be known that the workingmen of America will demand in the future a more equal share of the wealth their industry creates . . . and a more equal participation in the privileges and blessings of those free institutions, defended by their manhood on many a bloody field of battle."

The Negro people, whose troops had suffered thirty-five per cent greater casualties than any of their comrades-in-arms, also had their demands. "We are men; treat us as such!" said Louisiana Negroes in a petition to President Lincoln before his death and in South Carolina the former slaves, meeting in convention, demanded equality before the law, equality in schools, and equality in land.

On May 23–24, 1865, there was the Grand Review in Washington of Grant's Army of the Potomac, of Sherman's Army of the Tennessee. The endless clatter of cavalry, the crash and swell of military bands, the battle-torn banners, the queer silences in which the only sound was the scrape of marching feet and then a bugle curling far away as if sounding Taps for the vast dead silenced the onlookers with emotions too complex for cheering. And many wept when the marching men sang *The Battle Hymn of the Republic.*

"He has sounded forth the trumpet that shall never call retreat,
He is sifting out the hearts of men before his judgment seat,
Oh! be swift, my soul, to answer Him! be jubilant, my feet!"

The ragged, sinewy men, victors in history's fiercest war, swept endlessly by, their bayonets gleaming in the soft spring sunlight. Their thousand-voiced battle hymn faded into the distance and into history. But it echoed long on the air and everywhere the steps of men were jubilant.

And in the general confidence the foreign-born, the Abolitionists, and trade unionists hoped they had heard the last of the old, old charge that they were conspirators, foreign agents, intent on overthrowing the government by force and violence. All had fought on "many a bloody field of battle" against the real conspirators, the real users of force and violence, and these had not been the poor, but the ruling class that now ruled no more.

7. Gone the Glory

The age was fat and the glory was gone. Never before had there been such open, all-pervading corruption, such a universal fever for riches gained any way and anyhow. It was a time of lavish *soirées* and dark tenements, of high silk hats and cold hunger. The new tycoons were just beginning to import castles, stone by stone, from Europe as they cast uneasy eyes at culture and angled for titles and marriage for their daughters. And in the cold, outside the imported castles and elsewhere, the men in blue, no longer victorious members of the Army of the Potomac but desperate members of the army of the unemployed, wondered if it was for this they had fought.

Jubilee Jim Fisk, his fat hands studded with diamonds, his ample girth resplendent in flowing capes and fancy vests, was a public hero now in 1866 as he protected himself with a sword-cane from irate husbands and investors. In his late twenties at the end of the war, one of the band of youth that had made theirs while others were dying, Fisk was a pupil and ally of wily old Daniel Drew, owner of the Erie Railroad. So was young Jay Gould, of the dark beard and darker eye, soon to cheat old Cornelius Vanderbilt of $6,000,000 through the sale of counterfeit Erie bonds before robbing Drew himself of his railroad.

The plain living and high thinking of an Adams or Jefferson had become a quaint anachronism, as dead as the valor of Gettysburg. William H. Tweed, Tammany boss, was looting the New York City treasury of an estimated $200,000,000 while General George B. McClellan, erstwhile commander of the Union armies and Democratic nominee for the Presidency in 1864, was backing a $10,000,000 corporation built on a nonexistent ruby field in California. General Robert C. Schenck, author of a monograph on winning at poker and American minister to the Court of St. James, was contributing to Anglo-American friendship by defrauding his British friends of $50,000 through the sale of fraudulent stocks. Andrew Carnegie was already making so much money that he feared he was being debased for all time. As he wrote shortly after the war's close, "To continue much longer with most of my thoughts wholly upon the way to make more money in the shortest time, must degrade me beyond hope of permanent recovery."

Despite all this it was with jubilant feet that labor delegates poured into Baltimore on a hot and sultry day in August, 1866. They had a right to jubilance as they glanced up at a banner stretching the width of the Rayston Building and proclaiming, "Welcome to the Sons of Toil from North, South, East and West." In the face of the postwar depression and bitter employer attack, they were about to form the first successful nationwide labor organization, to succeed where similar attempts had failed in the thirties, forties, and fifties.

The year since victory had been a tough one, the new birth of freedom beginning with lockouts and the imprisonment of strike leaders in the North and the Memphis and New Orleans massacres of Negroes in the South. All during 1866 the labor press was filled with the refrain that labor must unite or die. Many locals had been shattered and the membership lists of national unions were low. "Capital is centralizing, organizing and becoming more powerful every day," warned the Rochester *Daily Union and Advertiser*, adding that only a national organization could "save the labor movement from destruction."

Everywhere employers were combining into associations to fight labor, locally as in New York City, Buffalo, St. Louis, and Boston, on a statewide basis as in Michigan, on a national scale in the case of foundry owners. The American National Stove Manufacturers and Iron Founders Association had been formed in 1866 when almost its first act was a lockout of the iron molders, starting in Albany and Troy and spreading westward until ten local unions were involved in a life-and-death fight.

As unemployment increased in the North with the sudden cessation of war contracts and with demobilization, Southern planters, intent on saving their system by replacing slavery with peonage through debt and vagrancy laws, had instigated mass killings of Negroes in Memphis on May 1, 2, and 3, 1866, when forty-six Negroes were taken from their homes and lynched. And as 5,000 iron molders, locked out in Pittsburgh, their leaders jailed on conspiracy charges, were entering their seventh month of semi-starvation, forty-five more Negroes were slain in New Orleans.

The paramount question facing every sector of the American people, but above all labor, was the fate of the Negro people. The question, simply put, was whether the Negro people were to be enslaved again after the bloody war to free them. As the delegates converged on Baltimore many labor voices were raised in the declaration that labor and the Negro people, both under mounting attack, must join together or be defeated separately. Sylvis, who had worked himself into exhaustion and a breakdown by his efforts to bring about the Baltimore founding convention, sent word that it should not only unite labor but organize an independent political party composed of labor, the Negro people, and the farmers.

Acutely conscious of the growing power of finance, Sylvis wrote of the Negro people, "If we can succeed in convincing these people to make common cause with us . . . we will have a power . . . that will shake

Wall Street out of its boots." To those trade unionists who were advocating rejecting Negro proffers of cooperation, he said:

"The line of demarcation is between the robbers and the robbed, no matter whether the wronged be the friendless widow, the skilled white mechanic or the ignorant black. Capital is no respecter of persons and it is in the very nature of things a sheer impossibility to degrade one class of labor without degrading all."

Labor should join hands with the Negro in basic self-interest, not for the sake of the former slave but for the benefit of the working white man, said the Boston *Daily Evening Voice* not long before the Baltimore convention. Indicting President Johnson's efforts to restore the Southern planters to power while denying the Negro people the vote, civil rights, and land, the labor paper declared:

"Capital knows no difference between white and black laborers; and labor cannot make any, without undermining its own platform and tearing down the walls of its defence. The whole united power of labor is necessary to the successful resistance of the united power of capital."[18]

But most delegates meeting in Baltimore's Rayston Building were unimpressed by these arguments. In the first place there was still much prejudice in labor's ranks against the Negro, but more important still the delegates were on fire with their demand for a shorter working day. An eight-hour day without decrease in pay was what they wanted above all else, wanting it so fiercely that almost every other plan or reform seemed academic and remote. Working from the darkness of early morning to the black of night, too exhausted when work was done to do anything but collapse into the bed from which they would too soon arise, they said that this demand, if won, would change them from drudges into men.

As the delegates milled about the lobby before the first session little Ira Steward, middle-aged Massachusetts mechanic whose private monomania for shorter hours had become a national crusade, was snatching at the lapels of his colleagues, trying to hold them still as he argued for the immediate passage of his resolution calling for the eight-hour day. Little argument was necessary but he talked on anyway about his reform as he had been doing for a decade. A brown, gnome-like man, Steward could speak of little else. "Meet him any day as he steams along the street," wrote a contrib-

18 The argument used by the Boston *Daily Evening Voice* was valid almost a century later. See Chapter VIII. As late as 1947 the median wage of white workers was $1,980; of non-white, chiefly Negro, $863, a difference of $1,117. Multiplying this difference by the number of Negro workers gainfully employed in 1947 (about 3,500,000), Victor Perlo in his book *American Imperialism* finds that monopoly extorts annually almost four billions of dollars from the Jim-Crow system (pp. 88–89). The unorganized South, which President Franklin D. Roosevelt called the nation's number one economic problem, still drags down all wages and the entire labor movement.

utor to the *American Workman,* ". . . and although he will apologize
and excuse himself if you talk of other affairs . . . if you will only introduce 'hours of labor' . . . he will stop and plead with you until night-fall."

"Whether you work by the piece or work by the day, decreasing the hours
increases the pay," the delegates, red-faced and sweating in the fierce
Baltimore heat, chanted in unison, their voices thundering through the hall.
The jingle had been written by Steward's wife, Mary. For Steward said,
and millions agreed, that reduction in hours without a decrease in pay
would necessitate a larger labor force resulting in increased purchasing
power which would end depressions, increase production, and usher in
Utopia. It would bring opportunity for learning and development to the
workingman, as well as sweet rest, while solving all the ills of society.

With a whoop and a holler the delegates passed their eight-hour resolution which declared:

"The first and great necessity of the present to free the labor of this country
from capitalistic slavery is the passing of the law by which eight hours shall be
the normal working day in all states of the American Union."

They did little else, for this was a panacea and little else was thought necessary. Their action launched a great movement which ran with express speed
from the Atlantic to the Pacific, from New England to California. Eight-
hour Leagues were established all over the country. In California alone
there would be more than fifty by 1868. Even farmers were joining Grand
Eight-hour Leagues; state organizations working for the reform had
already been established in Illinois, Indiana, Michigan, and Iowa while
nearly all the unions in New York City were represented in the Central
Eight-hour League formed there in 1866. Such was the massive organized
strength behind the measure that in 1868 the federal government passed an
eight-hour law for workers employed by it. Six states also enacted legislation
providing for the eight-hour day. For a time union members thought they
had won but it soon became apparent that the laws were only political
demagogy in statute form, containing so many loopholes that they were, as
they were meant to be, impossible of enforcement.

In appraising the founding of the National Labor Union, Sylvis criticized
the convention for its lack of action on Negro-labor solidarity. He deplored
the fact that not even a recommendation was made for inclusion of Negro
workers into existing trade unions. With others Sylvis drafted an appeal
addressed to "American Trade Unionists" which was issued by the National
Labor Union in 1867 and said in part:

"Negroes are four million strong and a greater proportion of them labor with
their hands than can be counted from the same number of any people on earth.
Can we afford to reject their proffered co-operation and make them enemies?
By committing such an act of folly we would inflict greater injury upon the
cause of labor reform than the combined efforts of capital could furnish. . . . So

capitalists north and south would foment discord between the whites and blacks and hurl one against the other as interest and occasion might require to maintain their ascendancy and continue their reign of oppression."

At the same time Sylvis was pressing for the admission of women into the trade union movement[14] and for affiliation of the NLU with the International Workingmen's Association. Every ally everywhere and anywhere was needed, he said, for the labor movement was being slowly strangled by the grip of business, ever centralizing and ever growing stronger. The Molders Union was fighting for its very life, the lockouts and strikes forced upon it between 1866 and 1868 costing the union almost $1,000,000 in strike funds. As the strikes continued draining the union treasury Sylvis began to think that something more than trade unions and independent political action was needed to protect the interests of the workingman.

As Sylvis read of Drew and Vanderbilt, Gould and Fisk making daily killings through the manipulation of stocks on Wall Street while poverty steadily spread, he was slowly concluding that fundamental action was needed to break what he called "the money power" and replace it with something other than the profit system. "Capital," he said, "blights and withers all it touches. It is a new aristocracy, proud, imperious, dishonest, seeking only profit and exploitation of the workers."

At about the time Sylvis uttered these words old Drew, the millionaire manipulator of Erie Railroad stocks, was making additional millions on

[14] Speaking on the subject of women in industry, Sylvis said: "As men struggling to maintain an equitable standard of wages and to dignify labor, we owe it to consistency if not to humanity to guard and protect the rights of female labor as well as our own. How can we hope to reach the social elevation for which we all aim without making women the companion of our advancement?" Nevertheless most men and most trade unions regarded women workers, whose numbers had mightily increased during the Civil War, as a menace who drove wages down by taking underpaid jobs when they should have remained at home.

Virtually every trade union refused to admit them, despite the fact that they had been pioneers in the labor movement, inaugurating the trade union press with such papers as *The Lowell Offering* and *The Factory Girl*. They had, moreover, conducted some of the earliest mass strikes in American history, 5,000 young women striking in September, 1845, for example, in the cotton mills of Pittsburgh and Allegheny City where they received $2.50 for a seventy-two-hour week and where they broke down the factory gates and hauled out scabs.

Under Sylvis' leadership the NLU voted to admit women as delegates to its conventions, passed a resolution asking that all trade unions admit women to membership, and others demanding equal pay for equal work and the eight-hour day for women. Kate Mullaney, president of the Collar Laundry Women's Union of Troy, N.Y., was appointed assistant secretary and national organizer for women.

Under the stimulus of the NLU the Cigar Makers International Union amended its constitution to admit women in 1867 and the National Typographical Union took similar action in 1872. Yet, despite all this, most trade unions continued to bar women. Labor leaders were active in the woman suffrage movement and Susan B. Anthony and Elizabeth Cady Stanton, pioneer fighters for women's rights, attended the NLU convention in 1868.

Wall Street by endlessly selling high and buying low, contriving to send the market up or down at his will, as he fed out or drew in his endless series of Erie stocks.[15] When he had a good day he was fond of making a contribution to some church but if his day was disappointing he would retire to his bedside with a bottle of whisky. There he would plop down on his knees, alternately beseeching God and swigging whisky.

His arch-antagonist was the great-domed Cornelius Vanderbilt, a bald and craggy old man with a genius for invective, possessor of the nation's largest fortune, which included the New York Central Railroad. Between them Drew and Vanderbilt spent millions in bribing the New York City Council and the New York State Legislature, each seeking special privileges for his railroad at the expense of the other. The law was good for little beyond a laugh. When a judge remonstrated with Vanderbilt for prostrating the country for his private profit, the old man said, "Can't I do what I want with my own?" Rival railroads, including Erie and the New York Central, were hiring armies of thugs and fighting pitched battles for the possession of lines coveted by both—the imperial Morgan, still young and always practical, directing one such army from afar against the forces of Jubilee Jim Fisk.

Despite gargantuan postwar corruption railroads were actually being built, increasing from 31,000 miles in 1860 to 53,000 in 1870, joining the nation together but also bringing it under the ruthless power of a small group of men. The postwar depression produced unemployment and hunger but it did not seem to retard seriously the progress of industry. Between 1860 and 1870 the total value of manufactured products alone increased by over 100 per cent, from 1.9 billions of dollars to 4.2 billions of dollars. Fixed capital invested in industry rose from $1,010,000,000 in 1859 to $1,695,000,000 in 1869. Fortunes were being made in oil, coal, iron, timber, copper, beef, gold, and silver but the country was being despoiled as eroded lands and dust bowls would prove some generations hence. As the robber barons ripped their billions from the lovely American earth, they left gaping wounds, treeless and bare to sun, wind, and rain.

Their colossal larceny impoverished the people, too. Foster Rhea Dulles, writing of the period's constantly growing fortunes, adds:

"Yet at the same time millions lived in abject poverty in densely packed slums. . . . They struggled merely to maintain their families above the level of brutal hunger and want . . . the great majority [working] such long hours for such little pay that their status was a tragic anomaly in the light of the prosperity generally enjoyed by business and industry."

Money, farmers said, was as scarce as hen's teeth. They were suffering from exorbitant freight rates while agricultural prices had fallen disastrously

[15] A Wall Street saying of the time concerning Daniel Drew and Erie stock was "Daniel says 'up'—Erie goes up. Daniel says 'down'—Erie goes down. Daniel says 'wiggle-waggle'—it bobs both ways!"

since the end of the Civil War. Many were in debt for binders and reapers bought during these years. Increasingly farmers, middle-class liberals, and labor leaders were demanding currency reform as the way out, the conviction becoming widespread that if more greenbacks were issued, if money was only easier to come by and uncontrolled by a financial oligarchy, the country's troubles would be over. As Sylvis, Trevellick, and other leaders of the NLU came under the sway of the greenback panacea, they also decided they would directly attack private ownership by having trade unions enter into business themselves as producers' cooperatives, dividing the profits among the workers in a given enterprise.

"Divide the profits," Sylvis said, "among those who produce them and drive the non-producers to honorable toil or starvation." After 1867 locals of the Molders Union, as well as unions of bakers, coachmakers, shipwrights, mechanics, blacksmiths, shoemakers, hatters, printers, and others, did in fact set up producers' cooperatives, particularly after they had been locked out. They were spectacularly successful for a time, not only dividing profits but instituting the eight-hour day while they paid the prevailing wage, but one by one they failed for lack of capital and credit. Sylvis was voicing the opinion of thousands of the NLU's members when he declared that the cooperatives were failing because of Wall Street's control of money and credit. This control could be broken, he declared, only by running an independent ticket in which labor, farmers, the Negro people, and the city middle classes backed a Greenback program of more and easier money.

In 1867 the convention of the NLU again avoided action on the admission of Negroes into the labor movement and in 1868, when Sylvis was elected president of the organization, it again side-stepped the issue. On the very eve of the 1869 convention Sylvis died suddenly at the age of forty-one. His family did not even have enough money to bury him and was forced to borrow one hundred dollars. But he had the fervent love of American labor and had himself said not long before he died, "It is a matter of honest pride to me to know that my humble efforts in the cause of humanity and social reform are appreciated by my fellow workingmen everywhere."

The convention of 1869 was in a way a monument to Sylvis. Labor leaders who could not be convinced by Sylvis alive were in their grief convinced by Sylvis dead. At long last Negroes were admitted to the convention, nine of the 142 delegates being Negroes, and a resolution was passed which declared:

"The National Labor Union knows no North, no South, no East, no West, neither color nor sex on the question of the rights of labor, and urges our colored fellow members to form organizations in all legitimate ways, and send their delegates from every state in the Union to the next congress."

For a moment it seemed as if the long cleavage, extending back through two hundred years of slavery, between black and white labor was to be no more. As Isaac Myers, Negro delegate from the Colored Caulkers Trade

Union of Baltimore, made a remarkable speech, it appeared as if surely the old policy of divide and conquer would be thenceforth fruitless. Describing slavery as the main cause of the degradation of white labor, Myers said:

"Gentlemen, silent but powerful and far-reaching is the revolution inaugurated by your act in taking the colored laborer by the hand and telling him that his interest is common with yours, and that he should have an equal chance in the race of life. . . .

"Slavery, or slave labor, the main cause of the degradation of white labor, is no more. And it is the proud boast of my life that the slave himself had a large share in the work of striking off the fetters that bound him by the ankle while the other end bound you by the neck."

Within six years of its birth the NLU was dead, killed by its abandonment of trade union principles, by its preoccupation with currency reform. Its program of greenbackism gradually drove from its ranks all but the cranks on money. As early as 1868 two-thirds of its membership of 600,000 were not members of the labor movement but doctors, lawyers, farmers, preachers, editors, and others of the middle class who were not interested in strikes and thought agitation for an eight-hour day or other labor goals were side issues. The only worthwhile aim, they said, was the reformation of all society. When the NLU's leaders declared after the 1869 convention that "no permanent reform can ever be established through the agency of the Trade Unions," the trade unions began to withdraw, the Bricklayers, the Cigar Makers, the National Typographical Union, and others. At the 1871 convention there were only two delegates from the labor movement.

The 1869 convention had authorized the formation of a third party, the National Labor Reform Party, and entry into the Presidential campaign of 1872 on a platform that provided little or nothing but currency reform. The platform and the election results dealt a fatal blow to the NLU, the new party polling a little less than 30,000 votes. The Negro people, whom Sylvis had hoped to enlist in the third party, found nothing in greenbackism which would aid them in gaining civil rights, land, jobs, and the right to vote. They remained loyal to the Republican Party, which in the late sixties was still backing their bloody fight for the democratic reconstruction of the plantation economy in the South but which was soon to betray them. Labor's demands for higher wages, shorter hours, and the right to organize found no real reflection in the program of the National Labor Reform Party. In 1872, after the election, only seven delegates attended the NLU convention and it never met again.

For those who had worked and sweated and hoped to bring the first national labor federation into being, its death was only one event in what they sometimes believed to be a universal defeat for all progress. Too harried by such events as the death of the NLU to see an underlying, basic progress, labor leaders sometimes forgot that slavery had been defeated and the conditions created for a great forward thrust of both capital and labor. The founding of the NLU, with its pioneer fight for Negro-labor solidarity, the rights of women, independent political activity, and international labor solidarity, had been a great step forward despite its weaknesses and despite its defeat. And the very existence of such a national labor center had done much to improve the conditions of wage earners throughout the country.

When the cost of living began to drop after the Civil War, organized labor did not permit money wages to follow suit. As a result of its militant strikes and other demonstrations of strength, it forced wages up so that by the end of the sixties they were over 60 per cent higher than at the beginning. In the building trades and mining, where unions could be found, wages were almost doubled and tripled respectively during the decade. In the mining industry union workers were receiving 40 per cent more than nonunion labor. In 1869 the real wages of workers (that is, what their wages could buy) were a little higher than in 1860. Organized labor also improved working conditions by lowering the hours of work. Furthermore, as a result of the NLU's agitation for an eight-hour day, the average working day for all labor was reduced from 11 hours in 1865 to 10.5 in 1870.

Yet it was true enough that labor and the Negro people, having failed in building an alliance, were each under a separate and growing attack and each increasingly without allies. In the South Negroes were being lynched by the Ku Klux Klan, one hundred being slaughtered in Kentucky alone in the single year of 1871. In the North wages were being generally slashed after having been slowly built up since the end of the Civil War. Perhaps the predominant note of a corrupt age had been sounded by Jubilee Jim Fisk who, after a Congressional investigation into his dishonesty in one deal, had jovially exclaimed, "Cheer up, my hearty! Nothing is lost save honor!" Graft and industry, ever pyramiding in strength, seemed triumphant, both booming as never before under the administration of General Grant, elected on the Republican ticket in 1868, re-elected in 1872.[16]

Stocks, bonds, and bribes had won the day. With the death of the National Labor Union, the assault on the working people of America increased in intensity and soon wages dropped to around a dollar a day.

16 Grant's entire administration was infested with graft. Cabinet officers, Congressmen, and even Grant's brother-in-law, Abel R. Corbin, helped Jay Gould corner the nation's gold supply in a speculation that made millions for Gould, Fisk, and their allies while ruining their competitors. W. A. Richardson, Secretary of the Treasury, hastily resigned to avoid Congressional censure. Schuyler Colfax, the Vice President; James A. Garfield, a future President; Senator Patterson of New Hampshire, and Representative Oakes Ames of Massachusetts were involved in bribes paid in connection with the construction of the transcontinental Union Pacific Railroad which had been completed on May 10, 1869. Grant's private secretary, O. E. Babcock, was involved in the so-called Whisky Ring of the time while W. W. Belknap, Secretary of War, resigned in 1876 to escape impeachment for bribe-taking.

CHAPTER II

"Give Them a Rifle Diet"

CHICAGO IN POSSESSION OF COMMUNISTS
New York Times, July 25, 1877

COMMUNISTS IN CHICAGO . . . THIRTEEN KILLED
New York Tribune, July 28, 1877

PITTSBURG SACKED: THE CITY COMPLETELY IN POWER
. . . OF DEVILISH SPIRIT OF COMMUNISM
New York World, July 22, 1877

1. End of the Great Barbecue

There were small warnings of the great disaster coming but for the most part, Mark Twain found, they were ignored. Instead, he wrote, "joy sat on every countenance, and there was a glad, almost fierce, intensity in every eye that told of money-getting schemes that were seething in every brain." Unnoted were the signs that the Great Barbecue was ending.[1] Lost was the significance of such a fact as that Boss Tweed had actually been indicted for his multimillioned graft; or that jet-bearded Jay Gould had been threatened with prison before he was ousted from the Erie, escaping to the West with other plans for plunder in his mind and several millions of dollars in his bags. Even the slaying of gaudy Jim Fisk who had jovially

[1] Vernon Louis Parrington in his *Main Currents in American Thought* describes the Civil War and postwar pillage of American resources by the robber barons as a great feast, a Great Barbecue, in which Congress served the already fat with course after course of the nation's best. He writes: "Congress had rich gifts to bestow—in lands, tariffs, subsidies, favors of all sorts; and when influential citizens made their wishes known to the reigning statesmen, the sympathetic politicians were quick to turn the government into the fairy godmother the voters wanted it to be. A huge barbecue was spread to which all were presumably invited. Not quite all, to be sure; inconspicuous persons who were at home on the farm or at work in the mills and offices, were overlooked; a good many indeed out of the total number of the American people. But all the important persons, leading bankers and promoters and businessmen, received invitations. There wasn't room for everybody and these were presumed to represent the whole. It was a splendid feast."

38

despoiled the public of millions and was shot and killed on Jan. 7, 1872, in a quarrel over love and blackmail, was not remarked upon for what it was—the end of an era.

Agricultural prices were down, wages were falling, but dividends were firm and everyone knew that endless expansion and ever greater prosperity were a permanent characteristic of the American way. To speak of possible panic or coming depression was unpatriotic. If there was any uneasiness it was ignored in the manner of the country's greatest banker, Jay Cooke, who patronizingly declared from his glided, rococo castle, Ogontz, outside of Philadelphia, "I feel an unfailing confidence in the God in whom we put our trust. I do not believe He will desert us."

In this belief, which was the country's, the mania for speculation became even more universal. "Gold was the favorite of the ladies," recalled a contemporary writer. "Clergymen affected mining and petroleum. Lawyers had a penchant for Erie." Even the judgment of the astute was weakened by the common lust. Tom Scott, president of the Pennsylvania Railroad, and the great Jay Cooke himself, were overextended and pressed for funds as European investors began to unload bonds through the sale of which Cooke and Scott were attempting to build great new railway systems, Scott in the Southwest, Cooke in the Northwest.

To the naked eye, however, the country seemed flourishing enough. Miners were digging coal and copper, iron manufacturers were planning to build huge steel mills, there was an ever-increased gold and silver flow from the Comstock Lode and great coke ovens were being operated in Pennsylvania's newly developed Connellsville area. The granaries of the nation were bulging with wheat and corn, factories were humming with activity—and then suddenly there was paralysis. The work of the nation stopped almost as abruptly, and nearly as completely, as if an evil spell had been placed upon it.

This life in death, which is a depression in an industrial society, was heralded by the closing on Sept. 18, 1873, of the great banking house of Jay Cooke and Co. on Third Street in Philadelphia. Cooke, who had not believed that God would desert him, heard about it as he ate breakfast in his castle with President Grant, the latter silent and bashful and yet quietly pleased by all the luxury about him. Cooke did not weep until he left the presence of the President—and then standing behind the closed doors of his bank he turned his face to the wall while the tears trickled from his bright blue eyes and ran in little rivulets down his blond beard.

The economic crisis of 1873, like those that were to follow it in cyclical succession, was due to the fact that private business enterprise, ever ready to increase its already swollen profits, overextended production with the result that there was an overproduction of machinery, iron, lumber, and other producers' goods and of wheat, cotton, textiles, woolens, and other basic commodities—all at the expense of the working people of the country. While employers kept workers' wages below even minimum living standards, they forced their laborers to increase production by working them excessively long hours and by introducing new speed-up techniques. More and more goods were produced at less and less cost with the result that profits went skyrocketing. Instead of more equitably distributing these in the form of higher wages and shorter hours, they took it for themselves, plowing part of it back into more machines and more plants in order to make more money. The consequence of capital taking too much and the people who produced the wealth getting too little was an economic glut that spelled disaster.

Disaster came in 1873 after a boom period unprecedented in American history. In commenting on the prosperous years following the end of the Civil War, Prof. Allan Nevins in his *Emergence of Modern America* writes: "More cotton spindles were set revolving, more iron furnaces were lighted, more steel was made, more coal and copper were mined, more lumber was sawed and hewed, more houses and shops were constructed and more manufacturies of different kinds were established, than during any equal period of our earlier history."

Then came the lean years, six long and terrible years. The textile factory whose very floors and windows had shaken with the endless vibrations of its clacking looms was now silent, its machines as still as if they had been frozen, its long vistas of floor space as empty of workers as a desert. Many mines were now but empty holes in which a shout echoed eerily away until one heard again in the growing silence the small and steady drip of seeping water, the only sound in the earth's blackness. Plows rusted in dusty fields and harvesters stood motionless and unused while corn and wheat withered on the stalk as the growing army of the unemployed called for food.

By 1877 there were as many as three million unemployed. It was estimated that at least one-fifth of the nation's working force would never again be on a payroll. Two-fifths of those employed were working no more than six to seven months a year and less than one-fifth was regularly working. And the wages of those employed had been cut as much as 45 per cent, often to little more than a dollar a day.

Of the thirty national trade unions that had been in being when the depression began, only eight or nine remained by 1877. Lockouts, blacklists, conspiracy charges, and the "loyalty oaths" of their day, the despised "yellow-dog contracts," in which employees were forced to swear they would never join a union, had done in the rest. A trade union member in the United States was "hunted like a mad dog." So a delegation of French trade unionists were told in 1876 when they came to attend the national celebration of the centennial of the Declaration of Independence. Trade unions still extant had been forced to become secret societies, with passwords and recognition signs, as was the case with the slowly growing Knights of Labor, destined soon to be the largest federation of trade unions the country had yet seen.

Great armies of unemployed drifted over the country searching for work while newspapers ceaselessly fulminated against "tramps," maintaining that the hungry could find work if only they wished to. "Half of those out of work could find it if they wanted it," the comfortable declared, but did not explain why the "other" half who wanted it, according to the calculation, could not find it either. In the main, press and clerics maintained it was not a breakdown in industry that was responsible for idleness but a breakdown in character, in the old American traits of making-out and making-do.

But not all was misery. Old Daniel Drew, speaking of the Civil War, had said complacently, "It's good to fish in troubled waters," and Andrew Carnegie, J. P. Morgan, John D. Rockefeller, and others found the remark equally true of depressions. Carnegie, for example, rapidly building his huge steel mills, profiting from the low cost of materials and labor, sententiously declared, "The man who has money during a panic is the wise and valuable citizen." From the depression's wreckage new figures arose, Rockefeller having absorbed hundreds of competitors, J. P. Morgan replacing Cooke as the nation's leading banker, while Henry C. Frick with the help of Andrew Mellon gobbled up the Connellsville coal region, and James J. Hill, Henry Villard, and Edward H. Harriman, profiting from the same general ruin, emerged as the new industrial titans, the possessors of railroads, land grants, and coal fields.

There were not many Fricks or Harrimans, however. All over the country men idled on street corners, sat listlessly in saloons nursing beer bought on the cuff, passed long hours in kitchens staring at the wall wondering what was wrong with themselves and the country. Millions of American men, with that terrible humility that comes when one cannot feed his kids nor withstand their questioning eyes, were deciding that they were failures.

And then a slow anger began to rise. Farmers in the West joined Granges and muttered against Wall Street. In the East there were demonstrations and riots such as that in New York's Tompkins Square whose signs proclaimed "The Unemployed Demand Work, Not Charity" and "When the Workingman Begins to Think, Monopoly Trembles."

At the height of the demonstration it was attacked by police who afterwards held that it was Communistic. "Police clubs," said a contemporary account, "rose and fell. Women and children ran screaming in all directions. Many of them were trampled underfoot. In the streets bystanders were ridden down and mercilessly clubbed by mounted officers." However, a *New York Times* reporter found the scene "not unamusing" and observed, "the persons arrested yesterday seem all to have been foreigners. . . . Communism is not a weed of native growth."

The anger mounted. In Chicago 20,000 workers marched on city hall demanding that the $700,000 which remained from the relief fund for victims of the Chicago fire now be used for victims of unemployment. After a prolonged dispute about 9,700 families were provided with some kind of subsistence from the fund.

"What changes in a century!" wrote one victim of the depression. "Look at our thousands of miles of railroads, our countless mills and factories, our mines and forges, our vast wealth! All created by labor in one century. And what has labor to show for its share in the good things it has produced? Literally nothing. It has neither railroad, factory, forge or mine. Capital has cunningly appropriated everything."

As men talked so their anger continued to rise and so did their needs. There were textile and coal strikes in 1874 and 1875 and as the militancy of the workers increased employers began to worry. Individuals working through the Republican Party began preparing for a new offensive against the trade union movement.

Their first move was to gain a new ally for themselves while denying it to labor. They lived in fear that labor, making common cause with restive farmers, would resurrect the Democratic Party and, in alliance with the South's planters, turn all Republicans out and, worse still, reverse their profit-breeding policies. To avert this they decided to make the Southern planters, stalwarts of the Democratic Party, their allies instead of their opponents. Since 1867 they had given support, however vacillating, to the Negro people in their fight against reenslavement through debtors' laws and for democratic rights in the South. The Republicans had divided the South into five military districts garrisoned by the United States Army, had armed the Negro people for defense of their rights, had disfranchised leading planters while aiding the fight which put more than 700,000 Negroes on the South's voting lists. They had backed, in short, a revolutionary upsurge in the South that had scored great democratic gains but now, pressed by the new threats of the depression, they were in a mood to make allies of their old opponents to prevent the formation of a new and radical Democratic Party. This they were soon to do in a fundamental realignment of political forces that increased the dangers facing labor.

The army that had garrisoned the South was soon to be withdrawn and thrown against Northern workers on strike against depression wage cuts. The Negroes in the meantime were left to the mercies of their ex-masters. Under the new alliance the Democratic Party in the South became to a large extent an appendage of the Republican Party in the North, at least economically, its platforms usually as conservative and as lacking in menace to the wealthy as those of the Republicans themselves. But as this was happening, Northern workers, intent on their own problems, did not connect their own plight with what was happening in the South. "During the years that textile workers and miners were suffering serious setbacks" in the North, James S. Allen writes, "the progressive governments in the South were being replaced by governments dominated by planters and industrialists."[2]

[2] Allen writes of this period in his *Reconstruction*, pp. 188–189: "In general, the temper of the Radical Republicans had changed. The prime obstacle to capitalist expansion had been removed with the abolition of chattel slavery. Restoration of the slave power had been effectively prevented and the financial-industrial bourgeoisie was well en-

Popular movements were being broken both North and South, separately and without either popular force aiding the other. Their enemies combined but the people's movements did not despite the many past warnings of Sylvis and others. Philip S. Foner, writing of reaction's attack, declares, "Preoccupied with their own struggles to gain higher wages and to halt employer offensives, organized workers of the North did not understand that their future was being influenced by the outcome of the struggle for democracy in the South."

The Republican Party's desertion of the Negro people, who fought gallantly on but were slaughtered by the hundreds, did not take place all at once. Rather it was a development over a period of four or five years. But in 1877, as the result of the Hayes-Tilden contest over the Presidency,[3] a formal agreement was made in which the Republicans contracted to permit conservative Southern Democrats to deal with the Negro people as they would. In return Southern Democrats agreed to support the Republican Hayes as well as to aid Northern industrialists against dissatisfied workers and revolting farmers. The Republicans had abandoned the Negroes in the South the better to deal with rising protest in the North—and as they did so they took effective action to prevent the Democratic Party from developing into a farmer-labor vehicle of protest. Thus it was that Negroes were being murdered in Columbia and Spartanburg, S.C.; in Livingston, Ala., and Greggs County, Tex., as troops were being called out against Massachusetts textile workers and Pennsylvania miners fighting through the country's severest depression.

2. The Killer King of the Reading

When Franklin B. Gowen, once known as the King of the Reading Valley in Southeastern Pennsylvania, committed suicide in a lonely Washington hotel room in 1889 it was suggested by some that perhaps his brilliance had verged on insanity throughout his dramatic career. Others said he had taken his life when he felt his powerful but erratic brain losing its grip on

---

trenched. The other tasks of the revolution in the South could be left to work themselves out, although it was a matter of first concern to the Radical Republicans that they maintain political hegemony. Not at the price, however, of social unrest and continued upheaval. Social peace was needed to obtain the full benefits of the new plantation production and the tremendous internal market. The revolt of the farmers and the workers was disquieting enough, and peace in the rear would relieve the bourgeoisie to meet new threats. If peace could be obtained at the price of the hard-won rights of the Negroes, this was but a slight concession to ask of the bourgeoisie. Their hearts, after all, were with the men of property and 'the substantial citizens.' If they could patch up a settlement with these in the South, which would assure peaceful exploitation, it would be much more to their liking."

[3] For further details of the Hayes-Tilden contest, in which Southern Democrats backed the Republican Hayes in exchange for a free hand with the Negroes and other considerations, see pages 58-59.

reality. It was hinted then, as men discussed his solitary ending, that he had been near insanity even as his fevered eloquence sent nineteen Pennsylvania union miners to their deaths.

But that was sixteen years after he had led employers in a rapidly rising trustified industry against one of the earliest of the nation's industrial unions. Then he was hailed as the foremost of industrial statesmen, the country's savior, described as a genius, and feted for his victory over labor even in far-off London.

Gowen's fame reached its greatest height during the depression of 1873. Then, as head of the country's first effective coal trust as well as of the Philadelphia and Reading Railroad, he had charged that the Workingmen's Benevolent Association, a militant industrial union that had been organized by Pennsylvania's anthracite miners, was in reality a foreign conspiracy to overthrow society by force and violence. That charge, and the trials that followed, had shattered the union, resulting in the execution, imprisonment, or banishment of all its leaders.

The story, which was to have a fatal ending for so many, including even Gowen, began, in a sense, on Sept. 6, 1869, when the whistle atop the colliery at the Avondale Mine in Pennsylvania's Luzerne County sent out the sharp, repeated blasts that told of accident. The miners lived, for the most part, on a long street facing the mine entry, and now their wives ran toward the mine shaft, their little children following. Great columns of smoke and fire were billowing out of the only shaft, the only entrance or exit, and the women and children knew that their husbands and fathers were dead men unless they could blast their way to life by forcing a second exit.

One hundred and seventy-nine men were down in the bowels of the earth frantically digging as the smoke choked and blinded them, perhaps thinking even in their frenzy of their wives and children waiting on the ground above. The wives stood there for hours saying little, some holding babies, their older children clutching at their skirts. They kept vigil through the long day, remaining there when night arrived and the flames from the only shaft leaped and licked against the blackness. Occasionally some went back to their cramped, damp, decrepit homes to prepare meals for the children before returning and resuming their long and lonely wait.

The next day the fire still blazed from the shaft opening and no help could descend. Thousands of miners from Luzerne and Schuylkill Counties were packed around the mine entrance, sometimes cursing, mostly silent, occasionally begging to be used in the rescue team that was blasting and tunneling forward in a frantic effort to reach the trapped men. "Thousands of Miners Gather Around the Fatal Shaft," said a *New York Tribune* headline on September 8. "Six Hundred Widows and Orphans Left Destitute." And the story continued, "All work is suspended and the whole force of miners have gone to Avondale until their brothers are brought out dead or alive."

They were brought out dead, all one hundred and seventy-nine, two days after the whistle had rent the air. Because the mine owners had refused to spend the comparatively few dollars needed to construct a second entrance, or escape exit, the men were dead, as so many others had been and would be in Luzerne, Schuylkill, and Carbon Counties in Pennsylvania's anthracite. As the bodies were brought up one by one Irish John Siney, the head of the recently formed Workingmen's Benevolent Association, got up on a wagon, his face contorted with grief, as thousands of miners crowded around. In the sudden hush the distant sound of weeping could be heard. It came from the houses into which the bodies were being carried.

"Men," said Siney when he could speak, "if you must die with your boots on, die for your families, your homes, your country, but do not longer consent to die like rats in a trap for those who have no more interest in you than in the pick you dig with." He paused and when he could go on again he gestured toward the edge of the crowd where the dead bodies were still being carried by and asked the miners to join the union. Thousands of them did so on that day.

The Workingmen's Benevolent Association of Schuylkill County had been formed the year before in 1868,[4] when it went on strike for the eight-hour day. The strike was lost and yet it seemed as if the Irishmen who largely composed the union had a special genius for organization. They spoke of independent political action and insisted upon industrial unionism long before many others spoke for it. They were emphatic in their belief that all those who worked in and about the mines should belong to one big union.

Most of the Irish members of the Workingmen's Benevolent Association had fled the famine and tyranny of their British oppressor. During the forties, fifties, and sixties some 20,000 Irishmen had made their way to Schuylkill County. It was a historic irony that they had stepped from one tyranny into another, from the hangings imposed by the British landlords to the hangings, shootings, and frame-ups inspired by the growing American coal corporations. They had left a green land but it was a black land that they had come to. It was a land of coal and of breakers and tipples and collieries, of soot and culm banks and burning slag and everything that was not black was a gritty gray. The smoke and grime and dirt had even climbed the mountain sides and stunted the greenery of such grim slabs as Sharp and Locust, Brood and Blue, whose precipitous sides loomed bleakly above the grimy coal patches and little cabins in which the miners and their families lived.

They knew what Siney meant when he inferred that joining the union might mean death but that it was better to die fighting for themselves and their union than like rats in the trap of some death-sealed mine. The blackened waters of the Schuylkill River, blue enough where it rose in the

[4] Four years before the Workingmen's Benevolent Society of Carbon County, Pa., was organized.

mountains before it curled through the mining country, had been crimsoned with miners' blood during strikes in the forties and fifties. In 1842 their union had been shot out of existence and when they started another in 1849 it too was smashed after a violent strike.[5] They knew that the powers of the time regarded unionism as a conspiracy in violation of the law, a conspiracy as criminal as a plan to rob a bank. They knew that trade unionists were as much beyond the protection of the law as bank robbers.

But by the time of the Avondale fire a turning point had been reached. Increasingly after that disaster miners flocked into the union. They had had enough. Base pay, according to statistics of the time, was between $11 and $12 weekly for work from dawn to dark. Children, according to a miners' joke, never saw their fathers except on Sundays, when they asked their mothers, "Who's that old man hanging around the house?"

Starvation, at least during strikes, and death from the cold of bitter winters, were not unusual, according to Andrew Roy, historian of the American coal miner. And P. F. McAndrews, clerk of the mining district including Schuylkill County, wrote in 1875, "The miners' occupation . . . is little better than semi-slavery."

Of Schuylkill's 22,000 working in the mines, 5,500 were children, boys between the ages of seven and sixteen who were paid between $1 and $3 a week for separating slate from the coal as it poured down the shoots in the breakers. Old men, or the injured, were sent back to the breakers after a lifetime of work, to end their lives as they had begun them.

But worse than all this was the killing accident rate. When a man left in the morning dark for the mine neither he nor his wife nor his children knew if they would ever see him again. Working up to his knees in water, the slow drip of falling drops soaking him as he labored, he never knew when he would hear the dreadful rip of cracking timbers as rotten scaffolds buckled under the weight of sliding tons of falling coal. Nor did he know at what instant he might see that flash of searing fire that began with an explosion of poisoned gas, the blaze leaping through the lethal air and flashing down the black tunnel until it enveloped and killed the working miners. He knew only that the mine owners without one single exception had refused over the years to install emergency exits, ventilating and pumping systems, or to make provision for sound scaffolding. In Schuylkill County alone 566 miners had been killed and 1,655 had been seriously injured over a seven-year period while in the single year of 1871 some 112 miners of that county were killed and 339 badly injured.

Besides insecurity to life and limb the miners were faced with a terrific

[5] "No part of the world ever presented so favorable an opportunity as the coal regions for the rich to oppress the poor workingman," observed a signed article in the *New York Herald* of June 22, 1877. "In many instances the opportunity was not neglected. The rapacity, extortion and refusal to pay the laborer his just wages are still remembered . . . [and] still exist. Any attempt on the part of the workers to ameliorate their condition was at all hazards immediately crushed. Those who took a prominent part in such movements . . . were 'marked,' 'blacklisted.' "

speed-up. So grueling was the pace that miners often went without food so as to complete their daily work. "A miner tells me," wrote an on-the-spot reporter for *Harper's New Monthly Magazine* (November, 1877), "that he has often brought his food uneaten out of the mine from want of time; for he must have his car loaded when the driver comes for it, or lose one of the seven car-loads which form his daily work."

Among those who joined the union at about this time was an unusual group of young miners who in the struggle that followed proved that their abilities were far above the ordinary. With all the wealth and all of the press, and all of the clergy against them; with the militia, vigilantes, the courts, and the operators' Coal and Iron Police assaulting them; with more than $4,000,000 spent in a mighty effort to crush them, they nevertheless came close to winning. Their abilities were a surprise to almost everyone, for when they later appeared in court as defendants it was seen by the powerful that their antagonists were only young miners. Their backs were bent in the familiar miners' stoop, their hands were calloused, and they had that occupational trait known as Miners' Knees—that is, hard car-buncles over kneecaps from swinging away hour after hour with their picks at the coal in positions so cramped they had to work on their knees. But that was the only time these men were ever on their knees.

Some of them had seen their friends hanged for the wearing of the green in Ireland, and all of them from the first had known that their venture in union-building might lead to as desperate an end. Of their number was big Tom Munley, who had fled Ireland in 1864 after fighting for its liberty, a miner of unusual size and strength with a great flaring mustache, bright red cheeks, and a wife and four children. Another was Mike Doyle, a "strongly built man" of thirty who had "the dogged, defiant expression of a prize fighter." The smiling Ed Kelly, smooth shaven in that age of mustaches and beards, was another who gave power to the new union and with Jim Carroll, Jack Kehoe, Hugh McGeehan, and Tom Duffy, was advocating that the union put up candidates in the county elections. All were members of the Irish fraternal order, the Ancient Order of Hibernians, found in all parts of the country and much like the Masons or the Oddfellows in their activities and ceremonies. In their lodge the group of young Irishmen gradually developed into a caucus that put pressure on Siney and other leaders of the WBA for straight-shooting trade union policies.

These young miners and their colleagues knew at the start that their chief adversary in building their union would be Franklin Benjamin Gowen, himself not much older than they were but whose extraordinary personality was already being felt in every corner of the Reading Valley. In 1869, not long before the Avondale fire, he had been elected, although only thirty-three, to the presidency of the Philadelphia and Reading Railroad which spread "like a giant octopus" over Southeastern Pennsylvania, controlling its economic life. At the same time he was elected president of the railroad's subsidiary, the Philadelphia Coal and Iron Company.

As Munley, Kehoe, Carroll, McGeehan, Doyle, and their friends were organizing coal miners into their union, young Mr. Gowen was also engaged in organizing of a different kind. He was bringing all of the mine operators into an employers' association, the Anthracite Board of Trade. But he was doing more than that. At the same time he was organizing a monopoly in coal, his railroad a powerful device for getting his way. If a rival operator failed to succumb to his terms he boosted his freight rate or even refused to haul his coal to market. Using these methods he had acquired two-thirds of the coal mines of southeastern Pennsylvania where all the important deposits of anthracite in this hemisphere are contained in 484 square miles.

More important than this to the miners in the Ancient Order of Hibernians, Gowen seemed to be bringing John Siney, president of the union, under the sway of his magnetic personality. They were seen together frequently and increasingly Siney began to talk of the harmful tendency inherent in strikes and of how arbitration was the proper policy for a trade union.

Gowen already had the reputation of being irresistible. He radiated a kind of animal charm and when he spoke people hung on his words as if hypnotized. It was said that he could convince the most stubborn that black was white and he had been good enough to wheedle several millions out of English investors for his Philadelphia and Reading Railroad. A plunger, a taker of chances, ever trying to expand, his ambition was as boundless as his confidence and many of his stockholders eyed him with distrust from the beginning.

Rather British in his affectations, he had participated in the first game of cricket ever played at Pottsville, capital of anthracite, where he had been the district attorney as a young man after buying a substitute to serve in his place in the Union Army during the Civil War. His father, an emigrant from Northern Ireland, had been a sympathizer with the South and slavery, sending his son to a private school attended by the sons of plantation owners and the ironmasters of Schuylkill County. One of Gowen's favorite pastimes was the writing of limericks and another was the translation of German poetry. There is ample evidence that he saw himself as a hero who was to ride to national fame by his demonstration to the country's employers of the proper way of handling the growing labor problem.

At first Gowen, working through Siney, welcomed the union. He believed he could use it to further his own plans. The price of coal was falling, Gowen believed, because of overproduction. A strike or two, he thought, would raise prices by decreasing the supply of coal on hand. There was a strike in 1869 which was terminated when the operators, under Gowen's leadership, recognized the union. It now had 30,000 members, or eighty-five per cent of the miners in Pennsylvania's anthracite, as well as a written agreement signed on July 29, 1870. This was the first written contract between organized miners and operators in the history of the United States.

But the miners made the mistake of tying their wages to the price of coal. They did, however, include a minimum below which wages could not be cut in the event the price of coal went down. If it fell to less than three dollars a ton there would be no further pay cuts. The miners were betting on a rise in coal prices, and therefore of wages, but they lost their bet. As the price plunged downward so did their wages, which were slashed in some instances by almost fifty per cent. When the price dipped below three dollars a ton, Gowen wished to continue wage cuts unhampered by the minimum wage provision. When the union resisted wage cuts below the minimum stipulated in the contract Gowen determined to smash the union.

With the arrival of the depression of 1873 Gowen's plight became serious. He needed some great event in which to play the part of hero to recoup his sagging prestige. Before his career was over, his biographer Schlegel reports, Gowen was to borrow "millions upon millions to make the Reading Railroad one of the largest corporations the world had ever known," and he was already overextended. "Hard times and investments of a questionable nature on the part of the Philadelphia and Reading had placed Gowen at a disadvantage in the eyes of the stockholders, but if he could deal a death blow to organized labor . . . he would amply redeem himself in the public eye."[6] In addition an antimonopoly league was being formed in which dealers were charging him with selling coal short-weight, withholding freight cars fom rivals, delaying their shipments, and conspiring to control production.

As he brooded over his troubles, still confident that he was a genius destined to conquer all, it seemed to him that the primary source of his difficulties was the miners' union. Only by greatly reducing wages could he buttress his shaky financial position. But more than the miners' union, it was that group of young Irish miners in the Ancient Order of Hibernians who were standing in his way. It was they who opposed Siney when he talked of a reasonable attitude and arbitration instead of strikes and it was they who advocated strike rather than suffer a cut below the contract's minimum wage. If Gowen could get rid of Munley, Doyle, McGeehan, Kelly, Carroll, Kehoe, Duffy, and the progressives they led in the miners' union, he could have clear sailing. At first he thought he would charge them with being Communists and, in fact, as late as 1875 he testified before a committee of the Pennsylvania legislature that the group was composed of foreign agents, "advocates of the Commune and emissaries of the International."

This charge was a queer slip on Gowen's part because two years before he had called in Allan Pinkerton of the detective agency and, in employing him and his agency to break the union and its progressive caucus in the

6 J. Walter Coleman, *The Molly Maguire Riots. Industrial Conflict in the Pennsylvania Coal Region*, pp. 70-71.

Ancient Order of Hibernians, he had told another story. Then, to Pinkerton, and usually later, although he occasionally reverted to his charge that the progressive miners were Communists, he said that the Irish miners were members of a secret Irish terroristic organization whose end was the destruction of society.

The progressive miners, he told Pinkerton, were members of a band, formed in Ireland and brought to the United States, known as the Molly Maguires. Their goal was the seizure of power, their method was murder. They were using both the Ancient Order of Hibernians and the miners' union to conceal and further their conspiracy.

A good number of historians now concede that there was never any organization in Pennsylvania known as the Molly Maguires—although any militant miner might have been called a Molly Maguire after the newspapers had spread Gowen's charge far and wide. But the Molly Maguires in fact were nothing but a fabrication of the Reading Valley's leading and most eccentric citizen. There was only the Ancient Order of Hibernians, usually called the AOH, its oaths and rituals demanding brotherhood and patriotism.

But as Gowen spoke of his creation to Pinkerton in 1873, his eloquence overcame him and, pacing up and down his office before the detective, he said, according to Pinkerton, that the Irish terroristic society not only dominated southeastern Pennsylvania but most of labor the country over. "Wherever in the United States iron is wrought," he said, according to the detective, "from Maine to Georgia, from ocean to ocean—wherever hard coal is used as fuel, there the Molly Maguire leaves his slimy trail and wields with deadly effect his two powerful levers, secrecy and combination."

Pinkerton, duly convinced, declared that he could not begin to consider the case without a retainer of $100,000.[7] His mind just could not function until stimulated by such a fee. After obtaining the necessary stimulation he told Gowen that the operative whom he would send into the coal fields

[7] Pinkerton, born in Scotland and once a radical himself, was the founder of modern industrial spying. His first clients were Gowen, Tom Scott of the Pennsylvania Railroad, and other railroad managements. His agency, inherited by his sons and still in existence, became larger and larger as strikes in the seventies and eighties made the hiring of labor spies big business. In the 1930's the La Follette Civil Liberties Committee revealed that the agency was still receiving hundreds of thousands of dollars yearly for supplying leading corporations with labor spies. According to the committee, the Pinkertons had a gross annual income of over two million dollars in 1934 and 1935 and Robert A. Pinkerton, the head of the agency, received from it in dividends alone $129,500 in 1935, a sum much in excess of the salary of the President of the United States. The author of some twenty books about his exploits, Allan Pinkerton wrote in 1878 of his literary work, "My extensive and perfected detective system has made this work easy for me where it would have been hardly possible for other writers; for since the strikes of '77, my agencies have been busily employed by great railway, manufacturing and other corporations, for the purpose of bringing the leaders and instigators [of strikes] to the punishment they so richly deserve. Hundreds have been punished. Hundreds more will be punished."

must be a man who would have no more doubts than Gowen. For, as Pinkerton stated in his book about the Molly Maguires, an ordinary operative might think that Gowen was engaged in "persecution for opinion's sake" or that his plan of breaking the miners' union was only "a conflict between capital on one side and labor on the other."

After considerable thought Pinkerton selected as his leading spy for the coal fields one James McParlan, a twenty-nine-year-old native of Ireland who Pinkerton felt sure would not be bothered by any feelings that his victims were being persecuted for their belief in trade unionism. McParlan seemed a merry fellow, ever ready for a fight or a frolic, until one looked into his eyes. They were as cold as a cobra's. He had red hair, a sweet tenor voice, a large capacity for whiskey, and a past said to include a murder in Buffalo. His assignment was to join the Ancient Order of Hibernians and get or manufacture evidence upon which such militant union members as Duffy, Carroll, McGeehan, Kehoe, Kelly, Munley, and their friends could be hanged. Since Gowen believed that the union miners were criminal conspirators, that trade unions themselves were criminal conspiracies, the Pinkerton operative was not particular as how he was to settle with men believed to be beyond the law.

For two years McParlan, using the name of McKenna and receiving $12 a week and expenses, traveled the coal fields but was unable to obtain any evidence of crime committed by the miners. He was successful, however, in joining the AOH. He spent most of his time in saloons, occasionally joining in a brawl, always suggesting violence as the only course against the operators, and now and again raising his voice in song.

But fine as McParlan was as a singer, he was discovering no murders. His expected frame-ups were slow in coming and in 1874 the union still stood firm against a paycut despite the falling price of coal. Gowen decided to force a strike and showdown. A contemporary writer and confidant of Gowen, one F. P. Dewees, later wrote that by 1873 "Mr. Gowen was fully impressed with the necessity of lessening the overgrown power of the 'Labor Union' and exterminating if possible the Molly Maguires." He could wait no longer on McParlan and in December, 1874, the operators, under Gowen's leadership, announced a twenty per cent cut. The miners went out on strike Jan. 1, 1875.

From the first it was war, Gowen trying for the absolute extermination upon which Dewees wrote he was determined. Led by the president of the Philadelphia and Reading, the operators unleashed a reign of terror, hiring and arming a band of vigilantes who took the name of the "Modocs" and who joined the corporation-owned Coal and Iron Police in waylaying, ambushing, and killing militant miners.

Edward Coyle, a leader of the union and of the Ancient Order of Hibernians, was murdered in March. Another member of the AOH was shot and killed by the Modocs led by one Bradley, a mine superintendent. Patrick Vary, a mine boss, fired into a group of miners and, according to the later boast of Gowen, as the miners "fled they left a long trail of blood behind them." At Tuscarora a meeting of miners was attacked by vigilantes who shot and killed one miner and wounded several others. Later terrorists attacked the home of Charles O'Donnell in Wiggins Patch, killing this militant mine worker and murdering Mrs. Charles McAllister.

The miners, under the leadership of the AOH, began to fight back. Soon the state militia patrolled the coal patches, augmenting the Coal and Iron Police, who were responsible to none but the corporations which paid them. Not long later the courts were used to jail mine leaders who were daily being excoriated by the press, each Sunday from altar and pulpit. On May 12 John Siney, who had favored arbitration and had been against calling the strike, was arrested at a mass meeting of strikers in Clearfield County called to protest the importation of strikebreakers.

Xeno Parkes, field organizer for the Miners' National Association with which the Schuylkill union was affiliated, was also arrested along with twenty-six other union officials. They were charged with conspiracy. In his charge to the jury Judge John Holden Owes, in the Siney-Parkes case, declared that "any agreement, combination or confederation to increase or depress the price of any vendible commodity, whether labor, merchandise, or anything else, is indictable as a conspiracy under the laws of Pennsylvania." In sentencing two officials of a local miners' union Judge Owes said, "I find you, Joyce, to be president of the Union, and you, Maloney, to be secretary, and therefore I sentence you to one year's imprisonment."

Although the union was nearly broken by the imprisonment of much of its leadership and the cold-blooded terror and murder of operator-inspired vigilantes, the fight went on, led almost exclusively now by the rank-and-file miners of the Ancient Order of Hibernians. Gowen, in his effort to smash them, deluged the newspapers with stories of murder and arson on the part of the Molly Maguires. The reporters were charmed by the great man who talked to them so freely and soon there was scarcely a strike in the country that was not being attributed to Irish terrorists. As the press inveighed against the alleged Irish secret society, carrying each one of Gowen's fabrications as if it were uncontested fact, it published stories of Molly Maguires inspiring strikes in Jersey City, the Ohio mine fields, and Illinois. The great sensation of the day was the murdering Molly Maguires, the evil laboring men who were out to overthrow society, and the average reader accepted the fabrication as he accepted the fact that the earth was round.

But in Schuylkill County hunger was defeating the miners. "Since I last saw you," wrote one striking miner to a friend, "I have buried my youngest child, and on the day before its death there was not one bit of victuals in the house with six children." And Andrew Roy, in his history of the American coal miner, wrote:

"The miners made heroic sacrifices such as they had never made before to win the strike. In the closing weeks of the contest there were exhibited scenes of woe and want and uncomplaining suffering seldom surpassed. Hundreds of families rose in the morning to breakfast on a crust of bread and a glass of water, who did not know where a bite of dinner was to come from. Day after day, men, women and children went to the adjoining woods to dig roots and pick up herbs to keep body and soul together. . . ."

Defeated after six long months of hunger and bloodshed, the miners went back to work. They were forced to accept the twenty per cent cut. The union was destroyed. Those who had led the strike were blacklisted and many were driven from the anthracite fields.

"We are beaten," admitted John Walsh, Civil War veteran and one of the union leaders who was exiled from the coal country, "forced by the unremitting necessity of wives and little ones to accept terms which we have already told the Coal Exchange and the public, we would never under any other circumstances have been forced to accept." And Joseph F. Patterson, another strike leader, later said, "The organization was broken. The heart was knocked out of the brave fellows who built it up and sustained it."

But the heart was not knocked out of McGeehan, Carroll, and Duffy, nor of Munley, Kehoe, and Doyle and the men they led in the AOH. They fought on, determined to restore miners' wages and rebuild their union. It was then that Gowen apparently decided that any measure was justified in dealing with those whom the courts had found were criminal conspirators in that they were trade unionists. "Many operators," writes Peter Roberts in his *Anthracite Coal Communities,* "then furnished arms to their foremen ... When labor in many instances sought relief, it was answered with an oath supplemented with the pointing of a revolver." Militant miners often disappeared, their bodies sometimes being found later in deserted mine shafts.

When the miners fought back, under the leadership of those in the AOH, Gowen in 1876 summoned McParlan to him. The spy in three years of effort had gathered in nothing but a certain amount of booze and pay. He had obtained no evidence. But Gowen felt, and frankly said, that his own campaign had borne fruit, that public sentiment was such that, "It was sufficient to hang a man to declare him a Molly Maguire."

McParlan agreed to testify, and did testify, that all those whom Gowen wanted removed had freely and voluntarily confessed to him that they had committed various murders. His word was to be corroborated by various prisoners at various of the county's jails, freedom the reward for corroboration. Among those who buttressed McParlan's testimony at the ensuing trials was a prisoner known as Kelly the Bum, who admitted that he had committed every crime in the calendar. Another prisoner was one Jimmy Kerrigan whose wife testified that he himself had committed the murder with which he was charging the miners of the AOH.

The first big trial got under way in May, 1876, when McGeehan, Carroll, and Duffy, as well as two other militant miners, James Boyle and James

Roarity, also members of the AOH, were charged with the murder of Benjamin Yost, a patrolman in the mining community of Tamaqua. Gowen, who ran the whole Reading Valley, saw nothing peculiar in the fact that he had had himself appointed as special prosecutor in this and other trials, his pleasant duty being to ask for the executions of his labor antagonists.

Never had he enjoyed himself so much, his voice sometimes a challenging baritone, sometimes a solemn whisper, his handsome profile thrilling his acquaintances who crowded around him during each court recess. Just as he dominated the anthracite fields, so did he dominate each of the half dozen trials, which resulted in the executions of nineteen miners. He had defense witnesses arrested for perjury as they stepped from the stand. He had the various courthouses and courtrooms filled with the bayonets of the militia while he contrived to give the impression that at any moment a rescue of the defendants might be attempted by Irish foreign agents dedicated to the forcible overthrow of society.

In the first trial, which charged the miners' leaders with the murder of Yost, the actual murderer was apparently Jimmy Kerrigan, who won his own freedom by testifying against the defendants. Kerrigan's wife testified from the stand during the trial that her husband had committed the murder and that he was testifying against the five miners in an agreement with the State and Gowen that he would go free if he aided in convicting the union leaders. Not even Gowen himself, who took over her cross-examination, could shake her story.

Q. You have never seen your husband since that time, have you?   A. No, sir.

Q. Have you refused to send him clothes?   A. Yes, sir.

Q. And do anything for him?   A. Yes, sir.

Q. Did you come down from Pottsville, voluntarily, and of your own will, some time ago, to make a statement or affidavit that your husband had killed Yost; did you not do that of your own motive?   A. I made my statement before I came to Pottsville.

Q. You made it before Squire O'Brien?   A. Yes.

Q. You went there voluntarily?   A. Of my own accord.

Q. To get your husband hung?   A. To tell the truth.

Q. To have the father of your children hung?   A. Not when I was telling the truth.

Q. Why did you not send him clothes when he was lying in prison?   A. Why, because he picked innocent men to suffer for his crime.

Q. Because he picked innocent men to suffer for his crime?   A. Yes, sir.

Q. Why did you refuse to go and see him when he had sent word that he wanted to see you?   A. Because any man that done such a crime that he done, why should I turn around then and—

Q. And what; go on.   A. That is all.

Q. What crime had he done?   A. What crime did he do?
Q. Yes.   A. The crime of Yost.
Q. The murder of Yost?   A. Yes, sir.

There was other testimony describing Kerrigan as the actual murderer of Yost. The only testimony against the five miners, all of whom had been active in the 1875 strike and later, was that of Kerrigan himself, and the Pinkerton spy McParlan, who was engaged to Kerrigan's sister-in-law, Mary Ann Higgins, and who swore that each of the five men had carelessly confessed to him. Little mention was made of the fact that McParlan and Pinkerton were in Gowen's pay although defense attorneys did declare that the trial was Gowen's revenge for the role the defendants had played in the strike of 1875. But such were the time's hysteria and Gowen's power that the jury sent five innocent miners to their deaths.

The same verdict of guilty was handed down in the cases of other innocent miners. Mike Doyle and Ed Kelly received the death sentence. Jack Kehoe was convicted for the murder of one Langdon, a breaker boss, who had been killed fourteen years before. Langdon had been stoned by a crowd of miners and died three days later. Despite Kehoe's own testimony that he had not been at the scene of the stoning, others said that he was in the crowd of miners although there was no testimony that he actually threw a stone. Yet the jury found him guilty of murder in the first degree.

Four other miners were tried and condemned to death for a murder of which they had been previously acquitted and declared innocent. The testimony against them came entirely from McParlan and Kelly the Bum. McParlan said that the four had also happened to confess to him. Kelly the Bum was brought to the stand from the cell where he was being held under a charge of murder, and where he had been heard to say, according to testimony, "I would squeal on Jesus Christ to get out of here." After his testimony the murder charge against him was dismissed.

Gowen had need of all his eloquence in the trial of big Tom Munley, one of the most militant of the union leaders, as there was virtually no evidence against him save McParlan's oft-repeated story of a defendant confessing to him. Even the state's own witnesses declined to identify Munley as the murderer of Thomas Sanger, a mine foreman, and his friend, William Uren, on Sept. 1, 1875. Richard Andrews, called by the state, had been an eyewitness to the slayings. He gave a detailed description of the murderer and was asked:

Q. Did you see his face?   A. I saw his face.
Q. How was his face as to whiskers?   A. He had a mustache; a small mustache.
Q. Can you tell the color of his hair or eyes?   A. No sir, I cannot.
Q. Had you ever seen that man before?   A. I never saw that man before that morning.
Q. Did you know him at all?   A. No, I did not know him at all.

Q. Have you ever seen him since?   A. Yes, sir.

Q. Munley, stand up. Is that the man? (*The defendant stands up and the witness looks long and hard at him before replying.*)   A. That is not the man I can recognize at all.

In addressing the jury Munley's attorney cried, "For God's sake give labor an equal chance. Do not crush it. Let it not perish under the imperial mandates of capital in a free country."

As Gowen advanced to the jury rail to make his final plea in Munley's case he must have known that he had to rise to real heights since there was scarcely any evidence against the defendant. He did. Never had he been in such fine form. He thundered and roared, quoted poetry and plays, took a noble stance facing the courtroom audience and defied the Molly Maguires to kill him then and there if they dared. He had been through much, he said, but he had not quailed in the face of danger and, continuing, he told the jury:

"I feel, indeed, that if I failed in my duty, if I should shrink from the task that was before me, that if I failed to speak, the very stones would cry out. Standing before you now with the bright beams of victory streaming over our banners, how well I can recall the feeling with which I entered upon the contest, which is now so near the end. Do not think it egotism if I say with the hero of romance,

" 'When first I took this venturous quest
I swore upon the rood,
Neither to turn to right nor left.
For evil or for good . . .
Forward lies faith and knightly fame
Behind are perjury and shame;
In life or death I keep my word.' "

It was magnificent, or so the jury apparently thought, and nothing could stand against it. Certainly not the life of an Irish miner. Munley, too, was sentenced to death and so it was with all the others until nineteen men faced the scaffold.

3. Hanged Heroes

Ten men were hanged on June 21, 1877, six at Pottsville and four at Mauch Chunk. Vast crowds of silent miners surrounded the two jail yards, in each of which a scaffold had been erected. State militia, their bayonets glinting wanly in misty sunlight, surrounded each jail, and others were deployed around the scaffolds. The miners, and their wives and children, began arriving at four in the morning for executions scheduled at eleven o'clock, some coming from as far as twenty miles away and walking through the night.

By nine the crowd in Pottsville stretched as far as one could see, standing silent through the long moments and dragging morning hours, and witnesses said that the silence was the people's way of paying tribute to those about to die. Only once was it broken and that was when an old woman began to weep and curse.

Inside the jail at Pottsville, the *New York Tribune* declared, "the scene was a trying one." The six condemned men were saying farewell to their wives, mothers, and children. Father McDermott, who had attended Carroll and Duffy, was telling reporters, "I know beyond all reasonable doubt that Duffy was not a partner to the murder of Policeman Yost. The same would apply with almost equal force to Carroll."

The aged and impoverished father of Munley, who had walked all the way from Gilbertson, a distance of thirteen miles, was telling his son that he knew he was innocent but the distracted Munley, soon to die with an air reporters described as "nonchalant and easy," was inquiring for his wife. She was outside, weeping hysterically and shaking the locked prison gates, demanding admission. It was refused. She had arrived after six, it was said, the last moment for the admission of relatives. She tried to explain that she had had to arrange things at home and that that had made her late, but a prison official shook his head and walked away. For a moment she seemed to go mad with grief, shrieking and flinging herself against the gate until she collapsed, crumpling to the ground outside the prison wall.

Inside her husband had regained his composure and the chaplain later recalled that he "had been a fine looking man and that he showed no fear." All six were handsome and young. They were freshly shaved, dressed in their best, and a prison guard told reporters, "They looked like they were going to a wedding."

Each had in his lapel a red rose. "At 10:55 o'clock, a creaking of the iron gates at the opposite end of the yard," said the *Tribune*, "caused all eyes to be turned there. Two minutes later two of the condemned men were brought out, McGeehan and Doyle. Their demeanor was one of entire self-possession. The degree of nerve of both men . . . was extraordinary." As they mounted the scaffold together they joined hands and a moment before the trap was sprung Doyle said to McGeehan, "Hughie, let's die like men."

And so they all died. Thomas Munley, James Carroll, James Roarity, Hugh McGeehan, James Boyle, Thomas Duffy, Michael J. Doyle, Edward J. Kelly, Alexander Campbell, John Donahue, Thomas P. Fisher, John Kehoe, Patrick Hester, Peter McHugh, Patrick Tully, Peter McManus, and Andrew Lanahan.

The last two of the nineteen miners, Charles Sharpe and James Mc-Donald, were hanged on Jan. 14, 1879, at Mauch Chunk. The condemned men knew that it was probable that they had been pardoned by the governor and that it was likely that a messenger with a reprieve was on the way.

But there was no delay in the executions. They were held on the precise minute scheduled but the condemned men neither begged nor flinched. It was then that the *New York World* reporter wrote, "The demeanor of the men on the scaffold, their resolute and yet quiet protestations of innocence . . . were things to stagger one's belief in their guilt. . . . They were arrested and arraigned at a time of great public excitement, and they were condemned and hanged on 'general principles.' " And he concluded his report by telling how a few minutes after the dead men had been cut from the dangling nooses, the governor's reprieve had arrived granting them life.

4. *"Lead for the Hungry"*

Tom Scott, head of the Pennsylvania Railroad which moved 31,000,000 tons of freight and reported net earnings of $22,000,000 in a depression year, was as imposing in his way as the brilliant Gowen. He is described as a man of "extraordinary charm, affable, friendly and strikingly handsome." He was a strong man, too, who believed in keeping labor in its place, and strong enough, moreover, to decide who would be President of the United States.

Scott's chance at President-making came in the election of 1876 when Samuel J. Tilden, Democrat, had 184 electoral votes and Rutherford B. Hayes, Republican, 165. With twenty electoral votes in dispute and both sides claiming them, the contest was thrown into Congress to be decided there. Hayes became President after Scott, and others, contrived to win enough votes in Congress to award the Republican candidate all of the disputed electoral votes. It came about in this wise.

For all of his eminence Scott was hard pressed by the panic of 1873. Heavily involved in his Texas and Pacific Railroad, still a project rather than an actuality, he decided that the only way he could avoid ruin was by having the United States government subsidize the Texas and Pacific through advancing him some $312,000,000 in government bonds, including interest over a fifty-year period. Scott promised Hayes the Presidency, if Hayes would promise him the subsidy after becoming President. The deal was made, according to C. Vann Woodward in *Union and Reaction.*

Scott was able to deliver and make Hayes President through his control of the votes of Southern Congressmen. They wanted the Texas and Pacific, as well as other internal improvements, almost as badly as Scott and upon being assured that Hayes would back such a program they double-crossed their own candidate, Tilden, and threw the election to Hayes.[8] This was one part of the complicated maneuvering in which the Republicans abandoned the Negro people in the South as another inducement for Southern Democratic votes in the Hayes-Tilden contest.

Thus the alliance between Northern industrialists and Southern planters

[8] Hayes, however, after using Scott to obtain the Presidency, doubled-crossed him and refused to back the proposed government subsidy for the Texas and Pacific.

was formalized in 1877. Reaction had established a united front at the expense of the Negro people in particular and the American people in general.

Under the circumstances reaction looked forward to the future with confidence. The radical governments in the South were no more and the militant leaders of the Pennsylvania coal miners were being liquidated through judicial murder. No wonder the *Commercial and Financial Chronicle* reported "labor is under control. . . ." This observation gained something of the quality of a slogan for the short month between June 21 when the ten miners were hanged and July 16 when the statement was proved definitely premature.

On that date the first nationwide strike in history broke out on the railroads, a strike which spread from state to state and city to city, from West Virginia to Kentucky and Ohio, from New York to Chicago, from St. Louis to San Francisco. As fast as the strike was broken in one place it appeared in another. American troops fired on American workingmen as regiments under General Phil Sheridan were recalled from fighting the Sioux and thrown against the workers of Chicago. There was the Battle of the Roundhouse in Pittsburgh, bloody street fighting between troops and workers in Baltimore, and skirmishes the country over in which scores of workers were killed and hundreds wounded.

From the first day of the strike the press declared it was a Communist conspiracy to overthrow the government by force and violence. It was not.[9] It was the depression exploding. It was four years of humiliation, joblessness, and hunger erupting in struggle.

Women were particularly valiant as the strike spread, hurling stones as they stood against the fire of United States regulars. Children were killed in Pittsburgh and elsewhere as they fought militia. Farmers came trooping in from the countryside to help the strikers, whose ranks were swollen by the unemployed, by coal miners, mill workers, by all the thousands whose lives had been made uncertain and bitter by depression.

The anger of the people mounted as the *New York Herald* declared that "the mob is a wild beast and needs to be shot down," and as the *New York Sun* advocated "a diet of lead for the hungry strikers." It increased

[9] In May, 1878, a committee of the Pennsylvania state legislature, after prolonged inquiry, formally reported that the Railroad Strike of 1877 was not a Communist insurrection but the result of specific grievances of railroad workers. "The railroad riots of 1877 have by some been called an insurrection," said the report. ". . . [They] were not a rising against civil or political authority; in their origin they were not intended by their movers as an open and active opposition to the execution of the law. . . . It was in no case an uprising against the law as such. . . . As before stated, there was a sort of epidemic of strikes running through the laboring classes of the country, more particularly those in the employ of large corporations, caused by the general depression of business, which followed the panic of 1873, by means whereof many men were thrown out of work, and the wages of those who could get work were reduced. . . ." (*Report of the Committee appointed to Investigate the [Pennsylvania] Railroad Riots in July, 1877*, Legislative Document No. 29, Harrisburg, 1878, p. 46.)

as day after day the charge was trumpeted that their strike to avert pay cuts and speed-up was a Communist conspiracy, although it is doubtful if many strikers knew what a Communist was. Gradually it became clear to the strikers that the Communist charge was leveled at their fellow strikers who were members of the just-organized Workingmen's Party which included many who believed that the nation's economy should be owned and democratically operated by the people for the benefit of the many instead of the profit of the few.

But strikers knew that their strike had not been called, that it had been spontaneous, spreading with the speed of prairie fire as the result of intolerable grievances. Wages of railroad workers had been cut so frequently that earnings averaged between $5 and $10 a week although railroad dividends remained high. There was work for but three or four days a week, the rest of the week being spent at the other end of the line, waiting over for the trip back, while paying a railroad hotel $1 a day. A man often arrived home with less than fifty cents to show for a week's work. In addition the number of cars in freight trains was being doubled.

The immediate cause of the strike was still another 10 per cent pay cut announced for June 1 on the Pennsylvania and for a month later on most other lines. It started outside of Baltimore early on the morning of July 16 when forty Baltimore & Ohio firemen and brakemen quit. An hour later it had spread to Martinsburg, W. Va., where 1,200 brakemen and firemen seized the depot, stopping all freight trains. As miners and Negro farm hands trooped into Martinsburg to help, the Mayor arrested the strike's leaders, then released them as the workers prepared to storm the jail. Governor Matthews of West Virginia dispatched the state militia to the scene and when they fraternized with the strikers he appealed for federal troops to President Hayes, who held his office through the help of Scott and his railroad lobby.

They arrived at six in the morning on July 19 under General French. "The mass of strikers and their friends received the regulars without demonstrations of any kind," wrote Joseph A. Dacus in a contemporary account. "At ten o'clock an attempt was made to start a freight train from Martinsburg toward Baltimore. A locomotive was fired up, while guarded by the military; a large company of strikers had assembled; the Sheriff was present with a posse; an engineer named Bedford was found willing to go and he mounted to the cab. But he did not run the train out. . . . Just as it was about to move away Bedford's wife rushed from the crowd, mounted the engine and with agonizing cries besought him to leave the position. The engineer heeded the entreaties, and departed from the engine, followed by the fireman, which conduct elicited prolonged cheers from the strikers and their sympathizers. . . ."

After arresting strike leaders General French wired Washington that he had broken the strike. He was wrong. It had spread to Ohio, Kentucky, and Maryland. In Baltimore the Fifth and Sixth Regiments were called out for service against the strikers outside of the city. As they marched to the railroad station they were halted by several thousand workmen who tried to prevent them from entraining. The militia fired into the crowd, killing twelve and wounding eighteen.

"Between Holiday and South Street," writes J. B. McCabe in another contemporary account, "the soldiers fired many times. There was little noise beyond that caused by the musketry fire. The firing was also brisk from South to Calvert Street. The excitement, afterward, when the dead and wounded were collected was intense."

Federal troops were sent also to Maryland and with their aid the trains began to run again. Any group of strikers who tried to halt the trains was immediately fired upon and any striker who tried to persuade a strikebreaker to join the strike's ranks was immediately arrested. The strike on the Baltimore & Ohio was smashed by July 22.

But again the strike spread, this time to the Pennsylvania, the New York Central, and the Erie and increasingly to other lines until scores of thousands were on strike in Pennsylvania, New York, New Jersey, Ohio, Indiana, Illinois, Texas, and California. Great numbers of strikers, miners, farmers, and unemployed crowded on the railroad tracks, preventing the trains from moving by the sheer weight of their massed numbers.

In Pittsburgh the strike against the Pennsylvania had the support even of businessmen, angry at the company because of extortionate freight rates. On July 21 Sheriff Fife read the riot act to the thousands massing on the railroad tracks but it was like reading to an ocean. The militia was called out when Tom Scott, who could make Presidents but who at that moment could not make trains move, advised giving the strikers "a rifle diet for a few days and see how they like that kind of bread." But the local militia refused to obey orders and instead joined the strikers.

The Philadelphia militia was sent for and as its members entrained they were heard boasting that they would clean out Pittsburgh in short order. Even the *Army Journal* admitted they were "spoiling for a fight." As they got off the trains and marched out of the station at Pittsburgh they were greeted by the hisses and groans of a large crowd. They fired into it, killing twenty men, women, and children and wounding twenty-nine. "The sight presented after the soldiers ceased firing was sickening," said *The New York Herald* of July 22 under the caption of "War for Wages." "Old men and boys attracted to the [scene] . . . lay writhing in the agonies of death, while numbers of children were killed outright. Yellowside, the neighborhood of the scene of the conflict, was actually dotted with the dead and dying; while weeping women, cursing loudly and deeply the instruments which had made them widows, were clinging to the bleeding corpses."

Miners and steel workers came pouring in from the outskirts of the city and as night fell the immense crowd proved so menacing to the soldiers that they retreated into a roundhouse. The next morning one of the soldiers told a *New York Herald* reporter, "I served in the War of the Rebellion, and have seen wild fighting . . . but a night of terror such as last night I never experienced before and hope to God I never will again."

He told of firing into the crowd after leaving the station and reported that several workers had "taken hold of our muskets saying, 'You would not shoot workingmen, would you?' " "Before dark," he continued, "when the dead and wounded had been carried off . . . we were ordered into the roundhouse, as affording us a protection for the night. . . . At dusk, peeking out of the windows of the roundhouse, we saw the wagons carrying our rations captured by the crowd. . . . As the crowd in the streets was augmented with the approach of night, all thoughts of sleep were given over.

"At midnight the crowd outside . . . had grown into many thousands and shots were fired at us. . . . Some few men I heard made their way out of [the roundhouse] in citizen's clothes and escaped from their perilous positions. We could see long lines of cars, one after the other burning. . . . The fire slowly but surely crept down on us. . . . Suddenly down the grade came one car after another laden with oil which was on fire and burning fiercely. . . . The heat was so intense that we were obliged to retire from the windows and gather in the center of the building. . . .

"It was better to run the risk of being shot down than burned to death, and so we filed out in a compact body. . . . It was lively times I tell you reaching the U.S. Arsenal. . . . I thought we should be all cut to pieces."

It was then that the *New York World,* under the headline "Pittsburgh Sacked," reported that the city was "in the hands of men dominated by the devilish spirit of Communism." Three days later, after the railroad strike hit Chicago with a walkout on the Michigan Central, the *New York Times* proclaimed, "City [Chicago] in Possession of Communists." It was here that Albert R. Parsons, a handsome young Texan who dreamed and worked for a world from which poverty and persecution were forever banished, went from meeting to meeting urging the strikers to be "peaceable but firm." It was here, too, that General Sheridan's cavalry charged a group of workers, killing twelve and wounding forty.

The strike spread to the Missouri-Pacific Railroad and to St. Louis where a general strike was proclaimed under the leadership of the Workingmen's Party, which was also directing the strike in Chicago. For a week not a train moved, not a factory opened, and even most stores were closed. A Negro on a white horse, according to the *St. Louis Republican,* which described the strike as revolution, had galloped from factory to factory, calling for employees to strike and they had.

St. Louis corporations were handing out pay raises and agreeing to the eight-hour day when the military arrived. Martial law was declared. The United States regulars were reinforced by state militia and armed vigilantes. Seventy-nine strike leaders were arrested, forty-four receiving jail sentences. With the crushing of the strike, the widely won pay raises and the eight-hour day went out the window.

By now the military was thoroughly mobilized, as was the business community. Overwhelming force was brought against the strikers at all points. One worker declared "We were shot back to work." By August 2 the strike was broken everywhere. Under the shadow of bayonets the strikers trudged back to roundhouses, freight and switchyards. Somehow they were not downhearted at all and there was a good deal of laughter and joking as they climbed aboard freight and passenger trains. Without any organization they had fought with bravery and skill and the country had been behind them. The strike had been as solid as it was spontaneous. There had been few desertions and few scabs. Next time, they said, they would have a strong union and adequate organization. Next time they would win.

The railroad strike of 1877 was a symptom of the depression, a symbol of the temper of the American people, even more than it was a contest over wages. Farmers, hating Wall Street and eager for currency reforms, had supplied strikers with food when they did not themselves stream to trouble points and the unemployed were everywhere evident. The unrest continued after the strike, expressed this time in the workers' political parties and the Greenback movements of the farmers which were springing up all over the country.

The two movements were merging in Pennsylvania, Ohio, and New York as early as 1877 and in the following year they put a national ticket into the field. In the fall of 1878 some 1,000,000 votes were cast for Greenback-Labor candidates for Congress, fifteen of whom were elected, six from the East, six from the Midwest, and three from the South. The Congressional vote for Greenback-Labor candidates in Pennsylvania was almost 100,000, 14 per cent of the total vote, and the largest part of it came from the so-called Molly Maguire counties in anthracite.

Again the miners were organizing in Schuylkill County, joining the Knights of Labor, founded in 1869 but only now beginning to grow on a nationwide basis. To make matters worse, Terence V. Powderly, soon to be Grand Master Workman of the Knights of Labor, was elected Mayor of Scranton on what was known as the "Molly Maguire ticket."

Gowen's work was rapidly being undone and the anthracite monopoly he had created was crumbling. He had destroyed the miners' union and there it was again, demanding negotiations with as much spirit as if the nineteen had never been hanged. The Philadelphia and Reading was in bankruptcy, Morgan taking over in the reorganization, one of his representatives declaring that Gowen was "a Napoleon being banished to St. Helena." He added, "The trouble with Mr. Gowen is that he wants to be fighting all the time. When he was after the Molly Maguires he was in his element but as a railroad manager he is a failure."

Stripped of his railroad, his mines, and activity by Morgan, Gowen sank into so deep a gloom that friends feared for his sanity. He could not stand the word "failure" but he heard it frequently now. The old magic that had always been his was gone and when he asked for new capital to fight Morgan he was met with silence or evasion. No longer did he enjoy his limericks and when he called on the charm that once had never failed him there was no response.

On Dec. 13, 1889, Gowen shot himself through the head.

CHAPTER III

The "Iron Heel"

"As we view the achievements of aggregated capital, we discover the existence of trusts, combinations and monopolies, while the citizen is struggling far in the rear or is trampled to death beneath an iron heel. Corporations, which should be the carefully restrained creatures of the law and the servants of the people, are fast becoming the people's masters. . . ."

PRESIDENT GROVER CLEVELAND, ANNUAL MESSAGE TO CONGRESS, 1888

"I can hire one half the working class to kill the other half."

JAY GOULD, RAILROAD MAGNATE, BEFORE THE 1886 STRIKE ON HIS SOUTHWESTERN SYSTEM

1. The Dream

On July 4, 1880, the orators postured and roared about love of country but they did not often mention those who loved it most. Seldom has a nation had such lovers as these United States. Of what other country did men and women dream thousands of miles away and then come to it, traveling with incredible difficulties over long vistas of sea and land, that they might be a part of it? In distant Bohemia, in far-off Albania, in Minsk and Kiev and Warsaw, along the Rhine and Danube, on the estates of Prussian junkers and Austrian noblemen, in Sicily and Sardinia, in Vienna, Budapest, Naples, Hamburg, Belfast, Rome, Glasgow, Munich, Liverpool, and Dublin, the word America had a grand majestic sound which in every language meant liberty and plenty. It was this dream of social justice that drew millions across the sea.

In the ten years beginning in 1880 some 5,246,613 new Americans landed in the United States. Many died during passage to the promised land. "The

65

steamship 'Ohio' of the Bremen line arrived on Friday," said a contemporary account, "with 1,342 passengers crowded into steerage [only 857 passengers allowed by law for this ship]. There were 272 children under ten years of age, 156 being infants less than a year old. There was much sickness among them; thirteen died during the passage, and one at Castle Garden after the immigrants landed. All of the deaths were sudden." The numbers crammed into a ship's hold, invariably packed to the point of suffocation, were limited only by "the avarice of owners of vessels and steamship companies," Dr. Thomas J. Turner, medical director of the United States Navy, declared in 1880. "This method," his report continued, "has no regard for the health and comfort of the emigrant, views him only as supplying so many dollars to the bank account, and is a marine inheritance from the slave trade with all the horrors of the 'middle passage.' . . ."

Thousands of new Americans began life in the United States as industrial serfs in mines, steel mills, and railroad construction under terms of contract labor. Such immigrants were paid little or nothing until they had reimbursed those who had imported them for their cost of passage and food. The method of importing this human labor supply is graphically told in the following contemporary account appearing in *John Swinton's Paper* of Dec. 30, 1883:

"The contractors make their appearance under the American flag among the half-starved mudsills in some of the most wretched districts of Hungary, Italy or Denmark, tell the stories of fabulous wages to be gotten in America, bamboozle the poor creatures, rope them in and make contracts with them to pay their passage across the sea, upon their agreeing to terms that few can understand. When they reach the districts of this country to which the contractors ship them, they find their golden dreams turned into nightmares, as they are put to work in mines, factories, or on railroads, at even lower wages than those of them whom they throw out of work. . . ."

In his issue of May 18, 1884, Swinton described how thousands of Hungarians were being imported to the Connellsville coke regions of Pennsylvania where a young Mr. Frick was making millions. Here, where it was not uncommon to find as many as sixteen or seventeen men and women living in shacks only twelve feet long and eight feet wide, the operators were "pitting the English against the Irish, and vice versa, and the German against both . . . keeping up a constant war of races. . . . The heartlessness of the operators was fully exhibited by the remark of one. . . . 'I would rather have two men killed than one mule.' "

The owners of mines, factories, and railroads used these industrial serfs as strikebreakers. During the Hocking Valley strike of Ohio coal miners a New York concern supplied Italian contract laborers at fifty cents a day per man. The money was paid to the contractor and how much he paid these impoverished immigrants is not of record. Of these poor Italian laborers John Swinton wrote: ". . . they are hired out and put to work in ignorance of their rights. . . . Honest-hearted, hard-working men . . . these poor fellows from impoverished Italy, would not play the part of blacklegs [strikebreakers] if they could help it." But they could not help it. Accordingly, they were frequently herded from steerage to a scene of nightmare violence where they passed between lines of struggling men, throwing stones and curses into the gates of a struck mill or mine, while riot raged outside.[1] The vicious snap of rifle fire was almost the first sound heard in America by many a bewildered immigrant.

The immigrant might also expect violence on the frontier. Here ranchers and homesteaders waged a bloody war throughout the eighties. Here, too, farmers, with guns in hand, fought railroads attempting through court orders to evict them from lands which they had settled and improved in the Dakotas and which railroader James J. Hill, the great "Empire Builder," claimed as his own.

Phenomenal growth, but growth only by violent struggle, seemed to be a law of American life. Farmers strained against the last frontier, clamoring for statehood in the Dakotas, Washington, Montana, Idaho, and Wyoming as they began to organize the powerful Farmers' Alliances soon to number hundreds of thousands of irate farmers, most of them trying to form a third party for the overthrow of Wall Street domination. In the East corporations were combining into great price-fixing, wage-fixing pools, containing the leading corporations of an industry; pools were advancing into huge monopolies known as trusts, more closely knit and centralized than the pools, but the advance was strewn with the wreckage of thousands of enterprises, ruined and cast aside in the fierce fight for monopolistic supremacy.

Nevertheless, to the undiscerning middle-class eye the country seemed peaceful enough. Its streets echoed with the lulling cloppity-clop of gently jogging horses and the click of croquet balls was all that disturbed the serenity of golden afternoons. There were residential districts of pleasant homes in which the most exciting event of the day was the arrival of the boy on the bicycle who reached upwards with a pole and lighted the gas street lamp just at dusk and then went on and on down the street until it was punctuated by dots of yellow in the twilight. There were rich farms,

[1] From the National Labor Union through the Knights of Labor, trade union conventions annually petitioned the government to abolish contract labor. It was largely due to the pressure of the Knights of Labor that Congress passed a law in 1885 prohibiting the importation of contract labor. This law, however, was defective, since it made no provision for the establishment of enforcement machinery. By an act of 1887 the Secretary of the Treasury was empowered to deport contract laborers and in 1891 Congress prohibited under penalty of fine the advertising for and solicitation of immigrants by American industrialists. Yet, in spite of these laws, contract laborers continued to be imported. As late as 1907 the U.S. Commissioner-General of Immigration was complaining in his official report of the "padrone system" under which foreign labor was still being "introduced under contract or agreement. . . ." (U.S. Immigration Commission, *Abstract of the Report on Contract Labor and Induced and Assisted Immigration*, Washington, 1911, p. 15.)

broad and sleek, and harvest dinners of hot biscuits, corn on the cob, fresh butter and cream, preserves and jellies, fried chicken, snowy mounds of mashed potatoes—but as the recovery of 1879 changed to the depression of 1883–85 what remained of all this was merely a false front, a limited segment of American life, concealing the ever-mounting numbers of unemployed and impoverished.

With the return of depression violence increased, accompanying a wave of strikes to avert pay cuts. There were the great railroad strikes of 1885 and 1886 on the Wabash, the Missouri-Kansas-Texas and other lines which combined to create Gould's Southwestern System. There were strikes of telegraphers and textile workers, strikes of Michigan lumbermen and New York street car employees. There were bloody battles in Ohio's Hocking Valley where coal miners were striking against a wage cut. A labor editor described the bloodshed in an article called "Hell in Hocking." Miners were killed at Cripple Creek in Colorado and in the fields of Connellsville in Pennsylvania. Striking McCormick workers were killed in Chicago. Strikers were shot down in Texas while the Illinois militia killed strikers during the eighties at La Salle, Vinden, Braidwood, and East St. Louis.

The various National Guards, the state militias strengthened and re-equipped with new weapons and great armories after the railroad strike of 1877, were called out with such frequency that Joseph R. Buchanan, labor editor, declared they were as much a part of the corporations as their accounting departments. But most of the murders and most of the blood came from the private army of the Pinkerton Agency, an agency which by the eighties had graduated into the ranks of big business. When Allan Pinkerton died in 1884 the work of the firm was carried on by William A. and Robert A. Pinkerton, heads of the Western and Eastern Agencies respectively, with headquarters in Chicago and New York. In 1885 these two gentlemen sent out a secret circular offering the union-busting services of their agency to "railroad companies and other corporations . . . to keep a close watch for designing men among their own employees, who in the interests of secret labor organizations, are influencing their employees to join these organizations and eventually cause a strike."

Pinkerton operatives were hired out to corporations for strike-breaking as well as espionage purposes. These mercenaries were divided into detachments of infantry, cavalry, and artillery. Writing of the use of this private army to break the 1885 railroad strike on Gould's Southwestern System, labor editor Swinton observed:

"This peculiar private armed force is not in the service of the United States Government nor of any State Government—it is kept for the service of such corporations or capitalists as may hire it for the suppression of such strikes as may be stirred by the turning of monopoly screws. In Ohio it has been under the pay of the Hocking Coal and Iron Company; in some parts of Pennsylvania last year, it was in the pay of the coal corporations; and in Missouri, at this time, it is in the pay of Our Lord Paramount, Jay Gould."

To this observation Swinton added the fact that Pinkertons were used not only as strikebreakers and spies but as *agents provocateurs*, deliberately creating violence which was often used to discredit the labor movement and frame up and imprison its members.

To the immigrant, and to many of the native-born, the decade seemed to be heading toward some cataclysmic showdown. The working class was clamoring for an eight-hour day even as industrialists were announcing that labor unions must be smashed once and for all, now and forever. The only force growing faster than labor was capital. On one hand the Knights of Labor had advanced from 28,000 members in 1880 to 700,000 in 1886 but on the other bankers and industrialists had never been so aggressively triumphant as they were in the eighties while extending their control from government and the two major parties to control of pulpit, professor, and university through gargantuan gifts.

The gifts were useful. The overwhelming tendency of white, prosperous, Protestant America was to admire Big Business and all of its ways. But princely endowments to church and college furnished comforting corroboration in the form of preachers who proved that the trusts were the fulfillment of God's law, in the shape of professors who demonstrated that corporation violence was scientifically inevitable, a part of Darwin's progress in which survival went to the most predatory.

The middle-class white American, with a few notable exceptions, lived in a psychologically airtight compartment, almost completely unaware of the true nature of the reality about him. As far as he knew anything about the people on the other side of the tracks, he concluded that they lived there as a result of some perversity that led them to prefer beer and saloons to right thinking and progress. Henry Cabot Lodge was typical enough when he wrote in his autobiography that he had been utterly unaware of the existence of people unlike himself and his class until the great fire of 1872 destroyed the Boston slums, suddenly revealing acres of hidden poverty behind Boston's respectably comfortable façade.

The only consistent attention paid to the working class and foreign-born took the form of journalistic abuse, particularly in times of strikes and unrest. The Red Scare, already old, had been elevated into an institution. What it lacked in exactitude it made up for in violence. To the newspapers every striker was a foreigner and every foreigner a Communist, Anarchist, or Socialist or Nihilist. The press was daily punctuated with threats of violence against the working class. Not untypical were these two excerpts from the public prints of 1885. "These brutal creatures," said the *New York Tribune*, "can understand no other reasoning than that of force and enough of it to be remembered among them for generations." And the *Chicago Times*, referring to a strike on the Great Lakes, declared, "Hand grenades should be thrown among these union sailors . . . as by such treatment they would be taught a valuable lesson, and other strikers could take warning from their fate."

Writing of the Chicago press and its treatment of the foreign-born, Harry Barnard has said:

"The unemployed, if they bore foreign names, were 'European scum.' If Americans, they were tramps, bummers and loafers. Discontented workingmen had no real grievances but were always dupes of foreign agitators or American knaves. The solution was clear—deport the foreign scum and rabble-rousers, suppress the home-grown variety, if necessary by liberal use of gatling guns and gallows. . . .

"The columns of the *Tribune* and *Times* were filled day after day with cruel and senseless attacks upon the foreign-born. A 'communist' was always a '(German Communist.' Strikes and labor demonstrations were always mobs composed of foreign scum, beersmelling Germans, ignorant Bohemians, uncouth Poles, wild-eyed Russians."

The fact that the foreign-born and the rest of the working class did the country's work completely escaped attention. Laboring twelve and fourteen hours a day before blast furnace and forge, or knee-deep in the water of dark and dangerous mines, constructing and running the railroads, building locomotives, bridges, and dams, tunneling through mountains, manning the factories, and supplying the nation's coal, steel, oil, and copper, the fact that the workers were the backbone of the country went unnoticed. As unemployment and violence increased with the depression of 1883–85, along with poverty and abuse, it might have been natural enough if the millions of new Americans had turned against their new land. But they held to their dream. The struggle for it made it doubly precious and the love of the foreign-born for America was stronger in that it was edged with pain.

The native-born workers brooded, too, on the American Dream, sired by Jefferson and Revolution, wondering how the dream's brightness had turned dark and sometimes even into nightmare. It was the old, old promise of the Declaration that "all men are created equal" with equal right to "life, liberty and the pursuit of happiness" that drew men from all over the world, that haunted men born to the American earth, and when they found the promise broken they were hurt as only those who love can be hurt.

2. *God's Gold*

Standing as a roadblock to the realization of the American dream were the growing concentration and control of American industry by a small but powerful group of men. Since the Civil War there had been this growth and centralization of capital. And there had also been resistance on the part of the people to it. Presidents came and went, sometimes Democratic, more often Republican, Johnson, Grant, Hayes and Garfield, Arthur, Cleveland, Harrison, Cleveland again, and McKinley, but the Morgans and the Rockefellers remained throughout, their rule unchanging. All through the eighties the people fought back, running independent labor candidates in a score of cities, building the Grange and Farmers' Alliances into a formidable movement of agrarian protest and the Knights of Labor into the largest labor organization the country had yet seen.

But the one paramount fact of the decade was the growth of monopoly and the beginning of the trusts. All else was a reflex action to that. Big Business was the central magnet which drew to it everything else, fastening even its antagonists to it, dictating the time and place of all opposition. A master of divide and conquer, business itself grew more unified as finance capital merged with industrial, such bankers as Morgan taking over direction of the new trusts. As monopoly increased, it grew more skillful in keeping its opposition fragmented, the labor movement divided, with the working class and the farmers, the Negro people and the foreign-born fighting valiantly but separately and alone.

The eighties, even more than most decades, contained the future as well as the present. Gene Debs was growing to a gangling, lanky manhood in Terre Haute, reading Racine and Schiller, painting commercial signs, and practicing oratory before his mirror. Young Theodore Roosevelt, flasher of a toothy smile and apostle of the strenuous life, was striving to make himself acceptable to western voters by becoming a rancher in the Badlands.

Thomas Edison at Menlo Park was perfecting the phonograph, the electric light, the motion picture; even the ubiquitous radio was taking on a dim and uncertain shape in scientists' minds as Heinrich Hertz confirmed the existence of radio waves in 1885. The telephone, the electric street car, and the rotary press were coming into more general use and as for the telegraph, it was already a corporate monopoly. Henry Ford was tinkering in his bicycle shop, ideas germinating within him that would play their part in changing the face of American life. The Wright brothers were boys who not many years hence would give man wings at Kitty Hawk. The dynamo and the conversion of falling tons of water into power and light for far-away cities, distant factories, and remote farms had come into being at Niagara Falls.

Joseph Pulitzer, soon to be joined by young William Randolph Hearst, was developing the dismal outlines of modern journalism. Woodrow Wilson was a young man and Franklin D. Roosevelt had been born, as had most of the men who would liberate the colossal energy of the atom.

The eighties were dotted with dramatic figures. Even the petulantly conservative, flashily dressed Terence V. Powderly, against strikes and hating his job as head of the Knights of Labor, but stubbornly clinging to it, was forced into drama as he deplored or sold out the strikes he was forced to lead.[2] Joe Buchanan, self-styled labor agitator with a hatchet nose, an aggressive chin, and a sensitive, vulnerable mouth, wrote poetry, essays, and editorials as he set type and edited a newspaper while directing the first successful strike against a major railroad, the Union Pacific, in 1885. Martin Irons, selfless and brave and an advocate of socialism, was blacklisted and impoverished, dying sick and penniless, as a result of his leadership of the railroad strike of 1886 when he and the southwest's railroad men challenged the great Gould, only to be sold out by Powderly.

And while this was going on the squat, stonefaced Sam Gompers, who had also been a Marxist in his youth, was helping Peter J. McGuire and others establish the American Federation of Labor. McGuire was also a founder of the Carpenters' Union, as well as of the English-speaking branch of the Socialist Labor Party.

But the men who called the tune to which others danced were not the leaders of labor. They merely reacted to what other men did, taking counteraction to pay cuts or discharges; fighting when forced to by their membership or when more influential men decided to eliminate trade unions. The men who called the tune were leaders of Big Business, such as Jay Gould, his black beard now streaked with gray. Since he had fled from New York and a possible penitentiary sentence after looting the Erie, he had grown a good deal older and richer. He did not sleep well of nights, often walking the streets until dawn, coughing, hacking, and spitting blood.

By the late eighties he had owned and pillaged the Union Pacific, the Wabash, the Missouri-Kansas-Texas, the Texas-Pacific, the Western Union Telegraph Company, the *New York World,* several steamship companies, and a number of shorter Eastern railroads. It was his practice to gain control of ruined railroads, usually through stock manipulation (most American railroads were in bankruptcy at some time or other during this period), make a pretense of profitable operation, and then sell stocks and bonds based on that pretense before getting out just as the property failed again. Using this technique, he made $20,000,000 on the Union Pacific alone. He was willing to spend huge sums with the Pinkertons to shoot down strikers but totally unwilling to increase pay and once said scornfully, when threatened with strike, "I can hire one half of the working class to kill the other half." His avarice was celebrated in a bit of popular doggerel called "Jay Gould's Modest Wants":

[2] In 1886 Powderly was so frightened by the rapid growth and strikes of the Knights of Labor that the organization of new assemblies was forbidden for a period of some forty days and secret orders were circulated that no assembly was to strike on May 1st for the eight-hour day. He was so embarrassed by the militancy of the body he headed that he was ready to resign. " 'I am neither physically nor mentally capable of performing the work required of me,' Powderly complained, and he proposed to resign, because the members of the Order were putting him in a false position before the public." (N. J. Ware, *The Labor Movement in the United States, 1860–1895,* New York, 1929, pp. 312–13.)

> "My wants are few; I scorn to be
> A querulous refiner;
> I only want America
> And a mortgage deed of China;
> And if a kind fate threw Europe in,
> And Africa and Asia,
> And a few islands of the sea,
> I'd ask no other treasure.
> Give me but these—they are enough
> To suit my notion—
> And I'll give up to other men
> All land beneath the ocean."

Gould, more than any other figure of his time, was the symbol of monopoly to the American people. But his monopoly was rudimentary. It was a kind of personal single-corporation monopoly in which one railroad, for example, would capture the commerce of an area. Occasionally he would join pools, the forerunners of the trust proper, but he would invariably violate the loose federation's agreement as to prices, wages, division of the market, or freight rates. The real monopolists who foreshadowed the future were Frick and Carnegie, who were establishing a vertical trust in the steel industry, absorbing coke mines, iron ore deposits, and rolling mills; shrewd and cunning Andrew Mellon, who was organizing a company to take care of the estates of the Pittsburgh millionaires, thus putting more capital at his command and thereby enabling him to branch out into industry; and the regal Morgan, who was beginning to reorganize one railroad after another, gaining control over them, uniting in the process bank and industrial capital, a new phenomenon.

Similarly the future was being foreshadowed by sanctimonious John D. Rockefeller, the slim little deacon from Cleveland who knew what he wanted with an intensity that was almost fierce. Secretive and soft-footed, he liked to whisper if it were possible, and he was mildness itself unless money was involved and then he was as savage as a tiger. He had "an instinct for conspiracy"; the fact that it was against the law bothered him not a whit when he founded the first modern trust in world history in 1882, the Standard Oil Company.

The trust he originated, both as a legal form and as a method of tying together all the far-flung processes of an industry, controlling the products from their extraction from the earth as raw materials to their sale to the public, was to serve as the method and the model for all American industry. The trust's aim was the narrowing and centralization of ownership while creating a vast monopoly which increased profits by fixing prices high while holding wages low. Rockefeller's trust was a blueprint of the future. Upon this foundation American monopoly built, constantly pyramiding in strength and narrowing in control, until it was at last to seek the whole world as its province.

To his competitors Rockefeller was a scourge. He took what he wanted of his rivals' properties and buried the rest as thoroughly as if they had been struck by an avalanche. He never doubted himself for an instant, for he said God had put him on earth to make money. Those who got in his way were obstructing God's will. He was the first great combiner of American industry, transforming "the pigmy property of the many into the Titan property of the few, transforming the individual and scattered means of production into socially concentrated forms."

Rockefeller's plan to fulfill God's wish that he grow rich had the simplicity of genius. He persuaded the railroads to charge him about half of what they were charging his rivals as freight rates in the transport of oil.[3] By secret rebates they returned to Rockefeller 15 cents of every 40 cents they charged others for the transporting of each barrel of crude oil from the Pennsylvania oil fields. Rockefeller paid 25 cents a barrel for this service, his competitors 40 cents. For the transportation of the refined product to the market he actually paid 40 cents less than his rivals; the prevailing rate per barrel was $1.30 but after his rebate Rockefeller paid only 90 cents per barrel. Later he got the railroads, all of it being written up in long complicated contracts, to give him a percentage of the freight rates paid by the companies competing with him so that he always made money out of whatever business remained to his competitors. In addition, the carriers engaged in espionage for him, reporting regularly to him to whom his rivals were selling their product, how much they sold, and at what price.

Thus armed, Rockefeller started making a tour of his weaker competitors with a mildly voiced declaration of war. Either sell out to him at his own price or be ruined. Already determined to control the oil business of the world, he intended to persuade his stronger rivals to join him in his plan while wiping out the others. A plant costing $40,000, for example, had a value of $15,000 to him as a small link in the grandiose idea that gave him no rest. He would make only one offer on a take-it-or-leave-it basis and if refused he would undersell his rival until the latter collapsed. Mrs. Backus, of Cleveland, described as "the mother of fatherless children," came to Rockefeller asking his protection after her husband, also an oil refiner, had died. Weeping at her plight, Rockefeller promised he would help her but later decided that his plan needed her property. He forced her to sell at $79,000 what had cost $200,000 to build.

[3] The Rockefeller group was able to obtain these advantageous agreements with the railroads by promising to give them all their business and using their influence to throw their way the business of other refineries. For 50 per cent of Standard's freight Jay Gould, acting on behalf of the Erie Railroad, turned over to the Rockefeller people the Weehawken terminal. William H. Vanderbilt saw to it that the New York Central, which he controlled, gave the Standard special freight rates, a concession not unconnected with the fact that Vanderbilt was a large stockholder in that company's vast oil empire.

Such incidents happened by the score and once, when reproached with them, Rockefeller said, "I had my plan clearly in mind. It was right. I knew it as a matter of conscience. It was right between me and my God. If I had to do it tomorrow, I would do it again in the same way—do it a hundred times."

So he prospered down the years, replacing what had been owned by hundreds of companies with one great trust. His first years were occupied with seizure and gathering together, and then he was not averse to dynamiting or wrecking the property of a rival. His later years were spent in rationalization of the industry, in controlling production in the oil fields, in retailing on a vast scale, in developing his export business to worldwide dimensions, in installing the most modern plants and equipment, and always and everywhere slashing wages in his passion for economy for everyone and everything save the profits of himself and his associates.

The conspiracy laws, forbidding the fixing of prices, and used so effectively against trade unions in connection with wages, were found to be powerless against Rockefeller. "During forty years," Josephson observes, "the Standard Oil men marched from trial to trial like habitual felons before the public was convinced that it was not dealing with the arch-criminals of the age, but destiny." No matter what the legal obstacles and despite public sentiment, Rockefeller never permitted himself a moment of doubt that he was serving the Lord in creating monopoly.

His first attempt, the South Improvement Company, was forced out of business when the railroads whose secret rebates were the crux of the pool's plan withdrew, frightened at the avalanche of a public opprobrium that bothered Rockefeller not at all. He merely set to work again and by 1881 had more than forty companies under his control through his creation of a new pool, its members drawn together by an exchange of stock.

But Rockefeller wanted more control, more centralization; authority, power, and the invention of the trust were the answer to his need. In 1882, acting secretly, as was his custom, Rockefeller pursuaded the stockholders of his associated companies to hand over their stock to nine trustees, receiving trust certificates in exchange, which included himself, his brother, and his friends, and with the stock to give the trustees absolute control in managing the whole vast enterprise. Thus one entity replaced more than forty and with that fact the trust was born.

Soon the organization moved to New York and with its invincible formula for monopoly it was not long until it had virtual airtight control of the American industry, as well as drawing mammoth profits from all quarters of the world.

Josephson writes: "From their headquarters in the small old-fashioned building at 140 Pearl Street the supreme council of an economic empire sat together in conference, like princes of the Roman Church. Here in utmost privacy, confidential news brought by agents or informers throughout the world was discussed, and business policies determined. . . . Freed of all moral scruples, curiously informed of everything, they were prompted by a sense of the world's realities which differed strangely from that of the man in the street. They were a major staff engaged in an eternal fight; now they scrapped unprofitable plants, acquiring and locating others; or now they gathered themselves for tremendous mobilizing feats during emergencies in trade. They found ways of effecting enormous economies, and always their profits mounted to grotesque figures; in 1879, on an invested capital of $3,500,000, dividends of $3,150,000 were paid; the value of the congeries of oil companies was then estimated as $55,000,000. Profits were overwhelmingly reinvested in new 'capital goods' and with the formation of the Trust, capitalization was set at $70,000,000. By 1886 net earnings had risen to $15,000,000 per annum."

Profits similar to these poured in all during the eighties to the new monopolists, most of them still members of industrial pools and only striving toward the newer trust. But those receiving the fortunes were not always as abstemious as John D. Rockefeller. Many wallowed in their new wealth with astonishing abandon and, according to the Beards, "supplied amazing sensations to the public in the ample days of Cleveland and Harrison. At a dinner eaten on horseback, the favorite steed was fed flowers and champagne; to a small black and tan dog wearing a diamond collar worth $15,000 a lavish banquet was tendered; at one function the cigarettes were wrapped in hundred dollar bills; at another fine black pearls were given to the diners in their oysters; at a third an elaborate feast was served to boon companions in a mine from which came the fortune of the host. Then weary of such limited diversions, the plutocracy contrived more freakish occasions—with monkeys seated between the guests, human gold fish swimming about in pools, chorus girls hopping out of pies. . . . Diamonds were set in teeth; a private carriage and personal valet were provided for a pet monkey; dogs were tied with ribbons to the back seats of Victorias and driven out in the park for airings; a necklace costing $600,000 was purchased for the daughter of Croesus; $65,000 was spent for a dressing table; $75,000 for a pair of opera glasses."

Living in such lordly splendor, the rich began to lose their caution, giving out the secrets of their statecraft. It made no difference to them, they said, whether a Republican or Democrat was elected. They owned both. It was common conversation among the captains of industry that presently they would settle with the labor unions, that the time was not far off when the growing Knights of Labor would be smashed. They became more determined as the move for the eight-hour day threatened the rights of the country's owners to control the conditions of employment.

So it was that the wealthy Frederick Townsend Martin frankly declared:

". . . It matters not one iota what political party is in power or what President holds the reins of office. We are not politicians or public thinkers; we are the rich; we own America; we got it, God knows how, but we intend to keep it if we can by throwing all the tremendous weight of our support, our influence, our money, our political connections, our purchased senators, our hungry congressmen, our public-speaking demagogues into the scale against any legislature, any political platform, any presidential campaign that threatens the integrity of our estate. . . . The class I represent cares nothing for politics. In a single season a plutocratic leader hurled his influence and his money into the scale to elect a Republican governor on the Pacific coast and a Democratic governor on the Atlantic coast."

And Mr. Havemeyer, head of the sugar trust formed in the late eighties, testified later in a federal inquiry that the monopoly gave money impartially to both the major parties. "The Sugar Trust is a Democrat in a Democratic state and a Republican in a Republican state?" asked a Senator. "As far as local matters are concerned, I think that is about it," Havemeyer replied. "The American Sugar Refining Company has no politics of any kind. . . . Only the politics of business."

These great American trusts whose only politics was the politics of business had by the early nineties grown into Frankenstein monsters. Their gigantic size was indicated by Henry D. Lloyd in his celebrated work *Wealth Against Commonwealth* published in 1894.

"Not less than five hundred million dollars is in the coal combination . . . that in oil has nearly if not quite two hundred millions. . . . Hundreds of millions of dollars are united in the railroads and elevators of the Northwest against the wheat-growers. In cattle and meat there are not less than one hundred millions; in whiskey, thirty-five millions . . . in sugar, seventy-five millions; in leather over a hundred millions; in gas, hundreds of millions. . . ."

With the burgeoning of corporations into pools and pools into trusts, the speed-up of industrial workers increased greatly. As an official government body, the Industrial Commission, put it: "Various authorities cited by Mr. David A. Welles in his *Recent Economic Changes,* published in 1889, show that the productiveness of labor in the industries was multiplied, on the average, not less than three or four times, and in some departments many fold in the brief period from 1865 to 1889."

Under the circumstances, labor became more than ever a commodity, its costs calculated with the same impersonality as depreciation or the cost of steel. Most monopolists agreed with Jay Gould that "labor is a commodity that will in the long run be governed absolutely by the law of supply and demand." Testifying before a Senate committee investigating relations between labor and capital in 1883, a worker said "The employer has pretty much the same feeling towards the men that he has toward his machinery. He wants to get as much as he can out of his men at the cheapest rate." And Samuel Gompers told the same Senate committee that a manufacturer had told him, "I regard my employees as I do a machine, to be used to my advantage, and when they are old and of no further use I cast them into the street."

That such an attitude on the part of the employers was widespread was the testimony of W. H. Foster, general secretary of the Federation of Organized Trades and Labor Unions of the United States and Canada, predecessor of the American Federation of Labor. "Sullen discontent," he said, was common to labor, and he added "They do not seem to have the courage to express openly what they think all the time." It was clear to many that the common use of Pinkertons and the state militias, the frequent breaking of strikes by bloodshed, the force and violence that was the general solution of employers when faced with labor's demands, were generating a wide resentment.

More than that, the worker's daily life was miserable because of low wages and shocking housing conditions in the slums, common to all the great cities. Federal Labor Commissioner Carroll D. Wright, in his first annual report in 1886, stated mildly enough that if the question were asked "has the wage-worker received his equitable share of the benefits derived from the introduction of machinery, the answer must be no." Average weekly wages ranged from $7.50 to $8 while carpenters in 1883 averaged $1.45 a day.

On Oct. 18, 1883, Thomas O'Donnell, a mule-spinner at Fall River, testified before the Senate Committee on Labor-Capital Relations:

"I have a brother who has four children besides his wife and himself. All he earns is $1.50 a day. He works in the iron works at Fall River. He only works about nine months out of twelve. There is generally three months of stoppage . . . and his wife and family all have to be supported for a year out of the wages of nine months—$1.50 a day for nine months to support six of them. It does not stand to reason that those children and he himself can have natural food and be naturally dressed. His children are often sick, and he has to call in doctors."

O'Donnell was asked how he supported his own family of four on wages of $133 a year. He replied:

"I got a couple of dollars worth of coal last winter, and the wood I picked up myself. I goes around with a shovel and picks up clams and wood."
Q. What do you do with the clams?   A. We eat them. I don't get them to sell but just to eat for the family. That is the way my brother lives, mostly. He lives close by us.
Q. How many live that way down there [Fall River]?   A. I could not count them, they are so numerous. I suppose there are one thousand down there.
Q. A thousand that live on $150 a year?   A. They live on less.

Speaking of Chicago, where conditions were typical of those found in most American cities, another witness before the committee said that "workers almost invariably live in filthy tenement houses or in cellars or garrets." The tenement houses, he continued, "in the thickly populated part of the city along Clark and State streets, occupied by the Italians generally . . . are in a terrible condition. They are really uninhabitable. Swarms of children go about the street nearly naked; they come and go in that way and they are growing up to be the worst part of the community. They have no education."

And for the privilege of living in these slum areas American workers were forced to pay $10 and even $15 a month rent out of meager wages averaging $7.50 to $8.00 a week. Such rentals assured landlords exorbitant returns. As the Committee on Tenement Houses of the Citizens' Association of Chicago put it in its report of September, 1884: ". . . for some of the wretched tenements they now occupy, they [the workers] are fleeced at a rate which returns 25 to 40 per cent per annum of the value of the property."

While the idle rich were forced to the dining of monkeys for amusement those fortunate enough to have work among the working class had no difficulty in filling their time. Working from dawn to dark, they divided all their time between factory and bed. Asked whether Chicago workers had time "to visit each other and to have social intercourse between their families," a witness before the Senate Committee replied: "An average mechanic who has to go to work at 7 o'clock in the morning—and in most instances they have to go three miles to their work . . . such a man would have to get up at half-past 5 o'clock in the morning . . . and getting up as early as that and returning to his home at half-past 7 o'clock or 8 o'clock in the evening, you may judge that his opportunities for mingling with his fellow-workmen in a social way would be limited."

The average work day, in some industries, according to contemporary studies, was between fourteen and eighteen hours, while in Minnesota a law was passed providing a fine for railroads which forced firemen or engineers to work more than eighteen hours daily. New York City bakers worked from eighty-four to one hundred and twenty hours a week and ninety to one hundred hours weekly was not uncommon.

Most of the conditions described before the Senate committee became worse as the depression deepened. Hard times began, after a boom period which was characterized by overexpansion and super-speculation. In the railroad industry alone the country's rail mileage was increased by 34 per cent "of which," writes Forrest Davis in his book *What Price Wall Street?* "not more than one-third was justified by existing business." Listening to the lure of Wall Street's gilt-edged 7 per cent bonds, American and European investors poured money into an already overextended industry. And what happened in rails happened in steel, oil, textiles, and other industries. In 1883 the bubble burst and another in a periodic series of depressions hit the country. According to Labor Commissioner Wright, there were almost

1,000,000 unemployed in 1885 but Powderly estimated the unemployed as high as 2,000,000.

But the new monopolists continued to amass profits and wealth, capitalizing on the depression by annexing weaker rivals. More than one-half the national income, according to government figures in the census of 1890, was being enjoyed by one-eighth of the nation's families. The richest 1 per cent received a larger total income than the poorest 50 per cent. Of the 12,-000,000 families in the country, 5,500,000 families had no property at all. It was such facts as these that forced President Cleveland to declare in his annual message to Congress, Dec. 3, 1888, that "trusts, combinations and monopolies" were trampling the citizen "to death beneath an iron heel."

3. Labor Editor

Long before President Cleveland came to this conclusion many an old Abolitionist had come to feel the same way about the matter. These unreconstructed mavericks had no more use for the iron heel of big business than they had for the lash whip of the slave power. Born before the glory of the first American Revolution had faded from men's minds, weaned on tales of fighting for freedom from grandfathers who had fought in the War for Independence, they were incurable advocates of the right of the people to alter or abolish the existing form of government and inveterate defenders of the right of anyone to express any idea anywhere anytime. They themselves had spent the best years of their lives in trying to overturn that central federal authority that had sponsored and spread human slavery.

The elegant James Russell Lowell, late minister to the Court of St. James and one-time traducer of the government, had not been tamed, as became apparent in 1884 when he declared that "Socialism is the practical application of Christianity and has in it the secret of orderly and benign reconstruction." The aristocrat Wendell Phillips, among the greatest of Abolitionists, who died in the year of Lowell's declaration, was demanding the abolition of capitalism and championing labor with almost his last breath.

Among this number of unreconstructed Abolitionists was the large and Falstaffian John Swinton, whose life and words illuminate better than most the quality of that brutal decade that was the eighties. He was chief editorial writer of the *New York Times* from 1860 to 1870 and later managing editor of Dana's *Sun*. A reporter for Brooklyn's *Daily Union* described Swinton's "large framed full-faced healthy complexion, big dark brown eyes" and "sandy gray mustache." "His head was bald," said the reporter, except for "a rim of gray on the outlying county of an immense cranium." He was described as a "man who gives expression with rapidity of utterance and eloquence, now and then illustrating his points with a story, an allusion to history or some passage in the classics."

One night, probably in 1880, John Swinton, then the pre-eminent New

York journalist, was the guest of honor at a banquet given him by the leaders of his craft. Someone who knew neither the press nor Swinton offered a toast to the Independent Press. Swinton outraged his colleagues by replying:

"There is no such thing in America as an independent press, unless it is in the small towns. You know it and I know it. There is not one of you who dares to write his honest opinions, and if you did you know beforehand that they would never appear in print. . . . The business of the New York journalist is to destroy the truth, to lie outright, to pervert, to vilify, to fawn at the feet of Mammon, and to sell his race and his country for his daily bread. You know this and I know it, and what folly is this to be toasting an 'Independent Press.' We are the tools and vassals of rich men behind the scenes. We are the jumping-jacks; they pull the strings and we dance. Our talents, our possibilities and our lives are all the property of other men. We are intellectual prostitutes."

His colleagues should not have been surprised. Even while respectably employed Swinton had strained that employment to the utmost by speaking truth as he saw it even though not allowed to write it. His entire history should have warned them that he was not a conventional guest of honor. When less than twenty he had risked his life in South Carolina where he subjected himself to the possibility of a prison sentence by teaching Negro slaves to read and write. The lessons took place at night in an underground vault. John Brown was his hero. He had gone to Kansas in an attempt to help Brown's fight against the proslavery Border Ruffians. Sometimes infuriated by those who said that times had changed, that it was easier for Brown to struggle in 1859 than it was to struggle now in the 1880's, he frequently spoke as in this excerpt from a speech:

"It needs that we recall the stupendous strength of the old slavery establishment—its bulwarks of constitutionalism, legality, politics, mercantilism, capitalism—and ecclesiasticism; it needs that we recall the power of the interests and passions that environed it, and the subserviency or timidity of even its opponents, with few exceptions, before we can comprehend the influence of the man [Brown] . . . who struck through them all, and struck to the heart."

John Swinton was brought to the labor movement as the result of the police assault on the unemployed at the Tompkins Square mass meeting in 1874 in New York. In his speeches he frequently referred to it and it was a popular subject all through the eighties when there were so many instances of similar police violence. Once during a time of tension and strikes his friends were sure that he was going to his death when he decided to address a mass meeting of workers. He began to think this was possible when he saw the platoons of armed police drawn up on all sides. Nevertheless he jauntily began his speech with the words, "With 8,000 rifles and 1,200 clubs drawn upon me . . . ." In a speech about the Tompkins Square outrage, he said:

"But now, about ten o'clock, when they were standing around peaceably, waiting for the mayor, platoons of police suddenly appeared, deployed into the Square, rushed without warning whatever on the helpless and unarmed multitudes, violently assailed them with their clubs, struck at heads right and left, wounded many, dragged off some thirty or forty who were flung into station houses, not unlike the Black Hole of Calcutta. . . . The editorial funks and intellectual policemen have roused prejudices against these, their victims, by saying they were Communists, in league with the impending earthquake! Gentlemen, be not alarmed by mysterious words, and let not the epithet 'Communist' stir up the same kind of hydrophobia that the epithet 'Abolitionist' once did. Suppose the ideas of these hapless people were the sort which editors and policemen call 'communistic,' does anybody suppose that the thing can be scribbled out of their hearts or clubbed out of their heads?"

Shortly after his response to the toast to the Independent Press Swinton resigned his editorship and started his own newspaper, a weekly called *John Swinton's Paper*. Its masthead carried this statement of principles: (1) Boldly upholding the Rights of Man in the American Way. (2) Battling against the accumulating wrongs of society and industry. (3) Striving for the organization and interests of workingmen, and giving the news of the Trades and Unions. (4) Warning the American people against the treasonable and crushing schemes of Millionaires, Monopolists and Plutocracy.

Swinton's articles were long and detailed, factual yet partisan. He inveighed against the robber barons of the day, fought stoutly against the use of contract labor and Pinkerton thugs, and opened the columns of his newspaper to labor's progress in organization, wages, and eight-hour-day agitation.

It is of interest to American labor that Swinton was a great admirer of Karl Marx.

Swinton was neither a Socialist nor Marxist but he had read Marx since the Civil War when Horace Greeley, owner of the *New York Tribune*, had commissioned Marx for a series of articles. While in Europe in 1880 Swinton had interviewed Marx and he described Marx thus:

"A man without desire for fame, caring nothing for the fanfaronade of life or the pretense, without haste and without rest, a man of strong, broad, elevated mind, full of far-reaching projects, logical methods and practical aims, he has stood and yet stands behind more of the earthquakes which have convulsed nations and destroyed thrones, and do now menace and appal crowned heads and established frauds, than any other man in Europe, not excepting Joseph Mazzini himself. The student of Berlin, the critic of Hegelianism, the editor of papers, the old-time correspondent of the New York *Tribune*, he showed his qualities and his spirit; the founder and master-spirit of the once dreaded International, and the author of *Capital*, he has been expelled from half the countries in Europe, proscribed in nearly all of them and for thirty years past has found refuge in London."

Marx's manner of speech, Swinton declared,

". . . reminded me of that of Socrates—so free, so sweeping, so creative, so incisive, so genuine—with its sardonic touches, its gleams of humor and its sportive merriment. He spoke of the political and popular movements of the various countries of Europe—the vast current of the spirit of Russia, the motions of the German mind, the action of France, the immobility of England—referring contemptuously to the 'atomistic' reforms over which liberals of the British parliament spend their time. Surveying the European world, country by country, indicating the features and the development and the personage of the surface, and under the surface, he showed that things were working toward ends which will assuredly be realized."

John Swinton was not the only American attracted to Marx. Since the Communist Manifesto of 1848, with its message, "Workingmen of all lands, unite! You have nothing to lose but your chains!" Marx's influence had been a force in America. "Within a short time," wrote Charles A. and Mary R. Beard in *The Rise of American Civilization*, "the Manifesto crossed the Atlantic. As far west as Illinois and Missouri, sermons were preached on the new articles of faith by German immigrants expelled from their fatherland in 1848." As a result of conditions in the United States during the seventies and eighties the Socialist concept spread rapidly that the people should own and operate the means of production for the benefit of themselves rather than private profit. "Another development," writes Harry Barnard in his biography of Governor John P. Altgeld of Illinois, "was the remarkable hold that socialism had upon the workers. Never before, nor since, has this doctrine of a New Society had so many converts among the laboring masses, both native and foreign-born."[4]

Perhaps Swinton told Marx something of this as they walked the beach

[4] Two books, best sellers in their day, converted many to the doctrines of the new society. One of these books, *Progress and Poverty*, written by Henry George and first published in 1879, suggested that the inequalities of wealth from which modern society suffered could be eradicated by the imposition of "the single tax," a tax on land. "We hold that to tax land values to their full amount will render it impossible for any man to exact from others a price for the privilege of using those bounties," George wrote, ". . . that it will provide opportunities of work for all men and secure to each the full reward of his labor; and that as a result involuntary poverty will be abolished, and the greed, intemperance and vice that spring from poverty will be swept away." *Progress and Poverty* was in such demand that it was soon translated into a dozen languages and George's followers organized "single-tax" clubs to spread the new gospel. Similarly, Edward Bellamy's *Looking Backward*, published in 1888, set forth the doctrines of the new society so convincingly that it quickly sold a million copies and served Bellamy Clubs as a bible. Picturing a utopian socialist society in the year 2000 A.D., Bellamy explained how socialism had grown out of the development of huge monopolies that had stifled competition. His citizens found it hard to understand why the people of the late 19th century tolerated "the imbecility of the system of private enterprise as a method of enriching a nation . . . in an age of such general poverty and want of everything," an age in which "workmen rioted and burned because they could find no work to do."

together at Ramsgate. It is known that he asked Marx what he saw for the future. "It seemed as though his mind were inverted for a moment," Swinton wrote, "while he looked upon the roaring sea in front and the restless multitude upon the beach. Marx's laconic reply came in a deep and solemn tone:

" *'Struggle!'* "

4. Mr. and Mrs. Parsons

Albert R. Parsons' life began with struggle and ended with it. Before he was fourteen he was in the Confederate Army and served with it in Texas for four years. Sentimental, a singer of songs and a reciter of poetry, he was small and slim, as combative as a bantam rooster, a hair-trigger product of the frontier. When he began life it seemed as if he might develop into a Typical Southern Gentleman, but instead he progressed into the owner of one of those annoyingly logical minds who ask if this is a land of liberty for all, why haven't we all got it and if we haven't got it how do we get it? An expert horseman, a crack shot, he was generous and vain. His wife was the best of all possible wives and his kids were the smartest. He was inordinately proud of the sweep and flair of his black mustache, which he periodically dyed after his hair had turned prematurely gray.

In some ways he was old-fashioned. When he had his picture taken he placed his right hand, up to the thumb, beneath his coat above his heart, and he believed in honor. When he sang, he liked the song to be sad and when he gave a speech he liked to end it with a poem. Proud, something of an actor, sometimes moody, he thought he had to fight any man who called him a liar. Curious and eager for knowledge, he believed that for an honest man there could be no division between thought and action. This was difficult because as he grew older his thoughts, if more strictly logical in his view, were more absolutely uncompromising. He was as high-strung as a race horse. Passionately loyal, when he gave his allegiance it was forever.

On his father's side Parsons was descended from the Rev. Jonathan Parsons, a fiery old Puritan who, from the pulpit of his church, recruited a company from his congregation and marched it off to Bunker Hill, where another Parsons lost an arm.

Albert Parsons' father married Elizabeth Tompkins and shortly after the wedding the two left New England for Montgomery, Ala., where Parsons was born on June 20, 1848. Considerably the youngest of three children, he went to live with his elder brother, William, on a ranch on the Brazos River in Texas when his parents died when he was five years old. A Negro slave, he said later, Aunt Esther, acted as mother to the five-year-old orphan. This fact Parsons believed had a vital influence on his life.

When he was eleven Albert was sent to Galveston, where he became a printer's apprentice on the *Daily News*. When he was thirteen the Civil

War began and the boy, still shorter than a musket, insisted so long and strenuously that he was the equal of any man that he succeeded in enlisting in the cavalry. He was still fighting four years later, taking part in the very last skirmish of the Civil War when he was seventeen.

He returned home a man, troubled with the growing conviction that he had fought on the wrong side. Aunt Esther, who, he said later, "had been my constant companion and had always given me a mother's love," was free now and he could not look her in the eyes. After a time they had a long talk. Parsons always believed that the talk had been instrumental in changing his life. He decided to establish a newspaper which would fight for the rights of the liberated slaves although his fellow veterans told him that if he did so he would not live a fortnight. He did so and for a year no Southern white person spoke to him. Threats arrived almost daily declaring that he was to be lynched, horsewhipped, tarred and feathered, or flogged. Nevertheless he kept on publishing his paper, which he called the *Spectator,* at Waco until he ran out of money, occasionally taking the stump and campaigning for Negro rights as a Reconstruction Republican. In short, he was what conservative historians of the Reconstruction period have been pleased to describe as a "scalawag."

He found the experience conducive to thought about white supremacy and a good many other things and he was still thinking as he saddled his horse and rode away to the northwest of Texas. In Johnson County he met a beautiful Mexican-Indian girl whose name was Lucy Eldine Gonzales and Parsons, who might have developed into a defender and celebrator of white womanhood, fell in love with her. She lived with an uncle who owned a large ranch on Buffalo Creek. For the next three years young Parsons divided his time between Buffalo Creek and Austin, the state capital, where his fight for Negro rights had earned him the position of reading secretary to the State Senate under the Reconstruction Republicans.

Lucy and Albert were married early in 1873, going first to Philadelphia and immediately afterwards to Chicago. They were very much in love and remained so until the end. There is a record of her having been scornfully referred to as a "colored woman," and while the histories touch not at all on this aspect of the Parsons' lives, it might have been one reason why after their arrival in Chicago they associated so exclusively with the foreign-born. The latter frequently have less prejudice than those who have been born in the land of the free.

The young couple arrived in Chicago just before the long depression of '73. Parsons was twenty-five, his wife younger.

Chicago then, according to Barnard's description of the time, had "endless regiments of smokestacks, vast slum areas." A writer from abroad summarized the city with the sentence: "An overwhelming pall of smoke; streets filled with busy, quick moving people; a vast aggregation of railways, vessels and traffic of all kinds; a paramount devotion to the Almighty Dollar; these are the prominent characteristics of Chicago."

But there was not much smoke after Sept. 18, 1873, the day the banking firm of Jay Cooke and Company suspended activities. No longer did the wind from the south, floating over strangely quiet stockyards, distress the senses. Weekly the layoffs, wage cuts, strikes, evictions, breadlines, and hunger increased. There was no public relief until the unemployed by organizing won the soon depleted remnants of the fund subscribed for the victims of the Chicago Fire. As the autumn days lengthened into bitter winter the Parsons saw a world that changed their lives. Entire families stood in a swirl of snow, homeless and evicted, the children crying in the cold of Lake Michigan's piercing wind. Thousands of desperate unemployed, their pleas for food ignored by city and state, paraded through the streets with crude, makeshift signs on which were rudely scrawled the words, "Bread or Blood."

Albert and Lucy Parsons stood on the sidewalk watching the demonstrators. They went to the Lake Front and heard the speeches, until speakers were hauled down and clubbed by police while the newspapers called the speakers Anarchists, Communists, and Socialists. The Parsons wondered about free speech and they wondered, too, what a Communist or Socialist or Anarchist was. The depression dragged on and on and before it was over Albert Parsons had seen men shot and killed when they struck for wages high enough to live on. He did not believe an American should stand idly by and see his country go to ruin. In 1876 he joined the Social Democratic Party, which advocated abolition of the capitalist system and its replacement by socialism.

The following year Parsons took an active part in the great railroad strike during the course of which he had an unusual twelve hours. After addressing a meeting of strikers in the morning, he found himself fired and blacklisted by afternoon when a newspaper described him as "leader of the American Commune." Later in the same afternoon he was taken at gun point to City Hall where Chief of Police Hickey interrogated him before a group of prominent business men who now and then interrupted with the observation that Parsons ought to be strung up. After two or three hours of this Parsons was ushered to the door of City Hall by the Police Chief who said before shoving him outside: "Your life is in danger. Those men in there belong to the Board of Trade and they would as leave hang you to a lamp-post as not. You'd better get out of town and get out quick."

But Parsons did not get out of town. He stayed and played his part in building a Chicago labor movement which was acknowledged to be the strongest of any in America. A certain flair for drama, his obvious sincerity, his practice of singing a song before beginning a speech impartially punctuated with verse and statistics, made him a favorite labor speaker. He and Lucy were determined to find out the reason for society's evils. They were very poor but they enjoyed life, each stimulating the other in a remarkable companionship. Together they read Buckle, Marx, and Morgan, and together, until the two children arrived, they appeared on picket lines and on speakers' platforms. The Texan was particularly a favorite of the foreign-born. His personality formed a kind of bridge between them and those native to the United States.

In 1884 Parsons was editor of the journal *Alarm,* to which Lucy was a frequent contributor. By 1886, when he was thirty-eight years old, he was a national figure, an experienced trade union organizer. For the past ten years he had traversed the country speaking at meetings large and small, "in personal contact," he said, "with hundreds of thousands of working men from Nebraska in the West to New York in the East." Sometimes he spoke as a representative of the Knights of Labor, which he had joined in 1876; sometimes as a representative of "a Socialistic organization," but always, he said, "as an organizer of the working men, always as a labor speaker at labor meetings."

In 1883 Parsons, Spies, and others the country over had organized the International Working People's Association, which had thrown all its resources into the fight for the eight-hour day. Parsons became the recording secretary of the Chicago Eight-Hour League. It was with great satisfaction that he saw the eight-hour movement sweeping the country in 1885 and 1886 with the fervor of a religious crusade. At the same time, as a result of the successful strike on the Wabash and Gould's Southwestern System in 1885, the membership of the Knights of Labor increased sevenfold within a year, from 100,000 in 1885 to 700,000 in 1886. This tremendous growth frightened many a monopolist, who decided that the time had come to try once again to break the labor movement. All that was needed was the opportunity. It arrived in Chicago.

5. Mr. Powderly and the Eight-Hour Madness

Events were moving too swiftly for slim, prim Terence V. Powderly, Grand Master Workman of the Knights of Labor, and he resented it. In the first place, the Knights of Labor, he believed, was growing too fast and with such rapidity that it was undermining his health. In the second place, the nation's workers were going insane, Powderly felt, over their demand for the eight-hour day, determined to strike for it on May 1, 1886.

Harassed beyond endurance, the final straw was a request that he speak at a picnic. He hated picnics because beer was drunk at them and he abhorred all alcoholic beverage. "I will talk at no picnics," he announced, "where the girls as well as the boys will swill beer. . . . If it comes to my attention that I am advertised to speak at picnics . . . I will prefer charges against the offenders for holding the executive head of the Order up to ridicule."

Powderly felt that he was a labor statesman compelled to waste his time on strikes when his proper duty was the rebuilding of society through education. Believing himself impressive, he dressed accordingly. Handsome enough despite worried eyes behind thick-lensed spectacles, he usually wore stiff, stand-up collars, a double-breasted broadcloth coat, and narrow pointed shoes.

Powderly frequently had his doubts about the horny-fisted sons of toil. They were too militant. Strikes were wrong and useless. Education was what was needed for the gradual replacement of capitalism by workers' producer cooperatives. In addition he often complained that he was unappreciated and ignored, called upon to do the work of ten men. An instance in point was the universal ignoring of his proposal that the workers, instead of striking May 1 for the eight-hour day, write letters showing its value to the country which would be sent to the newspapers on Washington's Birthday. Instead of even mentioning this statesmanlike proposal, assembly after assembly of the Knights had sent in resolutions backing the May 1 strike.

There were many others who agreed with Powderly that the singing, shouting, marching movement for the eight-hour day was an inexplicable and unprecedented social phenomenon. "There is eight-hour agitation everywhere," wrote John Swinton in his April 18, 1886, issue. Workers marched and sang from New York to San Francisco. The newspapers were virtually unanimous in some variation of the declaration that the movement was "communism, lurid and rampant." They declared that it would engender "lower wages, poverty and social degradation for the American worker," while inducing "loafing and gambling, rioting, debauchery and drunkenness." The *New York Times* on April 25, 1886, declared the movement "un-American," adding that "labor disturbances are brought about by foreigners."

The workers seemed unimpressed by such warnings. While wearing "Eight-Hour Shoes," footwear manufactured in establishments which had already granted the shorter workday, and smoking "Eight-Hour Tobacco," they everywhere shouted a song that echoed menacingly on the air, at least to employers' ears:

> "We mean to make things over
> We're tired of toil for nought
> But bare enough to live on; never
> An hour for thought.
> We want to feel the sunshine: we
> Want to smell the flowers
> We're sure that God has willed it
> And we mean to have eight hours.
> We're summoning our forces from
> Shipyard, shop and mill
> Eight hours for work, eight hours for rest
> Eight hours for what we will!"

Powderly felt that he was being borne along by a giant tide which drowned the cautious sense with which he sought to direct it. Acutely conscious of the irony of his position, he wrote, as strikes and membership increased throughout 1885 and 1886 when the order grew from 100,000 to 700,000, "Just think of it! Opposing strikes and always striking!" He ordered a moratorium on the receiving of new members but he was as powerless as King Canute. The tide of membership continued to engulf the machinery of the order, organizers ignoring his instructions as completely as the assemblies had ignored his injunction against setting May 1 as a date for striking.

Even the slogan of the order, "An injury to one is the concern of all," was rising to plague him, as members used it in defending the proposed strike. Sixty thousand Negroes had joined the order and Frank Ferrell, Negro leader of New York, was a national officer. The foreign-born and unskilled labor had rushed into the organization by the thousands, unimpressed by its goal of education for producers' cooperatives, but eager for pay raises and trade union protection. Women workers were increasingly active in its ranks under the direction of Leonora Barry. Now one of the largest labor organizations in all the world, many of its members were talking of forming a worldwide labor organization. On rare occasions Powderly himself felt an apprehensive moment of elation until his troubles again bore him down.

They were many. He was for labor peace and yet the newspapers pictured him as an unprincipled agitator intent on overthrowing the government by force and violence. And sometimes the great tide moved even him but when it did he regretted it. Appalled by employer violence in the Hocking Valley, he had been indiscreet enough to say, "I am anxious that each lodge should be provided with powder, shot and Winchester rifles when we intend to strike. If you strike, the troops are called out to put you down and you cannot defend yourselves with bare hands." Aghast at his indiscretion, he had quickly denied the statement but the damage had been done.

The Chicago Central Labor Union in 1885 had recommended to its locals that "the workers arm in answer to the employment of Pinkertons, police and militia by their employers." Trade unions and Socialist clubs, which were expelled from the party for the act, were forming defense companies, particularly in Chicago. Employers, not satisfied with the militia and Pinkertons, were also forming military companies. The *Alarm* reported in 1885, "Although the fact is not generally known even in this city [Chicago], in one large business house alone, there is an organization of 150 young men who have been armed with breech-loading rifles and pursue a regular course of drilling."

Another of Powderly's troubles was the growth of an organization which developed into the American Federation of Labor destined to outlive the Knights of Labor and for a half century practically monopolize the labor scene. Founded in 1881 as the Federation of Organized Trades and Labor

Unions of the United States and Canada, it had its base among the skilled workers of the nation. Organized along craft lines, it sought to build strong and well-knit national unions financially able to carry on strikes, if necessary, to secure increased wages, shorter hours, and improved working conditions.

Among its leaders were prominent Socialists, men like Adolph Strasser and Peter Maguire. Another of its leaders, the up-and-coming Samuel Gompers, regarded himself in those days as a Marxist. With such a leadership it was therefore not strange to find the new national labor center which became the American Federation of Labor in 1886 adopting the following preamble to its constitution:

"A struggle is going on in the nations of the world between the oppressors and oppressed of all countries, a struggle between capital and labor which must grow in intensity from year to year and work disastrous results to the toiling millions of all nations if not combined for mutual protection and benefit."

Accepting the class struggle and the strike as labor's most potent weapon, this new and fighting organization, then an uncertain infant, sought an issue upon which to rally the nation's workers. It found it in the eight-hour day. At its 1884 convention it unanimously adopted a resolution proposing that all labor join on May 1, 1886, to establish an eight-hour day. This action added to Powderly's difficulties, difficulties already great as members of the Knights of Labor, acting against his instructions, tied up the Gould Southwestern system in a strike against pay cuts and for union recognition.

Blood was shed by the National Guard and Pinkertons from Texas to St. Louis where 1,300 strikers were arrested for violating a federal court injunction. On April 7, across the Mississippi river in East St. Louis, seven workers were killed in a battle between strikers and deputy sheriffs, police, and militia.

The newspapers and industrialists were increasingly declaring that May 1 was in reality the date for a Communist working-class insurrection modeled on the Paris Commune. According to Melville E. Stone, head of the *Chicago Daily News*—described at the time as "the greatest money-making publication west of New York"— a "repetition of the Paris Communal riots was freely predicted" for May 1, 1886. On that very day the Chicago newspaper *Inter Ocean* announced: "The socialistic agitators have boasted that they would turn the demonstration in favor of the eight-hour rule to good account. . . . It is intimated that there will be in Chicago today some of the shrewdest wire-pullers of the socialistic movement."

In the meantime Powderly was trying behind the scenes to do all he could to torpedo the eight-hour strike movement. On March 13, 1886, he issued a secret circular which said: "No assembly of the Knights of Labor must strike for the eight-hour system on May 1st under the impression that they are obeying orders from headquarters, for such an order was not, and will not be given."

But workers inside as well as outside the Knights of Labor were not impressed by Powderly's sabotage of the eight-hour strike movement because they were thoroughly committed to what the newspapers termed "the eight-hour madness." Meetings, resolutions, conferences, and parades multiplied as May 1 neared. Torchlight processions were held and perhaps Powderly shuddered a little as he saw the workers march, the red flame lighting up their faces, and as he heard them sing:

> "Toiling millions now are waking
> See them marching on.
> All the tyrants now are shaking
> Ere their power's gone.
>
> Storm the fort, ye Knights of Labor
> Battle for your cause:
> Equal rights for every neighbor
> Down with tyrant laws."

6. Let the Voice of the People Be Heard

Chicago's industrialists even in normal times had more than a little reputation for savagery. Their police department, according to Henry David in his authoritative work *The Haymarket Affair,* was "long used as if it were a private force in the service of the employers." It broke up all meetings of workers as a matter of course and of policy, freely clubbing all within range, jailing labor leaders indiscriminately, and occasionally using their revolvers after smashing in the doors of trade union meetings. Most officials of the force, as well as many patrolmen, drew pay from the corporations as well as from the city. No industrialist was more convinced than the average officer that every striker was a foreign agent and that all foreign-born were Communists plotting the overthrow of the established order.

The local barons of beef, pork, press, merchandise, and farm machinery, the Armours, Swifts, Medills, Fields, and McCormicks, walked Chicago's earth with royal stride, regarding themselves of infinitely finer clay than the Bohemians, Poles, Irish, and Germans swelling the city and doing its work. Something of Chicago's spirit even before May 1, 1886, may be gained from an excerpt from the *Chicago Tribune* of Nov. 23, 1875, in commenting on a meeting of fifty unemployed protesting the policies of the Relief and Aid Society in distributing doles to the unemployed.

". . . There is no people so prone as the American to take the law into their own hands. Judge Lynch is an American by birth and character. . . . Every lamp-post in Chicago will be decorated with a communistic carcass if necessary to prevent wholesale incendiarism or prevent any attempt at it."

During the two months preceding May 1, David writes, "disturbances occurred repeatedly and it was a common sight to see patrolwagons filled with armed policemen dashing through the city." All through March and April tension rose, like a thermometer in the sun, as daily additional thousands were reported in the Chicago newspapers as pledging strike on May 1. All through March and April Albert R. Parsons and August Spies worked as they had never worked before, persuading local unions to favor May 1 action.

Parsons, an eloquent speaker, was a powerful advocate. An acknowledged leader now of Chicago labor, he was not only a member of the Knights of Labor but a founder and official of the Central Labor Union with 12,000 members.

In March Chicago locals of furniture makers, machinists, gas fitters, plumbers, iron molders, brickmakers, and freight handlers passed resolutions for a May 1st strike, if not given the eight-hour day before that date. Early in April 35,000 stockyard workers voted to join the walkout and as April days lengthened hod carriers, plasterers, butchers, toy makers, boot and shoe workers, dry goods clerks, and printers joined the giant movement. By the last week in April *Bradstreet's* estimated that 62,000 Chicago workers had pledged to strike on May 1, while by Friday, April 30, another 25,000 Chicago workers had demanded the eight-hour day without threatening strike, and 20,000 had already won the shorter day.

As employers made preparations to mobilize the National Guard, increase the force of Pinkertons, and deputize special police, labor held two large and militant mass meetings, the first a Knights of Labor rally on April 17 with 7,000 inside the Cavalry Armory and 14,000 outside, the second on Sunday, April 25, when Albert Parsons and August Spies addressed 25,000 workers.

The Chicago newspapers, with the *Tribune* often reverting to variations of its favorite theme of "a communistic carcass for every lamp post," concentrated their fire on Parsons and Spies, as the persons most responsible for the eight-hour movement in Chicago.

May 1 was a beautiful day in Chicago. The blustery wind from the Lake, often particularly piercing in spring, suddenly died away and the sun was strong. It was a quiet day in more ways than one, the factories still and empty, the warehouses closed, the teamsters idle, the streets deserted, construction halted, no columns of smoke ascending from factory chimneys, the stockyards silent.

It was Saturday, ordinarily a day of work. But crowds of workers, laughing, chatting, joking, and dressed in their best clothes, accompanied by their wives and children, were assembling for a parade on Michigan Avenue. The avenue was gay with a holiday spirit—great red-necked men, a little awkward in their store clothes, repeating with satisfaction, "Everybody's out in my place; even the cat," but on side streets and nearby roofs the atmosphere was grim.

Off the main route of the parade and on streets adjacent to it, companies of armed police and special officers were gathering ready to enforce "law and order." On strategic rooftops police, Pinkertons, and militia officers were stationed with rifles and other paraphernalia of war. In the state armories 1,350 members of the National Guard were mobilized and under arms, uniformed, equipped with Gatling guns, and ready to march on the instant. In a central office building were gathered leading members of the Citizens Committee who remained in continuous session throughout the day prepared to receive reports from all points of the impending conflict; the general staff that was to direct the battle to save Chicago from the Communistic eight-hour day.

Albert Parsons, his figure trim, felt good. Walking in the soft May sunlight with Lucy and the two children toward Michigan Avenue, his heart leaped within him as he saw the thousands on thousands of strikers forming for their parade. August Spies, his best friend, his yellow mustache quivering with excited pleasure, ran up with a copy of the *Chicago Mail*. Some 340,000 workmen were parading all over the country. About 190,000 had gone out on strike. In Chicago some 80,000 had walked out for the eight-hour day and most of them, said Spies, excitedly waving his arm, were right here waiting for the parade to begin. Almost as an afterthought, he indicated an editorial in the *Mail* which said in part:

"There are two dangerous ruffians at large in this city; two skulking cowards who are trying to create trouble. One of them is named Parsons; the other is named Spies. . . .

"Mark them for today. Keep them in view. Hold them personally responsible for any trouble that occurs. *Make an example of them if trouble does occur.*"

The parade was beginning, the thousands getting under way, each member of it feeling some surging emotion of quickened, joyful solidarity as he marched. The children sometimes broke away from their parents and skipped ahead. People laughed with a queer elation, continually looking back at the vast marching concourse which seemed a visible symbol of labor's power when unified. In its seemingly unending numbers were Knights of Labor and members of the American Federation of Labor; Bohemians, Germans, Poles, Russians, Irish, Italians, Negroes, and former cowboys who now worked at the stockyards. There were Catholics, Protestants, and Jews, Anarchists and Republicans, Communists and Democrats, Socialists, Single-Taxers, and just plain people all one and irresistible for the eight-hour day.

Parsons walked near the parade's head, holding hands with Lucy; Lulu, seven years old, held her father's hand, Albert, eight, his mother's. The parade turned into the Lake Front, gathering there for speeches in English, Bohemian, German, and Polish. Parsons spoke of the invincible might of united labor. Spies, thirty-one, editor of the German workers' paper, *Arbeiter-Zeitung,* and equally eloquent in his native tongue and in English, was a favorite of the crowd. He was extraordinarily striking in appearance with a classic, sensitive profile, blue eyes and a very white skin. The applause for Spies died away and May 1 was all over.[5]

There had been no bloodshed, no repetition of the Paris Commune. The militia demobilized, the excitement of the morning gone, its members looking a little sheepish as they skulked home, their uniforms unpleasantly prominent in the crowds of civilians, many of whom had paraded. The press apologetically minimized its many predictions of violence. The police went back to ordinary tours of duty.

Expecting Armageddon, Chicago felt a little cheated at getting only peace. The next day was Sunday and Parsons left for Cincinnati where he was to address a meeting. On Monday the strike spread and several thousand Chicago workmen actually gained the eight-hour day while the Citizens Committee continued to declare that something had to be done.

The police, exasperated by the futility of May 1 after such high expectations, gained some relief by clubbing the locked-out employees of the McCormick Harvester Works as they rushed in 300 scabs. At closing time a great crowd of the locked-out employees were waiting the exit of the scabs when police suddenly charged them with drawn revolvers. They retreated when police, according to a witness, "opened fire into their backs. Boys and men were killed as they ran." It was reported that six had been slain. Spies, who had been speaking at a nearby meeting of striking lumber workers, was a witness to the massacre and, after he had reported it to his colleagues, it was decided to call a protest meeting against police violence for the next evening at Haymarket Square.

Parsons had returned from Cincinnati, still in high spirits, still jubilant at reports that thousands of workers all over the country were gaining the eight-hour day. After he gave a detailed account of his trip, Lucy told him as they ate at noon in their Indiana Street home of the meeting called for Haymarket Square, but added that on Sunday, while he was gone, she had called together a meeting of sewing women who were anxious to organize. Excited by the prospect, Parsons decided to skip the Haymarket meeting and meet with Sam Fielden and other officials of the Working People's

[5] This great demonstration for the eight-hour day in the United States was not forgotten. "In 1888 the American Federation of Labor . . . voted to continue the eight-hour movement, fixing May 1, 1890, as the time for action. The following year leaders of the organized labor movement in various countries met in Paris to form an international association of working people. After hearing reports of what had happened in America, they voted to support the eight-hour fight and designate May 1, 1890, for an international eight-hour-day struggle. On that day workers all over Europe showed their solidarity with working people in America by taking part in parades, meetings and demonstrations for a shorter work day." (H. M. Morais & W. Cahn, *Gene Debs: The Story of a Fighting American,* New York, 1948, p. 27.) Thus, international May Day was born in America, growing out of the struggle for the eight-hour day.

Association at the office of the *Alarm*, 107 Fifth Avenue, to plan the organization of the women.

That evening the whole family, the two children and a Mrs. Holmes, assistant editor of the *Alarm*, walked down the street to take a street car to the office. Waiting for the street car, they met a group of newspaper reporters who asked them about the Haymarket meeting, one of the reporters saying, "We hear there's going to be trouble tonight."

Parsons smiled and said, "Are you armed for the battle?"

"No," said the reporter. "Have you any dynamite on you?"

The street car was coming and Parsons took his little girl up into his arms. Mrs. Parsons looked fondly at her husband and said to the reporter, "He's a very dangerous looking man, isn't he?"

They were debating various proposals for an organizing campaign when a messenger ran in breathless. "There's a big meeting over at Haymarket," he said, and "Spies is the only speaker. He wants you to come," he said to Parsons, "and you, too, Fielden."

The crowd had been too small for Haymarket Square and Spies, who had arrived first, had pushed an empty wagon into a corner of the cobble-stone street, a half block away, the wagon to serve as a speakers' platform. Near by was the Desplaines Street Police Station, under the command of Captain John "Clubber" Bonfield, where, unknown to Spies, 180 patrolmen were mobilized, ready to march on the meeting if the occasion called for it. Unknown also to him was the fact that Mayor Carter Harrison was in the crowd.

Spies was speaking from the wagon when he saw Parsons walk up with his wife and children. The crowd saw him, too, and began to applaud. After placing his wife and two children on another empty wagon, Parsons approached the improvised speakers' platform, crawled up, and was introduced. "I am not here for the purpose of inciting anybody," Parsons said, "but to speak out and tell the facts as they exist." The Mayor of Chicago picked his way out of the audience, making his way to the nearby police station where he told Captain Bonfield that the meeting was peaceable and that the mobilized patrolmen should be dismissed and sent back to regular duty.

Parsons finished speaking at ten. A cold wind had whipped in off the lake and there had been a few drops of rain. It looked as if there would be a storm. Many in the crowd left. Sam Fielden was speaking now but Parsons lifted his wife and children off the wagon where he had left them and with some others adjourned into a pleasant saloon on the corner known as Zepf's. Soon the group were laughing and telling stories over mugs of beer as Fielden outside, a pedestrian speaker, plowed on before a steadily dwindling crowd.

"Is it not a fact," he was saying, "that we have no control over our own lives, that others dictate the conditions of our existence, that—" Suddenly there were cries of urgent warning. "Look! The police!" Down the street, in regular military formation, their clubs drawn, came 180 patrolmen, led by Captain Bonfield and Captain Ward. The crowd began to run as Captain Ward stopped before the wagon and, addressing the astonished Fielden, said: "In the name of the people of the State of Illinois, I command this meeting immediately and peaceably to disperse."

"But Captain," gasped Fielden, "we are peaceable."

There was a moment of silence and in the blackness of night there was the sound of running feet. Then there was a flash of red and a terrific explosion. Someone had thrown a bomb. There was a terrible confusion in the darkness, police firing wildly in every direction, people falling, many being wounded, others running, cursing, moaning, being trampled upon and wildly clubbed by the maddened police, one of whose number had been killed outright, and seven of whom were fatally wounded.

The next day Chicago and the nation exploded into one great cry for vengeance. "With the blast of the bomb," David writes in his account of the Haymarket affair, "the press lost every vestige of objective accuracy. . . . A characteristic headline screamed 'NOW IT IS BLOOD! . . . A Bomb Thrown into [Police] Ranks Inaugurates the Work of Death.'"

The *New York Tribune* reported:

". . . The mob appeared crazed with a frantic desire for blood and holding its ground, poured volley after volley into the midst of the officers."

Although from the first there were more than a few who thought that the bomb had been thrown by a hired agent provocateur, a hypothesis which later gained a measure of police corroboration, it was not safe to say so on the morning of May 5 or for many a day thereafter. "I passed many groups of people whose excited conversations about the events of the preceding night I could not fail to overhear," writes a Chicagoan of that time. "Everybody assumed that the speakers at the meeting and other labor agitators were the perpetrators of the horrible crime. 'Hang them first and try them afterwards,' was an expression which I heard repeatedly. . . . The air was charged with anger, fear and hatred."

The nation's press was a unit in declaring that it made no difference whether Parsons, Spies, or Fielden had or had not thrown the bomb. They should be hanged for their political views, for their words and general activities and if more trouble makers were given to the hangman so much the better. "Public justice," said the *Chicago Tribune,* "demands that the European assassins August Spies, Michael Schwab [another member of the Working People's Association] and Samuel Fielden, shall be held, tried and hanged for murder. . . . Public justice demands that the assassin A. R. Parsons, who is said to disgrace this country by being born in it, shall be seized, tried and hanged for murder."

R. H. Baugh, writing in the *Spectator,* said that, while a conviction was inevitable, even if the unthinkable should happen and the accused men were acquitted that fact would not save them from death. If acquitted, he said, they would be hanged by a mob. "A Vigilance Committee," he wrote, "will take the law into their own hands, and restore social order, by suspending civilization for three days."

The police, urged on by the press and pulpit, by the great and the near great demanding immediate revenge, went wild, packing Chicago's jails with hosts of foreign-born, smashing into private homes, breaking down doors, wrecking the presses of foreign-language newspapers, raiding the headquarters and offices of trade unions and other working class organizations. ". . . Suspects were beaten and subjected to the third degree," writes Professor Harvey Wish, "individuals, ignorant of the meaning of socialism and anarchism were tortured by the police," and "sometimes bribed as well to act as witnesses for the state." "Make the raids first and look up the law afterwards," said Julius S. Grinnell, Chicago State's Attorney, who would prosecute the cases.

The reign of terror, soon to spread to other cities, had as its main target trade union leaders. In ensuing weeks the entire district executive board of the Knights of Labor in Milwaukee was arrested and charged with "rioting and conspiracy"; four officers of the Knights of Labor in Pittsburgh were arrested and charged with conspiracy while in New York the executive board of District Assembly 75 of the Knights of Labor was arrested and charged with conspiracy while directing the Third Avenue Elevated strike. John Swinton declared that the New York working class was living "under a reign of terror. Corrupt judges and police who are slaves of monopoly, are now dragging citizens to prison by the wholesale."

Parsons, feeling almost on the instant that the bomb had been thrown by a paid agent and that he was one of the prospective frame-up victims, managed to escape amid the confusion immediately after the crime at Haymarket. Within a few days he was indicted for conspiracy to murder Mathias J. Degan, the patrolman slain at Haymarket, as were Spies, Fielden, Michael Schwab, George Engel, Adolph Fischer, Louis Lingg, and Oscar Neebe. Of these only Spies and Fielden had been at the scene when the bomb exploded. Parsons, with his wife and two children, it will be recalled, had been at Zepf's saloon, and a few hours later Parsons was out of Chicago.

While police frantically searched the country for him, he was secure, spending day after day on the top of a hill overlooking a peaceful Wisconsin countryside. But he found peace and safety difficult to take while his associates were in peril. Knowing that he would be hanged if he returned, he nevertheless felt that he could not remain in safety while innocent friends were framed up and executed. Knowing, as Governor John P. Altgeld of Illinois later formally found to be a fact, that he would face a packed jury, perjured testimony, and a judge determined on hanging, he nevertheless insisted on surrendering, suddenly appearing in court on the trial's first day where he said, with something of a flourish, "I have come to stand trial, your Honor, with my innocent comrades."

And he told a friend, "I know what I have done. They will kill me. But I couldn't bear to be at liberty, knowing that my comrades were to suffer for a crime of which they are as innocent as I."

Proceedings began before Judge Joseph E. Gary on June 21. The jury, consisting largely of businessmen and their clerks, was a packed one and the trial judge prejudiced. According to the later findings of Governor Altgeld of Illinois, "when the trial judge in this case ruled that a relative of one of the men killed was a competent juror, and this after the man had candidly stated that he was deeply prejudiced . . . and when in a score of instances he ruled that men who candidly declared that they believed the defendants guilty . . . when in all these instances the trial judge ruled that these men were competent jurors . . . then the proceedings lost all semblance of a fair trial."

In addition, "much of the evidence given in the trial was pure fabrication," said the Governor, adding that testimony was gained from "terrorized, ignorant men" whom police had threatened "with torture if they refused to swear to anything desired. . . ."

It was these witnesses, all of them terrified and some of them paid, who testified that the defendants were part of a conspiracy to overthrow the government of the United States by force and violence and that the Haymarket bomb and Degan's murder were the first blow in what was to have been a general assault on all established order. But their testimony was so filled with contradictions that the state was compelled to shift its ground in the midst of the trial. The core of the state's charge then became the allegation that the unknown person who had thrown the bomb was inspired to do so by the words and ideas of the defendants.

Thus the trial was transformed into a trial of books and the written word, a procedure which was later to be repeated in the United States. Endless editorials by Parsons and Spies were read. Interminable speeches by the defendants were recited to the jury. Excerpts were torn from the context of involved works on the nature and philosophy of politics and described as damning evidence against the conspirators. The political platform of the Working People's Association, its resolutions and statements were regarded as evidence involving the defendants in the murder of Degan.

The trial was conducted with all the sensational histrionics, all the stage properties which so often transform American legal proceedings into lurid public spectacles. As usual in such matters, a massive armed guard was thrown around the courthouse with the announcement that at any moment an anarchist army would attempt a rescue. As usual, people fought for seats, those successful in gaining entry bringing their lunches, and afternoons were fragrant with the smell of oranges and slippery from banana peels on the courtroom floor. As usual, it became the smart thing to attend, and the city's select somehow found their places at the side of Judge Gary himself, where the august jurist laughed and chatted, conducting charming little games with paper and pencil with his friends, and even offering them candy as the defendants fought for their lives.

The press was there, of course, in all its glory, from every great city of the country. Thousands of words were printed daily in all parts of the country. From these dispatches we learn of the graceful, laughing society people beside Judge Gary on the bench, learn of the wives of the defendants, pale and haggard, their restless, bewildered children clinging to them, as they crowded together in the front row. We are informed that the courtroom was hot and suffocating, that the people packed together had scarcely room enough to wave the fans with which they had supplied themselves, and that the length of the trial, dragging on week after week, reflected the justice of American jurisprudence wherein even the guilty get all the impressive forms of the law before hanging.

The defendants are described again and again; the stolid Fielden, the debonair Spies, the melodramatic Parsons, the tall, pale Fischer, the consumptive Schwab, the defiant Lingg. "They have neither penitence or remorse," one reporter wrote, "and to their twisted minds it is society which is on trial and not themselves."

From press reports we learn of a young girl who gave a bouquet of flowers to each defendant as he came into the courtroom and of a poorly dressed man who sobbed as Fielden addressed the jury, later telling a reporter, "I've lived near him for years and a better neighbor nor an honester man never lived." We are told of the beautiful Nina Van Zandt, youthful heiress who fell in love with Spies as she watched him fight for his life and sacrificed a fortune to marry him by proxy in the futile hope that the wedding would somehow save him.

The verdict was almost a formality and the trial's big day arrived when the condemned men arose in court to accuse the accuser, to say why death sentence should not be passed upon them by Gary, and why it was not they but society that was guilty. They dominated the courtroom and they dominated the country that day. No newspaper was so conservative that it did not admit that the defendants in defying death and in defending the working class were both dignified and impressive.

Neebe, who received a sentence of fifteen years and was the only one of the defendants not condemned to death, was one of the first to address the court. He said in part:

"I saw that the bakers in this city were treated like dogs. . . . I helped organize them. That is a great crime. The men are now working ten hours a day instead of fourteen and sixteen hours. . . . That is another crime. And I committed a greater crime than that. I saw in the morning when I drove away with my team that the beer brewers of the city of Chicago went to work at four o'clock in the morning. They came home at seven or eight o'clock at night. They never saw their families or their children by daylight. . . . I went to work to organize them. . . . And, your Honor, I committed another crime. I saw the grocery clerks and other clerks of this city worked until ten and eleven o'clock in the evening. I issued a call . . . and today they are only working until seven o'clock in the evening and no Sunday work. That is a great crime. . . ."

Neebe concluded by asking that he also be condemned to death, declaring that he was no more innocent than his friends, that they all were innocent. Parsons spoke next, a flower in his lapel, poetry on his lips. He began by quoting:

> "Break thy slavery's want and dread;
> Bread is freedom, freedom bread."

Defiant and impassioned he was and there were some who thought him theatrical until they perceived that he was near collapse as he neared the end of a two-day effort to clear his name and his beliefs. He insisted again that he had never advocated force save as a reply to force first used by employers. Reading from a long list of newspaper editorials advocating the use of violence against strikers, he then documented his charge with instance after instance in which Pinkertons, police, and militia had shot and killed workers without provocation. He charged in addition that the thrower of the Haymarket bomb had been hired to throw it by industrialists intent on bombing the eight-hour day out of American life. Continuing, he said:

"For the past twenty years my life has been closely identified with, and I have actively participated in, what is known as the labor movement in America. . . . I am an Anarchist. Now strike! But hear me before you strike. What is Socialism or Anarchism? Briefly stated it is the right of the toiler to have the free and equal use of tools of production and the right of the producers to their product. That is Socialism.

"I am a Socialist. I am one of those, although myself a wage slave, who holds that it is wrong, wrong to myself, wrong to my neighbor, and unjust to my fellowmen for me to make my escape as a wage slave by becoming a master and an owner of slaves myself. . . . Had I chosen another path in life I might now be up on the avenue of the City of Chicago today, living in a beautiful home surrounded by my family with luxury and ease, with slaves to do my bidding. But I chose the other road, and I stand here today upon the scaffold. This is my crime.

"Were they [the monopolists] not the first to say 'Throw dynamite bombs among the strikers, and thereby make a warning to others'? Was it not Tom Scott [president of the Pennsylvania], who first said, 'Give them a rifle diet'? Was it not the *Chicago Tribune* which first said, 'Give them strychnine'? And they have done it . . . They have thrown bombs and the bomb of the fourth of May at Haymarket was thrown by the hands of a monopolist conspirator sent from the city of New York for the specific purpose of breaking up the eight-hour movement. . . . Your Honor, we are the victims of the foulest and blackest conspiracy that ever disgraced the annals of time."

But it was Spies who hit the highest note as he addressed Judge Gary:

"If you think by hanging us you can stamp out the labor movement . . . the movement from which the down-trodden millions, the millions who toil in want and misery, expect salvation—if this is your opinion, then hang us! Here you will tread upon a spark, but there and there, behind you and in front of you, and everywhere, flames blaze up. It is a subterranean fire. You cannot put it out. . . .

"And now these are my ideas. They constitute a part of myself. I cannot divest myself of them, nor would I, if I could. And if you think you can crush out these ideas that are gaining ground more and more every day, if you think you can crush them out by sending us to the gallows . . . if you would once more have people suffer the penalty of death because they have dared to tell the truth . . . then I will proudly and defiantly pay the costly price! Call your hangman! . . . Truth crucified in Socrates, in Christ, in Giordano Bruno, in Huss, in Galileo still lives—they and others whose number is legion have preceded us on this path. We are ready to follow!"

On October 9, 1886, the sentence of death was passed. Judge Gary's face, according to the report of the *New York Times* in describing the sentencing of Spies, "worked convulsively . . . and when he reached the word 'hanged,' he faltered and could with difficulty utter 'till you are dead.' The last words were scarcely audible."

Chicago was relieved. It was all over but the hanging. Lucy Parsons did not agree. Accompanied by her two small children, raising money wherever and however she could, she began a tour of the country, intent "on saving the lives of seven innocent men, one of whom I love dearer than life itself." While the case of her husband and his co-defendants was being fruitlessly appealed to the Supreme Court of Illinois and the Supreme Court of the United States, Lucy Parsons ceaselessly moved over the country for almost a year, addressing more than 200,000 people in sixteen states, speaking at night, traveling by day, caring always for her children, often insulted, sometimes prevented from speaking, as when she was arrested and thrown into jail at Columbus, Ohio.

Proud and dry-eyed until this incident, she began weeping wildly and uncontrollably as two beefy deputies bundled her roughly off to a cell after she had protested to the mayor of Columbus at being denied a permit to speak. "They jerked my shawl off my shoulders," she later said, "the better to grip my arms in a vise, and as they dragged me downstairs [I cried], 'You scoundrels! Does it take two of you to carry one little woman?'"

She wrote hundreds of letters to trade unions and prominent people both in the United States and abroad, and her passionate devotion was instrumental in creating what many considered a miracle. Starting from almost Lucy Parsons alone, a protest movement grew until it became worldwide and included millions. America's leading man of letters, William

Dean Howells, wrote "I have never believed them guilty of murder, or of anything but their opinions, and I do not think they were justly convicted. This case constitutes the greatest wrong that ever threatened our fame as a nation."

After the United States Supreme Court refused to examine the case, execution was set for Nov. 11, 1887. Now the only hope was that Governor Oglesby would commute the sentences to life imprisonment.

Robert Ingersoll, Henry Demarest Lloyd, John Brown, son of the great emancipator, hundreds of Chicago's leading citizens, scores of trade union leaders, including Samuel Gompers, and thousands of people the country over appealed to the Governor for clemency, declaring the men were being hanged for their political opinions.

In France the Chamber of Deputies asked the Governor for clemency, as did protest meetings of workers in Italy, France, Spain, Russia, Holland, and England, where George Bernard Shaw and William Morris worked to save the lives of the condemned men.

Fielden and Schwab had appealed for clemency, as had Spies, who regretted it when he heard there were some who interpreted it as a sign of cowardice. Parsons steadfastly refused to ask for mercy, declaring that such a request was an admission of guilt. Finally both he and Spies addressed communications to the Governor which were read at a hearing before the chief executive two days prior to the scheduled hangings. They were read to Governor Oglesby by Joe Buchanan, Denver labor editor and organizer. Spies' letter was an effort to undo his previous petition for clemency. It said:

"During our trial the desire of the prosecution to slaughter me and let off my co-defendants with slighter punishment was quite apparent and manifest. It seemed to me then, and to a great many others, that the prosecution would be satisfied with one life—namely mine. . . . Take this then; take my life. . . . If legal murder there must be, let one, let mine suffice."

As Buchanan read Parsons' message to the Governor, "the blood of the listeners turned cold."

"If I am guilty," Parsons had written, "and must be hanged because of my presence at the Haymarket meeting, then I hope a reprieve will be granted in my case until my wife and two children, who were also at the meeting, can be convicted and hanged with me."

"My God, this is terrible," Governor Oglesby exclaimed, hiding his face in his hands.

The day before the execution the Governor commuted the death sentences of Fielden and Schwab to life imprisonment. On the same day Lingg, only 22, unable to speak English and described as "not having a friend in the world outside of his native Germany," either committed suicide or was murdered in his cell.

Some time before Parsons had written this to "My poor, dear wife. . . . You, I bequeath to the people, a woman of the people. I have one request to make of you: Commit no rash act when I am gone, but take up the great cause of Socialism where I am compelled to lay it down."

The four condemned men, Spies, Fischer, Engel, and Parsons, did not sleep much their last night but they seemed relieved that their ordeal was nearly over. In a room not far removed from their cells carpenters were erecting the gallows and the hammering could be heard plainly throughout the night. They stopped in their work toward morning when Parsons began to sing "Marching to Liberty," his rich tenor voice swelling through the jail. And then, quite softly, as if to himself and perhaps to one other, he sang "Annie Laurie."

In the morning Sheriff Matson and his deputies came to the four cells, bound the legs and arms of each man, and dressed each in a flowing white shroud. As her husband was being prepared for execution Mrs. Parsons and her two children were frantically trying to gain entry to the jail to see Parsons one last time. She was prevented from passing a line of police thrown about the prison in the belief that anarchists were about to attempt a rescue. When she insisted, she was arrested and locked with her children in a cell.

The execution room was crowded with officials and reporters when the four men were led in. They stood straight and proud above their accusers, somehow seeming very tall in their white shrouds on the scaffold high above the heads of the witnesses. There was something exalted in their manner as they took their places, each beneath a dangling noose, and more than one witness likened them to John Brown and his men who also had died for mankind.

As a deputy pulled down a mask before the face of August Spies the condemned man spoke a single sentence.

"There will come a time," he said, "when our silence will be more powerful than the voices you strangle today."

"This is the happiest moment of my life." Fischer said and Engel shouted, "Hurrah for anarchy!"

Parsons' voice boomed out asking if he might speak. "Will I be allowed to speak, O men of America? Let me speak, Sheriff Matson! Let the voice of the people be heard!"

He tried to go on but the trap was sprung.

In hanging Parsons, Spies, Fischer, and Engel, the big monopolists of the day were directing their blows not so much at the men themselves or the movement they represented, but at the much more potent force of organized workingmen in the country. It was the labor movement in general and the Knights of Labor in particular that they were determined to crush. As a Chicago businessman declared in referring to Parsons and his associates:

"No, I don't consider these people to be guilty of any offense but they must be hanged. I am not afraid of anarchy; oh, no, it's the Utopian scheme of a few philanthropic cranks who are amiable withal, but I do consider that the labor movement must be crushed! The Knights of Labor will never dare to create discontent again if these men are hanged!"

If the industrialists had not hired the unknown person who threw the bomb at the Haymarket, they at any rate profited from its throwing, immediately and skillfully using it for a terrific assault against labor. "The bomb that was flung by unknown hands," wrote John Swinton, "has been a godsend to all the enemies of the labor movement. They have used it as an explosive against all the objects that the working people are bent on accomplishing and in defense of all the evils that capital is bent on maintaining."

"The historical perspective," wrote William Dean Howells, "is that this free Republic has killed four men for their opinions.

"All is over now except the judgment that begins at once for every unjust and evil deed, and goes on forever."

CHAPTER IV

"The Cross of Gold"

"You shall not press down upon the brow of labor this crown of thorns; you shall not crucify mankind upon a cross of gold."

WILLIAM JENNINGS BRYAN, 1896

"A declaration of war does not change the moral law. . . . Then, more than ever, it is the duty of the good citizen not to be silent, and in spite of obloquy, misrepresentation and abuse, to insist on being heard, and with sober counsel to maintain the everlasting principles of the moral law."

CHARLES ELIOT NORTON, 1898, IN OPPOSING THE SPANISH-AMERICAN WAR

1. Prelude to Battle

Memory softens the harshness of the past until men see it through a golden haze mellowing all that was unpleasant and quite hiding that which we wish to forget. So it is with the nineties in the United States when industrial monopoly graduated into imperialism. The conquest of Puerto Rico and the Philippines, the massacres of union men at Homestead and Coeur d'Alene are forgotten, replaced by some impression of a bicycle built for two, Sweet Adeline, and corpulent patrolmen with gray helmets and John L. Sullivan mustaches.

The fierce conflicts of Chicago and Colorado, the strikes of steel workers, metal miners, and railroad men, the jailing of literally thousands of labor's rank and file, the renascence in the South of lynch-enforced white supremacy are lost in the mists of the past—replaced by memories of the old swimming hole, the moonlight boat ride, and the beer garden with its singing waiters. But as a matter of fact they were cruel and bloody years that stretched between 1890 and 1900.

It was the decade that heard Senator Beveridge of Indiana declare that it was America's destiny to rule the world, bringing profits to Wall Street and order to lesser breeds, to the yellow, brown, and black men who he said needed the inspiration and control of the American Way. Its symbol, at least among the elite, was Teddy Roosevelt, charging at the head of his Rough Riders up San Juan Hill to make Cuba safe for the American Sugar Refining Company. It was the time in which American finance underwent a qualitative change, beginning to export its money and Marines into the Caribbean and the Pacific, grabbing Puerto Rico and the Philippines by force of arms, controlling Cuba as a protectorate, and annexing Hawaii outright.

And it was the decade which saw one more gallant effort by the common people, the workers and farmers, to wrest the country from the control of Wall Street through independent political action. It was the time of labor's tall Gene Debs and the miners' Big Bill Haywood, of Sockless Jerry Simpson and Mary Elizabeth Lease, who advised the nation's farmers to "raise less corn and more hell." It was a decade in which monopoly, steadily growing since the Civil War, pyramided into new heights of power and it was a decade of depression when the ragged regiments of Coxey's Army of unemployed marched on Washington with demands for relief.

It was the time of Boy Bryan who in 1896, as the youthful Democratic candidate for President, rode out of the West with such force and sweep that even the rich feared for a spell that the end of monopoly had arrived, replaced by the rule of the people. Their fear was based on the knowledge that capitalism was still regarded by brigades of farmers and hosts of workingmen as an evil. Even the American Federation of Labor had a powerful wing of Socialists and they had long debates over resolutions, that narrowly missed passage, which advocated the people's ownership of private industry, a proposal endorsed in referendum by twelve of the Federation's unions. And while the Knights of Labor had but a shadow of the power that was theirs before the assault of Haymarket, James R. Sovereign, who replaced Powderly as Grand Master Workman in 1893, still called for the abolition of the wage system and the establishment of an order whose factories, mines, mills, railroads, and utilities were owned and operated by the people.[1]

"Let the voice of the people be heard," said Albert Parsons with his last breath. It was heard throughout the nineties and in tones of thunder. The Haymarket martyrs were not forgotten. Gene Debs, after being released from imprisonment for his leadership of the railroad strike of 1894, visited their graves at Waldheim Cemetery in Chicago where he said that their

[1] The American Federation of Labor was the first national labor center in American history to endorse capitalism. For thirty important years in American history the two dominant national labor organizations, the National Labor Union and the Knights of Labor, called for the replacement of the capitalist system by an economy owned and operated by the whole people.

souls went marching on, giving life and strength to the American labor movement.

Even before their executions labor was surging ahead politically. With every newspaper predicting labor's demise as a result of the Haymarket bomb, the trade unions and Socialists of New York came close to winning the mayoralty election in the fall of 1886. Labor, as its opponents confidently waited for it to roll over and die, ran independent candidates for Congress in 1886 in Maine, Connecticut, New York, New Jersey, Pennsylvania, Ohio, Kentucky, Michigan, Illinois, Wisconsin, Arkansas, Kansas, and Washington. It entered independent labor candidates for the legislatures of most of these same states and ran candidates in municipal elections in a score of cities.[2]

Despite these political struggles, monopoly usually won the elections and monopoly steadily grew. Yet such was the public clamor against the growing power of the trusts, ever increasing their grip on every aspect of American life, that in 1890 the Sherman Anti-Trust Act was passed, designed to prevent price-fixing and monopoly control but destined to be used more successfully against labor than against the corporations.[3] As the 1890's began there were price-fixing, wage-fixing, trusts in oil, sugar, whiskey, iron and steel, cottonseed oil, lead, tobacco, meatpacking, agricultural machinery, telegraph, telephone, and railroads. And the great age of financial concentration, of the narrowing control of the few who reaped fabulous profits from the work of the many, had just begun.

It was a historic irony that just as a single corporation began to operate a multiplicity of plants and to control a long series of industrial operations,

[2] Organized labor's fight-back before and after the execution of the Haymarket martyrs brought with it higher wages and shorter hours for the working people of America, nonunion as well as union. In 1890 average wages for all nonagricultural workers were 12.3 per cent higher per day than in 1880. For those in the unionized building trades the increase was even greater; the 1890 figure was 20.9 per cent higher than the 1880 one. Organized labor's fight-back in the eighties also paid off in shorter hours. The eight-hour-day agitation in particular produced results; the average working week was reduced from 60 hours in 1880 to 58.4 hours in 1890 and the average working day from 10.3 hours to 10 hours. In this connection workers in organized occupations were again better off than those in unorganized fields. In the unionized building trades the average working day was lowered from 9.9 hours in 1880 to 9.6 hours in 1890. In that year workers in unionized manufacturing industries were working 7.8 hours less per week than in nonunionized ones.

[3] When the Sherman Anti-Trust Act was passed it was generally agreed that labor did not come within the scope of its provisions. However, judicial interpretation, or as Henry D. Lloyd so aptly put it "judicial lynch law," transformed the act into an anti-labor law. From 1892 to 1896 the government brought ten cases under the act before the courts. Of these ten cases five were against labor and five against corporations. The courts decided in favor of the government in four of the five cases against labor and in only one of the five cases against the trusts. It is significant to note that the first time the Sherman Anti-Trust Act was successfully used was in 1894-95 against Debs and other Pullman strike leaders.

one corporation hiring miners, railroaders, and steel workers as in the case of Carnegie Steel, labor began to fragment itself into craft unions whose initiation fees were so high that it was difficult for a worker to join them. At the moment industrial unions became a necessity, the prevailing method of labor organization became that of comparatively small and separate groups. With industry centralizing into huge empires, such as Standard Oil and the American Sugar Refining Company, with scores of factories sometimes under a single ownership, labor under the American Federation of Labor was separating itself into exclusive rival departments of skilled workers while completely ignoring the millions of unorganized, unskilled workers in mass industries, particularly Negroes and the foreign-born.

Under this system in which management could play off one union against another, where it was faced with any union organization at all, it was difficult to strike even a single factory since all the crafts except the one with a grievance would often continue to work. And when the workers of a factory did succeed in uniting and walking out, management was increasingly in the position of waiting out the strike without serious loss through forwarding the work to another factory under the same ownership.

While industrialists, as they amply proved, never gave up their plan of destroying labor unions, there was much that they liked about the American Federation of Labor. Not only was its craft system, in the eyes of business, preferable to industrial unions but Gompers' dictum that labor should not take independent political action was also pleasing. It was not from the American Federation of Labor that the country's owners expected trouble, but from the farmers.

2. *"Less Corn and More Hell"*

The owners of the country were right. The farmers, aided by the Knights of Labor, the United Mine Workers and a good many trade union locals, founded that independent political movement known as the People's Party, or the Populists, which the industrialists and financiers of the East described as a "wave of the socialist revolution" and as "an onslaught on the rights of property." Never had there been such a movement. It swept the West, a great impassioned fiery crusade, daily growing in strength and numbers. It flared into the South, blazed into the Northwest, consumed and destroyed for a time the two old parties in Kansas, Nebraska, Colorado, Minnesota, and Iowa. Its million or more proponents argued and shouted and came together and held conventions with the fervor of those moved by a new religion whose devil was Wall Street and whose hell, they said, was the impoverished land created by the trusts.

All over Kansas, Colorado and Iowa, Nebraska, Michigan and Illinois, Indiana, Georgia, Alabama and Texas, vast concourses of farmers came together, some riding on mules, some walking hundreds of miles for the privilege of getting up on their hind legs and telling the world what was wrong with the country. Great hosts of wagon teams were tied to trees in Western forests about conclaves attended by whole families and their dogs, which lasted all day and where men and women recounted their wrongs before huge assemblages which whooped and hollered and sang songs of revolt set to the tunes of old-time hymns.

Elizabeth Barr, writing of the period, declared: "It was a religious revival, a crusade, a pentecost of politics in which a tongue of flame sat upon every man and each spoke as the spirit gave him utterance." A resentment growing since the Civil War had burst into words and action. "There are three great crops raised in Nebraska," wrote a farm editor in August, 1890. "One is a crop of corn, one a crop of freight rates, and one a crop of interest. One is produced by farmers who by sweat and toil farm the land. The other two are produced by men who sit in their offices and behind their bank counters and farm the farmers."

With corn sinking to as low as ten cents a bushel, wheat dropping to forty-nine cents, and cotton dipping to a little less than six cents a pound,[4] farm foreclosures mounted all over the country as the new decade got under way. A mortgage of $1,450, which in 1867 could have been paid off with 1,000 bushels of wheat, in 1894 took 2,959 bushels to retire. In Kansas from 1889 to 1893 over 11,000 farm mortgages were foreclosed and in some counties as much as 90 per cent of the farm lands passed into the hands of the bankers. In Kansas and North Dakota in 1890 there was a mortgage for every two inhabitants while in Nebraska, South Dakota, and Minnesota there was one mortgage for every three persons.

During these years people who had come to Kansas and other lands of the West trekked eastward again, signs on their wagons proclaiming such messages as "In God we trusted; in Kansas we busted" and "Going Back to My Wife's Folks. In God We Trusted. Going Home." But others stuck it out and one of them wrote, "We can't keep going west. We got to stay now and fight. . . ."

With such conditions and such feelings common to all parts of the country, organizations known as Farmers' Alliances developed during the eighties. Now they were combining into regional associations, into the Northern Alliance and the Southern Alliance, their membership increasing by the thousands as the 1890's began and they prepared for a nationwide political campaign. They called for more currency, silver coinage, easier

[4] The downward trend of farm prices can be seen in the following official government figures given by the Department of Agriculture. From 1870 to 1873 the average price of wheat was $1.067 per bushel, corn 43¢ per bushel, and cotton 15.1¢ per pound; from 1886 to 1889 the average prices were 74.8¢, 35.9¢, and 8.3¢ respectively and from 1894 to 1897, 63.3¢, 29.7¢, and 5.8¢, respectively. These official government figures were actually higher than the price the farmer was paid for his products. The government figures are based on prices for December 1; the farmer had to sell long before that time when the market was glutted.

credit, lower interest rates, cheaper freight rates, government loans on crops, the regulation of people's ownership of the railroads, and always they insisted that their fight was labor's fight and labor's fight theirs. Increasingly their resolutions scored the use of Pinkertons and troops against strikers and called for the eight-hour day.

Sovereign, head of the Knights of Labor, and other trade union leaders were attending the farmers' meetings as they attempted to transform themselves into a national political party. In the South, in more than one state, white farmers were combining with Negro farmers in efforts at political action. By 1891 the Colored Farmers' National Alliance and Cooperative Union had 1,250,000 members and state organizations in twelve states.

Every state was developing dynamic leaders, many of them women. One of them was Mrs. Mary Elizabeth Lease, a native of Ireland and the mother of four children, who told the insurgent Kansas farmers: "Wall Street owns the country. It is no longer a government of the people, by the people, and for the people, but a government of Wall Street, by Wall Street, and for Wall Street. The great common people of the country are slaves, and monopoly is the master. . . . Money rules. . . . The common people are robbed to enrich their masters. . . . The people are at bay. Let the bloodhounds of money who have dogged us thus far beware."

And something of the crusade's temper may be gained from the words of Jay Burrows, a Civil War veteran and leader of the Nebraska Farmers' Alliance. "We send the plutocrats a grim warning," he said. "The twin of this oppression is rebellion. Rebellion will seek revenge with justice, that will bring with it Pandora's box, fire, rapine and blood. Unless there is a change made, a remedy found, this day is as inevitable as that God reigns, and it will come soon."

Few could put on a better show on the hustings than the Populist Tom Watson, revered of Georgia farmers, a quick and angry man who fought some mighty battles for the people until he sold out in his old age. In describing his energy someone said he was "a team of horses and the dog under the wagon besides." In his days of power he had advocated Negrowhite unity. When he became corrupted he was one of the Negro people's most bitter foes. But in 1891, when the People's Party was organized in Georgia, he insisted that Negroes should be put on its committees. On the relation between the white farmer and the Negro farmer, Watson wrote at that time:

"Now the People's Party says to these two men, 'You are kept apart that you may be separately fleeced of your earnings. You are made to hate each other because upon that hatred is rested the keystone of the arch of financial despotism which enslaves you both. You are deceived and blinded that you may not see how this race antagonism perpetuates a monetary system which beggars both.' "

The Populists' entry into the national campaign of 1892, when Benjamin Harrison was the Republican nominee and Grover Cleveland the Democratic, was no spontaneous event. Hundreds of pamphlets had been written and were circulated in millions of copies. There were great petition campaigns in the fight to get on the ballot. It took hard work, shrewd organizing, and a series of meetings, conferences, and conventions to reconcile the conflicting viewpoints of farmers and workers from all parts of the country. The first conference was held in St. Louis, the second at Oscala, Fla., while a third was held in Cincinnati. At the latter meeting Robert Schilling, trade union leader, president of the Coopers' Union, and member of the Knights of Labor, was named secretary of the new party's executive committee.

At St. Louis on Feb. 22, 1892, where delegates were present from more than twenty organizations, representatives of the Knights of Labor, the United Mine Workers of Ohio, and a scattering of other trade union organizations, took a prominent part in the proceedings. At this meeting Omaha was named as the place and July 4, 1892, as the date for a founding and nominating convention of the People's Party.

Some 1,300 delegates attended and launched the new party with an emotional fervor and a belief in the justice of their cause seldom matched in American politics. Quoting the Bible and singing hymns, their battle cry was the summons from Scripture, "Then to your tents, O Israel!" Their cause was to return the American land to the American people; to rescue the American earth and all the richness thereof from "predatory plutocracy"; to transform Americans from automatons and pawns in the hands of monopoly to principals with a voice in their own lives and their country's life.

The stage was decorated with red, white, and blue bunting and on it sat the leaders of the Farmers Alliance, the Knights of Labor, anti-monopolists, and Single-Taxers. Across the stage behind them stretched a banner saying, "We Do Not Ask for Sympathy or Pity: We Ask for Justice." The Populist paper, *The Great West*, became lyrical as it reported the militant hope of the convention, declaring: "The party of the common people, the child, is come, and it is a giant at birth. The blood is circulated in 10 million hearts which from the depths cry out for a better life. Its sledge hammer swings with the muscles of the toiling army. . . . This is your party. The thrones of despotism are trembling. . . . Get into the fight."

The convention adopted a preamble, drafted by Ignatius Donnelly, which read:

"We meet in the midst of a nation brought to the verge of moral, political and material ruin. Corruption dominates the ballot-box, the legislatures, the Congress, and touches even the ermine of the bench. . . . The newspapers are largely subsidized or muzzled; public opinion is silenced and business prostrated; our homes covered with mortgages; labor impoverished; and the land concentrating in the hands of the capitalists.

"The urban workers are denied the right of organization for self-protection . . . a hireling standing army, unrecognized by our laws, is established to shoot them down, and they are rapidly degenerating into European conditions. The fruits of the toil of millions are boldly stolen to build colossal fortunes for a few, unprecedented in the history of mankind; and the possessors of these in turn despise the republic and endanger liberty. From the same prolific womb of governmental injustice, we breed two great classes—paupers and millionaires."

The platform adopted at Omaha declared:

". . . Wealth belongs to him who creates it, and every dollar taken from industry without an equivalent is robbery. 'If any will not work, neither shall he eat.' The interests of rural and civil labor are the same; their enemies are identical.

". . . We believe that the time has come when the railroad corporations will either own the people or the people must own the railroads. . . . Transportation being a means of exchange and a public necessity, the government should own and operate the railroads in the interest of the people.

". . . The telegraph and telephone, like the post office system being a necessity for the transmission of news, should be owned and operated by the government in the interest of the people."

The convention signalized the reunion of the common people, North and South, by nominating for President the Union general, James Baird Weaver of Iowa, and for Vice President the Confederate general, James C. Field of Virginia. The delegates wept at this symbol of a reunited people.

As the delegates left Omaha, excited by their experience, they felt they had glimpsed the mighty power of a unified people and their ability to transform the nation into a country that produced happiness instead of profits.

But the killing of workers by Pinkertons and troops brought them back to reality. On July 6 300 Pinkertons had been imported to Carnegie's steel mills at Homestead, Pa., where the Amalgamated Association of Iron and Steel Workers had been locked out in Henry Frick's successful effort to smash the union and slash wages. In the ensuing battles seven workers had been killed, as were three Pinkertons. The Pennsylvania National Guard had been called out on July 11, the very day a pitched battle had been fought at Coeur D'Alene, Idaho, between miners fighting against a wage cut and strikebreakers. The regular army was dispatched to Idaho, where 1,200 strikers were imprisoned in a barbed-wire enclosure, while eighty-five miners were indicted for contempt of court, twelve being convicted. And the troops had been called to Buffalo, too, where 6,000 armed militia broke the strike of railroad switchmen against a pay cut.

Wages and farm prices, already low, were falling to new depths as the depression of 1893 drew nearer. But as thousands of workers and hundreds of thousands of farmers prepared for the Presidential election of 1892 they were certain that all this would be changed, that Pinkertons, foreclosures, and trusts would be engulfed by a people's victory in November.

3. *Eagle Forgotten*

Each night for six months the light burned late in the study of John Peter Altgeld, the German immigrant who had become Governor of Illinois. In response to petitions from trade unions and liberals that he pardon the three survivors of Haymarket, who had now served seven years in prison, he was studying the monumental record of the trial.

Even his study of it, when the fact became known, outraged the political nerves of members of his administration. It was midnight when one of them entered the study, staring accusingly for a moment at the little Governor, whose blue eyes were curiously alive in a chalk-white face.

"I know, I know," Altgeld said wearily. "If I do it I will be a dead man politically." He went back to his examination of the record and sometime later another friend warned him. This time the Governor hit the desk with his fist, an unusually emphatic action for him, and said, "By God, if I decide that these men are innocent I will pardon them if I never hold office for another day."

He did so decide. In a decision then characterized as the ravings of a madman but now recognized as a state paper of first rank, he said that the four Haymarket victims had been legally lynched for their political opinions and that the three survivors were being imprisoned not for their actions but for their beliefs.

Altgeld knew what was coming and he faced it without flinching. The next morning, and already there was the rumble of journalistic thunder, Brand Whitlock, the Governor's secretary, met the chief executive. "He was riding his horse," Whitlock writes, "and he bowed and smiled that faint, wan smile of his, and drew up to the curb a moment. There was, of course, but one subject then, and I said:

" 'Well, the storm will break now.'

" 'Oh yes,' he replied with a not wholly convincing air of throwing off a care, 'I was prepared for that. It was merely doing right.'

"I said something to him then to express my satisfaction in the great deed that was to be willfully, recklessly and cruelly misunderstood. I have wished since that I had said something that could perhaps have made a great burden a little easier for that brave and tortured soul. But he rode away with that wan, persistent smile. And the storm did break, and the abuse it rained on him broke his heart."

"And the storm did break" with a ferocity unparalleled in American annals. But the little German immigrant, his black suit fitting him at an angle that always suggested Ellis Island, did not break. Backed by labor and the people, Altgeld fought on against anti-labor injunctions, against child labor, for the rights of the foreign-born and trade union members.

The journalistic attack increased in intensity during the remainder of his lifetime. He seldom picked up a paper without seeing himself lampooned in a cruel cartoon, yet those who watched him never saw in his face the faintest flicker of pain.

Altgeld, his name still a sneer in the mouths of most historians, has been buried in oblivion, although it is said that a generation of fighters for labor and reform were inspired by his example. The poet Vachel Lindsay has written of him:

"Sleep softly . . . eagle forgotten . . . under the stone,
Time has its way with you there, and the clay has its own.
Sleep on, O brave-hearted, O wise man, that kindled the flame—
To live in mankind is far more than to live in a name,
To live in mankind, far, far more . . . than to live in a name."

4. The Conservative Mr. Debs

Folks thought of Abraham Lincoln when they saw Gene Debs. It was not only his lanky height and a certain power that emanated from his loose frame with its great bald head and aggressive slant of jaw. It was his connection with people. His strength came from them. His development was a result of their development. His growth was forced upon him by their needs.

He was the quintessence of the Middle West. He could recite most of the poetry of James Whitcomb Riley, celebrator of Middle Western joys and virtues, who was his friend. At his parents' wedding anniversaries he was fond of giving flamboyant toasts to Father and Mother. "There are two words in our language," he said on one such occasion, "forever sacred to memory—Mother and Home! Home, the heaven upon earth, and mother its presiding angel."

He recited poems about "Friendship" and "Love of Country" and such brave speeches as that of Patrick Henry demanding "Liberty or Death" and that of John Brown upon receiving sentence of death for what his accusers called treason. At the age of sixteen he was a locomotive fireman and, believing in self-improvement, as did most Americans then, he was also the president of a literary society and a member of a debating club. He liked nothing better than a good speech and, as a boy, by his own efforts brought to Terre Haute, Ind., where he was born, such famous Americans as Wendell Phillips, fighter for labor and against Negro slavery, and Robert Ingersoll, the well known agnostic, then described as the world's foremost orator.

At eighteen he was "six feet of wiry muscles, hard as a spike maul, accepted by veteran railroad men as a first-class 'rail.' "

By the time he was twenty-four he had been elected to public office and at thirty he was a member of the Indiana legislature. All his life his neighbors tried to run him for Congress and from his early manhood there were many who saw in him a future President of the United States. But as the fight against slavery formed Lincoln, the fight against monopoly shaped the life of Debs. Instead of bringing him to the White House, his career twice brought him to prison with the respectable and the rich assailing this native of the banks of the Wabash as a foreign agitator. Frequently, as we shall see, he was the target of the old, old charge of conspiring to overthrow the United States government by force and violence, the inspirer of what was called the "Debs' Rebellion."

Debs had a sentimental goodness about him that in another man might have been mawkish. Again and again over the years he would return to his home on a cold winter day without his overcoat, which he had given away to some shivering member of the unemployed. Once when a railroad worker told him he could get a promotion if only he had a watch, needed on the proposed new job, Debs gave him his own watch. He was always turning his pockets inside out, stripping them of what money they contained, as he gave it to those he thought needed it more. He had faults, too. He liked drink overmuch and his idea of a good time was to tell stories and recite poetry before a bar. Yet few men have ever worked so hard. Organizer, orator, editor, writer, strike leader, he counted the hours lost that he spent in sleeping. From his nineteenth year he was a union man and from that time on he gave most of his time and all of his energy to the working class.

"As a locomotive fireman," Debs wrote, "I learned of the hardships of the rail in snow, sleet and hail, of the ceaseless danger that lurks along the iron highway, the uncertainty of employment, scant wages and altogether trying lot of the workingman, so that from my very boyhood I was made to feel the wrongs of labor. . . ."

He was only nineteen when he quit the railroad because of the entreaties of his mother, who feared he might be a victim of one of the many fatal railroad accidents that were then common. But he could have said then, in quitting the work he loved, what he did say later: "When I rise it will be with the ranks and not from the ranks."

Young Debs became a grocery clerk. Hating the clerking, he hung around the freight yards and the roundhouse, anywhere he could find railroad men, and when a firemen's union was organized at Terre Haute he joined it, soon becoming its first secretary. It was in 1874 that he joined the Vigo Lodge of the Brotherhood of Locomotive Firemen. In common with most other members of the brotherhood he did not then believe in strikes. Feeling, as did virtually all of the members, that its chief function was to provide cheap insurance, he preferred the name of fraternal order to trade union.

Naturally conservative and a hater of violence, he was "confused and stunned" by the rioting and bloodshed that accompanied the railroad strike of 1877. Steadily rising in the brotherhood, he had this to say of the 1877 strike to a national convention of the firemen at Indianapolis:

"A strike at the present time signifies anarchy and revolution, and the one of but a few days ago will never be blotted from the records of memory."

Young Debs, who sat out and condemned the greatest railroad strike of the time, was pleased when a railroad president, Riley McKeen, head of the Vandalia Railroad, praised him for his speech at the Indianapolis convention. Convinced of the goodness of men, pleased by his own rapid rise in the union, he felt certain that industrial strife was unnecessary and that all railroad presidents were kindly gentlemen who would rectify abuses and raise wages when the true situation was made clear to them.

And yet the canker of doubt must already have been eating away at his fine faith. The 1877 strike had almost wiped out even the railroad brotherhoods, the engineers, firemen, and conductors, organizations which had not backed the strike. The blacklist and the "iron-clad" or yellow-dog contract were common.[5] Almost at the same time that he was denying the presence of a class conflict, Debs was describing the blacklist as "dirty in its very conception and damnable in every feature." For he was no pie card, intent on creating for himself a soft and easy job. It was a passion with him to serve faithfully his membership, and increasingly all his thought was directed to the problem of how all labor could improve its position.

He rapidly became indispensable. His energy was such that the union's headquarters were actually moved to Terre Haute so it could retain his services. In 1880 he was elected secretary-treasurer and appointed editor of the *Locomotive Firemen's Magazine*. At this point, with only sixty lodges and a debt of $6,000, many in the brotherhood wished to dissolve it. To Debs this was unthinkable. At the 1881 convention, buttonholing delegates everywhere, seeing them in their rooms, arguing before bars, pursuing them out into the street, Debs almost singlehandedly saved the union.

In 1881 the membership doubled. Militancy increased the following year as railroad employees became additionally restive under the blacklist and pay cuts, and again membership increased. In 1882 the brotherhood had 5,000 members and the circulation of the magazine was increasing from 3,000 monthly to what in a few years became 30,000 monthly.

Although Debs was City Clerk of Terre Haute, he was always on the move. Riding in cabooses when he was able, sometimes in the engineer's cab, often grabbing a freight, he traveled all over the country on organizing trips and all over Indiana investigating accidents so that insurance could be swiftly paid. Then he would dash back to Terre Haute, get out an issue of

[5] The blacklist is a weapon used by employers to keep active trade unionists or those sympathetic to trade union organization from employment. Coming into general use in the United States after the panic of 1837, it was an established practice in the 1880's. In his *Labor Movement in the United States,* published in 1886, Richard T. Ely remarked upon the widespread use of the blacklist, citing specific examples to illustrate the point. The "ironclad" contract, or, as it came to be called in the 20th century, the yellow-dog contract, was another favorite anti-union device used by employers. Introduced in the 1870's and 1880's, this employer-inspired contract made the worker signing it renounce his connection with a trade union.

the magazine, writing almost everything in it himself, and catching up on his accounts as city clerk. Speaking of those days later, he said:

"My grip was always packed. To tramp through a railroad yard in the rain, snow or sleet half the night, to be ordered out of the roundhouse for being an agitator or to be put off a train, were all in the program."

Back in Terre Haute, he wrote editorials, directed audits, participated in Democratic politics, and found time to organize locals of carpenters and printers.

When the union held its 1882 convention in Terre Haute it was generally agreed that Gene Debs had saved it. "When other men had wavered he had stood firm," Ray Ginger writes in his excellent biography of Debs. "He had brought to the labor movement a determination and concentrated force which astonished his fellow officers. He worked with an urgency that affected his colleagues and even his mother. Often Daisy went to her son's room long after midnight and found him asleep over a half-written letter. With silent reproach, she turned out the lamp and left him slumped across the desk. The next morning he usually began working again before he had even finished breakfast. The problems of the firemen were Debs' whole life—yellow-dog contracts, the blacklist, poverty, accidents, corporate arrogance and corporate greed.

"But Debs was still certain that labor disputes could be solved by reason and compromise."

The facts of life began to change Debs' mind in 1884 with the arrival of another of the periodic depressions which have punctuated American history on the average of every ten or dozen years. Adding to the pressure for a change in his viewpoint were the workers themselves. As wages dropped and unemployment mounted they saw little in a union that gave them only cheap insurance. "The delegates to the BLF convention of 1885," writes Ginger, "were tired of the blacklist, yellow-dog contracts, unemployment and long hours. They were fed-up with meek submission. They thought the time had come to fight. Their first act was to knock out the no-strike provision in their constitution. They did not want to strike, but by God they would if they had to; they proved this by providing a fifteen-thousand dollar strike fund."

Debs was learning that if he did not believe in strikes or the class conflict, the rank and file did. The convention of 1885 continued to revolt by throwing out the brotherhood's national officers who had declared against strikes, with the exception of Debs and one other. They saw sincerity, ability, and fight in Debs, insisting on keeping him even when he tried to resign. They also believed in unity, in federation of the separate railroad brotherhoods, instructing Debs to attend the New Orleans convention of the Brotherhood of Locomotive Engineers with proposals for joint action. He did and was refused the floor or entry to the convention, forced to view its proceedings as an outsider from a balcony.

From that time on Debs increasingly became an advocate of federation between the brotherhoods and of joint action on wages and disputes. As the great eight-hour movement involved hundreds of thousands of workers the country over, Debs' militancy increased, borne along by the rushing torrent of trade union organization. The killing of railroad workers in East St. Louis and Texas during the Gould strike of 1886 modified his ideas about the absence of a class conflict. He learned, too, from the sell-out tactics of Powderly, another trade union leader who did not believe in strikes, as he saw the Grand Master Workman of the Knights of Labor play his part in wrecking that organization by selling out strikers, making agreements behind the backs of the workers in both the Gould strike and the stockyard strike in Chicago.[6]

His education was furthered by the strike of engineers and firemen on the Chicago, Burlington & Quincy which began on Feb. 27, 1888. It had been called reluctantly at the demand of the rank and file after the company had stalled in negotiations for a wage raise for over two years. Pinkerton thugs, hired by the railroad, gave frequent demonstrations of the class conflict by assaulting strikers and Debs wrote of them:

"They are distorted, deformed, hideous mentally and morally. Their trade is treason, their breath pollution and yet the officials of the C.B.&Q. formed a conspiracy with these professional liars, perjurers, cut-throats and murderers to overcome a strike, the result of a policy of flagrant injustice."

Even worse than the Pinkertons was the strikebreaking of rival unions. As the switchmen continued at work and members of the Knights of Labor took strikers' places in locomotives, Debs began to have stronger feelings about labor unity. After frantic appeals he succeeded in gaining the support of both switchmen and the Knights and, as the strike became solid, he was certain of victory. Sleeping on desks, living on sandwiches, addressing hundreds of meetings hundreds of miles apart, Debs did not see home or bed for weeks on end. He was the vital motor of the strike, tireless, sleepless, never running down. Unable to break the strike, the railroad decided to apply for a court injunction.

Upon receiving this news P. M. Arthur, head of the engineers, became panic-stricken and announced that he was ordering the engineers back to

[6] In 1885 the Chicago packinghouse workers walked off their jobs, closing down the stockyards. Everything pointed to a victory. At this point Powderly opened negotiations with the employers and, before the workers realized it, he ordered the men back to work. Soon afterwards the strike was broken. During the 1886 strike on Gould's Southwest System Powderly injected himself into the situation in an almost identical fashion. Having made a no-strike agreement in 1885 with the lines, Powderly felt duty bound to stop the strike. He was able to get his executive board to order the men back to work. Unfortunately for him, however, the Gould railroads refused even to deal with the union. The men were forced to strike again but Powderly continued his behind-the-scene maneuvers and on May 4, 1886, the general executive board called the strike off "in the public interest."

work. The firemen struggled on alone for almost a year but they gained nothing but the blacklist.

Debs was bitter. A single union was helpless, he wrote, but the strike could have been won in a day "if from the first there had been federation between engineer and firemen, switchmen and brakemen on the C.B.&Q." Somehow he no longer believed that a strike signified "anarchy and revolution." Instead he declared:

"The strike is the weapon of the oppressed, of men capable of appreciating justice and having the courage to resist wrong and contend for principle. The nation had for its cornerstone a strike, and while arrogant injustice throws down the gauntlet and challenges the right to conflict, strikes will come, come by virtue of irrevocable laws, destined to have a wider sweep and greater power as men advance in intelligence and independence."

Debs was learning the hard way but life and history had sterner lessons in store. Devoting his whole time now to the fight for unity, he and like-minded colleagues succeeded at last in forming a federation of the brotherhood of brakemen, switchmen, and firemen on June 3, 1889. From the first, united action won every strike, prevented more, and put money into the pockets of the railroad workers. The trainmen's union was about to enter and pressure was strong for participation of engineers and conductors when the federation suddenly and completely collapsed in 1892 over a bitter but minor jurisdictional dispute.

Debs was as conservative politically as he had been as a trade unionist. A confirmed Democrat, he was moved by the stirring people's movement of 1892 when the Populists ran General Weaver with the backing of the Knights of Labor and the farmers, but he found their platform too radical. He was opposed to government ownership of the railroads. Yet he wrote in the firemen's magazine that the Populists might be the party which would "discard class legislation and inaugurate a reign of justice."

Despite this feeling he worked for Grover Cleveland, successful Democratic candidate and a former President, who two years later would be instrumental in sending him to prison. Defeated as to the Presidency, the Populists nevertheless scored stunning gains. They elected governors in Colorado, Kansas, North Dakota, and Wyoming, sending two Senators and eleven Congressmen to Washington, naming 354 representatives to legislatures in nineteen states, and polling 1,027,239 votes, the equivalent of 5,000,000 in an election today. Pinkertons, foreclosures, and trusts had not been eliminated but so many voters had favored their elimination that the radical wing of the Democratic Party began advocating the adoption of the Populist program for its own platform in 1896.

Debs did not sulk or quit after the defeat of his great plan for railroad unity. Beginning work all over again, he gradually decided that a completely different and new kind of labor organization was needed, one which would replace the rival railroad brotherhoods with one big union of all railroad employees. It was not, strictly speaking, his idea. Men everywhere were weary of the jurisdictional fights of rival crafts and were discussing the industrial union. The times themselves reinforced his plans.

As Debs, thirty-eight now and married, worked on his new plan in his home in Terre Haute, he was appalled by the depression. The Panic of '93 was one of the severest the country had experienced up to that time. "Before six months had passed," writes the historian John D. Hicks in his book, *The American Nation,* "no less than eight thousand bank failures, involving liabilities of $285,000,000, were recorded. Four hundred banks, most of them in the West and South, closed their doors. Railroads followed each other into receivership in a procession that ended only after fifty-six companies, among them the Erie, Union Pacific, and the Northern Pacific, had gone into bankruptcy. Panic conditions lasted throughout the summer, after which the country . . . [waited] out a depression that was to last four years."

However, these four years were no waiting period for big business tycoons. J. P. Morgan "reorganized" the Erie and the Southern Railway and fastened his grip on the Philadelphia and Reading, the New York, New Haven and Hartford, and the Northern Pacific. Rockefeller picked up the Mesabi iron ore range for a song, forming the Lake Superior Consolidated Ore Mines Company. Carnegie expanded his mill operations and with the help of Rockefeller drove out iron ore producers in the Lake Superior region. Schiff of Kuhn, Loeb acquired the Union Pacific, only to be forced out by Harriman, the "human dynamo," who added this property to his Baltimore and Ohio holdings.

While the big monopolists were growing richer the farmers and workers were growing poorer. Farm prices were hitting all-time lows as it became cheaper to burn corn for fuel on the farms than to ship it to the cities. Workers saw their already meager wages drastically cut and unemployment rising to the estimated trade union figure of 4,500,000. Armies of unemployed roamed the country. Unemployed demonstrations became the order of the day. Among the most famous of these was the one led by General Jacob S. Coxey of Massillon, Ohio, a Greenbacker and Populist. The march, begun Easter Sunday, 1894, reached Washington on May 1. The marchers, five hundred strong, determined to present their demand for jobs through public works projects to Congress, were stopped by police stationed at the end of Pennsylvania Avenue. Coxey and other leaders were quickly arrested for stepping on the grass and the demonstrators dispersed. Unable to deliver from the steps of the Capitol the speech he had prepared, Coxey issued the following public statement:

"Up these steps the lobbyists of trusts and corporations have passed unchallenged on their way to the Committee rooms, access to which we, the representatives of the toiling wealth producers, have been denied. We stand here today in behalf of millions of toilers whose petitions have been buried in Committee rooms, whose prayers have been unresponded to, and whose opportunities for honest, remunerative labor have been taken away from them by unjust legislation, which protects idlers, speculators and gamblers."

As to Coxey and countless others, so to Debs the depression was appalling. With millions unemployed, Debs wrote in 1893 that "the capitalist class, like a devilfish, has grasped workingmen with its tentacles and is dragging them down to fathomless depths of degradation." As he watched mothers and their children root about in garbage cans for food, saw swarms of unemployed and evicted tramping over the countryside, he became more determined to help build a type of union which would really protect the working class. He gave away his best suit and now, more than ever, he seldom walked a mile without giving away whatever money he had on him.

Once when delegates at a convention spoke of the sacrifices he had made for the labor movement, he said impatiently, "I have a heart for others and that is why I am in this work. When I see suffering about, I myself suffer. When I put forth my efforts to relieve others, I am simply helping myself. I do not consider that I have made any sacrifice whatever. No man does unless he violates his conscience."

His lanky height, balding dome, and jutting chin were rapidly becoming a trade mark for integrity. If he wore his heart on his sleeve, he had brains in his head—and used them. John A. Hill wrote in the *Locomotive Engineer* that Debs was "by far the ablest labor speaker and writer in America" and George Howard, during the brief period of federation, told the Brotherhood of Conductors in 1890, "The majority of our successes for the past year was brought about through Eugene V. Debs . . . that fearless champion of the rights of labor under any and all circumstances."

The crux of Debs' power was his closeness to the rank and file and his ability to learn from them and from experience. It was Debs' prestige, as well as the overwhelming need for unity that gained wide and immediate acceptance for his plan for a new kind of union; an industrial union which united all railroad workers into one organization instead of dividing them into separate and often hostile crafts. It was new for railroaders, and new enough generally, although the brewery workers and the coal miners were organized industrially, and the metal miners were organizing similarly into the Western Federation of Miners even as Debs was working out his plan.

The American Railway Union was born in Chicago on June 20, 1893. From the first it attracted national attention because industrialists feared an industrial basis of organization. Debs was elected president. L. W. Rogers was named editor of its proposed publications. Sylvester Keliher was elected secretary and George Howard vice president. Headquarters were in Chicago. Dues were a dollar a year and even miners and longshoremen were eligible providing they received their pay checks from a railroad company.

But the great and tragic weakness of the new union was its constitutional exclusion of Negroes, its denial at birth of its own fundamental principle of the absolute unity of all railroad employees. At its first national convention the following year Debs led a bitter fight for the admission of Negroes and almost won. Later, he said that the exclusion of Negroes had been an important factor in the union's defeat and death and that the fight to exclude them had been led by those who were proved to be spies in the pay of the railroads. "They proved subsequently," he said, speaking of the leaders of the anti-Negro group, "to have been traitors to the union, sent to the convention at the instigation of the corporations to defeat the unity of the working class."

But defeat was far from Debs' mind as American railroad workers stampeded into the new union with shouts of joy. This is what they had been waiting for, they said. It sometimes seemed as if all of the more than 600,-000 railroad employees of the country were trying to get in at once. "By November 15, charters had been issued to eighty-seven lodges," Ginger writes, "enabling the order to keep four organizers on the payroll. At the year's end the Union Pacific, the Santa Fe, the Denver & Rio Grande, the Rio Grande & Western, and several lesser roads were solidly organized. There were twenty-two ARU locals on the Northern Pacific and more than forty on the Southern Pacific. Debs was everywhere advising the workers to resist all wage cuts during the depression, because if wages were once cut it would take years to have them restored; but his advice was not needed. Never had he seen such a spirit among the railroaders."

The heads of the do-nothing Brotherhoods were bitter as their membership daily decreased. Sam Gompers attacked the infant union which was breaking all records for phenomenal growth. Daniel de Leon, head of the Socialist Labor Party, hailed the ARU as "a step in the direction of clasping hands with the whole working class in all other industries," but Debs was more pleased with the mighty rush into the union of the unskilled and underpaid, thousands of whom had not been eligible for the brotherhoods.

The first test was a fight against a wage cut on the Union Pacific, spectacularly and unexpectedly won without a strike when a federal court, acting as a receiver and reversing a previous decision, rescinded the proposed slash in wages. But the real baptism of fire came with the strike on the Great Northern, the property of James J. Hill, who owned most of the Northwest as well and who had started on the road to power and wealth during the Civil War. The strike was called April 13, 1894, after three wage cuts had been suffered. Average wages on the Great Northern were $40 a month. From the first the strike was solid; scarcely a man worked, not a train, freight, or locomotive moved. The brotherhoods ordered their members back but ordered in vain.

From the first Debs and his colleagues laid all their plans to avoid violence, knowing that violence would fill only the needs of management. The Great Northern posted signs the length of its track declaring that any interference with the mails would be penalized by two years in federal prison but few read the signs. The men were at home. After the railroad had been motionless for two weeks Hill, in a meeting with Debs at St. Paul, said he would negotiate if the brotherhoods were parties to the bargaining. "If the brotherhoods control your workers," Debs asked, "why can't they move your trains? The strike will be settled on our terms or not at all."

Hill's next move was to order his Governor of Minnesota, one Knute Nelson, to summon Debs to his office where he called Debs "a foreign agitator" and an "anarchist." Debs waited until the tirade was over when he said, "You can't bluff me. You wear Jim Hill's collar. I don't. You are acting under his orders. I am here to fight him." Before the end of the interview Hill's Governor was begging Debs not to misunderstand him. "The trouble," Debs told him, "is that I do understand you. I can see clear through you."

Debs stood fast, as did the rank-and-file worker on the Great Northern. After eighteen days Hill surrendered and the strike was over. It was one of the few unequivocal victories that had ever been scored against a major railroad. It made a tremendous nationwide impression. The absolute unity of the strikers, the complete unity of action of all crafts, and Debs' integrity and skill won employees an aggregate raise of $146,000 a month. As Debs' train left St. Paul to take him back to Terre Haute and home, thousands of railroad workers stood silently and bareheaded beside the tracks. It was their way of thanking and honoring their leader. Debs never forgot it and wrote long afterwards:

"The greatest tribute that was ever paid to me was that of the section men after the Great Northern strike. As my train pulled out of St. Paul, those men with shovels in hand and happiness fairly radiating from their faces, yet with tears in their eyes—those section men stood at attention. Their tribute was more precious to me than all of the banquets in the world."

Within two weeks a sequence of events began that was to bring against the new union all the resources that monopoly could throw against it—the United States government, the President of the United States, the United States Army, the Attorney General, the courts, the prisons, bullets, and the press which outdid itself in describing what it called the "Debs' Rebellion." No matter how it is viewed it is an extraordinary chapter in American history. Because a trade union, with unusual generosity, tried to help some starving factory workers, all the forces of the established order were released to crush it and imprison its leaders.

All of this began in Pullman, Ill., a company town and suburb of Chicago in which lived the 5,000 employees of George M. Pullman, manufacturer of the sleeping car. With unbelievable audacity, Pullman had sent out lit-

erature far and wide describing the feudal community of which he was
"absolute monarch" as Utopia, a model community. It was Utopia but
Utopia for Pullman, who had perfected a way of getting back, and at a
profit, virtually all of the scanty wages he paid his employees. Receiving
even in prosperous times less than the prevailing rate of wages, all employees of the Pullman factory were forced to live in Pullman's model town
where they paid rents 20 to 25 per cent higher than the rents paid for
similar accommodations in Chicago.[7] The cost to the Pullman Company of
illuminating gas was only 33 cents a thousand cubic feet but Pullman employees were forced to pay Pullman $2.25 for a thousand cubic feet. Chicago
supplied the Pullman Company with water at four cents a thousand gallons,
but the Pullman employees paid the company ten cents a thousand gallons.

All of these profiteering charges were automatically deducted from the
employees' pay. Saloons, trade unions, and public meetings, other than
church services conducted in a Pullman church, were prohibited in Utopia,
which was infested with spies paid for weekly reports. Any careless word
might bring arbitrary discharge after years of service. One employee declared, "We are born in a Pullman house, fed from the Pullman shop, taught
in the Pullman school, catechized in the Pullman church, and when we die
we shall be buried in the Pullman cemetery and go to the Pullman hell."

To the unorganized employees of Pullman, made bold by desperation, the
founding of the ARU offered an opportunity to change themselves from
vassals into human beings. They were eligible for membership because
Pullman, in addition to manufacturing railway equipment, operated a small
railroad.

In the spring of 1894 men and women met secretly in neighboring towns
to avoid the spies, whispering excitedly of at last fighting for their rights.
Even the whispering made them feel better and before the ARU lodge was
formed at Pullman men were holding up their heads once more while
the eyes of their wives held life again. There was a feeling of great relief at
taking action, any action. They felt they had changed into Americans again.
They had had enough. On May 7, 1894, they organized and on the same day
forty employees marched into the office of one Wickes, a vice president and
superintendent, who could scarcely have been more surprised if forty dogs
had walked in with demands. A demand in Pullman until that instant had
been as unknown as a snowstorm in July.

Wickes stalled them off and when they returned two days later stalled
them off again. The next night a meeting was held in the neighboring town

[7] On July 26, 1894, President Cleveland appointed a United States Strike Commission
to inquire into the causes of the Pullman strike and the subsequent strike of the
ARU. Its members were Carroll P. Wright, John D. Kernan, and Nicholas E. Worthington, who heard voluminous testimony and made their report to President Cleveland Nov. 14, 1894, in which they absolved the strikers, blamed Pullman and the
railroads for the conflict. Their report can be found in 53 Congr. 3d Sess., Senate
Exec. Docs., vol. ii, p. xiii ff.

of Kensington where officials of the ARU counseled them to go slow. But having experienced a taste of manhood and womanhood, they found they liked it and there was no stopping them. They voted strike on the third ballot and on May 11 the factory was closed down tight.

Debs arrived three days later. He spent the entire day talking to the strikers, their wives and children, listening to their stories, looking at their seven-cent pay checks, hearing of the spying and surveillance that made up their lives in Pullman's Utopia. Many were already suffering from hunger. That night, at a meeting, Debs told the strikers:

> "If it is a fact that after working for George M. Pullman for years you appear two weeks after your work stops, ragged and hungry, it only emphasizes the charge I made before this community, and Pullman stands before you a self-confessed robber. . . . The paternalism of Pullman is the same as the self-interest of a slave-holder in his human chattels. You are striking to avert slavery and degradation."

Debs brought the plight of the Pullman strikers before the first annual convention of the ARU, which opened June 12, 1894, for a two-week session in Uhlrich's Hall in Chicago. It was attended by more than 400 delegates representing 150,000 railroad workers in 465 locals. But before Debs mentioned the Pullman strike, he made a plea for labor unity and independent political action which brought the delegates to their feet, whistling, cheering, throwing their hats into the air.

Only after these matters were disposed of did Debs turn to the Pullman dispute. "It was work and poverty in Pullmantown, or Pullemdown," he said, "until patience ceasing to be a virtue and further forebearance becoming treason to life, liberty and the pursuit of happiness, the employees determined to strike to better their conditions." And then he read the delegates an appeal from the strikers which concluded with the declaration:

> "We struck because we were without hope. We joined the American Railway Union because it gave us a glimmer of hope. . . . We will make you proud of us, brothers, if you will give us the hand we need. Help us make our country better and more wholesome. . . . Teach arrogant grinders of the faces of the poor that there still is a God of Israel, and if need be, a Jehovah—a God of battles."

The delegates were deeply moved but their emotion rose to a higher pitch when the Rev. William H. Carwardine, a Pullman preacher who had revolted and sided with the strikers, declared that even as he spoke women and children in Pullman were hungry, on the verge of starvation. The anger of delegates became most intense after they had listened to the story of Jennie Curtis, president of woman's local No. 269 at Pullman. Thin and tired, a seamstress at Pullman, she said that when her father died, after working for Pullman for thirteen years, she was forced to pay $60 for her father's back rent which had piled up while he was ill and dying.

One of the delegates jumped up and moved that the American Railway Union boycott Pullman cars, that they refuse to move a single sleeping car until Pullman agreed to negotiate with his employees. A roar of approval filled the hall. Debs refused to entertain the motion, having no illusions as to the kind of fight that might be expected. The federal courts were increasingly issuing injunctions outlawing strikes while troops were increasingly being called out to enforce the injunctions, breaking unions as well as strikes and imprisoning their officers. He suggested that a committee be appointed from the convention, consisting of six strikers and six non-strikers, which would seek a meeting with the company with a proposal of arbitration. Wickes, the vice president, refused to see the committee, which returned and reported to the convention.

Again a boycott was proposed and again Debs sidetracked it with a proposal that a committee consisting entirely of Pullman employees ask for a meeting with the company and request arbitration. Wickes said "there was nothing to arbitrate," and when the committee returned Debs could no longer stem the tide. A boycott was unanimously voted to begin at noon on June 26 unless Pullman negotiated with his employees on or before that date. If any member of the ARU was discharged for refusing to move sleeping cars, all other members on the line concerned would strike.

The General Managers Association, composed of officials of the railroads centering in Chicago and one of the most powerful organizations in the country, saw in the boycott an opportunity to break the new and growing industrial union. A failure to break it would mean hundreds of thousands of dollars in increased wages, continued resistance to pay slashes scheduled. Failure to smash it would probably mean the swift and irresistible growth of industrial unionism on a nationwide scale and in all industries as a powerful counterweight to monopoly.

The managers welcomed the conflict, making sure it would develop by announcing that Pullman cars would be included in all trains and attaching them to mail cars wherever possible. Their confidence was based on their perfect faith that they could force entry of the federal government on the side of management. Their device would be the claim of interference with the United States mails. Their confidence derived, too, from the strength of their own organization. The General Managers Association represented twenty-four of the nation's largest railroads, had a combined capital of $818,-000,000, some 221,000 employees, and 41,000 miles of vital railroad track.

Moreover, their confidence was not lessened by the fact that a railroad corporation lawyer was the Attorney General of the United States who would be in charge of controlling the strike on a nationwide basis and who had more than a little influence with the man who had appointed him, President Cleveland. The Attorney General was Richard B. Olney, late counsel for a half dozen railroads and a member of the board of directors of the Chicago,

Burlington & Quincy, now involved in the ARU strike. Olney took his duties seriously. Before accepting the cabinet position he had cleared the matter with his superior, Charles E. Perkins, president of the C.B. & Q., asking if it would be "to the true interest of the C.B. & Q." if he accepted the position of Attorney General of the United States. Perkins said it would be.

Thus with a railroad lawyer handling the strike in Washington, D.C., it was natural enough that the General Managers Association wanted a railroad lawyer handling the strike for the United States Government in Chicago. Attorney General Olney was advised of this and upon the recommendation of the Association's attorneys proceeded to appoint Edwin Walker Special United States Attorney in Chicago in charge of prosecutions growing out of the strike. Described as "the Nestor of the local bar," Walker was a corporation lawyer associated with railroads and insurance companies and at the time law partner of W. Eddy, counsel of a railroad immediately involved in the strike, the Chicago, Milwaukee and St. Paul.

Both Olney and the managers knew that the crux of their job was the supplying of violence. Debs knew it too. He knew that the heart of his task was the prevention of violence, that the strike could be won only if it were peaceful.[8] It began on June 27 when 5,000 men left their jobs, tying up fifteen railroads. The next day 40,000 had quit. Debs' warnings for peace still ringing in their ears, and by that night there were the first claims that the strikers were stopping the United States mails. On June 29, 125,000 were out. Twenty railroads were still and had no traffic on them. But the railroad brotherhoods were already beginning to scab and P. M. Arthur of the Engineers disciplined 400 members of his order when they went out on strike on the Wabash.

On the next day, June 30, the railroads began the manufacture of violence. According to the testimony of the Superintendent of Chicago police, the deputy marshals who were sworn in were made up of "thugs, thieves and ex-convicts." These deputy marshals had the power to arrest as well as to shoot, both of which they promptly did. "They were armed and paid by the railroads, and acted in the double capacity of railroad employees and United States officers," said the official government report which was afterwards returned by President Cleveland's strike commission. "They were not under the direct control of any Government official while exercising authority. This is placing officers of the Government under the control of a combination of railroads. It is a bad precedent, that might well lead to serious consequences." It did.

[8] Said the official government report submitted to President Cleveland by the U.S. Strike Commission: "There is no evidence before the commission that the officers of the American Railway Union at any time participated in or advised intimidation, violence or destruction of property." The report made it clear that much of the blame for the disorders rested with the government "for not adequately controlling monopolies and corporations, and failing to reasonably protect the rights of labor and redress its wrongs."

That night there was violence when more than a thousand of the railroad's Deputy United States Marshals were unleashed in and around Chicago. Governor Waite of Colorado, speaking of these deputies, described them as "desperadoes" who had been hired "without any regard for their qualifications but simply for military purposes." Chicago Police Chief John Brennan, after the strike was all over, testified before the government commission that the railroad's government officials fired without provocation into unarmed and peaceful crowds. "Innocent men and women were killed by these shots," he said. "Several of these officials were arrested during the strike for stealing property from railroad cars. In one instance, two of them were found under suspicious circumstances near a freight car which had just been set on fire. They were dangerous to the lives of the citizens on account of their careless use of pistols."

Olney was getting his violence, bought and paid for by the railroads and stamped with the authority of the United States Government, despite all of Debs' efforts for peace. Debs was often working around the clock now. His doctor had warned him against a breakdown some months before the strike. But now he spent himself, pouring out his energy with the same carelessness that he gave away his money. Clarence Darrow, soon to become the attorney for the ARU, saw him push his way through ugly threatening crowds of hired provocateurs, deputies, and the curious, climbing up on wagons to speak his message of peace. Later Darrow said of Debs, "There may have lived some time, somewhere, a kindlier, gentler, more generous man than Eugene V. Debs, but I have never known him. . . . He was not only all that I have said but he was the bravest man I ever knew. He never felt fear. He had the courage of a babe who has no conception of the word or its meaning."

Despite the violence the strike was solid on July 1, the fifth day and Debs still thought they would win. At a meeting of strikers, he said:

"The struggle with the Pullman Company has developed into a contest between the producing classes and the money power of the country. . . . The fight was between the American Railway Union and the Pullman Company. . . . Then the railway corporations, through the General Manager's Association, came to the rescue, and in a series of whereases declared to the world that they would go into partnership with Pullman, so to speak, and stand by him in his devilish work of starving his employees to death."

The press was in full cry against Debs and the railroaders, performing its particular function in breaking the strike as faithfully as Walker, or Olney himself. The strike was often referred to as the "Debs' Rebellion," its leader frequently called "Director Debs." On June 30 the Chicago *Tribune* declared "Mob Is in Control" while another headline charged "Law Is Trampled On." Later its headline read "Strike Is Now War" and an editorial began:

"Six Days Shalt Thou Labor—BIBLE"
"Not Unless I Say So—Debs"

Virtually all of the nation's newspapers declared that Debs was leading a conspiracy to overthrow the United States government by force and violence. "The attitude of Debs and his followers is that of rebellion and anarchy," said the New York *Times* editorially on July 7. "Debs should be made to suffer the penalty of inciting violence and insurrection against the authority of the government." And the New York *Tribune* said on the same day, "This man [Debs] stands for Anarchy in the most dangerous form in which it has yet presented itself. He is at war, not with corporations, or with capital, but with the United States Government and all government." Typical headlines were "Panic Reigns in Chicago. . . . Now in a State of Terror. . . . But No General Uprising" in the New York *Herald* of July 9, and "Thirsty for Blood. . . . Violence at Every Hand" in the Chicago *Evening Post* of July 7.

With these and similar events as the background, the stage was amply set for the issuing of a sweeping federal injunction on July 2 forbidding all strike activity. It was issued by Federal Judges William A. Woods, who "had accepted such important favors from the railroads that his impartiality was doubtful," and Peter S. Grosscup, who on the previous Memorial Day had said in a speech, "The growth of labor organizations must be checked by law." The injunction, written by Walker with the express purpose of breaking the strike and strengthened by the two judges in a little private conference, was issued without the ARU having attorneys present or even knowing that the federal court was going through the pretense of holding a hearing on whether or not an injunction should be issued.

Events moved swiftly toward a climax when Debs and other ARU officials declared that they could not yield to the injunction and call off the strike without dealing the labor movement a blow that would set it back for years. On July 4, 1,936 federal troops were dispatched to Chicago on the authority of President Cleveland, and despite the protest of Governor John Peter Altgeld of Illinois who declared the move lawless and unconstitutional, a transparent government attempt to serve the railroads and break the strike. Soon 14,000 armed men were in Chicago, consisting of 6,000 troops, 5,000 of the railroads' deputy United States Marshals, and 3,000 police, and then violence did, indeed, break out, most of it resulting from the thugs hired by the railroads and clothed with the authority of the United States. Thirty men and women were killed and three times that number wounded in a series of riots in which innocent bystanders were the most frequent victims.

On July 10 a federal grand jury indicted Debs and other officials of the ARU for conspiracy against the government of the United States in interfering with interstate commerce in violation of the Sherman Anti-Trust

Act.[9] They were arrested and gave bail but still the strikers fought on against all the power of government, corporations, the Army, courts, press, and pulpit. For a day or so it seemed as if there might be a nationwide general strike.

The Central Labor Union of New York City scathingly condemned the strike-breaking of the brotherhoods and President Cleveland. Gompers, president of the American Federation of Labor, sent a wire of protest to the President. In Chicago labor's rank and file was calling for a general strike. Some 25,000 trade union members spontaneously and without authorization quit work in a sympathetic walk-out. All the locals of the city and seven national unions met in Uhlrich's Hall where they demanded that Gompers call a meeting in Chicago of the federation's executive council on July 12. It met but took no action.

On July 17 Debs and the other strike leaders were arrested again, this time charged with contempt of court and violation of the July 2 injunction. With leaders imprisoned in the Cook County jail, all direction of the strike behind bars, it was at last broken. The ARU was smashed and industrial unionism had been set back, as time proved, some forty years. Clarence Darrow, the young lawyer who had resigned from his job with the Chicago & Northwestern to defend the strikers, met his clients in the filthy jail. A guard, he reported later, led him down "a long hall with iron floor, ceiling and walls," then ushered him into a cell which contained Debs and five other prisoners not connected with the strike. Some, Darrow recalled, were "stripped to the waist, scratching the bites inflicted by all manner of nameless vermin, the blood trickling down their bare bodies in tiny red rivulets. Sewer rats as big as cats scurried back and forth over the floor."

Debs was calm enough, interested in the fact that his cell was near the one in which Parsons had been imprisoned. When Darrow said he might suffer a severe reprisal for leading the strike, he replied, "I broke into railroading as a fireman. I'm used to handling the stormy end of a scoop." His chief worry was the 120,000 men, many of whom were now to be blacklisted. He saw the future clearly enough, knew then that these men would wander the country over the years, separated from their families, using assumed names as they finally got jobs for a day or two before the blacklist caught up with them and again set them wandering.

He was learning now as he always had. At one of the last strike meetings he had read himself out of the Democratic Party he had supported for so

[9] While this indictment was being handed down, Senator Peffer of Kansas, a Populist, took the floor in the Senate to condemn the Pullman Company and its head and to defend the American Railway Union and the strikers. He charged George M. Pullman with being "heartless, soulless, conscienceless . . . [a] tyrant of the tyrants" and answered the critics of the ARU strike by asserting that the strike was not "a strike of lawbreakers" (*Congr. Record*, 53 Congress, 2nd Sess., vol. 26, Part 7, p. 7231). For his defense of the strikers and condemnation of the Pullman Company Senator Peffer was pictured in the press as an un-American, a defender of anarchy. (See *New York Herald*, July 11, 1894, and *New York Times*, July 11, 1894.)

long and whose President had a hand in imprisoning him and making many of 120,000 men homeless wanderers without jobs. "I am a Populist," Debs had declared "and I favor wiping out both old parties so they will never come into power again. I have been a Democrat all my life and I am ashamed to admit it."

He was capable of change. He could learn from experience. The process continued after the United States Supreme Court approved his contempt citation, sentencing him to six months' imprisonment at Woodstock, Ill. While there he read Henry Demarest Lloyd's *Wealth Against Commonwealth,* which to him seemed to prove conclusively that the country was not run for the benefit of its people but for the profit of the few who controlled the trusts. Victor Berger of Milwaukee sent him a copy of Marx's *Capital.* So it was here, behind the bars of Woodstock, learning from the past and planning for the future, that the mental processes began which made him say a few years later:

"The issue is Socialism versus Capitalism. I am for Socialism because I am for humanity. We have been cursed with the reign of gold long enough. Money constitutes no proper basis of civilization. The time has come to regenerate society—we are on the eve of a universal change."

Ten thousand Chicagoans journeyed to Woodstock to greet Debs as he emerged from prison. They fought to touch him, "wept, cheered, laughed and cried." Back in Chicago 100,000 people were present when he stepped from the train. They held a parade, packed an armory, again wept and cheered. He spoke a few weeks later in New York at Cooper Union and Swinton wrote:

"Debs in Cooper Union reminded me of Lincoln there. As Lincoln of Illinois became an efficient agent of freedom, so perchance might Debs, of Indiana, become in the impending conflict for the liberation of labor. Let us never forget Lincoln's great words, 'Liberty before property; the man before the dollar.' "

And many wondered if the government was placing property before liberty and the dollar before the man, and why it had found it necessary to imprison one of the best loved figures in America.

4. "The Blessings-of-Civilization Trust"

As Gene Debs fought rats in his cell in the Cook County jail, Andrew Carnegie may well have been inhaling the scent of a rose beside his castle in Scotland while the imperial Morgan enjoyed the lovely coloring of some Renaissance painting. Both were crowding sixty now.

Carnegie, particularly, hated violence and bloodshed. He had been frank in declaring his thankfulness that he was abroad when his steely lieutenant Frick had been forced to kill Carnegie employees at Homesteao in breaking their union and slashing wages 20 per cent in 1892. There had been despair in the hovels and hearts of those around Homestead but Carnegie, enjoying the beauties of Italy, had cabled the victorious Frick: "Congratulations all around—life worth living again—how pretty Italia."

Rockefeller, shrinking in physical size but not in fortune as the years pressed on, had also admired Frick's killings, sending him a telegram of congratulations as he increased his princely gifts to the Church. Morgan, long graduated to larger deals than selling his countrymen defective rifles, was now the leading Episcopal layman of the United States. He has been described as "a bull-necked, irascible man with small black magpie's eyes and a growth on his nose," but whatever his appearance he did not worry much about such as Debs. After all, he had outlived Sylvis, saw the fading of Powderly, the hanging of the Molly Maguires, the killing of Parsons and Spies, the imprisoning of Coxey who had led the unemployed, the passing of Martin Irons, leader of the railroad strike of 1886, now ill, broken, blacklisted, and even suffering hunger.

Presidents came and went, some Republicans and others Democrats. The only constant was Morgan, ever throwing together larger and larger aggregations of corporate power. Workers sometimes wondered how he did it. After long years of baking before the forge, sweating in the mines, creating by hard labor every single thing that man used, wore, or ate, ordinary men had only old age. But Morgan, the imperial Morgan, could walk into a room containing some twenty heads of industry and when he walked out two hours later the magic of combination, the rattling of some papers and plans for the sale of watered stock, had made every single man in the room richer by millions. For Morgan knew, if Gompers did not, the power and profit of unity.

When weary of creating his monopolies—there was so much paper work and so many lawyers—Morgan would escape to France, impartially enjoying its wines and women, his nose becoming more porous and red with the years until its blossoming was a respected symbol for pride and power. He agreed with George F. ("Divine Right") Baer, the coal operator, soon to say during a strike that God had given the rich the control of the country. "The rights and interests of the laboring man," Baer said, "will be protected and cared for . . . by the Christian men to whom God in His infinite wisdom has given the control of property interests in this country."

"How pretty Italia," Carnegie had said over the bodies of the Homestead dead. Morgan, himself, was to send a cable in similar if less poetic vein from his chateau at Aix-les-Bains in France. After interrupting his pleasure to make a quick decision as to the necessity for a low wage scale for the millions of Americans in basic industry, he added "Weather superb."[10]

[10] This cable was addressed to E. H. Gary and read at a meeting of the finance committee of the U. S. Steel Corp., April 27, 1909 and was printed in the *Final Report of the Commission on Industrial Relations,* an official government document, with the following comment: "The lives of millions of wage earners are . . . subject to the

In 1894 the Supreme Court of the United States found that the Sherman Anti-Trust Act did not apply to trusts. It applied only, it developed, to labor. Debs had been indicted for violation of the anti-trust act but no tycoon could suffer its penalties, according to the Supreme Court's decision in the Knight case. Following this decision a great host of trusts and combinations and holding companies, price-fixing, wage-fixing monopolies whatever their name, burgeoned immediately, many of them giants at birth. In the next five years more than 300 great monopolies came into being, aided by the holding company, authorized by the laws of New Jersey which permitted one corporation to dominate scores through holding their stock.

The process of centralization seemed to increase at almost a daily rate. The extent as well as the tempo of the process is indicated in an official government document called the *Final Report of the Industrial Commission,* published in 1902. The document presented the following pertinent facts:

"The total number of industrial combinations reported by the census [of 1900] is 183. . . . The rapidity of the recent movement toward combination is shown by the fact that only 63 of these corporations were organized prior to 1897, while no less than 79 were organized in 1899 alone. The nominal capitalization of the corporations was $3,607,539,200. . . . In many of the most important lines of industry combinations have secured control of a large percentage of the country's production. In many articles of steel a single corporation controls 75 to 80 percent of the output, and in some lines even more; in sugar, about 90 percent; in petroleum, at least 82 percent. . . . Since the return to prosperity in 1898, railroad consolidation on a scale hitherto unequalled has been under way. . . . More than half of the [railroad] mileage of the United States is now under the control of six financial interests, four of which at least each approach a limit of mileage of 20,000 miles."

The Rockefellers in oil, the Havemeyers in sugar, the Dukes in tobacco, the Mellons in aluminum, the Carnegies and Fricks in iron and steel, and the Morgans in the railroads and the newly rising electrical manufacturing industry were moved in their trust-building activities by a desire not only to eliminate competition and thereby fix prices at the most profitable levels, but also to beat down organized labor and thereby lower wages. They were fully aware that through "the power of added capital" they could take a more independent stand against the trade union movement, particularly in view of the fact that union organization was splintered along craft lines. As the Industrial Commission put it in its *Final Report:*

dictation of a relatively small number of men . . . [who] are totally ignorant of every aspect of the industries which they control, except the finances, and are totally unconcerned with regard to the working and living conditions of the employees in those industries." (p. 118.)

"There can be little doubt that in many cases the organizers of combinations have felt that through the power of added capital, and the possibility of filling orders from any of the various plants, they would be more independent in their dealings with trade unions. For example, in 1899, when there was a smelters' strike in Colorado the American Smelting and Refining Co. closed the plants in which the strikers had been employed, transferred the work to other plants, and in this way coerced the strikers to some extent. When workingmen are not organized throughout the whole industry, a combination is able in this way to secure an advantage."

This latter point, never lost sight of by big business, was ignored by virtually all of the top leadership of the craft-minded American Federation of Labor.

While the Rockefeller interests in the late nineties were rounding up gas and electric companies, traction corporations, interurban lines, copper concerns, iron ore mines, and railroads all over the country, Morgan, controller of some of the major railways and the recently created General Electric Company, was laying plans for taking over the steel industry. He used Elbert H. Gary, a Chicago lawyer, as his front in the familiar device of making big ones out of little ones. Gathering together a whole aggregate of independent steel companies, he made them one as the Federal Steel Company, capitalized at $200,000,000. While Morgan made additional millions by the sale of the new concern's stocks and bonds—his invariable practice in all mergers—he lusted mightily for Carnegie's empire, still dominant despite the new giant. In 1901 he succeeded in creating his masterpiece, a monopoly in steel combining his Federal Steel Company with Carnegie's giant properties, thus forming the largest and most powerful corporation that the world had ever seen, the United States Steel. Its total capitalization was more than a billion and a third dollars.

The imperial Morgan, who walked with stately tread in and out of directors' rooms, always coming out richer than when he went in, was the master merger of bank and industrial capital. In the opening years of the new century it was he and his associates who organized super-trusts in steel (U.S. Steel), shipping (International Mercantile Marine), and agricultural machinery (International Harvester). The Morgan group had its hands in other fields—the railroads (where with Hill of the Great Northern some 30,000 miles of railways were controlled), anthracite coal (where from two-thirds to three-quarters of the entire shipment was in Morgan hands); other Morgan monopolies included electrical machinery (General Electric), communications (American Telephone & Telegraph, Western Union), traction companies (Interborough Rapid Transit in New York, Hudson & Manhattan), and insurance (Equitable Life). Closely associated with Morgan in his manifold enterprises was George E. Baker, president of the First National Bank of New York.

The Rockefellers began their larger operations outside of oil in alliance with James Stillman, president of the powerful National City Bank, thenceforward known as the "Standard Oil Bank." Through Stillman they dominated a whole series of banks, among them the National City, the Farmers Loan and Trust, and the Second National. Moreover, according to John Moody, "the fifteen directors of the Standard Oil Company of New Jersey held directorships in innumerable banks, traction companies, electric light, gas and industrial concerns of every sort." In addition, they held huge slices of the country's resources not only in oil, but in coal, iron ore, and copper. The Colorado Fuel and Iron Company as well as the Amalgamated Copper Company gravitated within their orbit. They dominated, through their alliance with E. H. Harriman, whose operations they largely financed, the Union Pacific and the Southern Pacific and owned outright the Chicago, Milwaukee and St. Paul.

By the turn of the century the United States had become the leading industrial nation of the world, manufacturing almost twice as much as Great Britain, its nearest rival. The value of its manufactured products came to more than eleven billion dollars a year. The number of its workers in industry had increased from 1,310,000 in 1860 to 4,713,000 in 1900 while 14,000,000 immigrants were pouring into the country as the population increased from 31,443,321 to 75,994,575. It was this huge national plant that had come under the domination of a small financial oligarchy whose members controlled the banks as well as industry and who knew the power of unity even if the country's top labor leaders did not.

With this giant centralization, this increasing merger of bank and industrial capital into monopoly capital, something new came into American life. So colossal was the capital gathered together that it was becoming much more profitable to reinvest it in colonial areas.

Accordingly, the whole world increasingly became the scene of American enterprise and investment, American battleships and soldiers guaranteeing the investments. Monopoly's plant at home had grown too large, constantly over-producing and piling up surpluses which the American people, millions of whom were hungry and ragged enough, could not buy. Monopoly had grown to such gigantic size, spawned such mammoth profits that it had to expand or die, reinvest or wither. The export of capital and the sale of surpluses abroad had become a necessity.

Statesmen, always sensitive to the needs of their more prominent constituents, began to speak of it being the will of Almighty God that America should bring the blessings of civilization to the benighted inhabitants of the Caribbean, the Pacific, Latin America, and everywhere else that the heathen dwelled in darkness. God was telling the American people, so Senator Beveridge of Indiana declared, "Ye have been faithful over a few things; I will make you ruler over many things." But before the demand for expansion could swell to imperative proportions, the imperialists were interrupted for a space by the Presidential campaign of 1896.

The common people were bitter and their bitterness was enough to make even Morgan tremble for a time. The Populists had combined with the radical wing of the Democratic Party, at whose convention William Jennings Bryan had unexpectedly run away with the nomination when he had declared that laboring America could no longer be crucified upon a cross of gold. With hunger still stalking the land, farm prices lower than at any time since the Civil War, average factory wages of $406 a year, there were some millions who felt that in fact they were being nailed to Wall Street's golden cross by such phenomena as unemployment and mortgages. Again there was a pentecostal uprising. A fury seemed to blaze across the land which the Republicans worked to extinguish by a huge campaign fund of close to 16 million dollars, as well as threats of universal foreclosure of mortgages and closing of factories if Bryan was elected over their candidate, William McKinley. And when it was all over McKinley had received 7,035,638 votes; Bryan 6,467,946.[11]

McKinley had been in the White House a little over a year, as he afterwards reported, when he had dropped to his knees to ask God what he should do about the Philippines. "Take them," he reported that God had told him, take them and give them the blessings of civilization. "I walked the floor of the White House night after night," he said, "and I am not ashamed to tell you gentlemen, that I went down on my knees and prayed Almighty God. . . . And one night late it came to me this way. . . . There is nothing left to do but to take them all . . . uplift and civilize and Christianize them. . . ."

Senator Beveridge of Indiana, Senator Lodge of Massachusetts, Under Secretary of the Navy Theodore Roosevelt and a good many others also felt that God wished us to seize the Philippines as well as Cuba and Puerto Rico. All three were owned by Spain and when the battleship *Maine* mysteriously exploded in the harbor at Havana, war was declared against that country on April 25, 1898.

Two days after war was declared Senator Beveridge hailed it with a paean of joy, declaring it the beginning of world domination for the United States. "American factories," he said, "are making more than the American people can use; American soil is producing more than they can consume." (He did not mention the great depression of 1893-97.) "Fate has written our policy for us; the trade of the world must and shall be ours.

[11] The battle put up by the monied interests in 1896—and their relief when the final returns were counted—is reflected in the following observation of one of its leading representatives: "The great fight is won," wrote Mrs. Henry Cabot Lodge, "a fight conducted by trained and experienced and organized forces, with both hands full of money, with the full power of the press—and of prestige—on one side; on the other a disorganized mob, at first, out of which burst into sight, hearing, and force—one man . . . a Crusader, an inspired fanatic. . . . It has been marvellous. Hampered by such a following, such a platform . . . he almost won. We acknowledge to 7 millions campaign fund, against his 300,000. We had during the last week of the campaign 18,000 speakers on the stump. . . . It is over now, but the vote is 7 millions to 6 millions and a half."

And we will get it as our mother [England] told us how. . . . We will cover the ocean with our merchant marine. We will build a navy to the measure of our greatness. . . .

"Our institutions will follow our flag on the wings of our commerce. And American law, American order, American civilization, and the American flag will plant themselves on shores hitherto bloody and benighted. . . . If this means the Stars and Stripes over an Isthmian canal . . . over Hawaii . . . over Cuba and the southern seas . . . then let us meet that meaning with a mighty joy and make that meaning good, no matter what barbarism and all our foes may do or say."

Even more specific had been Senator Thurston of Nebraska, who had said a month before the declaration of war, "War with Spain would increase the business and earnings of every American railroad, it would increase the output of every American factory, it would stimulate every branch of industry and commerce. . . ." And several years before the sinking of the battleship *Maine* Senator Lodge had indicated which way the wind was blowing as he said: "For the sake of our commercial supremacy in the Pacific, we should control the Hawaiian Islands and maintain our interest in Samoa. Our immediate pecuniary interests in Cuba are great. Free Cuba would mean an excellent opportunity for American capital invited there by signal exemptions. . . ."

The war with Spain, "a splendid little war," according to Secretary of State John Hay, was over in 113 days, when all that was left of the Spanish Empire was handed over to American monopoly. Despite the frank statements of Senators Lodge, Thurston, and Beveridge, newspapers and orators declared the conflict a war for the liberation of the peoples struggling under Spain's autocracy. While the bands played "It'll Be a Hot Time in the Old Town Tonight," thousands of young men enlisted to bring freedom to their "little brown brothers."

Yet not all Americans fell for the fraud. The Anti-Imperialist League with more than 500,000 members was formed under Senator Hoar of Massachusetts. The Socialists and most trade unionists were against the war. As Aguinaldo, leader of the Philippine insurgents, continued to fight for independence against American troops, he was increasingly likened to George Washington who had also fought a foreign tyranny. It was recalled nostalgically that there had been a time when Americans themselves had fought for liberty.

Mark Twain excoriated the American slaughter during the "splendid little war" of unarmed natives, the massacres of defenseless men, women, and children, which were palmed off as gallant victories. "The Blessings-of-Civilization Trust, wisely and cautiously administered, is a Daisy," Mark Twain observed. "There is more money in it, more territory, more sovereignty and other emolument than there is in any other game that is played."

"There are thousands who are not swept from their feet by the war craze," Debs said. "They realize that war is national murder, that the poor furnish the victims and that whatever the outcome may be, the effect is always the same upon the toiling class.

"In 1894 the press denounced us [the railroad strikers] for the alleged reason that we were murderous and bloodthirsty, and now the same press opposes us because we are not.

"We are opposed to war, but if it ever becomes necessary for us to enlist in the murderous business, it will be to wipe out capitalism, the common enemy of the oppressed and down-trodden of all nations."

But freedom was forced to give way to "The Blessings-of-Civilization Trust." The war, which gained roughly 120,000 square miles of valuable raw materials and a subject population of 10,600,000 to exploit, proved to be just a beginning. With Cuba made an American protectorate—she still has American military installations on her soil—American investments there increased from $50,000,000 in 1898 to $159,000,000 eight years later. As the new American empire increased in size so did private investment abroad. A half billion dollars in 1898, it was more than five times that much by 1914. Guam and Hawaii furnished excellent opportunities and the gathering in of Samoa sent investments higher. They increased still more after China was forced open to foreign exploitation by an invasion of foreign troops which included American regulars and Marines. This was the so-called Boxer Rebellion of 1900.

Investments, and surpluses that the American people could not buy, flowed into Korea and Manchuria in sufficient volume to make the State Department under President Theodore Roosevelt particularly sensitive to freedom in the Orient. Senator Lodge thought that perhaps we should liberate the Chinese, the Koreans, and the Manchurians, writing to the President in 1903: "I have been thinking a great deal about Manchuria. Our trade there is assuming very large proportions and it seems to me that we ought to take very strong grounds. . . . I have letters from Lawrence, where some of the mills make cotton goods which go to Manchuria, urging the strongest possible action and then demanding that a fleet be sent. . . ."

With the United States a world power, American monopoly was soon successfully challenging monopolies abroad, forcing entry into cartels, insisting on a division of properties and the sharing of world markets. In 1902 the American Tobacco Company came to an agreement with the Imperial Tobacco Company of Great Britain to form the super British-American Tobacco Co., Ltd. The following year Morgan's International Mercantile Marine and German shipping interests buried the hatchet to divide between them some of the trans-Atlantic traffic. In 1907 the Morgan-dominated General Electric Company arrived at an understanding with the German General Electric Company, A.E.G. At about the same time Rockefeller's Standard Oil Company agreed to divide certain European markets with the Deutsche Bank.

Few were more impressed by the grandeur and strength of American monopoly than such labor leaders as Samuel Gompers. Convinced that it was folly to fight it, Gompers and other labor statesmen joined the National Civic Federation, formed in 1900, dominated by the country's largest monopolists. Its stated aim was "to bring together the three great interested forces of capital, labor and the general public to work out industrial problems through evolutionary rather than revolutionary processes." Its first president was "Dollar Mark" Hanna, national boss of the Republican Party and big Ohio industrialist. Its second president was August Belmont, Wall Street financier and president of the Morgan-dominated Interborough Rapid Transit Company.

The Federation itself was to settle all disputes about wages. Representing the "public" on its Executive Committee were Andrew Carnegie, ex-steel magnate; James Speyer, banker; Grover Cleveland, the President who broke the Pullman strike; and Isaac N. Seligman, banker. Capital was represented by Henry Phipps, director of U.S. Steel; Francis L. Robbins, president of the Pittsburgh Coal Co.; Frederick R. Fish, president of the American Bell Telephone Co.; and Lucius Tuttle, president of the Boston and Maine Railroad. Labor members included Gompers; John Mitchell, president of the United Mine Workers; John Tobin, president of the Boot and Shoe Workers Union; William D. Mahon, president of the Amalgamated Association of Street Railway Employees; and Warren S. Stone, Grand Chief of the International Brotherhood of Engineers.

Something of how the Federation worked was frankly described by Alton B. Parker, corporation lawyer, who succeeded August Belmont as president. Belmont's street-car employees were about to go on strike, Parker said in an address and, feeling that such a strike might embarrass Gompers and the other labor leaders, Belmont offered to resign as President of the Federation. But Gompers and his labor colleagues not only insisted that Belmont not resign, but said, Parker proudly reported, that they would forbid the strike. Thus relieved, Belmont kept his position and left for Florida.

"He had no more than reached his destination," said Parker in his speech, "than the whole Interborough System was tied up by a strike. Messrs. Gompers, Mitchell, Stone and Mahon, who were on the ground, immediately issued a public statement declaring that the strike was in direct violation of orders—aye, that there was no occasion for it. They ordered the men back to work, thus virtually breaking the strike and making good their promise to Mr. Belmont."

As one segment of industry sought for industrial peace through the National Civic Federation, another power group, the National Association of Manufacturers, founded in 1895, launched an open-shop crusade at its 1903 convention. Fearful of the tremendous upsurge of organized labor—union membership had risen from 447,000 in 1897 to 2,072,700 in 1904, a 363.7 per cent increase—the National Association of Manufacturers adopted a "Declaration of Labor Principles" which proclaimed the right of an employer to hire workers "at wages mutually satisfactory, without interference or dictation on the part of individuals or organizations not directly parties to such contracts." Having asserted its intention to stamp out the trade union movement, the convention listened to such anti-labor tirades as the following: "Organized labor knows only one law, and that is the law of physical force—the law of the Huns and Vandals. . . . Its history is stained with blood and ruin."

To the National Association of Manufacturers labor's demand for a shorter workday was "communistic." On December 1, 1904, its official publication, *American Industries,* declared:

"Since there is no economic difference between the shorter work day . . . and the proposition to divide up all property and start all over again, the sentimentalists and meddlers all array themselves, whether they mean it or not, on the side of the collectivists. . . . Whether they mean it or not, they chase the horizon of commonism [sic]. . . ."

As Gompers glowed at banquets, pleased beyond measure when Belmont or Mark Hanna called him Sam, the corporations were slaughtering metal miners at Cripple Creek, Telluride, Leadville, and Coeur d'Alene. In 1901 the strike of 62,000 steel workers was defeated and unionism was virtually eliminated from the mills of the United States Steel Corporation. During the same year another employers' association, the National Metal Trades, broke a strike of 58,000 machinists. At the same time employers' lobbies in Congress were successful in defeating bills providing for the eight-hour day and outlawing injunctions.

Vigilantes were smashing union halls and the drive for the open shop, supported by the millions of the National Association of Manufacturers, was gaining in power. So was the Sherman Anti-Trust Act as a device against labor. In 1908 it was used against the Danbury Hatters, a federal court levying fines of $234,000 against a group of Connecticut workers who had tried to force an open-shop employer into line by use of the boycott.

But Gompers thought things were going well enough. Wages for skilled workers were increasing. The American Federation of Labor was growing; in 1904 it had over 1,500,000 members. He did not worry about the vast majority of the more than 7,000,000 factory and transportation workers who were not organized at the time or about the vast majority of other wage earners among the more than 30,000,000 gainfully employed. For that matter neither did monopoly.

CHAPTER V

Hell in the Rockies

"The masters of the government of the United States are the combined capitalists and manufacturers of the United States."

PRESIDENT WOODROW WILSON IN
THE NEW FREEDOM, NEW YORK, 1913

"The astounding situation here in Colorado is that . . . the higher authorities, using the military arm of their government, are devoting practically all their attention to putting down the law. The prime insurrectionist . . . against the regularly established laws are the governor and his soldiers . . . representative of . . . the mining and smelting interests of Colorado. It is bayonet rule against the rule established by the ballot."

HENRY GEORGE, JR., IN THE NEW
YORK AMERICAN OF JUNE 12, 1904

1. The Socialists of Cripple Creek

The American people were soon to learn that reaction is indivisible, that conquest and violence abroad mean killing and union-busting at home. Massacres in the Philippines were related to terror in Colorado, and to the hard-rock miners of that state it became abundantly clear that the tie binding both was profit. As American Marines and battleships intervened during the early 1900's in Cuba, Nicaragua, and other Latin American countries, other American troops were repeatedly hurled against the Western Federation of Miners until actual civil war raged in the Rocky Mountain states.[1]

[1] As American armed forces assailed the colored peoples of Asia and Latin America, American reaction also stepped up its assault against the Negro people at home. From 1889 to 1901, according to the minimal count of Tuskegee Institute, there were 1,955 recorded lynchings of Negroes in the South. While Philippine villages were being

The violence thrown against the metal miners of the West as they fought for a living wage and the right to organize during these years of gunboat diplomacy is almost without precedent in American history. The sagebrush plains and alkali deserts of Utah, the little one-street mining camps high above the timber line in the Colorado Rockies, the gulches and canyons of northern Idaho, all heard the tramp of invading, strike-breaking troops. The regular army and the National Guards of the various states, particularly in Colorado and Idaho, were called out at least a dozen times in a dozen years.[2] Either federal or state troops were sent against the miners in the bloody strikes of Coeur d'Alene in 1892, of Leadville in 1896, at Salt Lake City and Coeur d'Alene again in 1899, at Telluride in 1901 and 1903, in Idaho Spring and Cripple Creek in 1903.

Thousands of miners were placed in barbed-wire camps, as at Coeur d'Alene in northern Idaho in 1892 and 1899, where they were held for months without trial or charges being placed against them. Other thousands were herded from their homes at the point of the bayonet, as at Cripple Creek and Telluride in Colorado in 1903, loaded into freight cars as if they were cattle, and deported by the military without trial or charge except that they were union men. In this great 1903–04 strike for the eight-hour day in Colorado 42 men were killed, 112 wounded, 1,345 arrested and imprisoned in bullpens, or military concentration camps, and 773 deported from the state, according to the incomplete contemporary calculations of the magazine *Current History*.

If there was a law that the mine owners and the State of Colorado did not break during this strike it has eluded the scrutiny of researchers. "The tragic part of this warfare," writes Irving Stone in his life of Clarence

---

burned by American troops, Colonel A. M. Wadell led an armed force against the Negro-white city administration of Wilmington, N. C., in November of 1898, slaughtering scores and announcing himself the new mayor after seizing the city hall in a pitched battle.

Disfranchisement laws were passed at the turn of the century depriving millions of native-born Americans of the vote; Louisiana in 1898, Alabama and North Carolina in 1901, Virginia in 1902, in Georgia in 1908, and in Oklahoma in 1910. Soon poll-tax laws had been passed in eight Southern states and almost 10,000,000 Americans were deprived of the vote, either because of their color or because they were too poor to pay for the privilege.

[2] According to *A Report on Labor Disturbances in the State of Colorado, From 1880 to 1904 Inclusive*, 58th Congr., 3rd Sess., Senate Doc. No. 122, Washington, 1905, troops were ordered out by the Governors of Colorado on ten different occasions in the twenty-five-year period ending in 1904. The expenses to the state for these military campaigns came to $1,042,260. "State Treasurer Whitney Newton in his annual report to the Governor on Jan. 2, 1905, gave the total amount of certificates of indebtedness issued in payment of military expenses during 1903 and 1904 as $776,464, and recommended that the general assembly authorize the issuance of 'insurrection bonds' to the amount of $800,000 payable in 25 years, and to draw no more than 3½ per cent interest annually." (p. 360.) In short, the taxpayers of Colorado, working people included, were called upon to finance the strike-breaking activities of corporate interests. The latter could buy the bonds issued and receive principal plus interest on their investment.

Darrow, "was that it had been caused in its entirety by the refusal of the state government to live up to and obey the law of its state."

But what was really notable about great eight-hour-day strikes in Colorado was not the violence of the legal authorities but the élan and drive with which the miners fought back. Under the guns of troops they gained allies, not only among other union men but from the ranks of farmers and the middle class. With bayonets on every side they distributed handbills and used the night to plaster whole communities with signs, placards, resolutions, and appeals. Deported from the mining camps on freight trains, they returned to their homes on the rods beneath the very freight cars that had taken them out. Guns in hand they defended their homes, forcing vigilantes to flee and more than once, when they had to, in self-defense, they shot it out with the operators' professional gunmen, blasting away toe to toe.

One reason for the bitterness of this Colorado strike was that the miners were not taking anything any more. Former cowboys, lumbermen, prospectors, trappers, and hunters for the most part, they did not take kindly to the blacklist nor to the slow starvation of the lockout. The mining camp, with its solitary street lined with saloons between the almost perpendicular walls of some Rocky Mountain canyon, was not a school for gentleness. Men who believed they were as good as the next man and probably better did not propose to accept endlessly mass imprisonments in concentration camps. It was in the camp at Coeur d'Alene during the strike of 1892 that the miners had first spoken of organizing an industrial union, the Western Federation of Miners, founded a year later. Twelve hundred had been held at Coeur d'Alene for six months. Many died while their families starved. Only twelve were ever charged with crime.

The Colorado metal miners had received, just prior to the strike of 1903, another demonstration that the law belonged to those who owned the mines, that the law was for the workers to obey and the owners to violate. Their latest lesson concerned the eight-hour day. Since 1894 the miners had fought for it. In most of their strikes eight hours had been one of their demands. Organizing politically, drawing the other trade unions, particularly the United Mine Workers, into the fight, they had been successful in getting an eight-hour law passed in 1899 by the Colorado legislature. But the Rockefellers, the Guggenheims, and the other mine owners, their workers found, were above and beyond the law. They universally violated it. The very tycoons who had spoken so piously of law and order during strikes now broke the eight-hour law and without compunction until their state supreme court, so often used in approving injunctions against the miners, made it unnecessary for them to violate it by declaring it unconstitutional in 1901.

With immense effort the miners and their allies had gained a state referendum on the proposition of amending the constitution so that an eight-hour day would be constitutional. Rallying a wide segment of the public, the miners gained another victory when the amendment passed by a majority of 47,000. Still the owners did not accede; still the ordinary workday was for twelve hours, seven days a week. In addition, smelter men, also members of the Western Federation of Miners, worked around the clock, twenty-four hours, every second Sunday. Labor then succeeded, by another mobilization of the voters, in electing a new legislature pledged to the passage of a new eight-hour law. But the bribery and influence of the owners proved stronger than the will of the people. A corrupt legislature refused to pass the law to which it was pledged. The miners and smelter men continued to work a minimum eighty-four-hour week, the smelter men receiving $1.80 a day, the miners often less than $3.[8] Weekly pay, after the usual deductions of company towns for food and rent, was often no more than $10 or $15.

As the great strike neared, the mine owners were additionally frightened by the fact that the miners were increasingly embracing socialism. The tenth annual convention of the Western Federation of Miners in 1902 adopted the following resolution: "We . . . do declare for a policy of independent political action, and do advise and recommend the adoption of the platform of the Socialist Party by the locals of the Federation. . . ." Eugene Debs, soon to gain more than 400,000 votes as Socialist candidate for President, was touring the mining camps and receiving a remarkable reception. The miners, it was apparent, were ready for Debs' message.

During the long winter nights in the bunkhouses, before pot-bellied stoves, they had been reading and arguing, reading dime novels and Marx and Henry George, talking about the Haymarket martyrs, the Knights of Labor, Coxey's Army, the great American Railway Union strike, the massacre at Homestead, and the whys and wherefores of depressions. As a man took a final stretch before turning in, looking at the great shadowy bulk of the mountains looming blackly beneath the stars, he couldn't help wondering as he thought of his buddies who had been held behind barbed wire why a few men had millions while millions of men had nothing.

Such men, as indigenous to the U.S.A. as the Rocky Mountains in which they lived, were announcing themselves for socialism. Ex-bronco busters and range riders, defrauded homesteaders and blacklisted railroad men turned miner from necessity, they were completely unimpressed when mine owners described them as un-American. Thousands of them cheered as Debs spoke such words as these:

"The earth for all the people. That is the demand.

"The machinery of production and distribution for all the people. That is the demand.

"The collective ownership and control of industry and its democratic management in the interest of all the people. That is the demand.

---

[8] Secretary-Treasurer Haywood told a reporter of the *Denver Post*, March 4, 1903, that "During the bitter cold weather the wives and children of many of the men were huddled together in tents because the wages paid would not suffice to pay back rent and provide other necessities."

"The elimination of rent, interest, profit and the production of wealth to satisfy the wants of all the people. That is the demand.

"Cooperative industry in which all shall work together in harmony as the basis of a new social order, a higher civilization, a real republic. That is the demand.

"The end of class struggles and class rule, of master and slave, of ignorance and vice, of poverty and shame, of cruelty and crime—the birth of freedom, the dawn of brotherhood, the beginning of MAN. That is the demand.

"This is socialism."

Even as Debs spoke it was apparent that more industrial warfare was in the offing. The miners and smeltermen were daily becoming more determined to get the eight-hour day, to get by strike what they had not been able to get through the use of political action and law. The Mine Owners' Association was equally determined that the time had arrived for a showdown, that the time had come to destroy the Western Federation of Miners, utterly and completely, root and branch. Their gunmen repeatedly threatened Debs. On his first visit to Colorado in 1896, where he had gone to help the striking miners of Leadville, he had been met by gunmen as he got off the train and told to leave now or he would leave later feet first.

"This will be either the beginning of organized labor in Colorado," Debs had said, "or the end of me." Debs did not leave then nor later feet first. But his friends were nervous. A tough, rough-hewn individual had trailed him for days and Debs' associates feared that he was a mine owner's thug. This proved to be a libel. When Debs accosted him, the man gruffly replied that he was guarding him. "I have decided that you are on the level with the workingman," he said. "Anybody touches you will be carried out this here region a corpse."

As new rifles and equipment were issued to the National Guard in 1901 the miners, too, began arming themselves, but with more than guns. The Cripple Creek miners had 8,000 volumes in their library, housed in a new union building. This fact was typical. The Western Federation of Miners had increased from 12,000 members in 1896 to 25,000 in 1901 and all over the Rocky Mountains they were building new union halls, conducting classes, holding debates and lectures on everything from the possibility of a nationwide industrial union to the drama and English literature. It was this sudden predilection for thinking on the part of men who felt they were as capable as any Americans living that frightened the mine owners more than the miners' determination to defend their homes and jobs.

They talked, too, in their new union halls of the terrible mine disasters which each year took a toll of hundreds of lives. The Smuggler-Union mine at Telluride seemed typical enough of miners' lives everywhere in Colorado. The miners there, as in many other mine and smelting towns, lived in tents and tin huts, unable to afford real homes. In January, 1901, they had been forced on strike against the contract system in which miners were denied regular wages or a minimum rate and paid instead on a speed-up system based on the amount of ore mined.

During the strike there had been starvation. There were killings, arrests, and imprisonments. Then, the strike won, there had been a fire on November 20 in which sixteen miners were burned to death and after that a snow-slide which killed seventeen. Three thousand miners filed by the mass grave in which the sixteen victims of the fire were buried and as each one passed he let fall in the grave a sprig of evergreen. When the miners wept as they passed the grave they were thinking of thousands and not of sixteen.

They applauded when Big Bill Haywood, their secretary-treasurer and only thirty-four years old when the 1903 strike began, told them that he had raised $25,000 for the coming struggle with one letter and added, "Now that we have to fight for the eight-hour day, it will be one strike after another." He expressed the feelings of the smelter men when he said, "The fires that smelt the ores, like the fires of hell, never cool. There are no rest days, no Sundays, no holidays." He spoke, too, of rich men in the East who had never seen a mine or touched a power drill but who were getting $24,-000,000 of mined gold each year from the miners' work in the Cripple Creek region alone. "The barbarous gold barons," he said, "they do not find the gold, they do not mine the gold, they do not mill the gold, but by some weird alchemy all the gold belongs to them."

2. Big Bill

It was Big Bill who led the strike. Perhaps we can understand both it and the miners better if we consider him a moment. Six feet two of aggressive muscle, he tipped the beam at a lean 225 pounds. Able to break a man's jaw with a single punch, he would weep when a poem moved him. He had something in his make-up of Paul Bunyan with a full pugnacious face, a shock of straw-colored hair, and only one good eye. He had an appetite for knowledge as well as justice and if it was difficult to say which was the stronger, he saw no contradiction between them.

He was no saint; he had his share of vanity, but he had no more quit in him than a bulldog. He fought his weaknesses like he fought a strike. If he had one bad day, he'd fight harder on the next. Sometimes as he lurched in and out of saloons, laughing, fighting, reciting poetry, taking on scabs and gunmen, he seemed no more than a brawling giant. Then the saloons would not see him for a year while he read Buckle and Morgan and Darwin and Marx, while he read above all his beloved Shakespeare. Occasionally he went on long fasts, not eating for days and drinking only water, on the theory that body and mind were cleansed and strengthened by these bouts of abstinence.

As a young man in the mines his toughness was legendary. But so was the gentleness with which he treated his invalided wife, Nevada Jane Minor, permanently injured as the result of a fall from a horse. Often, after twelve hours underground in the Blaine mine at Silver City in Nevada, Haywood would be seen carrying his wife and two children up a steep mountainside, his wife in his arms, the children clinging to his broad back, as he took all three to visit friends who lived high above the mining camp.

His life contained much of the West's story since the Civil War. Born among the Mormons in Salt Lake City just before the continent was joined by the Union Pacific in 1869, his first memory was of the death of his father, who had been a Pony Express rider. The three-year-old child always remembered lying on the fresh grave while his weeping mother stood above him as he dug his arm into the grave as far as he could, straining and straining downward, trying to touch the coffin.

His mother married again and the little family moved to the Utah mining camp of Ophir, their house on the edge of Dry Canyon near the Hidden Treasure Mining Camp. When seven years old Bill Haywood saw his first gun duel. "One morning I was going to school," he wrote years later, "which was only a short distance from our house, when I saw Mannie Mills across the street pull his gun from his pocket and shoot at Slippery Dick who was walking just ahead of me. Dick also began shooting and they exchanged several shots when Mills fell on his face dead. Slippery Dick blew into the barrel of his six-shooter, put it into his pocket and walked away."

When he was fifteen he saw a Negro lynched. Afterwards, retiring to a lonely spot and the sobs shaking his body, he resolved that he would fight that thing, the racial oppression of which he had seen other instances, with all the strength he had in him. In that same year—it was 1884 and two years before the Haymarket affair—he got a job, through his stepfather, in the Ohio Mine in the Eagle Creek Canyon of Nevada. Before leaving Salt Lake City, he says, "I bought an outfit consisting of overalls, jumper, blue shirt, mining boots, two pairs of blankets, a set of chessmen and a pair of boxing gloves."

"My first job," he later recalled in writing of the Ohio Mine, "was wheeling rock from a shaft that was being sunk at the end of an open cut." Exhausted by the end of the day, he could hardly drag himself to the bunkhouse.

Here in the bunkhouse the miners would gather around the table and by the flickering candlelight play cards or chess or read. For they "were all great readers. . . . I did not have many books of my own, but the miners all had some. One had a volume of Darwin; others had Voltaire, Shakespeare, Byron, Burns and Milton. . . . We all exchanged books and quite a valuable library could have been collected among these few men."

The boy's special friend was Pat Reynolds, "the oldest man on the job, tall, raw-boned, with a red chin-whisker, bushy eyebrows and a strawberry mark on the outer corner of his left eye. It was this old Irishman who gave me my first lessons in unionism."[4] The labor movement owes a lot to such men as Pat Reynolds. The West and its mining camps, for the most part, knew little of trade unions then. The gospel of organization, the religion of class unity, was spread by such unknown and anonymous working men as Reynolds. Often blacklisted refugees from the East, workers who had grown old as they were hounded from job to job, they planted seeds as surely as the more celebrated Johnny Appleseed planted apple trees in Ohio. Solemnly, haltingly, they spoke of strikes won and lives bettered through unity and when they said in their rusty old voices, "An injury to one is the concern of all," it somehow made men think.

Haywood was still working at the Ohio Mine when Parsons and Spies, Engel and Fischer were executed. For more than a year the case had been a passion with him and during the trial he had discussed every word of testimony with Pat Reynolds. Questions kept running through his mind. "Who threw the bomb? It was not Albert Parsons, or any one he knew; if it had been why did Albert Parsons walk into court and surrender himself? The last words of August Spies kept running through my mind: 'There will come a time when our silence will be more powerful than the voices you are strangling today.' It was a turning point in my life."

His next job was in the Brooklyn lead mines in Utah where for a time he fired the boilers running the top car, taking away the waste and ore that were sent to the surface. "A crowd of lead miners presents a ghastly appearance," he observed, "as their faces are ashen pale." Deaths from lead poisoning and accidents were frequent and he witnessed the death of a friend while working 1,400 feet under the surface in the Mormon stope. "I was working but a short distance from Louis Fontaine when he was killed by a slab of rock from the roof that crushed his head on the drill that he was holding. We got the body out of the *stope* on a timber truck, ran it to the station, and put all that was left of Louis in the skip. We rang three bells for the surface."

When he was about nineteen Big Bill married his sweetheart, Nevada Jane Minor, and went to work on the Hopin Ranch in Nevada as a cowboy. From the ranch the young couple moved to a deserted Nevada army post, Fort McDermott, and while there he delivered his wife of a baby girl. With a child, the young man was fired with ambition, particularly after the region around McDermott was thrown open to homesteaders, and Haywood began improving a place which he thought would always be his own. He loved it. To him and his wife it represented independence and escape from the mines.

They needed money so urgently for equipment and improvements that now and again Bill would go back to the mines for a space. After returning home in 1893 he was cutting fence posts and putting in head-gates when the

[4] All of the quotations from Haywood are taken from his autobiography, *Bill Haywood's Book*, New York, 1929.

little family was struck by "a fearful blow." The government decided that it wanted the land back for the Indians.

The Haywoods had to leave. Even worse, the depression of '93 had also arrived and Bill could not get a job. "It seemed as if a black curtain had pulled down on the future," he writes. "There was no ray of hope. I broke out in a spirit of desperation and said that we should not starve as long as I had the old Springfield rifle and there were cattle on the range. Shortly after I moved my wife and baby to Winnemucca. There was nothing left; no compensation for the work I had put into the homestead, for the house I had built, the fences I had run, the trees I had set out."

As he circulated over the West, grabbing freights, walking, sometimes riding in a buckboard with a friendly rancher, he found that he was but one of an army whose goal was work. As he lay out under the stars on frosty nights, hitching his blanket about him, he thought more and more of the talks that he had had as a boy with Pat Reynolds. What was wrong? Why was he hungry and why were thousands of others? What was this employer class that Pat Reynolds had talked so much about and why did it, without work, own the world?

Then came the American Railway Union strike of 1894 and "suddenly," Haywood wrote, "there came a great rift of light. Here I felt was a great power. The big thing was that they could stop the trains. It was a lesson of the Knights of Labor, an echo of the voice of the Haymarket martyrs."

He was on fire with the idea of unionism in 1896 when he got a job in the Blaine Mine at Silver City, Idaho. Shortly after his right hand was crushed when it was caught between a descending car and the side of the shaft, Ed Boyce, president of the Western Federation of Miners, came to Silver City on an organizing tour. Haywood was ready for him. With his hand crippled and his wife just having had a second baby girl, he was living off collections taken up for him by his fellow miners. None was more active than Haywood in organizing the one thousand miners of Silver City and he saw to it himself that two miners who would not join were forced from camp.

In 1898 Haywood was elected delegate from the Silver City Miners' Union to the WFM convention at Salt Lake City. The following year he was again elected to the convention and as he left for it he heard the news that federal troops had again been sent against the striking miners of Coeur d'Alene where 1,200, as has been told, were behind barbed wire. The troops had been requested by Governor Frank Steunenberg, a sheep rancher, who appealed to President McKinley after a mine, whose owners were paying starvation wages, had been blown up.

"More than 1,200 men were arrested without warrant and held for months in prison without any charge being preferred against them," Haywood writes. "There was no insurrection in the Coeur d'Alene, there was no interference in the function of the courts, yet hundreds of men were punished with months of imprisonment in the bull-pen, a structure unfit to house cattle, enclosed in a high barbed-wire fence. The miners of the West became embittered at the vicious treatment imposed upon their brothers in the lead mines of Idaho. Money was raised in every mining camp, in every smelter town, and in many other places and sent to the suffering women and children. It was shown that the mining company was responsible for the damage. Indignant resolutions condemning the outrages flooded Congress.

"At Salt Lake City, I found the shadow of the Coeur d'Alene pervading the convention. The delegates could think or talk of little else. Twelve hundred members were in prison, nine of them indicted for murder, women and children were living under the dark menace of martial law. The legislature, the courts and the army were against us. Every man brought the question home to himself. If this dreadful thing happened in Leadville in the Coeur d'Alene, how long before it happens in Butte, in the Black Hills, in Nevada? What is to stop it happening in the camp where I live? Must wages and the conditions under which we live and work always be subject to the will and whim of the boss?

"The only answer I could find in my own mind was to organize, to multiply our strength. As long as we were scattered and disjointed we could be victimized."

At this convention Haywood was elected a member of the union's executive board. The next year, in 1900, he was elected secretary-treasurer of the Western Federation of Miners, which moved its headquarters to Denver. The young miner rapidly became the union's key figure.

Up out of the mine's damp gloom, he seemed to develop like some giant plant hitherto deprived of sunlight. It was not only that surcease from the mine's maiming toil liberated his mind to sudden growth, but there were a pride and excitement in him as he became increasingly convinced that miners and all workingmen were the peers of any men anywhere and that by acting together they could solve any and all problems. In 1901 he and Ed Boyce, president of the union, joined the Socialist Party and from that time on they talked, particularly when Debs was in Denver, of a countrywide industrial union, its ultimate goal a society run for humans rather than for profit.

Those who had seen in Haywood only a wild and aggressive militant soon found themselves mistaken as he went about his job as secretary-treasurer. As he entered the Colorado political fight for the eight-hour day in 1900 and 1901, it was found that he could plan campaigns, raise money, attract allies, persuade opponents. A forceful writer and debater, attractive in his bold and easy approach to all men, he could get the miners' viewpoint into a press that had never received it before, and never received it after. He would bull his way into a bishop's parlor as readily as into a meeting of an American Federation of Labor Local and, once in, his rough logic was often effective.

He could, moreover, present the miners' case, particularly in regard to the eight-hour fight, with such convincing phrase and such knowledge of the divisions current among the employers that he persuaded Senator Patterson of Colorado, owner of the *Rocky Mountain News*, to present a 27,000-word statement of the miners' case both on the floor of the Senate and in the columns of his newspaper.

The miners somehow saw themselves in him and they felt that if they could only make speeches they would say what he said the way he said it. They believed him fearless and incorruptible and if he was smart, well, he wasn't fancy. But above all he had had his guts shaken by a bucking drill as they had and had seen and heard the rock rumble as the timbers buckled and splintered before miners could escape the falling tons that crushed them. He had starved and sweated, fought and got drunk, hoped and worried as they all had and they were well content that he would lead them in the strike being forced upon them—for the eight-hour day of which they had been brazenly cheated.

The Colorado strike in August, 1903, with smelter men and miners asking a minimum of $3 for an eight-hour day.[5] And yet it is doubtful if what ensued can be called a strike. It was civil convulsion, civil war in which there were no neutrals. All rules were off from the first as far as the mine owners were concerned, and so blatantly did they proceed on the theory that anything that killed or imprisoned a union man was proper that soon even conservative newspapers were protesting. Frame-ups of union members occurred almost weekly and were regarded as praiseworthy acts. Judges, when they favored the law or strikers, were overawed by military power, their very courts invaded by soldiers.

Newspapers, when they printed a word favorable to the union, were closed and their staffs imprisoned. Lawyers, after defending strikers, were assaulted and deported. Professional killers, such as Bob Meldrum, K. C. Sterling, Frank Varnick, D. C. Scott, Willard Runnels, and Walter Kinley, were imported by the score by the Mine Owners Association, which organized the Citizens' Alliance, vigilantes with 30,000 members in the state.[6]

[5] According to an official government report, wages and hours of smelters in the Grant and Globe plants of the American Smelting & Refining Co. in Denver were as follows: $1.75 per day minimum for common labor, 10 hours; roaster men's helpers, $2.50, 12 hours; roaster men, $2.70, 12 hours; wheelers to blast furnaces, $2.50 to $2.75, 12 hours; furnace men and tappers, $2.50 to $3.00, 12 hours; engineers, $3.50, 12 hours. (*A Report on Labor Disturbances in the State of Colorado, From 1880 to 1904 Inclusive*, 58th Congr., 3rd Sess., Senate Doc. 122, p. 133.)

[6] *A Report on Labor Disturbances in the State of Colorado, From 1880 to 1904 Inclusive*, 58th Congr., 3rd Sess., Sen. Doc. No. 122, Washington, 1905, p. 48. This official government report goes on to say that "many persons joined the alliance because they believed that if they did not, they would be boycotted by members of the alliance. . . . Not only as individuals, but as an organization, the Citizens' Alliance actively supported the policy of the Mine Owners' Association of refusing employment to any member of the Western Federation of Miners, and also the policy of deporting all members of the Federation. The alliance and the association alleged that the Federation was a 'socialist and criminal organization.' . . ." (pp. 49-50.)

Private detectives and hired spies from the Pinkerton and Thiel agencies[7] were almost as thick as the spurred and uniformed soldiers who jangled about, guns strapped to their legs and bayonets on rifles, demanding passes from citizens as they walked the streets of their own towns.

The strike had scarcely begun when 1,000 troops, under the command of General Sherman Bell, arrived in Cripple Creek, a like number climbing off trains at Telluride. There had been no disturbance but, with the approval of Governor Peabody, General Bell declared martial law at both places. Bell, a strutty little man with a deep voice and a narrow chest, who had been a Rough Rider with Roosevelt in Cuba, was on the payroll of the State of Colorado but he also was receiving, according to the Boston *Transcript* and a good many other papers, $3,200 additional a year from the mine owners.

Upon his arrival in Cripple Creek he seized a private building to use as his military headquarters and marched his troops on the city hall where he informed the Mayor and the chief of police they would obey orders or go to jail. After forcing the resignation of three regularly elected officials whom he believed friendly to the strikers—the sheriff, the county assessor, and treasurer—he established a military bullpen and threw into it every union man in the district, some 600, whom he held for weeks without charge and without trial. When a lawyer appeared with a writ of habeas corpus for some of his clients, the General snorted, "Habeas corpus, hell! We'll give 'em post mortems!"

After the soldiers, who according to the *Army and Navy Journal* and Ray Stannard Baker in *McClure's* were being paid by mine owners, disembarked at Cripple Creek they placed guns trained on the town on every hill surrounding the community, Cow Hill, Bull Hill, Pisgah, Nipple Hill, Squaw Hill, and St. Peter's Dome. Not long later the editor of the Victor *Record,* a little newspaper in a town neighboring Cripple Creek, ventured to criticize Bell's seizure of power but the paper had scarcely come off the press when a detachment of soldiers clamped it down, seized the editors, the staff, and the printers, and threw them into the bullpen behind barbed wire.

[7] Among the hired detectives were K. C. Sterling and D. C. Scott. During the trial of union leaders in the Florence and Cripple Creek derailing case it was proved that it was not they, but the mine owners' and railroad company's own detectives, Sterling and Scott, "who were guilty of the crime." (M. Friedman, *The Pinkerton Labor Spy,* New York, 1907, pp. 197–98.) Among the Pinkerton and Thiel hired spies the most notorious was George W. Riddell, Pinkerton Operative No. 36, who was sent to Telluride to discover the existence of the "Inner Circle." This brain-child of James Mc-Parlan, superintendent of the Pinkerton Denver office and framer of the "Molly Maguires," was the group alleged to be directing the "terroristic" activities of the Telluride local. After working on the "Inner Circle" case at Telluride for two years at an expense of over $7,000, Pinkerton operative Riddell was unable to bring to light any evidence of the existence of such a group. (*Ibid.,* pp. 118–119.) The only things the notorious Riddell did during his two-year "investigation" at Telluride was on one occasion to propose to one of his close friends, Joseph C. Barnes, that two kegs of dynamite be rolled into the Liberty Bell Mill and on another that the miners burn the town. (*The Miners Magazine,* July 11, 1907, vol. ix, no. 211, p. 10.)

Emma Langdon, the wife of one of the linotype operators jailed and herself a printer, got out the paper singlehanded the next night with a headline proclaiming, "Slightly Disfigured But Still in the Ring!"

Attorneys for the union, Edmund Richardson, and an old man, a Civil War veteran, General Engley, were still trying to liberate the illegally jailed miners, who had already been in the bullpen for some two weeks. Their application for a writ of habeas corpus was argued in the courtroom of Judge Seeds in Victor. General Bell filled the courtroom with armed troops and trained guns upon it from nearby hills and buildings before he marched some thirty of the prisoners into the courtroom where the writ for their liberation was to be considered. Judge Seeds ordered the prisoners liberated. Bell merely laughed, declared the writ of habeas corpus suspended in Colorado, and marched the "liberated" prisoners back to the bullpen. As Richardson left the courtroom, he was assaulted and beaten up by Walter Kinley, one of the operators' hired men.

Bell's next order was that every gun in the district should be turned in to the military for registration. Old General Engley responded to the order by walking ostentatiously down the streets, an unregistered shotgun on his arm, his whole demeanor saying come and get it. John Glover, another lawyer, wrote a letter to the newspapers declaring that he had two unregistered guns in his office which would remain unregistered. A squad of soldiers surrounded the office and the lawyer shot it out with them, not surrendering until he was wounded.

In the meantime similar scenes were being enacted at Telluride with the difference that hundreds of union men were being rounded up and deported on freight trains. When someone again mentioned the Constitution to General Bell, he said, "To hell with the Constitution! We're not following the Constitution!" All of Colorado was in an uproar. As the strike went on week after week, the miners' big problem became food. Haywood opened a series of union stores but they were wrecked by the vigilantes as fast as they were opened.[8]

The State Federation of Labor was threatening a general strike while the United Mine Workers were out already and martial law had been established at Trinidad and Pueblo. *Harper's Weekly* reported that the president of the Citizens' Alliance in Pueblo had said, "The Alliance will

[8] In addition Pinkerton operatives, masquerading as union men, sabotaged the distribution of relief to the striking miners to set the men against the union and at the same time against Haywood. One of these Pinkertons, A. G. Gratias, wrote in a report dated June 29, 1904, that he was again resuming his role of distributing relief to the strikers. "I will carry out the instructions I received from Mr. Cary [Pinkerton manager] in regard to putting down relief as much as possible, so as to cause dissatisfaction and get the men against the union. I will put the blame for not giving the men more relief as much as I can on William D. Haywood by saying that I carried out his instructions." (*The Miners Magazine,* July 11, 1907, vol. ix, no. 211, p. 8, reporting Pinkerton operatives' reports read by attorney Clarence Darrow during the Haywood-Moyer trial.)

not lay down its arms until the Western Federation of Miners and the United Mine Workers have left the state." At about the same time the head of the Alliance in Denver declared, "Unions should not strike; striking unions are not legitimate; the Federation must be destroyed."

Big Bill Haywood and Charles H. Moyer, who had been elected president of the Western Federation of Miners, were traveling from mining camp to mining camp, proceeding mostly at night, guns in their belts, meeting in darkness, often on a hilltop, sentries posted about to give warning of approaching spies or troops. It was perfectly well understood that Big Bill, at any rate, would not be taken without a fight and perhaps not taken alive. Something of the tension of the time is revealed in this incident told by Haywood, involving himself, Moyer, and Dan MacDonald, president of the American Labor Union. It took place in Denver during the strike and just as the three union men were leaving a saloon.

"As we were going out, we met a gang of deputy sheriffs, headed by a young man who was a nephew of Felix O'Neill, captain of the Denver police. They all wore badges. Moyer sarcastically remarked:

" 'Pretty badges!'

"O'Neill said sharply, 'Don't you like 'em?'

"Moyer replied, 'Indeed I do; I'd like to have one for my dog.'

"He no sooner said it than one of them struck him squarely between the eyes. The man must have had on brass knuckles. As Moyer fell, his head struck the stone threshold and he lay quivering. The captain's nephew whipped out a big six-shooter, swung at MacDonald and struck him across the forehead, lifting his scalp about three inches. As Mac fell he broke his arm.

"I knocked the young fellow back and then had the whole bunch to deal with. I had not time to think how desperate was the situation: it was a fight for life. One of them struck me on the head with a gun. I dropped on my knees off the curb of the sidewalk, and drew my revolver. The captain's nephew was rushing up to give me another blow; I shot him three times in quick succession."

Later, at the hospital, it was found that the captain's nephew was only badly wounded.

"I am sorry I hurt him so badly," said Big Bill, "but from now on I'll carry a stronger shooting gun."

Protest was rising to such an extent that the habeas corpus was being restored and miners liberated from the bullpens. General Bell retaliated by arresting them again on charges of vagrancy. But this time some of the vigilantes helping the troops were driven off by rifle fire when they came to miners' homes at night. Several vigilantes were killed. Despite the arrests and despite the hunger, the strike remained solid. The owners, or at least their private detectives and hired spies, turned increasingly to frame-ups.

There was an explosion at the Vindicator Mine near Cripple Creek. Although the mine was guarded by troops and the explosion took place six hundred feet beneath the ground, officials of the miners' union in Cripple Creek were arrested and charged with the murder of a scab and the mine superintendent, killed in the accident.

They had no sooner been acquitted for lack of evidence than they were arrested again, charged this time with attempting to wreck a train. The case did not even go to the jury. The judge ordered the defendants acquitted after the star witness of the prosecution, one McKinney, "a rounder and a pimp," confessed under cross-examination that he had been hired by detectives of the Thiel Agency to frame the union officials. He said he had worked with a certain Scott and Sterling, two private detectives in the employ of the Citizens Alliance.

The strike was still strong on June 4, 1904, when a small railroad depot at Independence, near Cripple Creek, was blown up, killing fourteen scabs. The Western Federation of Miners was instantly charged with the crime although the explosion in fact had been set off by Harry Orchard, a fat informer with a face like a red moon, who by his own later confession was working for the Mine Owners Association. Posing as a loyal union member, Orchard, according to his own confession, had been reporting union meetings to detectives Scott and Sterling throughout the strike.

A good many people knew this to be a fact long before Orchard confessed it. Despite the fact, a coroner's jury returned a verdict finding that "members and officials of the Western Federation of Miners were responsible" for the explosion. The verdict had not long been returned when a large and excited mob gathered in the streets of Cripple Creek. What happened thereafter was reported as follows by a committee of miners, members of the Western Federation of Miners:

"Hamlin, the secretary of the Mine Owners' Association, addressed the great mob, violently condemning the W.F.M. for the explosion, saying that fifty union men should be shot down and as many more strung to telegraph poles, and the rest of them driven over the hills for the death of the brave men who had been blown up in the depot. One of the strikers asked:

"'Who do you mean by them?' Then the riot broke loose. Several scabs and non-union men were killed, and many union men who had taken refuge in their hall were seriously injured by volleys of bullets that were fired in the windows and down the skylights. When the sheriff came to the hall, the union men surrendered and were taken to the armory, the quarters of the militia, which was afterwards called the bull-pen.

"The furniture and fittings of the union halls had been demolished. The hall of the engineers' union was a total wreck. On the blackboard was written this motto: 'For being a union man, deportation or death will be your fate.'"

In addition mobs wrecked the union stores at Anaconda, Goldfield, Victor, and Cripple Creek, pouring coal oil over vast quantities of flour,

sugar, meat, and other foodstuffs while "scabs carried away tons of goods."
Moyer, president of the WFM, was arrested and held on the grounds of
"military necessity" while warrants charging murder had been issued by
the authorities against Haywood in connection with the Independence station massacre. And with all this against them, the miners of the Cripple
Creek district held a giant parade on September 7, Labor Day, through the
bayonet-lined streets of Cripple Creek.

Daily deported miners were returning home, although most of them had
been taken as far as the state line of Kansas or New Mexico. One of them,
Joe Barnes, was in pretty bad shape. He had himself nailed up in a barrel
and despite air holes was not feeling very chipper when he was liberated
by his wife in the back yard of their Telluride home. Each night in both
Cripple Creek and Telluride union men were eluding troops and vigilantes
to paste on poles, walls, and store windows a poster written by Haywood
and signed by him and Moyer.

"Is Colorado in America?" the top line asked and beneath the question
was a large American flag. On each stripe of the flag was an incription,
some of which read: "Free Press Throttled in Colorado," "Soldiers Defy
the Courts in Colorado," "Militia Hired by Corporations to Break Strikes
in Colorado" and "Corporations Corrupt and Control Administration in
Colorado." The poster particularly outraged the military and Moyer, as a
result, was arrested again, this time in Telluride where he was charged
with desecration of the flag. Escorted by troops, he was taken to Denver,
where Haywood decided to go down to the station to meet him.

"We went to the station," Haywood writes, "and when the train pulled
in a detachment of twelve soldiers got off first, then Moyer alone, then
twelve more soldiers with officers following.

"I stepped in and shook hands with Moyer and was walking along with
him, hands clasped, when I felt a pressure on my shoulder, trying to force us
apart. I looked around. There was Captain Bulkeley Wells [a mine super-
intendent], the same Wells who a few months before had entered into an
agreement with us that would have brought the peaceful settlement of the
strike at Telluride. This thought flashed through my mind, and I wheeled
and struck him full in the face.

"It was a wild thing to do. In a flash the soldiers came to his rescue, and
with the butts of their guns they struck me over the head and knocked me
back between two cars. One pulled his gun down on me. I could see the
hole in the barrel. I said, 'Pull it, you son of a bitch, pull it!'

"One of the officers knocked up the barrel and said sharply:

"'Stand back, stand back!' Then addressing me, 'Haywood, go along
with Moyer!'

"I went along with Moyer and we marched to the Oxford Hotel. . . .
When we reached the Oxford Hotel, we marched in and Moyer sat down.
I was standing with my elbow on the counter when Walter Kinley, the
Telluride gunman, came up to me and said:

" 'Sit down!'

" 'I don't want to sit down.'

"He pulled out his six-shooter and made a swing at me, shouting:

" 'Sit down, God damn ye!'

"I hit him first and his gun did not strike me. Five or six soldiers rushed up and struck me several times, knocking me back against the wall. Kinley ran around to where he could get an opening, reached over and hit me on the head with the handle of his gun. About the same time a soldier made a jab at me, striking me on the cartilage just before the ribs. An officer came up swinging his six-shooter, shouting:

" 'Get back, you fellers, get back! How many does it take to handle this man?'

"Soon I was taken upstairs and two gunmen were left in the room with me. One of them was Kinley, who was complaining about having broken the pearl handle of his gun on my head. . . . An army surgeon came and dressed the cuts in my head, sewing back my right ear, which required seven stitches. . . ."

In November, 1904, Governor Peabody was defeated, defeated so badly that even the mine owners' state Supreme Court could not refurbish him. It attempted to rescue him by declaring that he had in reality won over his opponent but the court could not convince even Governor Peabody. After twenty hours of his second term he resigned.

On Dec. 1, 1904, the mine and smelter owners of the Telluride district surrendered. After fifteen months of struggle the miners and smelter men received what they had asked more than a year before—a three-dollar minimum for an eight-hour day. Elsewhere results were mixed and many miners in Cripple Creek were blacklisted from that time on, thousands of them moving on to Tonopah and Goldfield, Nev., where gold had been discovered and where authorities promised Colorado's miners "a chance to sleep without the overhanging thought of militia, gunmen, jails and bullpens."

On the whole, however, the conflict ended with a great victory for the Western Federation of Miners. Many of its members had the eight-hour day and instead of being destroyed the organization was daily growing in membership and strength. By 1905 it had 40,000 members as against 25,000 in 1901. But the Mine Owners' Association had not given up. It was soon to evolve another plan for the destruction of the miners' union.

3. The Harmless Mr. Orchard

The fat spy who was Harry Orchard, his round, red face shining like a benevolent harvest moon, decided that he would pay a visit to Caldwell, Idaho, late in November of 1905. He didn't quite know why, but times were a little difficult since the end of the Colorado miners' strike when he had been on the payroll of the Mine Owners' Association and had, in line of duty, killed fourteen men by blowing up the Independence station. Something might turn up in Caldwell. His suitcase was packed with burglars' tools as well as dynamite and plaster of paris, for one never knew when a bomb might be profitable again.

He had, moreover, a vague feeling that something advantageous might be worked out in connection with former Governor Frank Steunenberg who lived in Caldwell and was hated by many groups. It was not necessary for him to plan a crime. He could rely on his instinct to lead him to it. Corruption was so imbedded in him that he could afford to act spontaneously, to drift with events, serene in the knowledge that they would lead him to a position where he could sell out someone or something.

He was a character so crooked, as he later spent months in proving, that he himself sometimes didn't know which side he was on. In the employ of the Mine Owners' Association, he passed as a loyal union man and there were occasionally instants when he apparently momentarily thought he was one. Some Irish blood flowed through his veins and he often chose to pose as an honest and convivial Irishman, a little unworldly, a little overly tenderhearted. He posed so successfully that people frequently said of him, "Why, he wouldn't hurt a flea. He's got a heart as big as a barrel."

And so he rocked back and forth in the lobby of Caldwell's Saratoga Hotel where he had registered as Tom Hogan and where he let it be known he was a buyer of sheep. The boys in the back room liked to have him in for a little game of cards. They liked him but didn't take him seriously. This may have offended the round little man, for he had always had a persistent yearning to be at the center of events. One of the card players afterwards said, "He was a sociable, affable fellow, well liked, a whole-souled mick who wouldn't hurt anybody."

In this role he spent five weeks in the hotel, each evening rocking back and forth in a chair in the lobby, a cheery open sort of a man who one would never believe had in fact shot and killed a drunk in a dark alley, had burned down a factory for the insurance, had wooed and robbed any number of women, and had plotted to kidnap the child of a partner. There was nothing to indicate that the honest buyer of sheep was in reality a professional burglar and labor spy who was a habitual user of dynamite for profit. Instead he seemed the soul of innocent normalcy as he squeaked back and forth in his rocker, a kind of adventurous insanity simmering within him, his inoffensive eyes speculatively sliding over the large and dignified figure of former Governor Steunenberg, Caldwell's leading citizen and another daily frequenter of the Saratoga's lobby.

The Governor was a plain man with a strong profile and a weak conscience. The combination had brought him the governorship in 1896. It had also brought him numerous enemies who thought he had been bribed to sell them out. His only idiosyncrasy was a refusal to wear a tie or speak of his refusal, his only ornament the naked dot of gold that was his exposed collar button. It was his simple pleasure to drop in to the lobby for a short time each evening on his way home to supper from the Caldwell Bank, of which he was president. There he would read the newspapers, rocking back and forth in his favorite chair. He was admired by some for getting his while Governor and making every effort to break the Western Federation of Miners at Coeur d'Alene after he had been bribed by one of the largest mine owners.

If the Governor noticed another persistent rocker there, "the whole-souled mick who wouldn't hurt anybody," he never mentioned it. Doubtless he would have been considerably surprised to know that Orchard, alias Hogan, was gradually coming to the conviction that if he could kill the Governor he might parlay it into something. There ought to be something, he thought, in killing a man so many hated, and besides he just had a hunch he could work it into something good. Not that he had thought everything out. He made a practice of never examining his own thoughts too closely, for after all he didn't want to spy on himself and what he didn't know of his own plans he couldn't tell. And yet he may well have allowed himself the quick and passing flash that the mine owners could use Steunenberg's murder if it could be pinned on the union.

At any rate he had permitted himself to make a bomb in the privacy of his hotel room, number 19. It was ready on Dec. 30, 1905, and when the Governor stood up from his chair in the lobby, a slow-moving man preparing to leave for home and supper, Orchard quickly sidled upstairs to his room and his bomb. Concealing the bomb beneath his coat, he ran through the early darkness to Steunenberg's home, taking a short cut through snowy fields, while the Governor, who liked to think that he resembled a Roman senator, ambled sedately along the streets toward his death.

With swift and expert fingers, Orchard fastened his bomb behind Steunenberg's gate, rigging a fishing line before it in such fashion that the Governor's step must strike the string and pull the bomb's trigger as he entered the gate. Then he ran as fast as he could back toward the Saratoga Hotel. He was almost there when he and the whole town heard an explosion that rattled the windows and dishes all over Caldwell. The Governor, a huge hole blown in his back and side, was dying in the snow before his home. He spoke but once before he died when he asked those who carried him into his house, "Who shot me?"

As the Governor died, Harry Orchard was having a drink in the hotel bar. He had accomplished his design of killing the Governor without witnesses and now it was his peculiar purpose to be arrested for it. He tried so hard for the next two days that people thought he must be a blind, an accomplice of the actual murderer drawing attention from him while he escaped. Orchard, of course, made no move to flee but, on the contrary, talking loudly, put his nose into every group that was discussing Caldwell's tremendous sensation. It had drawn to the little town most of Idaho's great, including Governor Gooding.

A Citizens' Committee was organized, holding its first meeting on December 31, the day after the murder, and offering a reward of $25,000 for the apprehension of the murderer. Orchard attended the first meeting, declaring that he understood he was suspected of the slaying. This was news to most. However, his campaign for arrest was rewarded on Jan. 1, 1906, after two days of effort. He sang as he was put in his cell, giving every evidence of happiness, apparently undisturbed by the fact that the same materials that had gone into the murder bomb had been found in his hotel room.

Students of the case have long been puzzled by Orchard's extraordinary performance. His later confession to the murder offers little to illuminate his actions. Although he had frequently been in the pay of the Mine Owners' Association, the evidence indicates that Orchard's crime was, at this point, a private enterprise of his own. Most experts have concluded that Orchard, not overly bright for all his cunning, wanted the murder for purposes of speculation. He felt that the fact there had been no witnesses afforded him room for maneuver and he was apparently willing to gamble his own life, which he felt confident he could save, for the pleasures of notoriety and the possibility of profit. Thus he was seemingly happy in the Caldwell jail as he awaited developments. He was in the market with a murder for sale to the highest bidder.

4. Return of the Cobra

A good many mine owners immediately perceived the value of Orchard's property. On the day of Orchard's arrest General Sherman Bell, who had never been accused of misrepresenting the operators' viewpoint, declared in Denver that he was sure Orchard could be induced to confess to the murder "and name his accomplices."

"I think," he repeated, "that we will be able to convince Harry Orchard of the wisdom of naming his accomplices," and even as he spoke newspapers all over the West, including the Idaho *Daily Statesman* and the Denver *Republican*, were charging that Steunenberg's murder was the result of a conspiracy of the Western Federation of Miners.

But to James McParlan, the framer of the "Molly Maguires," Orchard's arrest was an opportunity for which he had long lusted. It was a chance for vindication, a chance to show that despite his years he was as good as he ever was. He was no longer the fine boy he once had been, ever ready for a fight or a frolic, and there were even traducers who were passing it around that he no longer had the artistry at frame-up that had once been his.

Old and crusty and embittered, he had to use a cane now to get over the streets, and his insensate unblinking eyes were warmed when he spoke of the glory that had been his in the old days when he had been young and had hanged the nineteen miners of Pennsylvania. Then the new detectives would crowd around the old fellow, boss of the Denver Pinkerton office, his hair silver gray, his scalp pink and bald, their young eyes shining with the inspiration and example that he gave them.

He was rich enough in worldly goods. As head of the Pinkerton Agency in Denver he brought in some $70,000 a year for supplying the mine owners with strikebreakers, guards, and spies. He was a success. He associated with the best people. Governor Peabody was his good friend.[9] He was the strong right arm of the Mine Owners' Association. There was not one of its officials who did not enjoy having him in of an evening where, smoking fine Havanas and sipping sound whiskey before the fire, the graying veteran of breaking unions would give advice on how to smash the Western Federation of Miners.

Call it a terroristic secret society, he had advised, thinking of his youthful success of so long ago. Say it is really an organization known to its initiates as the Inner Circle, devoted to murder and the overturning of society. They had done it, and the miners had only laughed. That was what he could not stand—the laughter. He did not mind when the miners called him "The Cobra" or even "The Father of all the Cobras," but it festered in him when he heard they laughed at him and said, "The old crook's in his dotage."

He saw from the first that Orchard's arrest was his great opportunity. He knew he was as good as he ever was, was confident that age had not weakened his ability to destroy labor organizations through the execution of their leaders. Not many minutes after hearing of Orchard's arrest he was in communication with his employers, the Mine Owners Association, having little trouble in convincing its leaders that here was the time, place, and means of slaying the Western Federation of Miners, thereby reducing labor cost and saving millions annually. Within a matter of hours McParlan was in the office of Governor Gooding at Boise, Idaho. Nor did he have trouble, representing the mine owners as he did, in convincing the Governor that he should be placed in complete charge of the case with all the power of the state behind him. The State of Idaho, incidentally, spent some $96,000 on the case, much of which went to McParlan.[10] Age had not withered his ability to collect twice for the same job, for he was also being paid by the Mine Owners' Association.

[9] In a letter to George D. Bangs, general manager of the Pinkerton Agency, James McParlan reported that Governor Peabody was "a good friend of the agency." Dated Jan. 10, 1905, the letter condoned the unconstitutional activities of the governor as follows: "While a great deal that was done by Governor Peabody in the emergency which existed for a year or more past is approved by me, by other officials of the agency and by many citizens all over the state, few are willing to admit that all he did was in accordance with the Constitution of the United States or the State of Colorado. . . ." (*The Miners Magazine,* July 11, 1907, vol. ix, no. 211, p. 8.)
[10] In addition, the cost of the trial to Canyon County was $25,000. (*New York Herald,* July 29, 1907.)

Having been appointed by the Governor as chief investigator, the old Pinkerton proceeded to Caldwell but did not speak to Orchard. Finding that the prisoner was still brash and confident, McParlan felt that he should be broken down a bit before negotiations were started with him. Although it was illegal, he had Orchard removed from the county jail at Caldwell to the state penitentiary at Boise where he was thrown into a disciplinary cell without light or other facilities and held in solitary confinement for ten days.

Daily the astounded Orchard received one small plate of moldy bread and one small cup of water from a guard who had been instructed to tell the fat little man that he would surely hang. The ten long days and nights in the cold darkness worked a remarkable transformation. Sick, half starved, frightened, believing he faced death, he was no longer brash when he was led into a bright and sunny room in the penitentiary where Warden Whitney introduced him to McParlan.

The detective dismissed the warden with a careless wave of the hand. In his other hand he held a Bible which he now solemnly opened. "It's an awful thing," he began, "slowly to strangle to death by hanging and then suffer the eternal, unspeakable tortures of Hell." Orchard, already weak, slumped into a chair, unable to meet McParlan's beady eyes. "He started in on my belief in the hereafter," Orchard later wrote in his autobiography, "and spoke of what an awful thing it was to live and die a sinful death and that every man ought to repent for his sins and that there was no sin that God would not forgive. He spoke of King David being a murderer, and also the Apostle Paul. He also told me of some cases where men had turned state's evidence and that when the state had used them for a witness they did not or could not prosecute them. He said that men might be thousands of miles away from where a murder took place and be guilty of that murder and be charged with conspiracy and that the man who committed the murder was not as guilty as the conspirators. He further said he was satisfied I had only been used as a tool, and he was sure the Western Federation of Miners was behind this, that they had carried on their work with a high hand but that their foundation had begun to crumble."

Luncheon was then served, the first good food that Orchard had tasted "for ten terrible days." As Orchard ate, the detective pointed out that the choice before him was simple: he could either say what McParlan wished him to say or he could hang. He must not only confess to murdering Steunenberg on the orders of the Western Federation of Miners but he must confess, too, to all of the robberies, swindles, arsons, murders, and confidence games that he had really committed so that he could not be impeached on cross-examination. And he must embrace God, be born again, come to Jesus and the Mercy Seat where his soul would be washed so spotless that no jury could fail to believe his every Christian word. He could do this and go free, the recipient of the rewards and honors of a grateful state, of a grateful Mine Owners Association, or he could refuse to do it and be strangled, dancing on air at the end of a rope.

With this pleasant choice before him Orchard was returned to the dripping darkness of his solitary cell. The more he thought the whole thing over, the more he thought he had better be redeemed. He had been, he could see now, a very sinful man. The next time out he told McParlan, who still had his Bible in his hand, that God had spoken to him in the darkness of his cell, had taken the scales from his eyes and showed him that the only Christian thing to do was to confess as McParlan wished him to.

McParlan was right. He, Harry Orchard, had murdered Steunenberg for $250 paid to him by Big Bill Haywood, Charles Moyer, the president of the miners' union, and a miner named Pettibone. They were in Denver, a thousand miles away, when he killed the Governor but it was on their instructions that he had done it. But that was not all that he had done. They had paid him also to murder Governor Peabody of Colorado, the Judges of the State Supreme Court of Colorado, General Sherman Bell, and a good many others, but he had never got around to these murders or had bungled them when he had tried. They had also paid him to blow up a whole series of mines.

Seldom had McParlan been so touched. He had saved a soul. He had also showed these sons-of-bitches who said he was all through. He was in his dotage, was he? He felt almost tenderly toward Orchard, who never again experienced the rigors of a cell. Instead he was given a charming little cottage outside the prison walls, sufficient spending money, new clothing, and plenty of his favorite cigars. Governor Gooding, who said he was proud to count Orchard his friend, frequently took him to lunch at his club. Men who a few weeks before had talked of lynching Orchard now were praising him. There could be no finer work, they said, than saving the West from the miners' union.

Day and night the two men, Orchard and McParlan, who were friends now, worked out the details of the confession. Each was pleased, it is said, when told he looked a little like the other. They worked steadily for a month and it turned out that there was scarcely an unsolved crime in Colorado or Idaho that Orchard had not committed while in the pay of the Western Federation of Miners. To McParlan it was a labor of love. He felt young again. He was in his dotage, was he? He regarded the new Orchard as his own artistic creation. Sometimes in moments of sentiment he felt that Orchard was even better than Kelley the Bum who had committed every crime in the calendar in the old days in Pennsylvania, and whose perjured testimony had helped McParlan hang the nineteen when he was young.

He was as good as ever and after warrants had been issued for Haywood, Moyer, and Pettibone, all of whom were in Denver, he set about writing a little release that he would give to the press after the arrests. "I worked single-handed in the Molly Maguire case, and single-handed in this, and I know the ins and outs of both gangs," he wrote. "These fellows thought I must be in my dotage. It will cost Moyer, Haywood and Pettibone their lives."

5. Trial at Murdertown

The mine owners felt that it was vital that Haywood and Moyer hang. Not only would it save Colorado, Idaho, and the West but it might save the whole country. It might even be the means of saving an increasingly menaced capitalist system which President Theodore Roosevelt was soon to say was under threat and which he strove mightily to defend against itself.[11] For Haywood and Moyer were repeating on a national scale what they had done in the West with their federation. They, with Gene Debs, Daniel De Leon, left-wing Socialists, and a few minor officials of the American Federation of Labor, had organized on June 27, 1905, in Chicago the Industrial Workers of the World, a nationwide industrial union.

It was an enthusiastic gathering that launched the new organization. The founding convention, called "The Continental Congress of the Working Class," was attended by more than 200 delegates representing close to 150,000 workers. On the stage of packed Brand's Hall in Chicago on that warm June day were William Haywood, Eugene Debs, Daniel De Leon, head of the Socialist Labor Party, Mother Jones, beloved union organizer, and Lucy Parsons, wife of the Haymarket martyr. Haywood, as president of the Western Federation of Miners, the backbone of the new federation, acted as chairman. He set the tone of the convention when he declared that "the aims and objects of this organization should be to put the working class in possession of the economic power, the means of life, in control of the machinery of production and distribution, without regard to capitalist masters."

The IWW was essentially a reaction against the craft union structure of the AFL and the conservative policies of its top leadership. The crushing of the steel workers' strike in 1901 showed how limited the craft union form of organization was in a struggle against a highly trustified industry. On the other hand, the victory of the United Mine Workers in the great coal strike of 1902 revealed what labor could do when organized along industrial lines. These lessons were not lost on the IWW leaders, who proceeded to organize

[11] Although historians have portrayed Theodore Roosevelt as a "trustbuster," he was basically far from being one. What he wanted to do was to save Wall Street and its practitioners from themselves. In a letter to Jacob Schiff, head of Kuhn, Loeb and Company, March 28, 1907, he wrote pathetically that he could not understand "why there should be this belief in Wall Street that I am a wild-eyed revolutionist." He went on to say that some day the men of Wall Street would realize that they were wrong in opposing him "even from the standpoint of their own interests; and that nothing better for them could be devised than the laws I have striven . . . to have enacted." (As quoted in M. Josephson, *The President Makers, 1896–1919*, New York, 1940, p. 259.)

all workers, regardless of skill, sex, or race, into industrial unions. Anticipating the CIO movement of the 1930's, it set out to organize the unorganized on the basis of the unity of the working people. The IWW opposed not only the craft unionism but also the safe and cautious approach of the AFL leadership to big business. Desiring to revive the militant class struggle of an earlier period, it advocated militancy on both the economic and political fronts. Said the preamble to its constitution:

". . . the working class and the employing class have nothing in common. There can be no peace as long as hunger and want are found among millions of working people and the few, who make up the employing class, have all the good things of life. Between these two classes a struggle must go on until all the toilers come together on the political as well as the industrial field. . . ."

It was, however, on the rock of political action that the IWW was rent asunder. At its 1908 convention it came out against affiliation or cooperation with any political party, advocating instead revolutionary industrial unionism with "direct action" as the principal weapon of the working class. This caused the De Leon Socialist Laborites to leave the IWW. Even before this defection the Western Federation of Miners had broken away from the new national labor center and Debs had grown lukewarm to it.

But all of this was in the future. Back in June, 1905, when the new organization was launched, all was hope and promise. Many believed that the newly created federation was destined to replace the American Federation of Labor. True, some opposed the new labor center on the ground that it was a dual organization which would drain all that was progressive from the AFL and leave it the helpless prey of those collaborating with big business in the National Civic Federation. But Haywood and Debs, among a good many others, were confident that the great majority of American workers would be in the revolutionary IWW raising wages through general strikes while moving for the replacement of capitalism through agitation for socialism.

In the West, where employers had experienced the prowess of the Western Federation of Miners, monopolists did not believe that the program of the IWW was only an impractical pipe dream. Believing they were faced with a potential national emergency, one that might be liquidated through the hanging of Haywood, Moyer, and Pettibone, the mine owners did not intend to let observance of the law deprive them of victory. It was decided to kidnap the three from Denver in the dead of night rather than run the chance, however remote, of their liberation in the extradition hearing that the law required before a defendant charged in one state could be taken for trial from another state. They had special guards and a special train ready for action at the Denver terminal one dark February night when the streets of Denver were deserted.

"On the night of February 17, 1906, Moyer, I and George Pettibone were arrested," Haywood writes. "Moyer at the depot where he was on his way to visit the Smeltermen's Union at Iola, Pettibone at his home and myself at a rooming house near the office. About eleven-thirty there was a knock at the door. I got up and asked who was there. A voice replied:

" 'I want to see you, Bill.' I opened the door, when I saw a deputy whom I knew. He said:

" 'I want you to come with me.' I asked him why.

"He said, 'I can't tell you now, but you must come.' We went down and got into a carriage. I asked him where we were going. He told me, 'To the county jail.'

" 'If you are arresting me,' I said, 'why didn't you come with a warrant?' " 'I have no warrant,' he replied.

"They put me in one of the Federal cells. A few minutes later the sheriff came around. I asked him what it all meant. He said:

" 'They're going to take you to Idaho. They've got you mixed up in the Steunenberg murder.'

" 'Are we to have no chance at all? You can't arrest a man without a warrant and transport him to another state without extradition papers.'

" 'It looks as though that's what they're prepared to do,' he admitted.

"About five in the morning I was taken with Moyer and Pettibone into the office. There were a lot of strange men there. We drove along quiet streets, each of us in a separate carriage with three guards. A train was ready and waiting. We were handcuffed and manacled together. We were going at terrific speed. The train took on coal and water at small stations and stopped at none of the larger towns along the route. When we arrived at Boise we were again put into separate conveyances. We drove to the penitentiary. There was a sign over the gate 'Admittance Twenty-five Cents,' but I was admitted without charge. We were then put in murderers' row in the death house."

The arrests were such an ostensible frame-up that the entire labor movement flared up in fury. And yet the protest was not spontaneous; it had to be organized. Demonstrations were held all over the country. Socialist and conservative, IWW and AFL, joined hands in a defense which collected thousands of dollars and employed one of the nation's rising young lawyers, Clarence Darrow, to head the defense. Gene Debs, writing in the *Appeal to Reason,* Socialist weekly with a circulation of 250,000 ranging from the steel mills of Braddock to the general stores of Nebraska, commented on Mc-Parlan's assertion that the three union men would "never leave Idaho alive." Under the headline, "AROUSE YE SLAVES!" Debs had written, "Well, by the gods, if they do not, the governors of Idaho and Colorado, and the masters from Wall Street, New York, to the Rocky Mountains, had better prepare to follow them." Continuing, he wrote:

"Nearly twenty years ago the capitalist tyrants put some innocent men to death for standing up for labor.

"They are now going to try it again. Let them dare! There have been twenty years of revolutionary education, agitation, and organization since the Haymarket tragedy, and if an attempt is made to repeat it, there will be a revolution and I will do all in my power to precipitate it. The crisis has come and we have to meet it. . . .

"If they attempt to murder Moyer, Haywood, and their brothers, a million revolutionists at least will meet them with guns."

In Idaho an editor said, "Let them come! We'll meet 'em at the border with guns." Such was the temper of the country as the trial neared after the three framed men had been held in prison for more than a year. In Boston 50,000 union men marched through the streets, their voices echoing through the quiet precincts of Beacon Hill as they chanted:

"If Moyer and Haywood die; if Moyer and Haywood die;
Twenty million workingmen will know the reason why."

In San Francisco, the largest crowd in California's history heard a series of speakers declare that the three miners were being murdered because they had reduced the hours and raised the wages of thousands. With the trial scheduled to open on May 9, 1907, 20,000 New Yorkers paraded from the East Side to Grand Central Palace where they cheered, wept, and hooted as John Chase, Morris Hillquit, and Joseph Wanhope denounced the frameup. On the very eve of the trial, with Debs still charging up and down the land and the *Appeal to Reason* issuing special editions of 1,000,000 copies, President Theodore Roosevelt used a White House press conference to arraign Debs, Moyer, and Haywood as "undesirable citizens." Overnight, thousands of men and women began appearing on the street with placards proclaiming "I AM AN UNDESIRABLE CITIZEN."

When the trial at last got under way on May 9 in Boise, that town was close to permanent hysteria. Darrow was not only ostracized by the better elements but his telephone was tapped, his mail opened, and his moves shadowed while he was the target of a never-ending series of threats. The state had elected to try Haywood first. Special prosecutors for the state, and admittedly paid by the Mine Owners' Association, were Senator William E. Borah, his jutting chin cleft by a deep dimple, just elected by the Idaho legislature to the United States Senate, and James Hawley, a pugnacious, rough and tumble attorney, six feet two in height, who resembled some courtroom Daniel Boone.

Some reporter called the city of Boise "murdertown," on the theory that all of its social and economic life revolved around the murder of Steunenberg and the resulting trial. It was true enough that the trial seemed to be the town's chief industry, its chief means of livelihood, its sole preoccupation, its one subject of discussion. Stores and hotels prospered through an avalanche of witnesses, experts, labor observers, reporters, magazine writers, and curious tourists. There was not a large newspaper in the country, not a prominent magazine, which did not have its representative present.

When not speaking of Steunenberg's murder, Orchard's remarkable spirituality since his conversion, or Haywood's coming execution, the inhabitants of Boise were whispering of rumors of other murders soon to arrive as a result of the trial. Darrow was said to have posted killers with high-powered rifles on a hill behind Orchard's cottage, their purpose the killing of Orchard and the slaying of the state's attorneys who came to the cottage to confer with him. Hawley sent word to Darrow that "if Orchard dies Darrow will be the next man killed."

Orchard was, of course, the key to the trial as Darrow was its great performer, but it was Big Bill's life which was at stake. His dignity and composure, his contempt for all the legal hocus-pocus and oratory, all the motions and countermotions, were so monumental that they impressed even his enemies, some of whom said that, silent, he dominated the courtroom. The writer for *McClure's* described him as "a powerfully built man, built with the physical strength of an ox. He has a big head and a square jaw. Risen from the mines himself, 'from the bowels of the earth,' as he describes it, this man has become a sort of religious zealot and Socialism is his religion. He is the type of man, not unfamiliar now in America, equipped with a good brain, who has come up struggling and fighting, giving blows and taking them who knowing deeply the wrongs of his class sees nothing beyond. . . ."

If Haywood was a fighter, Orchard, according to the State's attorneys, was the anointed of the Lord. For three days he testified to his sins, wallowing in a whole series of murders, perjuries, robberies, and frauds, but, said Hawley, the prosecutor, that was the old Orchard, before he had been born again and redeemed. In this sanctimonious rebirth which no man could doubt without somehow being against religion, Orchard said that he had killed Steunenberg on Haywood's orders, on Haywood's pay, and that he had plotted and planned the murder of many of the great of Colorado on the same directions and for pay that came from the same man.

Goaded beyond endurance by Orchard's constant use of the Lord as he tried to perjure a man to death, Darrow sprang to his feet and over objections of court roared out: "If Harry Orchard has religion now, I hope I may never get it. Before Orchard got religion he was bad enough, but it has remained to religion to make him totally depraved. What does religion mean? It means love; it means charity; it means kindliness. Would you have any confidence in religion if a man was as cruel, as heartless as he was before? I want you to say whether religion has changed the nature of this wretch, and I should expect that if any of you were interested in religion you would say he hadn't got it. You would have to say that to keep from giving up your own."

While defense attorneys were unable to shake the essentials of Orchard's well-drilled and oft-rehearsed story, they were successful in forcing him to admit that he had committed perjury in courts before and that he had confessed to other crimes that he had not in fact committed. Big Bill, fighting for his life, took the stand and made Senator Borah, his renowned cross-examiner, quail when he demanded that Borah stand in such a position that he, the witness, could look into his eyes. The demand seemed to upset the Senator, who afterwards confessed to a friend, "His request threw me off stride. As a matter of fact, it doubled me up like a jackknife."[12]

Nevertheless it was the common opinion that Haywood's life was not worth a plugged nickel. Everything depended on Darrow's address to the jury and, while eloquence was expected, so was a verdict of guilty. The warfare between the mine owners and the Western Federation of Miners had been transferred to the courtroom, where only the gullible thought that the owners could lose.

Tall, shambling, apparently discouraged, his thumbs stuck in his galluses, his eyes brooding, his tone sad and solemn, Darrow advanced to the jury box to begin his summation. He was in his shirt sleeves, for the weather was hot; although he came from Chicago, he seemed more of a plain Westerner, more of a countryman, than any of the jurors. Sometimes he roared, occasionally he advanced on tiptoe dramatically whispering, but always he insisted that what was involved here was not the murder of a man but capital's conspiracy to murder the labor movement.

He had spoken for eleven hours when he arrived at his peroration. "Mr. Haywood," he said, "is not my greatest concern. Other men have died before him. Wherever men have looked upward and onward, worked for the poor and the weak, they have been sacrificed. They have met their deaths and he can meet his. But you shortsighted men of the prosecution, you men of the Mine Owners' Association, you people who would cure hatred with hatred, you who think you can crush out the feelings and the hopes and the aspirations of men by tying a noose around his neck, you who are seeking to kill him, not because it is Haywood, but because he represents a class, don't be so blind; don't be so foolish as to believe you can strangle the Western Federation of Miners when you tie a rope around his neck. If at the behest of this mob you should kill Bill Haywood, he is mortal, he will die, but I want to say that a million men will grab up the banner of labor where at the open grave Haywood lays it down, and in spite of prisons or scaffold or fire, in spite of prosecution or jury or courts, these men of willing hands will carry it to victory in the end. . . .

"I speak for the poor, for the weak, for the weary, for that long line of men who, in darkness and despair, have borne the labors of the human race. Their eyes are upon you twelve men of Idaho tonight. If you kill Haywood your act will be applauded by many. In the railroad offices of our great

[12] According to the *New York Herald*, July 13, 1907, "the cross-examination of Haywood by Senator Borah was considered the most brilliant work that has marked the trial. It was a battle between two men of keen intellects, the one in a mind trained and skilled in handling witnesses, the other shrewd, astute, fighting for his life. The cross-examination was in keeping with the temperature. Without the courtroom the sun shone fiercely, and inside the spectators, jurors and lawyers sweltered, but all listened with interest to the verbal dual in progress. . .

cities men will applaud your names. If you decree his death, amongst the spiders of Wall Street will go up paeans of praise for these twelve good men and true. In every bank in the world, where men hate Haywood because he fights for the poor and against the accursed system upon which the favored live and grow rich and fat—from all these you will receive blessings and unstinted praise.

"But if your verdict should be 'not guilty' in this case, there are still those who will reverently bow their heads and thank these twelve men for the life and reputation you have saved. Out on our broad prairies where men toil with their hands, out on the broad ocean where men are tossed and buffeted on the waves, through our mills and factories and down deep under the earth, thousands of men and of women and children—men who labor, men who suffer, women and children weary with care and toil—these men and these women will kneel tonight and ask their God to guide your hearts."

It was ten at night as Darrow concluded in a courtroom packed and silent. Sinking back into his chair, his inherent pessimism increased by his exhaustion, he leaned wearily over to his client, whispering, "Brace yourself for a guilty verdict." After the court's instructions the jury filed out and the long hours of waiting began, not only in the courtroom but all over the United States.

Darrow did not quite appreciate, perhaps, that there was more fighting for acquittal than his eloquence and Haywood's innocence. At about five in the morning he heard that the jury stood eleven to one and writes that it was the bitterest hour of his career.

From then on, events moved rapidly. About seven in the morning word came that the jury had agreed. According to an Associated Press dispatch of July 29, 1907, "Judge Wood took his place at the bench at 7:54 o'clock and four minutes later the tired, bedraggled, worn-out jurors filed in. Haywood sat with his right elbow hung over the high back of his arm-chair—a characteristic attitude. As the clerk began to read the roll the silence in the courtroom was painful. The tick of the clock on the wall sounded like blows from a sledge. Then came the voice of Judge Wood asking 'Gentlemen of the jury have you agreed on a verdict?' 'We have,' came the response from Foreman Gess. Judge Wood glanced at it [the paper handed him] and tossed it to the clerk. 'We, of the jury, find the defendant, William D. Haywood, not guilty.'"

CHAPTER VI

Progress and the Wobblies

> "The great struggling unknown masses of the men who are at the base of everything are the dynamic force that is lifting the levels of society. A nation is as great, and only as great, as her rank and file."
>
> WOODROW WILSON, IN THE
> NEW FREEDOM, NEW YORK, 1913

> "Universal economic evils afflicting the working class can be eradicated only by a universal working-class movement. Such a movement of the working class is impossible while separate craft and wage agreements are made favoring the employer against other crafts in the same industry, and while energies are wasted in fruitless jurisdictional struggles which serve only to further the personal aggrandizement of union officials."
>
> FROM THE 1905 CALL TO THE FOUNDING CONVEN-
> TION OF INDUSTRIAL WORKERS OF THE WORLD

1. Free Speech and Free Men

It was primarily for the unskilled worker, unorganized and excluded from the American Federation of Labor, that the Industrial Workers of the World was formed. Never before or since has there been such an organization. Its members, at least in the West, were always on the go, moving from job to job, from state to state, from the Rio Grande to the Columbia, from Omaha to San Diego, hopping freights, riding the rods, traveling blind baggage to anywhere and everywhere. It was a union on wheels, iron wheels, and their clackety-clack, clackety-clack, their cadenced metallic waves of endless sound, the smell of cinders and smoke, the wail of the locomotive whistle in the night, were the common experience of almost every member. So were the constant fights between the Wobblies, as the union men were called, and the armed "shacks," or brakemen, sometimes on winter nights high in the Rockies, when being thrown from the train meant death.

The Wobblies probably never had more than 60,000 active members[1] but they influenced millions as they moved into strike situations all over the country from McKees Rocks, Pa., and Skowhegan, Maine, to Goldfield, Nev., and Portland, Ore. And as they led the huge mass strikes they were forever talking of one big union, of solidarity, of one for all and all for one; forever declaring that the working class, those who did the nation's work, should own the nation's industries. They did not put much stock in contracts, thought the workers' strength should guarantee gains won, and seldom tried to sign workers up in a permanent local union. They were for enforcing improved conditions by the constant threat of "pulling the pin," "hitting the bricks," by the constant threat of strike.

The most active of the Wobblies were young migratory workers, blacklisted railroad men and miners, lumberjacks, cowboys, construction workers. They were harvest hands, threshers of wheat, shockers of corn, workers in the beet fields of Utah, the lettuce fields and fruit orchards of California, they were unemployed sailors and longshoremen, and the vigor with which they charged into a strike or town seemed like revolution to the staid townsfolk. They had a magnificent contempt for stay-at-homes, whom they called "homeguards."

The Wobblies liked songs and stories. They were sentimental, almost old-fashioned in a way, and they liked to sing and talk as they sat around campfires, maybe in the desert near a railway water tank, maybe in the mountains at a junction point. They had hundreds of songs, most of them set to the tune of old hymns. Joe Hill, their poet laureate, afterwards framed and executed during a Utah strike,[2] was one of their best liked

[1] This was the figure in 1916. In 1917 the Government, in its indictment of William D. Haywood, credited the organization with a membership of 200,000 (P. F. Brissenden, *The I.W.W.: A Study in American Syndicalism*, New York, 1919, p. 357, Appendix IV).

[2] "Almost two years elapsed between the day of [Hill's] arrest and the day of execution," writes Barrie Stavis in the introduction to *The Man Who Never Died, A Play About Joe Hill.* 'During this period, Joe Hill's name became known to millions of people and his cause was embraced by hundreds of thousands who were convinced of his innocence. The adherents of Joe Hill say that he was framed; that he was shot by the State of Utah not for the murder of a grocer and his son, but because he was *Joe Hill,* labor's poet, the man who wrote songs expressing the deepest needs of the working class. . .

"In the early stages of his imprisonment, his defenders consisted almost entirely of the working class. . . . Only in the latter stages of the battle did the case reach out to wider sections of the population. At first in the United States, and then gradually all over the world, facts about the case became known and hundreds of thousands joined the fight to save Joe Hill.

"President Wilson intervened *twice* on behalf of Joe Hill; the Swedish government intervened; A.F. of L. delegates at their thirty-fifth annual convention unanimously adopted a resolution condemning the trial and demanding of Utah 'that he be given a new and fair trial'; a mass meeting of 30,000 Australian workers passed a resolution

members. A thousand Wobblies pouring off freights as they converged upon a strike was something to see. At the top of their lungs they would sing their song, "Tie 'Em Up" which went like this:

> "Why do you make agreements that divide you when you fight
> And let the bosses bluff you with the contract's 'sacred right'?
> Why stay at work when other crafts are battling with foe?
> You must all stick together, don't you know?

> "Tie 'em up! Tie 'em up! That's the way to win.
> Don't notify the bosses till hostilities begin.
> Don't furnish chance for gunmen, scabs and all their like,
> What you need is One Big Union and the One Big Strike."

From the first these men of the West were termed "foreign agents," "representatives of a vicious and alien philosophy." Typical was the outburst of the San Diego *Tribune* of March 4, 1912, which declared editorially, "Hanging is none too good for them. They would be much better dead. . . ."

The first great struggle of the IWW was for the free speech necessary to spread the word and organize. Free speech was free, the Wobblies found, only if what was said was what the bosses wanted the workers to hear. Otherwise it had to be paid for by a jail sentence and often by a slugging from police or vigilantes. It was generally held, particularly in the West, that the First Amendment did not apply to the IWW because its cowboys, lumberjacks, and miners were un-American. The IWW fought for free speech by exercising it, and exercising it on such a wholesale scale wherever it was threatened that the jails bulged and the streets echoed with the forbidden word until the authorities rued the day they had ever banned it.

The method of battle was for every Wobbly anywhere, and all Wobblies

---

demanding the immediate freedom of Joe Hill and threatened a boycott of goods manufactured in the United States unless the release was granted. And there were many others, individuals and organizations, who voiced their protest."

On the night before the execution of Joe Hill a speaker cried at a protest meeting: "Something is going to happen. Joe Hill will never die. You hear it everybody? Joe Hill will never die."

Hill's last words before his execution, Nov. 19, 1915, were, "Don't mourn for me—organize!" During the CIO organizing drive of the mid-thirties thousands sang the moving and beautiful song *Joe Hill* by Alfred Hayes and Earl Robinson:

> "I dreamed I saw Joe Hill last night
> Alive as you and me
> Says I, 'But Joe, you're ten years dead,'
> 'I never died,' says he.

> " 'Joe Hill ain't dead,' he says to me.
> 'Joe Hill ain't never died,
> Where workingmen are out on strike
> Joe Hill is at their side.' "

everywhere, to grab a freight and head for the city or town in which free speech had been banned. Thus literally thousands of them converged between 1909 and 1912 on Spokane, Fresno, Denver, Kansas City, Duluth, New Castle, San Diego, New Bedford, and Missoula, climbing on a soapbox upon arrival and promptly lifting their voices in cussing out the capitalists and inviting one and all, if they were workers, to join the IWW.

As soon as one was carted off to jail another took his place. Sometimes vigilantes and police clawed up at platforms, trying to pull down workers reading from the Declaration of Independence. Others were hauled down into the bloody embrace of "patriots" even as they read from the Constitution which holds that anyone anywhere has the right to say and think what his conscience dictates. Occasionally six would be speaking from six assorted soapboxes scattered over a town square and when these occupants, a bit bloody usually, had been removed six more Wobblies took their places.

Taxpayers began to complain that they were feeding whole armies of jailed Wobblies. The courts became so clogged they could handle little else but free speech cases. The fight for free speech became largely a question of endurance between the lungs and heads of the Wobblies and the stamina of the police. In Missoula and Spokane, as well as in most of the other towns where free speech fights were waged, any citizen could address any assemblage on any street on any subject at any time by the end of 1912.

The IWW leaders showed the same spirit in their leadership of strikes in the mining fields, on lumbering projects, in the construction camps of the Northwest; in Pacific coast canneries, eastern textile mills, midwestern steel and meat packing plants, and among streetcar workers, window cleaners, and longshoremen.

But the best known of all the strikes, and one of the best known strikes in American history, was that of the 23,000 textile workers in Lawrence, Mass., in 1912. As in all their strikes, the IWW leaders gave the strike to the strikers, in this case to the women and children, the foreign-born and Yankee mill hands who worked in Lawrence. They ran it. They decided every policy after long debate in more than a score of tongues and after Big Bill Haywood had explained the issues as he saw them. As in all of their strikes, the IWW leaders encouraged the workers to put on shows and entertainments, to hold dances and debates, and as for Big Bill he always used every strike as a kind of workers' university, a short and intense course in reality and the class struggle.

Almost every reporter covering the strike, and they came from everywhere, remarked on the sense of growth common to most strikers and many observed a queer happiness in the workers as they found in struggle what they had never found in the monotony of the mills. Something of the strike's quality can be gained from the words of Mary Heaton Vorse, the writer, who always regarded it as one of the decisive events of her life:

"It was a new kind of strike. There had never been any mass picketing in any New England town. Ten thousand workers picketed. It was the spirit of the workers that seemed dangerous. They were confident, gay, released and they sang. They were always marching and singing. The gray tired crowds ebbing and flowing perpetually into the mills had waked and opened their mouths to sing, the different nationalities all speaking one language when they sang together."

If there was any trickery or any violence or any fraud that was not used by the employers to smash the Lawrence strike it has never been discovered in all the lexicon of reaction. The strike began spontaneously when the average wage of $6 a week was even further lowered in the case of thousands of women and children when their work week was reduced by state law from fifty-six hours a week to fifty-four. As a result of the hours reduction, employers had speeded up the looms and when they cut pay, too, that was too much. "Short pay! Short pay!" echoed from loom to loom on Jan. 12, 1912, when the new pay scale was first handed out and then it echoed from factory to factory and from mill to mill until suddenly everyone was parading in the streets, no one quite knew how.

The National Guard was immediately on the scene and so were Elizabeth Gurley Flynn, twenty-one-year-old organizer for the IWW, and the more experienced IWW strike leaders, Joseph Ettor and Arturo Giovannitti, who was also a poet. Not only were twenty-two companies of militia called out but the employers imported fifty thugs from a Boston detective agency who masqueraded as strikers, overturned trolley cars, smashed windows, and assaulted people on the street.

The thugs planted dynamite near the strikers' headquarters. The strikers were charged with sabotage until one of the employers happened to get drunk and tell of the plot; he committed suicide to atone for his error after sobering up. And when police shot one of the strikers, a girl by the name of Annie Lo Pizzo, they arrested the strike leaders, Ettor and Giovannitti, on a murder charge.

The miracle of Lawrence was the vibrant triumphant spirit, like something alive and palpable, unweakened it seemed as February dragged into March while hunger and killings and frame-ups steadily continued. To Mary Heaton Vorse it seemed as if Elizabeth Gurley Flynn, one of the first American women to lead mass strikes, was the symbol of Lawrence and she wrote:

"When Elizabeth spoke, the excitement of the strikers became a visible thing. She stood up there, young, with her Irish blue eyes, her face magnolia white, and her cloud of black hair, the very picture of a youthful revolutionary girl leader. . . . It was as though a spurt of flame had gone through the audience, something stirring and powerful, a feeling which has made the liberation of people possible.

"For Elizabeth that winter of the strike there was ceaseless work, day and night, and she seldom slept. Speaking, sitting with the strike committee, going to visit the prisoners in jail, organizing their defense, and endlessly raising money. Speaking, speaking, speaking, taking trains only to run back to the town that was ramparted by prison-like mills before which soldiers with fixed bayonets paced all day long. She was the spirit of that strike."[3]

But Elizabeth's most important task was the gathering of food, for hunger was the chief enemy of the strikers. What hurt them most was to see their children daily become weaker for lack of food. By a great effort arrangements were made for hundreds of them to be sent to workers' homes in other cities for the duration of the strike. The groups of starving children seeking food and shelter made a tremendous impression throughout the nation. As a result, the city authorities of Lawrence stated that no more children would be allowed to leave the city. When the strike committee tried to send another group away, the children and their mothers were assaulted by police at the railroad station in Lawrence.

The Women's Committee of Philadelphia, whose members were to care for the children, described the ensuing scene in a report:

"The station itself was surrounded by police and militia. . . . When the time approached to depart the children, arranged in a long line, two by two in orderly procession, with their parents near at hand, were about to make their way to the train when the police, who had by that time stationed themselves along both sides of the door, closed in on us with their clubs, beating right and left, with no thought of the children, who were in the most desperate danger of being trampled to death. The mothers and children were thus hurled in a mass and bodily dragged to a military truck, and even then clubbed, irrespective of the cries of the panic-stricken women and children. . . ."

This was the turning point of the strike as Victor Berger, Socialist Congressman from Milwaukee, sought and obtained a Congressional investigation into the strike and its causes. On March 14 the textile manufacturers surrendered and the strikers, most of them women and children, returned victorious with, according to a federal government report, "an increase in wages of from 5 to 20 per cent; increased compensation for overtime; and the reduction of the premium period from four weeks to two weeks." Of this wage increase the highest percentage went to the unskilled workers. At the same time, indirectly as a result of the strike, "material increases in wages were granted," said the official government report, "to thousands of employees in other textile mills throughout New England."

"Lawrence was not an ordinary strike," writes P. F. Brissenden in his authoritative work on the IWW. "It was a social revolution *in parvo*." Lawrence showed "it was possible for the unskilled and unorganized

---

[3] Elizabeth Gurley Flynn was sixty-two years old when sentenced in February, 1953, as a Communist leader to three years in the penitentiary for alleged violation of the thought-control Smith Act.

workers (preponderantly immigrants of various nationalities) to carry on a successful struggle with their employers. It showed what latent power is in the great mass of semi-skilled and unskilled workers." And it made the IWW famous, giving it power and influence in the East and an opportunity to play a larger part in the labor movement of the country.

With the strike over, most of those jailed were released. But Ettor and Giovannitti were still held on a framed-up murder charge. As the weeks dragged on without trial, the workers once more went out in a great twenty-four-hour general strike which played its part in the subsequent trial and acquittal of the two IWW organizers.

"Let me tell you," said Giovannitti as he addressed the crowd greeting him on his release from prison, "that the first strike that breaks out again in this Commonwealth or any other place in America where the work and help and intelligence of Joseph J. Ettor and Arturo Giovannitti will be needed and necessary, there we shall go again, regardless of any fear or any threat. We shall return again to our humble efforts, obscure, unknown, misunderstood soldiers of this mighty army of the working class of the world, which, out of the shadows and darkness of the past, is striving towards the destined goal, which is the emancipation of human kind, which is the establishment of love and brotherhood and justice for every man and woman on this earth."

2. "The Progressive Era"

The period between 1901 and 1917, between the beginning of Theodore Roosevelt's administration and our entry into the First World War, is frequently called "The Progressive Era."

Largely a misnomer, it has, however, a certain validity in that labor's long fight was beginning to quicken, influence, and move the great middle class whose standards and ways of life have always been regarded as the country's. The martyrdom of the "Molly Maguries," the violence of the railroad strike of 1877, the hanging of the Haymarket victims in the eight-hour fight, were having a kind of delayed reaction. The Pullman strike, the so-called Debs' Rebellion, and the civil war in Colorado were causing increasing numbers of the middle class to wonder whether after all the whole subject of labor and strikes could be disposed of by the epithets "un-American" and "foreign agent."[4]

[4] The IWW had its share in creating the new climate, such as it was and however limited. "It spectacularly centered attention," the labor historian Foster Rhea Dulles writes, "on the desperate needs of vast numbers of unskilled workers." It educated by the shock treatment. When wages of $6 a week, such as those paid at Lawrence, failed to shock liberals into knowledge of the facts of life, the Wobblies' methods of struggle often succeeded. Their calm announcement during the McKees Rock strike in Pennsylvania, for example, that they would kill a policeman for every striker killed by police did more to call attention to the institution of police violence than any number of tracts.

The platforms of the Populists, like John Brown's soul, went marching on long after the Populists were forgotten, until their indictment of monopoly had such currency that it was the property of millions. Debs' campaigns for the Presidency on the Socialist ticket, in which he gained 97,000 votes in 1900, more than 420,000 in 1904, and twice that many in 1912, made men think about social problems as they had seldom thought before. Typical figures of the new ferment in ideas and politics were two Ohio mayors, Tom Johnson of Cleveland and Sam "Golden Rule" Jones of Toledo.

Both were backed by labor and both fought monopoly. Jones ran for mayor in Toledo in the early 1900's on the Golden Rule, his platform Christ's words, "Whatsoever things ye would that man should do to you, do ye even so unto them." He was elected three times by huge votes. For six years the Golden Rule was a political issue in Toledo. Some thought Jones had discovered the rule and there were impassioned arguments as to whether the new rule would work. Many a man won an argument in favoring the Golden Rule by knocking down his opponent.

Jones, a large, lusty, hairy man who always wore a cream-colored ten-gallon hat and a black flowing tie, thought the rule meant what it said. After being elected Toledo's mayor, he used it as a yardstick to judge every municipal question. In the name of the Golden Rule he lowered the tax rate for the poor, sided with labor in a strike, and fought against the renewal of a street-car franchise held by a powerful utility. All of the righteous were outraged at his application of the Golden Rule.

While Sam Jones was applying Christianity in Toledo, Tom Johnson in his battle against monopoly in Cleveland had "everyone against him but the people." Part of this fight revolved around his efforts to get a three-cent fare on a city-sponsored street-car line competing with Senator Hanna's company, which charged five cents. Every effort of the city was blocked by injunctions. At one point in the long fight, because of some legal technicality, it was necessary to get a city-sponsored street car over a quarter of a mile of injunction-blocked route. A crowd gathered about the trolley and, pushing it, hauling it, lifting it, somehow carried it over the injunction-blocked tracks and into the free territory.

Tom Johnson inspired this kind of spirit as he waged his campaign in a huge circus tent. His one plank declared that monopoly was running Cleveland and the country for its own profit and not in the interests of the people. After three terms he was defeated in a bitter campaign and it was, according to a friend, "his death blow." A short time before he died he was given a medal which held the inscription, "The truth . . . will find friends . . . those who will toil for it, if need be die for it."

This middle-class awakening, backed by labor and often brought into being by the struggles of labor and the farmers, was becoming common to the whole country by 1910. It was expressed in the exposures by those whom Theodore Roosevelt had derisively dubbed "muckrakers," journalists like

Ida Tarbell, Lincoln Steffens, and Ray Stannard Baker, who demonstrated again and again to millions of readers that American industry and American government had the common denominator of colossal graft. The Negro middle class and Negro intellectuals were a part of the new ferment, their demands reflected in the Niagara movement, founded by Dr. W. E. B. DuBois and the precursor to the National Association for the Advancement of Colored People. The age was reflected, too, in the new creed being adopted by intellectuals whose feelings were expressed by Herbert Croly when he wrote in 1909:

"A numerous and powerful group of reformers has been collecting whose whole political policy and action is based on the conviction that the common people have not been getting the Square Deal to which they are entitled under the American system and these reformers are carrying with them a constantly increasing body of public opinion.

"A considerable portion of the American people is beginning to exhibit economic and political, as well as personal, discontent. A generation ago the implication was that if a man remained poor and needy, his poverty was his own fault, because the American system was giving all its citizens a fair chance. Now, however, the discontented poor are beginning to charge their poverty to an unjust political and economic organization, and reforming agitators do not hesitate to support them in their contention."

It was under the impetus of all this, as well as of numerous strikes and widespread industrial unrest, that Theodore Roosevelt's "Square Deal" and Woodrow Wilson's "New Freedom" came into being, programs of protest forced on two conservative politicians by the increasing militance of the people. Both were efforts, often demagogic and consistently ineffective, to liberalize the two main parties by exerting a measure of control over Wall Street. Roosevelt, who in 1895 had demanded that Debs and Altgeld be "placed before a stone wall and shot," was scoring "malefactors of great wealth" after his election on the Republican ticket in 1904. Soon he was accused of being a "wild-eyed revolutionist" and some businessmen saw in him a traitor to his class as he campaigned on the rump Progressive ticket in 1912.[5] And Woodrow Wilson was declaring, as he sought and won the Presidency on the Democratic ticket in 1912, that "A nation is as great, and only as great, as her rank and file."

[5] However, not all businessmen in 1912 saw in Theodore Roosevelt a traitor to his class. In fact, George W. Perkins of the House of Morgan, Frank A. Munsey, a newspaper publisher, and H. H. Wilkinson, president of the Crucible Steel Company, "boomed" Roosevelt for the nomination on the Progressive ticket and financially backed his "Bull Moose" campaign. These big businessmen, fearful of the popular clamor against the trusts, got behind Roosevelt the better "to outflank Western radicalism [La Follette] and preserve 'benevolent trusts.'" (M. Josephson, *The President Makers*, p. 431.) They backed Roosevelt's campaign to eliminate the possibility, as one of them put it, "'of his children having to face revolution.'" (*Ibid.*, p. 431.)

It was not all demagogy. There was a new spirit in the air and it was reflected in both state and federal legislation. It was expressed in the growing number of states granting suffrage to women, their long and militant campaign at last beginning to bring results. It was exemplified by pure food and drug laws, by state laws providing for factory inspection, and by such federal attempts to regulate monopoly as the Clayton Act of 1914, which also declared that trade unions were not a conspiracy or a monopoly in restraint of trade.

By 1915 twenty-five states had passed laws limiting the working day while thousands of workmen had gained the eight-hour day through trade union action. Child labor laws, for which labor had agitated for nearly a century, placing restrictions on the age at which children could be employed and the hours which they could work, had been passed by thirty-eight states by 1912. In that year Massachusetts enacted the first minimum-wage law and was followed in 1913 by eight other states. By 1915 thirty-five states had passed laws providing for workmen's compensation after industrial accidents, another ancient demand of labor. In the same year Congress, spurred by union seamen, passed the La Follette Seamen's Act, an important step toward removing seamen from a serfdom in which ships' captains had absolute power and in which quitting a job during a voyage was a criminal offense. In the following year the Adamson Act was passed by Congress, after a strike threat by railroad workers, giving interstate railway employees the eight-hour day and time and a half for overtime.

3. The Old Oaken Gompers

Samuel Gompers, who liked to say "The Gompers are built of oak," president of the AFL for thirty-seven years,[6] hailed the "Progressive Era" as the beginning of the end of all of labor's troubles. The Clayton Act, he said, was labor's Magna Carta, the dawn of a new day. In his autobiography Gompers relates how he "sat tense" in the Senate gallery listening while the measure was being debated and how when it was finally passed his "emotion well-nigh overcame [him]. It was a great hour for labor. . . ." When, on Oct. 16, 1914, he received the pen President Wilson had used in signing the law, he saw to it that it was "framed and placed with a collection of other pens" equally celebrated in history.

A chunky, strutty little man, a big cigar usually protruding above a square jaw, he was fond of high silk hats and the company of the great. Even when the Supreme Court definitely revealed to all and sundry that

[6] Gompers was president of the AFL from its founding in 1886 to his death in 1924 with the exception of the year 1894 when the Socialists, refusing to support him any longer, joined others in electing John McBride of the United Mine Workers president by a vote of 1,170 to 976.

the Clayton Act meant virtually nothing to labor,[7] Mr. Gompers was neither abashed nor discouraged. Once known as "Stuttering Sam" but now a master of the orator's platitude if not of his art, he made a series of speeches about the accomplishments of the AFL.

These accomplishments were undeniably notable. The leading national trade union center since 1890, it had been the first to put American trade unionism on a sound and practical basis, using strict business principles in the collection of dues, in the raising of adequate strike funds, in the creation of old-age, sickness, and burial funds for its members. If its top leadership blessed private enterprise as the best of all possible systems, opposed independent political action, and frowned as sternly on government unemployment insurance and old age pensions as any industrialist, this course gained it a limited measure of employer acceptance. It had the support of the American worker who in the main regarded it, and not the IWW, as the pre-eminent American labor organization. Many of the millions of unskilled, denied entry into it, looked to it with hope.

What it lacked in vision it made up for in practical benefits to its members. It had by 1914 a membership of 2,021,000 workers for whom it had won higher wages, shorter hours, and increased security. From 1890, when it became the leading national labor center in the country, to 1914, when the European war broke out, the average full-time weekly earnings in union manufacturing industries and the building trades rose from $17.57 to $23.98, while the average working week in union manufacturing industries was reduced from 54.4 hours to 48.9. The higher wages and shorter hours won by organized labor during these years had the effect of raising the wages and reducing the hours of work of the great mass of unorganized workers. From 1890 to 1914 the average full-time weekly earnings of unorganized, unskilled laborers went up from $8.82 to $11.52, while the average working week in manufacturing industries went down from 62.2 hours to 55.6.

Yet, despite the wage and hour gains registered by American workers during these years, their real wages—that is, their ability to buy back the goods and services they produced—were lower in 1914 than during the 1890's. This was true with respect to unionized as well as nonunionized

[7] The Clayton Anti-Trust Act of 1914 was supposed to have given labor relief from action under the Sherman Law, especially the issuance of injunctions in labor disputes. The historians Louis M. Hacker and Benjamin B. Kendrick write: "Article 20 [of the Clayton Act] seemed to say that injunctions could not be issued to prevent persons from quitting work, from engaging in peaceful picketing, from carrying on primary and secondary boycotts, from collecting and paying out strike benefits, from assembling and, in fact, from doing all those things they could legally do in times of no industrial disputes." (*The United States Since 1865*, p. 720.) But in 1921 and after, the U.S. Supreme Court not only decreed otherwise but added to labor's woes. As the same authors put it, "Not only had the Clayton Act, the Supreme Court was to show, not freed organized labor from the weight of legal displeasure but it had even added an additional burden, to wit, that injunction proceedings could be brought against trade unions by private individuals instead of by the federal Department of Justice alone as under the Sherman Law." (p. 720.)

wage earners. Concerning the relative purchasing power of American workers from 1890 to 1914, Paul H. Douglas has this to say in his authoritative work on the subject:

"Taking the 15 years from 1900 to 1914 as a whole, the amounts by which the real earnings exceeded 100 [the average of 1890–99] were precisely equal to the amounts by which it fell below the average. . . . So far as the employed wage earners in manufacturing were concerned, they did not secure any permanent gains. Their increases in money income were swallowed up by commensurate increases in the cost of living."[8]

Had the AFL officials gone out to organize all the 9,600,000 workers in manufacturing and transportation in 1914 and the millions outside of those fields, this condition would not have existed to the extent it did. The fact that no wages can be really high while virtually all other wages are low did not seem to penetrate the consciousness of the top leadership of the AFL. Concerned with "job control," "craft pride" and "business unionism," they appeared to be totally unconcerned about the great mass of industrial employees who worked without the benefit or protection of trade unions.

The AFL produced a good many leaders in the image of the oaken Gompers, obsequious before the great of the National Civic Federation and hard on the membership whom they ruled with an iron hand. Settlements over the heads of the membership were not uncommon, bribes to business agents by employers were not unusual.

Nevertheless Gompers was personally honest and competent. If he liked the tycoons of the National Civic Federation, he also liked the beer gardens, the Atlantic City boardwalk, chorus girls, and an occasional glass of whiskey. Under his jealous eye the American Federation slowly but surely increased in size and stability. If it did not directly serve all of American labor it at least served its own restricted membership in its own restricted way.

Gompers liked to regard himself as a typical example of the American saga, poor boy makes good. Born in London in 1850, from childhood he was a maker of cigars as his father had been before him. Whatever education he acquired came as his fingers deftly rolled cigars in a dark and dusty loft while one of the workers, his pay made up by the contributions of his listeners, read aloud to them as they worked.

When he was thirteen his family moved from London's East End to New York's East Side. When he was twenty-three he saw the police assault the unemployed demonstrators at Tompkins Square, breaking heads and skulls with the justification that their owners were radicals. Until that time Gompers regarded himself as a radical, too, but although his own skull had been untouched, the very sight of the police clubs had an unmistakable effect on his thinking.

[8] Paul H. Douglas, *Real Wages in the United States, 1890–1926*, Boston, 1930, p. 232.

He was twenty-nine when the Cigar Makers International was reorganized on so-called business principles, eschewing all political goals and all ends except "a fair day's pay for a fair day's work." From that time until his death Gompers never deviated from "pure and simple trade unionism." Until the end he remained a fighter for an antiquated craft unionism even in the face of the growing number of industrial unions in the AFL such as the brewers, the United Mine Workers, the International Ladies Garment Workers' Union, and, later, the Amalgamated Clothing Workers. His main antagonist through the years was the considerable Socialist bloc in the AFL, always advocating independent political action and industrial unionism, which as late as 1912 received 27 per cent of the vote when Max Hayes ran for president against Gompers.

Only once did his faith in capitalism falter. That was in 1907 when the Buck's Stove and Range Company, headed by NAM president James Van Cleave, secured an injunction against him and other AFL officials for putting the company's products on the "We Don't Patronize" list of the *American Federationist.* He was hailed into court and sentenced to a year in jail by Justice Wright. Plaintively he writes in his autobiography: "The hour I spent in Justice Wright's court listening to him read his opinion and pronounce sentence upon us [himself, Mitchell, and Morrison] was one which burned itself into my soul. . . . We were called leaders of the 'rabble' who would 'unlaw' the land, 'public enemies' whose intent was to . . . subordinate the 'supremacy of the law' to 'anarchy and riot.' "

These were harsh words and they left a bitter taste in his mouth. He felt betrayed by the great tycoons who had called him Sam and had wined and dined him. He almost once again came to believe in the class struggle, all the more so as in 1909 his appeal was turned down by the Court of Appeals. Finally in 1911 the United States Supreme Court sent the case back "without prejudice" to the district court for contempt proceedings. With Justice Wright again presiding, Gompers was tried for contempt and the original jail sentence reaffirmed. Once more the shadow of prison aroused in him a momentary militance but there was still in it more of sorrow than of anger. Poor Sam was saved from jail only by the Statute of Limitations, the Supreme Court dismissing the case on that ground in 1914.

Later Gompers wrote of his seven-year travail as follows:

"In that period I was several times seriously ill. It was hard to reconcile myself to the thought that if the end should come, a blot would rest on my name which no amount of explanation could completely remove. The shadow of that prison sentence harassed my wife, my father, my children for seven years."

But with the Supreme Court decision everything was once again sweetness and light, Gompers basking in the sunshine of Big Business and the glories of the Progressive Era.

4. Reality and Massacre

Behind the legislation and fine words of the "Progressive Era" were the reality of child labor, the exploitation of women workers, contract labor and peonage,[9] bitter strikes, an increasing disparity between the poverty of the average American and the millions of dollars in profit being received by the few. As Wilson spoke of the "New Freedom," and Roosevelt of the "Square Deal," neither of these was much in evidence for workers harried by the open-shop drive of the National Association of Manufacturers, impartially using propaganda, guns, and spies in their ceaseless campaign to prevent union organization.

In 1910 some 2,000,000 children, according to government figures, were forced to work to supplement the family income, their average wage less than $2 a week in the clothing industry, less than $3 weekly in the glass and silk industries.[10] Women, more than one-fifth of the country's labor force in 1910, were earning for the most part an average of $6 a week in the textile and clothing industries, in glass and silk factories.

From two-thirds to three-quarters of all men employed in industry earned less than $15 weekly, according to the final report of the government Commission on Industrial Relations in 1915, and only about one-tenth of all men employed in American industry earned more than $20 a week. "Approximately 35,000 persons were killed last year [1914] in American industry," the report continued, "and at least one-half of these deaths were preventable." After declaring that the billionaires should be held responsible "for each of the 17,500 preventable deaths," the report stated that 700,-000 were injured annually in the nation's mines, mills, and factories.

Despite state legislation for the shorter working day, the Commission declared, working hours ranged up to twelve per day, seven days a week, in steel and railroads, with relatively few workers having the eight-hour day. As for housing, the commission stated, immigrant workers' homes were often little but bunkhouses, their occupants sleeping in shifts, using the beds by turns.

"Massed in millions at the other end of the social scale," this official government report continued, "are fortunes of a size never before dreamed of, whose very owners do not know the extent nor, without the aid of an in-

---

[9] See earlier chapters.

[10] According to an official government report, children worked "surprisingly long [hours]. Less than one-fifth of the boys whose hours were reported worked 8 hours or less, one-fourth were working 9 hours, and nearly one-half (45.9 per cent) worked 10 hours daily." (U.S. Dept. of Labor, Bureau of Labor Statistics, *Summary of the Report on Conditions of Women and Child Wage Earners in the United States,* Bulletin No. 175, Washington, 1916, p. 283.) The same government report, using a study of the causes of death among cotton mill workers in Fall River, revealed that tuberculosis among boys 15 to 19 employed in cotton mills was nearly double that of boys not so employed and among girls more than double. (p. 368.)

telligent clerk, even the sources of their incomes." Continuing, the report said of the concentration of wealth:

"Incapable of being spent in any legitimate manner, these fortunes are burdens, which can only be squandered, hoarded, put in so-called 'benefactions' which for the most part constitute a menace to the State, or put back into the industrial machine to pile up ever-increasing mountains of gold. We have, according to income tax returns, forty-four families with an income of $1,000,000 annually or more, whose members perform little or no useful service, but whose aggregate incomes, totalling at the very least fifty millions a year, are equivalent to the earnings of 100,000 wage earners at the average rate of $500."

As to the disparity between the rich and the poor, the official report declared:

"The ownership of wealth in the U.S. has become concentrated to a degree which is difficult to grasp. The 'Rich,' 2 per cent of the people, own 35 per cent of the wealth. The 'Middle Class,' 33 per cent of the people, own 35 per cent of the wealth. The 'Poor,' 65 per cent of the people, own 5 per cent of the wealth. The actual concentration, however, has been carried much further than these figures indicate. The largest private fortune in the U.S., estimated at one billion dollars, is equivalent to the aggregate wealth of 2,500,000 of those who are classed as 'poor,' who are shown . . . to own on the average about $400 each."

This Industrial Commission was in itself the "Progressive Era" at its best but it also revealed that the era was having little practical effect on an ever-increasing repression by an ever-growing monopoly. Authorized by Congress and appointed by President Wilson, it was headed by Frank P. Walsh, Kansas City attorney. As part of its work, it took evidence concerning one strike after another, a silk strike at Paterson, a rubber strike at Akron, lumber strikes in the northwest, the strikes of the metal and coal miners in the Rockies.

"Freedom does not exist either politically, industrially or socially" for workers on strike or trying to organize, the commission declared. It found, moreover, that the use of thugs, spies, and hired gunmen was general throughout the country in the employers' efforts to keep the open shop, adding, "the fiber of manhood will inevitably be destroyed by continuance of the existing situation." In particular it indicted the Rockefeller-controlled Colorado Fuel & Iron Company which it found dominated the state government and used the law for its own ends.

"Almost without exception the employees of large corporations are unorganized, as a result of the active and aggressive 'non-union' policy of the corporation managements," the commission continued. "Our Rockefellers, Morgans, Fricks, Vanderbilts and Astors can do no industrial wrong because all effective action and direct responsibility is shifted from them to executive officials. . . ."

In addition, the commission found, the Morgans, Rockefellers, and their allies were controlling the thoughts of Americans as well as their lives. Through monopoly ownership of influence, the press expressed monopoly's policies. Moreover, Wall Street was increasingly controlling public education, as well as colleges, universities, professors, and preachers through gifts, endowments, and foundations. The report continued:

"The domination by the men in whose hands the final control of a large part of American industry rests is not limited to their employees, but is being rapidly extended to control the education and 'social service' of the Nation. This control is being extended largely through the creation of enormous privately managed funds for indefinite purposes, hereinafter designated as 'foundations' by the endowment of colleges and universities, by the creation of funds for the pensioning of teachers, by contributions to private charities as well as through controlling or influencing the public press. . . .

"Apart from these foundations there is developing a degree of control over the teachings of professors in our colleges and universities which constitutes a serious menace. In June of this year [1915] two professors were dropped . . . [one] a professor of law in a state university, who had acted as counsel for the strikers in Colorado; the other, a professor of economics active in fights in behalf of child labor legislation and other progressive measures."

Turning to women workers, the commission declared that nearly one-half of them earned less than $6 weekly and asked:

"Six dollars a week—what does it mean to many? Three theater tickets, gasoline for the week, or the price of a dinner for two; a pair of shoes, three pairs of gloves, or the cost of an evening at bridge. To the [working] girl it means that every penny must be counted, every normal desire stifled, and every basic necessity of life barely satisfied by the sacrifice of some other necessity."

The conditions under which most women worked were described by Louise Marion Bosworth in 1911:

"In one factory of a well-known hat company the women stitch all day in a gloomy room with bare and dirty brick walls, the floor cluttered with crumbs, crusts and dirty cups from the brief lunch on the work tables. They work ten hours a day, only stopping long enough to heat some cold tea at noon. . . .

"In a box factory the girls take off their street suits and put on old skirts and waists matted with glue and dirt, in which they spend ten hours a day 'scoring,' cutting and snipping, wetting great sheets of paper with paste . . . lifting the heavy finished boxes back and forth, or deftly covering little ones and throwing them rapidly into a basket, at a few cents a day.

"In an overall factory, the light is so poor, and soot-caked windows make it so dim, that some of the women who work there say they cannot stand the eye-strain and will have to work elsewhere.

"In one shoe factory town many complaints are heard about the ventilators; in winter the windows are kept closed until the girls' shirt waists are wet with perspiration. Then at five they suddenly emerge into the winter air and consequently have perpetual coughs."

Thirty-seven per cent of working class mothers, according to the Industrial Commission, were forced to work for wages in addition to caring for their families.[11] On New York's East Side, where the sweatshops were filled with thousands of working women, the intolerable conditions under which they worked were brought to the attention of the public by the tragedy of the Triangle fire when one hundred and forty-six women were burned to death in a crowded, packed loft from which there was no effective escape.

Militant Jewish workers, most of them fresh from Czarist Russia and possessed of a rich tradition of struggle on behalf of labor organizations and against anti-Semitic pogroms, rose in revolt against sweatshop conditions in the needle trades at about this time. Herded together in broken-down tenements or in basements, the air saturated with dust and stench, they worked as many as fourteen hours a day at wages not enough to support themselves, much less their families, the helpless victims of a speed-up system that added to the wrecking of their health and vitality. Ill-ventilated and disease-breeding, the shops in which these workers toiled were more often than not firetraps, as illustrated by the tragic Triangle Waist Company fire.

It was against these sweatshop conditions with their low wages, killing speed-up and hazardous working set-up that tens of thousands of Jewish needle workers from New York's East Side revolted in a series of great strikes. In 1909 twenty thousand shirt-waist makers, four-fifths of whom were women, went out on strike. Their bravery and unity on the picket lines led the then not too militant Sam Gompers, AFL president, to make the following observation: "The girls were willing to go hungry and many of them did so; they braved the ruffianly police while peacefully picketing, went to imprisonment as part of their duty to their comrades when sentenced by unsympathetic magistrates, skillfully and energetically aroused a sentiment in their favor in the community, and finally convinced their employers that they had learned the merits of combination for their plainly just purposes."

The following year, 1910, saw over sixty thousand cloakmakers, the vast majority of them Jewish, go out on strike and after a courageous and militant struggle win a collective bargaining agreement. The signing of this "Protocol of Peace" established the International Ladies Garment Workers Union, founded ten years before, on a solid basis. From 1910 to 1920 the union spread to Chicago, Boston, Cleveland, and other cities and by 1920 had a membership of over 100,000.

[11] By 1910 there were 76,784 women trade union members and ten years later 379,000.

The uprisings of 1909–10 in the women's clothing industries had their repercussions in the men's clothing field. In 1910 the workers of Hart, Schaffner & Marx, the largest clothing manufacturing company in the country, went out in a city-wide strike in Chicago, the strike ending with the company recognizing the United Garment Workers Union. As more and more of the industry was organized, chiefly as a result of the militant strikes of tens of thousands of Jewish workers, a rank-and-file movement developed against the Rickert clique that dominated the Garment Workers. When in 1914 these rank-and-filers were refused seats at the Garment Workers Convention and their request for recognition was denied by the conservative AFL officialdom, they founded the Amalgamated Clothing Workers Union early in 1915. Within four years the militant leadership of the new union was able to organize a majority of the leading clothing manufacturers in the country.

Meanwhile unions were organizing women's auxiliaries. Annie Clemence, a Slav girl of about twenty-four, was president of the ladies' auxiliary of the Western Federation of Miners in Michigan's copper country. There 15,000 copper miners with an average pay of $1 a day were on strike against the Calumet and Hecla Mining Company. The officials of the company had announced a 400 per cent stockholders' dividend a short time before the strike was called, not long before Christmas of 1913. Annie Clemence had organized a Christmas party for the children of the strikers in a hall with only one exit and that at the foot of a long narrow stairway. A deputy, intent on breaking up the party, shouted "Fire!" when there was no fire.

Ella Reeve Bloor ("Mother Bloor"), then a Socialist organizer, was a witness. She writes:

"On Christmas eve the children gathered in a hall where Annie had fixed up a Christmas tree. First the children sang, and then the presents were given out. A little towheaded Finnish girl of about 13, with long braids down her back, sat down at the piano. She had started her piece when a man pushed the door open and shouted: 'Fire!'

"There was no fire. But at the cry the children started to rush out of the hall in terror. Annie and one of the mothers got up and said, "Don't be scared, children, there isn't any fire.' We around the platform did not realize how many had gone through the door, as the room was still crowded. We tried to keep the entertainment going. The little girl kept on playing.

"In about five minutes the door at the back of the room opened, and a man came into the room with a little limp figure in his arms. Another man followed, carrying another child. Then another, and another and another. They laid the little bodies in a row on the platform beneath the Christmas tree. The children were dead. . . . There were seventy-three of them. I can hardly tell about it or think about it even today.

"The people in the hall were deathly silent, frozen with horror. Then Annie screamed, 'Are there any more children dead?' And one of the deputies said, 'What's the matter with you? None of these children are yours, are they?'

"She cried out, tears streaming down her face, 'They are all mine—all my children. . . .'

"They kept bringing the children up the stairs, into the hall, as the people rushed forward in agony and fear to look for their own. Priests arrived and began to pray for the dead. Then Annie went wild and started pummelling the priests and pushed them away from the children, because these same priests had been preaching against the strike. 'Don't let these scab priests touch these children!' she cried. The deputies took her away and locked her up in the courthouse. Then they came for the bodies of the children, took them to the courthouse, and kept them there at night, until they could get undertakers."

The Morgans, Rockefellers, and their ilk who had not gone to war in 1861 were old men now. Their sons were overseeing the mammoth empires that they had acquired as the ruthless Robber Barons while, uncertain and sometimes not quite clear as to exactly what was happening, they doddered around, enjoying their simple hobbies. Old John D., who had shrunk until he resembled a mummy with bright bird-like eyes, had fastened on the innocent enjoyment of giving a single new dime to every person he met.

Morgan, his imperial mien now vanquished by illness, his black eyes rheumy with age, fumbled through the long lines of treasures he had collected from all the earth, a solitary figure moving through the medieval armor. Chinese porcelains, rare old books and manuscripts, jewels, and paintings stretching into the distance in the vast white marble palace he had built for them. He died in Rome on the last day of March in 1913.

Carnegie, now "a rosy, twinkling old man," had apparently forgotten the massacre at Homestead, so great was his delight in his baronial castle at Skibo on the coast of Scotland. He liked to have a bagpiper wake him at eight in the morning by skirling, first from a far distance and then nearer and nearer the castle. He had his private organist play for him each morning at breakfast and had constructed a miniature waterfall to tinkle outside his bedroom window. He died in his castle in 1919.

Old John D. outlived them all. Each day he was propped up and taken out to the golf course where a servant was posted to periodically shout at the man whose very glance had once made rivals quail, "Keep your head down! Keep your head down!" His son, John D. Rockefeller, Jr., liked to think that the old man's understanding was as mighty as ever, taking pleasure in telling him about the strike of Colorado coal miners in 1914 against the Rockefeller-dominated Colorado Fuel & Iron Company. "I know," he wrote L. M. Bowers, chairman of the company's board of directors, "that my father has followed the events of the last few months in connection with the fuel company with unusual interest and satisfaction."

The events that the old man was following with such unusual interest and satisfaction included the eviction of the strikers, members of the United Mine Workers of America, from their company-owned houses. The miners were living in tents at Ludlow, their colony surrounded by the National Guard. The militiamen occasionally shot into the colony, particularly at night. The women were terribly afraid that some of their children would be killed. They decided to dig a cave inside the largest tent. There they put thirteen children and a pregnant woman.

That night, it was in Easter, 1914, company-employed gunmen and members of the National Guard drenched the strikers' tents with oil. They ignited them after the miners and their families were asleep. When the miners, their wives, and children ran from the burning tents, they were machine-gunned. Most escaped in the darkness, many were wounded, but the thirteen children and the woman in the cave were all killed, some shot to death and others suffocated.

One of the Ludlow strikers, William Snyder, testified at the coroner's inquest. His eleven-year-old son had been killed, shot through the head.

"They set fire to the tent?" Snyder was asked.

"Yes, sir. My wife then said, 'For God's sake save my children.' "

"What did they say to you?"

"They said, 'What in the hell are you doing here?' I told them I was trying to save my children, and they said, 'You son of a bitch get out of there and get out damn quick at that.'

"My wife was out by that time. . . . I told them to hold on, I had a boy killed in there, and they told me to get out damn quick. I picked the boy up and laid him down outside so I could get a better hold of him.

"I asked some of these fellows to help me carry him to the depot, and he said, 'God damn you, aren't you big enough?' I said, 'I can't do it.' I took him on my shoulder, and sister on the other arm, and just then one of these militiamen stopped me and said, 'God damn you, you son of a bitch, I have a notion to kill you right now.' He said, 'You red-neck son of a bitch, I have a notion to kill you right now.' "

Another woman, and five men, all of them strikers, were killed that night in addition to the thirteen children. Perhaps old John D. was never told about it. The son took full responsibility for it, saying it was the unfortunate outcome of a principled fight he was bound to make for the protection of the workingman against trade unions. The Robber Barons were gone but their sons were following in their footsteps. J. P. Morgan's son and namesake, who later took a similar stand for the open shop, also proved himself worthy of his father.

But the miners felt differently about the Ludlow Massacre. They erected a monument which still stands. Carved in stone are the figures of a miner and his wife. At their feet lies their slain child.

The inscription reads:

"Erected by the United Mine Workers of America, to the memory of the men, women and little children who died in freedom's cause, April 20, 1914."

CHAPTER VII

Murder and Millions

"By 1917 the Allies had borrowed one billion, nine hundred million dollars through the House of Morgan: we went overseas for democracy and the flag;
"and by the end of the Peace Conference the phrase *J. P. Morgan* suggests had compulsion over a power of seventy-four billion dollars.
"J. P. Morgan is a silent man, not given to public utterances, but during the great steel strike, he wrote Gary: *Heartfelt congratulations on your stand for the open shop, with which I am, as you know, absolutely in accord. I believe American principles of liberty are deeply involved, and we must win if we stand firm.*"

JOHN DOS PASSOS IN U.S.A.

"The Debs idea will not die. To be sure, it was not his first at all. He carried on an older tradition. It will come to pass. There can be a brotherhood of man."

HEYWOOD BROUN, 1926

1. A Little "Industrial Rivalry"

Between July 28, 1914, and Nov. 11, 1918, some 10,000,000 young men were killed in that vast orgy of mass murder known as World War I. An estimated 20,000,000 more were maimed, crippled, burned, and wounded, their youth lost by mutilation. At the same time 13,000,000 civilians died in that great holocaust; there were 10,000,000 refugees, 5,000,000 war widows and 9,000,000 war orphans. The statistics may convey little but perhaps John Dos Passos may make them clearer with his single sentence: "The blood ran into the ground, the brains oozed out of the cracked skull and were licked up by trench-rats, the belly swelled and raised a generation of bluebottle flies . . ."

The economic cost of World War I has been estimated by a careful student, Professor E. L. Bogart, to have run to 331.6 billion dollars. Its cost to the United States alone has been officially put at 50 billion dollars, not including war loans abroad. According to Harry Elmer Barnes and Henry David in their book, *The History of Western Civilization,*

"The editor of the *Scholastic* [Nov. 10, 1934] made an effort to translate these figures of war costs in terms that we can visualize. He indicated that the cost of the World War would have been sufficient to furnish (1) every family in England, France, Belgium, Germany, Russia, the United States, Canada and Australia with a $2,500 house on a $500 one-acre lot, with $1,000 worth of furniture; (2) a $5,000,000 library for every community of 200,000 inhabitants in these countries; (3) a $10,000,000 university for every such community; (4) a fund that at 5 per cent interest would yield enough to pay indefinitely $1,000 a year to an army of 125,000 teachers and 125,000 nurses, and (5) still leave enough to buy every piece of property and all wealth in France and Belgium at a fair market price."

As the young men of World War I died many thought they were dying for a great ideal. It was only after it was all over that an increasingly large number of people came to the realization that the 10,000,000 had died for the private profit of monopoly—as a result of the conflict between two great groups of competing imperialists. Some 20,000 new millionaires in the United States alone came into being from the 10,000,000 dead.

Before American entry into the war on April 6, 1917, President Wilson told Walter Hines Page, according to this pro-war American ambassador to Britain, that there was little to choose between the belligerents, that the cause of the war was that "England owned the earth and Germany wanted it." President Wilson, the Beards declare, during the early years of the war regarded "the conflict as a war of commercial powers over the spoils of empire."

And after it was all over President Wilson himself wearily asked an audience on Sept. 5, 1919, "Is there any man here or woman—let me say is there any child—who does not know that the seed of war in the modern world is industrial and commercial rivalry?" Then he said explicitly, referring to the war just over, "This was a commercial and industrial war."

But in between he was forced to rally the nation for the war which was "to end war," and "make the world safe for democracy." When the European conflict broke out in August, 1914, he urged Americans to be "impartial in thought as well as in action" and his Secretary of State William Jennings Bryan condemned loans to any belligerent powers as contrary to the spirit of neutrality. Three months later Bryan's assistant, Robert Lansing, held a conference with an officer of the National City Bank who discussed Wall Street's need for short-term credits to European governments so that they could purchase supplies here. Writes Matthew Josephson in his *President Makers:*

"The gist of this conference was then summarized in a letter which was given Lansing and which he merely copied and showed President Wilson that same night, October 23, 1914 as representing his own views of the proper policy regarding the temporary banking credits. That night Lansing won Wilson's agreement to 'look the other way' at temporary credit accommodations that were being supplied the French and British treasuries. Wilson, who had earlier supported Bryan's position, now executed a strategic retreat from a position based upon the 'true spirit of neutrality' to one based upon 'strict legality.' "

In 1915 Lansing replaced Bryan as Secretary of State. By then Wall Street was agitating for long-term instead of short-term loans to England and France but all in the hush-hush atmosphere of the back rooms. H. P. Davison of the House of Morgan held a conference with Secretary of the Treasury McAdoo, the President's son-in-law, who became convinced that "to maintain our prosperity we must finance it." And financing it meant the approval of a huge Wall Street loan to Britain and France. With the new Secretary of State Lansing backing McAdoo's position, President Wilson, on Aug. 26, 1915, revoked Bryan's prohibition. Wilson's decision was never given out to the American people; it was, however, secretly conveyed to those entitled to know.

Thus in the end the Morgan lack of neutrality overcame Wilson's announced neutrality as if the Morgans were at the center of power and reality,[1] the government an unrealistic appendage which they were forced to bring into line. "Our firm," said Thomas W. Lamont, the Morgan partner, "had never for one moment been neutral. We didn't know how." And how could they, when billions of dollars were involved?

In September, 1915, the Morgan syndicate floated the first of the huge Anglo-French loans. It was for half a billion dollars, the greatest foreign loan yet floated in this country. In gross commissions alone the Morgan people made a cool 22 millions out of it. Loan followed loan so that by the election year of 1916, when Wilson ran on the slogan "He kept us out of war," we were in fact already in it. Allied purchases of munitions, food, steel, copper, and all the materiel of war had become the chief source of the country's economic life. The repayment of over two and a half billion dollars depended on an Allied victory while a German triumph would have plunged the country into panic and depression.

In the early part of 1917 things looked very dark for the Allies. Financially the Allied governments were finding it increasingly hard to carry on the war, making frantic appeals for more and more credit and loans. On March

[1] Concerning the power of these investment bankers, the future U.S. Supreme Court Justice Louis Brandeis had this to say in his book *Other People's Money and How the Bankers Use It* (New York, 1913), p. 4: ". . . these bankers bestride as masters America's business world, so that practically no large enterprise can be undertaken successfully without their participation or approval. The key to their power is Combination—concentration intensive and comprehensive."

5, 1917, Walter H. Page, American ambassador in London, sent a cable home in which he spoke of the perilous economic position of England and France. In this confidential cable (which was kept from public view until 1936), Page went on to say: "Perhaps our going to war is the only way in which our present prominent trade position can be maintained and a panic averted."

Just one month later President Wilson asked and received from Congress a declaration of war.

2. *The Fight for Peace*

"We are going into the war upon the command of gold," said Senator George W. Norris of Nebraska. "I feel that we are about to put a dollar sign on the American flag."

Senator Robert M. La Follette of Wisconsin was also declaring almost daily in the Senate throughout 1915 that we were on the verge of entering a war in which American boys would be slaughtered not for the national interest but for the profits of Wall Street. In September, 1915, the Senator's publication, *La Follette's Magazine,* declared:

"With the first clash in the great European War came President Wilson's solemn appeal, 'The U.S. must be neutral in fact as well as in name.' But when you can boom stocks 600 per cent in manufacturing munitions, to the Bottomless Pit with Neutrality! What do Morgan and Schwab [head of Bethlehem Steel] care for world peace when there are big profits in world war? The Schwab properties which stood at a market value of 7 millions before they began supplying the Allies are today given an aggregate 'value' of 49 millions. And now we are about to engage in furnishing the Allies funds. We are underwriting the success of the cause of the Allies. We have ceased to be 'neutral in fact as well as in name.' "

But the American people could not be easily rallied to a war for monopoly's profits. From 1914 on public opinion was divided, with much of it against the war. There was a strong pacifist tendency in the country which gravitated around Jane Addams, William Jennings Bryan, and Oswald G. Villard. Opposed to this tendency were the big army and navy advocates, who launched a preparedness movement. Most active in this connection was the National Security League, which was supported by Brady of New York Edison, Rogers of Standard Oil, du Pont of the munitions industry, Perkins of U. S. Steel, Guggenheim of the copper trust, J. P. Morgan, and John D. Rockefeller.

The campaign carried on by these "dollar scarred heroes" was designed to soften up the American people for entry into the war under the guise of increasing the size of the army and navy just in case, just to be prepared. Huge "Preparedness Day" parades were held in New York, Chicago, and

San Francisco as a fomented hysteria for war slowly began to take shape with strikes already declared unpatriotic.

As a result of one of the Preparedness Day parades, that in San Francisco on July 22, 1916, one of the grossest frame-ups in all American history was carried out. A bomb was thrown at the parade, killing nine and wounding forty. Without even trying to find the guilty, a corporation-owned district attorney, Charles M. Fickert, arrested young Tom Mooney, who had just led a bitter strike of San Francisco street car workers, fastened the bombing upon him through perjured testimony, and had him sentenced to death. Warren K. Billings, another youthful labor leader, was also framed and convicted of the bombing.

The case was scarcely over when key prosecution witnesses confessed to perjury, while it was proved that others had been paid for their testimony. Frank C. Oxman, star witness in the Mooney trial, was shown to have been a perjurer and one who had attempted to make another prospective witness testify falsely. Another key figure in the case, John McDonald, in an affidavit some years after the trial, admitted he had committed perjury. It was likewise established that William MacNevin, the chairman of the jury that convicted Mooney, was working hand in glove with Edward Cunha, the Assistant District Attorney.

Government investigations proved conclusively that Mooney had been framed because he was a labor leader. Said President Wilson's Mediation Commission, headed by future Supreme Court Justice Felix Frankfurter: "In the spring of 1916 Mooney and his wife were the leaders in the bitter and unsuccessful fight to organize the carmen of the United Railways in San Francisco. The utilities sought 'to get' Mooney. Their activities against him were directed by Martin Swanson, private detective. It was Swanson who engineered the investigation which resulted in Mooney's prosecution."

Said the official report of John B. Densmore to Secretary of Labor W. B. Wilson: "The basic motive underlying all the acts of the prosecution springs from a determination on the part of certain employer interests in the city of San Francisco to conduct their various business enterprises upon the principle of the open shop. There has been no other motive worth talking about."

Organized labor, recognizing the frame-up, sprang to the defense of Mooney and Billings. Mass protest meetings were held throughout the country. Similar demonstrations were organized by European workers. So great was the outcry that President Wilson was forced to intervene and save Mooney from execution.

His sentence commuted to life imprisonment, Mooney, then thirty-five, was to spend the following twenty-two years in jail. During all that time this fighting AFL organizer and militant Socialist never lost heart. And the labor movement did not forget him. Not only did the AFL call for his release, but the CIO, founded in the 1930's, did likewise. On January 7, 1939, he was freed by New Deal Governor Olsen of California and in September of the same year addressed the Springfield convention of the United Electrical, Radio and Machine Workers of America, an organization which contributed to the unionization of the workers of one of the very companies that had sent Mooney to jail.[2]

As the war hysteria steadily mounted, the number of similar anti-labor atrocities increased. Five members of the IWW, engaged in trying to organize the lumber industry, were killed in Everett, Wash., on Nov. 5, 1916. The strike in which these five died resulted in the eight-hour day in the lumber industry.

After war had been declared on April 6, 1917, and with the country mobilizing "to make the world safe for democracy," any strike or any word for peace was likely to bring mob action. In Tulsa, Okla., seventeen oil workers trying to organize their industry were kidnapped, tied to trees, "beaten with blacksnakes until their bodies dripped with blood." In July, 1917, during a strike of copper miners at Bisbee, Ariz., 2,000 strikers were routed from bed by armed vigilantes, taken at dawn under guns to cattle cars, and deported into the desert where they were abandoned without food or water and under threat of death if they returned to their homes and their families. On August 1 Frank Little, the Indian organizer for the IWW and a member of its executive board, was taken from his hotel, where he was suffering from a broken leg, and hanged by a mob from the trestle of a railway bridge.

While such events were taking place a committee on public information was being formed with George Creel at its head and with the purpose of "selling the war to America." Under Creel's direction were mobilized great hosts of advertising men, campaign directors, designers of posters, artists, professors, sales specialists, publishers, historians, journalists, publicity directors, public relations experts, motion picture producers, editors, and novelists. Presently bulletins, movies, speeches, posters, editorials, news stories, books, tracts, advertisements, leaflets, flyers, pictures, headlines, pamphlets were flooding the country. Their common message was that this was a war against tyranny, for the right of free speech and free thought, a crusade against German autocracy, to make the Bill of Rights and democracy safe.

In the meantime, Congress was passing a series of espionage and sedition laws that made it a crime to speak out, especially for peace. But despite the penalties of sedition laws and the terror of mobs, thousands of Americans were getting up on their hind legs and telling the world why they thought the war was wrong. Thousands of stickers were materializing in the night, on signboards and fences, in subways and on telephone poles, which proclaimed, "Don't be a soldier, be a man. Join the IWW and fight on the job for yourself and your class."

[2] It is interesting to note that William Sentner, then a vice president of the UE, yielded the floor to Mooney. Today Sentner himself is a victim of political persecution under the Smith Act.

198   **LABOR'S UNTOLD STORY**

As early as 1916 the IWW had come out against the war, announcing in a resolution, "We condemn all wars and for the prevention of such, we proclaim the anti-militarist propaganda in time of peace, thus promoting class solidarity among the workers of the entire world, and, in time of war, the General Strike in all industries."

Even labor's rank and file in the AFL were expressing dissatisfaction with the war as prices rose sharply while wages lagged.[8] There were 4,450 strikes in 1917 involving more than 2,300,000 workers. Most of them were pressed with vigor, and most of them were won, despite statements by press and employer that strikes were treason. The United Mine Workers, the Typographical Union, the Ladies Garment Workers, and the Journeymen Barbers refused to attend the prowar trade union conference called by Gompers on March 12, 1917. In addition there was strong anti-war spirit in many local unions, city labor councils, and state federations.

On April 7, the day after war was declared, the Socialist Party, with close to 100,000 members, met in emergency convention in St. Louis. Addressing the American public, it condemned the war, taking much the same line as Senators Norris and La Follette, declaring it was "instigated by the predatory capitalists of the United States," while describing it as "a crime against the people of the United States."

And then the raids and arrests began. On Sept. 5, 1917, IWW halls were raided in all parts of the country by Department of Justice men, aided by local vigilantes. A few days later the national headquarters of the Socialist Party was raided while dozens of newspapers were suppressed, including the New York *Call, The Masses,* and *The Appeal to Reason.* In February, 1918, there was another nationwide raid directed against the IWW, its entire executive board being arrested. By the end of the month 2,000 Wobblies were in jail awaiting trial. There were mass trials, 165 IWW members being tried in Chicago, 146 in Sacramento, 38 in Wichita, 7 in Tacoma, 27 in Omaha, and 28 in Spokane. Virtually all of the defendants, including Big Bill Haywood, were found guilty of opposing the war, most of them receiving prison sentences of ten to twenty years.

Of the Socialists, Charles E. Ruthenberg, Alfred Wagenknecht, both later founders of the Communist Party; Kate Richards O'Hare, J. O. Bentall, Scott Nearing, Rose Pastor Stokes, and scores of others were in prison for their fight for peace. Molly Steimer, a young girl, was given a fifteen-year sentence for distributing antiwar leaflets. The national executive committee of the Socialist Party was indicted: Victor Berger, Adolph Germer, J. Louis Engdahl, Irwin St. John Tucker, and William Kruse. Intolerance

[8] Despite wage increases during World War I the cost of living increased more rapidly. "From 1916 to 1920," writes Prof. J. M. Short, "wage-earners were subject to a positive disadvantage in buying power—their 'real wage' or actual buying power was on the average about 12 per cent less than in 1914." ("Women's Wages Compared with Living Costs and General Community Standards, 1914–1932," in *Reed College Bulletin,* vol. xii, January, 1933, pp. 5-6.)

flamed as vigilanteism was made an arm of the government and in East
St. Louis, Ill., thirty Negroes were killed in a race riot.[4]

It was then that Eugene Debs decided to take the stump again for peace.
An older man now, he was sixty-three in that summer of 1918; he did not
want prison but he could not endure liberty while the finest of his friends
were being jailed in their struggle for peace and human happiness. When
Kate O'Hare and Rose Pastor Stokes were sentenced to prison, the former
to five years and the latter to ten, Debs said, "I feel guilty to be at large."

Tired and often ill, his gaunt figure stooped with the years, great creases
across his forehead, his eyes so weak now that he always wore his gold-
rimmed spectacles, he found it hard to gird himself for prison, for he had
known cells before.

As early as 1915 he had toured the country warning against American
entry into the war. He had been surprised at the strength of peace sentiment. On June 11, 1915, he had written Frank O'Hare from Garrison,
N.D., "If you could only be here and see this demonstration! . . . The old
warehouse was packed as soon as the doors were open and hundreds
couldn't get in. . . . The farmers and their families have come from a hundred miles around—and they are red to the core."

Even before our entry into the war Debs had declared, "I am not a capitalist soldier; I am a proletarian revolutionist. . . . I am opposed to every war
but one; I am for that war with heart and soul, and that is the world-wide
war for the socialist revolution. In that war I am prepared to fight in any way
the ruling class may make necessary, even to the barricades. That is where
I stand, and believe the Socialist Party stands, or ought to stand, on the question of war."

He was miserable as he debated with himself in his Terre Haute home.
Should he suffer prison or enjoy the retirement he had earned? When he
made his decision he felt wonderful. By God, they would either arrest him
or he would rally the country for peace until all his jailed comrades were
free. He hated the thought of prison but he hated worse the thought that
he had sufficiently softened that the authorities felt it safe to ignore him
while imprisoning those who had never heard of Socialism until they heard
Eugene Debs speak for it.

"As he took the train eastward into Ohio, Debs was happier than he had

[4] The basic cause of the East St. Louis riots was to be found in the importation by employers of Negro labor for the purpose of depressing wages. The railroad and factory
employers showed little regard in respect to even the minimum necessities of life for
the 10,000 Negro workers so imported. According to the Report of the Special Committee *Authorized by Congress to Investigate the East St. Louis Riots*, July 15, 1918,
"It [was] a lamentable fact that the employers of labor paid too little heed to the
comfort or welfare of their [Negro employees]. They saw them crowded into
wretched cabins, without water or any of the conveniences of life." And when the employers "were through with them," they were left, the secretary of the Illinois State
Federation of Labor said, to shift for themselves "without any place to sleep or
live. . . ." (As quoted in S. D. Spero and A. L. Harris, *The Black Worker*, New York,
1931, pp. 162, 163.)

been for what seemed an eternity," Ray Ginger writes. "His own move would encourage similar action by other Socialists. At last he had resumed his customary post, at the head of the radical offensive. . . ."

His first speech on his new tour was at Canton, Ohio, on June 16, 1918. Before making his speech at Nimisilla Park, he dropped into the Stark County Workhouse near the park where h e visited the three leading Socialists of Ohio, who had been imprisoned there for their fight for peace. They were Charles E. Ruthenberg, Alfred Wagenknecht, and Charles Baker, who told Debs that they had been hung by the wrists from a rafter for two days when they protested discrimination used against them.

The day was scorching hot when Debs climbed up onto the platform at Nimisilla Park. In the large crowd was a government stenographer who scribbled frantically, sometimes falling behind, as Debs paid tribute to the Russian Revolution, denounced the war, spoke for Mooney who had just been convicted, for Haywood and the other Wobblies who were then on trial in Chicago, declaring that those who had been imprisoned were the real patriots, not the profiteers making millions and shouting for war. He continued, pointing to the near-by prison:

"I realize that, in speaking to you this afternoon, there are certain limitations placed on the right of free speech. . . . I may not be able to say all I think but I am not going to say anything that I do not think. I would a thousand times rather be a free soul in jail than a sycophant and coward in the streets. They may put those boys in jail—and some of the rest of us in jail—but they cannot put the Socialist movement in jail. . . .

"The master class has always declared the war; the subject class has always fought the battles. The master class has had all to gain and nothing to lose, while the subject class has had nothing to gain and all to lose—especially their lives. . . .

"Yes, in good time we are going to sweep into power in this nation and throughout the world. . . . The world is changing daily before our eyes. The sun of capitalism is setting; the sun of Socialism is rising. . . . In due time the hour will strike and this great cause triumphant—the greatest in history—will proclaim the emancipation of the working class and the brotherhood of all mankind."

On June 20, 1918, a federal indictment was returned against Debs for his use of free speech at Nimisilla Park. He was charged with ten crimes in his speech, ten different violations of the Sedition Act. His only defense at his trial in September was that any American and every American had the inalienable right to express his thoughts about his country's policies under the First Amendment in the Bill of Rights.

He did not present witnesses or contest the government's case insofar as it concerned his speech at Canton, but his gaunt figure dominated the courtroom. To some he was just an eloquent working man, elderly and failing in health, with a gleaming bald head and a ponderous chin, with

long gangly arms and great worker's hands. But somehow his years of
service to the working class had given him a stature that put him beyond
the attacks of the little politicians serving as federal attorneys.

On Sept. 14, 1918, he was sentenced to ten years in federal prison for
speaking his convictions about the war. But before he was sentenced he
addressed the court; and, writing of it later, Heywood Broun declared
that "tongues of fire danced upon his shoulders as he spoke":

"Your honor, years ago I recognized my kinship with all living beings,
and I made up my mind that I was not one bit better than the meanest on
earth. I said then, I say now, that while there is a lower class I am in it; while
there is a criminal element, I am of it; while there is a soul in prison, I am not
free. . . .

"Your honor, I have stated in this court that I am opposed to the form of our
present government; that I am opposed to the social system in which we live;
that I believed in the change of both—but by perfectly peaceable and orderly
means.

"In the struggle—the unceasing struggle—between the toilers and producers
and their exploiters, I have tried, as best I might, to serve those among whom
I was born, and with whom I expect to share my lot until the end of my days.

"I am thinking this morning of the men in the mills and factories; I am thinking of the women who, for a paltry wage, are compelled to work out their
lives; of the little children who, in this system, are robbed of their childhood,
and in their early, tender years, are seized in the remorseless grasp of Mammon,
and forced into the industrial dungeons, there to feed the machines while they
themselves are being starved body and soul. . . .

"Your honor, I ask no mercy, I plead for no immunity. I realize that finally
the right must prevail. I never more fully comprehended than now the great
struggle between the powers of greed on one hand and upon the other the rising
hosts of freedom. I can see the dawn of a better day of humanity. The people
are awakening. In due course of time they will come into their own.

"When the mariner, sailing over tropic seas, looks for relief from his weary
watch, he turns his eyes toward the Southern Cross, burning luridly above the
tempest-vexed ocean. As the midnight approaches the Southern Cross begins to
bend, and the whirling worlds change their places, and with starry finger-points
the Almighty marks the passage of Time upon the dial of the universe; and
though no bell may beat the glad tidings, the look-out knows that the midnight
is passing—that relief and rest are close at hand.

"Let the people take heart and hope everywhere, for the cross is bending,
the midnight is passing, and joy cometh with the morning."

There was a long silence. The judge, after characterizing the defendant's
stand as "anarchy pure and simple, and not according to my reading and
understanding of Socialism," sentenced Debs to ten years in jail.

The case was appealed to the United States Supreme Court on the sole
issue of free speech under the First Amendment. Debs, his body twisted

with rheumatism, waited the decision at Terre Haute. He seemed happier than he had been for years. In November, 1918, when American armies along with those of France, Britain, and Japan were invading the new country of Socialism, Debs sent greetings to Nikolai Lenin and his followers. He said:

"Comrades of the Russian Soviet and the Bolshevik Republic, we salute and honor you on this first anniversary of your great revolutionary triumph, the greatest in point of historic significance and far-reaching influence in the annals of the race. . . ."

Early in April, 1919, the Supreme Court said that free speech was not involved in the Debs case and rejected the appeal. Debs issued a statement:

"The decision is perfectly consistent with the character of the Supreme Court as a ruling class tribunal. It could not have been otherwise. So far as I am personally concerned, the decision is of small consequence. . . .

"Great issues are not decided by courts but by the people. I have no concern with what the coterie of begowned corporation lawyers in Washington may decide in my case. The court of final resort is the people, and that court will be heard from in due time. . . ."

On April 12 Debs left for prison. Some 200 workers were at the Terre Haute station as he climbed aboard a train. A coal miner pushed from the crowd, tears running down his cheeks, and said, "We're with you, Gene— by God, we're with you to the last man." Debs embraced the miner as he said, "You boys take care of the outside and I'll take care of the inside."

As the prison doors clanged shut on the working class leader, Bethlehem Steel was announcing a dividend of 200 per cent. The E. I. du Pont de Nemours Powder Company had paid 458 per cent on its common stock throughout a profitable war. And as the tall old man was being issued prison garb, the Calumet & Hecla Mining Company, where the 72 adults and children had died during the 1913 copper strike, was paying 800 per cent on its capital stock.

3. Big Steel

The war was over on Nov. 11, 1918. Out of the holocaust came two great earth-shaking historical changes. The first was the revolt of hundreds of millions of people against the misery, starvation, and death brought about by the war and the stirrings of hundreds of millions of others against colonial subjugation. In November, 1917, the Russian people eliminated the profit system and established socialism on one-sixth of the earth's surface. Inspired by this great revolutionary upheaval, the people of China under Sun Yat-sen moved forward to liberate their country. Similarly, the people of India under Mahatma Gandhi began a long and bitter struggle for liberation from British colonial rule.

The second great change was that out of the general weakening of the capitalist system the United States emerged as the leading capitalist power. During the war the position of the United States changed from a debtor to a creditor nation. Over a billion and a half dollars of European holdings in the United States was liquidated, while more than two and a half billion dollars of private capital and seven billion dollars of public capital were extended to the Allied powers in the form of loans. Practically all of this money was spent in the United States as war orders, flowing like an undreamed-of bonanza.

J. P. Morgan & Company together with three of its allies on Wall Street extended their imperial domain in America beyond the "341 directorships in 112 corporations having aggregate resources or capitalization of $22,245,-000,000," their holdings according to an official Congressional report submitted one year before the outbreak of the war. Meanwhile American big business, taking advantage of the preoccupation of its European rivals, transformed the Caribbean Sea region into an American lake and extended its sway over more of Latin America. Battleships, marines, and soldiers—all at the public expense—were sent to Haiti (1914-15), the Dominican Republic (1916); Cuba (1916-17), and Mexico (1914 and 1916). By the end of World War I the United States owned outright in the Caribbean Sea region Puerto Rico, the Canal Zone, and the Virgin Islands and held as protectorates Haiti, the Dominican Republic, Cuba, Nicaragua, and Panama.

The war marked the end of an era for the United States. Until American entry into the war there were many who still thought it possible somehow to return the country to a non-monopolistic middle way, some modern version of Jeffersonianism in which none was either very rich or very poor. However, with the war's end, there was small chance for a return to the simplicities of Jeffersonianism. For better or worse, American monopoly was in the saddle, stronger than ever before, its foreign rivals badly shaken and coming increasingly under its control through financial need. As never before, the whole world beckoned to it as a prize to be won. It was a dazzling prospect.

But at home the prospect was not so dazzling. The year 1919 was coming up—and there was a year! People all over the world including those in America were on the march. To stop this popular upsurge in the United States American monopoly trotted out the time-honored red scare. Seldom has it been used so widely and seldom have the people fought back so valiantly. The red scare was used against the overworked and underpaid Boston police department when its members went on strike in the summer of 1919. It was used against the 60,000 workers of Seattle during the general strike there in 1919. It was used against the general strike that year in Winnipeg. Every strike everywhere was said to be on the direct orders of the Kremlin.

It was true enough that Communists were active in strikes, just as they had been in the railroad strike of 1877 and the great eight-hour fight of

1886, but the direct and overwhelming cause of the wave of strikes in 1919 was the fact that the cost of living had doubled since 1914 while real wages were 14 per cent less in 1919 than in 1914. Communists were but one tenth of one per cent of the country's population but milk had jumped since 1914 from nine to fifteen cents a quart, eggs from thirty-seven to sixty-two cents a dozen, butter from thirty-two to sixty-one cents a pound, and sirloin steak from twenty-seven to forty-two cents a pound. This fact and not Bolshevism was the cause of a strike wave involving 4,000,000 American workers but the open-shop drive of the National Association of Manufacturers, using the red scare as its main weapon, convinced millions of the middle class that every strike was the beginning of revolution.

The historian Foster Rhea Dulles, writing of the period, observes that the "legitimate rights and justified grievances of the workers were forgotten in a fearful eagerness to make Bolshevism the cause of all labor unrest." Speaking of the general fear of instant revolution, Dulles continues:

"Employers made the most of these fears and alarms, waging a ceaseless campaign to identify all strikers as reds . . . labor found itself everywhere on the defensive, hard-pressed to maintain its position, let alone improve it.

"Moreover, the attempt of . . . employers to fasten the charge of Bolshevism on the labor movement as a whole could not have been wider of the mark. The leadership of the AF of L was as violently hostile to communism as the governing board of the National Association of Manufacturers. Gompers was in the very forefront of the red-baiters who were helping to create the hysterical intolerance of the period. . . . His irresponsible exaggeration of the red menace intensified the public's fears of social conflict and consequent demand for the forcible suppression of strikes."

Aided by the cries of such as Gompers,[5] the red scare rapidly became a racket used by every politician and every promoter to further his schemes. Frederick Lewis Allen observes:

"Innumerable . . . gentlemen now discovered they could defeat whatever they wanted to defeat by tarring it conspicuously with the Bolshevist brush. Big-navy men, believers in compulsory military service, drys, anti-cigarette campaigners, anti-evolution Fundamentalists, defenders of the moral order, book censors, Jew-haters, Negro-haters, landlords, manufacturers, utility executives, upholders of every sort of cause, good, bad and indifferent, all wrapped themselves in Old Glory and the mantle of the Founding Fathers, and allied

[5] Two editorials by Gompers which appeared in *The American Federationist*, February and March, 1920, were republished by the AFL in a pamphlet entitled *The Truth About Soviet Russia and Bolshevism*. It is significant to note that Gompers in these editorials lumps together "reds" and "liberals." "It is doubtful," he wrote, "whether the publications issued more or less directly by Russian Bolshevist agents have as great an effect in America as those publications which style themselves 'liberal' and which like to be known as 'journals of opinion,' such as the *Nation*, the *Dial*, and the *New Republic*. . . ." (p. 3.) Again, "The purple fringe of intellectual freakishness in America is for Bolshevism. It happens to be the mode. . . ." (pp. 13-14.)

their opponents with Lenin. The open shop, for example, became the 'American plan.' . . . A cloud of suspicion hung in the air, and intolerance became an American virtue."

It was against this background that the 4,000,000 were striking for higher wages and better working conditions. There were strikes among the long-shoremen, the stockyard workers, the shipyard men, subway workers, shoe employees, carpenters, and telephone operators, to name only a few of the groups. But the most important of them all, and one of the most important strikes in all American history, was the Great Steel Strike of 1919. If steel were organized, the great bulwark and fortress of the open shop, the symbol of the nearly 20,000,000 unorganized wage earners, if steel were organized, it was generally agreed on both sides, all American industry would soon be unionized. It was a crucial strike and recognized as such.

On Sept. 22, 1919, some 365,000 steel workers, organized under the direction of William Z. Foster in spite of every conceivable kind of terror in the fourteen months preceding, went on strike in fifty cities of ten states. Virtually every key plant of the United States Steel and the big independent producers was closed. Twenty-two were killed, including Fanny Sellins, an organizer of the United Mine Workers; hundreds were wounded or beaten up; several thousands were arrested, while over a million and a half men, women, and children "struggled and starved."

Although most of the strikers had been doing back-breaking, killing work for twelve hours a day at wages close to the starvation level, according to the report of the Interchurch World Movement Commission of Inquiry, the strike was immediately smeared in full-page newspaper advertisements run all over the nation as a Bolshevist plot to seize the steel industry.

Elbert H. Gary, chairman of the United States Steel, said that the strike was an effort "to sovietize the steel industry" and that one of its aims was the redistribution of wealth and property.[6]

Never has such colossal force been brought against strikers, never has a strike been so smeared as "red revolution," seldom have strikers fought more bravely. The regular army, under Major General Leonard Wood, was thrown against the strikers of Gary, Ind., where eighteen strikers were killed. Department of Justice men immediately entered the strike, arresting hundreds, many of them for deportation under the wartime deportation law which provided that any alien might be deported without trial on the charge that he believed in the overthrow of the government.

The Interchurch World Movement, which investigated the strike, declared in connection with these arrests that "the Federal Department of Justice seems to have placed undue reliance on cooperation with corpora-

[6] The actual demands of the strikers were for the right of collective bargaining, reinstatement of all men discharged for union activity, the eight-hour day, one day's rest in seven, abolition of the twenty-four-hour shift, increase in wages sufficient "to insure an American standard of living," seniority, overtime pay, and the abolition of company unions.

tions' secret services." Said a later report of the Senate Judiciary Committee, entitled "Charges of Illegal Practices of the Department of Justice," inserted into the *Congressional Record* by Senator Walsh of Montana:

"It was singularly unfortunate that the campaign . . . [against the 'reds'] should have synchronized with the steel strike of 1919–1920. . . . When they [strike leaders] were arrested and their followers from the ranks of the strikers were jailed by the hundred, it was quite reasonable that the great body of those honestly in the movement to secure shorter hours and better wages should have reached the conclusion that the Government had taken sides with their employers in an effort to break the strike and even that the arrests were made to that end."

In addition to troops, state constabulary, deputy sheriffs, veterans, private detective agencies, and hundreds of paid spies, thousands of vigilantes were deputized for action against the strikers. The *New York World* reported on September 22:

"In anticipation of the strike, what do we see? In the Pittsburgh region thousands of deputy sheriffs have been recruited at several of the larger plants. The Pennsylvania State Constabulary has been concentrated at commanding points. At other places the authorities have organized bodies of war veterans as special officers. At McKeesport alone 3,000 citizens have been sworn in as special police deputies subject to instant call. It is as though preparations were made for war."

And it was war, war against American citizens seeking a living wage. So widespread was the conviction that the strikers were trying to set up Russian Soviets in Pennsylvania, Illinois, and Indiana that the Interchurch group investigating the strike made every effort to show that intolerable conditions were the cause of the strike. It held hearings and took testimony. For a "minimum comfort level," the church group revealed, a weekly wage of $38.92 was necessary but common laborers in steel were getting only $34.19.[7] In a report it described work in the steel mills. Two of the jobs were described in these words:

"Job of the third helper, open hearth furnace: With other helpers he makes 'back wall' which means throwing heavy dolomite with a shovel across blazing furnaces to the back wall, to protect it for the next bath of hot steel. Heat above

[7] Using the weekly wage of $38.92 as the cost of maintaining a worker's family of five at a minimum "comfort" level in August, 1919, we find anthracite miners earning $29.98 a week; anthracite laborers, $26.90; soft coal laborers, $29.90; common laborers in the building trades, $22.88; carpenters, $34.56; painters, $32.61; book and job compositors, $26.28; railroad freight firemen, $28.80; railroad hostlers, $25.49; railroad shopmen, $34.56; shipyard laborers on the Atlantic coast $17.28 and on the Pacific coast $29.96; shipyard workers (including laborers), $34.90; and street-car workers from a low of $22.45 to a high of $28.09. (Interchurch World Movement, Commission of Inquiry, *Report on the Steel Strike of 1919*, pp. 262, 265–66.)

180 degrees at the distance from which the shovelful is thrown in; each shoveler wears smoked goggles and protects his face with his arm as he throws. After a back wall, it is necessary to rest at least 15 minutes. A man may have 4 or 5 hours to himself out of the 14 hour shift or he may work hard the whole turn. He may have two or three easy days or he may have a week of the most continuous and exhausting toil.

"The third helper fills large bays with coal to throw into a ladle at tap time; easy to burn your face off. Helps drill a 'bad' hole at tap time, work of the most exhausting kind; also must shovel dolomite into ladle of molten steel. This is the hottest job and certainly the most exposed to minor burns. Temperature around 180 degrees. Nearly every tap time leaves three or four small burns on neck, face, hands or legs. . . .

"On the blast furnaces. Job of the stove gang: Six to ten men in a gang keep the blast furnace stoves cleaned; as stove cools, gang cleans out hardened cinder in combustion chamber with pick and shovel. Men go inside the stove. Before going in the man puts on heavy wooden sandals, a jacket which fits the neck closely, and heavy cap with ear flaps; also goggles. Cleaning out the flue dust is not so hot, but men breathe dust-saturated air. Hardest job is 'poking her out,' ramming out the flue dust in checker work at top of stove. Large pieces of canvas tied over feet and legs to keep heat from coming up legs; two pairs of gloves needed, handkerchiefs cover all head except the eyes. Three minutes to ten minutes at a turn are the limit for work in the chamber at the top of the stove; very hard to breathe. Hours: twelve hours a day."

Foster, thirty-eight years old and leader of the strike, a tall, wiry, handsome man, was the target of every kind of threat and pressure as the great and crucial strike went solid into its second month. He traveled through the ten states, addressing strike meetings in the face of Legionaires and company gunmen. Again and again he was threatened with death if he addressed the steel workers but again and again he did address such meetings.

A former Wobbly, he had been imprisoned in the Spokane free speech fight. Foster had made his way to Europe as a young man to study the labor movement there. Frederick Lewis Allen describes him as the "most energetic and intelligent" of the current labor leaders while Dulles says of him that his "organizational skill was outstanding." Born in Taunton, Mass., and starting work at the age of ten, he had worked for twenty-six years in many industries including chemical, lumber, metal, meatpacking, agriculture, marine transport, railroad, and building construction; had worked all over the country, bumming his way from New York to California and from Florida to Washington. A student as well as a worker, he was an omnivorous reader. He had organized the packing industry in

1917, the first mass-production, trustified industry ever to be organized on the principle of industrial unionism.[8]

The steel strike was fought under the formal leadership of the AFL but because of its potential of mass industrial unions the country over, many of the conservative leaders, including Gompers, were frightened by its implications. They sabotaged it by refusing support, adequate finances, or a sufficient number of organizers. Despite Foster's organizational skill, the strike was lost after three and a half months of heroic struggle. The Interchurch World Movement said of the defeat in its report on the strike:

"The United States Steel Corporation was too big to be beaten by 300,000 workingmen. It had too large a cash surplus, too many allies among other businesses, too much support from government officers, local and national, too strong influence with social institutions such as the press and the pulpit, it spread over too much of the earth—still retaining absolutely centralized control—to be defeated by widely scattered workers of many minds, many fears, varying states of pocketbook and under a comparatively improvised leadership."

The Interchurch World Movement in its *Report on the Steel Strike of 1919* did not fail to mention the importance of employer and government espionage as a means of breaking the strike. After speaking of company-hired spies, the report said:

"These company-spy systems carry right through into the United States Government. Federal investigation officials testified to the Commission that raids and arrests for 'radicalism' were made especially in the Pittsburgh District on the denunciations and secret reports of the steel company 'under cover' men, and the prisoners turned over to the Department of Justice."

At that time the Department of Justice was headed by A. Mitchell Palmer, a business man associated with bank and public utility enterprises. On June 1, 1920, he was brought before the Committee of Rules of the House of Representatives to answer charges made against his department, particularly against the Bureau of Investigation headed by William J. Flynn, ex-private detective, and its Radical Division headed by J. Edgar Hoover, then an up-and-coming young man. Speaking of the steel strike, Attorney General Palmer testified:

"After various maneuvers of the American Federation of Labor, and with the assistance of various radical organizations, Foster was successful in bringing about a general strike of the steel workers in September, 1919, but through the action of the Department of Justice . . . this strike was terminated. . . ."

[8] On July 25, 1917, the Stock Yards Labor Council was organized under the jurisdiction of the Chicago Federation of Labor with William Z. Foster, John W. Johnstone, and John Fitzpatrick as organizers. By November between 35,000 and 40,000 workers were organized. In the process some 20,000 Negroes were unionized, about 10 per cent of the total number of Negroes who had been able to break through Jim Crow barriers and obtain union cards. (A. Herbst, *The Negro in the Slaughtering and Meat Industry in Chicago*, Boston, 1932, pp. 29, 42.)

On the stand A. Mitchell Palmer also spoke with pride about breaking the miners' strike and the Connecticut brass workers' strike. Said he:

"The Department of Justice, appreciating the efforts which the red elements were making in influencing the miners, had an injunction issued before Judge Anderson at Indianapolis, preventing further activities on the part of the miners."

*   *   *

"For some time prior to June, 1919, agitation and propaganda had been active in New Haven, Ansonia, Waterbury, and Bridgeport. On June 8 a strike was started in the Ansonia mill of the American Brass Company, being instituted entirely by foreigners through the organization of Russians, although several radical Americans participated. . . . It was necessary to adopt drastic methods by the state and city authorities, the department working in close cooperation. A number of the most active leaders at Ansonia were arrested on deportation warrants. . . . A black anarchist flag among other things was recovered. . . . However, a number of prominent agitators who were citizens continued their efforts. The strike failed after the federal and state prosecutions."

As a result of such strike-breaking activities by their government, millions of American workers had to suffer the low pay and long hours of the open shop for eighteen years more.

Monopoly rode the people in 1920 but uneasily, always knowing that at any instant the people's unity might toss it from the people's back. Monopoly was in the saddle but always it fought to keep its seat, never forgot that its position was precarious, always remembered that its exploitation would be over the day that 27,000,000 American workers found unity.[9]

But in 1920 that day was not yet. Monopoly's sure-fire formula for dividing the workers was about to be applied on a larger scale than ever before.

4. The Sure-Fire Formula

The employers' red scare was paying off handsomely. Because of it the organization of the mass industries was delayed a generation. Because of it millions of workers were getting less pay. Because of it steel, rubber, auto, packing, electrical, and many other industries were open shop and because of it AFL membership declined from a little over 4,000,000 in 1920 to a little under 3,000,000 three years later. It was the magic formula to break strikes. It was the sure recipe for low wages. It was the certain route of election to

[9] In 1920 there were 15,370,000 industrial workers (manufacturing, transportation, mining, construction, etc.), 7,930,000 other wage earners (servants, farm hands, etc.), and 3,715,000 clerical employees (office workers, salespeople, technicians, etc.)—in all, 27,015,000 workers (L. Corey, *Decline of American Capitalism*, New York, 1934, p. 560.)

office. It was the one way to divert attention from graft, as members of the Harding administration tried to demonstrate when accused of the mammoth oil steal of Teapot Dome.

The red scare made more money than speed-up, increased profits faster than new machinery or labor-saving devices. It was ageless and forever new. It had been used against Americans ever since the middle of the nineteenth century when even the Abolitionists had been called Communists. It had worked against the railroad strike of 1877. It hanged the eight-hourday advocates in 1887. It had been a mighty help against Debs and the Pullman strikers. It had smashed the steel strike of 1919. It divided workers almost as effectively as using white employees against Negro.[10]

The red scare was valuable in that it could be used with or without a Communist Party. But now, as two small Communist Parties were formed in 1919, the old scare got another shot in the arm. As the two tiny parties were organized, it was said louder than ever before that revolution was imminent. The newspapers were filled with stories of Moscow gold and Russian spies. Said the *New York Tribune* on June 4, 1919, "Nationwide Search for Reds Begins," while four days later the *New York Times* reported "Russian Reds Are Busy Here." On Jan. 2, 1920, presumably unconscious of the similar headline it had used forty-three years before, the *New York Times* proclaimed, "200 Reds Taken in Chicago. Wholesale Plot Hatched to Overthrow U.S. Government."[11]

[10] To quote Cayton and Mitchell, the employers have "found racial prejudice to be a profitable thing" (*Black Worker and the New Unions*, p. x), and have used it to break strikes and reduce wages. This employer tactic of dividing Negro and white workers was aided and abetted by "lily white" leaders in the AFL. As late as 1926 the constitutions and rituals of eleven unions affiliated with the AFL and thirteen unaffiliated unions limited membership to whites. (S. D. Spero and A. L. Harris, *The Black Worker*, p. 58.) The exclusion of Negroes by the unions opened the door to employers. During the great steel strike of 1919 the Commission of Inquiry of the Interchurch World Movement noted that the steel companies imported Negro workers and shifted them from plant to plant, pitting them off against white workers. " 'Negroes did it' was a not uncommon remark among company officers." (*Report of the Steel Strike of 1919;* pp. 177–78.) Years later, in 1934, an official of the Carnegie Steel Co. in an interview at Homestead said: "As far as I am concerned I believe the Negro has been a life saver to the steel company. When we have had labor disputes, or when we needed more men for expansion, we have gone to the South and brought up thousands of them. I don't know what this company would have done without Negroes." (Quoted in H. R. Cayton and G. S. Mitchell, *op. cit.*, p. 7.)

[11] The sense of imminent peril obscured the fact that there had been Communists in the United States since 1848 and that in all that time there had been no revolution except that which was involved in putting down the counter-revolution of the slaveholders. The first Communist organization was founded in New York in 1852. It was in fact an older American political organization than the Republican Party, formed in 1854. Americans had called themselves Communists long before the Russian Revolution was ever heard of. Communists had rallied the unemployed in the depression of 1857. They had served in the Civil War and President Lincoln had given a general's commission to their leader, Joseph Wedemeyer, friend of Karl Marx.

The genesis of the two rival Communist Parties in the United States could be traced,

By 1920 the red scare was the heart of the open-shop drive of the National Association of Manufacturers, which found the red menace, according to the official report of the La Follette Committee of the United States Senate, "in such demands as union recognition, shorter hours, higher wages, regulation of child labor, and of the wages and hours of women and children in industry." The recently formed American Legion worked with the NAM, its members vigilantes in the breaking of strikes, and in the saving of the country from the Bolshevism of the closed shop.[12]

The American trade union movement, said NAM president John Kirby in a pamphlet written in 1913, was "an un-American, illegal and infamous conspiracy." Attorney General Palmer agreed, and ran the Department of Justice as an appendage to the National Association of Manufacturers.

---

their adherents declared, from 1848 to the International Workingmen's Association, founded by Karl Marx in 1864, and organized in the United States in 1867; from the Socialist Labor Party of 1876-1900 to the Socialist Party of 1900 to the parties that had just been formed. Most of their founders, in fact, were members of the seceding left wing of the Socialists, reinforced by former members of the IWW. When the parties merged in 1920 into the Communist Party of the United States, Big Bill Haywood joined, as did William Z. Foster, at the present time the party's head, and at seventy-three under an indictment resulting from the thought-control Smith Act.

[12] In March, 1919, the American Legion was founded in Paris with some 463 delegates attending the first caucus. Among them were such future leaders of big business as David M. Goodrich of the rubber family; R. D. Patterson, radio executive; Franklin D'Olier, insurance company official; and Devereau Milburn, wealthy polo player. (R. S. Jones, *History of the American Legion*, New York, 1946, pp. 31-32.) When it was organized, the American Legion needed a quarter of a million dollars. "This money," writes Prof. W. Gellerman in his *American Legion as Educator*, p. 20, "was borrowed from 'friends of the Legion,' not all of them Legion members. . . ." Among these "friends of the Legion" were large corporations like Swift & Co. under whose letterhead appeared the following addressed to other big business outfits: "A national drive is being made for the Legion and the amount asked for Illinois is $100,000, Mr. James B. Forgan, Chairman of the First National Bank being treasurer of the fund for Illinois. We are interested in the Legion, the results it will obtain and the ultimate effect in helping to offset radicalism." (As quoted in M. Duffield, *King Legion*, p. 8.) "To offset radicalism" meant the breaking of strikes of workingmen for a living wage and improved working conditions. And this the Legion did, intervening in a street railway strike in Denver in August, 1919, and in Centralia in November, 1919. In April, 1920, there was talk of enlisting Legion members to break a strike which had closed down the port of New York. No wonder organized labor assailed the Legion; a speaker at the Butchers' Union meeting in Omaha called Legion members "Trained murderers opposed to organized labor."

In 1923 the Legion invited Mussolini to speak to its San Francisco convention. In January of the same year National Commander Alvin Owsley declared: "If ever needed, the American Legion stands ready to protect our country's institutions and ideals as the Fascisti dealt with the destructionists who menaced Italy. . . . Do not forget that the Fascisti are to Italy what the American Legion is to the United States." (As quoted in N. Hapgood, *Professional Patriots*, pp. 61-62.) This was the same Alvin Owsley who was invited in 1921 to speak before the AFL convention by its top leaders. In that year George Berry, head of the Pressmen's Union, was invited as a speaker to the American Legion Convention.

On the night of Jan. 2, 1920, 10,000 American workers, both aliens and citizens, most of them trade union members and many of them union officials, were hauled from their beds, dragged out of meetings, grabbed on the streets and from their homes, and thrown into prison by the federal police under the direction of Attorney General Palmer and his aide, J. Edgar Hoover. The raids, made simultaneously in seventy cities, purported to be for the purpose of seizing aliens for deportation, an iniquitous proceeding at best. But thousands of citizens also were seized.

Of the 10,000 arrested, according to the estimate of Senator Thomas I. Walsh of Montana, 6,500 were ultimately released without any charge whatsoever being placed against them. They were not aliens or were not eligible for deportation. It was all just an unfortunate mistake. Forget the beating. Forget jail. Forget the indignity. And of the 3,500 held for deportation or on other charges, the great majority were acquitted and freed.

But on the night of the raids acquittal and freedom were far away. It had not yet been discovered that the whole thing was a regrettable mistake—if it was a mistake. In Boston 400 workers were led through the streets, manacled and handcuffed, clanking with chains. Federal Judge George W. Anderson said that the manner of their arrest was for display and the creation of public prejudice. "A mob is a mob," he said, "whether made up of government officials acting under the instructions of the Department of Justice, or of criminals and loafers and the vicious classes."

Vigilantes and private detectives, employed by corporations to point out active trade unionists, aided the Department of Justice men in their round-up. Almost everywhere prisoners were manhandled and beaten while in Philadelphia, where 200 were arrested, the third degree was used on almost all. In Hartford, Conn., scores of workers were tortured by fierce, unbearable heat in "punishment rooms" while at least one victim had a rope placed around his neck by Justice Department men who said they would hang him if he did not give them names of other workers.

In Detroit the raid "marked a peak in brutality." Eight hundred men were packed in a narrow windowless corridor on the top floor of the Federal Building. They remained there, many ill and without food, for six full days until Mayor James Couzens said that the conditions under which they were being tortured were "intolerable in a civilized city." Then they were moved to a deserted army encampment at Fort Wayne where new methods of torture were devised. The wives and children of those imprisoned there were beaten in the sight of the prisoners. When Alexander Bukowetsky protested he was shot at by a guard, the shot wounding another prisoner.

According to a news item in the *New York Sun*, Jan. 9, 1920, one hundred "reds" in Chicago were beaten by "the respectable prisoners of the county jail yesterday. Those of the outraged respectability include a half a dozen safe-crackers, a quartet of auto bandits and a number of jewel thieves." The ringleader in the attack was one John Russo, charged with robbery and quoted as agreeing with the proposition that "What we want to see is patriotism reducing the Bolshevik life limit. The necessary instruments may be obtained at your hardware store." A similar lofty sentiment was to be expressed years later by the notorious Chicago gangster, Al Capone, America's Public Enemy Number 1. At Deer Island in Boston Harbor a prisoner committed suicide by hurling himself from a fifth-floor window. Many prisoners went insane.

In New York City 700 were seized. Describing the arrests there and elsewhere, L. F. Post, then the Assistant Secretary of Labor, wrote:

"Meetings wide open to the general public were roughly broken up. All persons present—citizens and aliens alike without discrimination—were arbitrarily taken into custody and searched as if they had been burglars caught in the criminal act. Without warrants for arrest men were carried off to police stations and other temporary prisons, subjected there to secret police-office inquisitions commonly known as the 'third degree,' their statements written categorically into mimeographed question blanks, and they required to swear to them regardless of their accuracy."

But it was not only men who were arrested. Old women, who could not speak the English language, were hauled into custody. A woman with an infant and girls in their teens were picked up. *The New York Tribune* in its issue of Jan. 3, 1920, described the scene in the New York offices of William J. Flynn, the veteran private detective who headed the Department of Justice's Bureau of Investigation. The *Tribune* said:

"All night long the process of questioning and sorting out the captives went on at the office of the Department of Justice. . . . Looking over the head of the motley crowd jammed into the offices . . . at midnight Mr. Flynn said, 'This is the breaking of the backbone of radicalism in America.'

"Green light was the prevailing color in the office. It came from a gigantic bulb used in photography. It was the first thing that popped into the eyes of the startled men and women as they struggled out of the elevator. Sixty to sixteen were the ages given by the women. . . . Just before midnight six old women, some of them with white hair, appeared among the file escorted in by the agents. Men, women and girls, and with them all the paraphernalia taken from the places where they were found, were crowded into the elevator and quickly carried upstairs."

Some of those arrested were veterans who had served in the armed forces of the United States during World War I. Many were heads of families. Senator Thomas J. Walsh of Montana read into the *Congressional Record* this description of the victims of the raids:

"Instances were not rare in which the victims were the fathers of families, including a number of children born in America, while sad to relate, not a few had enviable war records, having served in the Grand Army of that country whose government they were accused of trying to overthrow by force and violence. . . . Among those taken were skilled mechanics. . . .

"Mr. Barkley, a Detroit newspaperman, said of those arrested in Detroit, 'They seemed to be simple men, not perhaps very highly educated. They were clean. Most of them were fairly well dressed for workingmen, not dirty-looking fellows. They did not look like what we have been led to believe Bolsheviks look like—that is, when they were taken in there. After four or five days, of course, they had all grown a pretty good crop of beard. They were not permitted to shave and slept in their clothes. . . . No, they were reputable workmen. Their familes were very well clothed. They were skilled workmen.' "

Many of those arrested had been active in strikes and union affairs. A federal official, testifying before the Commission of Inquiry of the Interchurch World Movement, said that "ninety per cent of all radicals arrested and taken into custody were reported by one of the large corporations either of the steel or coal industry." Continuing, he said:

"I mean by that, that these corporations are loaded up with what they call 'under-cover' men who must earn their salaries. They go around and get into organizations and report the cases to the detectives for the larger companies. These detectives in turn report to the chiefs of police . . . generally . . . placed there by the corporations. The corporation orders an organization raided by the police department, the members are taken in, thrown into the police station and the Department of Justice is notified. . . ."

The Palmer raids were widely denounced as the most flagrant case of official lawlessness in American history. Such was the stand taken by the Chicago Federation of Labor, the Amalgamated Textile Workers at a mass meeting in Lawrence, and Jackson H. Ralston, general counsel of the AFL.

Such was the view of Senator Walsh of Montana after hearings before the Senate Judiciary Committee. Such was the declaration of Federal Judge George W. Anderson, Louis Post, Assistant Secretary of Labor, and Charles E. Hughes, Republican Presidential candidate in 1916 and later Chief Justice of the Supreme Court. Mr. Palmer, aided and abetted by William J. Flynn and J. Edgar Hoover,[13] had directed raids which flouted almost every provision of the Bill of Rights they were sworn to uphold, ac-

[13] In 1924 J. Edgar Hoover, then acting director of the Bureau of Investigation, virtually acknowledged that what was done during the Palmer Raids was not according to existing law. He is quoted by Homer Cummings, Attorney General under Franklin D. Roosevelt, and Carl McFarland, special assistant to the Attorney General, in their book *Federal Justice*, to have made the following acknowledgment: "It is, of course, to be remembered that the activities of the Communists and other ultra-radicals have not up to the present time [1924] constituted a violation of federal statutes." (pp. 430-431.)

cording to the findings published in the *Report Upon the Illegal Practices of the United States Department of Justice*.[14]

The raids were criticized as monumental lawlessness, as a wholesale trampling upon the people's rights, but in the main they served their purpose. They frightened people and dampened militancy. They weakened labor. They buttressed the open-shop drive. They played their part in keeping wages down. The old sure-fire formula had succeeded once again. Labor did not recover from the onslaught "against the reds" until the beginning of the New Deal.

5. The Fight Back

An old man in prison garb received the delegation in his Atlanta prison cell where the convict was notified that he had been nominated for the Presidency of the United States. The man was Eugene Debs, of course, the time was 1920, and the nomination was on the Socialist ticket. The first man in history to run for the Presidency while behind prison bars, Debs was not abashed by the honor but criticized the platform upon which he had been nominated.

It was not the place of the Socialists, he said, to use the bosses' game of divide and conquer through the red scare. "I was sorry," he said, "to read a speech of Victor Berger's the other day attacking the Communists. I have known many of the Communist comrades. They are as honest as we are." He pointed out that both of the Communist Parties were working for industrial unionism and recognized the class struggle, saying that he wished the Socialist platform had emphasized these two points to a greater degree. He decried criticism of the Russian revolution and told the committee, "I heartily support the Russian Revolution without reservation."

The convict polled almost a million votes in the election which gave victory to Republican Warren G. Harding, the tall and pleasant poker player from Marion, Ohio. The Debs vote, in addition to proving that many Americans were unimpressed by the red scare, provided impetus for the slowly growing campaign for amnesty for Debs and all other political prisoners.

It was becoming clear to many that the imprisonment of Debs and hundreds of others for political belief was part of the drive against labor. More and more trade unionists were seeing a relation between the Palmer Raids and long hours and inadequate pay. When hundreds were being arrested,

[14] This report was signed by twelve of the most eminent lawers in the United States: Zechariah Chafee, Jr., author of the classic book, *Freedom of Speech*; Felix Frankfurter, later Justice of the Supreme Court; Roscoe Pound, dean of the Harvard Law School; Francis Fisher Kane and David Wallerstein of Philadelphia; Alfred S. Niles of Baltimore; Ernst Freund of Chicago; Jackson H. Ralston of Washington, D.C.; Swinburne Hale and Frank P. Walsh of New York; Tyrrell Williams of St. Louis; and R. G. Brown of Memphis.

after being pointed out by the corporations as "reds," but in reality for militant trade union activity, such activity was bound to lessen. If only Chamber of Commerce types were on grievance committees, where there were such committees, there would not be much of a fight to right grievances.

Hundreds of thousands signed petitions asking that President Harding grant amnesty to Debs. The Chicago Federation of Labor led the fight. Scores of trade union locals passed resolutions demanding amnesty. Newspaper offices were flooded with letters favoring Presidential clemency. It was pointed out again and again that Debs was deprived of liberty for his thoughts and words and not for his acts. Finally even Sam Gompers came out for clemency, even visited Debs at Atlanta prison. Ray Ginger describes the scene:

". . . The Socialist leader had found his place with the unskilled workingmen, the unorganized farmers, the disinherited convicts, at the bottom of the social heap. Gompers had consciously chosen to speak for the skilled craft unionists. Now they met again: the squat and well-tailored confidant of industrialists and statesmen; the gaunt intimate of criminals, wearing his shabby prison stripes.

"Debs broke the silence with a curt greeting: 'How do you do, Mr. Gompers.'

" 'How do you do, Gene,' Gompers replied. Then stung by the formality of Debs' words, he hurried on: 'Many years ago you called me Sam. Can't we get back to those terms again?'

"Frigid and unforgiving, the prisoner replied: 'Perhaps some day we can.' The two men spoke of generalities a few minutes; then Debs returned to his duties in the hospital."

Despite the opposition of the American Legion, Debs and twenty-three other political prisoners were liberated by President Harding, who issued a Christmas amnesty on Dec. 23, 1921. The people, the unpredictable people were restive and it was thought better to humor them with Debs' release. At the same time labor's rank and file, often led by the militants who had organized packing and steel, began to fight back against the phenomenally successful open-shop offensive of the employers. The fight back took the form of so-called wildcat strikes, a rising cooperation between progressives and middle-of-the-roaders, a slowly growing movement for independent political action, and an increasing realization that Gompers' red-baiting was disarming labor in the face of its enemies.

Gompers and other AFL leaders took to red-baiting for a twofold reason. The first was their fear of being unseated and their policies reversed by the rising tide of militancy within the AFL. As L. L. Lorwin in his authoritative *History of the American Federation of Labor* put it, they used the cry of "Bolshevism" to check "the radical forces in the labor movement which threatened to make a sweep of established methods and policies." By crying "red" they thought they would be able to divert attention from the demands of the militants in the AFL for industrial unionism and more action on both the economic and political fronts.

Second, they used red-baiting to demonstrate that they and their organization were not "Bolshevist." Actually it did them little good, for despite their protestations of 100 per cent Americanism pamphlets appeared, such as the one written by Francis R. Welsh and entitled *America's Greatest Peril,* which charged "the red element" in the AFL with fraternizing with the IWW. To prove such charges were false Gompers and his associates went out of their way to play the employers' game by red-baiting everything and everyone stepping out of line.

Labor's anti-Communism was becoming a self-destroying luxury which it could not afford. The chief propaganda claim, as we have seen, of the National Association of Manufacturers in its fight against the trade unions was that the closed shop and the labor movement were Communist conspiracies. With Gompers himself seeing reds and plots on every hand, he and the AFL were in a poor position to fight the open-shop campaign. The AFL leaders had themselves admitted and taken over the chief point of the employers' anti-labor propaganda.

Aided by the great red scare, which the top AFL leadership itself had helped to encourage, the open shop became an American dogma, as holy to some as the Declaration of Independence and as little to be questioned. When the government broke the strike of 400,000 railroad shopmen in 1922 with one of the severest court injunctions ever issued, forbidding all strike activity on penalty of imprisonment, Attorney General Daugherty, afterwards indicted on a charge of receiving bribes and defrauding the government, made a statement widely praised as the sheerest patriotism. "So long and to the extent that I can speak for the government of the United States," he said, "I will use the power of the government within my control to prevent the labor unions of the country from destroying the open shop." The patriotic Attorney General, incidentally, claimed that he himself was a victim of the Red Conspiracy when he was indicted for raiding the public treasury.[15]

Not only the government but literally hundreds of powerful private organizations were devoted to the principle of no effective trade unions. As early as 1919 William H. Barr, president of the National Founders' Association, listed the organizations devoted to the open shop and the thesis that the trade union movement was a Communist conspiracy.

"A partial but careful survey of the irresistible activities in behalf of the open shop shows that 540 organizations in 247 cities of 44 states are engaged in promoting this American principle in employment relations," he said. "A total of 23 national industrial associations are included in these agencies. In

[15] "I was the first official," Daugherty wrote, "to be thrown to the wolves by the Red borers of America. Their ultimate success in my case was intended to intimidate every man who succeeded me, and make the American Republic thereafter cower under a reign of terror."

addition 1,655 local chambers of commerce are also pledged to the open shop."

Other open shop organizations, in addition to the National Association of Manufacturers, were the powerful National Metal Trades Association and the League for Industrial Rights. In New York State alone there were fifty employer associations whose sole function was opposition to trade unionism, activity carried on by means of the blacklist, hired spies, and continual and constant firings for union activity.

This huge campaign, in which millions of dollars were employed, was not for fun but to keep wages down and break strikes. It was doing both in the name of the American Way. Wages had been slashed between 25 and 50 per cent in 1921, a year of depression in which 3,500,000 were unemployed. The open-shop drive reached its climax in 1921–1922 when strikes in packing, textile, coal, and railroad were broken. Despite aggressive efforts on the part of the rank and file to break through the open shop citadel, unions in lumber, meatpacking, steel, and the maritime industry were virtually non-existent while established union organizations in coal, printing, textile, clothing, building, and railroad were badly hurt.

These reverses were stirring trade union militants and thousands of honest rank and filers into a fight for life. In November, 1920, the Trade Union Educational League was formed by militant trade unionists. Not a dual union but working within all unions, its members worked for the program of amalgamating craft unions into industrial unions, for independent political activity, and for the recognition of Soviet Russia by the United States government. From the first it scored striking successes, chiefly as a result of the coalition formed between the militants of the TUEL and middle-of-the-roaders in the AFL.

The TUEL itself expressed this unity of left and middle-of-the-roaders, its membership including Communists and non-Communists, progressives of every shade, and trade unionists whose only policy was disgust with the sell-out policies of Gompers and his colleagues. But what particularly gave it force was its united-front alliance with the Chicago Federation of Labor and its 350,000 members at the heart of the country's industry. When the Chicago Federation of Labor, the leading progressive labor center of the American trade union movement, went on record for the amalgamation of craft unions into industrial unions, for independent political action, and for recognition of Socialist Russia, it put the whole American labor movement into motion.

In 1922 and 1923, following the example of the Chicago Federation of Labor, a whole series of important labor organizations went on record for industrial unionism, independent political action, and recognition of Russia. Sixteen international unions endorsed amalgamation or industrial unionism. Seventeen state federations, including Pennsylvania, Ohio, Michigan, Minnesota, Indiana, and Washington, passed resolutions favoring amalgamation. Thousands of local unions favored it, including 3,377 in the railroad industry alone. There was similar action in Canada. In all some 2,000,000 trade unionists, more than half of the labor movement, went on record in favor of the industrial union.

As to independent political action, 7,000 local unions favored it in answering a referendum on the subject conducted by the TUEL. Many international unions went on record for recognition of Russia including the United Mine Workers, the Painters, Locomotive Engineers, Machinists, the Amalgamated Clothing Workers, and the Stationary Firemen. It was in response to this fight back of the rank-and-file, to this pressure from the united front of progressives and moderates, that Gompers and the AFL hierarchy reversed their traditional stand against independent political action and endorsed the independent farmer-labor candidacy of Senator Robert M. La Follette for the Presidency in 1924.

La Follette polled 4,822,856 votes, 16.6 per cent of the total vote cast, the largest vote polled by an independent in all American history. It was a good beginning, and obviously was an adequate basis for a permanent independent political party based on labor and the farmer. That, however, was the last event desired by the AFL hierarchy. The embryonic party was formally killed at Chicago on Feb. 21, 1925, by decision of its founders. The alliance of progressives and middle-of-the-roaders fell apart and once again the policies of Gompers were supreme.

Gompers died on Dec. 13, 1924, but there was no change in policies under William Green who succeeded him as president. Industrial unionism and independent political action were held back until progressives and forward-looking moderates combined to build the CIO during the days of the New Deal.

CHAPTER VIII

The Golden Insanity

> "O, let America be America again—
> The land that never has been yet—
> And yet must be—the land where every man is free.
> The land that's mine—the poorman's, Indians,
>   Negro's, ME
> Who made America,
> Whose sweat and blood, whose faith and pain,
> Whose hand at the foundry, whose plow in the rain,
> Must bring back our mighty dream again . . .
>
> "O, yes,
> I say it plain,
> America never was America to me,
> And yet I swear this oath—
> America will be!"

LANGSTON HUGHES

1. Hate, Inc.

In the aftermath of World War I, when all efforts were judged good or bad according to the profits they brought in, even the organization of hate became a profitable industry. Millions of dollars were made by those who knew how to manipulate, encourage, and increase the hatred of one part of the population for another part.

Sociologists explained the hate manifested by such organizations as the revived Ku Klux Klan by declaring that the government had brought into being as part of its win-the-war, hate-the-enemy campaign a vast fund of unexpended hate, unused because the war ended too quickly to exhaust it. Now smart promoters, it was said, were organizing this oceanic unexpended reservoir of meanness.

Perhaps a more accurate explanation rested in the fact that foreign-born and Negroes received about half the average wage of white native workers.[1] Billions of dollars in super-profits were obtained each year by employers, who were always ready to contribute to organizations which aided in the immensely profitable technique of divide and conquer—whereby huge groups were paid less for work than other groups.

The Ku Klux Klan, revived in 1915 in Atlanta, began appealing to the native-born millions in about 1920. Great organized public orgies of hate, disguised as patriotism, were stage-managed in the South and Middle West, long before Hitler organized similar manifestations with his storm troopers.

On scores of hillsides oil-soaked timber crosses burned in the night while around them gathered thousands in white robes, hoods concealing their faces, thrilling to such hymns as "Onward Christian Soldiers," glorying in a ritual in which drug store proprietors were "Kleagles" and real estate salesmen "Wizards."

The Klan was, its members said, 100 per cent American. It was against trade unions as a manifestation of Communism. It was against Roman Catholics as foreign agents representing an international conspiracy under the Pope, whose prime object was seizure of the White House by force and violence. It saw all Jews, too, as representatives of an international conspiracy.

Membership in the Klan cost $10. By 1924 its membership had reached a total of 4,500,000 and had contributed some $45,000,000 to its promoters, according to the careful researches of Stanley Frost. The Klan elected Congressmen, governors, mayors, state legislatures. It dominated the political scene as well as the governments of seven states, Indiana, Ohio, California, Texas, Oklahoma, Arkansas, and Oregon.

Its "white robe and hood, its flaming cross, its secrecy, and the preposterous vocabulary of its ritual could be made the vehicle for all that infantile love of hocus-pocus and mummery, that lust for secret adventure which survives in the adult whose lot is cast in drab places," writes Frederick Lewis Allen. "Here was a chance to dress up the village bigot and let him be a Knight of the Invisible Empire." And many a union organizer and many a Negro felt the lash of the village bigot's whip.

The 13,000,000 foreign-born, the 30,000,000 who were children of the foreign-born, did most of the nation's work in 1920, particularly in coal, steel, clothing, metal mining, construction, marine, and all kinds of manufacture, yet they were regarded by millions of native-born Americans as

[1] The United States Immigration Commission, in its *Abstract of the Report of Immigrants in Cities*, Washington, 1911, gives the yearly average in wages of foreign-born male workers as $385 and foreign-born female workers as $219 in contrast with $533 earned by native-born male workers and $275 by native-born female workers. (pp. 44, 45.) As late as 1950 the average annual wages of white male workers was $2,709 and of white female workers $1,062, while those of Negro male workers came to only $1,471 and Negro female workers to only $474. (*U.E. Fights for FEPC*, p. 3.)

potential spies, subversives, possible bomb throwers, and saboteurs. They were called kikes, wops, hunkies and dagoes, squareheads, heinies, greasers, and polaks. It was more than a little strange in that everyone in the United States, save the Indians, was either an immigrant or the descendant of immigrants.

The immigrants had come expecting a fair land and a fair deal and many had found instead a condition little better than slavery. Billions were made from their sweat, from the difference in wages paid them and native-born white workers. They did the hardest work for the least pay, always with the exception of Negroes, while living in the worst housing. The United States Immigration Commission found evidence of widespread peonage in 1910 among the foreign-born, a system of forced labor in which employees are not allowed to quit despite harsh treatment and starvation wages. This condition existed, the commission found, in every state of the Union except Oklahoma and Connecticut. In addition the Commissioner-General of Immigration reported in 1907 that thousands of Italians and Greeks "are practically enslaved by the padrones who effect their importation."

Members of the United States Immigration Commission reported forced labor general in the South as well as in the lumber and railroad camps of Minnesota and North Dakota. This report, published in 1911, declared of the Maine lumber industry:

"There has probably existed in Maine the most complete system of peonage in the entire country. . . . The employment agents misrepresent conditions in the woods. . . . Arriving at the outskirts of civilization, the laborers are driven in wagons a short distance into the forests and then have to walk, sometimes 60 or 70 miles, into the interior, the roads being impassable for vehicles. The men will then be kept in the heart of the forests for months throughout the winter. . . ."

And, as with Negroes, the foreign-born were on the one hand denied advantages and on the other scorned for being without them. Denied running water, they were said to be against bathing. Forced to live in dark and dilapidated tenements, they were accused of shiftlessness and a lack of neatness. Denied the vote, they were chargd with lacking public spirit. Confined to ghettoes, they were charged with clanishness, with being willfully un-American. Because most of them were laborers, they were held to lack intelligence. For years a ditch was regarded as the proper place for an Irishman; that is, if he was working and had a shovel in his hand. This view was later held as to Italians. Of the nation's miners in 1900 44.3 per cent were foreign-born while 61.2 per cent were of foreign parentage. Almost 36 per cent of iron and steel workers were foreign-born, 63 per cent of foreign parentage.

Despite grossly discriminatory pay and inferior living conditions, 14,531,-000 immigrants poured into the country between 1901 and 1920. From that prison home of nations that was Austria-Hungary 3,042,000 arrived between these years; 3,155,000 arrived from Italy, while 2,519,000 came from Czarist Russia.[2]

Typical were two Italian immigrants who arrived in 1908. They were both poor, both workmen, and they had, too, a certain love of learning, of music, of culture, an ancient humanist tradition which has been the great contribution of the immigrant to America. They were both completely anonymous, of course, as they landed, as were virtually all immigrants, and both were young, Bartolomeo Vanzetti, at twenty, arrived in New York, while Nicola Sacco was only seventeen when he came ashore in Boston. Vanzetti afterwards described his arrival:

"In the immigration station, I had my first surprise. I saw the steerage passengers handled by the officials like so many animals. Not a word of kindness, of encouragement, to lighten the burden of tears that rest heavily upon the newly arrived on American shores. How well I remember standing at the Battery in lower New York upon my arrival, alone, with a few poor belongings in the way of clothes, and very little money. Until yesterday I was among folks who understood me. This morning I seemed to have awakened in a land where my language meant little more to a native (as far as meaning is concerned) than the pitiful noises of a dumb animal. Where was I to go? What was I to do? Here was the promised land. The elevated rattled by and did not answer. The automobiles and the trolleys sped by heedless of me."

He stood there a long time in the growing dusk, the elevated an iron roar that keened into a screeching soprano as it grated around the Battery's curve. Vanzetti loved Puccini, knew Dante, had an honesty within him that made him try hard for truth no matter if it led to danger. For days he searched for a job and for days he knew the faintness of hunger and the hardness of the sidewalk when used for a bed. Finally he found a job as a dishwasher in a fashionable New York club and again his days were typical of the thousands who had just arrived from Europe. Later he wrote:

"I worked there for three months. The hours were long; the garret where we slept was suffocatingly hot; and the vermin did not permit me to close my eyes. . . . Leaving this place I found the same kind of employment in the Mouquin Restaurant—the pantry was horrible. There was not a single window in it. When the electric light was for some reason out, it was totally dark. The vapor of the boiling water where the plates, pans and silver were washed formed great drops of water on the ceiling, took up all the dust and grime there, then fell slowly one by one upon my head, as I worked below. During working hours the heat was terrific."

[2] In 1921 the 3 per cent quota act was passed in which immigration was permitted to the extent each year of 3 per cent of those of a given nationality who were already in the United States according to the census of 1910. In 1924 a 2 per cent quota was adopted and the census of 1890 was taken. At the same time Asian immigration was excluded.

Vanzetti worked there for eight months but even as he worked among the sewage he felt a greatness in him, not a greatness of self but the greatness of the working man. Often he did not finish work until two in the morning but then, lying on his cot in a cheap boarding house he would read until the light was gray and then firm and sunny. Reading books he thought would help in his study to find out why millions worked to exhaustion while a few clipped coupons. He wanted dignity and learning for his fellow man, not the garbage in which he and others were forced to live.

Vanzetti was a man who grew; his horizons and his knowledge broadened until the last day of his life. As he worked in the stone pits of Connecticut, as a laborer in Youngstown, as a steel worker in Pittsburgh, as a railroad section hand in Massachusetts, he continued to read because he had a thirst for knowledge and liberation. The two were one to him. He settled at last in Plymouth, Mass., and there he led a strike in 1916 at the cordage factory. By then he knew that study was only for the valiant, that trying to learn and express the truth held its own real danger.

At night, there where the Pilgrims had landed—immigrants seeking liberty of mind some 300 years before—he read books that might have brought him imprisonment or ostracism had Plymouth's now mighty known that he was reading them. He was reading Marx and Darwin, *Capital* and *Origin of the Species,* reading Hugo, Gorki, Tolstoi, Zola, Dante, Renan. "Ah, how many nights," he later wrote in his death cell, "I sat over some volume by a flickering gas jet, far into the morning hours. Barely had I laid my head upon the pillow when the whistle sounded and back I went to the factory or the stone pits." He had joined that army of working men—Parsons had been a member and so had Haywood—who have risked their lives by thinking, by turning their whole minds and beings to the effort to discover and act on truth.

"I learned," Vanzetti wrote in the Charlestown death cell, "that class-consciousness was not a phrase invented by propagandists, but was a real, vital force, and that those who felt its significance were no longer beasts of burden but human beings."

Vanzetti, who took to fish peddling after being blacklisted in the 1916 strike, became a close friend of his fellow countryman Nicola Sacco, as a result of the opposition of both to World War I. They had come to the same conclusion President Wilson was to come to when he termed the war "a commercial and industrial war," and rather than kill other human beings in such a conflict they joined a group of Italian anarchists who left the United States for Mexico during the duration of the war. They continued their friendship after returning to Massachusetts at the war's end.

Sacco was a skilled shoe worker. Short and muscular, he was a handsome young man with an unusual appetite for life. He loved the visual world, trees, flowers, the sky, with a real intensity, and was a gardener of skill, raising so many vegetables that he regularly distributed them to those in need of food. He had a lovely wife, Rosina, whose hair was a golden red, and at the time one small child, a boy, Dante. A later addition was a baby girl, Inez. The family, living in a pleasant rented cottage in a grove of oaks and beside a stream near Milford, was completely happy. Rosina, reporters afterwards said, was the kind of woman who, herself being good, could not understand evil—and the neighbors later told of often seeing Nicola and Rosina come from a Sunday walk in the woods, hand in hand.

But Sacco's views were such that he could not forget those less fortunate than himself. Despite long hours in his garden and a full day six days a week in a Milford shoe factory, he found time to help neighboring strikers and contributed money for the defense of such labor leaders as Ettor and Giovannitti, framed in the Lawerence strike of 1912. In 1916 he was arrested for taking part in a demonstration expressing sympathy for the strikers of the Mesabi Iron Range in Minnesota. Before that he had helped in the strike at the Draper Company in Hopedale, adjoining Milford.

In the same way that Sacco and Vanzetti had been active in strikes, so they were active in defense of the foreign-born when arrests and deportations became a holy crusade with the Palmer-Flynn-Hoover raids early in 1920. To be a foreigner was to be in danger as the mania ascended to the degree that the raids were regarded as saving America. As the Abolitionists once had been, the foreign-born were "hunted like partridges upon the mountainside." Sacco and Vanzetti raised money for defense, had handbills printed, organized protest meetings. They themselves were on the secret lists of the Department of Justice and as they tried to play the part of men, meeting the needs the time had placed upon them, they were often followed by hired federal spies, one of whom, a certain Shaughnessy, was later convicted for highway robbery.

When a friend of Vanzetti's, an Italian printer by the name of Andrea Salsedo, was arrested in New York, Vanzetti went there to try to find out what was happening to him. Scarcely had he returned on May 3, 1920, when Salsedo's crushed body was found beneath the fourteenth-story window of the Department of Justice in New York's Park Row Building. Held illegally in the offices for eight weeks, Salsedo had either jumped or been pushed from the offices of the Department of Justice. With this occurrence Vanzetti and Sacco began organizing a meeting to protest the death of Salsedo. It was to be in Brockton on May 9.

It was never held. On May 5, 1920, Sacco and Vanzetti were arrested, leaflets announcing the meeting in their hands. Picked up originally for "dangerous" radical activities, they soon found themselves charged with a payroll robbery in which two guards were killed at South Braintree, Mass., on April 15, 1920. Significantly, it was upon this charge and not on the one they had been arrested that Sacco and Vanzetti were sent to their death. In addition to the South Braintree murder, Vanzetti was charged with an unsuccessful attempt at a payroll robbery at Bridgewater, Mass., in December, 1919.

It is doubtful if anyone who carefully investigated the cases ever thought they were really guilty. That was irrelevant. In the first case, for example, the trial of Vanzetti for the payroll attempt at Bridgewater, Judge Webster Thayer had said in his instructions to the jury, "This man, although he may not have actually committed the crime attributed to him, is nevertheless morally culpable, because he is the enemy of our existing institutions." Vanzetti was found guilty and sentenced to from twelve to fifteen years in prison, a sentence whose purpose was to give Vanzetti a criminal record for the murder trial coming up.

That was also before Judge Thayer. It began at Dedham, Mass., on May 31, 1921. The defendants, manacled and loaded with chains, were taken into a heavily guarded courtroom and placed in a cage, according to the benevolent custom and law of Massachusetts. In an effort to give the impression that a red rescue was imminent the courthouse was guarded by armed police and everyone entering the courtroom was searched for weapons.

In his remarks, and later charge to the jury, Judge Thayer exhorted the jurors to act as soldiers on the battlefield serving their country against a foreign enemy. "You must remember the American soldier boy," he told the jurors, ". . . giving up his life on the battlefields of France. . . . I call upon you to render this service here with the same spirit of patriotism . . . as was exhibited by our soldier boys across the seas. . . ." The plain impression given by his remarks and attitude was that to kill the foreign-born defendants was to somehow serve the country as nobly as if the service had been given, not in the jury-box but upon the battlefield. The jury foreman, a former chief of police, ostentatiously faced the flag on the courtroom wall each morning as he entered the jury box and gave a military salute. The atmosphere was described by Felix Frankfurter in his book, *The Case of Sacco and Vanzetti*:

"By systematic exploitation of the defendants' alien blood, their imperfect knowledge of English, their unpopular social views and their opposition to the war, the district attorney invoked against them a riot of political passion and patriotic sentiment; and the trial judge connived at—one had almost written cooperated in—the process."

Both Sacco and Vanzetti took the stand in their own defense, but their broken English, their views on war and the profit system—above all, the fact that they were not Americans—made each syllable of their testimony tell against them. And it was more than the Commonwealth of Massachusetts that they were fighting.

Mr. Frankfurter, in his examination of the case published in 1927, wrote of the Department of Justice:

"Facts have been disclosed, and not denied by the prosecution, to show that the case against Sacco and Vanzetti for murder was part of a collusive effort between the district attorney and agents of the Department of Justice to rid the country of these Italians because of their Red activities."

Mr. Frankfurter was referring to two affidavits, one by Lawrence Letherman, head of the Department's office in Boston, and the other by Fred J. Weyand, special Department agent, both declaring that the federal authorities knew that Sacco and Vanzetti were innocent but were determined to see them executed because of their political convictions. Both affidavits were sworn to in 1926, a year before the executions, but their general content was known, of course, to those prosecuting at Dedham. Mr. Letherman declared under oath:

"The Department of Justice in Boston was anxious to get sufficient evidence against Sacco and Vanzetti to deport them but never succeeded in getting the kind and amount of evidence required for that purpose. It was the opinion of the Department agents here that a conviction of Sacco and Vanzetti for murder would be one way of disposing of these men. It was also the general opinion of such agents in Boston as had any knowledge of the Sacco and Vanzetti case, that Sacco and Vanzetti had nothing to do with the South Braintree crime. My opinion, and the opinion of most of the older men in Government service, has always been that the South Braintree crime was the work of professionals."

And Mr. Weyand declared in an affidavit:

"I am thoroughly convinced, and always have been, and I believe that is and always has been the opinion of such Boston agents of the Department of Justice as had any knowledge on the subject, that these men had nothing whatever to do with the South Braintree murders, and that their conviction was the result of the cooperation between the Boston agents of the Department of Justice and the District Attorney. It was the general opinion of the Boston agents that the South Braintree crime was committed by a gang of professional highwaymen."

But nothing indicating anything of this was permitted at the patriotic frame-up at Dedham. The main "eyewitnesses" testified in full, round voice that they had seen Sacco or Vanzetti or both shooting and robbing at South Braintree. One of them was "a woman of doubtful repute," who, according to testimony at the trial, "fingered" the defendants for the Government because she needed a job. Another "eyewitness," it was later brought out— and by that time it did not make any difference as to the conviction—was a fugitive from justice from another state and had given evidence under a false name.

Both Sacco and Vanzetti protested as best they could against the translations the court interpreter was making of their testimony. This man, one Joseph Ross, so warm a friend of Judge Thayer's that he named his son for the jurist, was later sentenced to prison for an attempt to bribe a judge. The chief law enforcement officer of the Commonwealth of Massachusetts, in fact, the Attorney General of the State and active in the prosecution, was later impeached and disbarred—not for aiding in the murder of Sacco and Vanzetti, but for blackmail of a Massachusetts concern.

The verdict, returned on July 14, 1921, could not have surprised the defendants. According to a later affidavit, a friend of the former chief of police, who was acting as foreman, revealed that even before any evidence in the trial had been given the foreman told him: "Sacco and Vanzetti should be hung." And George U. Crocker, a friend of Judge Thayer's, later swore that the judge had discussed the case with him during the trial. He said:

"He conveyed to me by his words and manner the distinct impression that he was bound to convict these men because they were 'Reds.' I remember Judge Thayer in substance said to me that we must stand together and protect ourselves against anarchists and 'Reds.'"

Sacco and Vanzetti, of course, did not hear these conversations but the spirit in the courtroom was unmistakable. On the thirty-seventh day of the trial, July 14, 1921, the verdict of guilty of murder in the first degree was pronounced, a verdict which automatically under Massachusetts law brought with it death in the electric chair.

"Sono innocente!" Sacco shouted from the steel cage in the courtroom.

"They kill innocent men," Vanzetti said quietly.

On Oct. 29, 1921, a motion was made to set aside the verdict. The following day the *New York Times* carried the news dispatch under the caption: "Court Under Guard as Radicals Plead. Precautions Against Outbreaks in Dedham. . . . Boston Is Also Under Guard." Three days earlier on October 27, the same newspaper under the heading "Say Radicals Plot to Bomb Many Cities" reported: "Federal agents have unearthed in Boston plans of an organized gang of radicals to spread a reign of terror over the whole United States for three days. . . . The plot, according to the investigators, is international in its organization and was to have been carried out by radicals to aid the cause of Sacco and Vanzetti. . . ."

Amid such synthetic hysteria, the battle to reverse the verdict of Judge Thayer's court was begun, a battle that was to continue for nearly six long years.

2. Revelry and Grief

Sacco was twenty-nine when arrested, Vanzetti thirty-two. For seven years their shadow fell across the land, scarcely perceptible at first but gradually lengthening and deepening as it became steadily more evident that they were innocent. Vanzetti's personality had impact. Although he was a quiet man, his still face, his serene bearing shouted so of innocence that presently it was echoing around the world. He was a fighter, too, and soon thousands were fighting for him and Sacco under the direction of Elizabeth Gurley

Flynn and other champions of workers' rights and of civil liberty. And while Sacco studied English in his cell, Vanzetti was reading political economy, philosophy, history, and science.

Harding was elected President in 1920, the year Sacco and Vanzetti were arrested. At about the time Vanzetti was demanding books, as if he would encompass all of life and understanding before both were taken from him, Warren Harding was also considering books in the White House but a bit less eagerly. "Almost unbelievably ill-informed," according to William Allen White, the poor President was suffering as he tried to understand what was beyond him. Once, trying to comprehend the gist of tax recommendations that required his decision, he cried to a secretary, "John, I can't make a damn thing out of this tax problem. . . . I know somewhere there is a book that will give me the truth, but hell, I couldn't read the book. . . ."

But there were not many parallels, even inverted, between the death cells at Charlestown prison in Boston and the White House on the Potomac. There the harried President and Nan Britton, according to her published story, were furtively flitting from room to room, concealing their shoddy little romance from Mrs. Harding.

One evening Sacco was writing a letter to his little girl, Inez, born shortly after his imprisonment. It was very still in his death cell at Charlestown prison. There was only the occasional footstep of a guard echoing down the iron corridor. It was difficult to see in the moldy light of the single bulb that hung above his cot. His English was a good deal better now but still it was hard to write, hard to explain to a little girl why her father was faced with death. She would have to read it again when she was older. He began by declaring that he and Vanzetti had been arrested because they were foreigners, active in strikes, known for their ideals and struggles for a better world, but soon he began to think of the little cottage beside the stream and under the trees where they had been so happy.

"I would like that you should understand," he wrote, "what I am going to say to you, and I wish I could write you so plain, for I long so much to have you hear all the heart-beat eagerness of your father, for I love you so much as you are the dearest little beloved one. . . .

"It was the greatest treasure and sweetness in my struggling life that I could have lived with you and your brother Dante and your mother in a neat little farm, and learn all your sincere words and tender affection. Then in the summertime to be sitting with you in the home nest under the oak tree shade—beginning to teach you of life and how to read and write, to see you running, laughing, crying and singing through the verdant fields picking the wild flowers here and there from one tree to another, and from the clear, vivid stream, to your mother's embrace.

"The same I have wished to see for other poor girls, and their brothers, happy with their mother and father as I dreamed for us—but it was not so and the nightmare of the lower classes saddened very badly your father's soul.

"For the things of beauty and of good in this life, mother nature gave to us all, for the conquest and joy of liberty. The men of this dying old society, they brutally have pulled me away from the embrace of your brother and your poor mother. But in spite of all the free spirit of your father's faith still survives, and I have lived for it and for the dream that some day I would have come back to life, to the embrace of your dear mother, among our friends and comrades again, but woe is me! . . ."

And yet the two prisoners sometimes seemed happier than the President. Great pouches had formed beneath Harding's eyes and his color was no longer ruddy, but an unhealthy purple. He could not sleep at night. The prisoners had no sense of guilt but the President, stories of colossal graft in his administration having come to his ears, lived with it. He had a horrible sense of insufficiency and perhaps cursed the day that Harry Micajah Daugherty, back in Ohio in the old days, had eyed Harding's floor walker's form and dignity with a speculative glance and exclaimed, "By God, you look like a President should look!"

Harding had always known that his dignity had concealed only a well-meaning hollowness and even then, back in Marion, he had answered Daugherty's exclamation with a doubtful, "Do you think I am a big enough man, Harry?"

And now even Daugherty, head of the Ohio Gang of politicians who had sold him to the monopoly interests running the Republican convention in 1920, had betrayed him. The Attorney General would soon be in the prisoner's dock for selling his influence for bribes. Albert B. Fall, his Secretary of the Interior and likewise a champion in the fight against the Red Menace, was also shortly to be imprisoned for taking bribes of at least $400,000 as payment for turning over the Navy's oil at Teapot Dome to private oil companies. His friend, Colonel Charles R. Forbes, head of the Veterans Bureau, was stealing together with his associates huge sums of money from the public till. He, too, was to be indicted and imprisoned. Harding's whole administration, the whole land since prohibition's arrival, was honeycombed with graft and the President could not face the coming exposure.

On Aug. 2, 1923, President Harding suddenly died under mysterious circumstances. Amid the rustic surroundings of his father's farmhouse at Plymouth, Vt., Calvin Coolidge, the Vice President, took the oath of office as President of the United States. The nation took comfort in the spartan simplicity of the ceremony as if it would somehow help rout the general atmosphere of graft and corruption. But instead the great inflation, the golden insanity in which even clerks bought Wall Street stocks on the installment plan called margin, was beginning to swell.

The great fleecing of the gullible many by the old shrewd few was about to begin. That the poor get poorer and the rich get richer was again to be demonstrated on the more monumental scale by Morgan & Company, Dillon Read, Brown Brothers, the Rockefeller interests, the National City Bank, and others of the Lords of Creation as they rigged markets, formed pools, and sold phony bond issues by the billion. In the spurious bubble of prosperity that was generated the Daffiness Era came into being with all its flagpole sitters, gold fish eaters, phonograph-record eaters, danceathons, walkathons, bathing beauties, Grover Whalen Broadway receptions of channel swimmers and aviators, bunion derbys, and million-dollar gates and stadiums.

People were still muttering, "Day by day in every way I am getting better and better," in accordance with Dr. Coué's formula for infallible success. Speakeasies were multiplying by the thousands, there was a still in every cellar and gin in every bathtub. Cocktail parties in homes and country clubs degenerated into brawls and petting parties and getting drunk was an American institution, the favorite indoor sport of thousands who had never touched a drop until prohibition gave them a holy cause and an ungodly thirst. The graft built on prohibition alone pyramided into hundreds of millions of dollars as the gangsters bought off chiefs of police, sheriffs, and federal government officials who sold them the contents of government warehouses. Hijackings, bandit raids on banks, machine gunnings in the street, gang warfare, and gang control of counties, cites, trade unions, and small industries became common while stocks were beginning the climb that would send the nation into mass hysteria, a feverish panting for riches.

There was prosperity of a kind, built on credit and installment buying, on the shifting sands of overexpansion. In 1920 there had been 7,000,000 passenger cars in the United States. By 1929 there were almost 24,000,000. Radio had blossomed into a major entertainment and a major industry. A total of $60,000,000 was spent in 1922 for radio sets, parts, and accessories. By 1929 $850,000,000 was spent on the same objects. Mass production and the belt line had come into their own.

Ford, with his gospel of what he called high pay and low prices, was regarded as a major prophet and the slogan "Not Marx but Ford!" rang through the land. The speed-up, increased production, and pay by piece work [3] became the be-all and end-all of American industry while trade unions became little more than an employer-controlled device to guarantee greater production.

[3] In 1929 the National Industrial Conference Board, an employer organization, found in a survey it had conducted that 97 per cent of the large plants were using either piece rates or special wage "incentive" plans. The stretch-out system in textiles and the "clean-up" system in soft coal mining were the order of the day. So prevalent was the speed-up in the eight years following World War I that the average output of workers, according to the *Annual Report of the Department of Commerce, 1027-28*, increased by 33 per cent or about double that of the twenty previous years.

The AFL hierarchy frankly and eagerly liquidated any and all policies that did not contribute to monopoly profit and seemed not dismayed when membership steadily continued to drop. Elbert H. Gary, chairman of the United States Steel, declared "Labor unions are no longer necessary!" and when company unions blossomed the AFL's only reply was that their unions could answer the employers' will even better that the company union. Its Executive Council formally declared in 1927 "there is nothing that a company union can do . . . that the trade union cannot accomplish more effectively."

Softened up by the red scare and the accompanying open-shop drive, there was no group in the country that embraced the new prosperity, the new American way, the way of Ford not Marx, more feverishly and firmly than the trade union bureaucrats. It became exceedingly common for trade unions to employ efficiency experts who vied with corporation experts in devising plans for increased production through speed-up. The sole function of the trade union seemed to be to increase the work of its membership.

In the Daffiness Days of the twenties many trade unions were investing their funds in stocks, bonds, real estate. They established investment houses, they handled securities, played the market, opened banks and insurance concerns, and had not the slightest thought of crash or 1929. Prosperity was permanent and if any gave warning they were called Communists and doubtless were. Again any mention of possible depression was unpatriotic and un-American.

As the mania spread, William Green, president of the AFL, declared that strikes were outmoded. H. V. Boswell, head of the Locomotive Engineers Bank of New York, expressed the new spirit when he said, "Who wants to be a bolshevik when he can be a capitalist instead? We have shown how to mix oil and water; how to reconcile capital and labor. Instead of standing on a street corner soapbox, screaming with rage because the capitalists own real estate, bank accounts and automobiles, the engineer has turned in and become a capitalist himself."

Prosperity, it was wonderful. Who could think of two innocent men in Charlestown prison when workers, so it was said, were buying silk shirts, when there was a chicken in every pot, a car in every garage, and a gangster in every local? Certainly not Calvin Coolidge in the White House, whose duties were such that he slept for two hours each afternoon, according to the later reminiscences of Ike Hoover, head White House usher. The Coolidge philosophy of the Presidency was to keep hands off while Big Business built universal happiness.

And there were so many more important matters than the two militant workers in 1925. For eighteen days the nation wept and prayed for Floyd Collins, his foot pinioned by rock in a Kentucky cave. The National Guard was called out to handle the crowds. Concessionaires did a thriving business and newspaper circulation increased by the hour. But Floyd died on

Feb. 17, 1925. Then there was the monkey trial in Tennessee when John Thomas Scopes was arrested for teaching high school students the theory of evolution and William Jennings Bryan, no longer the boy of the silver tongue, battled for the faith at the ensuing trail against Clarence Darrow, declaring evolution to be blasphemy.

And then a young criminal showed more compassion than all the great of Massachusetts. For it was generally recognized among them now that Sacco and Vanzetti were probably innocent but it was said, privately, of course, that the authority of the law and the Commonwealth of Massachusetts had to be vindicated by their murder. So Robert Lincoln O'Brien, owner of the Boston *Herald* and Boston *Traveler,* was saying to friends what later he declared in a privately published document: "The momentum of the established order required the execution of Sacco and Vanzetti."

But the young criminal, Celestino F. Madeiros, under death sentence on the charge of killing a cashier in a bank robbery, was not a pillar of society. His heart was moved when he saw Rosina Sacco, and the two children, Inez and Dante, visit Sacco. And although he had a chance to live, for his case was on appeal, he decided to give up the chance rather than see injustice done. For he knew that the agents of the Department of Justice were right when they said that the Braintree job had not been done by Sacco and Vanzetti but by professionals. It had been done by the notorious Morelli gang of Providence. He knew. He was there.

On Nov. 15, 1925, he sent Sacco a note which said, "I hereby confess to being in the South Braintree shoe company crime and Sacco and Vanzetti were not in said crime." He confessed in detail to William G. Thompson, Boston's foremost lawyer, who had taken up the case, and when his story was checked and rechecked Sacco and Vanzetti had been conclusively proved innocent. Now it seemed to millions that the Commonwealth of Massachusetts could not dishonor itself by killing them. And yet some wondered why young Madeiros had given up a possible chance for life that others might live. "I seen Sacco's wife come here with the kids," Madeiros explained, "and I felt sorry for the kids."

But the processes of law are long and cold and at every step they must be respected. All of the evidence, and it was voluminous, had to be written up in legal language and placed in a formal motion for a new trial. The authorities could not just open the prison doors. Due form must be respected. And so the motion, as argued before Judge Webster Thayer, was denied. Again he said that Sacco and Vanzetti must die. Once before, when denying another motion, Judge Thayer had excitedly asked Professor James P. Richardson of Dartmouth College, "Did you see what I did to those anarchist bastards the other day? I guess that will hold them for a while. . . ."

All over the world a shudder of rage and pain coursed through the veins of those who loved justice. The work of Elizabeth Gurley Flynn, of the left-wing journalist Art Shields, and of the defense committee was beginning to bear fruit. Heywood Broun was crying out in his column in the *New*

York World and the *St. Louis Post Dispatch* was protesting what it called a
legal lynching. Demonstrations were increasing before American embassies
and consulates in France, England, Italy, Russia, Germany, India, and
China and Brazil. [4] The needle trades unions in New York, Philadelphia
and Chicago were demanding a new trial. So were many locals of the United
Mine Workers. The central labor bodies of Detroit, Chicago, Minneapolis,
St. Paul, Seattle, Tacoma, Evansville and Salem were appealing for defense
funds. The Utah State Federation of Labor, the Pennsylvania State Federation of Labor, and finally the AFL itself, clamored for a new trial.

But in 1926 the great majority of Americans were not concerned over the
fate of Sacco and Vanzetti. Everybody, clerks, bricklayers, chauffeurs, stenographers, was buying stocks on margin, so the press reported. The sky was
the limit. Wealth was inevitable. Between 1910 and 1920 the number of
shares of stock that changed hands yearly had never been more than
312,000,000. In 1926 449,000,000 shares of stock were bought and sold. The
next year it was 576,000,000. During the week of Dec. 3, 1927, more shares
of stock changed hands than in any other previous week in the history of the
New York Stock Exchange. The amount of money loaned to brokers to
carry margin accounts had increased during the year from $2,815,561,000 to
$3,558,355,000.

Who could think of two Italians when American Can was going up,
when Tel & Tel had climbed ten points, when Anaconda, General Electric, General Motors were climbing almost by the hour? Don't sell America
short. If you got a good stock hang on to it. Sacco and Vanzetti? Haven't
seen them listed. All the big boys say it's just the beginnings. Money is as
near as your telephone. All you have to do is to reach out for it. You don't
have to pay for stock. Buy it on margin like you buy everything else. It's
going up . . . up . . . up. . . .

So it was in 1926 as Sacco and Vanzetti waited in their cell. So it was in
1927 as the Massachusetts Supreme Court turned down their appeal and
the date of execution was set for Aug. 23, 1927. The days went by and something stirred throughout the world and Vanzetti's strong waiting face behind the bars seemed a silent cry that must be answered with deliverance.
And as the day came nearer there were many men and women who suddenly knew they must do something. It could not happen. It must not happen. As July progressed into August, all over the land unknown men and
women suddenly rose in silent rooms deciding they must go to Boston.

[4] International demonstrations reached a crescendo after Gov. Alvin Fuller's refusal
of Aug. 3, 1927, to stop the execution of Sacco and Vanzetti. The following headlines
from only one issue of the *New York Times* (Aug. 10, 1927, p. 4) tell the story
graphically: "British Urge Mercy for Doomed Men," "50,000 Swedes Parade," "Berlin
Police Battle Reds at Our Embassy," "Argentine Strike Goes On," "Russian Appeals to
World," "Danes Threaten Legation," "French Protests Continue," "Uruguayan Deputies Plead," "Strike Proposed in Oslo," "Warsaw Mob Kept from Legation," "Dutch
Demonstration Broken Up," "Paraguay Press Urges Commutation," "Brussels Police
Rout Rioters," "Montreal Protest Meeting," "Guard Vancouver Offices."

There was a picket line before the gold-domed State House on Beacon Hill and daily, hourly it increased. Heywood Broun was there, and Edna St. Vincent Millay and John Dos Passos, all household names in American culture, and William L. Patterson and Art Shields and scores of others who grew to hundreds and then to thousands. And the two men waited in their cells, their faces strong and questioning. Delegations saw Governor Allan T. Fuller. He appointed three of the Commonwealth's greatest to sift the evidence, to decide whether the two should live or die. They were A. Lawrence Lowell, president of Harvard University, Samuel W. Stratton, president of the Massachusetts Institute of Technology, and Robert Grant, a retired probate judge, all old and of the quality.

As the three old men pondered there were protest rallies from coast to coast. As the date of execution drew near there were protest strikes. Protests were pouring into the State Department from all the world. Americans were declaring that if the Department of Justice framed up men for their lives on this occasion it would do so again. In Paris and London, Madrid, Havana, and Mexico City, in Buenos Aires, Bombay, and Moscow there were massive rallies. It seemed at times as if all humanity could see the waiting faces behind the bars and was determined to rescue them. Romain Rolland, George Bernard Shaw, Albert Einstein, John Galsworthy, Martin Anderson Nexo, Sinclair Lewis, H. G. Wells, and hundreds of others of the world's greatest, as Gene Debs and Anatole France had done before their deaths, sent impassioned appeals that the two lives be spared.

But sensible men knew that it was all a Red Plot and turned to the financial page to see with gratification that Tel & Tel was going up, that American Can had gained five points. Dempsey had signed for a return bout with Gene Tunney at Chicago and the gate was expected to exceed $2,000,000. Al Capone, Chicago overlord of crime, had organized the underworld into a big business mechanism. A staunch anti-communist, America's public Number 1 enemy was soon to warn that "Bolshevism is knocking at our gates. . . . We must keep the worker away from red literature and red ruses." And on August 3 the three old men of Massachusetts, Lowell, Stratton, and Grant, decided that the momentum of the established order required the execution of Sacco and Vanzetti.

The night of execution arrived and all over the earth men came together unbelieving. They stood in the market squares of little Italian towns. They packed the streets not only of Paris, New York, Berlin, and London, but in provincial towns along the Rhine, in the Alps, along the Mediterranean, in Rocky Mountain mining camps, and on the pampas of the Argentine. There were strikes in which hundreds of thousands participated, in New York, Pennsylvania, Colorado, Illinois, New Jersey. Police arrested demonstrators in Philadelphia and Chicago, clashed with 50,000 gathered in New York's Union Square.

In Boston it was raining as sobbing thousands, often clubbed by police, trudged through the night around the State House, formed a great solemn procession about the state prison, its walls punctuated with machine guns and guarded by the National Guard. Men and women, picket signs in their hands, walked on hour after hour beneath the prison walls, saying over and over again to themselves, "It can't happen. It can't happen."

In the death cell, Sacco was writing a last letter to his son, Dante:

"So, Son, instead of crying be strong, so as to be able to comfort your mother, and when you want to distract your mother from the discouraging soulness, I will tell you what I used to do. Take her for a long walk in the quiet country, gathering wild flowers here and there, resting under the shade trees, between the harmony of the vivid stream and the gentle tranquility of the mother-nature, and I am sure she will enjoy this very much, as you surely would be happy for it. But remember always Dante, in the play of happiness, don't use all for yourself only . . . help the weak ones that cry for help, help the persecuted and the victim because they are your better friends; they are the comrades that fight and fall as your father and Bartolomeo fought and fell . . . for the conquest of the joy of freedom for all. . . ."

Madeiros, the young criminal who had compassion denied the great, went first. Then Sacco, followed by Vanzetti.

After the execution Warden William Hendry made public the following telegram sent to the condemned men: "Take heart, men. It is justice that dies. Sacco and Vanzetti will live in history."

And live they did. As Vanzetti so aptly put it some four months before the execution:

"If it had not been for this thing I might have lived out my life among scorning men. I might have died unmarked, unknown, a failure. This is our career and our triumph. Never in our full life could we hope to do such work for tolerance, for justice, for man's understanding of man, as now we do by accident.

"Our words—our lives—our pains—nothing! The taking of our lives—the lives of a good shoemaker and a poor fish peddler—all!

"This last moment belongs to us—this last agony is our triumph!"

The prison lights dimmed three times, then flared firm again, and those outside knew it had been done. All over the world men wept in the belief that the earth had been made a poorer place, that humanity had been sullied.

The newspapers were filled with it the next morning[5] but there were many who glanced at the headlines, "then whipped open the paper to the financial page. . . . What was General Motors doing?"

[5] For example, the *New York Times* of Aug. 23, 1927, reported the execution of Sacco and Vanzetti under an eight-column page 1 headline and filled five to six of its pages with stories about the case. Contrast this with the way the same paper handled the case six years before. On July 15, 1921, the *New York Times* buried the story on page 6 under the caption "Find Italians Guilty of Paymaster Murder." A scant fifty-two lines were given to this news item giving the verdict of the court.

3. Behind the Mirage

During the Daffiness Days of the Golden Insanity every kind of nonsense was devoutly believed. Bankers and brokers were paragons of virtue, their honesty exceeded only by their wisdom. Businessmen were statesmen whose views of the world were as accurate as science, as undebatable as Scripture. When they said in 1928 that what was good for business was good for the country it had the force of one of the Ten Commandments. And yet within a matter of months it would be discovered that their ignorance was exceeded only by their dishonesty, that they had plundered the American public of billions with no more morals or compunction than a common pickpocket.

But let us first examine the legend of general prosperity during the golden perfection of the boom days of the 1920's. At its very crest, when a golden glow, it was said, shed its radiance on every man, almost 60 per cent, according to the figures of the conservative Brookings Institution, did not receive sufficient income to buy "the basic necessities" of life. In 1929 an income of $2,000 was needed by an average family "to supply only the basic necessities." But in that year, the richest year until that time in all American history, 16,354,000 American families, 59.6 per cent of the American population, received less than $2,000 a year. Nearly 6,000,000 families received less than $1,000 a year while 12,000,000 families or 42 per cent of the population received less than $1,500 and 20,000,000 families or 71 per cent received less than $2,500 a year. One tenth of one per cent of the families on top received as much as 42 per cent of the families at the bottom.

Before the crisis of 1929 the 33,000,000 wage earners in the United States received an average of $25 a week. More than half of the country's workers fell below the average and less than one-tenth were earning as much as $40 a week. As for women workers, the highest median[6] wage in any of thirteen states surveyed by the United States Women's Bureau was $16.36 per week in Rhode Island and the lowest was $8.29 in Mississippi.

Hours of work and speed-up soared during the Golden Age. According to the findings of the government's Hoover Committee on Recent Economic Changes speed-up and new machinery had increased productivity per worker by 53.5 per cent in the eight years ending in 1927 in manufacturing and by 17 per cent on railroads. Only 1,000,000 workers out of 33,000,000 were on the five-day week in 1929 while a work week was 54.6 hours in iron and steel, 53.4 hours in textile, and 60 hours in street laboring.

Speed-up, which was the really predominant characteristic of the Golden Era, also increased unemployment and industrial accidents. In "normal" times before World War I, according to government statistics, there were usually at least 1,000,000 unemployed but during the great prosperity the number was pushed up to about 4,000,000. And, according to the United

[6] By median is meant that half earn more and half earn less than the stated amount. It is therefore a kind of average.

States Bureau of Labor Statistics, there were about 25,000 workers killed annually in America during the 1920's while 100,000 were permanently disabled and between 2,500,000 and 3,000,000 annually were injured.

While the stockmarket soared and Dillon Read, Brown Brothers, J. P. Morgan & Company, Chase Securities, National City, Kuhn, Loeb, and others of the élite pried billions from investors, 2,000,000 New Yorkers lived in fire-trap apartments which had been condemned in 1901 as unfit for human beings. Over 100,000 New Yorkers occupied damp, dark, windowless basements. In company towns throughout the country workers lived in unpainted wooden shacks without running water or plumbing.

As for the nation's farmers their plight had been so bad since the end of World War I that even the ballyhoo artists of the Coolidge-Hoover prosperity had been hard put in representing them as basking in rich contentment. The total value of the country's farm property had dropped from $77,924,000,000 in 1920 to $57,604,000,000 in 1929 while gross income from farm production in the same years had decreased from $13,566,000,000 to $11,918,000,000. Of the nation's 6,000,000 farmers less than 600,000 were raising products valued at $4,000 or better a year. "Put baldly and bluntly," wrote L. M. Hacker, "fully half of the farmers in the country in 1929 . . . could boast of an annual average money income not much in excess of $350 a year." And the farmer hadn't seen anything yet.

But the age was golden, mighty golden, for investment bankers. They took the country like Gould took the Erie and by much the same methods. A total of $2,928,000,000 in profits from speculation on Wall Street was recorded for 1928 in tax returns. Most of it went to the one-tenth of one per cent of the population which was getting richer, the remainder to a stock-buying middle class which was then in the process of being taken. From 1925 through 1929 investment houses and bankers put stocks and bonds upon the market totaling 46 billions of dollars and cleared in commissions, assuming a two or two and a half per cent return, from $920,000,000 to $1,190,000,000. From 1922 to 1928 inclusive 36.5 billions of dollars was paid out in cash dividends while 7.3 billions was paid out in stock dividends.[7] Salaries and bonuses, voted by corporation officials to themselves, totaled more than three billions of dollars in 1928. But the greatest amount of money gained in these bonanza days by bankers and brokers was made in the old way of Drew and Vanderbilt, playing the market, forming pools, driving stocks up, selling high and getting out before a stock collapsed.

[7] On April 29, 1938, Pres. Franklin D. Roosevelt, in citing the following figures in respect to concentration of stock ownership, indicated who received the dividends which big business ladled out. "The year 1929 was a banner year for the distribution of stock ownership. But in that year three-tenths of one per cent of our population received 78 per cent of the dividends reported by individuals. This has roughly the same effect as if, out of every 300 persons in our population, one person received 78 cents of every dollar of corporate dividends while the other 299 persons divided up the 22 cents between them." (Message to Congress, *Senate Document* No. 173, 75th Congr., 3d Sess., p. 2.)

To the plucked the ways of the great seemed the ways of the con man. But a really artistic criminal is so crooked that he believes he is honest and so it was with the Mitchells and the Whitneys, the Morgan partners and the representatives of the National City Company, Dillon Read, Lee, Higginson, and Chase Securities as they testified before the Senate Committee on Banking and Currency in 1933 and 1934. For example, in 1927 and 1928 National City Company and other Wall Street investment banking houses floated three bond issues to the amount of $90,000,000 for the Republic of Peru at a profit to themselves of $4,500,000. In 1931 all three issues were in default as had been the case with Peruvian bonds in the past.

"The public never had a chance," writes Ferdinand Pecora, counsel for the Senate Committee, in his book *Wall Street Under Oath*, "The prospectus prepared for its benefit contained an impressive list of the various Peruvian governmental borrowings, but never even mentioned that there had ever been a default on any of their debts." Years after the Peruvian bonds had been defaulted Hugh Baker, president of the National City Company, was put on the witness stand by the United States Senate Committee on Banking and Currency. Asked Mr. Pecora, its counsel: "Do you think that the public would have subscribed to the bonds at 91½ if they had been told in the circular that Mr. Durrell [the National City Company's overseas manager] in July, 1927, advised the company that 'Peru's political situation is equally uncertain. I have no great faith in any material betterment of Peru's economic conditions in the near future'?" To which banker Baker replied, "I doubt if they would."

To Mr. Baker and his associates in the banking fraternity there was nothing wrong in the above transaction. It seemed only the normal functioning of private enterprise. Was it their concern if bonds were defaulted or stock market prices collapsed and millions of "suckers" not "in the know" were ruined? Their function was to float loans, form pools, drive securities up and make a killing.

That such was the case can be seen in testimony concerning the stock of the Kolster Radio Corporation. In 1928 the corporation was on the verge of bankruptcy, its earnings virtually nil. Rudolph Spreckels, chairman of the company and a sound businessman, saw his failure as a golden opportunity if handled according to Wall Street standards. He called in George Breen, "the hero of a hundred pools" and a figure of great respectability, who by a few simple routine moves cheated the public of millions of dollars while handing Spreckles a profit of $19,000,000 on its sale of worthless stock.

Mr. Breen, testifying before the Senate Committee, was very modest. He really hadn't done anything that everybody didn't do and it was really a very minor transaction scarcely worth the Senate's interest. First he had formed a pool, letting his friends in on a good thing. They all knew the stock was worthless but they all started rumors of "highly favorable developments at Kolster Radio." He had hired a publicity man who sent out releases about another opportunity to "invest in America's prosperity" and presently the newspaper financial columns were filled with favorable notices for Kolster Radio.

Then members of the pool started "the big push" to force up the price of the stock which was lifted twenty-two points, from seventy-four to ninety-six, at which point members of the pool unloaded with handsome profits. A short time later Kolster Radio went into bankruptcy. "The naïve public had lost millions of dollars," comments one historian in describing the little adventure but Mr. Breen was indignant at any innuendo of wrongdoing. He said that he had merely "stabilized" the market.

There were hundreds of such "stabilizations" and they made millions for their promoters. Such figures as Charles E. Mitchell, of the National City Bank, John D. Ryan, and Thomas E. Bragg took the public for a $160,-000,000 loss while they made a correspondingly large profit through forming a pool in support of the Anaconda Copper Company. Richard Whitney, president of the New York Stock Exchange but soon to be a Sing Sing prisoner, testified before the Senate Committee, describing the way J. P. Morgan and Company forced up the price of German bonds through the activities of a pool while the bond issue was being sold to the public. As soon as the bonds were sold, the syndicate keeping the price up withdrew its support and the bonds fell until on the day of Mr. Whitney's testimony they were bringing thirty-five cents on the dollar. Mr. Whitney, somehow offended at Senatorial innuendo that there had been dishonesty somewhere, protested that this technique of bond selling was "an absolutely usual and customary method of merchandising and distributing securities."

By such "usual and customary" methods the usual and customary concentration of wealth into fewer and fewer hands continued as it had continued since the Civil War. In 1929, for example, there were 300,000 non-financial corporations in the country but of this number 200 giants, less than seven one-hundredths of one per cent, controlled 49.2 per cent of corporate wealth of the country. And the controllers of the 200 giants were the Morgan-Rockefeller-Mellon interests. In 1929, for example, J. P. Morgan and his seventeen partners alone held ninety-nine directorships in seventy-two of the largest corporations in the country with combined assets of twenty billions of dollars. When the directorships of the Morgan allies were added, Morgan interests controlled assets of approximately 74 billions of dollars, sufficient to give them an adequate voice in the country's policies.

The Morgans, their allies, the Rockefeller and Mellon interests, as well as more than a few others, had investments of some 16 billions of dollars abroad. American financiers were quick to point out that they were not engaged in imperialism, that no Americans ever were, but were merely developing backward countries for the good of all concerned. As with their operations on the stock market, they were only doing good by accepted business methods and if some hundreds of thousands of colonials were killed and starved and sweated in the process, charges of imperialism were as difficult to understand as the charges of graft in connection with Wall Street pools.

The American capitalists found that dollar-control could be more successfully hidden than outright political control of foreign territory. It was more satisfactory to rule through a Haitian puppet, a complaisant Cuban government, or a bought and paid for president of the Dominican Republic or Nicaragua than to rule through the actual annexation of other nations. Ruling thus, American imperialists were in a position where they could denounce and deny imperialism while praising the self-determination and independence of peoples. They could have all the fruits of imperialism while condemning it, particularly the imperialism of their British rivals which they hoped to displace with their own more streamlined brand.

Nevertheless throughout the 1920's American armed force always followed American investments, ousting governments favoring repudiation of Wall Street loans, guarding American oil properties from expropriation, squelching all attempts at genuine independence through the machine gun and bomb. Hundreds of Latin American patriots have died on the bayonets of American imperialism with scarcely anyone knowing or caring in the United States. Major General Smedley Butler, of the United States Marine Corps, later told how American bayonets were used and how American boys died in the protection of Wall Street investments abroad. General Butler wrote:

"I spent thirty-three years and four months in active service as a member of our country's most agile military force—the Marine Corps. I served in all the commissioned ranks from second lieutenant to major-general. And during that period I spent most of my time being a high class muscle man for Big Business, for Wall Street, and for the bankers. In short, I was a racketeer for capitalism.

"Thus, I helped make Mexico and especially Tampico safe for the American oil interests in 1914. I helped make Haiti and Cuba a decent place for the National City Bank to collect revenues in. I helped purify Nicaragua for the international banking house of Brown Brothers in 1909–1912. I brought light to the Dominican Republic for American sugar interests in 1916. I helped make Honduras 'right' for the American fruit companies in 1903. In China in 1927, I helped to see to it that Standard Oil went its way unmolested."

While such force and violence were being practiced upon helpless people abroad the same thing was being done to native-born Americans at home, the impoverished Negro people who in 1920 numbered some 10,000,000. The object of the force and violence at home was the same as its object abroad—corporate profit. Between 1910 and 1930 more than 1,000,000 Negroes moved north, where most of them entered industry and where a development of great historical importance took place when they made contact with the progressive trade union movement. Thousands of them were active in the Chicago stockyards strike of 1917 and other thousands participated in the great steel strike of 1919.

The differential in wages between white workers and Negroes, a difference which meant literally billions of dollars to the employers, was being menaced. To save these billions in corporate profits, to perpetuate the division between white and black and thus keep all wages lower, industrialists consistently pursued policies that pitted white workers against Negro workers and frequently resulted in race riots.

Such riots took place in Detroit, East St. Louis, Washington, and Chicago. In the latter city the newly organized Chicago Stockyards Labor Council, founded by William Z. Foster and headed then by J. W. Johnstone, branded the riots of 1919 as an attempt to drive a wedge between the white and Negro laborers of the stockyards and break the new industrial union there.

On July 6 the Labor Council organized an impressive Negro-white unity parade of packinghouse workers which marched through the Negro district, where agents of the packers were already fomenting violence.[8] Despite this attempt to forestall the outbreak the race riot developed and virtual civil war raged in Chicago for two weeks while 30,000 white trade unionists from the stockyards expressed solidarity with their "Negro brothers," demanding the withdrawal of troops from the Negro district.

Similar progress was made in the great steel strike of 1919 when Foster insisted on hiring Negro organizers and absolute equality for Negro strikers. In addition Negro workers and intellectuals were themselves organizing to strengthen the Negro's position as a part of the trade union movement. *The Messenger,* an advanced Negro publication, consistently exposed the Jim-Crow policies of the AFL bureaucracy, while the group around *The Messenger* organized the United Brotherhood of Elevator and Switchboard Operators, the Brotherhood of Sleeping Car Porters, the Brotherhood of Dining Car Employees, the National Association for the Promotion of Labor Unionism among Negroes.

In 1925 the American Negro Labor Council was formed, leading a number of strikes of Negro workers, its chief purpose the fighting of Negro discrimination in the labor movement. Later, in 1930, the League of Struggle for Negro Rights, led by Harry Haywood, was established and did important organizing work among Negro workers in the South.

But in general the trade union movement, under the policies of Gompers and Green, collaborated with employers in refusing employment or trade union membership to Negro workers. The declarations of Sylvis and the

---

[8] The Negro people, of course, were no stranger to violence nor in fighting back against it. Not only had there been the bloody tyranny of 250 years of chattel slavery, with its 250 insurrections, and the terror of the Klan during Reconstruction; in 1917 some 38 Negroes were lynched while the following year 58 were lynched and in 1919 at least 70 were thus murdered; between 1885 and 1930 there were 3,256 lynchings of Negroes.

Knights of Labor that organized labor could not prosper unless it included the Negro were apparently forgotten. The top leadership of the AFL co-operated with finance and industry in their policy of using Negroes only as strikebreakers or in those jobs so exhausting and poorly paid that even the foreign-born would not take them. But through great bravery and endurance, through fighting for the smallest opportunity, often despised by others, Negro workers slowly made their way, despite every obstacle, into American production. By 1930 they were part of the labor force in virtually every significant industry. In that year they made up 7.3 per cent of the total number of workers in manufacturing and mechanical industry. They constituted 22.7 per cent of construction workers, 16.2 per cent of unskilled steel laborers and 25 per cent of the unskilled workers in meat packing.

However, the labor movement was seriously retarded and weakened, and still is, by the Jim-Crow policies of many trade unions.[9] It was only half a

[9] As late as 1947 a list quoted by the National Association for the Advancement of Colored People of the trade unions practicing some form of discrimination against Negro workers read as follows:

I. Unions which exclude Negroes by provision in ritual: Machinists, International Association of (AFL)

II. Unions which exclude Negroes by provision in constitution:

    A. AFL Affiliates

    Airline Pilots' Association; Masters, Mates and Pilots, National Organization; Railroad Telegraphers, Order of; Railway Mail Association; Switchmen's Union of North America; Wire Weavers' Protective Association, American.

    B. Unaffiliated Organizations

    Locomotive Engineers, Brotherhood of; Locomotive Firemen and Enginemen, Brotherhood of; Railroad Trainmen, Brotherhood of; Railroad Yardmasters of America; Railroad Yardmasters of North America; Railway Conductors, Order of; Train Dispatchers, American.

III. Unions which habitually exclude Negroes by tacit consent:

    A. AFL Affiliates

    Asbestos Workers, Heat and Frost Insulators; Electrical Workers, International Brotherhood of; Flint Glass Workers' Union, American; Granite Cutters' International Association; Plumbers and Steamfitters United Association of Journeymen; Seafarers' Int'l Union.

    B. Unaffiliated Organizations

    Marine, Firemen, Oilers, Watertenders and Wipers' Association, Pacific Coast; Railroad Shop Crafts, Brotherhood of

IV. Unions which afford Negroes only segregated auxiliary status:

    A. AFL Affiliates

    Blacksmiths, Drop Forgers and Helpers, Brotherhood of; Boilermakers, Iron Shipbuilders, Welders and Helpers, Brotherhood of; Maintenance of Way Employees, Brotherhood of; Railway Carmen of America; Rural Letter Carriers, Federation of; Sheet Metal Workers International Association.

    B. Unaffiliated Organizations

    Railroad Workers, American Federation of; Rural Letter Carriers' Association.

Other craft unions such as the United Brotherhood of Carpenters and Joiners and the Brotherhood of Painters, Decorators and Paperhangers, both AFL, which have

movement as long as the South, constantly growing in industrial capacity, was virtually completely unorganized, its low wage scale a brake on wages all over the country, as is still the fact today. Every pay envelope of a white worker contained a good deal less than it would have contained had it not been for the fact that Negroes were paid approximately half as much as white workers. During the 1920's the Trade Union Educational League and other progressives frequently pointed out that the Jim-Crow policies of labor were aiding none but the corporations while injuring the white worker along with the Negro. Repeatedly they spoke such words as those Sylvis uttered in 1867:

"A greater proportion of them [Negroes] labor with their hands than can be counted from the same number of any people on earth. Can we afford to reject their proffered cooperation and make them enemies? By committing such an act of folly we would inflict greater injury upon the cause of labor reform than the combined efforts of capital could furnish. . . . So capitalists north and south would foment discord between the whites and blacks and hurl one against the other as interest and occasion might require to maintain their ascendancy and continue their reign of oppression."

The stock market continued to soar, Flagpole Kellys continued to sit on poles all over the nation, and more trade unions were hiring efficiency experts to speed up their members. "What is American Can doing?" was the first question of newspaper readers unless they were drawn to Kolster Radio or some other sure thing such as Morgan's German bonds. Luscious Peaches Heenan was suing old Daddy Browning for doing things, the tabloids said, that an old man, or any other man, should not think of doing. The New Unionism, as it was called, was triumphant with its labor banks and investment houses, and the long fight for industrial unionism was, or so it seemed, as dead as the IWW.

"The country," said President Coolidge on Dec. 4, 1928, in his last message to Congress, "can regard the present with satisfaction and anticipate the future with optimism."

---

no discriminatory rules, nevertheless commonly relegate Negroes to an inferior status in segregated locals. Machinations by unions against Negro workingmen sank to an all-time low when, in 1941, the Brotherhood of Locomotive Firemen and Enginemen and twenty-one railroad companies entered into an agreement to completely eliminate colored firemen from the industry.

The constitution of the CIO states that one of its objectives is to "bring about the effective organization of workingmen and women of America regardless of race, color, creed or nationality." While the practices of some CIO locals are discriminatory, in general CIO unions have non-discriminatory policies. In the AFL the United Mine Workers and International Ladies' Garment Workers Union are non-discriminatory.

Among independent unions, the United Electrical, Radio and Machine Workers of America; the Fur and Leather Workers Union and the International Union of Mine, Mill and Smelter Workers, not only do not practice racial discrimination but actively fight it.

And Herbert Hoover, in his successful campaign for the Presidency against Democrat Al Smith, declared on July 27, 1928, "The outlook for the world today is for the greatest era of commercial expansion in our history."

Bruce Barton was describing Christ as the First Big Business Man, declaring that American business was only practical Christianity. The Rev. Christian Reisner, of New York's Broadway Temple, said he "loved big business men" and that they were the highest expression of spiritual development. Big Business had won the day. It was supreme. Jefferson and Sylvis, the Molly Maguires, the Populists, Parsons, and Debs were only forgotten dust in a glorious present. And nothing was more dead than a vital labor movement.

Many trade unionists gave up the ghost as far as industrial unionism was concerned. The fight of a half century or more seemed lost. But far beneath surface appearances, and unnoticed amid the general hossanah to a victorious Big Business, men and events were steadily combining into necessary new patterns that would not be fully evident for almost a decade. Members of the Trade Union Educational League in auto, railroad, rubber, marine, steel, coal, packing, textile, machinists, printing, and the needle trades were talking to their shopmates about industrial unionism, about an end to discrimination, an end to the competing, futile craft set-up, an end to sell-outs, gangsters, and bureaucracy. The overwhelming needs of the time gave force to their words, power to their initiative.

Members of the Trade Union Educational League, that effective meeting place of radicals and middle-of-the-roaders, of Communists and moderates who could not stand the sell-out policies of the AFL, led a whole series of important strikes. The TUEL was the source of the militant trade union activity of the time. Workers rallied to it by the tens of thousands, as the only instrument of getting sorely needed raises, fighting not only the employers, but gangsters, goons, and police, who attacked their drive for improved working conditions with the old cry of "Red!" During the late 1920's the top leaders of the AFL did all in their power to smash the broad united front movements within their organization, calling them Moscow conspiracies. Not long after they repeated these tactics in their fight against the CIO.

The Trade Union Educational League, often including elements far to the right and backed by the broadest possible groupings of rank and file, led strikes in textile, coal, and the needle trades. The AFL officials, still clinging to their no-strike policies, fought the militants so remorselessly, openly sabotaging huge struggles for pay raises and shorter hours while expelling literally thousands on thousands of their own members, that the inevitable result was the founding of new independent unions in textile, coal, and the needle trades. These were formed under the TUEL and later under the Trade Union Unity League, established by broad united front forces in 1929 with Foster as secretary.

While AFL officials were cooperating with employers by acting as a brake upon their membership, the TUEL was leading the famous Passaic strike of New Jersey textile workers in 1926. It was leading the walkout of 26,000 cotton workers in New Bedford, and the most notable textile strike of the period, the Gastonia strike of 1929 in North Carolina.

The Gastonia strikers, earning as little as $10 a week and almost half of them women from North Carolina farms, were attacked as agents of Moscow. The governor, owner of a textile mill, called out the National Guard to protect the state against what he called a foreign conspiracy. Attacked by police, deputy sheriffs, militia, and American Legion vigilantes, the men and women of the textile factories fought with such fury that on more than one occasion they routed their attackers.

On April 18, vigilantes attacked the union hall and wrecked it, wounding several workers. On June 7 the vigilantes returned, led by Chief of Police Aderholt, who was killed in the battle. Ella May Wiggin, a mother and one of the most beloved of the strike leaders was also killed. Seven strike leaders were sentenced to prison, some for twenty years.

Thousands of coal miners, rebelling against the passivity of the United Mine Workers under an employer assault which was losing the union huge areas in Pennsylvania, West Virginia, Ohio, Kentucky, and Alabama, formed a Save The Union Committee under the TUEL. It had the militant backing of at least half of the membership of UMW as it organized the unorganized and became the heart of the 1927 miners' bituminous strike. During the strike the committee had more than 100,000 members but when the strike was lost mass expulsion of the militants followed, further weakening a sick union in a sick industry. It was then that the National Miners Union was organized in Pittsburgh in 1928.

The most important and violent of all the strikes of this period took place on the sidewalks of New York. There the fur and needle trades workers, many of them women, the majority of them Jewish but also including Negroes, Greeks, Hungarians, Slavs, and Italians, fought gangsters and police, both urged on by the leadership of their own AFL unions, with a bravery equal to that of the Colorado metal miners. Women, many of them far from young, shawls around their heads, battled with club-swinging police while their men folk struggled with armed gangsters. Both police and gangsters shouted against communism as they slugged, clubbed, stabbed, and shot. But when the 1926 strike of the furriers, led by Ben Gold and the TUEL, was all over the people of the sidewalks of New York had won a forty-hour five-day week.

The furriers' union, like the International Ladies' Garment Workers Union, was led by right-wing Socialists who had formed an alliance with the most reactionary of the AFL hierarchy. The furriers' union, particularly, had become little more than an employment agency for the manufacturers, who dominated the union as effectively as they dominated the underpaid industry whose 12,000 workers had nothing to say about their conditions of work or the operation of their union. Pay averaged $18 a week—when the furriers were working—in a seasonal, chaotic, sweatshop industry characterized by mass lay-offs and arbitrary discharge.

Gangsters policed sell-out contracts, slugged any who objected or questioned union policy. "In no union in the American labor movement," wrote a newspaper reporter in the early 1920's, "is gangsterism such a big factor as in the Furriers Union. The officialdom of the furriers outbid every other officialdom in the extent of using violence to gain and hold control of the organization." It was an ironclad rule that no member of the union was allowed to question or criticize the administration. Any attempt to do so was invariably met with a slugging from the hired gangsters who kept order at all union meetings. "Do you know," asked a letter to the progressive Jewish paper, *Freiheit,* "that no member dares criticize the administration lest he be beaten mercilessly . . . that almost every week a worker is beaten?"

It was to fight such conditions that the Furriers Section of the TUEL was born in 1922. A typical incident of the time was the stabbing and beating of Ben Gold at an open union meeting when he dared to ask Morris Kaufman, president of the international, for details as to a contract that had just been signed. "Whoever asks questions tonight," announced President Kaufman, "will pay for it with his blood." When Gold and Max Suroff persisted, the goons jumped into action with knives, chairs, and the butt end of revolvers. Gold's head required eleven stitches but it was he who was arrested for assault.

Such attacks, however, only strengthened the TUEL leadership, and while the manufacturers and AFL officials shouted "Moscow plot!" New York's whole rank and file in fur soon rallied behind Gold and others in a broad united front. The progressive forces took over the New York leadership of the furriers' union, being overwhelmingly elected to the New York Joint Board in 1925, the controlling and administrating body in New York City.

The great 1926 strike came when the furriers demanded the five-day forty-hour week and a 25 per cent increase in wages. The first day of the seventeen-week strike is described by Philip S. Foner in his history of the Fur and Leather Workers Union:

"Ten thousand strikers responded to Gold's call on Monday, March 8. The police lunged into the mass of workers and beat down hundreds of strikers, men and women. The workers fought back. Frail girls leaped up fearlessly and returned blows squarely in the policemen's faces. As the line of strikers continued to forge ahead, police in patrol cars drove with breakneck speed into large numbers of workers on the sidewalk. Still the mass of strikers did not budge. In spite of every new assault by mounted police and motorized squads, the line grew. In the face of this immovable force the police were powerless. Finally the great mass of pickets broke through completely and marched triumphantly to the strike halls. Besides the hundreds of strikers beaten up in that single demonstration, one hundred men and twenty-five women were arrested."

Such scenes were repeated almost every day until thousands had been injured, hundreds arrested, scores sentenced to prison. But the virtually unanimous militancy of the strikers behind Gold prevented defeat, and a 10 per cent wage increase and the unprecedented five-day work week resulted.

But that was just the beginning of the struggle. The AFL expelled the 12,000 victorious strikers and their leaders. The International, aided by Green, Matthew Woll, and Ed McGrady, induced the manufacturers to break the 1926 contract and deal with the old and repudiated leadership of the furriers. Gold and others of the united front who had won the strike were arrested and some were imprisoned, under the charge of forcing entry into a manufacturer's establishment; the real charge, thoroughly aired at the so-called trial, was that the strike was only a rehearsal for Red Revolution. Wages went back to $18 and hours up to fifty. In 1927 the strike had to be fought all over again to enforce the 1926 contract. A. C. Sedgwick described the treatment of arrested strikers in *The New York Times:*

"One detective takes a piece of rubber hose, which is part of the equipment of the detectives bureau and is favored because it leaves no marks. Another takes out his blackjack. Others grab for anything—blackjacks and nightsticks. The prisoners fall to the floor. The blood pours from their faces. They spit and cough blood. The detectives, still in a rage, look at them. A young policeman in a uniform pokes his head in. 'You fellers is easy with 'em,' he says. 'Is that so?' roars a detective and kicks a prisoner in the face, pulls him to his feet, props him against the desk, then with the butt end of his revolver makes a gash in his head. . . ."

But this strike, too, was won. The forty-hour five-day week was restored, as was the wage increase. There were similar struggles in the International Ladies' Garment Workers, the rank and file fighting for democratic trade unionism and better conditions against a leadership allied with the bureaucracy of the AFL. Such struggles as these were the reality of American life behind all the golden froth of the Golden Twenties. It was men and women fighting for a better life amid conditions that would have discouraged those less brave that was remarkable—not the rise of American Can and the stock market.

4. Disaster

The Golden Insanity built on red scares and graft, on the open shop and wild gambling, ended where all refusals to face reality end.

In late October of 1929 the bubble burst. Its symbol was the tumbling stock market where nearly 25 billions of dollars in stock market values were wiped out almost overnight. Its reality was the fact that big monopoly, ever eager to increase its already swollen profits, expanded plant capacity and production to such an extent that there was an overproduction of producers' goods (machinery, factories, iron and steel) and consumer commodities (cotton, wheat, textiles)—all at the expense of the American people. While employers kept the wages of most Americans below the minimum needed to supply even the basic necessities of life, they drove their workers to speed up production, thus producing more and more at less and less cost to themselves. As a result of such speed-up and low wage policies, employers saw their profits zooming and instead of more equitably distributing these, regularly plowed part of them back into production. Under the circumstances the American people were unable to buy back what they had produced.

As banker Frank Vanderlip admitted: "Capital kept too much and labor did not have enough to buy its share of things." In short, the depression of '29, like those of '73, '84, '93, '07, and '21, was the result of the inherent contradiction between an industry socially operated and privately owned; between an economy operated by the many who received little and owned by the few who received almost everything. And, for that matter, the Federal Government itself was soon to declare in its famous TNEC report on monopoly, "A more nearly perfect mechanism for making the poor poorer and the rich richer or for making depressions could scarcely be devised."

And so the whole vast economy of the nation, its mills, factories, mines, its stores, transport, and distribution, came to a slow, grinding stop or at the best proceeded at about half speed. Some 5,761 banks failed. Gross farm income dropped from 12 billions of dollars to a little over five billions. Wage cuts came one after the other until they averaged forty-five per cent for all industry. Industrial production dropped by almost fifty per cent. By 1933 there were anywhere from 12,000,000 to 17,000,000 unemployed.

There was food, millions of tons of it. But people soon were starving as the food was destroyed or left to rot because it could not be sold at a profit. There was clothing, warehouses filled with it, and millions were shivering for lack of it as the depression continued but the clothing could not be used to keep the people warm because the people had no money to buy it.

There were warm houses, thousands of them, but empty now, as thousands of evicted suffered cold, rain, wind, and snow in the leaky tarpaper shacks in the Hoovervilles built on garbage dumps that became a common feature of the American scene.

And yet as the breadlines and apple stands of the unemployed increased in number, leaders of the country were not dismayed. The great thinkers and statesmen of business, finance and industry were well nigh unanimous in declaring that there was nothing to worry about. Not long before the crash President Hoover had declared, "We in America today are nearer to the final triumph over poverty than ever before in the history of any land. The poorhouse is vanishing from among us."

As the suffering of the depression deepened the country's leaders were daily stripped more bare. Revered as the repositories of all wisdom and virtue, they seemed determined to prove that they had neither. One of the country's leading crusaders against communism, Andrew Mellon, "the greatest secretary of the treasury since Alexander Hamilton," on May 5, 1931, declared there should be no pay cuts in industry. On October 1 of the same year he reduced the wages of all his thousands of employees in the Mellon-dominated Aluminum Company by 10 per cent.

On March 18, 1931, Henry Ford, who had spent millions in fighting what he called the Jewish conspiracy, declared that the depression came about because "The average man won't really do a day's work unless he is caught and cannot get out of it. There is plenty of work to do if people would do it." A few weeks later he closed down the Ford plant, throwing 75,000 men out of work.

On Dec. 1, 1930, Charles M. Schwab, leader of the steel industry and a staunch opponent of trade unions, declared, "I know that our normal trend is upward and onward" and not long later Bethlehem and United States Steel ordered a 10 per cent wage cut. In November, 1930, Alfred P. Sloan, Jr., chairman of General Motors and a fighter for the open shop, said, "I see no reason why 1931 should not be an extremely good year." When the year arrived, he ordered 10 to 20 per cent reductions in wages.

By 1932 there were 10,000,000 unemployed and people began to wonder if it was really the reds that had been menacing them. It was easy enough to see the menace in testimony before the Senate Subcommittee of the Committee on Manufacturing investigating unemployment relief. But it was a little difficult for most to see how that menace came from the Communists. On Jan. 4, 1932, Governor Pinchot of Pennsylvania was testifying before the committee. He read into the record a whole series of letters from the unemployed and their families which were typical of conditions all over the United States.

Some of the letters follow:

"This is the first time in my life that I have asked for help, but the way things are now I must. I have been out of work for a long time and my wife is sick in bed and needs medicine, and no money to buy nothing to eat and what is a fellow going to do. I don't want to steal but I won't let my wife and boy cry for something to eat.

"I owe $200 in the building loan association and they are coming to take our home. . . . How is a fellow going to pay when he hasn't got any money? I am willing to work anywhere at anything, but can not find nothing. How long is this going to keep up? O, if God would only open a way. I am sorry I have to ask you but hunger drives me to do this. I will ask before I steal, as Governor of our State, I beg for help. I am drove to this being out of work, and no money. What is wrong with this country, anyway?"

And a second letter said:

"There are nine of us in the family. My father is out of work for a couple of months and we haven't got a thing eat in the house. Mother is getting $12 a month of the county. If mother don't get any more help we will have to starve to death. I am a little girl 10 years old. I go to school every day. My other sister hain't got any shoes or clothes to wear to go to school. My mother goes in her bare feet and she crys every night that we don't have the help. I guess that is all, hoping to hear from you."

Another letter had informed the Governor:

"My four motherless children and I, the father, are on the verge of freezing and starving. Being several months out of work, I have no money to buy coal, food or winter clothes for my school children. Being many months back with my rent the landlord attempts to evict me from his premises. Two of my children are ill. So please, Mr. Governor, be kind and render your assistance as soon as possible, for my children are hungry and I with them; please assist us from cold and hunger, Mr. Gov. Pinchot."

Testifying before the same Senate committee, Prentice Murphy, director of the Children's Bureau of Philadelphia, said:

"If the modern state is to rest upon a firm foundation, its citizens must not be allowed to starve. Some of them do. They do not die quickly. You can starve for a long time without dying."

Other testimony before the committee told of no fewer than two hundred women sleeping in Grant and Lincoln Parks in Chicago during September, 1931; and of 478 men and 17 women living in a small Pittsburgh park, among them a war veteran, his wife, and their four-month-old infant. A Chicago committee, investigating city garbage dumps, reported, "Around the truck which was unloading garbage and other refuse were about 35 men, women and children. As soon as the truck pulled away from the pile all of them started digging with sticks, some with their hands, grabbing bits of food and vegetables."

By 1933 a third of the nation, some 40,000,000 men, women, and children, were living without benefit of industrial or other normal income, each one having his own individual story of suffering and blasted hopes. Perhaps the children suffered most. By August of 1932 according to the Children's Bureau of the Department of Labor, 200,000 of them were wandering across the country searching for food. President Hoover himself stated that "there are at least 10,000,000 deficient children in this country." In 1932 a municipal hospital spokesman wrote, "This week we have had four children admitted with the diagnosis of starvation. One, who was found eating out of a garbage can, has died since admission."

And *The New York Times* of June 6, 1932, had this item:

"Eugene Olsen, 16 years old, a senior at George Washington High School, standing high in his classes and especially interested in scientific studies, committed suicide by hanging himself with a dumbwaiter cord in the basement storeroom that was his home. His father, a carpenter, had been out of work for several months. Unable to pay the rent, the family had been evicted and were occupying a basement storeroom rent-free. The father said the only reason he could give for the boy's suicide was worry over their financial condition."

Hundreds of small businessmen committed suicide as their concerns failed. but Big Business grew steadily larger as President Franklin Delano Roosevelt told Congress in 1938 when he said, "in time of depression bigger business has opportunities to grow bigger still at the expense of smaller competitors." Thousands of men, with the old feeling that they were failures, holding themselves personally accountable for a national calamity, sat silently in kitchens as their grandfathers had done in the depression of 1873, maddening desperation simmering within them. Thousands of young married people went home to their parents, who were often also unemployed, and people sleeping in the living room, in the kitchen, on the floor everywhere were a common mark of the depression.

"For a farmer to buy a good toothbrush," said John A. Simpson, president of the National Farmers' Union, in 1932, "he would have to sell eight dozen eggs and he then would owe two cents. A farmer must sell forty pounds of cotton to buy a good shirt." On April 4, 1932, Senator Huey Long of Louisiana told the Senate that 504 super-millionaires made more money in 1929 than the combined income of 2,300,000 farmers raising wheat and cotton. Thousands of farmers were being "tractored" out of their homes after foreclosure, a tractor hired by a bank or loan company crumpling the rickety old homestead as the ousted family stood by. Then they took to the road in a battered jalopy, loaded with a crazy pile of pathetic furniture, often heading for nowhere, often for California.

Sometimes it seemed as if the whole nation was on the road, searching for a job and a square meal, scrawny children peering out of wheezingly decrepit cars at those fortunate enough to have homes and food. Freight trains swarmed with an army of young people, who long since had left broken homes and now moved over the country, living in hobo jungles and empty boxcars. Thousands of young people graduated from school into long years of morale-shattering unemployment.

In at least a quarter of the nation's industries women received less pay than men for the same work, according to a government study under Robert S. Keebler. Wages of $5, $6, and $7 a week for full-time work for women were common. The wages of Negro women, the most oppressed of all workers, were even lower than those of white women. In Virginia, for example, in 1932, white women received 21 cents an hour in the food industries while Negro women were receiving 16½ cents an hour, and 27 cents an hour in textile while Negro women received 16 cents.

And according to an old American custom the wages of white workers were kept low by paying Negroes even less. Through a similar custom, in which Negroes are always the last to be hired and the first to be fired, a higher percentage of Negroes were without work than any other group. Three-quarters of Negro wage earners in New Jersey, for example, were unemployed on Jan. 15, 1934. The destitution of the nation's Negro families was twice as great as that of white families, according to an unemployment relief census taken by the federal government in October, 1933.

The appointment of committees and commissions was President Hoover's way of dealing with the depression. He took no action to help the unemployed, backed the wage cuts, and favored "staggered employment," that is, part-time employment in an effort to spread jobs. Feeling that it was the employers who needed help, he organized the Reconstruction Finance Corporation, which loaned two billions of the taxpayers' money to industry and finance on the theory that their prosperity would "trickle down" to the common people. It did not.

In general the officials of the American Federation of Labor backed the President. They did not oppose the wage-cutting program nor did they offer any program of their own for the relief of the unemployed. There were virtually no AF of L strikes in resistance to wage cuts as William Green, Matthew Woll and others of the hierarchy joined President Hoover in assuring the workers that "prosperity was just around the corner." Following the lead of the National Association of Manufacturers and the United States Chamber of Commerce, the AF of L, one year after the crisis began, went on record against unemployment insurance. Green characterized unemployment insurance as "a hindrance to progress," "a dole" which would degrade "the dignity of the workingman" and "subsidize idleness." As Green took his stand, the United States Chamber of Commerce described unemployment insurance as Communism, declared those fighting for it were un-Americans "trying to sap the initiative of the American people."

Within a year of the depression's beginning American workers were beginning to realize that they would gain nothing from Hoover or the AFL top leadership, nothing that they did not win by their own united struggles. By 1930 there were great hunger marches demanding public aid, huge demonstrations against unemployment, mass fights against evictions. Farmers were coming together to oppose evictions and mortgage sales, to withhold produce from the market in strikes against prices that were less than the cost of production.

At one of their darkest hours the American people, fighting, suffering, and learning, began the great struggles that were to culminate in great victories.

CHAPTER IX

Grapes of Wrath

> "If you think by hanging us you can stamp out the
> labor movement . . . the movement from which the
> down-trodden millions, the millions who toil in want
> and misery, expect salvation, if this is your opinion,
> then hang us!
>
> "Here you will tread upon a spark, but there and there,
> behind you and in front of you, and everywhere, flames
> blaze up. It is a subterranean fire. You cannot put it
> out."
>
> AUGUST SPIES, BEFORE BEING SENTENCED TO
> DEATH IN THE EIGHT-HOUR-DAY FRAME-UP IN
> CHICAGO, 1886.

1. The Fall and Rise of Mr. Grossup

The triumph that the Molly Maguires had never found, that had eluded
Parsons and been denied to Debs, was about to arrive and it was sweet
when it came at last.

Almost a hundred years of struggle was on the point of merging with
the necessity of the moment. The spur of wage cuts and unemployment was
driving men to a painful progress. The seed of industrial unionism, watered
by the blood of Spies and countless members of the Knights of Labor and
the Industrial Workers of the World, was beginning to grow.

What argument could not prove the developing facts of life revealed.
Persuasion had not been able to convince most workers of the value of industrial unionism but great new battles on the picket line did convince
them. The nightstick and tear gas are great educators and they were freely
used throughout the thirties. A cop's club on the skull inclines one to believe in the class conflict. Confinement in a cell for shouting "Scab!" often
makes one wonder if the law is really neutral. Retching from the effects of

vomiting gas, as the troops advance with bayonets, the victim sometimes doubts whether the sole function of the military is national defense.

Such occurrences as these, and they happened everywhere during the six years preceding formation of the CIO, prepared the soil for it. Solidarity, it was found, was not a noble sentiment but a rock-bottom requirement for living during the most severe depression in history. When the CIO exploded over the land in 1936, organizing on an industrial basis the great open-shop citadels of steel, coal, glass, rubber, auto, marine, electrical, and other mass industries almost overnight, it sometimes seemed as if the great event had occurred as suddenly as a flash of lightning.

But the subterranean fire of which Spies spoke had been smoldering. The CIO was the leaping flame suddenly blazing bright in the long night of the open shop. There was in fact a sudden boiling over of the American working class. But there had been a six-year simmering, six years of learning, six years of preparation through hunger marches and struggles of the unemployed; through battles against evictions and pay cuts and for unemployment insurance; through struggles of the new industrial unions which the AFL bureaucrats were everywhere trying to break up into crafts.

Unity was just a word used by agitators until actuality made it a necessity for survival. It was this unity, searched for and pursued down many a blind path during the years immediately preceding the CIO, that was the basis for that organization's triumph. But it came slowly. It had to be fought for. It was gained through painful experience, often personally suffered.

The depression was like some natural physical catastrophe, a flood, tornado, or hurricane, bringing monumental hardship in its wake. It was understood as little by the average man as if it had been some arbitrary disaster of nature. But, unlike a hurricane, it did not blow itself out. It continued year after year, 1929, 1930, 1931, 1932, 1933, getting worse and worse, stronger and stronger, stripping millions of jobs and shelter, forcing millions to the homeless road; spreading to Latin America and Europe, enveloping nations and continents, the proud empire of Britain, France, Germany, Italy, Austria, the Balkans, all of Africa and Asia. World production fell by 42 per cent while world trade decreased by 65 per cent. There were some fifty millions of unemployed in all parts of the world.

But the Red Cross did not come after the depression struck. There was no rallying of forces or coming together to care for the sick and hungry although their number, increasing daily, was far greater than those injured or made homeless by tornado or earthquake. At first each man was alone, often sitting silently in his home, hiding his unemployment and growing poverty as if it were a shameful disease. Unlike a hurricane, the ravages of the depression could not be seen clearly in a well-defined path of destruction. Instead it was everywhere, and for a long time things looked almost as usual. But behind the cold, expressionless fronts of tenements, houses, and apartments, inside and concealed from the public gaze, men and women struggled alone at first, viewing their plight as personal, private disasters, a slow and dreadful panic rising within them.

Such was the position of Peter Grossup,[1] a tall, slim man of fifty-five, with a white, cliff-like face and a habit of comfortable silence. A skilled cabinetmaker, he had worked for twenty-six years for the Tonti Custom Furniture Company in a Middlewestern city of 300,000. Until he was laid off on Jan. 1, 1930, he had always regarded himself and his life with quiet satisfaction. He liked what was his. He liked his house, on which he owed only $1,800 on a first mortgage, and he liked his wife and two children. Mary, seventeen, attended the Sacred Heart Academy, and George, nineteen, was about to complete his first year at the state university.

Those times after supper in the easy chair were the times he liked best. He never said much but he'd rattle *The Daily Record* open and read, half listening to the radio. He liked that Cameron fellow on the Ford Hour. A lot of sense. A man got what he earned. You got no more out of life than you put into it. After such a thought he'd sneak a look at Fanny in the kitchen, usually wearing her old gray sweater, and sometimes when the dishes were done she'd sit for a time beside him on the little leather seat that went with his chair. Occasionally he would fumble for her work-roughened fingers and turn them around so that he could see the plain band, the wedding ring he had given her twenty-one years before. He liked that ring.

That's the way evenings had been before he had been fired on Jan. 1, 1930. Eighteen months later, in the summer of 1931, they weren't much like that. Mr. Grossup still sat in his easy chair but he sat there all day now, turning things over in his mind, trying to see where he had made his mistake. Maybe if he had gone into electrical engineering, something with a future, things would not have gone this way.

It hadn't been so bad at first. Sometimes he would leave the house, all dressed up in his best, and then he'd walk fast with his back very straight, his face carefully held to bright alertness, trying to look as if he were hurrying to a business appointment. But he always ended up in the park. "Something will turn up," he had told his wife, "the President himself says so." He had $312.62 in the First National Bank when he was laid off. After that went he cashed in a $5,000 insurance policy and got $1,900 for it. If it hadn't been for payments on the mortgage, $58.50 a month, it would have lasted longer.

He had hated to part with his watch and was still always groping for it. It gave him an empty feeling, just like his vacant pocket, when his hand reached in for what wasn't there. He'd received only $15 for it and Fanny had received even less for her wedding ring. "Trying to make a fool out of me," he asked, "pawning your own wedding ring? I suppose you wish

[1] This case history is based on an interview. For obvious reasons the exact name of the town or its location is not indicated.

you'd married somebody else?" Seemed like he'd fly off the handle these days just for anything. Like when she asked him why he didn't go for a walk and he went god-damning around that a man couldn't stay in his own home without being driven out.

Maybe if he had gone into radio things wouldn't have come out this way, Mr. Grossup sometimes thought as he sat in his chair and stared at the opposite wall. He could hear his wife stirring in the kitchen, making the small, rustling noises of a mouse as if she were afraid any louder noise might irritate him. The house was very still now. The two children were gone.

George had had to quit the state university. First he went to Chicago, then to St. Louis, later to Dallas, looking for work. He wished Fanny wouldn't worry so about the boy. He wouldn't fall under any freight. The last time they heard he was in San Diego, bumming his way from Dallas. He missed his daughter Mary. She had married. Mr. Grossup didn't like Mary's husband. Sometimes he even feared that she had gotten out of the house just to make things easier. No money and the man of the house just sitting there doing nothing.

For the last six months notices had been coming from the bank about the lapsed mortgage payments. Any day now. Any day now. He didn't let himself complete the thought. *The Record* was right, of course, when it pointed out that no one with get-up-and-go, no one with real initiative and enterprise, was on relief.

Going down to the county relief office had been the worst. He had had to stand in line with Negroes, and foreigners and people ragged enough to be bums. As a taxpayer and solid citizen he had never believed in the dole. Sure he was a union man but the AFL didn't believe in it either. Well, he hadn't gone there until Fanny and he had been hungry.

He had tried to explain to the social worker at county relief that his case was different. He wasn't a bum. When he got on his feet again—but she had just given him a tired smile, meant to be friendly but seeming mocking to Mr. Grossup, before saying, "Next!" It was hard for two people to live on $12 a month.

If he could only borrow some money for the mortgage. He called the bank but they said it was too late now. The case was in the courts. There would be a judgment any day now.

His wife was standing in the kitchen door looking at him. He pretended not to see her.

"Peter," she said, "I just have to talk to you."

Still he didn't look at her. There was nothing to talk about.

"Peter, we just have to do something!"

"Do something? Do you think I sit here because I like to?"

Mrs. Grossup's mouth quivered.

"Peter, you never used to talk to me that way."

He glared at her. She did not retreat but eyed him firmly.

"I've been talking to Mrs. Flaherty next door. She says if you'd go down to the Unemployment Council on Spear Street we wouldn't be evicted."

Mr. Grossup was honestly shocked.

"Go down to that bunch of Communists? I'd die first!"

"Mr. Flaherty's a member of it. We've got to do something. The sheriff will be here any day now." In his excitement Mr. Grossup rose from his chair and stood grandly alone.

"*The Record* says that bunch is Communistic!"

"They can take my house," he said and his voice broke queerly, "but I am asking no help from any Communist!"

They came the next day. Mr. Grossup couldn't believe it. Even as they began taking down the beds, clumping through the house, moving the old sofa out into the street, he still couldn't believe it. They were robbing him and he was alone. There was no one to help him. There was no police to call on for they were the ones that were doing it. Or at least they were deputy sheriffs.

Mrs. Grossup stood in the kitchen, huddled in a corner so as to be out of the way, her face still and crumpled. Mr. Grossup, like a troubled shadow, followed the deputies in and out, grabbing at furniture that he thought might fall or be scratched. Out on the street he stood bewildered, surrounded by the property which had made his days, the refrigerator, the Atwater Kent, pots and pans, their wedding picture, a framed photograph of George with his high school baseball team, the beds and mattresses upon which they had slept, the dishes from which they had eaten. A deputy was speculatively examining some of Mrs. Grossup's best linen. Neighbors were standing around but Mr. Grossup could not meet their sympathy or even know it was that.

Coming through the door, tottering in the grasp of two deputies who found it hard to grasp securely, was his easy chair and, as Mr. Grossup ran to help, one of the deputies stumbled and the chair crashed down the steps.

"My God!" Mr. Grossup cried, "you can't do that!"

He was conscious of Mr. Flaherty plucking at his sleeve and trying to speak to him but his outrage was so intense that he did not answer him. The deputies were standing on the porch now looking at a group of men and women who had suddenly appeared. A tall Negro, apparently in charge, stood next to Mr. Flaherty.

"Good God!" Mr. Grossup cried again, trying to right his chair and restore the big leather cushion, "you can't treat a man's property that way!"

He looked around, his face twitching. Mr. Flaherty pulled at him again and said, "We're from the Unemployed Council. We want to help."

"Well, my God," shrieked Mr. Grossup, "if you want to help, do something then!"

The tall Negro looked briefly at the five deputies on the porch and then at his thirty unemployed.

"Move it back," he said.

In an instant before Mr. Grossup's very eyes all of his prized possessions, his easy chair, even the big refrigerator, the bed posts, the pictures, everything was streaming back into his home. The neighbors began grabbing pots and pans and mattresses and stumbling a little and laughing wildly and calling out in excited tones, clumping up onto the porch and into the house. There was a little scuffle once on the porch with the deputies but more and more neighbors were helping and they just pressed in.

Mr. Grossup never knew how it all happened. It was a happy blur. He had his home again. He had strength. He had friends. His chair was in its place. His wife seemed suddenly to have grown younger. Police reinforcements appeared but left after looking at the increasing crowd outside. Someone was making coffee and sandwiches in the kitchen.

It was like a party. Everyone was shouting and laughing and Mr. Grossup shook hands with at least two dozen men he had never met before. The Negro leader of the unemployed, Hugh Henderson, a sandwich in his hand, was making a speech from the front porch.

Mr. Grossup somehow found himself making a speech too. "After a life of hard work," he said. "Taking a man's home. It isn't right. They put my chair, everything, out on the street. Worked hard all my life. It isn't right."

There were cheers. Some of the crowd went away but more seemed inside the house. "We'll stay awhile," Mr. Henderson said, "to be sure the police don't come back."

A great tension, an awful loneliness, was slowly seeping from Mr. Grossup's veins. He hadn't known how miserable he had been. A man couldn't do anything by himself. He hadn't known how many people had been going through the same things he had.

Something had happened to him. He felt as if he had broken from the prison of his baffled self. No longer did he sit in his home all day. Still there were times on the picket line or while defying police as he helped move someone else's furniture back in that he wondered at the tight, little inturned man he once had been. And it hadn't been much fun. He was growing under the impact of adversity and most of America was growing similarly.

2. The Battle Cry of Poverty

Hundreds of thousands of Mr. and Mrs. Grossups of every age, trade, creed, national origin, and political belief were coming together to fight the depression in 1932. As they changed, they changed the country. They transformed America from a place of despair to a country of struggle. They astonished themselves, not only by their courage and their militance but by the swiftness with which they learned, throwing aside old beliefs and habits which had brought them nothing but disaster. There were times that a man learned more in an hour about what makes the world go than he had learned previously in a lifetime.

The slow boil was beginning that reached its climax with the CIO. The country was punctuated by picket lines, hunger marches, meetings demanding unemployment insurance and adequate relief. The unemployed had left their tenements and kitchens, the four walls in which they had hidden what they thought was their private shame, and their slogan now was "Don't Starve—Fight!"

Everyone was learning and experience was the teacher. In struggles against evictions and foreclosures, for food and shelter, the social power of people united—a power difficult to come by but absolutely irresistible when achieved—was being slowly perceived. The great lesson might be learned by such a simple occurrence as a man pleading for more relief, separately and alone, and being refused, and then winning the increase a week later when he returned with 5,000 members of the Unemployed Council.

There were Mr. Grossups who were Iowa farmers, crowding around an auctioneer selling a foreclosed homestead, law-abiding, conservative men who now grimly menaced anyone who bid more than a penny for the foreclosed farm. Pushing about a banker or real estate man about to buy the farm, the farmers often suggestively handled a rope as one of their number made the penny purchase and then returned the farm to its foreclosed owner. Despite the aid of neighbors and penny sales, between 1929 and 1933 some 1,000,000 farmers lost their property through foreclosure.

There were Mr. Grossups who were veterans of World War I, already planning their march on Washington to demand the adjusted service pay due them, often called the bonus. But the country hadn't seen anything yet. Police were assaulting hunger marchers, fifteen were killed in such demonstrations in 1932 and eight others were killed upon the picket line, but the great social upheaval in behalf of the common man was just beginning. Through trial and error it was being found that anything that divided was the cardinal sin. Through experience it was being slowly discovered that the spy and stool pigeon were everywhere, and that a man must be judged by performance and not by what newspaper, stool pigeon, or Congressman said of him.

The weapon of the jobless, the organization with which they fought and defended themselves, was the National Unemployed Council. It was organized in Chicago on July 4, 1930, at a convention attended by 1,320 delegates. Until the advent of the CIO it was perhaps the most vital and necessary of all American organizations.[2] It had councils and branches in forty-six states as well as in almost every town and city of the nation.

For the first time in history there was virtually no scabbing during a depression, the unemployed instead appearing on the picket line behind the banner of the Unemployed Council helping win the strikes of those fortu-

[2] In April, 1936, the Unemployed Council merged with the Socialist Workers Alliance and the National Unemployed League. In 1938 it had a membership of 80c,000.

nate enough to be employed. Its primary function was agitation and mass demonstrations to the end that people might be fed. It increased the relief allotments of literally millions, campaigned for public works and unemployment insurance.

Negroes, hardest hit of any section of the population, were among the most active in the Council, which fought militantly against every form of racist discrimination. Such was the Council's power that the AFL reversed its position against unemployment insurance.[8] The fact of its existence prevented the nation from ignoring or forgetting the 12,000,000 to 17,000,000 who were jobless by 1933.

One of the Unemployed Council's big jobs in all parts of the country was the preventing of evictions. Some indication of the vast size of this job can be gained from the fact that in five industrial cities of Ohio alone eviction orders were issued against nearly 100,000 families in the two and a half years beginning in January, 1930. In Chicago 3,611 families, including 26,515 children, were evicted during the year beginning in December, 1931. During the eight months ending June 30, 1932, some 185,794 families in New York City were served with dispossess notices. But 77,000 of these families were moved back into their premises by the people of the Unemployed Council.

On Feb. 2, 1932, the *New York Times* described the eviction of three families in the Bronx:

"Probably because of the cold, the crowd numbered only 1,000, although in unruliness it equalled the throng of 4,000 that stormed the police in the first disorder of a similar nature on January 22. On Thursday a dozen more families are to be evicted unless they pay back rents.

"Inspector Joseph Leonary deployed a force of fifty detectives and mounted and foot patrolmen through the street as Marshal Louis Novick led ten furniture movers into the building. Their appearance was the signal for a great clamor. Women shrieked from the windows, the different sections of the crowd hissed and booed and shouted invectives. Fighting began simultaneously in the house and in the street. The marshal's men were rushed on the stairs and only got to work after the policemen had driven the tenants back into their apartments."

And on February 27 the *New York Times* described a similar scene under the headline, "1,500 Fight Police To Aid Rent Strike."

[8] Louis Weinstock of the Painters' Union did as much as any man to make unemployment insurance an actuality for the American worker. He headed the AFL Committee for Unemployment Insurance and Relief. This committee won the support for unemployment insurance of five international unions, thirty-five city central councils, six state federations, and almost 3,000 local unions. In 1953 Weinstock was sentenced to three years in prison for alleged violation of the thought-control Smith Act.

From the first the Unemployed Council was attacked as a Communist organization, and it was true enough that Communists gave it their backing
and were active in it. From the first hundreds of thousands of non-Communists in the Unemployed Councils were faced with the question of
whether they should leave an organization fighting militantly in their behalf or continue fighting for themselves in its ranks. They rejected all incite-
ments toward witch hunts, declared that division through political purges
meant weakness and further hardship for the unemployed, condemned
Matthew Woll, AFL leader, who charged that the unemployed movement
was only a Kremlin conspiracy.

From the first, too, the demonstrations and hunger marches were regarded by police and government as initial steps in revolution. The police
in a score of cities jailed and clubbed the unemployed with an almost unprecedented ferocity, justifying their actions on the grounds that the jobless
were trying to overthrow the government.

The first nationwide protest against unemployment was called by the
Trade Union Unity League and the Communist Party on March 6, 1930.
On that date huge meetings were held in all parts of the country, an esti-
mated 1,250,000 unemployed participating in them. More than 100,000
demonstrators gathered in Detroit. Some 50,000 came together in Chicago.
A like number met in Pittsburgh and there were huge crowds of unem-
ployed at meetings in Milwaukee, Cleveland, Los Angeles, San Francisco,
Denver, Seattle, and Philadelphia.

In New York 110,000 packed Union Square. Suddenly the vast throng
was attacked by 25,000 police. Hundreds were beaten to the ground with
nightsticks, scores trampled by the charge of mounted police. The police
went as insane as they had fifty-six years before when they clubbed the
unemployed at New York's Tompkins Square, and their excuse in 1930
was identical with that of 1874. The jobless, they said, were Communists.

A *New York World* reporter, describing the assault at Union Square, told
of:

". . . women struck in the face with blackjacks, boys beaten by gangs of
seven and eight policemen, and an old man backed into a doorway and knocked
down time after time, only to be dragged to his feet and struck with fist and
club.

". . . detectives, some wearing reporters' cards in hat bands, many wearing no badges, running wildly through the crowd, screaming as they beat those
who looked like Communists.

". . . . men with blood streaming down their faces dragged into the temporary police headquarters and flung down to await the patrol wagons to cart
them away."

Hundreds of the unemployed were arrested as was the case in Detroit, too,
where police also attacked the demonstration.

But the unemployed movement strengthened and grew; the demand for unemployed insurance became increasingly irresistible.

Even the notorious Fish Committee created in 1930 to investigate Communism could not frighten the American people with the time-hallowed cry of "Red." Said Congressman Fiorello H. La Guardia of New York, attacking the Fish Committee on the floor of Congress:

"I would sooner spend that money [money to be used to investigate Communism] for something necessary, for something constructive in the way of solving the unemployment problem. Remove the cause of discontent and there will be no danger of Communistic activity. But if there is unemployment, if there is want, suffering and hunger, no investigation by Congress on communism will stifle resentment. Every open shopper will call everyone who seeks to protect the interests of the workers a bolshevik. Let us not be enticed away on an appeal for security into a movement for the open shop, to destroy labor unions in this country."

Fish Committee or no Fish Committee, demonstrations of the unemployed went on. Three thousand members of the Unemployed Council marching in St. Louis forced the passage at city hall of two relief bills. In Chicago 5,000 members of the Council forced the improvement of conditions involving 20,000 jobless living in municipal lodgings. With most cities approaching bankruptcy, with President Hoover still staunchly against federal relief, unemployment insurance, or anything except loans to Big Business, such demonstrations were necessary to avoid starvation. Their value is attested by Mauritz H. Hallgren, who wrote in his *Seeds of Revolt:*

"Social workers everywhere told me that without street demonstrations and hunger marches of the Unemployed Councils no relief whatever would have been provided in some communities, while in others even less help than that which had been extended, would have been forthcoming."

As banks continued to fail while factories increasingly closed down and unemployment continued to rise, the prestige of the National Unemployed Council steadily mounted. Its leaders had a program—federal relief, unemployed insurance, public works, the elimination of discrimination against the Negro people—which was more than could be said for the frightened leaders of business and government, baffled and chastened by a disaster which they could neither understand nor control. Day by day the world seemed to grow more topsy-turvy, a world in which the jobless acted with increasing unity and confidence, in which the great sulked in semiretirement.

In December, 1932, the Unemployed Council organized a national hunger march on Washington while stout, silver-haired old gentlemen in various Union Leagues and other exclusive clubs whispered again of the threat of revolution and of the guillotine. As columns from all over the country, their approach synchronized by careful organization, converged on Washington, coming on foot, on freights, in broken-down jalopies, panic seized Senators and lobbyists, Cabinet members and retired admirals. Congressmen demanded protection, prophesied revolution, and as the tattered army marched down Pennsylvania Avenue troops were mobilized for instant action at forts and installations encircling the nation's capital.

There were only 3,000 of the hungry, but they were the menacing representatives of millions like themselves. The police had arrested Coxey in 1894, during a similar Washington demonstration, for walking on the grass, but there were no arrests in 1932. The parade was flanked by three times as many police as the number in the line of march and there was consternation when the marchers' band played on the steps of the Capitol.

A delegation was received by crusty Charlie Curtis, Republican Vice President and politician from Kansas, who trembled with rage at the duty forced upon him. "Don't cast any reflections on me!" he cried in a querulous, old man's voice. "You just hand me your petition; you needn't make any speech. I have only a few minutes time."

Cactus Jack Garner, Democratic Speaker of the House, equally testy and equally reluctant to receive the delegation, addressed the chairman as Mr. Levinsky. When the chairman said his name was Levinson, Mr. Garner said, "What's the difference?" He waited impatiently for the petition for unemployment insurance and then hurried away without a word, obviously feeling that the starving should starve quietly, without benefit of bands, marches, and petitions.

But the starving were not quiet in 1932. In the South Negro and white sharecropper were coming together in the Sharecroppers Union. Ralph Gray, its Negro leader in Alabama, was lynched by a mob after the union passed resolutions hailing the international fight to save nine Negro youths, the Scottsboro Boys, condemned to death on a charge of rape although even one of the women allegedly raped said that it was a frame-up and no attack had ever taken place. The Negro people were in motion to an extent in excess of anything since Reconstruction. Almost half of the hunger marchers in the Washington demonstration had been Negroes and their initiative and courage were manifest in all of the actions of the unemployed.

As the sharecroppers of the South fought off mobs and violence in 1932, the farmers of Iowa, Illinois, North Dakota, Nebraska, and New York were grabbing pitchforks and wrenches, setting up roadblocks and barricades upon the routes that led to markets. Thousands of them were on strike against prices so low that crops were being sold for less than cost. They were following the old advice of the Populists to "raise less corn and more hell!" Stones crashed through the windshields of farmers who sought to run the blockades and sell their produce. Milk was dumped, trucks were wrecked, their drivers beaten, vegetables and grain scattered to the roadside. The *New York Times* reported on Aug. 16, 1932, from Sioux City, Iowa:

"Scores of trucks loaded with milk, farm products and livestock headed for Sioux City have been turned back today on nearly every highway after the drivers have been warned in no uncertain terms.

"More than forty trucks were halted . . . north of the city, where hundreds of farmers had gathered.

"A few trucks crashed through a steel cable which was stretched across a bridge, but were blocked a second time when railroad ties were thrown under the wheels."

Other trucks were stopped when pitchforks were used to puncture tires. Still others by stretched barbed wire, boards with nails, and barricades of logs. At Leeds, Iowa, according to the *New York Times,* "one milk truck went through the farmers' lines, but pickets smashed the windshield with sticks and rocks."

As the farmers of Iowa were planning their strike early in 1932, thousands of unemployed Ford workers in Detroit, led by the Unemployed Council, were also planning action to better their condition. In February Edsel Ford, son of Henry, had issued a statement in which he had apparently generously offered to help unemployed Ford workers, of whom there were then 85,000. Taking him at his word, his former employees decided to march to the plant at Dearborn on March 7, 1932, when they were to present a program through which they could be re-employed.

Philip Bonosky writes of the hunger march to Dearborn which ended in massacre by Ford police of Ford workers:

"It was early, it was cold when the first of the unemployed Ford workers (many of whom had been laid off only the day before) arrived at Baby Creek Bridge. They were a small gray group, and they stood slapping their sides, warding off the cold, and wondering if they alone would come. And then, one by one, emerging with hunched shoulders from Miller Road, others joined them; and then suddenly a hundred workers with banners came briskly marching, and cheers and singing broke forth.

"Then truckloads rolled in from Dearborn, Lincoln Park, Melvindale, Ercorse—yes, from Inkster, too. As each arrived, the marchers were greeted with more cheers, with louder and more triumphant songs, with great laughter. Old friends found old friends; there were hugs and handshakes, and a great impatience to get going.

"The leaders arrived: Al Goetz, Communist and chairman of the Michigan Unemployed Council; Joe York, district organizer of the Young Communist League, a fresh, strong-faced boy of barely nineteen; James Ashford, young Negro worker, active in the organization of the unemployed and in the campaign to free the Scottsboro Boys. (He carried a banner: FREE THE SCOTTSBORO BOYS!) There were others—names that would never be forgotten, but now only simple, ordinary people: young Joe Bussell, Joe DeBlasio, Coleman Leny. . . ."

The army of unemployed Ford workers, their banners shining in the uncertain sunlight of the late winter morning, advances toward the great stern plant in which most had spent years of their lives building Ford cars and one of the greatest American fortunes. But their fortune is unemployment. As they approach the Dearborn city line, the city owned by Ford, Al Goetz climbs up on a truck and cries, "Remember we don't want any violence! A committee will present our demands. No trouble. No fighting. Stay in line."

Now the Dearborn police are drawn across the roadway but the great press of marchers, extending for blocks behind the Dearborn boundary and unconscious of the armed police there, push ahead and thrust those leading through the line of police. Hundreds of Ford gangsters, the Ford service men under command of Ford's Harry Bennett, protected by fences, from behind buildings, send a deadly fire into the ranks of the marching men as they approach the plant with their plan for re-employment. Bonosky writes:

"Then came the bullets. They whistled past Bill's ears, and he remembered his days in the trenches in France, and shuddered . . . men and women fell before him as though suddenly broken. Young James Ashford, his FREE THE SCOTTSBORO BOYS tumbling, pitched to the ground with a bullet in his leg. In front Joe York fell. Some ran screaming with blood flowing from wounds in chest and shoulders; others writhed on the ground, staring at the bones of their shattered legs.

"The marchers fell back; but again, the incredible courage of them surged up. They picked up their wounded—there were almost 60—these men and women who had never seen wounded before; but they did not run in panic. Blood soaked the road. . . . A machine gun, inside the gates, sent out a roar of death. . . . More marchers fell. Their shocked faces were thrown to the sky and they collapsed on the ground, holding their empty, defenseless hands to their bleeding stomachs. Three more lay dead; Joe Bussell, Coleman Leny, and Joe DeBlasio. Twenty-three others lay seriously wounded."

That was the Ford Massacre. But it was too late to stop the American people with bullets.

3. MacArthur Wins a Battle

The veterans of World War I were about to show how late it was. Thousands of them, under a Congressional Act of 1923, had $50 or $100 coming to them under a provision for adjusted service pay. The money, however, would not be paid until 1945. But in 1932 $50 or $100 seemed a fortune, meant the difference between eating and not eating if only for a matter of weeks. Under the spur of want a strange, spontaneous movement got under way in which, with almost no organization, detachments of veterans, many accompanied by their wives and children, headed toward Washington, getting there any way and any how with a demand to Congress for pay now.

It all began in April, 1932, when Communist leaders of the Workers Ex-Servicemen's League, Peter Cacchione, James W. Ford, and Emanuel Levin, testified before the House Ways and Means Committee, demanding immdiate payment of the so-called bonus; the adjusted service pay which provided for additional pay of $1 a day for World War I service in the armed forces at home, $1.25 for service overseas, but with payment deferred for thirteen years. When the Congressional committee scorned the demand, the Communists issued a call for a march of veterans on Washington but few thought that a call issued under such auspices would result in much.

For many of the influential did not realize the humiliation of the depression, a humiliation particularly marked in those who had once been hailed as heroes and told that they had made the world safe for democracy. They had saved their country, the veterans said, and what had they got? Evictions, joblessness, hunger, sickness, sometimes lack of shelter save for Hoovervilles.[4] The call for the march had scarcely been issued when veterans who wouldn't have known a Communist from a Mohammedan began their remarkable trek to Washington.

In jalopies and on foot, in broken-down trucks and on freights, stopping passenger trains and demanding free rides, the veterans started their Bonus March. They came from Alaska, some 4,000 miles. Three stowed away in a ship sailing from Honolulu to San Francisco and then advanced, thumbing rides, hopping freights. They converged on Washington in groups as large as 1,000; single families trudged northward on Alabama roads, the father holding a baby in his arms, the mother herding her young before her; groups would clatter into town in a wheezy truck, half-starved and half-frozen from the spring rains, demanding food and gasoline, singing and shouting, filled with disrespect and a strange recklessness.

The first contingent left early in May from Portland, Ore., its membership including 200 veterans and a number of women and children. The prominent there had tried to deter them, pointing out that it had been Communists who had called for the march, but veterans were reported to have declared, "We don't give a damn who called it. We want our money. Money isn't Communist."

As over the land they moved, coming from every direction, from Little Rock, Ark., and Niles Center, Ill., and Peru, Ind., and Dubuque, Iowa,

---

[4] These Hoovervilles, named by the jobless in honor of President Hoover, were to be found in almost all of the large cities of the country. Here in nondescript shelters lived the destitute and homeless, tens of thousands of men, women, and children. The squalor and misery surrounding them may be gleaned from the following: "An expectant mother lives in Hoovertown, on the edge of the industrial section of Los Angeles, with no shelter except a piece of canvas stretched over the bed. She and her husband have been out of work for months. For food they eat the decaying vegetables given away by the wholesale markets as unfit for sale." (Letter from a Los Angeles worker quoted in G. Hutchins, *Women Who Work*, p. 3)

and Grays Harbor, Wash., always moving closer to Washington, from north, south, east, and west, so strange and reckless and insistent, a queer hysteria began to rise in the ranks of the great and respectable. They must be turned back, the newspapers said, they must be dispersed, forced back to their homes.

Several thousand arrived in Cleveland where they took over the switch-yards, preventing the moving of traffic until a freight had been made up for them. Nine hundred had left from Chicago, 600 from New Orleans, 700 from Philadelphia, while 200 wounded, many of them on crutches, some with horrible mutilations from the battlefields of France, were coming from the National Soldiers Home at Johnson City, Tenn.

And always they carried their bitter signs, "Heroes in 1917—Bums in 1932," and "We Fought for Democracy—Where Is It?" The Negro veterans, of whom there were many, virtually always carried signs about Jim Crow and discrimination, signs reminding those who saw them that the Negroes had fought to make the world safe for democracy fourteen years before.

They must be turned back, declared General Pelham Glassford, chief of police of Washington, D.C. He sent telegrams in all directions with this demand, to governors and chiefs of police, to mayors and sheriffs, but one might as well have tried to turn back the tide. By June there were more than 20,000 veterans in Washington, streaming through the corridors of Congress, buttonholing Representatives and Senators, demanding that a bill be passed granting them their money now, not thirteen years from 1932.

The first veterans to arrive took shelter in an abandoned building at Third Street and Pennsylvania Avenue. Others built a little village of huts in a nearby open space. As the hosts of unkempt men, soiled from traveling and hardship, continued to stream into Washington, often accompanied by tired wives and whimpering children, they were directed across the Potomac to a flat and dreary stretch of land known as Anacostia Flats. By June 15 almost 25,000 were living in as strange a community as has ever been seen upon the North American continent, living in caves and holes in the ground, in shacks constructed of packing boxes, in tents and lean-tos and in nothing at all save for blankets beneath the sky. And all in the very heart of the nation, not far from the Capitol and the White House, democratic symbols of the people's power.

By June 15, according to the later statement of Police Chief General Glassford, it had been decided that the men who had fought for their country and who were now petitioning Congress must be dispersed. Demands that this be done, General Glassford said, had rolled in from the respectable everywhere. "Some members of the wealthy classes," said General Glassford, "looked upon the occupation of the nation's capital as a revolutionary action." As a consequence of this concern, General Glassford went on, troops and Marines in and about Washington began in June to receive special instructions in the use of tear gas and "maneuvers incident to dispersing crowds."

"Some members of the wealthy classes" had also decided that the veterans should not receive their adjusted pay and they so informed Congress through their National Economy League. This organization, formed at about the time the bonus army began to gather in the spring of 1932, threw all of its weight against payments to the veterans. Its weight was considerable since it was financed by such figures as John D. Rockefeller, Jr., Marshall Field, Mrs. H. P. Davison, widow of a Morgan partner, Edward S. Harkness, of the Standard Oil, and others of similar stature.[5]

Congress adjourned on July 17 without taking action on the veterans' petitions, its members swiftly scurrying out of town. On July 28 Washington police under General Glassford ordered several hundred veterans out of the building at Third Street and Pennsylvania Avenue, and when they refused police advanced with drawn guns. The veterans fought. Two of them were killed and word of their killing was dispatched to the White House as the veterans rallied for a stand before their shacks near Pennsylvania Avenue.

President Hoover, who had not acted effectively during almost three years of depression, now acted with dispatch. He called out the United States Army against the former members of the United States Army, their wives, and children. There was a little delay while General Douglas MacArthur, Chief of Staff who was to command this assault against Americans, sent to a nearby fort for his uniform. He was joined by Colonel Dwight D. Eisenhower and Major George O. Patton. General Glassford, as he later reported, visited General MacArthur and told him there were women and children among the bonus marchers at Anacostia Flats. "I know it," General MacArthur said, according to the chief of police.

The troops were drawn up in Pennsylvania Avenue when General MacArthur and Colonel Eisenhower arrived at about 4 P.M. Some of the bonus marchers were barricaded at Third Street, where there was a shanty village of veterans, and it was decided to oust them before advancing to the Battle of Anacostia Flats. The *New York Times* reported:

[5] Concerning Archibald B. Roosevelt, secretary of the National Economy League, as well as some others in it, Congressman Patman told the House on Jan. 3, 1933: "Archibald Roosevelt is interested in getting a sold million dollars a year subsidy from the Government on one of these Government ocean and steamship lines, when a canary bird could fly across the ocean on Christmas Day carrying all the mail they carry. Admiral Byrd, another active member of this outlaw group, is drawing $4,600 a year from the Government, not because of any service-connected disability incurred during the war. Then there is our friend, General Pershing, who draws $21,000 a year from the Government, another member of this outlaw organization. He is very much aggrieved and disturbed because some of these ex-buck privates who served under him are now drawing $12 a month for 49 per cent disability." (*Congressional Record*, 72:2, p. 1232.)

"Down Pennsylvania Avenue . . . the regulars came, the cavalry leading the way, and after them the tanks, the machinegunners and the infantry. . . . There was a wait of maybe half an hour while the Army officers talked it over with the police and the bonus marchers shouted defiance. . . .

"Twenty steel-helmeted soldiers led the way with revolvers in their hands until 200 were in position in front of the 'bonus fort.' Then the mounted men charged. They rode downstreet clearing the path with their sabres, striking those within reach with the flat of their blades.

"The action was precise, well-executed from a military standpoint, but not pretty to the thoughtful in the crowd. There were those who resisted the troops, fought back, cursed, kicked at the horses. . . .

"Amidst scenes reminiscent of the mopping up of a town in the World War, Federal troops . . . drove the army of bonus seekers from the shanty village near Pennsylvania Avenue."

As the cavalrymen, swinging their sabres, cleared the barricade, infantrymen, gas masks on their faces, advanced on the pathetic, makeshift group of packing-box huts, the women and children running shrieking before their country's soldiers who lobbed tear gas bombs after them.

Mrs. John Meyers, an eleven-week-old infant in her arms, was one of those fleeing. "I simply did not know which way to turn," she later said. "We ran up a porch and the gas came down. Then a family across the street called to us to come into their house. The troops came up the hill, driving the people ahead of them. As they passed the house, one of them threw a bomb over the fence and into the front yard, just a few feet from the door. The house was filled with smoke and we all began to cry. We got wet towels and put them over the faces of the children. An hour later my baby began to vomit. . . . Next day it turned black and blue and we took it to the hospital." There the eleven-week-old baby died, a casualty of the United States Army.

The victorious army, its cavalrymen and tanks, its infantry and machine-gun detachments, pressed on to Anacostia Flats as the summer evening deepened into dusk. There the veterans had gathered for a last stand at the entrance of their encampment, some timber mattresses, chairs, boxes, and tables thrown before them for protection, their wives and children behind anxiously watching from the caves and huts that had lodged them.

At one end of the barricade a tall Negro veteran held an American flag while other veterans crouched near him. Among them was a relative of Abraham Lincoln, a sixth cousin, now facing his country's troops, Charles Frederick Lincoln, described as "a slight man, deeply tanned by the exposure of the march." He had come with a Pacific Coast contingent from Los Angeles. Nearby was John Pace, a "hard-boned gangly American veteran . . . whose ancestors fought in the Revolutionary War, the War of 1812, and Civil War and whose father, a farmer like his own father, had served in the Spanish-American War."

The battle was swift and savage. The cavalry charged, sabres swinging, and again the infantry moved in with gas masks and gas bombs. Soon the pathetic city of the veterans was ashes, soldiers putting the huts and small belongings to the torch. Their jalopies, too, were destroyed. Again men, women, and children fled, pursued by their country's troops, blinded by gas, staggering through the streets of nearby neighborhoods.

The United States Army was again victorious. Master of the field, General MacArthur was being interviewed by reporters when one of them said that he had seen a cavalryman use his sabre to slash off a veteran's ear. But that was quite impossible, said the General, a little amused. "You don't slash with a sabre. You lunge." He took a noble pose and lunged forward, illustrating the proper form.

"The mob was a bad-looking one," General MacArthur continued. "It was one marked by signs of revolution. The gentleness and consideration with which they had been treated they had mistaken for weakness."

Flushed with victory, President Hoover issued a proud and ringing statement. "A challenge to the authority of the United States has been met swiftly and firmly," he said. "After months of patient indulgence, the government met overt lawlessness as it always must be met. . . . The first obligation of my office is to uphold and defend the Constitution and the authority of the law. This I propose always to do."

All that night and the next day the former members of the United States army poured out of their capital in retreat. Some carried children, some were limping, some occasionally vomited by the roadside from the effects of the gas. There was a good deal of confusion. Children were lost and crying. Women passed down columns looking for their husbands from whom they had become separated.

South into Virginia, north into Pennsylvania, over into Maryland, the 25,000 fled from their government and its army. A few were on crutches, some were cursing, and many were weeping with anger and shame. They had exercised their constitutional right of petitioning Congress, and the army in which they had proudly fought had been turned against them; their own army in battle dress had attacked their wives and children.

Well might they weep.

But they did not weep long. A hard anger seized the people, the common people, the working people, and it was to flare strong on many a picket line that built the CIO. And, along this road, the bonus was won.

4. Tear Gas and Solidarity

In that summer of 1932 Franklin Delano Roosevelt, Governor of New York, graduate of Groton and Harvard, product of a background of wealth and aristocracy, was campaigning on the Democratic ticket for the Presidency against Republican Herbert Hoover. Conservative enough when nominated by the Democratic convention at Chicago, the pressures of the time and the rank and file of the American people were already impelling him to growth. Time was to come when Liberty Leaguers, Christian Fronters, and America Firsters were to charge that he, the President of the United States, was himself a Communist or at least a fellow traveler. But now the land's reactionaries were speaking softly when they spoke at all.

Definitive disaster, complete breakdown, seemed increasingly inevitable. The Democratic candidate, receiving reports from all parts of the country, felt that armed revolution of the American people was a possibility unless immediate measures were taken to relieve three years of suffering.

In an interview with Emile Gauvreau, editor and publisher of the *New York Graphic,* Governor Roosevelt said that he proposed American recognition of the Soviet Union, reversing the policy of hostility that had been directed against Russia by every American administration since 1917. He quickly passed, however, to the alarming situation at home.

"Our people have to be put back on their feet," he said. "It will have to be soon. They are getting restless. Coming back from the West last week, I talked to an old friend who runs a great western railroad. 'Fred,' I asked him, 'what are the people talking about out here?' I can hear him answer even now. 'Frank,' he replied, 'I'm sorry to say that men out here are talking revolution.' "

The people of the world were on the move and monopoly the world over was afraid. Five weeks before Franklin Delano Roosevelt was sworn in as President of the United States, after having been elected by a 7,000,000 majority and carrying all but six of our forty-eight states, Adolf Hitler came to power in Germany as the representative of German monopoly. Immediately Hitler disbanded the trade unions, formed a monopoly-dominated government front of labor, moved against every people's organization with the charge that it was a Communist conspiracy. Within a matter of months thousands of trade unionists, Communists, Jews, Socialists, churchmen, and progressives were either executed or in concentration camps where they lamented the lack of unity that had brought Hitler into power. Thirty thousand German Communists had lost their lives in the fight against Hitler and reaction during the 1920's.

During the long preliminary fight against the rise of Hitler, many had believed that German monopoly's attack against the Communists would be limited to the Communists. They did not know that it was only a prelude to their own destruction, as events proved, and the destruction of all German liberty won by the trade unions and labor over long, hard years of struggle. Hamstrung and paralyzed by Hitler's red scare, a campaign that went on day after day and year after year, almost every German newspaper filled with "spy" stories and allegations of Communist conspiracies against the state, the German people had been unable to unite while the very Nazi-monopoly forces which had declared that Communists were about to seize the country took the country over themselves.

By a similar device, and similarly with employers' backing, Mussolini had seized power in Italy in 1922. Now both Hitler and Mussolini, the latter about to assault Ethiopia, were eying democratic Spain, determined that it would be their first joint victim in the Fascist drive to "save the world from Communism" by armed conquest. Wages in both Italy and Germany plunged to unparalleled lows while speed-up and hours of labor reached new heights as the industries of both countries boomed with the profits of munitions and armaments. They were necessary, the dictators said, for self-defense against the Soviet Union.

But in the United States the militant people, constantly increasing their unity as they largely ignored the growing shout of "Red!" had brought forth a democratic leader. There was hope even though the new President, sworn in on March 4, 1933, began his administration on a day that seemed to mark the complete breakdown of the economic life of the United States.

During February, 1933, with Roosevelt elected but Hoover still in the White House, runs on banks, bank failures, and bank closings in state after state had brought the financial system of the country to a virtual standstill. Money was disappearing. Wages could not be paid. Purchases could not be made. Food could not be bought. Checks were not honored. Vast crowds, ruined by the bank closings, clamored, wept, and rioted before silent, vacant savings institutions in every large city, their life savings gone they knew not where. Bankers, pillars of the community, were everywhere confessing, or being forced to confess by overwhelming facts, that they had lost their depositors' money in buying Wall Street's worthless securities and foreign bonds.

State after state, beginning with Michigan and spreading to Ohio, Indiana, Illinois, New York, Massachusetts, California, Texas, ordered all banks closed, froze their assets, if any, forbade any withdrawal of funds. By March 4, the day of F.D.R.'s inauguration, about three-fourths of the states had closed all banks, had suspended bank withdrawals and instituted what was called a Bank Holiday.

City funds were frozen everywhere. City services often came to a halt. Schools were closing. In many places they had been closed for weeks due to lack of municipal funds. Department stores and factories, grocery stores and butchers, mines and steel mills could not meet their payrolls nor could their customers make payments. New currencies were invented by corporations and cities but no one wanted the worthless paper.

Now the great of the country were naked. The open-shoppers stood stripped and the Red Peril did not seem the peril at all. The peril had been the conspiracy of Wall Street. The omniscient industrialist, the great financier, the all-wise businessman were revealed for dishonest incompetents. They were neither honest nor wise. The country had come to a total standstill because of their policies.

"What a mess for the new President to step into," virtually everyone was saying as they approached their radios that noon of March 4 to hear the inaugural of Franklin D. Roosevelt.

With almost the first syllable there was relief. Within a matter of moments there was courage. The confident lilting voice was facing facts, calling a spade a spade, heaping the country's scorn on the wealthy who had betrayed the people for love of profit. "We must drive the money-changers from the temple," the curiously alive and confident voice declared, and people everywhere leaned nearer their radios, intent on not missing a word.

"There must be an end to speculation with other people's money. . . ."

"Values have shrunk to fantastic levels, the withered leaves of industrial enterprise lie on every side; farmers find no markets for their produce; the savings of many years in thousands of families are gone. More important, a host of unemployed citizens face the grim problems of existence, and an equally great number toil with little return. Our great primary task is to put people to work. I am prepared under my constitutional duty to recommend the measures that a stricken nation in the midst of a stricken world may require."

A permanent excitement seized the land, almost a gladness, in those early days of the New Deal when, after years of government idleness in respect to the welfare of the people, act followed act, and law followed law, each one designed to meet the emergency. Relief, recovery, reform were the watchwords of the New Deal as huge public works were got under way in the sending of thousands back to work and wages. First there was the Emergency Banking Act in which all banks were forced to remain closed until given federal approval or until they were reorganized under federal supervision. Immediately laws were passed designed to prevent the widespread misrepresentation and dishonesty in the sale of securities and the use of other people's money in speculation on Wall Street.

There was the CCC, the Civilian Conservation Corps, to give employment to the impoverished youth of the country; there was the AAA, the Agricultural Adjustment Act, to help the hard-pressed farmers of the nation; there was the NIRA, the National Industrial Recovery Act with its Section 7(A), the opening wedge for workers to organize in unions of their own choosing; there was the Wagner Act or National Labor Relations Act, to guarantee wage earners for the first time the right to bargain collectively and the right to strike by prohibiting specifically coercive anti-union activities on the part of employers; and there was the Fair Labor Standards Act, to prescribe maximum hours of work and minimum wages and regulate child labor in interstate commerce.

The purpose of F.D.R. and his New Deal was the saving of the menaced capitalist system and yet in a very real sense it was a people's movement, too. It was the militance and unity of the people, particularly labor, farmers, and the Negro people, that drove the New Deal forward. A high point in American democracy, the New Deal was the necessary answer to the people's insistent demands. F.D.R. became a world figure because he moved to meet the people's needs.

There was an élan to all his acts, a shining challenge that rallied labor, farmers, and the Negro people to a fighting unity in which there was neither witch hunt nor red scare. His Fireside Chats, frequent reports to the people over the radio, seemed to bring the President of the United States into every home, almost as if he were a friendly neighbor. There was excitement in the fact that at long last there was a man in the White House, a human being of ability, and there was a great surge of hope stemming from the fact that here was a President who actually talked sense. It seemed unprecedented.

He spoke of peace not war, of friendliness among the nations of the earth, of an end to conquest and imperialism, of collective security which he increasingly saw as joint action of the United States, the Soviet Union, Great Britain, and France, for the purpose of restraining the rising fascism of Germany, Italy, and imperial Japan. The people loved him for the enemies he made. Wall Street was against him to a man.

Among the first actions of the New Deal, as has been said, was the passage in 1933 of the National Industrial Recovery Act. In the hullabaloo of setting up the vast organization, the country seethed with activity. It seemed good to be alive. Action was a tonic that made life worth living. Everywhere people gathered in meetings, chastened businessmen and eager workers, drawing up plans for the NIRA codes that were to restore and revivify American life.

Recovery was to be gained through the self-organization of each industry which would restore itself under government supervision through eliminating cutthroat competition, through setting up fair practices and fair standards, through increasing purchasing power by higher wages, through agreeing on minimum wages and hours. But the heart of the act, as far as labor was concerned, was Section 7(A), which stipulated as a matter of solemn law that workers were to be allowed to bargain collectively through representatives of their own choosing.

The average worker at first saw in the NIRA only the chance of getting a raise and better hours as well as a trade union to protect both. Everybody else, he said, was getting something out of the NIRA and he was damned if he was going to stand aside, an untouchable who got nothing. Newspapermen and clerks, white-collar workers who had never thought of trade unions, began to wonder if their clean hands and white collars were sufficient recompense for having nothing to say but "yes sir" about their hours, pay, and conditions.

The workers in auto, electrical manufacturing, rubber, glass and marine, in Westinghouse, RCA and Standard Oil, in General Electric and United States Steel, began to wonder if the American Plan, the open shop, that made the workers voiceless and powerless as to the conditions of their own lives, was really the last word in patriotism.

The law now said that an employer *had* to bargain collectively with unions, and millions of workers were suddenly becoming fanatically determined that employers would do just that. It became more imperative to them when the gains of the NIRA as to wages and hours proved in the overwhelming majority of cases to be unsatisfactory. And when company unions were set up, their members often determined to capture them and transform them into real unions.

And it was on the picket lines that the workers struggled with their employers to make Section 7(A) of the NIRA mean something. In 1933 more than 900,000 workers went on strike for union recognition and wage increases, three times more than the previous year. Trade union membership zoomed as 775,000 workers flocked into labor oragnizations, 500,000 into the AFL, 150,000 into independent unions, and 125,000 into the Trade Union Unity League. The latter organization led strikes in steel, auto, coal mining, meat packing, and the beet sugar industry. In 1933 alone the TUUL conducted strikes of 16,000 auto workers in Detroit, 5,000 to 6,000 steel workers in Ambridge, Pa., and 2,700 meat packers in Pittsburgh.[6]

The strike wave continued into 1934, when mass picket lines increased to nearly 1,500,000 workers. More than 450,000 textile workers went on strike after sixteen were killed on their picket lines. The year 1935 saw 1,150,000 on strike fighting for union recognition and improved working conditions. Some 18,000 workers were dragged from the picket lines, arrested, and jailed. From 1934 to 1936 eighty-eight workers lost their lives in strikes.

While workers were being killed and arrested on picket lines, great locals were being formed in steel, textile, auto, glass, rubber, and the electrical industry. The workers formed industrial unions, knowing that it would be obtuse and weak to separate and divide a plant's strength by fragmenting it into a score of competing craft unions.

Unwillingly, throughout 1934 and 1935, the AFL granted membership to these massive industrial unions that had formed themselves almost spontaneously in response to Section 7(A) of the NIRA. With worry and apprehension the Old Guard of the AFL issued what they termed federal charters, frankly declaring that as soon as they had time the new industrial unions would be divided among the crafts.

But that was not their only worry. As soon as the unions were formed, almost before they were formed, their new members wanted action, strikes, results. AFL organizers were dispatched all over the country, to Akron, Toledo, Gary, Chicago, Pittsburgh, Detroit, San Francisco, their mission not organization but preventing strikes and checking the torrent of militance everywhere growing.

Such was the aggressive spirit of the workers that this was no easy job. It took two years to accomplish it and even as the unprecedented movement

[6] The Trade Union Unity League was led in 1933 by Jack Stachel, who was later to be sentenced to a five-year prison term under the thought-control Smith Act.

was brought to a standstill by the Old Guard of the AFL, its own ranks
were being increasingly divided by those favoring industrial unionism, by
those aghast at the AFL's failure to take advantage of the golden opportunity to organize the mass industries.

The workers moved into the AFL federal locals, which increased from
307 in 1932 to 1,788 in 1934. Most of them outraged every tenet and every
rule of AFL procedure and practice.

The new unions adopted the methods of militancy, of the IWW and the
Trade Union Unity League, with giant, mass picket lines; with singing and
forums, debates and meetings; with the women organized into auxiliaries
and active members of every strike; with sitdowns and slowdowns and
demonstrations and flying squadrons that sped from point to point in fast
cars when there was trouble.

They inaugurated the use of sound trucks, of the loud-speaker booming
instructions over an amplifier from an auto, the great voice sounding im-
pressively over whole square miles as it directed picket lines and maneuvers
of actual battle when troops or police assaulted the lines.

The new union militants, soundly indicting the bosses, purchased time on
the radio, full-page advertisements in the newspapers, organized wide
citizens committees backing the strike, brought the issues of the strike to
the public in understandable terms. And always they held mass meetings
where a democratic majority vote was necessary before any union policy,
including union contracts, could come into being.

All over West Virginia, Pennsylvania, Illinois, and Kentucky, a now
fighting John L. Lewis, president of the United Mine Workers, had signs
put up declaring, "President Roosevelt Wants You To Join the Union!"
All through the Middle West handbills containing the same message were
appearing in factory washrooms, in factory restaurants, even coming down
the assembly line, a handbill tucked into each auto or tire or other article
moving by the workers on the conveyor belt.

Meanwhile big business was launching an anti-union drive of unprecedented proportions. Some of the breadth of this drive, almost always disguised as a fight against Communism, can be seen from the 1936 report of
the National Association of Manufacturers. The report, made by Harry A.
Bullis, described the scope of the Association's propaganda as follows:

> *Press*—Industrial Press Service—reaches 5,300 weekly newspapers every
> week. Weekly cartoon service—sent to 2,000 weekly newspapers.
> "Uncle Abner Says"—comic cartoon appearing in 309 daily papers with a
> total circulation of 2,000,000 readers.
> "You and Your Nation's Affairs"—daily articles by well known economists
> appearing in 260 newspapers with a total circulation of over 4,500,000.
> Factual bulletin—monthly exposition of industry's viewpoint sent to every
> newspaper editor in the country.
> For Foreign-born citizens—weekly press service, translated into German,

Hungarian, Polish and Italian, printed in papers with a total circulation of almost 2,500,000.

Nationwide Advertising—6 full page ads about the "American System" of which 500 newspapers have carried one or more.

Radio—"The American Family Robinson"—program heard from coast to coast over 222 radio stations once a week, and over 176 stations twice a week. Foreign language—1,188 programs in 6 languages over 79 radio stations.

Movies—Two 10-minute films for general distribution, seen by over 2,000,000 people.

Public Meetings—70 meetings featuring 8 professional speakers.

Employee Information Service—Leaflets—a series of 25 distributed to over 11,000,000 workers.

Posters—over 300,000 for a series of 24 for bulletin boards in plants throughout the country.

Films—10 sound slide films for showing in plants.

Outdoor advertising—60,000 billboard ads scheduled for 1937.

Pamphlets—"You and Industry Library"—over 1,000,000 copies of a series of seven pamphlets distributed to libraries, colleges, businessmen, lawyers and educators.

In addition the NAM distributed thousands of copies of a booklet endorsing the Mohawk Valley strike-breaking method as well as 10,000 copies, at a later date, of the booklet called *Join the CIO and help build a Soviet America.* The United States Chamber of Commerce, with a membership of 700,-000, sponsored propaganda activities whose extent was as wide as that of the NAM.

In 1934, in a futile effort to ward off union organization American industry began spending an estimated $80,000,000 yearly for the purchase of spies, their duties reporting on the activities of employees and their unions, building blacklists, framing trade union officials, and breaking up trade unions. According to the later researches of the La Follette Senate Committee, which in 1936 began an investigation into industry's purchase of violence and espionage, 230 detective agencies furnished the largest American corporations with 100,000 spies, who were thought to have penetrated every one of the country's 48,000 local trade unions. Many of the spies became officials of the trade unions and an increasing number of active trade unionists were fingered and fired.

General Motors officials, testifying before the Senate Committee, blandly admitted that they had spent hundreds of thousands of dollars for spies in an effort to violate, or circumvent, the law providing for collective bargaining. In the purchase of spies General Motors had spent $419,850.10 with the Pinkertons[7] alone between January, 1934, and July, 1936, when they spent

_____

[7] In recent years Pinkerton's industrial spying has fallen off, much of the finger work being taken over by the Federal Bureau of Investigation. Discharges of union militants are now often carried out through the device of Congressional hearings, often held just before labor board elections.

a total of $994,855.68 with all agencies hired during that period. Similar sums for spies were spent by the Radio Corporation of America, Westinghouse Electric, Aluminum Company of America, Chrysler, Firestone, Standard Oil, New York Edison, Bethlehem Steel, Libby-Owens-Ford Glass Co., United Shoe Machinery, Carnegie-Illinois Steel, Western Union, Continental Can, and a half a hundred other of the leading American corporations.

It was also in 1934, according to testimony before the La Follette Senate Committee, that American industry began spending hundreds of thousands of dollars for tear gas, shot guns, automatic pistols, armored cars, fragmentation bombs, sub-machine guns with which to attack employees in the strikes that were clearly looming. Even as American big business executives talked of law and order, of Communist plots to employ force and violence, they were spending a total of $1,040,621.14 between 1933 and 1936 with only three of the many companies manufacturing armaments for the private wars of corporations against their workers.

The Federal Laboratories, Inc., began to do a land office business. Its president, John W. Young, testifying before a Senate Committee, said that he was really a humanitarian at heart since he sold more gas than bullets to the corporations and it was "better to gas a striker than to kill him." Jubilant because of an abundance of what one of his representatives called "nice, juicy strikes," Young sent salesmen wherever a strike loomed, with large orders invariably resulting. Usually his salesmen set up gas guns right on the spot, discharging them into picket lines as part of the free demonstration.

Young loved strikes, which he often called Communist insurrections. Joseph M. Roush, star salesman for the Federal Laboratories, hustled across the country from Pittsburgh in the summer of 1934 with a varied assortment of gas guns and gas when the newspapers carried reports that there was to be a strike of San Francisco maritime workers. In addition to his weapons he carried with him, as all Federal salesmen did, copies of Elizabeth Dilling's *The Red Network* and pamphlets entitled *The Red Line of Crime and Civil Disorder*. It was his contention, increasingly popular, that all strikes were caused by Communists.

Roush arrived in San Francisco just in time for the maritime strike of 1934, where he gave a practical demonstration of the worth of his product. He wrote his home office:

"The evening of July 2, Sergeant McInerney and Officer Myron Gernea . . . asked me if I would go with them in the Headquarters' car the next morning and take some of my gas equipment. They said they expected considerable rioting and would appreciate my experience in the use of gas. . . . We started to do battle with [gas] equipment and two shotguns. We did not have long to wait. The first riot started early in the morning and we went in with short range shells and grenades. . . .

"I might mention that during one of the riots, I shot a long range projectile into a group, the shell hitting one man and causing a fracture of the skull from which he has since died. As he was a Communist, I have had no feeling in the matter and I am sorry that I did not get more."

After this demonstration, Roush wrote, "It was a landslide business for us. Immediately following . . . came orders for gas and machine guns from the surrounding territory." He continued:

"Please convey my thanks to all the members of the company that made this business possible for us. I can think of no greater inspiration to get out and get more business than the knowledge of how firmly the factory and its personnel are behind me. . . .

"I shall make San Francisco my permanent headquarters. . . . I find it so practical and pleasant I shall continue to live here. . . ."

Trying to regain the offensive, industry evolved an elaborate strike-breaking formula known as the Mohawk Valley Formula, the creation of James H. Rand, Jr., of the Remington Rand Company. Circulated widely by the National Association of Manufacturers, the plan had as its first point, according to the findings of the La Follette Senate Committee, the branding of any strike anywhere and every strike everywhere as a Communist plot. Other points provided for complete domination of local police, full-page advertisements in the newspapers, the widespread use of armed vigilantes and citizens' committees, the formation of "loyal employee groups," and a back-to-work movement which was to smash through picket lines by means of tear gas, clubs, and machine guns employed by police and vigilantes. All violence, the La Follette Committee found, was to be charged to out-of-town agitators and Reds.

At the same time the American Legion launched a mammoth drive against "the menace of Communism" under the leadership of its national commander, one Frank N. Belgrano, Jr., president of the Pacific National Fire Insurance Company and the American Security Insurance Corporation, and vice president of the Bank of America National Trust and Savings Association and the Occidental Life Insurance Company. A few months before the inauguration of their drive against Communism, wealthy Legion members visited General Smedley Butler, according to his testimony before a Congressional committee, offering to elect him national commander of the Legion if he would lead a fascist march on Washington for the ousting of the Roosevelt administration and a fascist seizure of power.

In 1934 the Ku Klux Klan was revived under Dr. Hiram W. Evans of Dallas, its prey union organizers, its fake purpose the saving of the nation from Communism. In the same year the Sentinels of the Republic, financially backed by Atwater Kent and the Pew oil millions, launched a campaign against trade unions, Roosevelt, and Communism. The American

Liberty League was formed in 1934, its members controlling investments totaling thirty-seven billions of dollars, its goal the open shop and the destruction of the New Deal, its method the campaign against Communism.

A secret organization known as the Special Conference Committee, made up of the twelve biggest corporations in the country—General Motors, Standard Oil of New Jersey, General Electric, Goodyear, Westinghouse, American Telephone and Telegraph, Du Pont, U.S. Rubber, Bethlehem, International Harvester, U.S. Steel, and Irving Trust—considered itself a mysterious, unknown General Staff of the counteroffensive against labor and the New Deal. In an effort to pressure the Government E. S. Cowdrick, secretary of the committee, wrote to the Assistant Secretary of Commerce on Dec. 20, 1935, that business confidence in the administration would be restored if there would be "definite opposition to such measures as the 30-hour bill, the Walsh government contract bill." Sometime later another letter was sent by Cowdrick to the same Commerce Department official suggesting that "it might be well also to call off the La Follette [labor spy] investigation."

H. W. Anderson, General Motors vice president in charge of personnel, writing to a colleague in the Special Conference Committee troubled by union organization, according to the La Follette Committee, suggested, "Maybe you could use a little Black Legion down in your country. It might help."

The Black Legion to which Anderson of General Motors referred was a Northern version of the Ku Klux Klan. Springing up during the depression in the Detroit and Flint areas, it had more than a thousand members who rigged themselves up in a blackhooded regalia and armed themselves with whips, blacksnakes, and revolvers. They kidnapped scores of automobile workers active in attempts at union organization in 1934 and 1935, flogged them, tortured them, and killed at least ten with the allegation in each instance that the men were Communists. Governor George H. Earle of Pennsylvania made the public charge that the Black Legion was being financed by the du Ponts of Delaware, General Motors, and the tycoons of the Liberty League.

In all the long history of the Red Drive, reaching back to 1877 and ascending to high points at Haymarket, the Pullman Strike of 1894, and the Palmer Raids of 1919–20, there had never been so many organizations with so many millions of dollars devoted to the breaking of labor and reform through the charge of Communism. But somehow it didn't take. The economic royalists had overplayed their hand. In the first place the government as expressed in the Roosevelt administration and the New Deal was hostile to red-baiting since the New Deal, itself, was so often the victim of it. Moreover, the tycoons persistently whispered that Roosevelt, himself, was an agent of the Kremlin and this to most seemed merely ridiculous. A Communist scare, to be successful, needs all the power of government behind it.

Officials of the New Deal knew that it was only a dodge to divide and confuse the people.

By 1934 labor solidarity, "an injury to one is an injury to all," had soared to a general acceptance by local unions the country over. When one union's picket lines were attacked by police all unions in a given locality threatened general strike. This happened again and again in 1934 and 1935. It happened in Milwaukee in February, 1934. It happened in Minneapolis in May of that year. It happened in Pekin, Ill. Everywhere workers were saying to police and goons, "If you smash that picket line every union in the city is going out."

In Toledo eighty-three of ninety-one local unions voted a general strike when violence was used against 3,000 striking metal workers. In Terre Haute 26,000 workers went out on a two-day general strike in support of 600 police-assaulted metal workers. But the greatest demonstration of solidarity, and one of the greatest strikes in all American history, was the general strike that made San Francisco as silent and still and unmoving as death itself in the summer of 1934 when all the city's unions rallied to the help of the hard pressed maritime workers.

5. Solidarity on the Embarcadero

San Francisco is a busy city of 600,000, its heart the waterfront, the chief source of its life. And yet the men who kept the city alive, who did its most important work, the longshoremen who loaded and unloaded the vessels that made the city prosperous with trade, the seamen who manned the ships, received in 1933 little more than $10 a week. To be precise, the average weekly wage of longshoremen was $10.45, while able seamen received $53 a month and ordinary seamen $36.

And yet even more important was the fact that the maritime workers were voiceless serfs in an industrial autocracy, powerless employees of a shipping industry which received millions on millions of dollars, according to the Black Senatorial Investigation, in subsidies from the federal government. A few seamen belonged to a corrupt, sell-out organization, the International Seamen's Union, and still fewer to the militant Marine Workers Industrial Union (TUUL), but to all practical purposes they were unorganized. The longshoremen, since 1919, had been dragooned into a creature of the shipping industry known as the Blue Book Union, an employers' organization controlled by gangsters who forced the underpaid longshoremen to bribe them for jobs.

The shape-up, that is, a crowd of longshoremen packing around a foreman on the street, each one hoping that he would be chosen for work, was the common method of hiring. There was usually a three- or four-day search or wait for work between jobs but once gained a longshoreman might work twenty-four to thirty-six hours at a stretch on a single shift. Seamen, after they had once shipped out, too, had long periods of unemployment, worked on an average of between fourteen and sixteen hours a day.

In 1933, under the impetus of NIRA and Section 7(A) as well as the spur of intolerable conditions, longshoremen in San Francisco and up and down the Pacific coast began flocking into the International Longshoremen's Association, AFL. Knowing something of Joseph P. Ryan,[8] its president, they were determined on rank-and-file control. One of their leaders was a sharp-featured, sharp-witted longshoreman by the name of Harry Bridges. A tough and rugged character, his assets were an impregnable honesty and a stout belief in the ability and right of the rank-and-file to govern themselves.

Although federal law made it mandatory that the shipping magnates negotiate in collective bargaining with any union that their employees chose, they unhesitatingly broke the law by refusing to so negotiate. Instead, in September, 1933, they discharged four rank-and-file leaders of the union. When the regional labor board ordered their reinstatement, the longshoremen surged into the ILA with such unanimity that the Blue Book Union "became little more than an office with a telephone number."

After the employers had refused to negotiate or recognize the union over a period of months 12,000 longshoremen went out on strike at 8 p.m. on May 9, 1934, in San Francisco, Seattle, Tacoma, Portland, San Pedro, San Diego, Stockton, Bellingham, Aberdeen, Grays Harbor, Astoria, and all other Pacific coast ports. The Marine Workers Industrial Union followed suit and by May 23 eight maritime unions and 35,000 workers were out on strike up and down the coast.

It was primarily unprecedented police brutality that turned the seamen's strike into a general strike of 127,000 San Francisco workers that in an instant transformed the city into a ghost town in which there was no movement. The police took their line from the Industrial Association, the combination of San Francisco's most powerful tycoons, organized in 1919 as a Law and Order Committee to break a waterfront strike and developing until it was the real ruler of San Francisco. The slightest utterance of its officials became newspaper headlines. The employer organization was almost decisive in the election of mayors, governors, Congressmen. It maintained a powerful lobby in Washington. It was the Pacific coast's most powerful group, its members owning shipping companies, piers, warehouses, railroads, banks, utility companies, land, insurance corporations, and public officials.

From 8 P.M. on May 9 officials of the Industrial Association and the San Francisco Chamber of Commerce said there was nothing to negotiate. There was only a Communist insurrection to put down. Typical of the statements that filled the newspapers was that of J. M. Maillard, Jr., president of the Chamber of Commerce:

[8] In 1953 Joseph P. Ryan was ousted as president of the International Longshoremen's Association and indicted for stealing union funds which he had earmarked to fight Communism.

"The San Francisco waterfront strike is out of hand. It is not a conflict between employer and employee—between capital and labor—it is a conflict which is rapidly spreading between American principles and un-American radicalism . . . the welfare of business and industry and the entire public is at stake in the outcome of this crisis."

The port, officials of the employers' organizations declared, must be opened. The police must break and clear the mass picket lines from before the piers.

The longshoremen had drawn up a list of demands, pay of $1 an hour, a six-hour day, a thirty-hour week, a union hiring hall, but officials of the Industrial Association declared there was no issue at stake but the suppression of a Red Revolt. Press, pulpit, and radio combined with tireless unanimity to whip up hysteria against workers striving to better their lives. Not unusual was the first-page story of the *Chronicle,* "Red Army Marching on City." The story read in part:

"The reports stated the communist army planned the destruction of railroad and highway facilities to paralyze transportation and later, communication, while San Francisco and the Bay Area were made a focal point in a red struggle for control of government.

"First warning communist forces were nearing the Northern California border was relayed from J. R. Given, Southern Pacific superintendent at Dunsmuir, to District State Highway Engineer Fred W. Hazelwood who immediately reported to State Director of Public Works Earl Lee Kelly."

Bumbling Joseph P. Ryan, president of the International Longshoremen's Association but in league with the gangsters of New York, was rushed from New York to quiet the strikers. Long known as an ardent fighter against Communism, he did his part as expected when unable to sell out the maritime workers. He said the strike was a Communist Plot and again the headlines shrieked. Then Edward F. McGrady, Assistant Secretary of Labor whose part in breaking the furriers' strike in New York may be recalled, was rushed from Washington and when he, too, could not succeed in forcing the longshoremen to give up their demand for a union hiring hall, he, too, said the strike was Red Revolution.

With the stage set and the police eager, the employers announced that they would smash the picket lines before the piers on the Embarcadero on July 3, 1934. At 1:27 P.M., with thousands of pickets massed before the piers, the steel rolling doors on Pier 38 went up and five trucks loaded with cargo, preceded by eight police radio patrol cars, moved out. Mike Quin in his history of the strike tells what happened:

"A deafening roar went up from the pickets. Standing on the running board of a patrol car at the head of the caravan, Police Captain Thomas M. Hoertkorn flourished a revolver and shouted, 'The port is open!'

"With single accord the great mass of pickets surged forward. The Embarcadero became a vast tangle of fighting men. Bricks flew and clubs battered skulls. The police opened fire with revolvers and riot guns. Clouds of tear gas swept the picket lines and sent the men choking in defeat. Mounted police were dragged from their saddles and beaten to the pavement.

"The cobblestones of the Embarcadero were littered with fallen men, bright puddles of blood colored the gray expanse.

"Squads of police who looked like Martian monsters in their special helmets and gas masks led the way, flinging gas bombs ahead of them. . . ."

The fighting continued for four hours before a vast gallery of San Franciscans, perhaps half of the city watching it from the hills which loom above the waterfront. Two airplanes, packed with the curious, circled low over the bloody battle area. The battle was fierce but it was only the prelude to Bloody Thursday. The next day, after the initial attack of the police, was July 4, and by common consent there was a one-day truce before the battle resumed on Thursday, July 5. Quin writes:

"There were no preliminaries this time. They just took up where they left off. . . . Teeming thousands covered the hillsides. Many high school and college boys, unknown to their parents, had put on old clothes and gone down to fight with the union men. Hundreds of working men started for work, then changed their minds and went down to the picket lines."

At 8 A.M. police went into action. One newspaper reported:

"Vomiting gas was used in many cases, instead of the comparatively innocuous tear gas, and scores of dreadfully nauseated strikers and civilians were incapacitated. There was no sham about the battles yesterday. Police ran into action with drawn revolvers. Scores of rounds of ammunition were fired, and riot guns were barking throughout the day."

But the strikers and their thousands of sympathizers fought on with their bare hands against bullets and bombs. Their only weapons were bricks and stones. Hundreds were badly wounded. Two, Nick Bordoise and Howard Sperry, were killed. Sperry was a longshoreman; Bordoise was a culinary worker, a member of the Cooks' Union and of the Communist Party. A reporter for the *Chronicle* in describing the bloodshed wrote:

"Don't think of this as a riot. It was a hundred riots big and little. Don't think of it as one battle, but a dozen battles."

All day the battle raged and all day reinforcements from other unions poured into the riddled picket lines, workers declaring, "If they win this, there'll never be another union in Frisco!" The police, clubbing and injuring literally hundreds of passersby and bystanders, charged into the union headquarters of the longshoremen and wrecked it. At the close of the day Governor Merriam ordered in the National Guard, two thousand of them with full equipment, and Harry Bridges said, "We cannot stand up against police, machine guns, and National Guard bayonets."

The employers thought they had won. They had not. The strike was just beginning. "That night," writes Quin, "San Francisco vibrated to intense conversation. Every home or gathering place in town hummed with talk. Doorbells and telephones rang. Neighbors came in from next door. . . . Men had been shot down in cold blood. Authority had taken the shape of force and violence. Bedtime came and went but still the city talked. . . . A General Strike was being forged in the firesides of San Francisco."

The Painters' Union, Local 1158, sent out a call for a general strike and it had scarcely been issued when the Machinists Union, Local 68, took up the demand. But first labor had to bury its dead. More than 35,000 workers walked behind the coffins. There were no police about as the stern-faced workers marched through the heart of the city. One newspaperman wrote of the slain men:

"In life they wouldn't have commanded a second glance on the streets of San Francisco, but in death they were borne the length of Market Street in a stupendous and reverent procession that astounded the city."

And Quin writes of the funeral:

"A union band struck up the slow cadence of the Beethoven funeral march. The great composer's music never applied more fittingly to human suffering. Slowly—barely creeping—the trucks moved out into Market Street. With slow, rhythmic steps the giant procession followed. Faces were hard and serious. Hats were held proudly across chests. Slow-pouring, like thick liquid, the great mass flowed onto Market Street.

"Streetcarmen stopped their cars along the line of march, and stood silently, holding their uniform caps across their chests, holding their heads high and firm.

"Not one smile in the endless blocks of marching men. Crowds on the sidewalk, for the most part, stood with heads erect and hats removed. Others watched the procession with fear and alarm. Here and there well dressed businessmen . . . stood amazed and impressed but with their hats still on their heads. Sharp voices shot out from the line of march. 'Take your hats off!'

"The tone of voice was extraordinary. The reaction was immediate. With quick, nervous gestures the businessmen obeyed. Hours went by, but the marchers still poured onto Market Street."

Now locals were meeting all over the city, one after another voting for a general strike. In the debates it was admitted that Communists were active in the struggle of the maritime workers. For that matter, it was said, they, or other Marxists, had been active in every big strike since the railroad strike of 1877. Trade unionist after trade unionist declared that for the San Francisco labor movement to fall for the employers' red scare was to agree to its own division, to less pay, longer hours. On July 10 the Alameda Labor Council went on record for a general strike. On July 12 the powerful locals of the teamsters' union in San Francisco and Oakland issued a call for union and solidarity, favored the general strike.

William Green sent telegrams forbidding the strike, but by July 15 some 160 local AFL unions, with a membership of 127,000 workers, had voted general strike effective the following day.

The typographical workers and powerhouse employees stayed in but with these two exceptions members of every union walked out on the morning of July 16. Quin writes:

"The paralysis was effective beyond all expectation. To all intents and purposes industry was at a complete standstill. The great factories were empty and deserted. No streetcars were running. Virtually all stores were closed. The giant apparatus of commerce was a lifeless, helpless hulk.

"Labor had withdrawn its hand. The workers had drained out of the shops and plants like life-blood, leaving only a silent framework embodying millions of dollars worth of invested capital. In the absence of labor, the giant machinery loomed as so much idle junk. . . .

"Everything was there, all intact as the workers had left it—instruments, equipment, tools, machinery, raw materials and the buildings themselves. When the men walked out they took only what belonged to them—their labor. And when they took that they might as well have taken everything, because all the elaborate apparatus they left behind was worthless and meaningless without their hand. The machinery was a mere extension of labor, created by and dependent upon labor.

"Labor held the life-blood and enegry. The owners remained in possession of the corpse.

"Highways leading into the city bristled with picket lines. Nothing moved except by permission of the strike committee. Labor was in control. Employers, however, controlled an important factor. Through the 'conservative wing' they held the balance of power within the General Strike Committee. But this 'conservative wing' had to buck a strong progressive minority, and dared not move too obviously contrary to the will of the masses."

Three thousand additional troops were dispatched to the strikebound city but that turned not a wheel. Mobs of vigilantes were sworn in as special police, armed with clubs and guns, but the workers were at home, with a new consciousness of their power and dignity. When they ceased working the world stopped. And all of the silk hats, dollars, and guns could not start it again without them.

The vigilantes swung into an orgy of lawlessness, wrecking union halls, raiding clubs of the foreign-born, beating their occupants, destroying progressive book stores, scattering all the volumes and pamphlets to the street. The police looked on as the vigilantes destroyed the offices of the *Western Worker,* Communist paper backing the strike. They watched as they wrecked the headquarters of the Communist Party, the Marine Workers' Industrial Union, the ILA soup kitchen, the Workers' Ex-Servicemen's League, the Mission Workers' Neighborhood House.

Then the police themselves moved into lawlessness as they arrested 500 old men, members of the unemployed, the helpless down-and-out, and charged that those hauled in were Communist conspirators. "The Communist Party is through in San Francisco," announced Captain J. J. O'Meara, head of the police radical squad, before it was found that not one of the old men was a Communist. They were finally released.

But the force and violence of police and vigilantes moved not a wheel. The city was like a tomb all of July 16. Nothing moved on July 17. San Francisco was a ghost on July 18. Yet on each of these days "the conservative wing" had succeeded in loosening the strike's grip. Restaurants were allowed to open on one day. It was extended to some trucking the next day. More exceptions were made the next. Rumors were spread that the strike was over. One of the biggest demonstrations in the history of American labor ended on July 19 when Deal, Vandeleur, and Kidwell, conservative AFL officials, refusing a rollcall vote, announced that the central labor body had ended the general strike by a standing vote of 191 to 174.

But the workers returned as if celebrating a victory. They put their hands to switch, throttle, wheel, and assembly line and death became life. The maritime workers, rejecting all attempts to divide the eight unions out on strike, remained on their picket line but with an increased strength. No police assaulted their lines now. National Guardsmen stayed their distance. Labor had demonstrated its power and the tycoons of the Industrial Association, fighting now among themselves, did not want another taste of labor's unity.

On July 30 the 35,000 maritime workers went back to work. Within a matter of weeks the longshoremen had gained, as a direct result of the strike, the six-hour day, a thirty-hour week, and time and a half for overtime. Wages were raised to a basis of ninety-five cents an hour, $1.40 for overtime. But above all they had won the basis for the union hiring hall, a method for democratic rotary hiring without which the union would have been powerless to protect its gains.

The seamen returned under conditions which granted recognition to the International Seamen's Union. But because the union was in the control of a reactionary clique subservient to the shipping interests the seamen won little substantial gain. On the other hand, because the longshoremen's local was run by its rank and file its members' gains were persistently extended.

Harry Bridges, the rank-and-file leader, was elected president of the San Francisco local of the International Longshoremen's Association and later he was elected to the presidency of the entire West Coast District. From then on he was a marked man. He had committed the unpardonable sin. He had raised wages. He had lowered hours. He had put more wages in pay envelopes. He had transformed employees into men with a voice in the decisions governing their own hire. If he had not done all these things himself, he at least had played an important part in accomplishing these worthy ends.

From the moment the Bridges leadership played a vital role in raising wages, Bridges was a Communist in the eyes of the powerful Industrial Association of San Francisco. He could be neither bought nor frightened, bribed nor bullied, and with that established the employers marked him for destruction. Whether he was a Communist or not made not a whit of difference. He had worked with Communists and he was incorruptible.

On four separate occasions they have gathered together a choice selection of paid spies, perjurers, and criminals to testify as told or face prison. On four different occasions federal authority or juries have found that Bridges is not a Communist, has not been a Communist, but has instead been persecuted as few men in history in an implacable plot to frame him. Even the Supreme Court of the United States so ruled. Despite this, powerful interests on the Pacific coast are now engaged in a fifth attempt to frame Harry Bridges.[9]

But workingmen know that all the endless frame-up attempts against Bridges stem from his leadership of the San Francisco General Strike of 1934, a demonstration of iron-clad unity which inspired all American labor. It was an important factor in increased wages at points far from San Francisco. It was the prelude to even greater battles and greater victories.

[9] "A monument to man's intolerance to man," were the words with which the late Supreme Court Justice Frank Murphy described the persecution of Bridges. And Supreme Court Justice Douglas found in 1945 that Bridges was responsible only "for a militant advocacy of trade unionism" and that he had never been guilty of "Subversive conduct condemned by the statute."

Dean James Landis of the Harvard Law School found after hearings in 1939 that Bridges "is not a member nor affiliated with the Communist Party." He described one witness against Bridges as "a self-confessed liar," "pathological," "corrupt," and others as "prejudiced, intemperate and overbearing."

CHAPTER X

Victory

"Let him who will, be he economic tyrant or sordid mercenary, pit his strength against this mighty surge of human sentiment now being crystallized in the hearts of thirty millions of workers who clamor for the establishment of industrial democracy and for participation in its tangible fruits. He is a madman or fool who believes that this river of human sentiment, flowing as it does from the hearts of these thirty millions, who with their dependents constitute two-thirds of the population of the United States of America, can be dammed or impounded by the erection of arbitrary barriers of restraint."

JOHN L. LEWIS, JULY 6, 1936

1. CIO

Now the climax, the boiling over, was moving nearer. It was as if the entire history of the American labor movement had been only a mere introduction to the great crusade that was the CIO. "Hundreds of thousands of men mad with anger and frustration leaped to the battle. They would stop at nothing and nothing would stop them."[1] It was a revolutionary, apocalyptic time. What generations had battled in vain to accomplish was accomplished now in a matter of weeks or days. The impossible was achieved daily. Of a sudden, or so it seemed, labor could not lose.

It was a time of youth and growth but above all it was a time of blazing, unified action. The new was not feared but welcomed. The red scare was laughed at. A man could feel himself grow in stature and capability, in resource and in courage, and when his abilities were merged with the abilities of literally millions, who felt as he did, the unity that resulted was irresistible, It pushed aside hoary institutions, such as the open shop, as a cyclone

[1] Saul Alinsky, *John L. Lewis, An Unauthorized Biography*, G. P. Putnam's Sons, New York, 1949.

might a straw. It assaulted and reduced what had been unconquerable, the strongest aggregations of corporate power, armed with guns, spies, and billions, that the world had ever seen.

The very air was tonic. Courage was contagious. It multiplied by the industry and city, by the shop, by the county and the state; it pyramided daily to new heights as each edition of each newspaper carried new accounts of new thousands moving in their own behalf. One could almost feel and see the common people by the millions, taking new heart and new resolve, as they read of the unprecedented sit-downs that were reducing the proud, billion-dollar open-shop fortress that was General Motors. It was good to be alive. It was better to be winning, for when had labor ever won before on such a scale as this? It was good to release in triumphant mass action the long-pent-up bitterness, the helplessness, the defeats, the humiliations, not only of the depression but of the generations.

It was as if the thousands on the singing picket lines somehow knew of the nineteen executed union miners of 1877, of the framing and hanging of Parsons and the other fighters for the eight-hour day, of the imprisonment of Debs, of the long travail of Haywood, of the endless discrimination against Negroes, women, the foreign-born, and unskilled, of the thousands of strikers beaten and arrested, framed and slain, in all the lost strikes of long ago. They had a sense of history in that all felt strongly that the time of long defeat was coming to an end. But, however imperfectly they knew of their labor predecessors, they knew in unforgettable detail what had happened to themselves, knew the evictions and the joblessness they had suffered, knew of unemployed demonstrators shot down as at Ford's in 1932, knew of the veterans attacked by the army of their own country, knew of the killings of union men in San Francisco.

The workers were in an explosive mood. The NRA, they said, had proved the National-Run-Around as far as they were concerned. By 1935 more than 600 federal locals had been disbanded in disgust. Wages in steel averaged $560 annually, a little more than a third of the $1,500 necessary, according to government figures, to maintain a family on a minimum level. The average hourly rate in the electrical industry was only 50 cents and a pay check of $10 for a week's work was a common occurrence. In auto, in 1934, the average yearly wage was less than $1,000.

In 1935 the NRA was declared unconstitutional and in the same year the Wagner Labor Act was passed. This Act, as had the NRA, gave labor the right to collective bargaining through unions of its own choosing, but labor knew now that this right would be only as effective as labor made it on the picket line. The time of illusion was over. A law was something to break, employers knew, if it increased costs. They would obey it only if forced to do so by strong unions.

There were 35,000,000 organizable workers, most of them clamoring for the protection of a union. The AFL had in 1935 a membership of but 3,045,347. Another 571,000 were in independent unions for a total of 3,616,-

847, only 10.6 per cent of those awaiting organization. But the AFL did not move to take advantage of the greatest opportunity in the history of labor to organize the unorganized.

So it was that when John L. Lewis, his eyebrows twitching aggressively, his burly form hunched forward, strode across the AFL convention hall at Atlantic City in October, 1935, and punched William Hutcheson of the Carpenters square on the nose, the rank and file of the labor movement were delighted. Hutcheson, along with Green, Woll, and Frey, had been the very symbol of the AFL's refusal to organize the millions industrially and thousands of workers had ached to do what Lewis had done. The act was symbolic of a growing split between eight AFL unions, embracing a membership of 1,000,000, whose officials were demanding the industrial organization of the unorganized, and the stand-pat, do-nothing policy of the Old Guard controlling the remainder of the AFL.

As the pale-faced, histrionic Lewis, his eyes a baleful glare, moved to assault the 300-pound Hutcheson, one might have thought that it was the spontaneous flare-up of an angry man. But never did a man move with more premeditated deliberation. In a later statement to Saul Alinsky, as described in Alinsky's excellent biography of Lewis, the latter said he had carefully planned the assault in an effort to further the break that eventuated in the CIO.

"It was Bill Hutcheson's supporters and associates in the AFL who successfully blocked every single move that was made in the direction of industrial unionism," Lewis told Alinsky. "All I will say is that I never walked across an aisle so slowly and grimly as I did that day in the 1935 convention. An act of some kind, an act dramatic to the degree that it would inspire and enthuse the workers of this country was necessary. Did I say necessary? It was essential. With this in mind, I laid my plans. The 1935 convention of the American Federation of Labor was to be the scene and Bill Hutcheson, unknowingly, was to be one of the main actors of the cast. The reason for this selection and this plan was to be found in the background of Hutcheson and myself in the previous AFL conventions."

As the two labor chieftains rolled on the floor, thumping and thwacking each other, one might not have known that one was witnessing an act of high industrial statesmanship on the part of Lewis. But such it was. The breach between the two factions now could not be healed and the Committee for Industrial Organization was a virtual fact within a matter of hours. At that very convention the Lewis adherents, the partisans of industrial organization of the unorganized, met and planned an organizing meeting for the new committee for Nov. 10, 1935, in Washington.

At that meeting were Lewis; Charles P. Howard, of the Typographical Union; Sidney Hillman, of the Amalgamated Clothing Workers; Thomas McMahon of the United Textile Workers; Thomas Brown, of the Mine, Mill and Smelter Workers; Harvey Fremming, of the Oil Field, Gas Well and Refinery Workers; David Dubinsky, of the International Ladies' Garment Workers Union; and Max Zaritsky, of the Hat, Cap and Millinery Workers.

At that meeting the CIO, the Committee for Industrial Organization, was born with the announced purpose of working within the AFL rather than establishing an independent organization.[2] For the first time in history a drive to organize the millions of unskilled workers in basic industry was to get under way backed by established organizations with millions of dollars and adequate experience. When the zeal of youth and the ardor of a mass crusade were added to the experience and money the combination was to prove irresistible.

The very announcement of the new organization seemed to be a spring which released the energy of millions. Before the CIO could open offices or send organizers into the field the boiling over had begun. The long simmering was at an end. In December, 1936, and January, 1937, the staffs of most of the hotels of New York City walked out, leaving the guests to climb to their rooms, make their beds, do their cooking, and wait on themselves. At the same time Works Progress Administration artists were battling police as they began one of the first of the "stay-in strikes," refusing to be ejected from WPA headquarters. As oil painters and sculptors bit and clawed, striking AFL glaziers threw stove bolts through plate glass windows in all parts of the city. There was a strike on the waterfront as the seamen, about to form the National Maritime Union, battled against tear guns, bombs, machine guns, and nightsticks.

The torrent of strikes became nationwide. Many of them flowed from the example and inspiration of the first great sitdown in American industry, a weapon that seemed absolutely new and hit the employers with atomic force. The device was simple enough, consisting of staying inside the struck plant beside the machines and the assembly line, after going on strike without notice or warning, but it had all the elements of genius. Safe and secure inside, protected from rain or snow, cold or heat, the strikers were also safe from the assaults of police and vigilantes against picket lines. They held their places before their machines and so long as they were there no strike-breakers could take their jobs. The factory was a fort, sometimes relatively easy to defend because of the owner's fear that his machines would be injured if the workers were attacked.

And yet the new technique took courage to put into effect, especially for the first time in the United States on a large scale.[3] It happened in rubber

[2] The new organization specifically declared: "The purpose of the Committee is . . . [the] organization of unorganized workers in the mass production and other industries upon an industrial basis . . . [and] to bring them under the banner and in affiliation with the American Federation of Labor."

[3] Sit-down strikes had taken place in American history prior to the great demonstrations of 1936–37. In 1906 the IWW inspired an effective folded-arms strike in the huge General Electric plant in Schenectady which lasted for sixty-five hours. In 1910 women garment workers in New York carried on a similar demonstration.

at Akron, Ohio, in the Firestone Tire Plant No. 1. The night shift there had decided to pull the switch and stop the clattering roar of the assembly line at 2 A.M. It was Jan. 29, 1936. They had tried everything else from company unions to AFL federal unions but nothing had stopped the speed-up or resulted in a living wage. Now many were in the CIO although many were still unorganized. Now they would try this new strategy. Perhaps some of them had read that it had been successfully used recently by French workers.

As the night dragged on and 2 A.M. drew nearer, the tension increased. One could feel it in the air. Even though the foreman had no inkling of what was coming he, too, somehow knew that something big was going to happen. Ruth McKenney describes the beginning of the first big sit-down in the United States:

"The foreman paced slowly past his workmen, his eyes darting in and out of the machines, eager for any betraying gesture. He heard no word, and saw no gesture. The hands flashed, the backs bent, the arms reached out in monotonous perfection. The foreman went back to his little desk and sat squirming on the smooth-seated swivel chair. He felt profoundly disturbed. Something, he knew, was coming off. But what? For God's sake, what?

"It was 1:57 A.M., January 29, 1936.

"The tirebuilders worked in smooth frenzy, sweat around their necks, under their arms. The belt clattered, the insufferable racket and din and monotonous clash and uproar went on in steady rhythm. The clock on the south wall, a big plain clock, hesitated, its minute hand jumped to two. A tirebuilder at the end of the line looked up, saw the hand jump. The foreman was sitting quietly staring at the lines of men working under the vast pools of light. Outside, in the winter night, the streets were empty, and the whir of the factory sounded faintly on the snow.

"The tirebuilder at the end of the line gulped. His hands stopped their quick weaving motions. Every man on the line stiffened. All over the vast room, hands hesitated. The foreman saw the falter, felt it instantly. He jumped up, but he stood beside his desk, his eyes darting quickly from one line to another.

"This was it, then. But what was happening? Where was it starting? He stood perfectly still, his heart banging furiously, his throat feeling dry, watching the hesitating hands, watching the broken rhythm.

"Then the tirebuilder at the end of the line walked three steps to the master switch, and drawing a deep breath, he pulled up the heavy wooden handle. With this signal, in perfect synchronization, with the rhythm they had learned in a great mass-production industry, the tirebuilders stepped back from their machines.

"Instantly the noise stopped. The whole room lay in perfect silence. The tirebuilders stood in long lines, touching each other, perfectly motionless, deafened by the silence. A moment ago there had been the weaving hands, the revolving wheels, the clanking belt, the moving hooks, the flashing tire tools. Now there was absolute stillness, no motion, no sound.

"Out of the terrifying quiet came the wondering voice of a big tirebuilder near the windows: 'Jesus Christ, it's like the end of the world.'

"He broke the spell, the magic moment of stillness. For now his awed words said the same thing to every man. 'We done it! We stopped the belt! By God, we done it!' And men began to cheer hysterically, to shout and howl in the fresh silence. Men wrapped long sinewy arms around their neighbors' shoulders, screaming, 'We done it! We done it!' "[4]

They had done it all right and they stayed in. Within three days they had won. The speed-up was lessened, the base rate of pay increased. What the AFL could not do the sit-down had done. What argument and negotiation and what passed for collective bargaining could not accomplish they had accomplished through the sit-down. What the NIRA and the federal government failed to do they had done through the sit-down.

They had done it all right and soon workers everywhere seemed to be doing the same.[5] They sat down and as they sat they joined the CIO. CIO offices were flooded with telephone calls from excited workers who shouted, "We've sat down! Send someone over to organize us!" Even high school students the country over were sitting down and staying in, protesting bad teachers and bad food. Prisoners sat down in prisons from Pennsylvania to Alabama. The silversmiths of Greenfield, Mass., sat down, as did electric storage battery workers, dressmakers, and hosiery workers in Philadelphia.

City workers in Chicago went on a sit-down leaving the city's bridges open and up, cutting the city in two at the Chicago River. Workers everywhere, sitting down and standing up, staying in and staying out, were going on strike. Within a bare six months the CIO had 2,000,000 members, 1,000,000 having just joined, the other half coming in with the eight founding unions. The workers were apparently impressed not at all when on Aug. 4, 1936, the AFL Executive Council suspended the CIO unions, later expelling them.[6] At about the same time striking subway workers, also join-

---

[4] Ruth McKenney, *Industrial Valley,* Harcourt, Brace & Co. N.Y., 1939, pp. 261, 262.
[5] From September, 1936, through May, 1937, some 485,000 workers engaged in sit-down strikes. The strikes succeeded in closing down plants employing 600,000 other workers. The following song by Maurice Sugar, UAW counsel, epitomized the spirit of the sit-down period:

"When they tie the can to a union man,
    Sit down! Sit down!
When they give him the sack, they'll take him back,
    Sit down! Sit down!
When the speed-up comes, just twiddle your thumbs,
    Sit down! Sit down!
When the boss won't talk, don't take a walk,
    Sit down! Sit down!

[6] The steps taken by the AFL in the expulsion of the CIO unions were as follows: (1) The suspension order of Aug. 4, 1936, gave the organizations associated with the CIO until September 5 to sever their connections. When they did nothing to comply with the order, they were automatically suspended. The constitutionality of their suspension was seriously questioned within the AFL since the Federation's constitution provided at the time for the expulsion of member unions only by a vote of the

ing the CIO, seized the power plants of the BMT in New York, paralyzing the great city for a matter of hours. And still the country hadn't seen anything yet.

Top AFL leaders warned workers that the CIO was a Communistic plot but they continued flocking in, unimpressed. Although the formal charge made by the AFL against the CIO was dual unionism and refusal to abide by majority rule, its leaders never tired in associating the new organization with Moscow.

On August 13, 15, and 16, 1938, John P. Frey, president of the AFL Metal Trades Department, testified at public hearings of the Dies un-American Activities Committee that the CIO was Communist-dominated. Already reaction in its fight against the New Deal had sufficiently recovered to take over a part of government, beginning with this creation of the Dies anti-labor Congressional committee. Frey's testimony marked the beginning of a government-sponsored blacklist, inaugurating in recent times the Big Business use of government to destroy labor via the red scare.

Frey's testimony was eagerly seized upon by the press, the *New York Times* of August 14 heading its story, "Communists Rule the CIO, Frey of AFL Testifies. He Names 248 Reds." Most CIO officials were so branded including those who in 1955 were still being hounded on Frey's charge. He was the pioneer of much that was to come. In the light of Frey's charges against them it was somewhat ironic that a little more than a decade later CIO top leaders were to hurl identical charges at fellow trade unionists and proceed to expel a number of unions from their organization on Frey's ancient accusation that they were Communist-dominated.

But then, in 1936, as the CIO was getting under way with the force of an earthquake, all was action. Unity, not splitting, was the battle cry. The mammoth electrical industry, including General Electric, Westinghouse, and Philco, was being organized, often on the picket line. Federal locals, independent unions, and the International Association of Machinists, AFL, under Jim Matles, a young organizer of extraordinary ability and energy, were coming together in a unity that was sweeping all before them. The United Electrical, Radio and Machine Workers of America, destined to be one of the country's largest and best run unions, was organized in March, 1936. By May of that year a department at General Electric's vast plant at Schenectady had scored gains in one of the earliest sit-downs.

convention but said nothing about suspensions. (2) In November, 1936, the Tampa convention of the AFL sustained the Executive Council's suspension order by a vote of 21,679 to 2,043. The suspended CIO unions were not present at the convention. (3) In February, 1937, the AFL Executive Council ordered the expulsion of all CIO unions from city central and state federations. (4) In October, 1937, the Denver convention of the AFL authorized the Executive Council by a vote of 25,616 to 1,227 to revoke at its discretion the charters of all CIO unions. (5) In January, 1938, the Executive Council revoked the charters of three CIO unions and three months later of four others.

Such was the quality of the times that everything, even including attacks and unfavorable publicity, seemed to contribute to the UE's growth. For example, Governor Hoffman of New Jersey, later to leave a deathbed confession that he had embezzled hundreds of thousands of dollars in state funds, went on the air in a nationwide broadcast in which he assailed the young union then beginning to organize in his state. "There will be no insurrections in New Jersey," he told the country. "If the UE tries any sit-downs the whole power of the state, military and legal, will be used to eject them."

When the Governor made his attack the UE's main office was a little hole in the wall at 26th Street and Broadway, New York City, for which the rent was $27.50 a month. Membership lists were low, funds were hard to come by, and hundreds of thousands of electrical workers had never heard of the budding union. Working there some eighteen hours a day was Julius Emspak, secretary-treasurer, still a little awed by the big city and fresh from the assembly line at GE's Schenectady plant where he had worked as a tool maker for $1.14 an hour. A worker since childhood but a college graduate, too, majoring in philosophy, Emspak as well as Matles was typical of a new kind of union leadership.

When Governor Hoffman attacked the union, Emspak demanded and received the same amount of time and the same prominence in a nationwide radio hook-up to answer the Governor's charges. Thousands of electrical workers heard of the young union for the first time and thousands joined as the result of the Governor's attack.

The biggest strike that summer of 1936 was a UE strike, the bloody, gallant fight at the Radio Corporation of America's plant at Camden. The young men of UE, workers on assembly lines but a few months before, perhaps seemed a little awkward as they entered the sumptuous paneled office of David Sarnoff in New York's huge Rockefeller Center on Fifth Avenue. They asked for bargaining and union recognition for the workers of the RCA plant at Camden, N.J.

"I won't negotiate," said Sarnoff, the head of RCA, with the calm confidence of a great tycoon, "under this kind of pressure. I won't negotiate with a gun at my head. Anyway, you boys can't call a strike. John L. Lewis has personally given me assurance that there will be no strike."

Sarnoff apparently felt as he dismissed the young trade union officials that he had them successfully checkmated through going over their heads to their superior. But they could not believe that Lewis had promised no strike action. At the pace and with the energy typical of those days, they jumped into a car and drove all night until they finally located John L. Lewis just as he was leaving a hotel at Hazleton, Pa. Lewis, ringed around by his militant constituents, denied that he had ever said that there would be no strike.

The next morning 6,000 workers at the RCA plant in Camden went out on strike for recognition, hundreds joining up and signing cards as they walked out. Their mass picket lines were daily attacked by 1,000 city police, state troopers, armed finks, thugs, and criminals, the latter rented out to RCA by the Sherwood Detective Agency. The corporation spent at least $244,930, according to the researches of the Twentieth Century Fund, in fighting the strike and much of that amount went to the Sherwood Detective Agency as payment for armed thugs, guards, and strikebreakers.

Some 175 of the RCA strikers were arrested and jailed, held in bail that totaled $2,000,000. Each day the ambulance clanged up to the battered picket line, sped the injured to the hospital. The strikers knew that they were fighting not only for their own demands but for the whole labor movement. On one occasion, when CIO organizer Powers Hapgood was jailed, 5,000 strikers advanced on the Camden jail. The sheriff glanced out at them, massed as far as he could see around the jail, then turned and ordered Hapgood to be released immediately.

Almost daily Judge Neutz of Camden, in sentencing strikers to prison terms, charged that the strike and the union were a Communist plot. The strikers, many of whom received less than $10 weekly, branded the charge an attempt to divide and defeat them. They won, after four long and bloody weeks, and began the struggle which resulted in wage increases in the electrical industry of fifty-nine cents an hour over the next ten years. In the fifteen years preceding the formation of the union the industry had raised hourly rates by only five cents. But things changed after the RCA victory. That strike put the UE on the map.

In September, 1936, the UE and the shipyard workers joined the CIO. Their joining made a crucial difference in that organization, proving it could attract new and growing mass unions, could attract others than the original AFL unions which had formed it. Before the end of the year UE had organized the General Electric plant at Schenectady. This was a vital step in a growth that was to continue until UE included 358 local unions with collective bargaining contracts covering 600,000 workers in 1,375 plants. About the same time that the UE joined the CIO the new national labor center's numbers were increased by the Flat Glass Workers; the Amalgamated Association of Iron, Steel and Tin Workers, which was taken over by the Steel Workers Organizing Committee; the United Automobile Workers of America; and the United Rubber Workers. Daily, weekly, new unions added their strength to Lewis' 600,000 mine workers and to the 400,000 who composed the membership of the seven other founding unions.

2. Sit-down at Flint

The strategists of the CIO had intended to organize the union-breaking steel industry first, as the heart of the open shop since the Homestead Battle of 1892, but the great spontaneous surge of organization and the new sit-down tactic forced them to change their plans. The workers in auto had taken all they could and all they would. Speed-up had become a killer in Detroit, Pontiac, Flint, and Dearborn. Men were through, drained out, and cast aside before they were forty. On hot days, as the belt moved at ever faster tempo, its clatter an all-enveloping roar, each worker pushing himself to the point of desperation, men up and down the line dropped to the floor from exhaustion.

It was particularly bad during the summer of 1936 and Henry Kraus writes:

"During July, a torrid heat wave sent the thermometer boiling to over 100 degrees for a week straight. But the assembly lines pounded away mercilessly while many workers fell at their stations like flies. Deaths in the state's auto centers ran into the hundreds within three or four days, and the clang of hospital ambulances was heard incessantly to and from the factories in Detroit, Pontiac and Flint."

Each time the workers, by superhuman effort, mastered an increased rate of speed-up, the rates of the piece-work system under which they were paid were lowered. No matter how much faster they worked, pay remained the same. Clayton W. Fountain, in his book *Union Guy*, declares:

"Our major gripe was the piecework system. I don't recall exactly what our piece rate per cushion was at the time, but we made something like $6.50 or $7.00 a day. According to the theory of incentive pay, the harder and faster you worked, the more pay you received. The employer, however, reserved the right to change the rules. We would start out with a new rate, arbitrarily set by the company time-study man and work like hell for a couple of weeks, boosting our pay a little each day. Then, bingo, the timekeeper would come along one morning and tell us that we had another new rate, a penny or two per cushion less than it had been the day before."[7]

But that wasn't all. Wages were as low as twenty cents an hour in some plants. Terror and espionage were used against the auto workers to an unprecedented degree by tycoons receiving salaries of between $150,000 and

[7] There was virtually no difference between the speed-up in vogue in the middle 1930's and the one in vogue in the early 1900's. An official government study in 1908 showed that in the incandescent lamp industry the employers "as the result of a carefully planned policy" to speed up production would appoint a worker to act as "a pacemaker," urging her (since most electric lamp workers were women) "to increase her own production and that of her group by being paid five cents more than the average of the entire group." The study continues: "After this system has been in vogue for a short time and the girls have become accustomed to work at their maximum efficiency, the 'leader' is removed, the bonuses discarded, and according to the testimony of many of the girls, the piece rate is cut to such a point that the average wage level is as it was when the employees were producing less. By this means the production is said in several cases to have been doubled within a short time." (U.S. Dept. of Labor, Bureau of Labor Statistics, *Summary of the Report on the Condition of Women and Child Wage Earners in the United States*, Bulletin No. 175, Washington, 1916, pp. 155-156.)

$500,000 a year who had not the slightest intention of obeying the nation's law, the Wagner Act, making it mandatory for them to negotiate with their employees' union. Workers who attempted union organization were ruthlessly fired and often beaten up. Men were discharged for merely smiling, and sometimes for absolutely no reason at all, on the theory that sudden and arbitrary discharge would keep men docile.

Criminals were hired by the hundreds to bully and cow employees, many of them by the so-called Service Department under Harry Bennett at Ford's. Even lunch boxes were searched. A policy of silence, an absolute absence of human communication, was induced by terror, particularly at Dearborn, where spies were almost as thick as Ford cars. And outside of the auto plants there was the Black Legion—about which H. W. Anderson of General Motors spoke—its mission prevention of unionization through murder and torture.

But all of the terror and repression succeeded only in filling the auto workers with a dammed-up bitterness soon to break forth. Even in the twenties there had been attempts at organization under the Trade Union Educational League and by the early thirties unity had been forged among militants, as organizers moved through the night, signing up auto workers in their homes for the union, exercising a caution similar to that used by trade unionists in Hitler's Germany. And often down assembly lines, tucked into each half-built car, came leaflets urging organization.

In 1930 the Auto Workers Union, led by the TUUL, struck the huge General Motor's Fisher Body Plant Number One at Flint. The strike was defeated, the strikers blacklisted. In 1933 the Skilled Tool and Die Makers walked out. They were defeated. They were blacklisted. Early in 1935, under the stimulus of Section 7(A) of the NIRA, soon to be declared unconstitutional, the auto workers flooded into a new AFL federal union. Now the industry's 400,000 workers were sure they would have the opportunity of striking back. But the AFL officials abjectly capitulated to the giant auto industry, even agreeing to no union recognition. Thousands of auto workers, as the rubber workers had previously done, tore up their union books while other thousands threw theirs into bonfires.

In May, 1936, the Auto Workers Union withdrew from the AFL, shortly afterwards joining the CIO as the United Automobile Workers of America. As the wave of sit-downs hit the country in the wake of the Akron strike, a new surge of bitter determination seized the auto workers, particularly those of General Motors, the billion-dollar, world-famed corporation that had heretofore broken every attempt of its employees at union organization with contemptuous ease. Its officials were confident that they could do so again. A billion dollars had strength.

The confidence of the General Motors executives did not seem misplaced as the crisis of 1937 neared with "the curtain about to go up on one of the greatest upheavals in the history of labor in America." The corporation had on its rolls 261,977 employees, more than one half of the 400,000 employed in the auto industry. In 1937 it produced and sold 2,116,897 cars, had a capitalization of $1,040,655,000 and large plants in fifty-seven cities and towns that dotted the whole United States from Michigan to Georgia, from New Jersey to California.

It owned as well, to all intents and purposes, many of the towns in which it had plants, their courts, their police, their whole city officialdom. As for the town of Flint, Mich., the heart of the General Motors empire where the Buick and the Chevrolet were largely assembled, Alinsky writes:

". . . General Motors owned it body and soul. The newspaper and local radio station carried out General Motors' bidding, not only editorially and by biased news reporting but even by refusing to carry ads of the new CIO union. The police, the politicians and the judges were not the only ones genuflecting to the great god General Motors. So with few exceptions did the ministers, the priests and the school officials. General Motors owned everything in Flint, except the people; all they owned of them was their implacable hatred."

This mass hatred, and an accompanying aspiration to be something more than a unit on an assembly line, began to break through in the form of sit-down strikes late in 1936. The occasion, in almost every instance, was intolerable speed-up and management's refusal to bargain with the UAW. On November 18 there was a sit-down in the GM plant at Atlanta. On December 15 the General Motors plant at Kansas City sat down. On December 19 young Homer Martin, president of the UAW, former preacher and hop, skip and jump champion, sped to Washington where he conferred with John L. Lewis on the developing situation.

"It is the hope of the United Automobile Workers," Lewis said in a public statement, "that General Motors will agree to meet peaceably and work out these questions without any disturbance of production. Collective bargaining is the law of the land and we think General Motors should now do a little collective bargaining."

General Motors was not impressed by the law of the land. They were going to do no more bargaining than they were forced to. William Knudsen, executive vice president of GM, said that nationwide bargaining was out. They were willing and eager to meet with their employees but only on a plant basis. Any grievance should be taken up with any of the fifty-seven plant managers in whose plant the grievance had occurred.

Knudsen received his reply on December 28 when the GM plant in Cleveland sat down. At the same time Wyndham Mortimer, militant vice president of the UAW, served notice that the Cleveland sit-down could be settled only as part of a nationwide settlement that included the entire GM empire. On December 30 there were four major GM sit-downs, including decisive ones at the very heart of the GM system in Flint, in the gigantic Chevrolet Number Four, in Fisher Body Plant Number One, and in Fisher Body Plant Number Two.

By January 4 the sit-downers were in possession of the GM plants at

Cleveland, Ohio; Atlanta, Ga.; Anderson, Ind.; Norwood, Ohio; Kansas City, and, above all, at Flint, Mich.

By January 4 all hell had broken loose.

Flint was a town gripped by imminent civil war. Officials of the Flint Alliance, a General Motors vigilante "citizens' group" organized by George Boyeson, a former Buick paymaster, threatened to turn Chevy Four into a scene of mass murder. In response to the threats union men were coming by the thousands from all over the Middle West, flying squadrons, as the defenders called themselves, who sped in fast cars to Flint from Toledo, Gary, and Chicago, from Detroit, Akron, and Cleveland.

The thousands sitting down in the two Fisher Body plants, in Chevrolet Four, each instant expecting a bloody attack by troops, were reinforced by giant picket lines outside the plants, surrounding them, protecting them with a wall of human flesh, picket lines in which thousands of women and children massed to protect their husbands, fathers, sons, sitting down inside the plants. Day and night the huge mass picket lines, guided and instructed by the earth-filling voice that came from the sound car, surged back and forth, often in the light of fires that weakly assailed the cold of winter nights, its members determined that the men inside should not be attacked.

The thousands of men in the three plants, excellently organized into emergency communities which maintained perfect order day after day, seemed to be the beating heart of the country. From their determination came the impulse that for more than a month dominated the nation's life. Sleeping in half-completed cars on silent assembly lines, organizing "police departments" and jazz bands, the sit-downers at Flint were surely the nation's center then and would be for forty-four long days in which every instant seemed likely to bring the attack of troops and police.

Every normal recourse of society seemed powerless against them. They laughed at the orders of police. They hooted at court injunctions. They fraternized with the armed militia drawn up outside the factory gates, waiting for the zero hour in which the militia would be sent in with gas bombs and machine guns. But even as the sit-downers fraternized they built up piles of bolts and auto parts with which they meant to defend themselves.

The men just sat, day after day, their beards black and stubbly and growing longer, playing cards, writing letters, governing and running the strange new communities beside the motionless assembly lines. But it was their united force that sent President Roosevelt into action, caused Frances Perkins, Secretary of Labor, to make frantic and futile efforts to induce General Motors to obey the law of the land and negotiate. It was their presence, massed by the thousands beside the silent assembly lines, day after day and night after night, that brought John L. Lewis from Washington and Detroit, determined to make Sloan and Knudsen negotiate.

It was their presence that imperiled the political career of gallant Frank

Murphy, just sworn in as the new governor of Michigan, the target of a thousand demands for the use of force, a hundred threats that he would be impeached. It was the refusal of the sit-down strikers to work or to leave that filled column on column in every newspaper in the country, that caused speeches and screeches in the halls of Congress.

It was their firmness that built the CIO, that made a hundred other unions possible, that cracked the open shop, that filled the common people, the working people, with a great thrill and resolve. Workers everywhere snatched the editions of the papers as they came off the press. "Were they still in? Were they holding out?" And when the people read that the strikers still were holding firm, their eyes sometimes filled with tears and they felt a sudden surge of pride. Invisible impulses connected the sit-downers in Flint with every member of the working class in the United States.

There had been a low growl from press and politician as the sit-down progressed in 1936 but, hoping that it was only a passing fad, like the yo-yo top or flagpole sitting, they had not let out all the stops. But this was a different matter. Sitting down in General Motors, the pride and pomp, the power and glory, the very apex of the American Way and Private Property, this was unspeakable sacrilege. This was revolution. This was gigantic theft. This was wholesale trespass. This was flouting of law and order. This was Red Insurrection. This was a Communist attempt, said Alfred P. Sloan, head of General Motors, "to Sovietize" the auto industry, as "a dress rehearsal for Sovietizing the entire country."

Never in the history of the country has there been such an outraged, universal howl of horror as greeted the GM sit-downs. Thousands of the respectable agreed with Representative Clare Hoffman of Michigan that the sit-downers must be shot out of the plants.

John L. Lewis did not think so. He said that a charge of violation of the law came with poor grace from the country's largest corporation which was itself refusing to obey the law of the land, the Wagner Labor Act. While virtually every public figure, including labor leaders, shrank from the enormity of occupying private property, John L. Lewis said firmly as he arrived in Detroit to bargain with General Motors, "The CIO stands squarely behind these sit-downs."

For Lewis knew that the new technique gave him the only bargaining power he had. With the men out of the Flint plants, the arrogant GM officials would not so much as speak to him. With them in, he felt, they would not only speak but in the end would bargain collectively.

Governor Murphy, still holding out against the universal demand of the powerful that he use force and troops in ejecting the sit-downers, brought the GM officials and Lewis together. Of the three principals, Knudsen, Murphy, and Lewis, two were suffering acutely. Knudsen, a production man, had a passion for assembly lines and machinery. It was not that he loved humans less but that he understood machinery better. He could not stand the thought of the miracle that was GM production, over which he had slaved and sweated in his own executive way, being wrecked in a battle attempting to eject the sit-downers.

One injunction ordering the forcible ousting of the sit-downers had been declared void when it was found that the judge who had issued it was himself a large GM stockholder, thus violating a Michigan law that a judge shall have no interest in any case decided by him. Now another injunction for eviction of the sit-downers had been issued.

It was difficult to say who hated the injunction and its approaching enforcement most, Murphy or Knudsen. Murphy feared bloodshed. Knudsen feared damage to the plant. And the attitude of the Flint sit-downers was clear as they called from the plants, "Damn the injunction, damn the courts, damn the army, and double damn General Motors!" On the tenth day of the strike they issued a statement declaring they would fight to the last man if force were used against them. The Governor, a self-announced Irish revolutionary and the possessor of pronounced working class sympathies—his grandfather had been hanged by the British—nevertheless believed that his oath of office obliged him to enforce the injunction, by armed force if necessary.

With Murphy and Knudsen sweating, John L. Lewis was comparatively relaxed. In the endless silent sessions of mock collective bargaining, held together only by Murphy's determination, he sometimes amused himself by goading the dour, silent executives of General Motors. Once he asked John Thomas Smith, a monument of stern, sour dignity who had sat for hours without opening his mouth, if he would be so good as to move his chair closer to him, say no further than three inches away.

"Smith looked down at the space between our chairs," Lewis told Alinsky, "and ejaculated, 'Move it closer to you? Why we're practically sitting in each other's laps right now, Mr. Lewis. My chair is only about six inches away from your chair. Why should you want me to move closer to your chair?'

"I then stared at him and with a wistful tone, I said, 'You see, Mr. Smith, for the past hour I have been thinking about how some day in the future I would be able to tell my grandchildren about how one time I sat just six inches away from one and a half billion dollars, but I would like to tell them that I sat only three inches away! Please, do you mind moving your chair a little bit closer?' "

Such approaches would occasionally force yelps of protest from the GM executives, and then, if they didn't watch themselves, they would find themselves slipping into talk about the issues. But they did watch themselves. As the days progressed, the eleventh, the twelfth, the thirteenth, fourteenth, a whole slow week and then it was January 21, it became clear that Knudsen and his associates were on a sit-down of their own.

Their real interest was in Flint, not in John L. Lewis. The contest was not across the collective bargaining table but between the sit-downers and a management determined to sit down on bargaining. The issue was who would quit sitting down first. Knudsen decided to discourage his opposing sit-downers by turning off the heat in the three Flint plants. He would freeze his antagonists out. But the sit-downers, somehow informed of certain GM insurance contracts, threw open the windows, threatening plant fire-fighting equipment with freezing, an act which voided the insurance contracts. Mr. Knudsen, in the utmost anguish, ordered the heat turned back on.

Then it was decided to starve out the Flint sit-downers. The effort precipitated a battle between police and women, who had each day for almost a month brought food to their men, and were wildly determined that they should not be stopped. The conflict, in which fourteen fell from gunshot wounds, was later called "The Battle of Bulls Run." It was called this, writes Mary Heaton Vorse, because the bulls ran. She continues:

"Preparatory to the battle the street had been cleared. Motorists had been warned to drive elsewhere. The police stationed themselves around the plant armed with tear gas and guns. They had gas masks on when the women came with the evening meal. The door through which they usually passed the food was blocked. The women began passing the food through the windows. . . . Then came the tear gas. One shell was shot inside the plant, one into the crowd. But the men and women with streaming eyes persisted in getting the food in. They fought back. Telling about it later, the women said:

" 'Nothing was going to stop us getting food in to our men.' The first shot crashed through the air. . . . Inside the plant the heavy fire hoses were played on the police and on the tear gas bombs. . . . The police were firing pointblank into the crowd that included women. Union sympathizers were retaliating with the only means of defense—they had stones, lumps of coal, steel hinges, milk bottles. That, and their courage, were their only weapons. Yet they held their ground.

"The sound truck came into play. Its calm, great voice directed the battle; advised the men where the attack would come from; encouraged them to stand firm. After two hours of battle the police began to weaken. . . ."

Now the climax was coming fast. The state police were called, and the militia mobilized. There was a battle before Chevrolet Nine, where a good many of the women's Auxiliary were gassed. A rumor that police and militia now in the streets of Flint were about to enter Chevy Four brought a vast crowd, women, children, strike sympathizers, members of flying squadrons from all over the Middle West, who formed a mammoth picket line about the plant. A woman's voice addressed the great picket line from the sound wagon. Mrs. Vorse tells of it:

"She told the crowd that the women had gone to the Hall [Pengally Hall, the union headquarters] to wipe their eyes clear from tear gas and would soon be back. 'We don't want any violence; we don't want any trouble. We are going to do everything we can to keep from trouble, but we are going to protect our husbands.'

"Down the hill presently came a procession, preceded by an American flag. The women's bright red caps showed dramatically in the dark crowd. They were singing 'Hold the Fort.'

"To all the crowd there was something moving about seeing the women return to the picket line after having been gassed in front of plant number 9.

"It was getting dark, the crowd had grown denser. A black fringe of pickets and spectators was silhouetted against the brilliant green lights of the plant windows. . . . When later in the evening I went down to Chevrolet Number Four, a cordon of militia men had been thrown about the great plant. We could not pass. Far down in the hollow the salamanders glowed. You could see the faithful picket line moving back and forth. At half past three in the morning a dozen women of the Emergency Brigade were on duty in the first-aid room in Pengally Hall."

The thirtieth day of the strike came and went. The sit-downers felt as if they had always lived beside the motionless conveyer belts; that there had never been any other kind of life. A whole new way of living evolved, no wives, no kids, no whiskey, no gambling, no beds, nothing but waiting, waiting, waiting for a settlement or for the entry of armed troops. They had little to comfort them but unconquerable determination.

On the thirty-fifth day the Flint authorities began arming hundreds of vigilantes as special police who said they were going to clear the three plants. Now the tension was becoming unbearable. Each day members of the Flint Alliance announced they were going in shooting. Each hour brought rumors that Governor Murphy had at last ordered the troops to clear the plants. Each day proved the rumors wrong but on the fortieth day the sit-downers sent this telegram to Governor Murphy:

"Unarmed as we are, the introduction of the militia, sheriffs or police with murderous weapons will mean a blood-bath of unarmed workers. . . . The police of the City of Flint belong to General Motors. The Sheriff of Genesee County belongs to General Motors. The judges of Genesee County belong to General Motors. It remains to be seen whether the Governor of the State also belongs to General Motors.

"Governor, we have decided to stay in the plant. . . . We fully expect that if a violent effort is made to oust us many of us will be killed and we take this means of making it known to our wives, to our children, to the people of the State of Michigan and the country, that if this result follows from the attempt to eject us, you are the one who must be held responsible for our deaths!"

Governor Murphy must have groaned as he read the telegram and Knudsen's ruddy face may have paled. The Governor was still desperately sparring for time but he could not hold out much longer. Every newspaper and radio station, every citizen of substance in the state and nation, with the exception of President Roosevelt and members of the New Deal, were demanding that he live up to his oath of office. He contrived by frantic efforts to keep the so-called negotiations in progress. Sometimes he thought Knudsen was weakening, sometimes John L. Lewis. But right now John L. was thundering, accusing his GM opponents of conspiring at mass murder, of insisting on the wreckage of Knudsen's beloved machinery.

The forty-second day of the strike arrived and had nearly passed. It was almost midnight when there was a knock on the door of the hotel room of John L. Lewis. There stood a miserable Governor Murphy. He had succumbed at last. He, not Knudsen, had been the first to break. In his hand was an order to the troops of the National Guard to clear the plants on the following morning.

John L., who had been ill, now gathered himself for a final effort. He turned all his scorn and eloquence upon the suffering Governor who had said that he must "uphold the law." Alinsky describes the scene:

"Lewis continued with his voice rising with each sentence. 'Governor Murphy, when you gave ardent support to the Irish revolutionary movement against the British Empire, you were not doing that because of your high regard for law and order. You did not then say "Uphold the law!" When your father, Governor Murphy, was imprisoned by the British authorities for his activities as an Irish revolutionary, you did not sing forth with hosannas and say "The law cannot be wrong. The law must be supported. It is right and just that my father be put into prison! Praised be the law!"

" 'And when the British government took your grandfather as an Irish revolutionary and hanged him by the neck until he was dead, you did not get down on your knees and burst forth in praise for the sanctity and the glory and the purity of the law, the law that must be upheld at all costs!

" 'But here, Governor Murphy, you do. You want my answer, sir? I give it to you. Tomorrow morning I shall personally enter General Motors Plant Chevrolet Number 4. I shall order the men to disregard your order, to stand fast. I shall then walk to the largest window in the plant, open it, divest myself of my outer raiment, remove my shirt and bare my bosom. Then when you order your troops to fire, mine will be the first breast those bullets will strike!'

"Then Lewis lowered his voice. 'And as my body falls from the window to the ground, you listen to the voice of your grandfather as he whispers in your ear, "Frank are you sure you are doing the right thing?" ' "

The Governor, white and trembling, turned and fled. When morning came he could not make himself issue the order. He was not the only one pacing the floor. Knudsen, too, was suffering. If the assault was made the public might hold General Motors responsible for bloodshed while stockholders might hold him responsible for a long, long interruption in production. The market was being taken away from GM, day by day and week by week, by its unfeeling rivals, Chrysler and Ford. Knudsen and his associates wrestled with their agonizing problem all that day, the forty-third day of the strike. If they surrendered it was possible that steel, and all American industry would be forced to surrender. Damn the union, damn

Lewis, and double damn this new sit-down business. If the workers would only quit the plants. GM had tried the red scare, tried the courts, the police, vigilantes, but still the workers sat as unmovable as the Rocky Mountains. All night the GM officials discussed, debated, worried.

At 2:45 A.M. on the morning of the forty-fourth day of the strike, Thursday, February 11, General Motors surrendered. They announced they would recognize the union, negotiate nationally as to hours, wages, speed-up.

The sit-downers at first refused to believe it. It was a trick to get them out. Then, as the morning progressed, they could hear cheering swelling higher and higher, coming nearer and nearer, louder and louder. Looking out the windows they could see thousands outside, mad with joy, dancing, embracing, shouting, weeping. Then they received authoritative word from union leaders. They had won—won not only for themselves and their families, won not only over the country's greatest industry, but won for all American labor. They had not been divided by the red scare or any other kind of scare.

The sit-downers felt queer and weak as the great strain slowly ebbed from their taut nerves. They cheered and howled for a time and then looked dazedly around at the vast expanse, still echoing with their victory shouts, that had been their homes for forty-four days. Slowly they began to pack their things. They would march out together. John Thrasher, of Fisher Number One, later told of their feelings:

"As the exhilaration of our first union victory wore off the gang was occupied with the thoughts of leaving the silent factory which for days had been our home. One found himself wondering what home life would be like again. What will it be like to go home—and to come back again tomorrow with motors running and the long-silenced machines roaring again? But that is for the future.

"One must pack. In a paper shopping bag I place the things which helped make my 'house' a place to live in: house slippers, extra shirt, sox and underwear; razor and shaving equipment; two books, a reading lamp; and the picture of my wife that hung above my bed. It is near time to go. Already there is a goodly number of cars and people outside, brother workers who have come to escort us from the plant. The first victory has been ours but the war is not over. We were strong enough to win over all the combined forces of our enemies and we shall continue to win only if we remember that through *solidarity* we have been made free. Now the door is opening."

Henry Kraus, in his book *The Many and the Few*, continues the story of leaving Fisher Number One:

"The factory whistle blew a full blast and the men began marching to the door. The crowd of thousands that was gathered ouside let out a great hurrah as Bud Simmons appeared heading the line. Every striker toted a big bundle on his back. The lines formed immediately in the street for the two-mile parade to the other plant where the celebration was scheduled. Four color bearers with large American flags were in the lead. Tiny flags were carried in every hat. The massive jam of sit-downers, sympathizers and hundreds of autos began their singing, cheering, honking way toward town.

"Night was beginning to close down on Chevrolet Avenue when the Fisher One contingent appeared at the crest of the hill. A combined roar from the two crowds down the street . . . greeted the long-awaited marchers. The Chevy Four leaders were standing on the high landing above the gate, a tall American flag on each side, and their men were gathering inside the doors. As the Fisher One parade reached the plant, great flares suddenly lit up, confetti flew and the enormous gates of the plant opened slowly.

"Lungs that were already spent with cheering found new strength as the brave men began to descend the stairs. They looked haggard with exaustion. As they came out, wives and children rushed to husbands and fathers who had not been seen for . . . days. Strong, heavily-bearded men were unashamed of tears. Then someone began to sing 'Solidarity' and as all joined in, the moment was carried beyond its almost unbearable tenseness and emotion."

Within a year wages in the auto industry had been increased by $300,000,-000, in many instances from thirty and forty cents an hour to one dollar. Within a year the UAW had grown from 30,000 members to 500,000 and had written agreements with 4,000 automobile and auto parts concerns. It was as if the victorious marchers already knew all this and Mary Heaton Vorse writes that as they marched they chanted "Freedom! Freedom! Freedom!"

"Men and women from the cars and marchers shouted to the groups of other working people who lined the streets, 'Join the union! We are free!' . . . Homer Martin, Wyndham Mortimer, Bob Travis and other strike leaders addressed the roaring crowds. . . . The joy of victory tore through Flint. . . . The working people of Flint had begun to forge a new life out of their historic victory."

And so also the working people of America.

3. Triumph

Now the back of the open shop was broken. A great cry of joy ascended from the country's working people as they heard of the surrender of General Motors. Ford would be next, the auto workers said, and, although it took four more years, it was done.

In the aftermath of Flint sit-downs came like snowflakes in a blizzard. The storm moved from Flint to Detroit, to Chicago and Milwaukee, paralyzing stores, factories, and hotels. It sped to Denver, roared on to the West Coast and back again to the Atlantic. It hit St. Louis with one of the longest sit-downs on record when 2,000 UE workers at the Emerson Electric

Company won union recognition and pay increases after fifty-three days of staying in.

What had been a labor tactic seemed to become a universal mania. To the élite the sit-downs seemed like some horrible disease, an inexplicable plague that harried them wherever they went. Woolworth girls jitterbugged in the aisles of stores closed tight as a result of sit-downs. Waiters in exclusive clubs, sitting down in the seats of the mighty, stared coldly and impassively at bankers demanding service and their chairs.

A new set of standards seemed suddenly to blossom in the American people. The old wisdom of Sylvis, Parsons, Debs, and Haywood, once as a whisper in a gale, now was on the lips of everyone. Even architects and engineers, chemists and scientists, teachers and professors were saying as they organized, "Never pass a picket line," "In unity there is strength," and "An injury to one is an injury to all."

One might walk into a barber shop and find the barbers sitting down, go to lunch and find the restaurant occupied by sit-down cooks and waitresses. Teachers, WPA workers, artists, bus boys, bellboys, municipal employees, clerks, stenographers, cooks, steel workers, longshoremen, garment workers, fur workers, waiters, bartenders, miners, sailors, firemen, power house workers, lumberjacks, sharecroppers, salesmen, thousands who had scarcely heard of unions before, were talking solidarity as they organized, sat down, got contracts, raised wages. Society people were rolling their eyes and shuddering from California's Gold Coast to Maine's Bar Harbor as they recounted tales of horror suffered at the hands of those who had suddenly forgotten their places.

With this tidal wave of pro-union sentiment as an aid and background in the organizing of heavy industry, the CIO moved fast. In auto, Chrysler followed General Motors, surrendering in short order to another massive sit-down. Steel, proud steel, was crumbling. Steel, Big Steel, the historic foundation of the open shop in the United States, was finding that its traditional murder and terror, as in 1892 and later in 1919, did not work when it was faced with CIO.

The forty huge plants (now ninety-three) of the Morgan-dominated General Electric, largest electrical trust in the world, which had successfully fought off effective union organization since 1892, were now being organized, one by one.

The great upheaval was thrusting up a new kind of union leader, young, militant, capable, as different from the old-time business agent as a jet plane from a covered wagon.

This new kind of labor leader was sometimes in a cell one day and the guest of honor at a banquet the next. More than one turned up at the conference table with a black eye, or an arm in a sling, the result of an attack by police or goons. In auto Wyndham Mortimer, Bob Travis, the Reuther brothers, Richard Frankensteen, such rank-and-file leaders as Bud Simmons and Bill McKie, were bringing into their union additional thousands.

On the West Coast Harry Bridges, J. R. Robertson, Lou Goldblatt, Germain Bulke, Charles "Chili" Duarte, Henry Schmidt, and a strong rank and file were strengthening the International Longshoremen's and Warehousemen's Union in their famous march inland, signing up the employees of warehouse after warehouse.

In Lynn, Mass., Albert J. Fitzgerald, later to become president of the United Electrical, Radio and Machine Workers of America (UE), was working with others day and night organizing the huge GE plant. James Matles, Julius Emspak, James Carey were bringing the UE into being while Ernest De Maio, Ernest Thompson, and William Sentner[7] were organizing in the Middle West. Joseph Curran, Ferdinand Smith, Al Lannon,[8] Blackie Myers, Howard McKenzie, and a militant rank and file were organizing the seamen. Quill, Hogan, Santo[9] and McMahon were leading the organization of transport while Ben Gold and Irving Potash[10] were uniting fur and leather workers into a powerful CIO union. Everywhere the rank and file, the real organizers of CIO, were developing such new leaders as John Clark, Maurice E. Travis, Orville Larsen, and Asbury Howard of Mine, Mill and Smelter.

But by far the most important of all organizing drives was that in steel which was now rocketing along, carrying everything before it. Steel workers, workers everywhere, had jumped into the labor movement with an almost religious zeal.

Labor, in the year 1937, was not just a program of economic improvement. It was a way of life, a holy creed, a passionate belief, a blazing crusade for which thousands were ready to give their lives. Tough veterans of the United Mine Workers, Socialists, Communists and non-Communists, old-time steel unionists who had seen their organizations shot out and blacklisted out of the mills, took to the steel circuit. They boldly pushed into steel's company towns, defied the dreaded police, appeared in mills at Braddock, Homestead, Aliquippa, McKeesport, traveling up and down the Monongahela, the Ohio, the Mahoning, the Allegheny, advancing into Youngstown in Ohio, into Gary and Chicago. They traveled the dark valleys of the steel country where the Bill of Rights had been a mockery for workingmen for almost a century.

---

[7] Sentner, who has done as much as anyone to raise wages of Middle Western electrical workers, now faces prison for his political beliefs under the thought-control Smith Act.

[8] Al Lannon, one of the founders of the National Maritime Union, is under three-year prison sentence for alleged violation of the thought-control Smith Act.

[9] John Santo, brilliant negotiator and another raiser of wages, has been deported to his native Hungary.

[10] Another victim of the Smith Act was Irving Potash, vice president of the Fur and Leather Workers Union. He is perhaps more responsible than anyone, with the possible exception of Gold and Samuel Burt, for the freeing of the fur workers from the Lepke-Gurrah Gang. Potash, with Gold, played a principal part in the raising of wages.

There were more than 5,000 volunteer organizers in steel. To their ardor made hot by the sit-downs in auto were added experience, know-how, all the resources of the United Mine Workers, largest and strongest union in the country. The Steel Workers Organizing Committee, headed by Philip Murray and established in June, 1936, immediately opened up three vast, streamlined regional offices, in Pittsburgh, Chicago, and Birmingham. They had publicity men, statisticians, batteries of lawyers, as well as such astute veterans as John Brophy, Van A. Bittner, Bill Mitch, and David McDonald, later head of the steel union. SWOC had thirty-five subregional offices, 158 field directors and full-time organizers, eighty part-time organizers. The veterans of the Great Steel Strike sometimes came and gaped at the rows of stenographers' elegant glass-topped desks, the files, the lawyers, and shook their heads sadly in recalling the unaided poverty-stricken days of 1919 when a man had only himself and his fists.

The drive began, a drive described by Phil Murray at the time as "the biggest task ever undertaken by organized labor within the memory of man. It is the most important job ever undertaken in the history of the labor movement." At first the going was hard. If there were thousands filled with courage, there were other thousands in the steel mills, long the object of unrelenting persecution, who were filled with fear. By November the SWOC had some 82,000 members. But during the Flint sit-downs thousands flocked in and at the time of the victory against General Motors there were 150,000 members of the Steel Workers Organizing Committee.

The steel workers were not the only ones impressed by the triumph over General Motors. So, among others, was Myron C. Taylor, chairman of the Board of Directors of United States Steel.

Taylor had been conferring with John L. Lewis, who had all the prestige of his General Motors victory fresh upon him. Suddenly, without a strike and without warning, the largest steel company in the world surrendered. The foe that the CIO had thought would be the toughest succumbed without a struggle. By a mere show of strength the SWOC had won a 10 per cent wage increase, a forty-hour week, and union recognition for the thousands of steel workers employed by United States Steel.

It would be difficult to say who was most surprised at U.S. Steel's capitulation, the workers or the tycoons who operated "Little Steel," the misleading designation for a group of independent steel mills, representing about a quarter of the nation's steel production. Tom Girdler, of Republic Steel, said that the industry had been betrayed by Taylor. As for himself, he said, he would resign and grow apples before he would sign with CIO. It was not for him, he grandly declared, to play any part in handing America over to Communism.

Forming "an unholy alliance," as Phil Murray called it, with Youngstown Sheet and Tube and Inland Steel, Republic and its adherents brazenly violated the Wagner Labor Act as they stocked up on munitions in preparation for war against their employees. In the immediate weeks before the strike called by SWOC in the spring of 1937, Little Steel prepared for it by spending $43,901.88, according to the La Follete Committee, for machine guns, rifles, revolvers, tear gas, and bombs.

Little Steel's war was not long in coming, blazing out in May—in Cleveland and Massillon, in Youngstown and Chicago—reaching its climax at the Memorial Day Massacre where ten were killed and scores wounded as they tried peaceably to picket before the Republic plant. Mary Heaton Vorse, herself injured in an attack by Republic Steel police at Youngstown, lists some of Little Steel's dead strikers:

"Let the dead walk before you and acquaint yourselves with their names. There is Earl Handley, dead of hemorrhage because his wounds were not treated. Workers got him into a car and the police dragged him out and he bled to death.

"Otis Jones had his spinal cord severed by a bullet in the back.

"Kenneth Reed bled to death in a patrol wagon. A bullet had sliced through his back and into his abdomen.

"Joe Rothmund was shot far down in his back.

"Lee Tisdale died of blood poisoning from a wound.

"Anthony Tagliori also died from a bullet in the back.

"Hilding Anderson died of peritonitis.

"Alfred Causey was shot four times and he died.

"Leon Francesco was another shot in the back.

"Sam Popovitch was not shot but his skull was battered to pieces by police clubs as he ran, an old man, bald, trying in vain to shield himself. The police ran after him and they beat him when he was down. You can see him in the Paramount film yourself, a little scared old figure flying from the failing clubs.

"But these folks are not all the dead. There are others to be added to this procession of workers with their mashed heads, dead of blood poisoning, dead of wounds in the back, dead of peritonitis.

"George Bagavitch of Youngstown belongs with these Chicago workers.

"James Eperjessi, also of Youngstown, was killed there by deputies on Saturday night, June 19.

"George Mike belongs with this long list of dead.

"Chris Lopez, beaten to death, was said to have died from heart disease.

"Fulgencio Calzada of Massillon was shot in the back of the head on the night of July 11, when the deputies fired into a crowd.

"Nick Vadios was shot through the abdomen and mortally wounded by these deputies.

"A man in Cleveland was killed on the picket line when the troops tried to open the mills.

"Seventeen are dead and ten more are seriously wounded. The number of minor wounds in the steel area goes far above one hundred and fifty. These are the treated hospital cases. The record of the smaller wounds, the gassings, will never be known."

The Paramount film of the Memorial Day massacre in Chicago might well stand for every such assault on labor from New York's Tompkins Square in 1874 to the Ludlow Massacre of 1914 to the most recent strike. After such affairs the press baldly states that a number were killed and injured but in this film the statistics come to life, change into human beings fighting for their very lives against murderous police breaking the Bill of Rights and the nation's most fundamental law. On June 17, the St. Louis *Post Dispatch* described the Paramount film which never was released for public showing:

". . . Those who saw it [the film] were shocked and amazed by scenes showing scores of uniformed police firing their revolvers pointblank into a dense crowd of men, women and children, and then pursuing and clubbing the survivors unmercifully as they made frantic efforts to escape.

"The impression produced by these fearful scenes was heightened by the sound record which accompanies the picture, reproducing the roar of police fire and the screams of the victims. . . .

"A vivid close-up shows the head of the parade being halted at the police line. The flag-bearers are in front. Behind them the placards are massed. They bear such devices as 'Come on Out, Help Win the Strike;' 'Republic vs. the People' and 'CIO.' Between the flag-bearers is the marchers' spokesman, a muscular young man in shirt sleeves, with a CIO button on the band of his felt hat. . . .

"Then suddenly, without apparent warning, there is a terrific roar of pistol shots, and men in the front ranks of the marchers go down like grass before a scythe. The camera catches approximately a dozen falling simultaneously in a heap. The massive, sustained roar of the pistol shots lasts perhaps two or three seconds.

"Instantly the police charge on the marchers with riot sticks flying. At the same time tear gas grenades are seen sailing into the mass of demonstrators, and clouds of gas rise over them. Most of the crowd is now in flight. . . .

"In a manner which is appallingly businesslike, groups af policemen close in on those isolated individuals [Those who did not run]: They go to work on them with their clubs. In several instances, from two to four policemen are seen beating one man. One strikes him horizontally across the face, using his club as he would wield a baseball bat. Another crashed it down on top of his head, and still another is whipping him across the back.

"These men try to protect their heads with their arms, but it is only a matter of a second or two until they go down. In one such scene, directly in the foreground, a policeman gives the fallen man a final smash on the head, before moving on to the next job."

Everywhere the camera moves, the reporter says, men and women are literally having their brains beaten out. He describes a girl, "not more than five feet tall, who can hardly weigh more than 100 pounds . . . she is seen going down under a quick blow from a policeman's club, delivered from behind. She gets up and staggers around. A few minutes later she is shown being shoved into a patrol wagon, as blood cascades down her face and spreads over her clothing."

The camera catches "a husky, middle-aged, bare-headed man" cornered by the police. Cut off, he decides to run directly through them, to run the gauntlet of the flying clubs. He is surprisingly agile as he twists and dodges.

"The scene is bursting with a frightful sort of drama. Will he make it? The suspense is almost intolerable to those who watch. It begins to look as if he will get through. But no! The police in front have turned around now, and are waiting for him. Still trying desperately he swings to the right. He puts his hands up, and is holding them high above his head as he runs.

"It is no use. There are police on the right. He is cornered. He turns, still holding high his hands. Quickly the bluecoats close in, and the night sticks fly— above his head, from the sides and from the rear. His upraised arms fall limply under the failing blows, and he slumps to the ground in a twisting fall, as the clubs continue to rain on him. . . .

"Ensuing scenes are hardly less poignant. A man shot through the back is paralyzed from the waist. Two policemen try to make him stand up, to get into a patrol wagon, but when they let him go his legs crumple, and he falls with his face in the dirt. . . . A man over whose white shirt front the blood is spreading perceptibly, is dragged to the side of the road. There is plain intimation he is dying. . . .

"There is continuous talking, but it is difficult to distinguish anything, with one exception—out of the babble there rises this clear and distinct ejaculation:

" 'God Almighty!' "

Amid such scenes was the CIO built.

Girdler was once asked about his buying of munitions and cheerfully replied: "Sure we got guns!"[11]

But Otis Jones and Kenneth Reed, Nick Vadios and Chris Lopez, did not die in vain in the Republic strike. Nor did Tom Duffy and Ed Kelly, James Carrol or Michael Doyle, the Irish miners hanged by Pennsylvania in 1877, die in vain. Out of their deaths came the organization of Republic and Little Steel, ten per cent raises for thousands of their brother unionists, recognition of the union and the five-day, forty-hour week. Out of their deaths, and the deaths of others like them, out of the unity of millions, came the triumph that was CIO.

For the first time in history thousands on thousands of Negro workers, who had fought for admission into the labor movement since 1869 and the great plea of Isaac Myers before the National Labor Union, were or-

11 "The Republic Steel Corporation," said the La Follette Committee Report, "has a uniformed police force of nearly 400 men whom it has equipped not only with revolvers, rifles, and shotguns, but also with more tear and sickening gas and gas equipment than has been purchased . . . by any law-enforcement body, local, State or Federal in the country. It has loosed its guards, thus armed, to shoot down citizens on the streets and highways." (*Hearings before the Subcommittee of the Committee on Education and Labor*, U. S. Senate, 76th Congr., 1st Sess., p.29.)

ganized on a basis of equality into the nation's trade unions, into the new industrial CIO. Their efforts in organizing steel, auto, packing, and marine were vital and their influence was decisive in drafting CIO union constitutions which barred no one from membership because of "sex, race, creed or national origin."

For the first time in history, with the exception of textile and the needle trades, thousands of working women were admitted into such mass industrial unions as the United Electrical Workers, packing and others, dedicated to the principle of equal pay for equal work. Sylvis in the sixties, Susan B. Anthony, and Elizabeth Cady Stanton had not fought in vain for this advance.

For the first time in history the dream of Parsons, the goal of Haywood, Debs, and Foster, had become an actuality. The heart of monopoly, of trustified industry, was at last organized industrially.

Nor was this all the CIO accomplished as it grew from 1,000,000 to 2,000,000, from 3,000,000 to nearly 4,000,000. In 1938 it changed its name from the Committee for Industrial Organization to the Congress of Industrial Organizations, becoming a permanent organization.

Such was the impetus of its growth, with 600,000 coal miners, 400,000 automobile workers, 375,000 steel workers, 300,000 textile workers, 250,000 ladies' garment workers, 200,000 electrical workers, 100,000 agricultural and packing workers, that it even spurred the AFL into vigorous action. Machinists, teamsters, hotel and restaurant workers, and boilermakers launched successful organizing drives that increased the AFL's membership by more than 1,000,000. By 1940 the AFL had 4,247,443 members, the CIO 3,810,318, independent unions some 2,000,000 more. In four years labor, with about 10,000,000 members, had almost tripled its growth.

Moreover, the eight-hour day, fought for and died for since 1866, was at last reality in much of industry. Parts of the open-shop South, particularly in textile, were penetrated and organized by CIO men and women who were flogged, tarred and feathered—some killed by the Ku Klux Klan—but who stayed in the South, organizing.

Independent political action, the dream of Sylvis and the labor-Populists of the nineties, was at least a limited reality as Labor's Non-Partisan League campaigned to re-elect Roosevelt in 1936, and as CIO's Political Action Committee, under Sidney Hillman, later rallied millions to the New Deal standard. The American Labor Party in New York, the Washington Commonwealth Federation on the Pacific Coast, the Farmer-Labor Party in Minnesota, were other examples of labor's independent political action during this period.

The CIO's story in 1940 was a story of victory. It was a story of changed lives. Thousands whose days had been dominated by the clatter of the assembly line alone were now getting up in union meetings and making speeches, serving on committees, checking over union books, writing leaflets, growing and developing in a hundred ways as they acted democratically to control the vital decisions of their own lives. Thousands had faced danger and conquered it. A striker who had faced cops and troops and had felt the rulings of the courts would never be quite the same again. By their own efforts American workers had increased their pay, their leisure, their dignity as human beings. They had made their country a better place, and that is a big thing to do.

Philip Murray was speaking of all this when he said at the 1939 CIO convention in San Francisco:

"The wage increases that you have gotten out of industry during the past three years for all the workers affiliated with CIO organizations in America, plus the indirect wage increases that have gone to millions of unorganized wage earners in this country . . . have increased the national purchasing power of the workers in the United States approximately $5,000,000,000 each year.

"You know, I have a faint notion that this is service; that this is doing something for this country; that that is providing for more clothing, better advantages for education, and better food.

"What greater contribution can we render society than that?"

4. The Know-How of Victory

When the dam of the open shop broke at last, releasing titanic energies that had been repressed and held back for more than sixty years, the CIO was swiftly built but it was not easily built. It was hit and hit hard by the charge of Communist conspiracy, thundered with all the power of ninety-eight per cent of the nation's press and radio, with all the force that the world's largest aggregate of monopoly capital could muster.

It was hit from within the labor movement and it was hit from without. The fact that the high point of the New Deal had been reached and passed by the end of 1937 aided the offensive. By 1938 monopoly had sufficiently recovered to take its first step in its long fight to regain ownership of the national government so that it might use it against labor and for itself. That first step was the setting up of the House un-American Committee and government blacklists of union men under the direction of Martin Dies, the Representative from Texas.

The committee held hearings in 1938 before labor board elections all over the country in an effort to swing them to the AFL by the cry of Red. Day in and day out, the CIO was charged with fomenting Red violence as vigilantes smashed its picket lines, declaring they were only saving the country from Moscow. We have seen how Sloan described the great General Motors strike as an attempt to sovietize the auto industry. Some 2,220,000 copies of *Join the CIO and Help Build a Soviet America*[12] were distributed by the National Association of Manufacturers as it progressed in its long

[12] Joseph P. Kamp, of the pro-fascist Constitutional Educational League, is the author of *Join the CIO and Help Build a Soviet America*. In his checkered career he has been indicted for conspiracy to undermine the morale of the nation's armed forces during

drive toward the election of such a figure as Eisenhower and the liquidation of the New Deal.

In the face of charges of Communism that in the panicky hysteria of today would disrupt with the power of an atom bomb, CIO workers and officials were largely unmoved. There were no purges, no expulsions, no weakening of the CIO by the CIO although the charge of Red mounted ever higher over a four-year period. CIO officials declined to do the job of the enemy for the enemy. They and the rank and file of the CIO continued the immensely difficult job of organizing the unorganized, most never forgetting for an instant that all differences could and would be healed if all groups united on this primary reason for the existence of any labor organization. And they never forgot that eighty per cent of American workers were still unorganized.

In describing the ever-growing attack against the CIO's unity and very life, John L. Lewis, its president and moving spirit, declared that those who said it was Communist-dominated "lie in their beard and they lie in their bowels." Lewis described reaction's attack at the CIO's first constitutional convention in 1938 when it was reconstituted as the Congress of Industrial Organizations. He said:

"Our people in this movement know how hard it is to preserve their rights and their liberty—even within democracy. They have battled against violence, brutality and calumny. The forces of public order have been perverted against them. And yet our people have not faltered in their conviction that they have rights which must not be destroyed.

"The agencies of public information have boiled with jeremiads against the Committee for Industrial Organization. On no other occasion of modern times has the American ideal of a free press been so sullied. The loyalty of the members and friends of the CIO through these storms of falsity shows again that American people will not be misled by cynical untruths and bitter misrepresentations. . . .

"To millions, because of this movement, the word 'liberty' has acquired new meaning. Often those who seek only license for their plundering, cry 'liberty.' In the guise of this old American ideal, men of vast economic domain would destroy what little liberty remains to those who toil. The liberty we seek is different. It is liberty for common people—freedom from economic bondage, freedom from the oppressions of the vast bureaucracies of great corporations, freedom to regain again some human initiative, freedom that arises from economic security and human self-respect."

World War II, and for contempt of Congress but has never served time. When Charles A. Hanson, secretary-treasurer of the Constitutional Educational League, was examined by the La Follette Committee, he could tell little if anything about the content or the history of the Constitution. This defender of the Constitution, educating the country about its meaning, did not know how many amendments there were to the Constitution nor could he give any information about the Bill of Rights.

Before examining the reasons for the CIO's continued growth, from 1,000,000 members in 1936 to nearly 4,000,000 in 1940, to 6,000,000 in 1945, in the face of charges that today have paralyzed the labor movement, perhaps we should look into the general background of the red scare that failed. It did not fail because monopoly was weaker. On the contrary, as President Roosevelt warned in 1938, the depression which had meant suffering for the people had meant opportunity for the great corporations. Monopoly was steadily increasing in power and concentration. On April 29 the President told Congress:

"The statistical history of modern times proves that in times of depression concentration of business speeds up. Bigger business then has larger opportunities to grow still bigger at the expense of smaller competitors who are weakened by financial adversity."

Just as Gould and Rockefeller and associated robber barons had grabbed competitors' and the nation's resources during the panic of 1873, so had their successors, on an immensely larger scale, fattened themselves on the depression beginning in 1929. As a result, the President said, using government figures of 1935, one-tenth of one per cent of all the nation's corporations took 50 per cent of total net profits. And less than four per cent of the corporations, the real giants who were attacking the CIO, had received 84 per cent of all the profits of all the nation's corporations. He continued:

". . . 47 per cent of all American families and individuals living alone had incomes of less than $1,000 for the year; and at the other end of the ladder a little less than 1½ per cent of the Nation's families received incomes which in dollars and cents reached the same total as the incomes of the 47 per cent at the bottom. . . ."

Turning to the immense and growing concentration of capital, the President said that many corporations pretending to be independent were in fact a part of secret trustified combinations.

"Close financial control, through interlocking spheres of influence over channels of investment, and through the use of financial devices like holding companies and strategic minority interests, creates close control of the business policies of enterprise which masquerade as independent units. That heavy hand of integrated financial and management control lies upon the strategic areas of American industry. Private enterprise is ceasing to be free enterprise and is becoming a cluster of private collectivisms; masking itself as a system of free enterprise after the American model, it is fast becoming a concealed cartel system after the European model."[13]

[13] The government National Resources Committee reported in 1939 that the nation's economy was largely controlled by eight comparatively small groups of men "by no means independent of each other." The eight groups, controlling $61,000,000,000 of investments in industrial corporations, railroads, banks, and public utilities, were Morgan-First National, Rockefeller, Kuhn, Loeb, Mellon, du Pont, the Chicago group, the Cleveland group, and the Boston group.

And yet the CIO was defeating this giant. Despite its roar of protest, labor was taking from it, as Murray proudly pointed out, five billions of dollars each year in increased wages. Since the beginning of time there are not many cases on record in which employers have willingly acquiesced in transforming profits for themselves into pay raises for their employees. There are few calamities that cause the owner deeper anguish than to increase costs by increasing pay.

No policy, if official United States Senate hearings are an accurate gauge, is too degraded, no means too brutal, no frame-up too heartless, to be discarded by monopoly in the drive to prevent or liquidate increased payroll costs. To prevent such a calamity the greatest American corporations had been spending, as we have seen, $80,000,000 yearly in the purchase of spies and thugs to prevent unionization, and additional thousands for munitions to shoot them out of being when organization succeeded. By 1937 representatives of the strongest aggregation of capital in the world were prepared to do whatever was necessary to turn back the clock of progress and destroy the CIO. The blacklists and violence of half a century indicated that they would not be too squeamish in their methods.

The techniques they employed against the President of the United States were added indication that their methods against labor, and the leaders of labor who could not be bought, bribed, or bullied would not be overly tender.[14] As a matter of fact many of them were becoming intrigued with the methods of Hitler and talk of fascist seizures of power, beginning on the lunatic fringe of the Christian Front, the German-American Bund, and other organizations, was increasingly being repeated by industrial leaders of substance and prestige. Henry Ford, T. J. Watson, president of International Business Machines, and a host of lesser tycoons accepted decorations from Hitler, who was fast becoming the hero of much of American business. "American business might be forced to turn to some form of disguised Fascistic dictatorship," announced H. W. Prentiss, former president of the National Association of Manufacturers.

Covert talk of a fascist seizure of power was general in many quarters by 1938 when General Butler's testimony that he had been urged to lead such a fascist coup revealed that it might be more than just talk. The President himself took note of it by declaring that "the liberty of a democ-

[14] Who does not remember the sly, back-room whispering, spread by Liberty Leaguers and various other alleged defenders of the Constitution, to the effect that one of the greatest of American Presidents was actually insane? Who does not remember the rumors assiduously spread that the President was suffering from some foul disease, the reports of his breaking into hysterical, mad laughter at White House conferences?
In them was the germ of current efforts to brand the late President as a traitor, who, under the influence of the Kremlin, sold out the United States by needlessly bringing it into war against Hitler; in them the beginning of the smear that charged former President Truman with knowingly promoting a "Soviet spy" to high position. After this what trade unionist can be astonished by corporate or political attacks on honest trade union leadership?

racy is not safe if the people tolerate the growth of private power to a point where it becomes stronger than their democratic state itself. That, in its essence, is fascism. . . ." As early as 1936, according to the researches of Dr. Birkhead, there were "119 pro-fascist organizations in the United States . . . having connections with 5,000,000 people."[15] Most of these organizations, despite the approval of the Hearsts, McCormicks, Pelleys, Coughlins, Smiths, and Huey Longs, did not amount to much but by 1940 the powerful pro-Hitler America First Committee contained representatives of much of American industry.

The fact that after Hitler there were no trade unions in Germany made a powerful impression on many American industrialists. Payroll costs were not rising there where monopoly controlled a state in which all democratic opposition had been eliminated. From the first it was apparent that in reaction's blueprint for a fascist America the Communists were only incidental. They would be the first victims but the non-Communists who were increasing the costs of production by diverting billions into the people's pay envelopes, the non-Communists who were building the New Deal would be the real targets. The progress of the red scare, if it proceeded according to the schedule enunciated first by the crackpots of the Christian Front and German-American Bund but increasingly by men of substance and power, would be from the smearing of the New Deal as a Communist plot to the destruction of the labor movement.

As a matter of fact they proceeded on both fronts at once. But they were swimming against the stream, forced to wait for success until the time of Presidents Truman and Eisenhower. The world situation favored them no more than the situation at home. The Soviet Union, instead of urging war and revolution, was trying to organize a collective security that would prevent war and contain the fascist powers.

Reaction's covert attacks on Roosevelt as a Communist, usually by innuendo, succeeded only in convincing many that the CIO was no more Communist than the President. One might call John L. Lewis many things, and most industrialists did, but to call him a Communist was only laughable.

Moreover, working men and other anti-fascists were uniting by the millions in France, China, and above all, in Spain, into democratic fronts against fascism's Big Lie and attempt at world conquest. Thousands of working men, from the United States and the world over, went to Spain after 1936, when Hitler and Mussolini invaded that country, helping a democratically elected New Deal republic in its battle against Franco, Hitler and Mussolini.

While some industrialists talked of the possibility of a fascist seizure of power during 1937 and 1938, more attempted, according to the charge of John L. Lewis, to thwart the New Deal by going on a sit-down strike against it through trying to induce an artificially created depression. This

---

[15] A. B. Magil and Henry Stevens, *The Peril of Fascism*, New York, 1938.

was the way, they apparently thought, to turn back the surging labor movement, to liquidate the Wagner Act and the whole New Deal. A little unemployment would bring workers to their senses. One result was the depression of 1938 and another was a series of strikes, most of which were won and many of which were provoked by attempts to break unions through slashing wages.

Typical of these victories was that t Philco where 8,000 Philadelphia electrical workers not only resisted a wage cut but won a five-cent-an-hour increase after a twenty-nine-day strike which was neither divided nor weakened by the charge that it was Red insurrection.

Even more significant, indicating as it did the shape of things to come, was the Maytag strike in Newton, Iowa, where 1,400 UE workers walked out in protest against a 10 per cent wage cut and where sixteen of their leaders were arrested, charged with sedition, attempting to overthrow the government, and criminal syndicalism. Many of these charged were but recently off Iowa farms. Nevertheless they were described as "Red Revolutionaries" as the state militia was ordered into the little Iowa town where martial law was declared and where union men "were hunted like partridges on the mountainside."

William Sentner, leader of the strike and later to be imprisoned under the thought-control Smith Act, was seized by the military and held without bail as he attempted to negotiate with Maytag's owners.

For ninety-eight days the strikers fought on against vigilantes and citizens' committees, against back-to-work movements and charges of Moscow plot, against wholesale arrests by the military, and injunctions and contempt citations by the courts. On Aug. 4, 1938, they returned to work, walking down elm-lined streets flanked with steel-helmeted, bayonet-carrying soldiery, machine guns posted before the factory gates and at every street intersection. Virtually none had deserted in the face of the greatest display of force and falsity in the entire history of Iowa. They knew that their strike was not the result of Reds but of wage cuts and they knew the source of force and violence.

As members of the Newton union, still a strong organization despite the attempt to destroy it, returned to work, one labor reporter predicted that "their brave stand against red baiting and a wage cut may bring an abrupt halt to the wage slashing plans now current throughout the nation. If they have lost for themselves, they have won for others. Few bosses want a 90-day fight." And the Newton union, Local 116 of the UE, issued this statement as its members returned under the guns of the National Guard:

"Our membership is returning to work under the compulsion of military force, but we are confident that the law which gives us the right of collective bargaining, is mightier than armed force and military tribunals. We do not waive these rights in any way and will steadfastly maintain our organization for the protection of these rights."

It was this kind of spirit that defeated American reaction's revived effort in 1937 and 1938 to mount a bigger and better red scare. The decisive element in the defeat was the refusal of the CIO and the common people of America to be confused or divided. The refusal averted what might have been a really serious attempt at an American fascism in the late thirties. Instead Roosevelt was elected in 1940 for a third term, receiving 449 electoral votes to 82 for Wendell L. Willkie. But this is not to say that there was not often real danger that monopoly would succeed in its attempt to divide and weaken the CIO by use of Hitler's refurbished technique of the Big Lie. There was danger, acute danger, particularly when the international situation shifted so as to place the Soviet Union in general disfavor in the United States as after the non-aggression pact between Germany and Russia in 1939 and the Finnish War of 1940. It was at those moments that the unity of the CIO was particularly threatened. It was those moments that were made to order for reaction's plot to divide.

Monopoly's plot was thwarted by the positive CIO policy that had brought it into being in the face of the red scare and carried it to phenomenal growth in numbers and power even as the charge of Communist domination increased in intensity from 1936 to 1941. The heart of that policy was that organization of the unorganized and struggle for substantial wage increases were basic and that everything else was secondary. The crux of that policy was that loyalty was to be judged by successful action in the organizing of the unorganized and in the winning of pay raises and not by what hired spies said were the political beliefs of a CIO member or a CIO official or a CIO union. The foundation of that policy was unity, unity on the necessity of organizing the unorganized and winning substantial wage boosts, and autonomy for each constituent union on all other matters.

This policy was the formula of victory and under it billions of dollars in yearly wage increases flowed into the pockets of the workers. Because of this policy CIO refused to divide itself and decrease its numbers and strength by its own action, refused to penalize its members, as monopoly dearly wished. Under this policy what never had been organized *was* organized and labor grew and flourished as never in history. This was the policy that resulted in mass picket lines, in universal militance, in a crusading spirit that swept all before it, that conquered the open shop in steel, auto, rubber, glass, electrical, transport, packing, communications, in all of American basic industry.

This know-how of victory, this unity on the vital matter of organizing the unorganized regardless of the politics of the organizer, was a characteristic of the CIO from its first exciting beginning. When auto and steel and electrical and marine were being organized, everyone from Lewis and Murray to the janitor wanted everyone to organize who could sign up union members and they didn't care if the man who did the signing up was a Republican or a Hottentot. They were in a fight and they wanted results.

Because they wanted results many of the first CIO organizers hired were former members of the Trade Union Unity League who, under Foster, had been through this fight before and knew all there was to know about mass picket lines and vigilante attacks. Some of these organizers were Communists, others not, but Lewis and Murray had only one criterion for loyalty. That was loyalty to the CIO proved by the concrete action of carrying out its policy of pay raises and organization of the unorganized. In the stress of blazing actions, when the whole country was aflame, a coalition grew up within the CIO that was to carry it to unprecedented success, a coalition between the left and center, between progressives and Communists and middle-of-the-roaders. This coalition, founded in the knowledge that no one benefits from purges and division but the monopoly that seeks them, was an organizational expression of the formula for victory, unity on the fundamental of organizing the unorganized, autonomy for member unions in other matters.

Writing of the Communist role at the beginning of this coalition, the New Dealer Alinsky says in his life of Lewis, written in close collaboration with the latter:

"Then, as is now commonly known, the Communists worked indefatigably, with no job being too menial or unimportant. They literally poured themselves completely into their assignments. The Communist Party gave its complete support to the CIO. The fact is that the Communist Party made a major contribution in the organization of the unorganized for the CIO."

But this unity was not easy to come by. Always it was menaced and always it had to be consciously fought for on the premise that without it there could be little progress. The attack against it was so continuous and constant, and invariably in the guise of the fight against Communism, that the La Follette Senatorial Committee declared in 1939 that the National Association of Manufacturers saw "Communism behind every move designed to improve the lot of labor." The Committee added that the employer "cloaks his hostility to labor" under "the pretext that he is defending himself and the country against Communism." Tom Girdler spoke as many of his colleagues were speaking when he asked, after his employees in the CIO demanded pay raises, "Must Republic Steel and its men submit to the Communistic dictates and terrorism of the CIO? If America is to remain a free country the answer is No."

From the first employers made valuable use of the House un-American Activities Committee in its effort to split the CIO by the charge of red. Then an underling on the committee, J. Parnell Thomas, later to be imprisoned for payroll padding, told industrialists in a speech that their un-American Committee was serving employers well by the gathering together of a huge blacklist. He said on January 6, 1941:

"There is material of vast value to management in the files of the Dies Committee. We have the names of thousands of men whom we have reasons to suspect because of their connections past or present with subversive organizations. These files are available to you."

Typical of employer propaganda filling the newspapers and flooding the country was a pamphlet by Representative Clare E. Hoffman of Michigan, in which state the CIO had increased annual wages by millions of dollars, which declared that the CIO was only an arm of Moscow's conspiracy to build a Soviet America. In his pamphlet, which he called *Battalions of Death*, the Michigan Representative wrote:

"The CIO probably boasts that, under its leadership, under the CIO banner, labor is on the march. Let us look at the color of the banner, examine . . . the goal toward which they are marching. The banner is the red banner of Soviet Russia. . . . Their goal, 'Carry on the fight for a Soviet America.' "

And yet, in the full flood of this deluge of red baiting, the CIO stood firm, increasing its numbers, increasing pay, winning union recognition, contracts, grievance committees, and the shop steward system. It won paid vacations, paid holidays, seniority, overtime, a lessening of speed-up, and the five-day forty-hour week in industries and areas that had scarcely heard of such improvements before the CIO. Its members met the red scare head-on, lived through it, conquered it, and in doing so bettered their lives and the lives of their families.

Despite the return of depression in 1938, which was to continue until industry revived through munitions and matériel contracts of World War II, the CIO in that first year of a new recession added over a million people to its membership rolls and gained, directly and indirectly, five billions of dollars in increased wages for American workers.

Every abortive attempt within the CIO, and there were always such employer-inspired attempts, however unsuccessful, to destroy that organization's left-center coalition for victory, was drowned by cries of "Organize the unorganized!" Said the veteran John Brophy, who from its founding held a series of leading positions in the CIO:

"Red-baiting, lies, slanders, raising the cry of 'Communist' against militant and progressive union leaders make up nothing more than a smokescreen for the real objective of the people that use them. The real objective is to kill the CIO, to destroy collective bargaining, to destroy the unity of the organized and unorganized workers, that the CIO is building throughout the nation."

Said Walter Reuther, who was to become head of the CIO:

"Many years ago in this country when the bosses wanted to keep the workers from forming a strong union, they tried starting scares of various kinds. One scare that the bosses raised was the Catholic against the Protestant. Another scare they used very successfully was the American-born against the foreign-born. . . . Now the bosses . . . are raising a new scare, the red scare. They pay stools to go whispering around that so-and-so, usually a militant union leader, is a red. They think that will turn other workers against him. What the bosses really mean, however, is not that he is really red; they mean that they do not like him because he is a loyal, dependable union man, a fighter who helps his union brothers and sisters and is not afraid of the boss.

"So let's all be careful that we don't play the bosses' game by falling for the red scare. Let's stand by our union and fellow-unionists. No union man, worthy of the name, will play the bosses' game. Some may do so through ignorance. But those who peddle the red scare and know what they are doing are dangerous enemies of the union."

James Carey, later to turn against his own union, the UE, and form a rival, raiding organization, declared that the red scare was the creation of reactionaries, that "Dies, and the other mouthpieces who scream red at everything progressive are only their tools."

And Philip Murray, in a reminiscent mood about the founding of the CIO, declared in 1944 that the charges then being made against the United Electrical, Radio and Machine Workers of America were exactly the charges that had been leveled against the CIO in 1935 and 1936 and which unity had defeated. In an address before the Tenth Convention of the UE he said on September 25:

"These same interests did exactly the same thing when the CIO was born eight or nine years ago—exactly the same interests, exactly the same newspapers, exactly the same people did the same job nine years ago when you were at the plant gates doing your missionary work to get men to join your labor union. Yes, they said it would be a mistake for you to join a union. They said that to join a union would be subversive and not to the best interest of your family or yourselves or your country. Sure, they said that about 2,000 years ago—they said that about Jesus Christ. They have never missed a day, they have never missed an hour since the beginning of time, the same interests, to do exactly the same job that they are trying to do today."

As for the old lion of the labor movement, John L. Lewis, he met each and every attempt to shatter unity with the roar of "Organize the Unorganized!" At the 1939 CIO convention he cried as he had so many times before:

"Organize the unorganized! There are millions clamoring for admission to our movement as economic conditions permit them to hazard their jobs, or find ways and means to associate themselves with us. . . .

"The end is not yet, because your job is not done. We must not glue ourselves too closely to the bottom of our swivel chairs. That goes for me as well as you. We must leave them at times and go out . . . and carry the philosophy and ideals of labor to the waiting millions in many industries who are waiting for your help."

And even in the Lewis swan song before the 1940 convention, where the first serious cracks in CIO unity began to appear, the labor chieftain pleaded for a unity which would organize the unorganized. It was at this convention that muttering against so-called "reds" rose higher than it ever had before over the dispute of whether or not the United States should enter World War II, although the dispute did not reach its climax until a year later and then was quickly healed, at least ostensibly, with the American declaration of war. Even though Lewis resigned as president of the CIO, and later withdrew his United Mine Workers, because CIO would not follow him in his support of Willkie against Roosevelt, he called for organization instead of bickering. He said:

". . . there are 52,000,000 people in this country who do not have enough to eat. . . . Well, what are you going to do about it? You are well fed; so am I. You are not hungry; neither am I. What are we going to do? We might be doing something on that subject rather than spend our time in bickering and dissension."

The four-year unity of the CIO against the Big Lie, to be continued for five more years after the interruption in 1940-41, was not only the formula for CIO success. It played a vital role in advancing the larger coalition, itself an alliance of left and center, that was the New Deal supported by the Negro people, the farmers, labor, white collar workers, and small businessmen. Under the leadership of the CIO, these powerful groups also rejected red-baiting and moved forward with labor to gain and enforce the Social Security Act, the Minimum Wage Law, unemployment compensation, and a whole series of substantial gains for the common people.

Typical of the powerful allies gained for labor by CIO's stand was Cardinal Mundelein of Chicago. In an address before the Holy Name Society of that city, he said on Jan. 12, 1938:

"The trouble with us in the past has been that we were too often drawn into an alliance with the wrong side. Selfish employers of labor have flattered the Church by calling it the great conservative force, and then called upon it to act as a police force while they paid but a pittance of wage to those who worked for them.

"Don't let others use communism as a cloak to cover corrupt practices when they cry out against communism, and they themselves practice social injustice; when they fight against a minimum wage and we find girls and women trying to live on ten and fifteen cents an hour."

President Roosevelt himself indicted the Dies Committee for its wholesale use of the Red Smear, calling its methods "a sordid procedure." The *New World,* important Catholic journal, declared the Red Menace a myth created by the Liberty League, the United States Chamber of Commerce, and the National Association of Manufacturers. If the Dies Committee "is really a committee to investigate 'un-American activities,'" the Catholic publication declared, "it really should begin with itself and the first witness should be the un-American Mr. Dies himself."

CIO's coalition of left and center faltered, as has been told, in 1940–41 before American entry into World War II. But when monopoly suddenly found itself at the beginning of the war the unwilling ally of the Communism it had so long condemned, the red scare went out the window. The alliance of progressive and middle-of-the-roader continued to lead the CIO to victory after victory until by 1945 it had 6,000,000 members and the proudest record of tangible accomplishment in all the history of American labor.

But the men of Wall Street did not give up after the red scare that failed. There would be another time and other days for another attempt to destroy the labor movement. The memory of Hitler's monopoly state, without trade unions and without the brake of democratic opposition, remained to haunt them long after Hitler was no more. Mr. Prentiss, of the National Association of Manufacturers, continued to talk about the advantages of "some form of disguised Fascistic dictatorship." Neither he nor his colleagues could forget that there had been a time under Coolidge and Hoover when the most prominent of labor leaders did their bidding by shouting "red!" That time might come again.

CHAPTER XI

War—Hot and Cold

"We seek peace—enduring peace. More than an end to war, we want an end to the beginning of all wars—yes, an end to this brutal, inhuman and thoroughly impractical method of settling the differences between governments. . . .

"Today as we move against the terrible scourge of war—as we go forward toward the greatest contribution that any generation of human beings can make in this world—the contribution of lasting peace, I ask you to keep up your faith. . . . The only limit to our realization of tomorrow will be our doubts of today. Let us move forward with strong and active faith."

FRANKLIN DELANO ROOSEVELT; WRITTEN APRIL 11, 1945, THE NIGHT BEFORE HIS DEATH.

1. Blood and Gold Again

The parallels of history can be stretched unduly and yet, as we near our story's end with World War II and its aftermath, there is much that reminds us of our story's beginning. Both the Civil War and World War II were revolutionary wars but both resulted in the unprecedented strengthening of American capital, the first on a continental basis, the second on a scope that was worldwide.[1]

Both wars were of a hitherto unknown scope and ferocity, the American Civil War, still the bloodiest conflict that has ever raged in the Western Hemisphere, extending from the Mississippi to the Atlantic, World War II having the earth itself as its battlefront. It blazed its cataclysmic destruction

[1] In the latter instance, however, American capital's position contained new elements of weakness despite its growth. This stemmed in part from a general weakening of world capital as the result of one-third of the earth's population taking the path to socialism. In addition colonial struggles for independence were reducing the area of colonial exploitation.

from mud and sky, from on the sea and beneath it, from Asia and the Pacific to Africa, Italy and France, from atolls of the tropics to the slums of London, from China, Malay, and the Philippines to an eastern front that stretched in Russia from the Baltic to the Black Sea. Some 100,000,000 people were killed in battles, bombings, by disease and war-borne famine, or through Hitler's policy of coldly executing millions of human beings in the name of "racial supremacy."

Each war on one side had as a goal the enslavement of peoples based on race. The South fought in the Civil War for the perpetuation of the Negro slavery that held 4,000,000 Americans in bondage. Hitler actually made slaves of millions of Jews, Poles, French, Czechs, Serbs, Russians, Rumanians, and others, aside from the millions executed, on the grounds that they were lesser breeds, fit only to serve the needs of the Nazi Aryan.

Because both wars were for the liberation of the people from brutal reaction, both resulted in huge gains for labor, the American Negro people, and American women. Because both wars were progressive, Big Business, on the one hand, enjoyed the gold it harvested as millions died, but, on the other hand, was fearful of the great popular movements that the wars had brought into being. In each case big capital tried to turn back the clock, undo the great reforms won, cut wages, destroy the trade union movement, shift the costs of an approaching depression to the people, separate labor from the Negro people. In each case the aftermath of war found Congress giving away the people's resources to Big Business, the public lands of the West being given to the Robber Barons after the Civil War, public power and all the people's wealth of tidelands oil, amounting to untold billions, being presented to the new Robber Barons after World War II.

The war began for the United States on Dec. 7, 1941, with the Japanese sneak attack at Pearl Harbor, the American Pacific fleet being destroyed even as John Foster Dulles, later Secretary of State, and his like-minded associates of the America First Committee, were declaring there was no danger of a fascist attack.[2] From the first, important segements of Ameri-

---

[2] John Foster Dulles, one of the prime architects of the cold war, who made important financial contributions to the Hitler regime, told the Economic Club of New York in 1939: "There is no reason to believe that any of the totalitarian states, either separately or collectively, would attempt to attack the United States. Only hysteria entertains the idea that Germany, Italy or Japan contemplates war against us. . . ."

All during the middle and late thirties Dulles paid extravagant compliments to Hitler, Mussolini, and the Japanese imperialists. He defended the Nazi seizure of Czechoslovakia on March 19, 1939, declaring, "I dislike isolation, but I prefer it to identification with a senseless repetition of the cyclical struggle between the dynamic and static forces of the world." He considered Nazism "dynamic," and wrote, "We have to welcome and nurture the desire of the new Germany to find for her energies a new outlet."

The Dulles law firm of Cromwell and Sullivan was deeply involved in the financing of Nazi rearmament in preparation for World War II. In 1933, representing New York banks, he went to Berlin, where one billion dollars of German debt was canceled, providing the Nazis with a new credit for rearmament. In addition the Dulles law firm

can monopoly, much of it in the Middle West, were dazed and resentful, and even those dominant sections believing that German imperialism had to be contained were often worried by the fear that it was the wrong war in the wrong place against the wrong foe. If the war was an anti-fascist war as far as the people were concerned, it was a war for profit as far as monopoly was concerned, and it was concerned all right.

Only a redistribution of wealth on a monumental scale, taxing the American people to the tune of billions that were handed to monopoly in the shape of government war contracts and huge tax-free war plants, induced Wall Street's tycoons to participate in a national unity that made them uneasy even as it made them rich almost beyond counting. Some 117 billions of dollars in war contracts—117 billions in money taken from the taxpayer— went to one hundred of the largest corporations in the country.[8] Corporate profits soared to an all-time high, 250 per cent higher than the prewar level, while prices rose 45 per cent and wages were frozen at 15 per cent above the 1941 level.

Even with these incredible profits clearly looming before it, Big Business, according to more than one government agency, refused to cooperate in the war effort until it had secured its own terms both as to profiteering and control of the people's billions used by government in war production. A TNEC report had predicted this state of affairs in 1940 when it declared:

"Speaking bluntly, the Government and the public are 'over the barrel' when it comes to dealing with business in time of war. The experience of World War I,

---

was instrumental in placing American capital at the service of the German industrialists financing Hitler, chiefly through the Anglo-American banking firm of J. Henry Schroeder & Company. Cromwell and Sullivan drew up the incorporation papers of the pro-Nazi America First Committee, of which Dulles was a member and a contributor.

[8] It was during World War II that American Big Business, already the world's strongest aggregate of capital, made another phenomenal leap in additional billions and power, centralizing so swiftly into an ever smaller group that it was beyond dispute the primary source of power in the United States. A report of the Smaller War Plants Corp. to the U.S. Senate Committee on Small Business (79th Congress, 2d Sess. Document #206) describes the process:

"The increase in concentration which took place during the war was due largely to the distribution of the great bulk of the war contracts to a small number of great firms," the report says in calling attention to the 117 billions of dollars in war contracts given to the one hundred firms. But in addition, the report continues, 26 billions of dollars were put into new plants and new equipment, directly from Federal funds. "No less than 83.4 per cent of the value of the privately operated publicly financed industrial facilities were operated by 168 corporations. The hundred largest corporations operated exactly 75 per cent of the value of the Government owned facilities. Nearly half (49.3 per cent) were operated by the top 25 corporations" (p. 49). In addition nearly two billions of dollars of the taxpayers' money was given American corporations for research, exclusive of the atom bomb. Sixty-eight of the largest corporations received two-thirds of the two billions.

At the end of the war the 250 largest corporations took formal title to about 70 per cent of the new plants built with the taxpayers' dollars. They paid, after making billions in profits from their use, about sixty per cent of the original cost.

now apparently being repeated, indicates that business will use this control [the planned economy being set up in anticipation of war] only if it is 'paid properly.' In effect this is blackmail."

TNEC's prophecy concerning blackmail proved accurate as the steel, electrical, auto, and chemical industries, among others, converted from civilian to war production slowly if at all during 1941 and the first quarter of 1942. In an effort to end monopoly's sit-down, knowing that the life of the country was at stake, President Roosevelt was forced to load his administration with the representatives of Wall Street. They took over.

Edward Stettinius, chairman of the board of United States Steel and vice president of General Motors, became Secretary of State while Bernard Baruch, Nelson Rockefeller, Dean Acheson, Marriner S. Eccles and Lewis W. Douglas, as well as scores of oil executives, dozens of vice presidents of steel and auto, and hundreds of other businessmen and their lawyers took over positions of control in the awarding of war contracts and the deciding of policies.

With the cost plus contracts, special bonuses, and fat incentives, with billions of the people's taxes being spent to build plants from which the industrialists drew huge profits, Big Business at last consented to join the war and national unity. Even then the pursuit of profit took precedence over the pursuit of victory, according to a report of a committee of the United States Senate of which Senator Harry S. Truman of Missouri was chairman. This report, issued on June 18, 1942, declared:

"This committee has repeatedly concluded that the work of the Office of Production Management and War Production Board has been hampered by the extent to which their personnel was predominantly drawn from big business groups. . . . The attitudes and associations which these men have acquired through the years . . . make it undesirable to rely upon them exclusively for the war production programs."

Despite such facts, the great majority of the American people gave everything they had of sweat, will, and bravery to the winning of victory. The youth of the land streamed aboard transports and warships for bloody battle at the ends of the earth, on many a distant sea and island. Airplane flights over the broad Pacific, the North Atlantic seemed to become almost as common as bus rides and everyone's neighbors were serving in India, Sicily, at Anzio and Normandy, on the Burma Road, and at Guadalcanal. Acts of valor and the overcoming of incredible hardship became a mass phenomenon as a new spirit seized the American people. Most regarded the war as a crusade against slavery and racism, a war against those who would destroy trade unions and all democracy in the name of monopoly profit.

Some 12,500,000 Americans, men and women of every faith, national origin, color, creed, and political belief, joined the armed services, fighting and dying from Kasserine Pass in Africa to the Coral Sea in the Pacific. Before the war was over some 300,000 Americans were killed or missing in action and 700,000 were wounded. Never had there been such a universal social convulsion with whole peoples fighting for liberty, Catholic and Communist joining together in the undergrounds behind the enemy lines. Almost nightly Americans under cover of darkness parachuted down behind the enemy lines to fight and die with Communist patriots and Catholic martyrs executed by Hitler's firing squads.

Across 2,000 miles of battle front in the Soviet Union blazed the fiercest battles in all the history of mankind. Such was the tremendous power of the Nazi assault thrown against the Soviet Union on June 22, 1941, when 6,000,000 troops, then thought to be invincible, plunged into Russia, that Winston Churchill said that no other government "ever formed among men" would have survived the shock. Over six million Russian soldiers died in battle as hundreds of thousands of Russian civilians acted as partisans behind the enemy lines, ambushing, trapping, harrying the Nazi foe, the overwhelming part of whose army was on the Russian front.

Mile by blood-stained mile, the Russian army and the Russian people drove back the Nazi armies from the wrecked and devastated Soviet land, the whole world conscious that its fate was here being decided, until even General Douglas MacArthur said, "The scale and grandeur of the effort mark it as the greatest military achievement in all history." And Prime Minister Churchill added, "Future generations will acknowledge their debt to the Red Army as unreservedly as we do who have lived to witness these proud achievements."

The war was won by the same kind of coalition on a vastly larger scale that built the CIO and the New Deal, an earth-encircling alliance, containing British and Chinese conservatives under Churchill and Chiang-Kai-shek, the American center, itself a coalition of left and right, under Roosevelt, and the Communists of Russia and China under Stalin and Mao Tse-tung. And of all who participated in this huge international coalition for victory, few, if any, had a more important role than American labor. Without its mammoth contribution, the war could not have been won.

Again, as in the Civil War, the American armed forces were preponderantly made up of workingmen and farmers, and the sons and daughters of workingmen and farmers. More than 3,250,000 union men and women were in uniform, millions more in the armed services came from union families and a union background. Thousands of trade unionists shed their blood on land, sea, and air while Big Business safe at home made an average twenty-two billions of dollars of profits each year of the war, then the highest profits in history. They were more than twice the profits of 1929, which until the war had been the all-time high for profit in American industry.

The bombs at Pearl Harbor were still echoing when labor, AFL, CIO, and independent unions pledged not to strike for the duration of the war, an act as fundamental as if Big Business had pledged to produce for the country at the same rate of profit that obtained in 1940. Prodigies of labor valor were performed on the production lines as labor generally went on a basic 48-hour week.

More than 300,000 planes were turned out, more than 5,000 merchant ships were built, while 65,000 naval craft, large and small, left the shipyards. Three million machine guns were manufactured. Factories, mines, and mills worked the clock around on three-shift schedules, thousands working sixty and seventy hours a week, as 6,500,000 rifles, over 75,000 tanks, 5,500,000 carbines, over 2,000,000 sub-machine guns and nearly 1,000,000 trucks were produced. Men and women worked to exhaustion, as the accident rate steadily mounted before the always moving assembly lines, turning out 73,000,000 rounds of mortar shells, over 40,000,000,000 rounds of small gun ammunition, nearly 400,000,000 anti-aircraft shells.

Trade unionists not only made the weapons of war, but they delivered them to the far-flung battle lines. Almost 5,000 union seamen were killed by enemy action while delivering tons upon tons of planes, tanks, trucks, guns, TNT, gasoline, jeeps, bombs, food, shells, steamshovels, and soldiers to the world's fighting fronts. At home, despite the fact that many workers were forced to live in trailers and crowded, rented rooms as a result of a housing shortage, worker morale had seldom been so high.

It was workers, rather than the management, who pressed through their unions for ever greater feats of production. It was the trade unionists, ignoring all management provocation, who were determined that production must flow on uninterruptedly until victory was gained over a fascism enslaving millions of fellow-workers and threatening to enslave more. The world suddenly seemed topsy-turvy and upside down to many a straw boss and America First executive who stood around with nothing to do while the unions and the workers supplied their own disciplines of production.

While the working people of America were giving everything to the anti-fascist war effort, that effort was being hindered by international cartel agreements of big business. Not only did these trade alliances result in "the transmission of strategically important industrial information to German citizens and presumably to the German government to the detriment of the military security of other nations." We are further told by a subcommittee of the Senate Committee on Military Affairs that the "effect of [these] various cartel agreements in strategic industries was also to prevent the development outside of Germany of a substantial production of some of the most important new materials of war."

For example, there was the agreement between General Electric and German Krupp with respect to tungsten carbide, an agreement which created a bottleneck in the production of this hard-metal composition so important in cutting tools and dies. According to testimony before the Senate Committee on Patents, "In contrast with the situation in Germany, the present drastic shortage of this essential material in this country is notorious . . . [and] has constituted one of the principal bottlenecks in our present production program." That was in 1942. Six years later, after the war was over, General Electric, International General Electric, Krupp, and several General Electric and Carboloy officials were found guilty of conspiracy and fined $53,000, a mere bagatelle for a billion-dollar corporation whose loyalty to monetary gain transcended loyalty to country.

Yet, in spite of facts such as these as well as soaring prices, frozen wages, speed-up, and long hours, the American worker persisted in his course. He saw not only victory over the enemy ahead but a bright new world of peace and prosperity which labor would have an ever-increasing share in building.

An anti-fascist war cannot be fought with reactionary policies at home and as a consequence the frontiers of freedom were daily expanding as the American war effort surged forward. That half of the country composed of women, historically the object of a discrimination so traditional that it is almost unconscious, made a great leap forward, millions doing the work of men in industry as their number increased from 13,000,000 employed in 1940 to 18,150,000 in 1944 when women composed more than a third of the nation's working force.

In the aircraft industry approximately 500,000 women were building bombers, transport and pursuit planes, dressed in overalls and handling the riveting machines as if they had been born to it. The number of women in metal, chemical and rubber increased by over 460 per cent between the prewar years and 1944. Ten per cent of all workers in shipyards, for example, were women although virtually no women had been employed in that industry before Pearl Harbor. Women's membership in trade unions more than quadrupled. Some 3,500,000 were members at the end of 1944 although there had been only 800,000 women in the trade unions in 1938.

Both the need for manpower and the dynamics of a war for liberation did more to give the Negro people economic freedom than any event since the Civil War and Reconstruction. In 1940 more than 1,000,000 Negro workers were unemployed, still the object of discrimination, still, as traditionally, the last hired and the first fired, still for the most part barred from skilled occupations and outside of the labor movement. By 1944 Negroes were employed by the thousands in skilled industries that had never before accepted them. Their number in manufacturing and processing had increased from 500,000 in 1940 to 1,250,000 in 1944.

As a great Negro migration from the South got under way, some 120,000 Negroes were being employed in auto and aircraft factories, 190,000 in shipyards, 100,000 in electrical machinery and equipment, plants from which they had been entirely excluded before the war. Many Negro women found employment in industry for the first time during the war. An important impetus to Negro employment was the President's Fair Employment Practices Commission, the FEPC, established by executive order. By 1944 there were 850,000 Negro trade union members.

As working people continued their miracles of production, *at a cost of*

88,100 killed and 11,112,600 injured during the five years of war,[4] organized labor increased from 8,980,400 in 1940 to 14,776,000 in 1945. As a result some 56,000,000 Americans, including the families of trade union members, were influenced by organized labor's viewpoint and friendly to its program. Its word was powerful in the councils of the nation. It promised to become the most potent political force in the country, its program increasingly attracting allies since it was designed to improve the well-being of the entire American people.

Its representatives, for the most part, had the confidence of the President, meeting with him frequently as members of the Combined Labor War Board[5] while Sidney Hillman, president of the Amalgamated Clothing Workers, served as co-director of the important Office of Production Management. Labor was also represented on the War Manpower Commission, the Office of Price Administration, the Office of Civilian Defense, and the Economic Stabilization Board.

And everywhere labor's rank and file, including its members in the armed forces, were looking forward to a peaceful postwar world, declaring that if American industry could advance to prosperity and full employment by means of war, it could, should, and must be able to achieve it by producing for the people in time of peace.

Everywhere it was pointed out that it had taken war to finally cure the depression that had begun in 1929 and had hit again in 1937-38 and everywhere it was being said that the system would have to prove that it could serve the American people by full employment based on peace not war. And this was one of the President's great objectives.

In the face of all this the nation's Big Businessmen were suffering from a peculiar dichotomy, a peculiar division of spirit and mind. Their opportunities for the present and future were great but so were the dangers confronting them. Victory would bring them an almost complete domination of the capitalist world, financial control of the economies and the colonies of their smashed or crippled rivals in Great Britain, Germany, France, Italy, and Japan. But it was also bringing the fact that the demand for socialism was rising all over Europe and Asia, the people insisting on the public ownership of the banks, factories, mines, and mills which they said their labor and skill had operated so long for the profit of a restricted few.

Profits were rolling into the American trusts in a golden flood, monopoly

[4] See *Handbook of Labor Statistics, 1947,* Bulletin No. 916, U.S. Bureau of Labor Statistics, p. 164. This total of 11,200,000 workers killed and injured in major manufacturing and non-manufacturing industries from 1941 to 1945 inclusive was approximately eleven times as large as total United States casualties of 1,058,000 sustained in World War II.

[5] CIO representatives on the Combined Labor War Board or, as it was more popularly called, the Labor Victory Committee, consisted of Philip Murray, Julius Emspak of the United Electrical, Radio and Machine Workers, and R. J. Thomas of the United Automobile Workers. The AFL representatives were William Green, George Meany, and Daniel J. Tobin of the Teamsters.

was constantly devouring its weaker competitors as more than 2,450 manufacturing and mining companies of the United States were absorbed by the ever growing corporate giants. The assets of the defeated corporations, taken over during the war and in the years immediately following, amounted to more than five billions of dollars.

This was good but the worldwide prestige of the Soviet Union, rising constantly higher as it rolled back the Nazi Army, was not comforting to American tycoons. In addition the phenomenal rise in the members, power, and influence of organized labor was as alarming to finance as the rise of Soviet influence abroad. The most virulent of reactionaries regarded it as the common rise of the same force. To the whispering about the alleged Communist domination of the New Deal, there was now added whispering about the next war against the Soviet Union although the war against Hitler was yet to be won.

Under Secretary of the Navy James V. Forrestal, foremost architect of the Cold War to come, and former president of Dillon, Read and Company, which had frequently floated loans for German cartelists, was doubtless already dreaming of the next war in which American monopoly, entrenched at home through iron control of labor, would destroy the Soviet Union and dominate the world.[6]

But more immediately alarming to Big Business was the spectacularly successful political campaign of the CIO and its allies for the re-election of Roosevelt to an unprecedented fourth term as well as for the election of a wide number of win-the-war, pro-labor Congressmen, governors, and mayors. Through the Political Action Committee, led by Sidney Hillman, the labor movement put millions of Americans into motion in a broad coalition fighting for victory in the war and progress at home. In its radio broadcasts, advertisements, literature, and massive door-to-door campaigning, reaction saw the menace of a future independent people's coalition, led by labor, which would change the whole course of the country, ending monopoly's rule for monopoly's benefit. The increasing size of the trade unions and the world situation seemed to indicate that PAC might remain a force until it evolved into an independent labor party with powerful allies.

PAC's streamlined election methods in 1944 impressed friend and foe alike and even *Time* magazine declared its posters, broadcasts, and pamphlets were by "far and wide the slickest political propaganda produced in the United States for a generation."[7] They proved so effective that a howl

[6] Regardless of Forrestal's probable dreams he was actively planning for war against Russia as early as February, 1946, Walter Millis, editor of the *Forrestal Diaries,* indicates. By that date, Millis writes, Forrestal "felt increasingly that policy could not be founded on the assumption that a peaceful solution of the Russian problem was possible." For a brilliant, soundly documented exposition of the Cold War, and Forrestal's part in it, see Carl Marzani, *We Can Be Friends,* New York, 1952.

[7] The CIO Political Action Committee consisted of Hillman, UE's Fitzgerald, rubber's Dalrymple, Rieve of textile, Green of the Shipbuilders, McDonald of steel, Thomas of auto, and Van Bittner, representing the CIO national organization.

of protest rose from the Republicans, who had nominated Thomas E. Dewey for President, and from poll-tax Democrats opposing the President. The red scare, which had gone underground during the war save for the steady whispering campaign, was vociferously revived. Thirteen Republican Congressmen printed 3,000,000 copies of a document alleging that the Roosevelt administration was part of a gigantic conspiracy to betray the United States to the Communists. They added th it the "red spectre of communism is stalking the country from East to West, from North to South."[8]

PAC, repeated Dewey and Martin Dies, with tireless energy if no great originality, was a Communist conspiracy. Dies declared in a 215-page report of the House Un-American Activities Committee released in March of that election year:

". . . In other words, the political views of the Communist Party and the CIO Political Action Committee coincide in every detail."

The heart of F.D.R.'s campaign for a fourth term was victory in the war and peace in the postwar world through continuing the alliance between the United States, the Soviet Union, Britain, France, and China. Of equal importance to this foreign policy, and indeed a basic part of it, were full employment and full production in a peaceful American economy providing for ever rising standard of living for the American people. Knowing that depression at home adds to the menace of world war, President Roosevelt declared, "Unless there is security at home there cannot be lasting peace in the world."

Possessed by a practical vision of an ever expanding American economy in a world whose peace rested on Soviet-American friendship, the President proposed an Economic Bill of Rights for the American people. On January 11, 1944, he told Congress:

". . . In our day these economic truths have become accepted as self-evident. We have accepted, so to speak, a second Bill of Rights under which a new basis of security and prosperity may be established for all—regardless of station, race, or creed. Among these are:

"The right to a useful and remunerative job in the industries, or shops or farms or mines of the Nation;

"The right to earn enough to provide adequate food and clothing and recreation;

"The right of every farmer to raise and sell his products at a return which will give him and his family a decent living;

[8] On Oct. 5, 1944, President Roosevelt answered this red-baiting campaign as follows: "This form of fear propaganda is not new among rabble rousers and fomentors of class hatred who seek to destroy democracy itself. It was used by Mussolini's Black Shirts and Hitler's Brown Shirts. It has been used before in this country by the Silver Shirts and others on the lunatic fringe. But the sound democratic instincts of the American people rebel against its use, particularly by their own Congressmen—and at the taxpayer's expense."

"The right of every businessman, large and small, to trade in an atmosphere of freedom from unfair competition and domination by monopolies at home or abroad:

"The right of every family to a decent home;

"The right to adequate medical care and the opportunity to achieve and enjoy good health;

"The right to adequate protection from economic fears of old age, sickness, accident, and unemployment;

"The right to a good education."

All of these rights, including a right to a job, were to go by the board, to be lost, at least temporarily, along with free speech and free opinion, as labor became confused and divided by later red scares and war scares. But at the time the American people yearned for those eight provisions of security and felt that with the President re-elected they would form a practical program. He was reelected and PAC was a mighty contributor to his victory. In addition PAC was an important factor in electing 120 Representatives to Congress, seventeen Senators, and six governors.

But reaction, which never surrenders although it sometimes waits, now pulled itself together for a great effort. It determined to drive a wedge between the soldiers and sailors on the fighting fronts and the workers struggling at home to produce the tools of war. Newspaper, press, and radio combined to give the fighting forces a picture of labor whose members were constantly on strike as they became fat on the blood of their countrymen.

The truth, according to the United States Bureau of Labor Statistics, was that union labor had honored its no-strike pledge with virtual unanimity, only one-hundredth of one per cent of scheduled working hours having been lost through strike. The truth was that with wages frozen at 15 per cent increase over 1941 wages, prices had soared by 45 per cent while profits were increasing by 250 per cent.

And yet the campaign was largely successful. If many soldiers remained unimpressed, almost all Congressmen were highly impressed. They believed, if the soldiers did not. They proved it in June, 1943. Angered by the strikes of coal miners, who had been forced to call a halt in production because of the high cost of living, Congress passed the repressive Smith-Connolly Labor Act, forerunner of the Taft-Hartley Law, over the veto of President Roosevelt.

While the representatives of Big Business, steadily infiltrating the Roosevelt Administration, speaking increasingly of the next war, could hamper the tremendous thrust forward of the people, could delay the speed of victory, they could not halt the great historical forces unleashed by the war against German monopoly. On June 4, 1944, Rome was liberated by the American Army. On June 6, the long delayed second front, promised Russia in 1942, promised again in 1943, smashed into France with tremendous power, winning great victories from the first as it steadily fought its way toward Germany, everywhere being helped and greeted by armed French partisans.

As the Americans, British, and French ground forward on the western front, the Russians, who had been advancing ever since the capture of the Sixth German Army at Stalingrad on Feb. 2, 1943, launched a general offensive for the liberation of Poland and were soon in East Germany as the Allies closed in from both east and west. On April 12, President Roosevelt died on the very eve of the victory he had done so much to achieve. On April 28, 1945, Mussolini, front man for Italian monopoly, was killed by Italian partisans. On May 1—traditional working class holiday—Berlin fell and monopoly's Hitler committed suicide in the isolated bunker holding all that remained of the glory that was to have lasted for a thousand years.

On August 14, Japan surrendered and World War II was at an end. The people had been victorious. All over Europe, the people were armed, men and women, farmers, trade unionists, and fighting youth, conservatives and Communists alike, they thronged the streets of towns and cities, demanding that monopoly's collaborators with fascism be executed. Pétain, marshal of the French Army, was soon to be in prison, and Laval, the French premier who had handed his country over to the Nazis, was executed along with some of the greatest generals of Prussia. From Manila to Peking to Warsaw to Prague and Budapest, the rich collaborators with fascism were fleeing as their huge estates and factories were taken over by the people.

Yet, worse than all this, from the standpoint of American monopolists, was that their Nazi counterparts, the Krupps, the Thyssens, and the Farbens, were being tried and convicted, charged with financing Hitler and instigating world war for the billions in profits it brought them. Representatives of the Soviet Union, along with representatives of the New Deal, were particularly active in securing the conviction of Nazi monopolists, many of them with connections with American bankers. It was this worldwide revolutionary trend, this placing of businessmen in the dock and charging them with fomenting war for profit, which had to be reversed. It was then that the cold war, already under way, came into more active being, its goal the turning back of democratic forces surging forward both at home and abroad.

2. The Cold War Against Labor

The chief victims of the cold war were the American people. It was their trade unions which came under attack, their pockets which were robbed of billions to pay for monopoly's cold war contracts at home and abroad. It was their liberties which were destroyed, their lives which were menaced by atomic war. It was their weekly real wages which fell by 5 per cent under the impact of the cold war while corporate net profits increased by 69 per cent. It was their sons and brothers who died on Korean battlefields half a world away in a war which no statesman has been able to explain to the satisfaction of the American people.

Their sweat and their money, taken by taxation, created the 113.3 billions of dollars of net profit reported by American corporations during the five years beginning in 1947. The bulk of the 300 billions of dollars spent by the government for cold war mobilization came preponderantly from the working people, and went preponderantly to the corporations.

A number of historians date the cold war's beginning with the dropping of the world's first atomic bomb on already defeated Japan. It was released by order of President Truman over the city of Hiroshima on August 6, 1945, while the Japanese government was in the process of trying to arrange armistice negotiations. Although it killed or injured 160,000 men, women, and children in those horse-and-buggy days of atomic weapons, their deaths, according to Professor P. M. S. Blackett, were only incidental to demonstrating to the Soviet Union that she had better adjust to the desires of American monopoly. "The dropping of the atomic bombs," he writes, referring also to the one dropped on Nagasaki on August 9, "was not so much the last military act of the second World War, as the first major operation of the cold diplomatic war with Russia now in progress."

And yet even before the Hiroshima massacre, with the war still in progress, there was a good deal of talk of attacking the Soviet Union. The knowledge that we had the atom bomb and that Russia did not was already filling some with visions of a preventive war. In May, 1945, with Russia preparing to aid the American drive on Japan, "A complete diplomatic break with Russia, with war not far off, was . . . privately predicted by certain Washington officials—one of them, at least, on the White House staff," according to Albert Z. Carr, a Washington observer.

If such a person with such views was on the President's staff it was not remarkable. It was merely a reflection of the President's views, who even as a Senator had said, when informed of the Nazi invasion of Russia, "If we see that Germany is winning we ought to help Russia and if Russia is winning we ought to help Germany and that way let them kill as many as possible. . . ."

Having such views it was not difficult for Wall Street's James V. Forrestal, the first Secretary of Defense, to recruit the President in the growing camp of those who believed with Forrestal that war with the Soviet Union was inevitable. The quicker such a war came the better, Forrestal thought; in view of our atomic monopoly. On Dec. 8, 1947, he wrote: "The years before any possible power can . . . attack us with weapons of mass destruction are our years of opportunity." Forrestal was literally to give his life to the cold war, driving himself with such unfeeling energy that he cracked under the strain, leaping from an "unguarded window" of the Naval Hospital in Bethesda, Md., to which he had gone in 1949 during his last illness.

The President, even if he had wanted to, could not withstand such driving energy, whether insane or inspired. Forrestal spoke with the voice of authority, representing as he did the very center of American financial power. Within two weeks of Roosevelt's death Truman, in his own words, had reversed the heart of Roosevelt's policy by telling "the Russians to go to hell." Before the United Nations was founded at San Francisco in 1945 the foreign policy of F.D.R. had been further abandoned and handed over to John Foster Dulles and the equally reactionary Senator Arthur Vandenberg, one of Roosevelt's most implacable foes.

The cold war, from its inception, had everything on its side but the people. The American people, and above all the labor movement, approaching a strength of 16,000,000, were still solidly behind the policies of President Roosevelt. They knew, as Sumner Welles, former Under Secretary of State, wrote in 1946 to Franklin Roosevelt, a firm agreement with the Soviet Union was the indispensable foundation for peace in the future. They enthusiastically favored in their great majority President Roosevelt's plan for an expanding economy based on production for peace.

It was clear to Forrestal and Dulles that before the cold war could be effective it would be necessary to scare the people into it. Forrestal in his unending briefing of financiers and industrialists found willing listeners when he sang his siren song of the inevitability of war with the Soviet Union. He was only extending, only implementing a variation of what had long been the staple policy of the National Association of Manufacturers and the United States Chamber of Commerce, namely, the danger of the Red Menace.

Now, with official sanction, patriotism and self-interest merged and became one. What had been a selfish employer plot, at least in the eyes of some, was now a holy crusade, blessed and urged by the United States government. With war inevitable, it became a necessary and patriotic duty to fulfill profitable new armament contracts while seeing to it that labor could not strike or complain during preparations for the great new war coming. Generals talked, when on this subject of labor, of "the necessity of securing the home front for the war abroad," and the industrialists understood perfectly. Never was there such a fortunate merger, from the standpoint of Big Business, of high moral purpose and the necessities of monopoly.

But so wedded were the people to F.D.R.'s policies of peace and security, so popular was the Soviet Union for its battle against overwhelming odds, that a super-colossal scare would be needed which would banish every vestige of reason in general, all-pervading fear. It had been tried before, during the rise of the CIO, and then it had failed. But that was in the palmy days of the New Deal when President Roosevelt and the government stood between industry and its desire of panicking the people.

Now the New Deal was as dead as its protagonist, virtually all of its members having been moved out of the Truman administration, replaced by the presidents and vice presidents of Wall Street. Now more typical of the new time was a brashly ambitious freshman Senator from Wisconsin, one Joseph Raymond McCarthy, elected with the help of a fascist organization in 1946.[9] Almost his first act, upon election, was his protest against efforts to punish the Nazis who had perpetrated the Malmédy Massacre of American troops during the Battle of the Bulge in 1944.

Now monopoly was not on the defensive. With Roosevelt, its enemy, dead, its foreign rivals crippled, the whole capitalist world owing it money or depending on its favors, it would raise a war scare and a red scare that would make history. It was decided to launch such a scare with all the prestige and billions of the United States government behind it. Cyrus L. Sulzberger, a leading correspondent of the *New York Times,* wrote in that paper on March 21, 1946:

". . . the momentum of the pro-Soviet feeling worked up during the war to support the Grand Alliance had continued too heavily after the armistice. This made it difficult for the administration to carry out the stiffer diplomatic policy required now. For this reason, these observers believe, a campaign was worked up to obtain a better psychological balance of public opinion."

If the cold war began on the diplomatic front in 1945 with the dropping of the atom bomb, it began on the home front late in 1945 and early in 1946 as the employer answer to the great strikes against the wage freeze. From then on a curious parallelism developed: every move in the cold war abroad was matched by a move against civil liberties and the labor movement at home. The great strikes of 1945-46 frightened monopoly, convincing its leaders that the cold war was a heaven-sent opportunity to defeat a labor movement that was constantly growing in size, militancy, and unity.

The employer cold war offensive against labor was revealed first, at least to those with a discerning eye, at the so-called Labor-Management Conference called by President Truman in November, 1945.[10] Here was clearly indicated the shape of things to come. Here it was clear enough, as labor representatives listened to the statements of such business leaders as Eric A. Johnston, William M. Rand, Charles E. Wilson, David Sarnoff, Ira Mosher, and W. W. Prentis, Jr., that industry was determined to repeal the Wagner Labor Act, equally determined to grant no relief to labor suffering from a frozen wage scale and an ascending cost of living.

With Roosevelt dead, the world their oyster, their profits and power the greatest in world history, the American tycoons were fat and sassy. Already they were eager "to secure the home front" for a possible war against Rus-

[9] McCarthy was elected with the aid of American Action, Inc., whose members included Colonel Robert McCormick, owner of the Chicago *Tribune,* and General Robert E. Wood, former chairman of the America First Committee. Representative Wright Patman, of Texas, described the members of American Action as "fascists seeking to preserve property rights and ignoring human rights."
[10] Trade union officials at the Labor-Management Conference were Green, Woll, and Harrison of the AFL, Lewis of the United Mine Workers, and Murray, Thomas, Fitzgerald, and Emspak of the CIO.

344   LABOR'S UNTOLD STORY

sia and were demanding of labor "the sweetheart role" of class cooperation
in which labor would surrender its independent position. If labor didn't it
could take the consequences, for the whole punitive power of government
was soon to belong to American monopoly.

But the rank and file of labor were eager to fight. In fact, wages and prices
were such that it had to fight. In the face of the fact that the Special Conference Committee, "the secret general staff of American Big Business,"[11]
had met in New York and decided on a unified policy of fighting any and
all wage increases, 3,500,000 trade unionists in 1945 and 4,600,000 in 1946
went out on strike. This was more than ever before in all American labor
history and this was one of the highest points in that history.

Many of the strikers were still in uniform. Bearing such picket signs as
"One Front Now—For a Living Wage" and "From Bullets to Bull," the
strikers brought into play all they had learned in the building of the New
Deal and the CIO. Such were their skill, initiative, and unity that they won
substantial raises over bitter, determined employer opposition in coal, auto,
steel, electrical, maritime, and packing, among a good many others.

Their signs and placards, their radio talks and newspaper advertisements,
their citizens committees gaining wide community support, proclaimed
the facts of life far and wide, above all the fact that wages had been held to
a raise of 15 per cent of the 1941 scale while prices had soared by 45 per cent
and profits by 250 per cent. Other facts of life included 4,000,000 unemployed
as veterans returned to an economy that seemed prosperous only during
war or threat of war.

Unity paid off with money in the pocket. General Motors and General
Electric were forced to grant wage increases of eighteen and a half cents
an hour, Westinghouse nineteen cents an hour, all three forced to give
increased union security. Most of the remainder of basic industry was forced
to settle for similar raises. Seldom had labor scored such gains in the face
of growing unemployment and a threatened depression resulting from the
transformation of a wartime into a peacetime economy.

Employers, seeking a weapon to curb labor's advance, saw its answer in
the new cold war and the old red scare. The two could be combined into an
all-purpose weapon; a weapon that would result in war orders, thus delaying a threatened depression and at the same time being the means of dividing and weakening the trade unions as it menaced the Soviet Union. What
could be more perfect?

C. E. Wilson, head of General Electric, was frank enough in declaring
that the cold war had two targets, the American labor movement at home,
the Soviet Union abroad. One of the hundreds of executives about to be

---

[11] The Special Conference Committee, composed of representatives of twelve billion-
dollar corporations, was termed "the secret general staff" of America's ruling oligarchy
by Senator Elbert Thomas of Utah during the La Follette Civil Liberties Committee
Investigation.

drawn into the Truman administration, Wilson said on Oct. 10, 1946, "The problems of the United States can be captiously summed up in two words: Russia abroad, Labor at home." But, unfortunately, he was not being captious, as the policies of the NAM and the United States Chamber of Commerce, as well as those of the federal government, abundantly proved over the years.

As the employers opened their cold war offensive it was sometimes difficult to say who was its chief architect, the obsession-driven Forrestal or the officials of the United States Chamber of Commerce. Forrestal continued his briefing of key figures in key industries on his theme that war was imminent and that all must be subjected to the necessities of its approach. But the Chamber of Commerce, determined to prevent a repetition of the 1946 strikes, put out the first of five widely circulated brochures in that year, all furthering the cold war and all of whose recommendations have since become government law or policy.

The first of the series, *Communist Infiltration in the United States: Its Nature and How to Combat It,* said that radio, motion pictures, publishing houses, the theater, and television had been captured by Moscow. It suggested that Congressional committees act in this field. Before the year was out the House un-American Activities Committee was preparing to call the first of a long series of writers, professors, artists, doctors, producers, and actors to lose their jobs and be imprisoned. The formal charge was contempt of Congress, the actual offense the possession of political beliefs unacceptable to the Chamber of Commerce.

In 1947 the Chamber of Commerce published *Communists in the Government, The Facts and a Program,* blueprint for the charge that the New Deal was only a Communist conspiracy, destined to become the Bible and inspiration of Senator McCarthy. In the same year it published *Communists Within the Labor Movement, Facts and Countermeasures.*[12] This was the first gun in the battle to pass the Taft-Hartley Act, which became law that same year.

As the campaign to create the proper climate for passage of the Taft-

[12] The other two Chamber of Commerce pamphlets were *A Program For Community Anti-Communist Action* and *Communism: Where We Do Stand Today.* The same financiers and industrialists who control the NAM also control the United States Chamber of Commerce which NAM founded. The membership of the two organizations is in many instances identical. Members of the NAM control 3,000 corporations employing one out of every four American workers. The Chamber's views on Communism and its relation to the labor movement are indicated by the membership of its Committee on Socialism and Communism. Among the members of this committee since 1946 have been Francis P. Matthews, Truman's Secretary of the Navy and chairman of the Securities Acceptance Corporation; Thomas C. Boushall, president of the Bank of Virginia; Richard K. Lane, president of the Public Service Company of Oklahoma; Fred L. Conklin, president of the Provident Life Insurance Company; Powell C. Groner, president of the Kansas City Public Service Company; Frank W. Jenks, vice president of the International Harvester Company, and Chase M. Smith, general counsel of the Lumbermen's Mutual Casualty Company.

Hartley Act got under way, it became additionally clear that an attack on the trade union movement was merely the other side of the coin of the drive for war through raising the most stupendous red scare of all time. As the Chamber of Commerce was preparing its early anti-communist brochures, President Truman was breaking the national railroad strike by recommending the drafting of all strikers into the United States Army. As Eugene Dennis, general secretary of the Communist Party, was sentenced to a year's imprisonment in 1947 for defying the un-American Activities Committee, the President announced his Truman Doctrine, breaking the revolt of the Greek people against their fascist king, and the Chamber of Commerce and the NAM demanded that Congress pass the Taft-Hartley Act to rid labor of "Communist domination."

To compare the red scares of the past with this one, which, starting in 1946, continued day after day, week after week, and year after year, is like comparing a cap pistol with an atom bomb. With the press properly briefed and oriented by Forrestal,[13] it was not long until every page of every edition of every newspaper teemed with the alleged doings of the devilish foe at home and abroad.

The most alarming news began to appear. In the press and over the air the American people were told that the Red Army was mobilizing for the invasion of Iran one day, Turkey the next, and western Europe on the third. Red submarines were seen off the coast of California. There were Red Army plots to seize Yugoslavia and even Detroit, according to a witness at a later trial of alleged reds. The only thing that saved us was our monopoly of the atomic bomb and there was increasing talk of dropping it on Moscow and thus solving all.

No improbability was too wild for serious treatment by press or radio, particularly just before the Army or Navy asked for additional billions before Congressional appropriation committees. If an airplane crashed, it was Communist sabotage. If a murder was committed, it was Communist terror, and still the country hadn't seen anything yet.

President Truman, apparently convinced by the Chamber of Commerce brochure on Communist penetration of the government, was preparing to order loyalty tests for 2,000,000 government employees. In accordance with

[13] At one of his first briefing conferences Forrestal summoned before him some twenty-four of the country's most important publishers and editors, and told them that "no peaceful solution of the Russian problem was possible," and had Generals Marshall and Bradley give them the reasons. Such conferences, as well as those with working reporters, became an institution until the press lost what little independence it had had, becoming a government-coordinated instrument of Wall Street's national policy. Thenceforth the handouts and briefings of government officials were palmed off as objective reporting while reporters and editors largely surrendered the right of criticism and independent inquiry. Thus any brain-child of a McCarthy or a Dulles, of a stool pigeon or labor spy, went unchallenged in the press as long as it seemed to serve the cold war.

the spirit of the times, none of the government servants was to be allowed to know the identity of his accuser or the specific charge against him.

In the midst of all this the attorneys, officials, and lobbyists of the National Association of Manufacturers and the Chamber of Commerce were happily drafting the Taft-Hartley Law to repeal the Wagner Labor Act and in the name of fairness to return labor to the mercies of the employers. Although the measure, which John L. Lewis called "the first ugly, savage thrust of Fascism in America," bore the names of Senator Taft and Representative Hartley, it was presented by them to Congress only after it was presented to them by Big Business.

"The bill was written sentence by sentence, paragraph by paragraph, page by page, by the National Association of Manufacturers," said Representative Donald L. O'Toole of New York while Representative John McCormack of Massachusetts said the drive for its passage was "the most vicious kind of demonstration of corporate lobbying." He revealed that the bill had not been written by Congressmen or Senators but by such enemies of labor as William Ingles, a registered lobbyist for General Electric, Allis-Chalmers, Inland Steel, and J. I. Case and Company; Theodore Isserman, lawyer for the Chrysler Corporation; Mark Jones, a promoter said to be connected with the Rockefeller interests; and Jerry Morgan, a corporation lawer. This battery of corporate reaction was advised and helped by lawyers and consultants of the NAM and the Chamber of Commerce. Senator Joseph N. Ball of Minnesota tacitly admitted that the bill might go far in destroying labor, declaring, "The bill will bear most heavily on unions. I see no point in trying to dodge that fact." And Senator Taft of Ohio said: "The bill is not a milk toast bill."

The bill was passed by Congress in June, 1947. President Truman, soon to use the law a total of nine times in preventing strikes for higher wages, was in no position effectively to veto it or rally opposition against it after his action of breaking the railroad strike the year before by his threatened drafting of strikers into the Army. He registered a formal veto but Congress swiftly passed it over his ineffective protest. Most of the bill's supporters justified their stand by the cold war, concentrating on the anti-Communist provisions of the law, all union officers being forced to take oaths that they were not Communists. At the same time the cold war gutted opposition to the law from the first, many unions and union members being increasingly afraid that they would be smeared as "reds" if they effectively fought what was described as an anti-Communist measure.

The provisions of the Taft-Hartley were many and deadly and all geared to the destruction of labor as an independent force controlled by its members and responsible to them. Virtually repealing the Wagner Law and the Norris-La Guardia Anti-Injunction Act of 1932, both the fruit of years of labor struggle, the Taft-Hartley Act was a time-bomb scheduled to explode during a depression or at any other time employers needed it most. Although its full force was not immediately thrown against labor, within a matter of months it had brought the trade union movement to a complete standstill in organizing, afflicted it with paralysis, subjected it to the loss of literally millions of dollars in damage suits and fines, paved the way for union raids against each other, and subjected an increasing number of union leaders to indictment and imprisonment.

It was natural enough that Big Business took permanent delight in this victory over labor. "A New Deal for America's Employers," *Business Week* announced immediately after the law's passage. Six years later *U.S. News & World Report* asked with satisfaction, "Are Unions Slipping? No Growth in Six Years." A glance at the specific provisions of Taft-Hartley reveals both the reason for employer ecstasy and the halting of union advance in membership or appreciably higher pay.

The Taft-Hartley reinstituted injunctions, gave courts the power to fine for alleged violations. It established a sixty-day cooling off period in which strikes could not be declared. It outlawed mass picketing. It provided for the suing of labor for "unfair labor practices." It denied trade unions the right to contribute to political campaigns. It abolished the closed shop, went far toward building the conditions for a return of the old open-shop days that preceded the CIO. It authorized employer interference in attempts of his employees to join a trade union. It prohibited secondary boycotts. It authorized and encouraged the passage of state anti-union, "right-to-work" laws.

Through these provisions an employer could break a strike through injunctions against picketing and other standard strike procedure. He could refuse to bargain collectively, even by shutting down his plant to prevent negotiations. He could destroy union treasuries by suit, keep the open shop by legal threats against his workers, put company spies back into unions powerless to eject them under the law as long as they paid their dues. The employer could circumvent union democracy by charging any effective trade unionist with being a Communist, making his election unlikely, and laying the basis of perjury proceedings if he was elected.

Thus, if Dennis and other Communists had been victim number one of the cold war and the red scare, organized labor became victim number two with passage of the Taft-Hartley Act. As the cost of living rose to an all-time high some 16,000,000 trade unionists daily felt the law in their pockets and sometimes in their bellies. Their muscles, wearied by the ever-increasing speed-up, which always follows weakened unions, also told of the law. In addition the 232,000 trade union officials who signed the non-Communist oath were in daily danger of employer-inspired perjury indictments, the word of any hired stool pigeon being sufficient in days of cold war to send almost any of them to prison.

Their danger was attested by the case of Clinton Jencks, of Mine, Mill and Smelter, who, on the word of a stool-pigeon who later swore that he had committed perjury, was sentenced to five years in prison for allegedly falsely signing the oath. It was attested by the *Wall Street Journal* and the Chamber of Commerce,[14] both of which declared that non-Communist trade unionists were often as dangerous as if they were Communists. It was indicated by the perjury indictments in connection with the non-Communist oath against Hugh Bryson, president of the Marine Cooks and Stewards, and against Ben Gold, president of the International Fur and Leather Workers Union, both of whom had been instrumental in raising pay by millions of dollars.

Yet despite gargantuan war orders and the Taft-Hartley Act the country was skidding toward depression in 1949. Unemployment climbed to an estimated 5,000,000 that year as total gross private investment in the country fell off by 23 per cent, the index of industrial production dropped from 192 to 176, and net personal savings were cut from a rate of over 12 billions of dollars a year in the first quarter of 1949 to a rate of a little less than 6 billions a year in the third and fourth quarters.

Neither cold war nor huge armaments contracts proved sufficient to avoid the growing decline but *U.S. News & World Report* was confident that additional war scares would set things right. "War scares are easy to create," it observed on February 17, 1950, "and are nearly sure fire producers of money for more arms. . . ." And on the eve of the Korean War that publication said:

"Government planners figure they have found the magic formula for almost endless good times. They are now beginning to wonder if there may not be something to perpetual motion after all. . . . Cold War is the catalyst. Cold war is an automatic pump-primer. Turn the spigot, and the public clamors for more arms spending. Turn another, the clamor ceases. . . . Cold war demands, if fully exploited, are almost limitless."

But "the magic formula" was not working as the economic decline of 1949 deepened. It never does. Pump-priming for war, either hot or cold, may delay depression while it guarantees its inevitable approach and additional severity.[15] Monopoly was fortuitously rescued from its plight by

[14] The *Wall Street Journal* in its issue of April 9, 1952, declared ". . . Green, Murray and other such piously anti-Communist leaders [are] actually playing, unintentionally we hope, Russia's game by striking or threatening to strike. . . ." The Chamber of Commerce in its fifth report on Communism said that the real danger came from non-Communists, "those who engage in pro-Communist activities" such as fighting for higher wages, housing, or the repeal of the thought-control Smith Act. "The danger," said the Chamber in its report, comes from "ostensibly non-Communist individuals and organizations."

[15] During the great depression of 1929 Sir John Maynard Keynes, a noted British economist, advanced the theory that periodic depressions and mass unemployment could be prevented and the capitalist system saved from revolution by "pump-priming" that is, by government stimulation of business, particularly the subsidization of it. Almost at once the theory was widely accepted. Big business took it to its bosom in President Hoover's "trickle-down" theory expressed in the Reconstruction Finance Corporation while liberals and Social Democratic elements espoused it in the form of

President Truman's sudden declaration of "police action" in Korea in June, 1950. War orders and munitions contracts were doubled and wages were frozen as monopoly's profits before taxes leaped to an average of forty-three billions a year during the first two years of the Korean War.

Full production returned for a time as the wheels of American industry were turned by the flood of blood being shed in Korea. But as they turned, bringing in annual profits after taxes twice as large as those of World War II,[16] they also brought steadily nearer an economic decline which was soon to put an estimated four to five million American workers into the army of the unemployed. For always at the end of the road, beyond the war scares and the red scares, beyond the swollen profits of the few and the super-exploitation of the many, lies the mass misery of depression.

3. The CIO Divides Itself

To an unprejudiced reader it might seem incredible that the CIO, which had itself been expelled from the AFL on charges that it was a Communist conspiracy indulging in dual unionism, would proceed to divide and weaken itself by expelling CIO unions on essentially the same charge. Nevertheless, in 1949, in line with the policies of the Chamber of Commerce, Wall Street banker Forrestal, and the NAM, the CIO's dominant leadership deliberately diminished the CIO's strength by expelling eleven

---

President Roosevelt's "New Deal" which, in addition to continuing the RFC, introduced reforms designed to help directly those below. However, by failing to do away with the basic causes of depression and mass unemployment inherent in capitalism, Keynesism, in the form of both "trickle-down" and "trickle-up," failed to work; in 1937-38 there was a sharp economic breakdown and only the advent of World War II pulled the country out of the crisis.

After World War II Keynesism was revived and became accepted government policy in western Europe as well as in the United States. The initiation of the cold war resulted in government subsidization of industry through the purchase of gigantic armaments at public expense. In line with big business policies to dominate the world the Keynesian theory well fitted the needs of American imperialism. Under the impetus of war scares and red scares, the huge armaments program with its "trickle-down" theory of prosperity superseded any "Fair Deal" or "welfare state" approach to the problem of depression and mass unemployment as liberal and labor leaders with few exceptions went along with the program. But again Keynesism failed to prevent the economic breakdown of 1949-50. Only the hot war in Korea temporarily pulled the country out of the depression and when that "police action" was over the nation was faced by the so-called rolling recession of 1953-54 with its millions of unemployed and its millions of young men siphoned off into military service.

[16] Profits in the postwar period of the cold and hot wars dwarfed the bumper profits of the World War II years. From 1947 to 1952 profits before taxes totaled 213.6 billions of dollars as against 116.7 billions from 1940 to 1945, while profits after taxes came to 113.3 billions of dollars as compared with 55.1 billions. Profits per production worker in manufacturing rose from $957 in 1944 to $1,756 in 1952, an illustration of how monopoly was able to squeeze ever greater profits out of workers through increased speed-up, skyrocketing prices, and juicy war contracts.

of its own unions on accusations similar to those that the AFL's Green, Frey, and Woll had directed against the CIO itself more than ten years earlier. The libel of Communist domination which had been repelled over the years as a splitting device of the employer was adopted in 1949 by the CIO top leadership as it undertook a self-division approaching the suicidal.

The plot to divide the CIO was at all times a design of the CIO's cold-war leadership. It never had the approval of the CIO rank-and-file, who were to struggle for bargaining unity with the very unions which the CIO bureaucracy had expelled in scores of wage fights all over the country. No one knew better than the average union member that when one union is replaced by two or even more in a plant or industry, which was the inevitable result of the expulsions, the product is always decreased wages and heightened speed-up for the workers.

The self-destruction of the CIO is a study in cold-war hysteria. So shrill and constant had been the cry of "red" that down-to-earth common sense went out the window at CIO conventions, everything progressive being described as a Communist conspiracy. Advocacy of world peace became advocacy of treason. Proposals for the banning of atomic slaughter were regarded as the sure mark of the Communist. Warnings of inevitable depression brought on by cold-war armaments, fantastic profits, and shrinking real wages were considered Kremlin propaganda. Refusal to red-bait and witch hunt, to divide and weaken, was thought a tacit confession of Moscow domination.

Any discredited fiction could be passed off as truth during the CIO's campaign to destroy itself. There were no classes, said Philip Murray, who had succeeded Lewis as head of the CIO in 1940, and the interests of the man on the assembly line and Morgan were identical.[17] The war scare was not a method of further enriching the already wealthy, despite the repeated admissions of *U.S. News & World Report,* the *Wall Street Journal,* and other Big Business publications, but a holy crusade to save the world from evil. The red scare was not an employer-inspired splitting device, even though endlessly promoted by the Chamber of Commerce and the NAM in their campaign to pass the Taft-Hartley Act and other similar measures, but a tactic to be used by labor itself. Patriotism was following the prowar line of the NAM, treason was fighting for world peace and to save the American people from policies that might result in their atomic destruction. All traditional American values had been turned upside down.

From the first the United Electrical Workers, whose contracts and wage policies covering over a half million members were a standard for the whole CIO, was a main target of the CIO forces intent on transforming the CIO into an automatic rubber stamp approving each and every move of monop-

---

[17] "We have no classes in this country," Murray wrote in the *American Magazine,* June, 1948. "We are all workers here. And in the final analysis the interests of farmers, factory hands, business and professional people, and white collar workers prove to be the same."

oly's war policies. In January, 1948, the CIO Executive Board, attempting to make endorsement of the cold war a condition of membership, ruled it mandatory for all CIO unions to agree to back the nominee and the policies of the Democratic national convention six months away, certain that the nominee would be Truman, the policies more cold war.

The UE took the position that only its membership, acting by majority vote in convention, could bind the union to a political stand or any other kind of stand. It resented what it considered an attempt at outside political domination that would set aside the rank-and-file control of its membership. And that membership insisted on remaining loyal to the policies of Franklin D. Roosevelt providing for big-power unity and an expanding national economy based on world peace.[18]

The drive for political uniformity in the CIO got under way with differences of opinion arising in respect to the Marshall Plan. Launched in mid-1947 by Secretary of State George Marshall, this instrument of cold war policy was enacted into law in April, 1948, as the Economic Cooperation Act. Providing for the "rehabilitation" and "recovery" of Europe through a huge appropriation of about 20 billions of dollars spread over a four-year period, the Marshall Plan was criticized as a method of bringing the European economy under the domination of Wall Street and as in no way a help to Europe's workers. Such criticism made by UE, Fur and Leather, Longshoremen, and many other CIO affiliates in 1948 was regarded as akin to treason but, ironically enough, by 1950 CIO officials were saying the same things in even stronger terms.

John W. Livingston, for example, was an advocate of the Marshall Plan

[18] After the January edict of the CIO Executive Board, put out in violation of the CIO constitution providing for autonomy for member unions, Albert J. Fitzgerald, president of UE, and Julius Emspak, secretary-treasurer, sent a letter of resignation from PAC, the political arm of the CIO. Some UE members wanted to back the peace and labor policies of F.D.R. as represented by Henry Wallace, former Vice President of the United States under Roosevelt, heading a new third party in 1948. However, the UE convention of that year took no action with respect to Wallace, refusing to dictate to UE membership for whom it should vote. As it would not presume itself to dictate to its membership, so it would not permit an outside body, the CIO Executive Board, to rob its membership of political independence by an arbitrary ukase. The 1948 UE convention declared:

"There are some who would go so far as to deny the right of the new party to exist, who would outlaw any form of independent political expression in America, and who seek to impose their own political views upon union members by threats, coercion and expulsions. We condemn all such efforts, and although this convention endorses no presidential candidate, we expressly assert the right of any member, local or district of the UE to work for the advancement of the new Progressive Party, or any other political party. We condemn as well the despicable attempts that are being made to substitute red-baiting for democratic and open discussion of the issues of the presidential campaign by the American people.

"We urge our locals to promote such discussion, with confidence that our membership will reject all efforts at political coercion and despise all appeals to rancor and prejudice."

in the CIO conventions which resulted in the expulsion of the progressive unions. But in 1950, after the expulsions and after he visited Europe, this vice president of the United Auto Workers said:

"The Marshall Plan has been a 'miserable failure' insofar as skilled wage earners in Germany, Italy and France are concerned. Huge profits of companies whose plants have been rebuilt and rehabilitated by Marshall Plan funds and extremely low wages have lowered worker morale to make effective and convincing Communist propaganda."

And Jacob Potofsky, president of the Amalgamated Clothing Workers, CIO, also once an advocate of expulsion and the Marshall Plan, had also changed his mind, at any rate about the latter. In 1951 he said:

"Our money has been used primarily to strengthen the governments in power and the industrialists. The rich grow richer and the poor poorer. European industry has retained the time-honored theory of unbelievably high profits and low wages. Labor has not had the benefit of improved conditions since the end of the war."

And the views of William Belandger, of the Textile Workers Union, CIO; Harold Gibbons, of the AFL Teamsters; and Carmen Lucia, of the Hatters Union, AFL, were described in the *CIO News* of August 21, 1950:

"The American unionists, fresh from French industrial centers, voiced frank alarm about the economic hardship endured by French workers' families. All three were shocked to find that prices had been rising steadily in France during recent years while wages have been held down."

When a labor organization divides and weakens itself by its own action, it is proof positive that its leadership has been taken over by those who stand to profit most by such division. The self-division and self-weakening of the CIO were no exception. Its leadership had been recruited for the employers' cold war, just as the leadership of the AFL had been recruited in the 1920's for the employers' open shop. All facets of American life were rapidly becoming instruments of Wall Street's national policy—industry, banking, farming, the press, the movies, radio, television, education, and science—and the labor movement was not to escape monopoly's general mobilization. The CIO's policies were to be henceforth largely directed by the State Department, many CIO officials actually entering State Department service in a futile attempt to sell the Marshall Plan to European labor. [19]

[19] Lush jobs as Marshall Plan administrators and consultants were given to top AFL and CIO officials. Clinton Golden of the CIO was given a $15,000-a-year salary. Bert Jewell of the AFL drew down a like sum. George Meany and James Carey, members of the ECA advisory board, were given $50 a day for their services. Leland Buckmaster of the CIO Rubber Workers and Harvey Brown of the IAM, as members of the Anglo-American Productivity Council—an outfit designed to introduce American speed-up techniques in British mills and plants—got a de luxe ocean trip and $50 a day besides when they went to Britain on "official" business.

The assault on the CIO, that is, monopoly's pressure on it to make it purge and divide itself, began with an assault on Philip Murray's mind and spirit. He was the key in reaction's opinion, to forcing CIO to new policies since it was the alliance of center forces under Murray with the left that had made CIO the most successful labor organization in American history. This coalition had to be broken if CIO was to be broken and Murray had to be broken first of all as far as his stand for unity was concerned.

For three years he was urged by a steady procession of the great and near great, by prelates and Cabinet members, by editors and editorials, industrialists and right-wing labor leaders with an axe to grind, to split the CIO by purging the reds. Forrestal himself met with Murray, as the Wall Street cabinet officer recorded in his diary,[20] urging the cold-war policy upon him. At first Murray fought back. He did not surrender without a struggle. All his alliances, all his relationships and habits of thought throughout most of CIO history, welled up in him to make him reject at first the technique of red-baiting, split, purge, division. After all, the very heart of the labor movement is unity and it takes the corrupt to connive easily at shattering this absolutely fundamental tenet of trade unionism.

For years the right wing of the CIO, led by Reuther of Auto, Rieve of Textile, and Green of the Shipbuilders, aided and abetted by ACTU, the Association of Catholic Trade Unionists, had tried to break Murray away from the alliance of center and left that was the CIO's formula for victory. But Murray, at first with Lewis at his side and later alone, had stood firm over the years, declaring explicitly that purge and split was the method of death and destruction.

The AFL was easy enough for Forrestal and his associates to take over for it had a long tradition of accommodation and collaboration to the wishes of monopoly. Nevertheless John L. Lewis could not stomach the AFL's abject surrender and he withdrew himself and his miners, only recently returned to the fold, two months after the AFL's 1947 convention in San Francisco. The AFL, Lewis said at that convention, had even decided to accept the most vicious law ever directed against labor, the Taft-Hartley statute, "the first ugly savage thrust of fascism in America." He said further:

". . . You know, if you grovel enough in this convention, you will probably have more to grovel for next January and March, because when the Congress and the enemies of labor find out how easy you are they will give you more to grovel for. . . . Hadn't you better fight a little now than fight more down the road [to Fascism] or would you rather run?

"Well, gentlemen of the convention, I represent an organization. They pay me and they are not going to run with you. They don't like to run. I will say this, that those of the membership don't hesitate to tell me that they don't pay me to run either, in the wrong direction.

"We are not going to run with you. . . . If they [Congress] see that we are on

20 W. Millis, ed., *Forrestal Diaries*, p. 406.

the run . . . conceivably they might pass a bill . . . charge us with treason or high crimes and misdemeanors. That is the next logical step. That is what happened in Italy and Germany, didn't it? . . . If you don't resist, the power of the state, the central government, will be used against you that much more quickly, because they won't lose any sleep at night worrying about a labor movement that is fleeing before the storm. . . ."

But Murray and his allies did not surrender quite as quickly to the cold-war demands of monopoly as did the top hierarchy of the AFL. All through 1946 and 1947, even as he was being softened up, Murray nevertheless managed to make ringing statements against the policy of purge and divide. The pressure against him was increased in direct ratio to the pressure of what was from monopoly's standpoint a deteriorating world situation. The Chinese Revolution, involving some 500,000,000 people, was steadily advancing toward victory as it removed ever greater areas of China from the influence of Wall Street and the control of Chiang Kai-shek. Liberation movements all over Asia, Africa, and Latin America were driving monopoly from its colonial vantage points. The working men and women of Europe were resisting the drive to war, declaring that their countries were losing their independence under the domination of Wall Street and its Marshall Plan.

Almost daily, as Forrestal's diary indicates, Murray was subjected to false talk about putting his country before the trade union movement, as if it can be done without injury to the country, even phonier talk about possible sabotage by trade unionists in the face of war and attempted Russian invasion. As the pressure against Murray continued, the red scare pyramided, became louder and louder, stronger and stronger until Murray and his associates could see that they themselves would be in real danger if they stood firm for unity within the CIO in the face of all the power of organized reaction. It was easy enough to foresee, as reactionary forces reiterated, that non-Communists were often more dangerous than Communists, that the drive was going to continue until everyone who stood in the way of war and reaction, whether he be New Dealer or labor leader, would be engulfed.

If Murray needed the lesson underlined it was done for him by Louis Budenz, Communist renegade who was proving in testimony before Congressional committees, in 1948 and 1949 that the charge of Communist was wide enough to include everyone. Budenz solemnly declared in testimony solemnly received and solemnly praised that the fact that a man denied he was a Communist might prove he was a Communist since all Communists had instructions to deny it.

As a result of this testimony, Professor Owen D. Lattimore was indicted for perjury after he had sworn he was not a Communist. Budenz added that anything a man said might, as a matter of fact, prove he was a Communist since Communists spoke in a queer double-talk, in so-called "Aesopian" language. Thus, according to Budenz's testimony, if a man said, "I am not a Communist and I favor peace," he might really be saying in Aesopian language, "I am a Communist and I favor war." With this formula, generally acclaimed, no one was safe, least of all the leader of a militant labor center costing employers billions a year in wage raises.

Under this ever increasing pressure Murray, as his statements show, tried to do two things at once, to stand firm against dividing the CIO and to move nearer to the right and those supporting such division. During 1946 and 1947 he repeatedly urged unity, repeatedly rejected the demands of those who advocated amending the CIO constitution so as to remove all autonomy of member unions. Over and over again he said such an amendment would destroy the most basic provision of CIO and probably the CIO itself.

Rigid wages and rising living costs were daily emphasizing the necessity for unity. But even as Murray boldly challenged those who, he said, would destroy CIO and lower the workers' wages by political witch-hunting, he was in the process of moving nearer to their position, as later events were to show.

At the 1946 convention Murray challenged the Reuther-Green-Rieve-ACTU forces with this militant declaration for unity:

"Let no one create conflict within this movement. . . . I should say to you at this moment that this mighty organization, the CIO, is not going to be divided by anybody. It has been a united movement and will continue to be one throughout its existence, I hope. . . . We have our divisions of opinion and we, I suppose, in the years to come, will be susceptible to divisions of opinion. That is mighty healthy. If we were all united in the sense that we had one opinion on every subject I imagine that we might become a little rusty. . . ."

And at the steel workers' convention in 1946 he was even more emphatic:

"We ask no man his national origin, his color, his religion, his beliefs. It is enough for us that he is a steel worker and that he believes in trade unionism. . . . Our union has not been and will not be an instrument of repression. It is a vehicle for economic and social progress. . . . As a democratic institution we engage in no purges, no witch hunts. We do not dictate a man's thoughts or beliefs. Most important of all we do not permit ourselves to be stampeded into courses of action which create division among our members and sow the disunity which is sought by those false prophets and hypocritical advisers from without who mean us no good."

And in the very citadel of the Reuther forces, he rejected the counsel of those who wished to change the CIO constitution for the purposes of expelling those who did not agree with surrender to Wall Street's cold-war policies. Speaking before the convention of the United Automobile Workers in 1947, he said:

"We never determine the course of action of our affiliates. . . . They are sovereign, autonomous unions, and in matters of great moment we got together and we considered and advised with each other, but in the end we left the ultimate decision to each of the international unions for important policy decisions. There is a reason for that. I hope the day never comes in the history of the CIO when it shall take upon itself the power to dictate or to rule or to provide by policy methods of dictation and ruling that run counter to the very principles of true democracy."

At the Boston convention of the CIO in 1947 Murray again declared definitively and unequivocally against the policy of expulsions through amendment of the CIO constitution which was being ceaselessly urged upon him by Reuther and the ACTU. Declaring that all the lessons of history prove that expulsions or enforced conformity rob trade unionists of control of their own unions, he further said:

"They have in the constitution of the American Federation of Labor, and they have within the structure of their policy-making, power in the heads of that organization, the power to expel unions when they don't comply with the decrees of the people who occupy positions of authority at the top of the American Federation of Labor.

"The CIO in those days resented that idea. At its first constitutional convention held in Pittsburgh in 1938, they were careful to incorporate a provision which prevented officers of the National CIO or the National Executive Board from having the power to expel. Repeatedly since that time, questions have developed within the Council of the CIO. Questions of a more or less serious nature, but the CIO has the framework within its own democratic institutions to resolve these issues without the use of the sword or the axe. We decreed in 1938 that each union affiliated with the Congress of Industrial Organizations should and must exercise certain autonomous rights, and those rights could not be abridged by dictum issued by the President of this organization or by its Executive Board. And we have acted accordingly ever since. Therefore, the affiliated unions attached to this organization exercise the greatest possible degrees of autonomy. That is a democratic process."

With Murray temporarily standing staunchly for a continuation of center-left unity, the 1946 CIO convention continued to back F.D.R.'s policies of expanding production at home and Big Three unity abroad between the United States, Great Britain, and the Soviet Union. "We reject," said the main resolution in 1946, "all proposals for American participation in any bloc or alliance which would destroy the unity of the Big Three." But by the 1947 Boston convention of the CIO cracks were beginning to show in CIO unity, despite Murray's continued rejection of the tactic of expelling on the grounds that they were Communist conspirators, all those who disagreed with the policy of cold war.

By 1948 Murray had surrendered. It was not only the pressure of the

Reuther-Green-Rieve forces, the urgings of Forrestal, the Taft-Hartley Act, and the hue and cry of press, church, and radio that caused him to reverse the policies that had made CIO a symbol for working class victory and triumph. It was rather the whole overwhelming direction of events. It was the increasing danger that faced all dissent and dissenters to monopoly's policies, the ever mounting risk confronting all those brave enough to fight for trade union policies rather than Wall Street's policies.

The McCarran Bill, for example, providing that under certain conditions any American or American organization advocating anything the Communists advocated from rent control to higher wages to world peace could be criminally prosecuted, was before Congress and soon to be passed. The bill and its proponents were in themselves lessons not without result on Murray and others. In addition, the Attorney General by his own fiat, by his own executive order and without hearings, was declaring hundreds of private organizations[21] disloyal, their thousands of members "security risks."

No longer could Americans join any organization they saw fit to join but only those approved by the government. If private belief and individual conviction were becoming dangerous, as everyone knew they were, it was becoming even more dangerous for people with common views to associate in organization. It sometimes seemed, upon examination of the Attorney General's catalogue of *verboten* organizations, that any defense of American rights, particularly the right of advocating peace and speaking out against mass atomic destruction of human beings, was regarded as only a Kremlin conspiracy. Guilt by association and innuendo, guilt for political beliefs as attributed to people by informers, had replaced the old American rule of judging guilt on the basis of specific overt *acts* charged, the accusation to be tried by a jury.

It was in this climate that the CIO Executive Council in January, 1948, issued its ukase declaring that all affiliated unions had to favor the policies and vote for the political candidates that the Executive Council decided they should favor and vote for. It was in this climate that the 1948 CIO convention declared that those unions which refused to knuckle under to this violation of the CIO constitution were "through Communist domination serving the purposes of Soviet foreign policy." The purposes and well-being of the American people had been forgotten.

As the largest of the unions attacked, UE's response may be taken as an example of the thinking in the militant unions. Said the UE General Executive Board:

"Some labor officials have subordinated the interests of the membership of their unions to the dictates of the [Truman] Administration on domestic and foreign policy. This perverts the purpose for which unions were organized. We

[21] By June, 1954, 256 organizations were listed as "subversive" by the Attorney General.

have many times declared that the first function of a union is to serve the economic interests of its members. When these interests are placed first, the legislative and political programs which come from the union strengthen the national economy and promote democracy. When the policies of the unions are subordinated to the desires of American big business to run the world, the interests of the membership suffer." [22]

With the Chamber of Commerce, the NAM, and the press applauding, the CIO met in convention at Cleveland on Oct. 31, 1949, patriotically determined on suicide or at the very least considerable self-maiming. Again it

[22] Replying to the charge that its opposition to the anti-Roosevelt policies of cold war made it a Kremlin agent, the UE said in effect in 1948 and specifically in 1952 before the Senate Committee on Labor and Public Welfare:

"In 1947 the split that began between UE and the rest of CIO, insofar as it involved foreign policy, resulted not from a change in UE policy, but in a change of CIO policy. Without deviation, the UE has followed the policy developed by the late Franklin D. Roosevelt and enunciated as our national policy in the Yalta and Potsdam Declarations at the end of World War II. A close inspection of the issues of this period shows that only the application of the most extreme McCarthyism in the trade union field can lead to allegations of 'service to Soviet foreign policy' by the UE. . . .

"Conformity with the policies of the ruling clique is not Americanism. It is subversive of the Constitution to try to enforce such conformity. And when those policies have undermined the security of our people, it is the height of patriotism for Americans to work to change them.

"Had the members of this union declared that war profiteering is fine, we would not be here today. Some of us might have even been chosen to help hand out the government funds to the profiteers and grafters.

"If our members had put their stamp of approval on the tax-price-wage squeeze that is wrecking the country's living standards, we would not be charged with endangering the country's security.

"Had we called for atomic war, for 60 billion dollar arms budgets, for distributing America's wealth to corrupt dictators like Franco and Chiang Kai-shek, we would not be under attack. . . ."

As to UE's opposition to the Marshall Plan, later known as the ERP, or European Recovery Program, the union said:

"When this union said that the policy was a big business scheme, we were reviled by others in the labor movement. Refusal to beat the drums for ERP was used as one of the excuses for splitting the CIO.

"But that this union was right is admitted now by even those who carried the torch for bankrupt policies. Returning from Europe last fall [1951] AFL Boilermakers President Charles J. MacGowan said: 'Marshall Plan aid has done more to strengthen monopolies in western Europe than to aid the workers.' . . .

"American corporations, including many in the electrical, radio and machine industry, have used ERP backing to set up in cheap wage areas overseas, leaving American workers without employment.

"The program has proven a boon to big business here and its friends in other countries. Total foreign investments by U.S. corporations increased from $16.9 billion in 1947 to $20.7 billion in 1950.

"The American people have paid tens of billions of dollars in taxes for a program which has added to their cost of living; increased economic instability of the common people in other countries; made greater the danger of atomic war.

"Those who favor such policies are harming our country."

was passionately asserted that the Marshall Plan was only an idealistic method of feeding Europe's poor and that anyone who denied it was a traitorous Moscow conspirator. No sacrifice was too great to prove to monopoly that the CIO was as enthusiastic for cold war as Wall Street itself. War appropriations, their mammoth proportions built by the taxes of labor and the American people, were approaching fifty billions yearly. Approximately seventy per cent of each annual government budget was being spent for wars, hot and cold, past and future. But there was slight mention of this fact at the 1949 convention or of the fact that unemployment in 1949 had grown to 5,000,000, that 10,000,000 were working part-time, and that 500,000 steel workers and 320,000 coal miners were out in crucial strikes.

Instead Murray declared that the single issue before the convention was the expulsions. To carry out the suicidal policy it was necessary for Murray to eat his own words warning that such a policy was the road to destruction. He did it—to the cheers of the Reuther-Rieve-Green faction and his own admirers. It was necessary to amend basic provisions of the CIO constitution which expressly prohibited expulsion through witch-hunting. The constitution was amended amid the hoots, catcalls, and jeers directed at those who warned that if the amendment was for expulsion, it was also for lower wages, more speed-up, and an employer-controlled labor movement.

Patriotism demanded, it was said, the expulsion of the left unions. It was in vain that delegates from the left pointed out that real patriotism could not ask that unions be expelled whose only sin was that their members had decided by democratic vote to remain faithful to the peace policies of F.D.R. Real patriotism, delegates from the left declared, was not throwing your hat into the air every time a millionaire general addressed a CIO convention, but fighting for organization of the South, the repeal of the Taft-Hartley Act, the thirty-hour week, a higher minimum wage, Negro rights, the unity of the labor movement, and the right of any American anywhere any time saying any word he believed.

Fake patriotism, they said, was forcing Americans, forcing trade unions to back that which they believed would hurt the American people under penalty of expulsion if they did not. Real patriotism, said the delegates from the left, was not trying to court popularity with the State Department and Pentagon, but fighting for pork chops, for dollars-and-cents improvements in the lot of the American people, even though that fight was not popular with Big Business. It was fighting for world peace particularly when the alternative might be world destruction. Real patriotism demanded unending fight against labor becoming only the tail of reaction's kite. It required that real patriots fight such programs as the Marshall Plan under which billions of dollars were taken from the American taxpayer to enable Wall Street to capture control of European industry as a part of the drive toward war.

Such words were said but they were not often heard amid the jeers and catcalls. Thus was the amendment passed, and the convention proceeded to the next order of business, to the expulsion of the United Electrical Workers. Pietro Lucchi, secretary-treasurer of the Fur and Leather Workers, warned once more of the expulsions, said that he had participated in such fights between left and right before and that the only result had been lower wages and weakened unions. "I fought with the lefts for ten long years," he said. "What happened during those ten years? The fur workers and the union paid very, very dearly. Only the employers profited. . . ."

Not only was UE expelled, but the Fur and Leather Workers Union, the Mine, Mill and Smelter Workers Union, and the International Long-shoremen's and Warehousemen's Union—all of the pace-setters for the whole trade union movement by reason of wage scales and conditions won, by virtue of rank-and-file democratic control, and sound trade union prac-tice based not on Wall Street's needs but the needs of their memberships and the American people.

The process did not cease until almost 1,000,000 CIO members had been purged for their belief that unions should be run by and for the member-ship and not by cold-war cliques for the benefit of big business. The orders of the Chamber of Commerce had been successfully carried out within three years from the time they were issued. Other unions expelled were the United Farm Equipment Workers; Food, Tobacco and Agricultural Workers; United Office and Professional Workers; the United Public Workers; the American Communications Association; the National Union of Marine Cooks and Stewards, and the International Fishermen and Allied Workers.

Thus was the formula for victory shattered and since then the victories have been few and far between for all of labor. The expelled unions were the soul of the CIO. Since their expulsion it has been a body without a spirit. They were the CIO's fighters and pioneers. They ceaselessly agitated and pressed for advance, tirelessly fought all wage programs that tied wages to cost of living and employer profits, forever pressed for organization of the unorganized regardless of race, creed, color, political belief, or sex.

Always they opposed back-door approaches to the employer in collective bargaining, always insisted on membership control in drawing up contracts, in declaring strikes or settling them. It was the expelled unions which had fought for world peace and the Bill of Rights, had warned of mass atomic destruction and an approaching depression unless the cold war policies of Big Business were reversed for the policies of F.D.R. It was these unions that had fought the hardest for Negro employment, Negro upgrading, Negro representation in trade union offices. It was they that had led the fight for equal pay for equal work for women and it was they that had fought for the rights of such minorities as Puerto Ricans and Mexican miners. And what organization had been accomplished in the South had been done mostly by them.

In the aftermath of the self-division, the CIO began to feed on what had once been itself. Officials of the Steel Workers Union, for example, joined employer attacks on Mine, Mill and Smelter, the gallant successor to the Western Federation of Miners. Maurice Travis, secretary-treasurer of the hard rock miners and smeltermen, was slugged and blinded in one eye by goons hired by the raiding union. Reuther's union joined employers in attempting to divide UE's farm equipment and electrical workers through raiding while millions of unorganized workers in the South dragged down the entire American wage scale as Northern industry increasingly ran away to that haven of the open shop and low pay. [23]

The new, divided CIO might well have been exemplified by James Carey, Secretary-Treasurer of the organization. The difference between the old CIO and the new was reflected in the fact that at times Carey was more often abroad on State Department missions than he was at home fighting for the workers' demands. Whether in Europe or America, Carey and other "labor statesmen" of the CIO now talked eagerly of an approaching war. [24] Whether in France or Italy, Schenectady or Lynn, Carey blithely played the Administration's game. His target in Europe was the World Federation of Trade Unions whose stand for peace was regarded as inimical to Wall Street policy. His target in Lynn, Schenectady, and most other places in the United States was the United Electrical Workers whose policies were also against dragging the American people into war.

Both Wall Street and the CIO were now an integral part of government, the only trouble being that Big Business ran the administration which the CIO bureaucracy obeyed. Approximately a hundred representatives of Big

[23] The run-away-plant movement—the moving of plants and jobs to non-unionized, low-wage areas—has become the accepted policy of big business. Under the high-sounding name of "decentralization," big business, aided by a government tax-amortization program, has taken to the hinterlands. On Sept. 20, 1950, a secret conspiratorial meeting of fourteen persons including Charles E. Wilson of General Electric was held in New York City. This meeting, the proceedings of which were disclosed in part in Henry Luce's magazine *Architectural Forum* (September 30), discussed the ins and outs of the so-called decentralization program. According to GE's Wilson, who three months later turned up as Defense Mobilizer in the Truman Administration, the days of the large plants of 20,000 to 40,000 workers were over. Instead there were to be small plants of 3,000 to 3,500 workers. The run-away-plant movement was to have a twofold effect: the attainment of maximum profits through lower wages in newer areas and weakening of unions through unemployment in older areas. The run-away-plant movement was underwritten by the government which under the Defense Production Act allowed the issuance of "certificates of necessity" carrying a high amortization tax so that the plants could be paid for out of untaxed profits. Nine months after Defense Mobilizer Charles E. Wilson took office, 15 billion dollars worth of "certificates of necessity" were issued, more than during the whole five-year period of World War II. Of course, the cold war was used to justify this union-busting run-away-plant program, the rationalization being the need to spread American industry in case of atom-bomb attack.

[24] Carey, for example, according to the New York *Herald Tribune* of January 29, 1950, said, "In the last war we joined with the Communists to fight the Fascists; in another war we will join the Fascists to defeat the Communists."

Business[25] ran Truman's administration, directing the spending of the government's fifty-billon-dollar war budget. The CIO found itself not only taking orders from the State Department but a part of the government apparatus that was directing billions in profits to the corporations as it imposed a wage freeze on workers while lifting price controls on food and rent. If Carey, for example, ran cold war errands for the administration in Europe, it was C. E. Wilson, head of General Electric and the government Defense Mobilizer, and others like him, who sent Carey on his errands. And if there were errands also to be run at home, it was only natural.[26]

Under these circumstances it was inevitable that many of the CIO's resolutions and actions increasingly became little more than an echo of monopoly-controlled government policy. The CIO's bureaucracy found that it could not carry out reactionary policy abroad without surrendering important positions to that policy at home. As a result the CIO's wage policy steadily degenerated into an acceptance of employer wage formulas. Typical were the five-year contracts in auto tied into the cost of living, or what the government claimed the cost of living was, designed to keep the worker working at the lowest possible wage.[27] Such wage policies, geared to the employer's needs and not to labor's and guaranteed to keep wages at only a minimum subsistence level, had not been openly mentioned, outside of company unions, since 1939 when the CIO specifically condemned them in a resolution offered by the United Electrical Workers. By 1953 real wages had declined by 25 per cent from 1939 while profits had risen from six and one-half billions to forty-five billions. By 1954 auto workers, as at Studebaker, were agreeing to 15 per cent wage cuts proposed by management under threat of closing down and moving South to non-union areas.

The CIO, whose unity had once made it the leader of militant millions gaining wage increases at the rate of five billions a year, had now become

[25] According to Republican Senator Homer E. Capehart, himself a big industrialist and so an authority on the subject, some 100 big business men were drafted into the government in the war and postwar years for policy jobs. Senator Capehart has listed the names of these big business representatives and their industrial and financial connections in six pages of fine type in the *Congressional Record*, 82:2, pp. 5555-5561, May 20, 1952.

[26] It was natural, too, that Carey felt that his cold-war services for the government abroad entitled him to help from the government at home in dragooning electrical workers into his new union. If he served Big Business and government abroad, Big Business and government could help him and themselves by lending Carey a hand at home. Congressional investigations, grand jury inquiries, company-inspired McCarthy frame-ups, and the electioneering of Truman cabinet officials became the new CIO method of organizing as the government threw its weight against the independent unions.

[27] An example of how this auto contract worked was given in the *New York Times* of Feb. 27, 1954, in a story announcing a rise in the cost of living and a pay cut for almost 1,000,000 employees of the auto industry. On Feb. 27 prices rose to within 0.2 point of an all-time high. At the same time wages in auto were cut by one cent an hour because prices had fallen during previous months—before they went up again and before the cut became effective.

the almost tame creature of monopoly, largely abandoning an independent position based on the needs of its membership. During World War II and the CIO's left-center coalition, it had been about as large as the AFL. But red-baiting had reduced its membership and power as surely and inevitably as it had the AFL's in the early 1920's. By 1954 CIO membership was around 4,600,000 as against 6,300,000 in 1946.

While the CIO's membership decreased in the ten years following the end of World War II, the AFL's increased. In 1945 this oldest labor center in the United States reported a membership of 6,900,000. The following year saw it go over the seven-million mark for the first time in its long history. At its 65th annual convention in Chicago, Oct. 7–17, 1946, it claimed some 7,100,000 members and called for an organizing drive to bring that figure up to ten million. It was not until eight years later that this goal was achieved. In 1954 the AFL was said to have 10,200,000 members in 99 national and international unions, 4 departments, 42 state branches, 146 local central bodies, and 44 local trade and federal labor unions. The Teamsters Union alone, largest of its affiliates, had 1,300,000 members, more than double the 1946 figure.

The growing numerical strength of the AFL in the postwar decade was due more to reshuffling in the trade union movement than to organizing unorganized workers. Just as the CIO raided the progressive unions affiliated with it prior to 1950 and afterward outside of it, so did AFL unions prey on the CIO and the independents. From 1951 to 1953 alone there were as many as 1,245 raids between AFL and CIO unions, this exclusive of raids made by either on the independents. Through such tactics the AFL was able to increase its membership. There was, of course, during this period some AFL organization of the unorganized, but for the most part it fell far short of the proposed goal. In April, 1946, President Green announced an intensive drive in the South where millions of workers were ready and willing to join unions. The campaign, whch aimed at enrolling a million new members, was officially launched on May 11 at the third biennial meeting of the Southern Labor Conference in Asheville, N. C. In the thirteen-month period ended July 31, 1947, the AFL reported that its Southern organizing drive had netted 425,000 new members. Since then its campaign has ground to a halt with millions of Southern workers still waiting to be unionized.

The stalling of the Southern drive may be attributed partly to the fear still prevailing among many of the craft-minded leaders of the AFL of organizing unorganized semi-skilled and unskilled workers. This fear is part of the cautious position of Samuel Gompers, a position which William Green adopted from the time he became president of the federation in 1924 to the year of his death in 1952. But Green lived in a different world from Gompers. He and other top AFL leaders had to assume a more positive and militant approach during the postwar period to the question of higher wages, shorter hours, and improved working conditions. This had to be done in view of the fact that from 1945 to 1955 there were more than 43,000 strikes involving over 27,000,000 American workers—AFL as well as CIO and independents. Similarly, the realities of the situation compelled Green and his associates to accept the proposition that the unorganized ought to be organized, that industrial unions were here to stay, and that organic labor unity should be established.

4. The Attack Widens

The CIO did not save itself from further attack by its expulsion of eleven unions in 1949-50. Rather it encouraged such attacks on the entire labor movement. The CIO was itself declaring what the enemies of labor had always claimed—that some union struggles for higher wages and better conditions were only a Kremlin conspiracy. It was demonstrated again that an offensive against some unions encourages attacks against all unions. It was shown once more that if some unions are attacked as red, reactionaries promptly declare that all unions are red. The CIO's formula for expelling unions as Communist-dominated was immediately seized upon by Congressional labor-haters as reinforcement of their own idea of expelling all unions from American life on the allegation that all are Communist-dominated.

Stimulated by CIO's expulsions, Big Business Congressmen began to prepare bills, such as the Goldwater-Rhodes Bill and the Butler Bill, making it possible for any union to be denied certification for collective bargaining on the mere unproved allegation that its policies were "parallel" to Communist policies. Speaking of the Goldwater-Rhodes Bill, George Meany, the new president of the AFL, said "It would put Communist-dominated unions out of business, just like it would put all other unions out of business." And Glen Slaughter, of the AFL's Labor League for Political Education, added, "It could order out of business any union that ever advocated anything the Communist Party advocated, including income taxes and schools." Or world peace and a ban on atomic slaughter. In 1954 the principles of the Goldwater-Rhodes Bill were approved by the Eisenhower administration and passed by Congress under the guise of being only anti-Communist.

It did not take long to prove that the CIO's self-maiming had not saved it from the charge of red. The expulsions merely whetted the appetite of the Chamber of Commerce. The CIO had obediently expelled all the unions named as red by the Chamber of Commerce in its pamphlet of 1947 called *Communists Within the Labor Movement*. Now the Chamber of Commerce raised the ante, perhaps in the hope that the purified CIO would dissolve itself.

In 1952 it issued another brochure called *Communism: Where Do We Stand Today?* The CIO's work, the pamphlet indicated, had all been in vain. The cleansed organization was still infected. The Chamber of Commerce declared that the CIO had again been infiltrated by Communists, offering as proof the CIO's condemnation of the Smith Act. Speaking in similar vein, *The American Machinist* of Feb. 16, 1953, quoting a study of the CIO by the Timken Roller Bearing Company, observed that the purified CIO in economic matters "follows the Communist Party line with the persistence of a shadow."

Everywhere in employer circles the CIO's expulsions were being pointed to as proof that most unions were in fact Communist-dominated. The Textile Workers Union of America, led by Rieve, one of the chief architects of the CIO's anti-Communist purge, was itself being called Communist by employers even as they moved their plants from New England to the South which the CIO had failed to organize. The charge of red was too precious an asset in union-fighting for employers to give it up simply because the CIO had done some expelling. Murray himself was not saved from the charge of red by his part in expelling those whom he had charged were red. His patriotism was questioned by Clarence Randall, president of Inland Steel, during the 1952 steel strike when Randall declared Murray's "subversive" actions were aiding Communism and "threatening the safety of American soldiers in Korea."

Encouraged by their successes within the CIO, employers extended their red charge to the AFL. L. S. Boulware, vice president of General Electric stated that two AFL unions were "just as much help to Joe Stalin as if they were in fact Communist agents." Others, such as the Akron *Beacon-Journal*, declared that any union, Communist-dominated or not, was a "potential danger." It said:

"Actually a union doesn't need to be communist-dominated or to be led by communists to constitute a potential danger to industrial society."

The charge that the CIO unions which had voted to expel the allegedly Communist-dominated unions were themselves Communist-dominated became so general that Senator Hubert H. Humphrey of Minnesota was moved to protest. He said that employers were using the charge so indiscriminately that a non-Communist union was as likely to be accused of Communist-domination as a Communist union.

He did not explain as to how he decided which employer to believe. As head of the Senate Subcommittee on Labor and Public Welfare, he was holding hearings on proposals to give government licenses only to those trade unions which could prove they were not Communist. Feeling that the widespread charge of red against all unions was making his task difficult, he said, according to *U.S. News & World Report* of Dec. 28, 1951:

"Let me give you an example: the Textile Workers Union of the CIO. If any union in the country is clearly most anti-Communist this is it. Yet, I, as chairman of the Subcommittee, have held hearings where I heard employer representatives branding the Textile Workers Union as a Communist union because of the union's attempt to do some organizing."[28]

So general became the charge of red that when the Supreme Court of the United States upheld the Smith Act conviction of eleven Communist leaders on June 4, 1951, not for any acts, nor indeed for their beliefs but for what paid government witnesses and informers said were their beliefs, non-Communist officials of many CIO unions began to feel themselves in danger. They pondered the dissent of Justice Hugo Black who wrote:

"I want to emphasize what the crime involved in this case is, and what it is not. These petitioners [defendants] were not charged with an attempt to overthrow the government. They were not charged with overt acts of any kind designed to overthrow the government. They were not even charged with saying anything or writing anything designed to overthrow the government. The charge was that they agreed to assemble and to talk and publish certain ideas at a later date. . . ."[29]

[28] On June 27 and July 8, 1952, James Matles, UE director of organization, and Russ Nixon, UE Washington representative, testified before Senator Humphrey's committee in opposition to proposals to outlaw unions which were not given the stamp of government approval, preventing them from being certified as bargaining agencies. Commenting on Senator Humphrey's complaint that the Textile Union was charged with being Communist, Matles said: "To whatever degree any union attempts to serve the interests of its membership, it too will be red-baited, and it too [under Senator Humphrey's proposed legislation] will be outlawed in its turn. . . . Certainly the present experiences of the Textile Workers Union with the employers in the textile industry prove that no union, no matter how subservient to the interests of the employers it may be, or how obligingly it joins them in red-baiting the rest of the labor movement, is ensured thereby of safety from employer attack."

[29] Some 110 men and women have been either indicted or convicted under the thought-control Smith Act, about half of them trade union leaders. Among them were Jack Hall, of the International Longshoremen's and Warehousemen's Union; Irving Potash, vice president of the Fur and Leather Workers Union; William Sentner, a leader of the UE in the Middle West; Louis Weinstock, of the Painters Union and perhaps more responsible than any other single individual for unemployment compensation; Elizabeth Gurley Flynn, a leader of the Lawrence strike and a veteran of almost a half century in the American labor movement; Al Lannon, a founder of the National Maritime Union; George Myers, former president of the Maryland CIO; Philip M. Connelly, former president of the California CIO; Jack Stachel, former head of the Trade Union Unity League, pioneer fighter for industrial unionism. Others convicted include Robert Thompson, winner of the Distinguished Service Cross for gallantry in action during World War II's Pacific campaign; Eugene Dennis, former teamster and seaman and general secretary of the Communist Party; Benjamin J. Davis, Negro leader, former New York City Councilman, and John Gates, editor of the Daily Worker. Among other early victims of the anti-labor drive were Harold Christophel, former president of Local 248, UAW, the Allis-Chalmers local in Milwaukee, sentenced to three years in prison for alleged perjury when he contradicted the words of a paid stool pigeon; and James Lustig of the UE sentenced to prison, and now the victim of deportation proceedings, for refusal to hand over the names of the Joint Anti-Fascist Refugee Committee to a Congressional committee.

The organ of the Textile Workers Union, *Textile Labor,* in the past eager to cry red as it demanded the CIO expulsions, now expressed the fear that officials of the textile union might be charged under the Smith Act. Said *Textile Labor* on July 7, 1951:

"Sending men to prison on this basis could be dangerous to all of us. For example, there is no doubt that a whole segment of American society (including most southern mill owners), consider unions in general and T.W.U.A. in particular, 'subversive' and 'un-American.' "

And *Labor Sentinel,* a publication of Inland Steel Local 1010 of the United Steelworkers Union, CIO, said in July, 1951:

"In plain words a person doesn't have to be a member of the Communist Party to be prosecuted under this law. Every local steel leader and the union membership which engages in any kind of a militant fight can also be persecuted. And of course that's one of the main reasons the bill was passed."

The CIO *Packinghouse Worker* remarked on July 13, 1951, that labor had "learned the hard way" that when Communists were under attack it was scheduled for the next victim. Labor was given another lesson to ponder when the McCarran Internal Security Act was passed on Sept. 23, 1950, providing for the round-up of all the hundreds of thousands on the FBI's lists in event of war or national emergency. FBI director J. Edgar Hoover, that veteran of the Palmer Raids, appearing before a congressional appropriations committee in 1951, spoke about the possibility of throwing some 500,000 Americans into concentration camps in event of war. The McCarran Act also provided for long prison terms for the officers of non-Communist organizations which had "parallel aims" to those of the Communist Party, in the opinion of a Subversive Activities Control Board, if they did not register as officers of "Communist fronts."

In 1952 the McCarran-Walter Immigration Act was passed forcing 3,000,-000 non-citizens to carry registration cards in a Nazi-like system of identification and threatening 11,000,000 naturalized citizens with the possibility of denaturalization and deportation on charges that they might be "Reds." In its issue of August, 1953, *March of Labor* showed how this law could be and is being used against labor:

"A big strike is on. The workers are out solid. It looks like they're going to win that wage increase. Then suddenly the strike leader is thrown in jail, charged with being a 'subversive alien' and held indefinitely for possible deportation.

"Sounds like the answer to a boss's dream, doesn't it? But it's no dream. It's the McCarran-Walter law in operation. It's what actually happened not long ago to a group of striking bus drivers in Long Island."[30]

[30] Gordon A. Barrager, former president of Local 252, CIO Transport Workers, was negotiating a strike settlement for Long Island, New York, bus drivers demanding shorter hours and a wage boost, when immigration agents grabbed him from the bargaining table and rushed him to Ellis Island. There he was held under the Mc-

As the attacks on all unions increased in ferocity, at least some of the CIO bureaucracy were perhaps forced to see that instead of buying security by its expulsions it had instead opened the floodgates. The charges that it had thrown against the United Electrical Workers and the ten other progressive unions were now in some circles being extended to the entire labor movement. Senator Butler, speaking in support of Senate Bill 1606 to license government approved unions, made it clear that unions containing "liberals" or New Dealers would not be licensed, that he not only proposed the destruction of anti-Communist unions but the destruction of any and all unions that did not endorse the policies of the Chamber of Commerce and the NAM. [31]

In the meantime the rank and file of CIO, of the expelled independents, and of the AFL were struggling for unity, for joint negotiations in the bargaining fight all over the country. In addition John L. Lewis, unimpressed by the CIO's expulsions, called once again for organic labor unity in one organization of all trade unions which had contracts with the corporations of the country. In the oil industry twenty-two unions, AFL, CIO, and independents, succeeded in forging bargaining unity in 1951 that won a fifteen-cent-an-hour raise. In Erie, Pa., the United Electrical Workers, five CIO unions, Mine, Mill and Smelter, and two AFL unions joined together in a fight against the wage freeze.

In 1954 Lewis made another important move for labor unity. Joining with Dave Beck of the AFL Teamsters and David J. McDonald of the CIO Steelworkers, the three formed a Triple Alliance embracing nearly 3,000,000 wage earners. Criticizing the slowness of the AFL and CIO to seek organic unity, the three labor leaders announced that their unions would develop united labor action against unemployment and for repeal of the Taft-Hartley Act. So insistent did rank-and-file demands for basic labor unity become late in 1954 that George Meany of the AFL and Walter Reuther of the CIO issued a statement declaring that their two organizations would endeavor to become one by 1955.

Carran-Walter law for deportation to Canada. Said the CIO Transport Workers Union: "Congress should investigate whether the U.S. Immigration Service is being used as a strike-breaking weapon." Hundreds of union members have been arrested and face deportation, many of them without warrants, warning or legal procedure, since the law reads, "Any officer or employee of the Service . . . shall have power without warrant . . . to arrest any alien in the U.S. . . . ." Thousands of union leaders on all levels are naturalized Americans and subject to the law.

[31] Butler was frank in declaring that anyone with liberal and pro-union ideas who didn't agree with a one hundred per cent reactionary employer program was disloyal and should be suppressed. Butler claimed that the labor movement was filled with hidden Socialists and that they were more dangerous than Communists. "They are always liberals," he said, speaking of "the hidden Socialists," "and it is always in the name of liberalism that they speak and act. . . . In the field of labor, which next to foreign affairs is the most sensitive and fertile field for socialist infiltration, collectivist attitudes manifest themselves primarily in a pro-union, anti-management bias."

Then on Feb. 9, 1955, the AFL and CIO signed a merger agreement at Miami Beach for the creation of a single trade union center which would "preserve the integrity of each affiliated national and international union." By the terms of the agreement the thirty-four unions in the CIO, headed by Walter P. Reuther since Philip Murray's death in 1952, will go into the new labor center as the Council of Industrial Organizations. The backbone of this Council will be—as it was in the CIO—the Auto Workers with 1,400,-000 dues-paying members and the Steelworkers with its 1,157,000 members. The rank-and-file of these two unions have a fighting tradition that goes back to the early days of the CIO and has continued to the present, as the seven-week nation-wide strike of 600,000 steelworkers in 1952 attests and as the stoppages of auto workers at Chrysler, Ford, Briggs, and others in the recent past demonstrate.

The new national labor center brings together over 145 unions with a membership of 15,000,000 workers. Although nearly 2,000,000 organized workers—600,000 Mine Workers, 400,000 Railroad Brotherhood Workers and the rest in other independent unions like the United Electrical, Mine, Mill, Longshore and Warehouse—are still outside the new federation, the possibility exists of uniting the entire labor movement, thus achieving that unity of action which big business recognizes as its most potent weapon in the fight against labor.

CHAPTER XII

"The More Glorious the Triumph"

> "The summer soldier and the sunshine patriot will, in
> this crisis, shrink from the service of their country; but
> he that stands it now deserves the love and thanks of
> men and women. Tyranny, like hell, is not easily con-
> quered; yet we have this consolation with us, the harder
> the sacrifice, the more glorious the triumph."
>
> TOM PAINE, 1776

1. The Tide Begins to Turn

In 1952 General of the Army Dwight D. Eisenhower was elected President of the United States on the Republican ticket, the near unanimous
choice of Big Business and all other enemies of labor. It seemed to many as
if the story had come full circle and as if the days of "Give them a rifle diet
and see how they like that kind of bread," might return again so far as
labor was concerned.

At any rate, it was said, the New Deal, an uneasy ghost under Truman,
was now definitely buried. Reaction was in the saddle again and it was
back to the normalcy of Harding, if not Grant and the Robber Barons who
looted a country. The cold war would be warmed to hot by experts unim-
peded by Truman's vestiges of the New Deal, by way of the Red Scare and
Mr. Dulles' "massive retaliation."

And yet the Eisenhower administration saw the organic unity of organized labor, the coming together again of the AFL and CIO, the dream of a
generation realized, a basic condition for further progress fulfilled. There
was no shooting down of pickets, for the country, heading an alliance termed
democratic, was on world view and could not afford widespread violence.
Similarly the sight of Americans persecuted because of race and color could
not easily be endured and the Supreme Court's decision against Negro
segregation in the nation's schools was partially the result of world-wide
revulsion.

371

Even the old weapons, the Red Scare and the war scare, queerly enough, had a new tendency to turn in the hand and to become increasingly outmoded. Threats of war frightened allies abroad and alienated the support of the American people at home. The fact was that General Eisenhower and the Republicans had come to power at a time of profound world crisis, a crisis coloring each of their acts, and often eliminating the effectiveness of personal desire. The crux of the problem rested on the fact that with much of world production, and particularly American production, geared for war, war was becoming an impossibility if the human race were to live. The pursuit of life was perhaps beginning to take precedence over the pursuit of profit.

With American policy, propelled by the Red Scare and the cold war, heading inevitably towards a war that humanity did not want because it desired life, a good many changes were called for both in policy and production if humanity were not to die beneath a rain of hydrogen bombs, only one of which could kill a city. President Eisenhower, himself, under the spur of the mass desire for peace and life came in time to say that some Americans would have to "rethink" the nation's problems. Pushed by the peoples of the world, for even verbal changes seldom come easily, he spoke of world trade that included even Russia and China, sounding a new note with his declaration, "We can have prosperity without war production." And with something of the fervor of a New Dealer he recommended a great government road-building program.

None of this had been planned that way, of course. It resulted from gigantic objective facts, primarily the unprecedented, organized demand of the world's people for world peace, that pulled the policies of even the unwilling into accordance with it like some giant, irresistible magnet. Even those determined on war had to further their designs within this imposed framework of peace. If the Red Scare began to wear thin, paying ever diminishing returns, it was because its continued use might mean the end of more than the Bill of Rights. It might mean the end of man. It began to be dimly realized that calls for Communist destruction were only a disguised call for the destruction of American cities, that, as Bertrand Russell said, "If we cannot live together, we may die together." So many millions backed that statement that it perhaps presaged a great age of unity and coalition—and opportunity for American labor.

But the Eisenhower administration did not begin with surprises. Whatever changes that later arrived were forced upon it by public opinion as the administration moved slowly and painfully, and with many draw-backs and contradictions, into nearer accord with the great facts of life. Even in the administration's first days it quickly became apparent that rather than amend the Taft-Hartley Act, the Eisenhower administration would use it more fully than ever before unless labor knuckled under and made its use superfluous.

Under the guise of outlawing the Communist Party, the Eisenhower administration, aided and abettered by many Democrats, passed a law also providing in effect for the government licensing of trade unions. Not only did the law outlaw a political party for the first time in American history, thus telling the American people what they could think and could not think, who they could vote for and who they could not. In addition it provided for the destruction of trade unions which were charged with "Communist infiltration," by employers during a strike or by anyone else at any other time.

Thus another time-bomb was added to the anti-labor arsenal to be used if and when the proper moment arrived. As in the case of the Taft-Hartley Act, with its non-Communist oath provisions, another law ostensibly directed only against Communists was directed in reality against all of labor. Both George Meany, president of the AFL, and Walter Reuther, head of the CIO, said of the principles embodied in the new law that they could be used not only to destroy left unions but any and all unions. But, as in the case of the Taft-Hartley Act, labor was prevented from full mobilization against the anti-labor law by those of its leaders who feared that labor would be smeared as Communist if it acted in its own interest. And that was precisely the design of labor's enemies.

The New Deal had become only a symbol under Truman but under Eisenhower it became a synonym for treason. In an effort to undo what President Eisenhower called the "creeping socialism" of the New Deal, offshore oil, government-owned synthetic rubber plants, public lands, public power and atomic installations were handed over to the glories of private profit. Resources and enterprises estimated to be worth more than fifty billions of dollars were turned over to Standard Oil, General Electric, the du Ponts and other huge monopolies in deals which made the Robber Barons of Grant's day seem like pygmies.

As the New Deal's "socialism" was being reversed by the government's give-away programs for the benefit of corporations, Senator Joseph R. McCarthy was charging up and down the land accusing millions of Americans and virtually every Democrat of favoring or approving what he called "Twenty Years of Treason." President Roosevelt, McCarthy and other right-wing Republicans inferred, had deliberately sold out his own country to the Communists at the Yalta conference. Under McCarthy's ministrations the ancient Red Scare blossomed, like some ever-growing evil plant that was pulling all of society into its tentacles, until generals, the highest of government officials, the greatest of scientists, such as Dr. J. Robert Oppenheimer, the chief creator of the atomic killer, were smeared and ruined by the ever-expanding charge.

To the remainder of the world it seemed as if Americans had succumbed to mass insanity when McCarthy and Attorney General Brownell actually charged that former President Truman was himself a part of the so-called Communist conspiracy. He had knowingly, they said, promoted a Soviet spy to a high international post. "Why have we grown afraid of ourselves?" asked Adlai Stevenson, Democratic aspirant for the Presidency, speaking at Columbia University, in 1954. "We are acting," he said, "as though the whole of this nation was a security risk." But almost as he spoke the Eisenhower administration was announcing that it had discharged 7,000 government employees as possible Reds or as some other kind of security risk. Thousands of other Americans had lost their jobs, many of them trade unionists accused by McCarthy, were exiles in their own country because someone had whispered they had improper thoughts or associations. Thousands more had lost the power of protest, once the birthright of every American, had been paralyzed into silence by the general hysteria.

But not all were fearful and not all surrendered and slowly their ranks increased, helped once more by the world-wide will for peace. McCarthy had been as strong for war as he was against those whom he called Reds, and after every McCarthy speech there was protest and pain both from the world's foreign offices and from the world's press. He became an obvious liability to the administration and to the American people and both dumped him, at least for the moment, the first withdrawing support, the latter censuring him through a formal vote of the United States Senate.

There were other factors in the eclipse of McCarthy, whether temporary or permanent, not the least of which was one Harvey M. Matusow. An employee of McCarthy and the Department of Justice, one of the time's chief finger men, he confessed in his memoirs, *False Witness,* that he had been instrumental in convicting a score of persons, Communist and non-Communist, as well as trade union leaders, on perjury testimony bought and paid for by the government. Federal Judge Dimock formally found that Matusow had lied in testifying that George Blake Charney and Alexander Trachtenberg had advocated the violent overthrow of the government. Judge Dimock granted the Communist leaders new trials and in so doing placed an uneasy idea in the American conscience, the fear that all the Smith Act trials had been frame-ups.

With Matusow's confession, the Department of Justice's entire structure of paid stool-pigeon testimony seemed threatened with collapse. The Department announced, after repeated judicial rebuffs, that it was dropping the perjury case against Dr. Owen Lattimore, Far Eastern expert from Johns Hopkins University, a case built almost entirely on the charges of the Department's chief stool pigeon, Louis Budenz. Another of its stars, Elizabeth Bentley, one of the principal proponents of the Communist spy thesis, was characterized as a fraud by William Henry Taylor, a high official of the International Monetary Fund, as he demanded that the Senate Judiciary Committee allow him to confront those who accused him of disloyalty. And when a jury refused to believe Harry Gold, whose testimony was torn to shreds, and who with Bentley had been among the chief accusers of the Rosenbergs, was it any wonder that Americans began to wonder about the executed man and wife, about Morton Sobell, sentenced to thirty years in Alcatraz?

At about the same time the Supreme Court condemned the informer system, under which labor is a chief sufferer, in the case of Dr. John Punnett Peters. It declared he had been wrongfully fired for disloyalty when as senior professor of medicine at Yale University he had also served as a part-time consultant to the federal Public Health Service. Justice William O. Douglas wrote:

"Dr. Peters was condemned by faceless informers, some of whom were not known even to the [loyalty] board that condemned him. Some of these informers were not even under oath. None of them had to submit to cross examination. None had to face Dr. Peters. So far as we or the board know, they may be venal people or psychopaths, like Titus Oates, who revel in being informers. They may bear old grudges. Under cross-examination their stories might disappear like bubbles. Their whispered confidences might turn out to be yarns conceived by twisted minds or by people who, though sincere, have poor faculties of observation and memory.

". . . The practice of using faceless informers has apparently spread through a vast domain. It is used not only to get rid of employes in the Government, but also employes who work for private firms having contracts with the Government . . .

"It has touched countless hundreds of men and women and ruined many. It is an un-American practice, which we should condemn. It deprives men of 'liberty' within the meaning of the Fifth Amendment, for one of man's most precious liberties is his right to work."

That right to work had been taken from a good many trade union members without trial after sessions before McCarthy, as was the case at General Electric when McCarthy held hearings, usually just before Labor Board elections. Later, however, and after the discharges, the courts, always sensitive barometers to changes in public opinion, began to sound a more liberal note.

The Supreme Court, for example, reversed the contempt conviction against Julius Emspak, secretary-treasurer of the United Electrical Workers, which followed his refusal to allow a hostile congressional committee to pry into the affairs of his union. (Previously James Matles, UE director of organization, had been acquitted on a similar charge.) The Circuit Court of Appeals in Washington declared that the State Department could not withhold passports for travel abroad either on its own arbitrary whim or on the unsubstantiated and unrevealed accusations of informers. The same court in another jurisdiction in a minority opinion handed down by the Negro jurist, Judge William Hastie, declared that the government had not shown in a Smith Act trial of Communists that they were guilty of anything save their political opinions. Thus, he said, they were convicted in violation of the First Amendment.

None of this happened in a vacuum. It was of interest to labor for reasons other than the fact that labor has been a historic victim of the spy and informer, the frame-up and the perjurer. It was also of interest because it perhaps indicated the beginnings of a new political realignment in which the American people would insist on production for peace, would insist on the Bill of Rights and a life free from the menace of the hydrogen bomb. If the initial impetus of all this had been the Matusow confession, the more basic underlying cause was the lessening of world tensions, the world-wide demand for peace, the most important single phenomenon of the times which had a gravitational pull on all things and all events. It became increasingly clear as the courts slowly began to re-affirm the liberties guaranteed by the Bill of Rights, and as the State Department faced new realities in the decline of the Cold War atmosphere throughout the world, that red baiting as a technique against all democratic forces was increasingly difficult to employ.

2. The Tide Rises

The Eisenhower administration began in contradiction. From the first it foundered on the Gibraltar of immutable objective fact. Thus many of its supporters felt that the five-star General would lead to preventive war and the American century, but the American people so wanted peace that to gain the White House monopoly's candidate had to promise peace in Korea. Once in, one of President Eisenhower's first acts was the threat "to unleash" Chiang Kai-shek, who was to reconquer China, with American aid, but such was the uproar of allies abroad and Americans at home that the threat was quickly forgotten.

Not long later Vice President Nixon loosed "a trial balloon," declaring that the United States might intervene in the Indo-Chinese War. The balloon was punctured by an unprecedented protest that went up from churches, fraternal orders, political organizations, trade unions, Americans everywhere of every degree and class. When Congress authorized the President to defend the off-shore islands of China even, if necessary, by hot pursuit and atomic weapons against the Chinese people, virtually the whole world joined in protest, even including the closest of allies, fearful that it would precipitate the dreaded atomic world war.

If any one single fact impelled overwhelmingly towards peace, it was the terrible fact of the hydrogen bomb. Scientists and statesmen everywhere, including President Eisenhower, universally agreed that a war using this weapon would wipe out civilization and be a war in which there were no victors, a war in which scores of millions of civilians would be the casualties. As a result of the hydrogen bomb's discovery and development in both the United States and the Soviet Union, even right-led unions began taking unequivocal stands for world peace in the spring of 1954. The Amalgamated Clothing Workers, third largest union in the CIO, called for negotiations to avert nuclear war, pointing out that there could be no labor movement if there was no world.

Officials of the United Packinghouse Workers, addressing that union's convention, spoke of reassessing the international situation in the light "of the awful glare of the hydrogen bomb," and declared "our end being peace, our means must be negotiation." The Textile Workers of America, one of the nation's large unions, called for negotiations for world peace, pointed out that McCarthyism was the road to fascism and atomic destruction. The powerful United Mine Workers and officials of the AFL's Butchers' Union demanded peace and co-existence. Typical of labor's new drive for world peace was the report of the General Executive Board of the Amalgamated Clothing Workers. After declaring that the hydrogen bomb made it "more necessary than ever before that the differences between men and nations be reconciled by negotiations," the Board continued:

"Our entire thinking in the international field has been jolted by the development of the hydrogen bomb, which has altered drastically all earlier concepts of modern warfare.

"Until now it has been possible for some to think in terms of limited wars, of isolated military situations. With the hydrogen bomb, however, military victory is no longer possible, for this new weapon, if used, can destroy the entire world and civilization, as we have known it. Unless mankind wishes to destroy itself, world peace *must* be maintained. It may now be either peace or annihilation."

All over the world men were speaking thus with increased urgency and increased unanimity, demanding in Churchill's words, "a meeting at the summit," of government heads, its design the averting of atomic war. Peace became the dominant political issue in every domestic campaign the world over and equally paramount in world affairs. In Bandoeng official representatives of half the people on the earth, the inhabitants of Asia and Africa, met together for the first time, demanding co-existence and world peace through negotiation. In San Francisco in the summer of 1955 the tenth anniversary meeting of the United Nations at San Francisco, the delegates of sixty-six nations attending, became one great cry for peace. In Finland's capital of Helsinki, 2000 delegates from ninety countries demanded negotiations and world peace at the World Peace Assembly which also asked, as did most of the other conferences, for disarmament and the banning of nuclear weapons.

All of this was something new under the sun, a fact even more powerful perhaps than the hydrogen bomb. The most truculent of statesmen was forced to include in his calculations the almost unanimous demand of mankind for peace. It was then that President Eisenhower began to speak of prosperity through production for peace not war, saying it was possible after all, and it was then that a meeting at "the summit" between representatives of the United States, the Soviet Union, France and Great Britain was agreed upon and subsequently held at Geneva.

In a time of narrowing choice between life and death, it became additionally apparent as days and weeks went by that facts rather than the personal desires of individuals were increasingly dictating the course of men.

As regards the merger between the AFL and the CIO, the objective fact of a strong, united American labor center seemed more liable to determine the course of the new organization than those who might like to make it a kind of Hitlerian labor front for monopoly. Gravity pulls to earth no matter what the desire of the falling object and great facts have a similar pull. It seemed probable that the organic unity of American labor might in the long run have a dynamic of its own, forcing greater militance and higher wage scales, bringing organization of the South, a guaranteed annual wage, protection from automation, and independent political action, regardless of the bureaucrats, and derived, in part, from the rank and file conviction that a united labor should be a stronger labor that got results.

George Meany, president of the united labor organization, or perhaps some successor, might finally understand that peace for America had to include peace for the Soviet Union, too, and that if President Eisenhower could confer with the Prime Minister of Russia, it might be possible for the powers that be to include co-existence with the Bill of Rights and American dissent. But regardless of that, one gigantic truth seemed increasingly evident, that the peace and happiness of American labor and the American people depended upon the peace and happiness of the world.

Out of that great fact came hope, and some evidence, of new developments that might lead to a new coalition of the American people, a political realignment under a united labor that would save the country from the menace of depression and the catastrophe of war. And it was equally apparent that such a coalition could not be built until monopoly's Red Scare was buried in oblivion along with its counterpart, Hitler's Big Lie.

3. Epilogue

The Chinese ideograph for the word "crisis" is formed by two characters, one representing "opportunity," and the other representing "danger." The American labor movement, confronted with world crisis, as is every movement and every person, is faced with danger on one hand and opportunity on the other. The danger is atomic war, the opportunity the leading of the American people in making our economy work for peace instead of war. The danger is universal devastation and definitive ruin. The opportunity is the creation of unprecedented plenty and content through operating the huge American economy without the dangerous crutch of vast armaments and war orders, without the deadly narcotic of millions of tons of the weapons of death, useless and unproductive save for the creation of limitless misery and suffering.

As we said in the beginning, fundamentally labor's story is the story of the American people. Never has it lived in isolation or progressed without allies. Always it has been in the mainstream of American life with none more concerned than it, nor with more at stake, as to the course on which monopoly was leading the country. In the past labor has reached its greatest heights only in coalition as when it joined hands with farmers, small businessmen and the Negro people in the epic Populist revolts in the 1890's against the growing power of Wall Street. And again it was such a coalition that raised labor to the triumphs of the New Deal.

As East and West, capitalism and socialism, move towards a necessary peace, it becomes the historic role of labor to head a new coalition of the American people which will build an economy that can produce peace and happiness without benefit of war scare or Red Scare. As red baiting declines as official government policy, one discovers anew the lesson of American history, namely, that it is ever an effective technique of reaction unless openly exposed and strongly challenged. Eventually, despite vacillations, retreats and confusions, labor and the American people will accept this challenge and meet it just as both accepted and met the challenge of the depression years. In the long run, despite every difficulty, every democratic element in American life will rally to labor's leadership in solving the grave problems confronting the nation not with war and fascism but through peace and democracy.

And when the people unite under the leadership of labor, "there is no power of wrong," as Sylvis said at this story's beginning, "that we cannot openly defy." Labor united, and united with its allies, is an absolutely irresistible social force that can return this rich and lovely American land to the American people whose sweat and blood have made it great. The people's unity has a power in excess of any hydrogen bomb; a power that cannot be thwarted unless the people remain divided and weakened by monopoly's stale old cry of Red.

Labor's story gives every reason for confidence that the time will come when war and poverty and persecution for opinion's sake are only memories of a cruel past. There was once a time when Edmund Ruffin thought that human slavery was eternal and when the courts held that all trade unions were only foreign conspiracies. The path since the day of Sylvis has been long but in the end, despite all difficulties and all reverses, it has always led forward.

Big Bill Haywood, shooting it out with hired gunmen in the mine wars of the Rockies, did not fight in vain nor did Parsons die in vain as he cried with his last breath, "Let the voice of the people be heard!" It will be heard. Those who looked back at labor's history, recalling the Molly Maguires and Gene Debs and above all, the bravery and unity of the millions who triumphed with the CIO and the New Deal, could be nothing but confident of the future.

They knew there were great battles ahead and some dark days. But beyond the darkness they could glimpse the splendid light of a bright new day. And they had "this consolation," that "the harder the sacrifice, the more glorious the triumph."

NOTES ON SOURCES

Much primary and secondary material is available for the writing of a work covering so extended a period and so comprehensive a subject as labor's story from 1860 to the present.

The authors of this work have relied to a considerable extent on primary source material. Particularly helpful in this connection have been Government documents giving an insight into the conditions of labor, such as the *Report of the [Education and Labor] Committee of the Senate on the Relations of Labor and Capital* (1885), the various reports of the United States Immigration Commission (1910–11), the United States Bureau of Labor's *Summary of the Report on Conditions of Women and Child Wage-Earners in the United States* (1911) and the voluminous *Hearings* of the La Follette sub-committee of the Senate Committee on Education and Labor (late 1930's). Equally useful for first-hand information on labor's story have been the press, both union and commercial, the proceedings of labor organizations and the autobiographiess (in particular, Bill Haywood's book) and writings of labor leaders. For the development of monopoly—the other side of the labor coin—the authors have found the following primary source material to be especially helpful: the *Final Report of the Industrial Commission* (1902), the so-called Pujo Committee *Report . . . on the Concentration of Control of Money and Credit* (1913), the *Final Report of the Commission on Industrial Relations* (1915), *The Structure of the American Economy* published by the National Resources Committee (1939), the various monographs of the Temporary National Economic Committee investigating the concentration of economic power (1941) and the report of the Smaller War Plants Corporation on *Economic Concentration and World War II* (1946).

In addition to original sources, the authors have relied on the work of competent secondary authorities. Among the many consulted the writers wish to acknowledge their special indebtedness to Philip S. Foner, *History of the Labor Movement in the United States* (New York, 1947), James S. Allen, *Reconstruction: The Battle for Democracy in the South* (New York, 1937), Matthew Josephson, *The Robber Barons: The Great American Capitalists, 1861–1901* (New York, 1934), Henry David, *Haymarket Affair. Fifty Years After* (New York, 1936), Anna Rochester, *Rulers of America* (New York, 1936), Ray Ginger, *The Bending Cross. A Biography of Eugene Victor Debs* (New Brunswick, 1949), Mike Quin, *The Big Strike* (Olema, Cal., 1949) and Carl Marzani, *We Can Be Friends. The Origins of the Cold War* (New York, 1952).

The following bibliography is selective and only primary sources and
secondary authorities which have been specifically used in the text have
been mentioned.

Primary Sources

GOVERNMENT DOCUMENTS

ANNUAL REPORT OF THE ATTORNEY-GENERAL OF THE UNITED STATES FOR THE YEAR
1920, Washington, 1920
CONGRESSIONAL RECORD, 53:2, 67:4, 71:2, 72:2, 73:1, 82:2
DENSMORE REPORT, House Document No. 157, 60th Congr., 1st Sess.
Federal Trade Commission, THE MERGER MOVEMENT, Washington, 1948
FIFTH ANNUAL REPORT OF THE COMMISSIONER OF LABOR, 1889, RAILROAD LABOR, 51st
Congr. 1st Sess., House of Rep., Executive Doc. No. 336, Washington, 1890
FINAL REPORT OF THE COMMISSION ON INDUSTRIAL RELATIONS, Washington, 1915
FINAL REPORT OF THE INDUSTRIAL COMMISSION, vol. xix, 57th Congr., 1st Sess., House
of Rep., Doc. 380, Washington, 1902
FOURTH ANNUAL MESSAGE, Pres. Grover Cleveland, December 3, 1888, Miscel. Doc. 210,
Part 8, 53rd Congr., 2 Sess., House of Rep.
HEARINGS BEFORE THE COMMITTEE ON EDUCATION AND LABOR, U.S. Senate, 65th Congr.,
3rd Sess., "Social and Industrial Conditions in the United States," Washington, 1919
HEARINGS BEFORE THE COMMITTEE ON RULES, House of Rep., 66th Congr., 2nd Sess.
"Attorney-General A. Mitchell Palmer on Charges Made Against the Department
of Justice by Louis F. Post and Others," Washington, 1920, Part I
HEARINGS BEFORE A SUBCOMMITTEE OF THE SENATE COMMITTEE ON EDUCATION AND
LABOR, 75th Congr., 3rd Sess., Washington, 1938, 76th Congr., 1st Sess., Washington,
1939
HEARINGS ON UNEMPLOYMENT RELIEF, Subcommittee of the U.S. Senate Committee on
Manufactures, 72nd Congr., 1st Sess., Washington, 1932
INVESTIGATION AND STUDY OF PRESENT ECONOMIC PROBLEMS OF THE UNITED STATES,
U.S. Senate Finance Committee, 72nd Congr., 2nd Sess., Washington, 1933
MESSAGE TO CONGRESS, Pres. Franklin D. Roosevelt, April 29, 1938, Senate Doc. No.
173, 75th Congr., 3rd Sess.
National Resources Committee, THE STRUCTURE OF THE AMERICAN ECONOMY, Wash-
ington, 1939
President's Committee on Civil Rights, TO SECURE THESE RIGHTS, New York, 1947
REPORT OF THE COMMITTEE APPOINTED TO INVESTIGATE THE [PENNSYLVANIA] RAILROAD
RIOTS In July 1877, Harrisburg, 1878, Leg. Doc. No. 29
REPORT OF THE [EDUCATION AND LABOR] COMMITTEE OF THE SENATE ON THE RELATIONS
BETWEEN LABOR AND CAPITAL, Washington, 1885
REPORT OF LABOR DISTURBANCES IN THE STATE OF COLORADO FROM 1880 to 1904, INCLU-
SIVE, 58th Congr., 3rd Sess., Senate Doc. No. 122, Washington, 1905
REPORT OF THE COMMITTEE APPOINTED . . . TO INVESTIGATE THE CONCENTRATION OF
CONTROL OF MONEY AND CREDIT, 62nd Congr., 3rd Sess., House of Rep. Report No.
1593, Washington, 1913.
REPORT OF THE SENATE COMMITTEE ON EDUCATION AND LABOR, 76th Congr., 1st Sess.,
"Labor Policies of Employers' Associations, Part III, The National Association of
Manufacturers," Washington, 1939
REPORT OF THE SMALLER WAR PLANTS CORP. TO THE U.S. SENATE COMMITTEE ON SMALL
BUSINESS, 79th Congr., 2nd Sess., "Economic Concentration and World War II,"
Doc. No. 206
REPORT OF THE SUBCOMMITTEE OF THE U.S. SENATE COMMITTEE ON MILITARY AFFAIRS,

78th Congr., 2nd Sess., "Economic and Political Aspects of International Cartels," Washington, 1944

REPORT ON THE CIO POLITICAL ACTION COMMITTEE, Special Committee on Un-American Activities, 76th Congr., 2nd Sess., House Report No. 311

Temporary National Economic Committee, INVESTIGATION OF CONCENTRATION OF ECONOMIC POWER, Monograph No. 26, "Economic Power and Political Pressures," 76th Congr., 3rd Sess., Senate, Washington, 1941

U.S. Bureau of Labor, SUMMARY OF THE REPORT ON CONDITIONS OF WOMEN AND CHILD WAGE-EARNERS IN THE UNITED STATES, Bulletin No. 175, Washington, 1911

U.S. Bureau of Labor Statistics, HANDBOOK OF LABOR STATISTICS, 1947, Bulletin No. 916

U.S. Department of Commerce, Bureau of Census, HISTORICAL STATISTICS OF THE UNITED STATES, 1789–1945, Washington, 1949

———, STATISTICAL ABSTRACT OF THE UNITED STATES, 1938, 1947

U.S. Department of Labor, Women's Bureau, WOMEN WORKERS AND THEIR DEPENDENTS, Bulletin No. 239, Washington, 1952

U.S. Department of the Treasury, Bureau of Internal Revenue, STATISTICS OF INCOME FOR 1942, Part I

U.S. Immigration Commission, ABSTRACT OF THE REPORT ON CONTRACT LABOR AND INDUCED AND ASSISTED IMMIGRATION, Washington, 1911

———, PEONAGE AND THE TREATMENT AND CONDITIONS OF WORK OF IMMIGRANTS, Washington, 1911

———, ABSTRACT OF THE REPORT ON IMMIGRANTS IN CITIES, Washington, 1911

———, ABSTRACT OF THE REPORT ON STEERAGE CONDITIONS, Washington, 1910

U.S. Strike Commission, REPORT OF THE CHICAGO STRIKE OF JUNE–JULY 1894 WITH APPENDICES CONTAINING TESTIMONY, PROCEEDINGS AND RECOMMENDATIONS, 53rd Congr., 3rd Sess., Senate Executive Document, No. 7, Washington, 1895

PERIODICALS

American Federationist, 1920
CIO News, 1944, 1945, 1946, 1949, 1950
Daily Miners' Journal, Pottsville, 1877
Harpers' Monthly Magazine, 1877
Harpers' Weekly, 1894
John Swinton's Paper, 1883, 1887
Labor Clarion, 1916, 1917
Leslie's Weekly, 1877, 1894
Locomotive Firemen's Magazine, 1893, 1894
Machinist Monthly Review, 1945
March of Labor, 1952, 1953
Miners' Magazine, 1907
Monthly Labor Review, 1950
New York Daily Compass, 1952
New York Daily Tribune, 1865, 1869, 1877
New York Herald, 1876, 1877, 1886, 1894, 1895, 1907, 1918, 1920, 1921
New York Herald Tribune, 1927, 1937
New York Tribune, 1887, 1894, 1920
New York Times, 1877, 1886, 1887, 1894, 1895, 1907, 1919, 1920, 1921, 1927, 1937, 1948
The Nation, 1952, 1953
UE News, 1945, 1950

AUTOBIOGRAPHIES AND COLLECTED WORKS

Berkman, A., *Prison Memoirs of an Anarchist*, New York, 1912
Buchanan, J., *The Story of a Labor Agitator*, New York, 1903

Bloor, E. R., *We Are Many. An Autobiography*, New York, 1940
Chicago Martyrs. Famous Speeches of the Eight Anarchists in Judge Gary's Court and Altgeld's Reasons for Pardoning Fielden, Niebe and Schwab, San Francisco, 1899
Clews, H., *Fifty Years in Wall Street*, New York, 1908
Coyne, F. E., *In Reminiscence. Highlights of Men and Events in the History of Chicago*, Chicago, 1941
Darrow, C., *The Story of My Life*, New York, 1932
Debs: His Life, Writings and Speeches with a Department of Appreciations and a "Life of Eugene V. Debs" by S. M. Reynolds, Girard, Kansas, 1908
Foner, P. S., ed., *The Life and Writings of Frederick Douglass*, New York, 1952
Foster, W. Z., *Pages from a Worker's Life*, New York, 1939
———, *From Bryan to Stalin*, New York, 1937
Frankfurter, M. D. & Jackson, G., ed., *The Letters of Sacco and Vanzetti*, New York, 1928
Gompers, S., *Seventy Years of Life and Labor*, New York, 1925
Haywood, W. D., *Bill Haywood's Book. The Autobiography of William D. Haywood*, New York, 1929
Long, E. B., ed., *Personal Memoirs of U. S. Grant*, Cleveland, 1952
Powderly, T. V., *Thirty Years of Labor* (1859-1889), Cleveland, 1889
———, *The Path I Trod*, New York, 1940
Rosenman, S. I., ed., *Papers and Addresses of Franklin D. Roosevelt*, New York, 1938
Spies, A., Autobiography. *His Speech in Court and General Notes*, Chicago, 1887
Stone, M., *Fifty Years of Journalism*, New York, 1921.
Trachtenberg, A., ed., *Speeches of Eugene V. Debs with a Critical Introduction*, New York, 1928.
Vanzetti, B., *The Story of a Proletarian Life*, translated by E. Lyons, Boston, 1923
Vorse, M. H., *A Footnote to Folly: Reminiscences*, New York, 1935

OTHER PRIMARY MATERIAL

Abbott, E., ed., *Immigration. Select Documents and Case Records*, Chicago, 1924.
American Federation of Labor, *Proceedings*, 1935, 1936, 1937, 1938
Aptheker, H., ed., *A Documentary History of the Negro People*, New York, 1951.
Commager, H. S., *The Blue and the Gray. The Story of the Civil War as Told by Participants*, Indianapolis, 1950
Commager, H. S. & Nevins, A., *The Heritage of America. Readings in American History*, Boston, 1939
Congress of Industrial Organizations, *Proceedings*, 1938, 1939, 1947, 1948, 1949
Dacus, J. A., *Annals of the Great Strikes in the United States*, Chicago, 1877
Foster, W. Z., *The Great Steel Strike and its Lessons*, New York, 1920
Gaer, J., ed., *Our Lives, American Labor Stories*, New York, 1948
Interchurch World Movement, Commission of Inquiry, *Report on the Steel Strike of 1919*, New York, 1920
International Union of Mine, Mill and Smelter Workers, *Proceedings*, 1951
Kahn, A. E., ed., *McCarthy on Trial*, New York, 1954
Lloyd, H. D., *Wealth Against Commonwealth*, New York, 1902
Marx, K. & Engels, F., *The Civil War in the United States*, New York, 1937
Material in Connection with the Mooney Case, New York Public Library Collection, 7 vols.
McCabe, J. D., *The History of the Great Riots*, Philadelphia, 1877
Millis, W., ed., *The Forrestal Diaries*, New York, 1951
National Civic Federation, *Its Methods and Aims*, New York, 1905
Pinkerton, A., *The Molly Maguires and the Detectives*, New York, 1877
———, *Strikers, Communists, Tramps and Detectives*, New York, 1878

Report of the Committee on Tenement Houses of the Citizens' Association of Chicago, Chicago, 1884

Sacco-Vanzetti Case. Transcript of the Record of the Trial, New York Public Library, vols. ii, iii, iv, v

Smith, B., ed., *The Democratic Spirit. A Collection of American Writings from the Earliest Times to the Present Day,* New York, 1941

Van Doran, M., ed., *The Portable Walt Whitman,* New York, 1945

United Electrical, Radio and Machine Workers of America, *Proceedings,* 1947–1951

United Nations, Department of Economic Affairs, *Economic Development in Selected Countries,* Lake Success, N.Y., 1947

Secondary Authorities

Abbott, E., *Women in Industry,* New York, 1910

Abt, J., *The People vs. McCarthyism,* Civil Rights Congress, New York, 1952

Adamic, L., *Dynamite. The Story of Class Violence in America,* New York, 1934

Alinsky, S., *John L. Lewis, An Unauthorized Biography,* New York, 1949

Allen, F. L., *The Lords of Creation,* New York, 1935

———, *Only Yesterday, An Informal History of the 1920's,* New York, 1931

Allen, J. S., *Reconstruction, The Battle for Democracy in the South,* New York, 1937

Ambruster, H. W., *Treason's Peace. German Dyes and American Dupes,* New York, 1947

Angly, E., *Oh Yeah?* Compiled from newspapers and public records, New York, 1931

Aptheker, H., *American Negro Slave Revolts,* New York, 1943

———, *To Be Free, Studies in American Negro History,* New York, 1948

Austin, A., *The Labor Story. A Popular History of American Labor, 1786–1949,* New York, 1949

Beard, C. A. & Beard, M. R., *The Rise of American Civilization,* New York, 1927-1939, 3 vols.

Berge, W., *Cartels: Challenge to a Free World,* Washington, 1946

Beane, M. D., *A Short History of the American Labor Movement,* New York, 1925

Berle, A. A. & Means, G., *The Modern Corporation and Private Property,* New York, 1932

Berman, E., *Labor and the Sherman Act,* New York, 1930

Bernheimer, L., *The Trial of Sacco and Vanzetti. A Summary of the Outstanding Testimony,* New York, 1927

Bimba, A., *The Molly Maguires,* New York, 1932

Blackett, P. M. S., *Fear, War and the Bomb,* New York, 1948

Blanshard, P., *Labor in Southern Cotton Mills,* New York, 1927

Bonofsky, P., *Brother Bill McKee. Building the Union at Ford,* New York, 1953

Bosworth, L. M., ed., *The Living Wage of Women Workers,* New York, 1911

Boyer, R. O., *Magician of the Law,* New York, 1932

———, *The Dark Ship,* Boston, 1947

———, "Gestapo USA" in *Masses and Mainstream,* January 1951

———, "The Story of a Working Class Leader" in *Masses and Mainstream,* December, 1951

———, "Elizabeth Gurley Flynn" in *Masses and Mainstream,* May 1952

Brandeis, L., *Other People's Money and How The Bankers Use It,* New York, 1913

Brissenden, P. F., *The I.W.W. A Study in American Syndicalism,* New York, 1920

Cahill, M. C., *Shorter Hours: A Study of the Movement Since the Civil War,* New York, 1932

Cahn, W., *Mill Town,* New York, 1954

Calmer, A., *Labor Agitator. The Story of Albert R. Parsons,* New York, 1937

Cavan, R. S. & Ranck, H., *The Family and the Depression. A Study of One Hundred Chicago Families*, Chicago, 1938

Cayton, H. R. & Mitchell, G. S., *Black Worker and the New Unions*, Chapel Hill, 1939

Chafee, Z., *Freedom of Speech*, New York, 1920

Chase, S., *Prosperity, Fact or Myth*, New York, 1929

Cole, A. C., *The Irrepressible Conflict, 1850–1865*, New York, 1934

Coleman, J. W., *The Molly Maguire Riots. Industrial Conflict in the Pennsylvania Coal Region*, Richmond, 1936

Commons, J. R. and Associates, *History of Labor in the United States*, New York, 1918–35, 4 vols

Conrad, E., *Harriet Tubman*, Washington, 1943

Corey, L., *Decline of American Capitalism*, New York, 1934

———, *The House of Morgan. A Social Biography of the Masters of Money*, New York, 1930

Croly, H. D., *The Promise of American Life*, New York, 1909

Crane, M., ed. *The Roosevelt Era*, New York, 1947

Cross, C., *A Picture of America. The Photo Story of America as It Is and What It Might Be*, New York, 1932

Cummings, H. & McFarland, C., *Federal Justice. Chapters in the History of Justice and The Federal Executive*, New York, 1937

Daugherty, C. R., *Labor Under the NRA*, Boston, 1934

David, H., *Haymarket Affair. Fifty Years After*, New York, 1936

Davies, J. E., *Mission to Moscow*, New York, 1941

Davis, J., *Capitalism and Its Culture*, New York, 1935

Davis, F., *What Price Wall Street?* New York, 1932

De Mond, A. L., *Certain Aspects of the Economic Development of the American Negro*, Washington, 1945

Douglas, J., *Veterans on the March*, New York, 1934

Douglas, P. H., *Real Wages in the United States, 1890–1926*, New York, 1930

DuBois, W. E. B., *Black Reconstruction*, New York, 1935

Duffield, M., *King Legion*, New York, 1931

Dulles, F. R., *Labor in America*, New York, 1947

Dunn, R. W., *Company Unions*, New York, 1927

Dunn, R. W., ed. *The Palmer Raids*, New York, 1948

Faulkner, H. U., *American Economic History*, New York, 1924

Fay, S. B., *The Origins of the World War*, New York, 1928

Filley, J. & Mitchell, T., *Consider the Laundry Workers*, New York, 1937

Fine, N., *Labor and Farmer Parties in the United States, 1828–1928*, New York, 1928

Flynn, E. G., *Debs, Haywood and Ruthenberg*, New York, 1939

Flynn, J., *God's Gold, The Story of Rockefeller and His Times*, New York, 1932

Foner, P. S., *History of Labor in the United States*, New York, 1947

———, *The Fur and Leather Workers Union*, Newark, 1950

Foster, W. Z., *History of the Communist Party of the United States*, New York, 1952

———, *The Negro People in American History*, New York, 1954

Fountain, C. W., *Union Guy*, New York, 1949

Frankfurter, F., *The Case of Sacco and Vanzetti*, Boston, 1927

Frankfurter, F. & Green, N., *The Labor Injunction*, New York, 1930

Friedman, M., *The Pinkerton Labor Spy*, New York, 1907

Fuller, R. H., *Jubilee Jim. The Life of Colonel James Fisk Jr.*, New York, 1928

Gaer, J., *The First Round, The Story of the CIO Political Action Committee*, New York, 1944

Gambs, J. S., *The Decline of the I.W.W.*, New York, 1932

Gellerman, W., *The American Legion as Educator*, New York, 1938

Ginger, R., *The Bending Cross. A Biography of Eugene Victor Debs*, New Brunswick, 1949

Grattan, C. H., *Why We Fought*, New York, 1929

Hacker, L. M., & Kendrick, B. B., *United States Since 1865*, New York, 1932

Hacker, L. M., Modley, R. & Taylor, G. R., *The United States: A Graphic History*, New York, 1937

Hallgren, M. H., *Seeds of Revolt*, New York, 1933

Hapgood, N., *Professional Patriots*, New York, 1927

Hansen, M. L., *The Immigrant in American History*, Cambridge, 1940

Haywood, H., *Negro Liberation*, New York, 1948

Herbst, A., *The Negro and the Slaughtering and Meatpacking Industry in Chicago*, Boston, 1932

Hicks, J., *The American Nation. A History of the United States from 1865 to the Present*, Boston, 1941

———, *The Populist Revolt. A History of the Farmers' Alliance and the People's Party*, Minneapolis, 1931

Hillquit, M., *History of Socialism in the United States*, New York, 1910

Hopkins, J. A. & Alexander, M., *Machine Gun Diplomacy*, New York, 1928

Hourwich, I. A., *Immigration and Labor*, New York, 1912

Hoxie, R. F., *Trade Unionism in the United States*, New York, 1917

Huberman, L., *America, Inc. Recent Economic History of the United States*, New York, 1940

———, *The Great Bus Strike*, New York, 1941

———, *The Labor Spy Racket*, New York, 1937

———, *The NMU. What It Is and What It Does*, New York, 1944

———, *Storm Over Bridges*, San Francisco, 1941

Hutchins, G., *Children Under Capitalism*, New York, 1933

———, *Women Who Work*, New York, 1932

Johnson, S. C., *A History of Emigration from the United Kingdom to North America 1763-1912*, London, 1913

Jones, R. S., *A History of the American Legion*, New York, 1946

Josephson, H., *The Golden Threads. New England's Mill Girls and Magnates*, New York, 1949

Josephson, M., *The Politicos*, New York, 1938

———, *The President Makers. The Culture of Politics and Leadership, 1896-1919*, New York, 1940

———, *The Robber Barons. The Great American Capitalists, 1861-1901*, New York, 1934

Kahn, A. E., *High Treason*, New York, 1950

———, *The Game of Death. Effects of the Cold War on Our Children*, New York, 1953

Kahn, A. E. & Sayers, M., *The Great Conspiracy*, Boston, 1946

Karsner, D., *Debs: His Authorized Life and Letters*, New York, c. 1919

Korson, G., *Black Land. The Way of Life in the Coal Fields*, Evanston, 1941

Kraus, H., *The Many and the Few*, Los Angeles, 1947

Kuczynski, J., *A Short History of Labour Conditions Under Industrial Capitalism*, vol. ii, *The United States of America, 1789 to the Present Day*, London, 1943

Labor Fact Book, published by the Labor Research Association, vols. i to xi inclusive

Labor Research Association, *Monopoly Today*, New York, 1950

———, *History of the Shorter Work Week*, New York, 1942

Laidler, H. W., *Concentration of Control in American Industry*, New York, 1931

Langdon, E. F., *The Cripple Creek Strike. A History of Industrial War in Colorado, 1903-4-5*, Denver, 1904-5

Leeds, J., "Mother Jones" in *Masses and Mainstream*, March, 1950

LeSueur, M., *North Star Country*, New York, 1945

Leven, M., Moulton, H. G., and Warburton, C., *America's Capacity to Consume*, Washington, 1934

Levinson, E., *Labor on the March*, New York, 1938

——, *I Break Strikes. The Technique of Pearl L. Bergoff*, New York, 1935

Lindley, E. K., *The Roosevelt Revolution, First Phase*, New York, 1933

Lloyd, C., *Henry Demarest Lloyd, 1847–1903*, New York, 1912

Lorwin, L. L., *The American Federation of Labor, History, Policies and Practices*, Washington, 1933

Lowenthal, M., *The Federal Bureau of Investigation*, New York, 1950

Lynch, D. T., *Grover Cleveland*, New York, 1932

Lyons, E., *The Life and Death of Sacco and Vanzetti*, New York, 1927

McCarthy: A Documented Record in The Progressive, April, 1954

McKenney, R., *Industrial Valley*, New York, 1939

McWilliams, C., *Witch Hunt, the Revival of Heresy*, Boston, 1950

——, *A Mask for Privilege: Anti-Semitism in America*, Boston, 1948

Magil, A. B. & Stevens, H., *The Peril of Fascism*, New York, 1938

Marzani, C., *We Can Be Friends. The Origins of the Cold War*, New York, 1952

Means, G. B., *The Strange Death of President Harding*, New York, 1930

Mecklin, J. M., *The Ku Klux Klan: A Study of the American Mind*, New York, 1924

Meyer, H. D., *The Last Illusion. America's Plan for World Domination*, New York, 1954

Millis, W., *The Martial Spirit: A Study of Our War With Spain*, Boston, 1931

——, *The Road to War: America 1914–17*, Boston, 1935

Mills, H. A. & Montgomery, R. E., *Organized Labor*, New York, 1945

Minton, B. & Stuart, J., *The Fat Years and the Lean*, New York, 1940

Mitchell, B. & Mitchell, S. G., *Industrial Revolution in the South*, Baltimore, 1930

Moody, J., *The Truth About the Trusts*, New York, 1904

Morais, H. M. & Cahn, W., *Gene Debs: The Story of a Fighting American*, New York, 1948

Morris, G., *Where Is the CIO Going?* New York, 1947

——, *Conspiracy to Strangle Labor*, New York, 1951

Morton, J., *McCarthy: The Man and the Ism*, San Francisco, 1954

Myers, G., *History of Great American Fortunes*, New York, 1937

Nearing, S. & Freeman, J., *Dollar Diplomacy, A Study in American Imperialism*, New York, 1925

Negro Year Book, 1947, ed. Jessie Parkhurst Guzman, Tuskegee Institute, 1947

Nevins, A., *Emergence of Modern America, 1865–1878*, New York, 1927

——, *Grover Cleveland. A Study in Courage*, New York, 1932

Noyes, A. D., *The War Period in American Finance, 1908–1925*, New York, 1926

Oberholtzer, E. P., *A History of the United States since the Civil War*, New York, 1917-37, 5 vols.

Obermann, K., *Joseph Weydemeyer, Pioneer of American Socialism*, New York, 1947

O'Connor, H., *Mellon's Millions. The Biography of a Fortune*, New York, 1933

Ogden, A. R., *The Dies Committee*, Washington, 1945

Orth, S. P., *The Armies of Labor, A Chronicle of the Organized Wage-Earners*, New Haven, 1921

Palmer, J., ed., *The Bench and Bar of Illinois*, Chicago, 1899

Parrington, V. L., *Main Currents in American Thought*, vol. iii, *The Beginnings of Critical Realism in America*, New York, 1930

Parsons, L. E., *Life of Albert R. Parsons with a Brief History of the Labor Movement in America*, Chicago, 1889

Pecora, F., *Wall Street Under Oath. The Story of Our Modern Money Changers*, New York, 1939

Perlman, S., *History of Trade Unionism in the United States*, New York, 1922

Perlo, V., *American Imperialism*, New York, 1951

Piller, E. A., *Time Bomb*, New York, 1945

Pratt, J. W., *Expanionists of 1898*, Baltimore, 1936

Pruette, L., ed. *Women Workers through the Depression*, New York, 1934

Quarles, B., *The Negro and the Civil War*, Boston, 1953

Quin, M., *The Big Strike*, Olema, Cal., 1949

Riegel, R. E., *The Story of the Western Railroads*, New York, 1926

Rochester, A., *The Populist Movement in the United States*, New York, 1943

———, *Rulers of America*, New York, 1936

Rowan, R. W., *The Pinkertons. A Detective Dynasty*, Boston, 1931

Roy, A., *A History of the Coal Miners of the United States*, Columbus, 1902

Saposs, D. J., *Left Wing Unionism*, New York, 1926

Schappes, M. U., "Jews and the American Labor Movement, 1850–1880," *Jewish Life*, July 1954

———, "Beginning of the Jewish Labor Movement," *ibid.*, September 1954

Schlegal, M. W., *Ruler of the Reading: The Life of Franklin B. Gowen, 1836–1889*, Harrisburg, 1947

Schuman, F. L., *American Policy Toward Russia Since 1917*, New York, 1928

Seldes, G., *Witch Hunt: The Technique and Profits of Red Baiting*, New York, 1940

Seldes, G. V., *The Years of the Locust. America, 1929–1932*, Boston, 1933

Shannon, F. A., *Economic History of the People of the United States*, New York, 1934

Short, J. M., "Women's Wages Compared with Living Costs and General Community Standards, 1916–1932," *Reed College Bulletin*, vol. xii, no. 1, January 1933

Spero, S. D. & Harris, A. L., *The Black Worker. The Negro in the Labor Movement*, New York, 1931

Spivak, J., *America Faces the Barricades*, New York, 1935

———, *Patterns of American Fascism*, New York, 1947

Sprigle, R., *In the Land of Jim Crow*, New York, 1949

Stavis, B., *The Man Who Never Died. A Play about Joe Hill with notes on Joe Hill and His Times*, New York, 1954

Steuben, J., *Labor in Wartime*, New York, 1940

Stone, I., *Clarence Darrow for the Defence*, Garden City, 1943

Sylvis, J. C., *The Life, Speeches, Labors and Essays of William H. Sylvis*, Philadelphia, 1872

Symes, L., *Our American Dreyfus Case*, Los Angeles, 1935

Tansill, C. C., *America Goes to War*, Boston, 1938

Tarbell, I., *The History of the Standard Oil Company*, New York, 1925

The Law and Harry Bridges, Bridges-Robertson-Schmidt Defense Committee, San Francisco, 1952

Todes, C., *William H. Sylvis and the National Labor Union*, New York, 1942

Trachtenberg, A. *The History of Legislation for the Protection of Coal Miners in Pennsylvania, 1824–1915*, New York, 1942

United Electrical, Radio and Machine Workers of America, *The UE Record*, Publication #93

———, *Industry's Law Against the People*, Publication #109

———, *Operation Intimidation*, Publication #238

———, *UE Fights for FEPC!* Publication #229

———, *UE Fights for Women Workers*, Publication #232

———, *In Defense of Labor*, Publication #240

Veblen, T., *The Theory of the Leisure Class, An Economic Study in the Evolution of Institutions*, New York, 1899

Vorse, M. H., *Labor's New Millions*, New York, 1938

Walsh, J. R., *CIO: Industrial Unionism in Action*, New York, 1937

Wanhope, J., *The Haywood-Moyer Outrage. The Story of their Illegal Arrest and Deportation from the State of Colorado*, New York, 1907(?)

Ward, E. E., *Harry Bridges on Trial*, New York, 1940

Ware, N. J., *The Labor Movement in the United States, 1860–1895*, New York, 1929

Warshow, R. I., *The Story of Wall Street*, New York, 1929

Wesley, C. H., *Negro Labor in the United States, 1850–1925*, New York, 1926

"What is McCarthyism?" in *UE Steward*, September, 1953

Wiley, B. I., *The Life of Billy Yank the Common Soldier of the Union*, Indianapolis, 1952

Wilson, W., *Forced Labor in the United States*, New York, 1933

Winkler, M., *Investments of United States Capital in Latin America*, Boston, 1928

Wolman, L., *The Growth of American Trade Unions*, New York, 1924

Woodson, C., *The Negro in Our History*, Washington, 1922

Woodward, C. V., *Reunion and Reaction. The Compromise of 1877 and the End of Reconstruction*, Boston, 1951

Yellen, S., *American Labor Struggles*, New York, 1936

Index

A